Principles of Macroeconomics

About the Author

John B. Taylor is one of the field's most inspiring teachers. As the Raymond Professor of Economics at Stanford University, his distinctive instructional methods have made him a legend among introductory economics students and have won him both the Hoagland and Rhodes prizes for teaching excellence. Described by the *Wall Street Journal,* Taylor's "sober appearance . . . belies a somewhat zany teaching style." Few of his students forget how he first illustrated a shift of the demand curve—by dressing up as a California raisin and dancing to "Heard It Through the Grapevine," or how he proved that the supply and demand model actually works—by having student buyers and sellers call out live bids to him in the classroom. It is this gift for clear explanations and memorable illustrations that makes his textbook so useful to students around the country.

Professor Taylor is also widely recognized for his research. He has created formulas for wage and price setting and models for economic policy evaluation. One of his well-known research contributions is a rule—now widely called the Taylor Rule—used at central banks around the world. The *U.S. News and World Report* wrote about his rule, "Amaze Your Friends! Predict the Fed's Next Move!" His latest research focuses on why economic expansions have gotten longer.

Taylor has had an active public service career. On leave from Stanford, he now serves as the Under Secretary for International Affairs at the U.S. Department of the Treasury. He has also served as economic adviser to the governor of his state (California), to the U.S. Congressional Budget Office, and to the president of the United States.

Professor Taylor began his career at Princeton, where he graduated with highest honors in economics. He then received his Ph.D. from Stanford and taught at Columbia, Yale, and Princeton before returning to Stanford.

Principles of Macroeconomics

FOURTH EDITION

John B. Taylor

Houghton Mifflin Company   **Boston**   **New York**

Publisher: Charles Hartford
Editor in Chief: Jean L. Woy
Sponsoring Editor: Ann West
Editorial Associate: Tonya Lobato
Project Editor: Paula Kmetz
Senior Production/Design Coordinator: Carol Merrigan
Senior Manufacturing Coordinator: Priscilla J. Bailey
Executive Marketing Manager: Andy Fisher

Cover photo © Mike Zens/Corbis

Printed in the U.S.A.

Library of Congress Control Number: 2002109684

ISBN: 0-618-23003-3

1 2 3 4 5 6 7 8 9-VH-07 06 05 04 03

Brief Contents

Contents

PART TWO Principles of Macroeconomics 83

CHAPTER 4 # Macroeconomics: The Big Picture 84

CHAPTER 8   # Productivity and Economic Growth   176

Labor and Capital Without Technology   178
Labor Alone   178
Diminishing Returns to Labor 178
Labor and Capital Alone   180
Diminishing Returns to Capital 181

Technology: The Engine of Growth   182
What Is Technology?   183
Invention, Innovation, and Diffusion 183 • Organization and Specialization 184 • Human Capital 185
The Production of Technology: The Invention Factory   185
Special Features of the Technology Market   186

Measuring Technology   188
The Formula and Its Coefficient   188
Using the Formula   188

Case Study   Growth Accounting in Practice   190
The 1970s Productivity Growth Slowdown   190
The 1990s Rebound and the New Economy   190
Demise of the Soviet Union   191

Technology Policy   193
Policy to Encourage Investment in Human Capital   193
Policy to Encourage Research and Innovation   193
Technology Embodied in New Capital   194
Is Government Intervention Appropriate?   194

APPENDIX TO CHAPTER 8   # Deriving the Growth Accounting Formula   198

PART THREE Economic Fluctuations and Macroeconomic Policy 223

CHAPTER 14   # Monetary Policy   318

PART FOUR Trade and Global Markets 365

Preface

I love economics and I enjoy sharing my love of it with others. The goal of this book has been to present modern economics in a form that is intuitive, relevant, and memorable to students who have had no prior exposure to the subject. I have been gratified by the positive responses I've received to the first three editions from economists who teach introductory economics. But most rewarding have been the kind thank-you's from students—frequently by email from colleges around the country—for the clarity of the presentation and for the one-on-one teacher–student focus of the writing.

Standing on the Shoulders of Giants

When I took the introductory economics course in college in the 1960s, I found the course and the textbook (Paul Samuelson's) fascinating. People called 1960s-vintage economics the "new economics," because many new ideas, including those put forth by John Maynard Keynes, were being applied for the first time in public policy. But during the 1970s, the 1980s, and the 1990s, economics underwent another tremendous wave of change. Now at the beginning of the 21st century, economics places much greater emphasis on incentives, expectations, long-run fundamentals, individual experiences, institutions, and the importance of stable, predictable economic policies. These new ideas are of great relevance to real-world economic policy and confirm to students that economic ideas do indeed affect people's lives.

I believe that this book has achieved the right mix of old and new. I know from experience that its "newness" and the knowledge that the ideas are actually used in practice make economics more interesting to students, thereby making learning economics easier.

Changes to the Fourth Edition

Many of this text's adopters have commented on how much they and their students enjoy reading the book and appreciate the graphs, real-world examples, and modern approach to economic policy. In the previous two revisions, I focused my efforts on streamlining and clarifying difficult concepts, expanding introductory chapter vignettes to be sure they clearly (and dramatically) motivated the ideas in each chapter, reviewing (and in some cases, revising) the flow of ideas both within chapters and from chapter to chapter, and adding interesting examples, many in the form of longer case studies that follow the flow of the chapters and help clarify difficult material just presented.

With many of the organizational and presentation challenges solved, this revision focuses on addressing specific points brought up by our reviewers and updating the content to reflect the latest trends in the world's economy. Several new case studies help illustrate key ideas and many new or revised chapter-opening vignettes keep the "drama" alive. In addition, many new examples of economic concepts appear in the "Economics in Action" and "Reading the News About . . ." boxes. In response to popular demand, the appendixes once again directly follow the chapters they supplement.

The world economy has changed radically in recent years. Following two back-to-back record-breaking expansions, the U.S. economy—the largest in the world—went into recession. The second and third largest economies in the world, Japan and Germany, are also facing an economic slowdown, making this a challenging time for the world economy. Yet, there are many reasons to be optimistic. Market economies are now the preferred choice of virtually all countries around the world. The two most populous countries of the world, India and China, have opened up their economies and are experiencing rapid economic growth. Billions of people are linked together through international trade in this "new economy." With these changes, economics is now more fascinating and more relevant than ever.

The strategy for revising the third edition was to give these changes a prominent, clearly explained place within the basic tradition of economics upon which they stand. Emphasis is placed on the central ideas of economics: that people make purposeful choices with scarce resources and interact with other people when they make these choices. There are also demonstrations showing how a market economy works and a thorough explanation of why markets are efficient when incentives are right and inefficient when incentives are wrong. Long-run fundamentals are given prominent attention along with real-world public policy issues where the short run matters, too.

Content Changes

A detailed account of the chapter-by-chapter changes in the text can be found in the Transition Guide available in the Instructor's Resource Manual or on the book's web site. Here are just a few highlights:

- The revised macroeconomics chapters improve on the new approach to teaching modern macroeconomics that was introduced with the first edition nearly ten years ago. That approach starts with long-run fundamentals about unemployment, economic growth, and the composition of spending. It stresses that the United States is part of the world economy. It shows how the Fed's decisions about the interest rate are intended both to keep inflation in control and to prevent or mitigate recessions. The recent recession has provided some interesting new data to explore in this regard, and key economic data have been updated throughout these chapters.

- Chapter 4, "Macroeconomics: The Big Picture," addresses the macroeconomic impact of September 11 and contains an expanded discussion of the role that macroeconomic policy (both fiscal and monetary) plays in the economy.

- In Chapter 6, the discussion of the impact of interest rate changes on consumption and investment has been clarified and now includes discussion of how to find the equilibrium interest rate using the spending allocation model.

- The section on Malthusian equilibrium found in Chapter 8, "Productivity and Economic Growth," has been streamlined, with a more prominent role given to the discussion of technology as a driver of economic growth. A new "Reading the News About . . ." box in this chapter focuses on the recent spurt in productivity growth.

- Chapter 9, "Money and Inflation," has been revised to illuminate the role that money plays in the economy; in addition, the notation in the section on the money multiplier has been clarified.

- Chapter 10, "The Nature and Causes of Economic Fluctuations," now includes discussion of the most recent business cycle, and coverage of the simple model where consumption and income are interrelated has been clarified.

- In Chapter 11, "The Economic Fluctuations Model", the structure of the model is presented so that it explicitly incorporates the real interest rate. The Fed's policy rule is presented in terms of the real interest rate being changed in response to changes in inflation. The text makes clear that the Fed does not directly control the real interest rate but instead manipulates the nominal interest rate to influence the real interest rate. The derivation of the real interest rule is explained using additional graphs. Finally, the "Reading the News About . . ." box was changed to reflect more recent policy decisions by the Fed.

- The case study in Chapter 12, "Using the Economic Fluctuations Model," now covers the recent recession, including an explanation of how the *AD-IA* model can be used to understand this recession.

- The introduction to Chapter 13, "Fiscal Policy," now focuses on the recent rapid reversal of the government's budget situation from deficit to surplus and back again. The "Reading the News About . . ." box in this chapter was changed to focus on the impact of the recession and tax cuts on budget balance. A brief discussion of the Economic Growth and Tax Relief Reconciliation Act of 2001 has also been added.

- The introduction to Chapter 14, "Monetary Policy," talks about the challenges that faced the Fed in 2002 and includes an updated discussion about Argentina in the section on the effects of fixed exchange rates on monetary policy. There is also a new "Reading the News About . . ." box about the economic situation in Argentina.

- The discussion of international trade in Chapter 18 has been updated to include current trade policies.

Enhanced Teaching and Learning Package for Students and Instructors

The array of teaching and learning aids provided with this text (and described below) has also been revised and contains several new options, including a **Student Technology Package**—automatically shrinkwrapped with most new texts. The Student Technology Package is comprised of a new, highly interactive Tutorial CD-ROM; access to SmarThinking™, a live online tutoring service with e-structors qualified in economics; and a print Technology Guide to help students integrate into their study schedules all the technology options available with the text.

For instructors, an instructor CD, HMClassPrep with HMTesting, includes computerized testing, PowerPoint slides, and instructor materials—providing in one place all the teaching resources and tools a principles instructor or teaching assistant might need.

A Brief Tour

Principles of Economics is designed for a one-term course. Recognizing that teachers use a great variety of sequences and syllabi, the text allows for alternative plans of coverage. International economic issues are considered throughout the text, with separate chapters on international economic policy.

The basic workings of markets and the reasons they improve people's lives are the subjects of Part One. Chapter 1 outlines the unifying themes of economics: scarcity, choice, and economic interaction. The role of prices, the inherent international aspect of economics, the importance of property rights and incentives, and the difference between central planning and markets are some of the key ideas in this chapter. Chapter 2 introduces the field of economics through a case study showing how economists observe and explain economic puzzles. Chapter 3 covers the basic supply and demand model and introduces elasticity. The goal of these chapters is to show how to use the supply and demand model and to learn to "think like an economist."

The study of macroeconomics begins with Chapter 4. This chapter is an overview of the facts emphasizing that macroeconomics is concerned with the growth and fluctuations in the economy as a whole. Chapter 5 shows how GDP and other variables are measured.

Chapter 6 starts with the first macro model to determine the long-run shares of GDP. Chapter 7 gives an analysis of how the level of unemployment in the economy as a whole is determined. Labor, capital, and technology are then presented in Chapter 8 as the fundamental determinants of the economy's growth path. One clear advantage of this approach is that it allows students to focus first on issues about which there is general agreement among economists. Moreover, this ordering helps students better understand short-term economic fluctuations. Similarly, the long-run treatment of money, presented in Chapter 9, sets the stage for economic fluctuations.

As shown in Part Three (Chapters 10 through 15), the economy does fluctuate as it grows over time. Declines in production and increases in unemployment (characteristics of recessions) have not vanished from the landscape as long-term growth issues have come to the fore. Part Three delves into the causes of these fluctuations and proposes an analysis of why they end. It begins by explaining why shifts in aggregate demand may cause the economy to fluctuate and ends by showing that price adjustment plays a significant role in the end of recessions.

Countries have tried a variety of approaches to deal with economic growth and economic fluctuations. Part Four examines these approaches to policy, about which there are many differing opinions. Areas of agreement are also stressed.

Pedagogical Features

The following pedagogical features are designed to help students learn economics.

Examples within the text. Illustrations of real-world situations help explain economic ideas and models. A wide variety of these examples are included throughout the text. Examples include the health care case study in Chapter 2, an exploration of unemployment among young people around the world in Chapter 7, and a case study examining the recent recession in Chapter 12. Many other examples are simply woven into the text.

Boxed examples to give real-life perspectives. "Reading the News About . . ." boxes explain how to decipher recent news stories about economic policy and in this edition include a look at the recent spurt in productivity growth and Argentina's current economic situation. "Economics in Action" boxes examine the contributions of the great economists, such as Adam Smith, or notable current events, such as the macroeconomic impact of the September 11th attacks.

Stimulating vignettes at the beginning of each chapter. Examples of opening vignettes include the opportunity costs of college for Tiger Woods in Chapter 1, the work of health-care economist Mark McClellan in Chapter 2, and finding a job in 2003 in Chapter 7.

Functional use of full color. Color is used to distinguish between curves and to show how the curves shift dynamically over time. An example of the effective use of multiple colors can be found in the equilibrium price and equilibrium quantity figure in Chapter 3 (Figure 3.8).

Complete captions and small conversation boxes in graphs. The captions and small yellow-shaded conversation boxes make many of the figures completely self-contained. In some graphs, sequential numbering of these conversation boxes stresses the dynamic nature of the curves. Again, Figure 3.8 provides a good example.

Conversation boxes in text margins. These appear where an additional explanation or reminder might help students more easily grasp a new concept.

Use of photos and cartoons to illustrate abstract ideas. Special care has gone into the search for and selection of photos and cartoons to illustrate difficult economic ideas such as inelastic supply curves or opportunity costs. Each text photo (many consisting of two or three parts) has a short title and caption to explain its relevance to the text discussion.

Key term definitions. Definitions of key terms appear in the margins and in the alphabetized glossary at the end of the book. The key terms are listed at the end of every chapter and appendix.

Brief reviews at the end of each major section. About four per chapter, these reviews summarize the key points in abbreviated form as the chapter evolves; they are useful for preliminary skim reading as well as for review.

Questions for review at the end of every chapter. These are tests of recall and require only short answers; they can be used for oral review or as a quick self-check.

Problems. An essential tool in learning economics, the problems have been carefully selected, revised, and tested for this edition. An ample supply of these appear at the end of every chapter and appendix. Some of the problems ask the reader to work out examples that are slightly different from the ones in the text; others require a more critical thinking approach. A second set of problems parallels those in the text and is included in the accompanying test bank and on the instructor's HMClassPrep with HMTesting CD. This problem set is also available to instructors via the web site.

A Complete Package of Teaching and Learning Aids

The highly effective teaching and learning package prepared to accompany this text has been completely revised, updated, and expanded. It provides a full range of support for students and instructors.

Student Technology Package. This package is available with all new texts and is also available for sale separately. The package includes:

- **Tutorial and Simulation Software.** A brand-new, interactive computerized tutorial parallels the content in the fourth edition and provides a unique way for students to review basic concepts covered in the text. Interacting directly with the graphs relevant to each chapter, students can observe how changes affect curves and test themselves on what they've learned. A glossary and context-sensitive help are always at students' fingertips. The simulation component of the software includes more than 60 years of data on more than 20 key economic indicators. The software allows students to plot data, compare various measurement instruments in table or graph form, and print out their results.

- **SmarThinking™ Online Tutoring Service.** A live tutoring service allows students to interact online with an experienced SmarThinking e-structor (online tutor) between 9:00 P.M and 1:00 A.M. EST every Sunday through Thursday. SmarThinking provides state-of-the-art communication tools, such as chat technology and virtual whiteboards designed for easy rendering of economic formulas and graphs, to help students absorb key concepts and learn to think economically.
- **Student Technology Guide.** A printed guide to all available resources.

Principles of Macroeconomics Study Guide. Revised and updated by David Papell of the University of Houston and Wm. Stewart Mounts, Jr. of Mercer University, this study guide provides a wonderful learning opportunity that many students will value. Each chapter contains an overview, informal chapter review, and a section called "Zeroing In," which harnesses students' intuition to explain the chapter's most important concepts. The study guide also provides ample means for practice in using the economic ideas and graphs introduced in each text chapter and suit a variety of learning needs through graph-based questions and problems as well as multiple-choice practice tests. A section called "Working it Out" provides worked problems that take the student step by step through the analytical process needed to solve real-world applications of core concepts covered in the chapter. These are followed by practice problems that require students to use the same analytical tools on their own. Detailed answers are provided for all review and practice questions. End-of-part quizzes offer students yet another chance to test their retention of material before taking in-class exams.

Web Site (http://college.hmco.com/ ; select "economics"). The Taylor *Economics* web site provides an extended learning environment for students and a rich store of teaching resources for instructors who are using the text. Materials are carefully developed to complement and supplement each chapter. The student will find key economic links as well as numerous opportunities to test their mastery of chapter content—including both objective-type quizzes and more extended web-based assignments developed by John Kane of SUNY, Oswego. Instructors will find an additional set of guided web activities that relate to the key concepts of each chapter of the textbook. Prepared by John S. Min of Northern Virginia Community College, the Economics W.I.R.E.D. web links are accompanied by brief suggestions to the instructor regarding their use in the classroom as well as discussion questions or exercises for assessing student learning. In addition, the instructor web site contains a complete set of parallel questions (and solutions) matching the end-of-chapter problems from the text.

Principles of Macroeconomics Test Bank. A reliable test bank is the most important resource for efficient and effective teaching and learning. The test bank to accompany this text was prepared by Jim Lee of Texas A & M, Corpus Christi and Stuart Glosser of The University of Wisconsin—Whitewater. It contains more than 3,000 test questions—including multiple choice, true/false, short answer, and problems—many of which are based on graphs. The questions are coded for correct answer, question type, level of difficulty, and text topic. The test bank also includes a set of parallel problems that match the end-of-chapter problems from the text and are conveniently available in both printed and computerized form.

Instructor's Resource Manual. Prepared and revised by Wm. Stewart Mounts, Jr. of Mercer University and Sarah Culver of the University of Alabama at Birmingham, the Instructor's Resource Manual provides both first-time and experienced instructors with a variety of additional resources for use with the text. Each chapter contains a brief overview, teaching objectives, key terms from the text, a section that orients instructors to the text's unique approach, and a suggested lecture outline with teaching tips that provide additional examples not found in the text as well as hints for teaching more difficult material. Discussion topics and solutions to end-of-chapter text problems are also provided.

PowerPoint Slides. A complete set of downloadable PowerPoint slides is available to adopters of the text on the fourth edition web site. To gain access to the web site's instructor resources, obtain a user name and password from your Houghton Mifflin sales representative. The slides will also be available to adopters of the fourth edition on the HMClassPrep with HMTesting CD-ROM.

HMClassPrep with HMTesting CD-ROM. Organized by chapter for easy reference and class planning, this all-in-one instructor CD contains a wealth of resources, including lecture outlines, teaching objectives and tips, solutions to text problems, a set of parallel problems and solutions, video footage, and in-class experiment and discussion ideas. PowerPoint slides for most of the figures in the text are also contained on this CD, as are *all the questions* found in the two test banks. Using the sophisticated and user-friendly HMTesting program, instructors can quickly create tests according to various selection criteria, including random selection. The program prints graphs and tables in addition to the text part of each question. Instructors can scramble the questions and answer choices, edit questions, add their own questions to the pool, and customize their exams in various other ways. HMTesting provides a complete testing solution, including classroom administration and online testing features in addition to test generation. The program is available in Windows and Mac versions.

Overhead Transparencies. Overhead transparencies for key figures from the text are available to adopters of *Economics, Principles of Microeconomics,* and *Principles of Macroeconomics.* I usually use two overhead projectors in class so that more than one figure or table can be shown simultaneously.

Experimental Economics Lab Manual. Instructors who would like to incorporate experiments into their classroom teaching should request a copy of the experiments manual prepared by Greg Delemeester of Marietta College and John Neral of Frostburg State University. Written for instructors who are both new to and experienced in the use of experiments in class, this manual provides detailed instructor support, including an overview of the experiment and its purpose, necessary materials, step-by-step instructions for conducting the experiment, and any relevant worksheets.

WebCT WebCourselet and Blackboard Course Cartridge. These resources provide text-specific student study aids in customizable, Internet-based education platforms. Both platforms provide a full array of content delivery and course management features for instructors who wish to incorporate educational technology in their traditional classrooms or for those who are creating distance-learning courses.

Acknowledgments

Completing a project like this is a team effort. I have always been fortunate to work with some very talented economists at Stanford—colleagues and students—who have provided me with many ideas and feedback through every edition. But in the case of the fourth edition, I acknowledge with very special gratitude the substantial contributions of two of my former graduate students, Marcelo Clerici-Arias and Akila Weerapana. Both Marcelo and Akila have become extraordinary educators in their own right. Marcelo helped in the creation and management of the Introductory Economics Center at Stanford University, where he served as associate director for several years. He is currently the Associate Director for Social Sciences and Technology at Stanford's Center for Teaching and Learning and regularly teaches undergraduate courses in the economics department. Marcelo has been involved in this book from its very beginning—both as a sounding board and as an experienced teacher.

Akila Weerapana demonstrated his extraordinary research and teaching skills even before completing his Ph.D. at Stanford. He provided an enormous amount of useful feedback on this book. After receiving his Ph.D., Akila joined the faculty at Wellesley College, where he has taught the principles course over many semesters and further established his reputation for teaching excellence. Akila and Marcelo have both played essential roles in the completion of this fourth edition, including researching new data, writing up new examples and other material, and making critical decisions about topics they felt needed more attention.

Many college teachers have taken the time to write with questions or comments about the text and ideas for improvement that have come from their own teaching. In particular, I would like to mention John Constantine, University of California at Davis, who was extremely generous in providing his thoughts on improving material in several macro chapters. I would also like to especially mention the in-depth reviews received from Laurie J. Bates, Bryant College; Mark L. Burkey, North Carolina A&T State University; Chiuping Chen, American River College; Eric D. Craft, University of Richmond; Gregory Green, Idaho State University; Murat F. Iyigun, University of Colorado, Boulder; Bridget Lyons, Sacred Heart University; A. Cristina Cunha Parsons, Trinity College, Washington D.C.; Robert J. Rossana, Wayne State University; Sarah L. Stafford, College of William and Mary; and Shaianne T.O. Warner, Ithaca College. These instructors provided comments and suggestions that were critical to the development of the fourth edition. I would also like to thank Jim Lee, Texas A&M University, who reviewed the text for accuracy.

I am grateful to the authors of the fourth edition supplements, including Wm. Stewart Mounts, Jr., Sarah Culver, David Papell, Cliff Sowell, Jim Lee, and Stuart Glosser. Their careful attention to text changes both small and large has resulted in ancillaries that match the text in content and spirit.

I am grateful to the excellent team of professionals at Houghton Mifflin working on this fourth edition, including Ann West, Paula Kmetz, and Tonya Lobato. I am grateful to them for their help and encouragement. I would also like to thank Priscilla Bailey, Nancy Doherty-Schmitt, Andy Fisher, Charline Lake, Carol Merrigan, Henry Rachlin, Elizabeth Santiago, and Jean Woy for their many contributions to this project.

Reviewers

This book would not exist without the help of all the reviewers and readers who have provided suggestions incorporated into each revision.

Mark D. Agee
Pennsylvania State University, Altoona

James Alm
University of Colorado at Boulder

Lee J. Alston
University of Illinois

Christine Amsler
Michigan State University

Lisa Anderson
College of William and Mary

Dean Baim
Pepperdine University

R. J. Ballman, Jr.
Augustana College

Raymond S. Barnstone
Northeastern University and Lesley College

Laurie J. Bates
Bryant College

Kari Battaglia
University of North Texas

Klaus G. Becker
Texas Tech University

Valerie R. Bencivenga
Cornell University

Sidney M. Blummer
California Polytechnic University

William M. Boal
Drake University

Roger Bowles
University of Bath

Paula Bracy
University of Toledo

Jozell Brister
Abilene Christian University

Robert Brown
Texas Technical University

Robert Buchele
Smith College

Mark L. Burkey
North Carolina A&T State University

Michael R. Butler
Texas Christian University

Richard Call
American River College

Leonard Carlson
Emory University

Michael J. Carter
University of Massachusetts, Lowell

William E. Chapel
University of Mississippi

Chiuping Chen
American River College

Kenneth Chinn
Southeastern Oklahoma State University

Stephen L. Cobb
University of North Texas

Mike Cohick
Collin County Community College

Kathy L. Combs
California State University, Los Angeles

Joyce Cooper
Boston University

Eric D. Craft
University of Richmond

Steven Craig
University of Houston

Sarah Culver
University of Alabama, Birmingham

Ward S. Curran
Trinity College

Joseph Daniels
Marquette University

Audrey Davidson
University of Louisville

Gregg Davis
Marshall University

Gregory E. DeFreitas
Hofstra University

David N. DeJong
University of Pittsburgh

David Denslow
University of Florida

Enrica Detragiache
Johns Hopkins University

Michael Devereux
University of British Columbia

Michael Dowd
University of Toledo

Douglas Downing
Seattle Pacific University

Dean Dudley
United States Military Academy

Mary E. Edwards
St. Cloud State University

Ken Farr
Georgia College

David Figlio
University of Oregon

Gerald Friedman
University of Massachusetts, Amherst

Edwin T. Fujii
University of Hawaii

Charles Geiss
University of Missouri

Janet Gerson
University of Michigan

J. Robert Gillette
University of Kentucky

Donna Ginther
Southern Methodist College

Mark Glick
University of Utah

Stuart M. Glosser
University of Wisconsin, Whitewater

Phil Graves
University of Colorado, Boulder

Gregory Green
Idaho State University

Paul W. Grimes
Mississippi State University

Lorna S. Gross
Worcester State College

Shoshana Grossbard-Shechtman
San Diego State University

Robin Hahnel
American University

Alan Haight
Bowling Green State University

David R. Hakes
University of Northern Iowa

Greg Hamilton
Marist College

David Hansen
Linfield College

Mehdi Haririan
Bloomsburg University

Richard Harper
University of West Florida

Mitchell Harwitz
State University of New York, Buffalo

Mary Ann Hendryson
Western Washington University

James B. Herendeen
University of Texas, El Paso

Pershing J. Hill
University of Alaska, Anchorage

Denise Hixson
Midlands Technical College

Gail Mitchell Hoyt
University of Richmond

Jim Hvidding
Kutztown University

Beth Ingram
University of Iowa

Murat F. Iyigun
University of Colorado, Boulder

Joyce Jacobsen
Wesleyan University

Syed Jafri
Tarleton State University

David Jaques
California Polytech University, Pomona

Allan Jenkins
University of Nebraska

David Johnson
Wilfred Laurier University

Charles W. Johnston
University of Michigan, Flint

Nake Kamrany
University of Southern California

John Kane
State University of New York, Oswego

Manfred Keil
Claremont McKenna College

Kristen Keith
University of Alaska

Elizabeth Kelly
University of Wisconsin—Madison

John Klein
Georgia State University

Harry T. Kolendrianos
Danville Community College

Margaret Landman
Bridgewater State College

Philip J. Lane
Fairfield University

William Lang
Rutgers University

William D. Lastrapes
University of Georgia

Jim Lee
Texas A & M University

Lawrence A. Leger
Loughborough University

David Li
University of Michigan

Susan Linz
Michigan State University

John K. Lodewijks
University of New South Wales

R. Ashley Lyman
University of Idaho

Bridget Lyons
Sacred Heart University

Craig MacPhee
University of Nebraska, Lincoln

Michael Magura
University of Toledo

Robert A. Margo
Vanderbilt University

John D. Mason
Gordon College

Robert McAuliffe
Babson College

Henry N. McCarl
University of Alabama, Birmingham

Laurence C. McCulloch
Ohio State University

Rob Roy McGregor
University of North Carolina, Charlotte

Richard McIntyre
University of Rhode Island

Mark McLeod
Virginia Tech

Gaminie Meepagala
Howard University

Micke Meurs
American University

Khan A. Mohabbat
Northern Illinois University

Douglas W. Morgan
University of California, Santa Barbara

Norma Morgan
Curry College

Peter Morgan
*State University of New York
at Buffalo*

Wm. Stewart Mounts, Jr.
Mercer University

Vai-Lam Mui
University of Southern California

David C. Murphy
Boston College

Andrew Narwold
University of San Diego

Ronald C. Necoechea
Ball State University

Rebecca Neumann
University of Colorado at Boulder

Hong V. Nguyen
University of Scranton

Lou Noyd
Northern Kentucky University

Rachel Nugent
Pacific Lutheran University

Anthony Patrick O'Brien
Lehigh University

William C. O'Connor
Western Montana College

Eliot S. Orton
New Mexico State University

Jan Palmer
Ohio University

David Papell
University of Houston

Walter Park
American University

Charles Parker
Wayne State College

A. Cristina Cunha Parsons
Trinity College, Washington D.C.

James Payne
Eastern Kentucky University

David Petersen
American River College, Sacramento

E. Charles Pflanz
Scottsdale Community College

William A. Phillips
University of Southern Maine

Charles Plott
California Institute of Technology

Lidija Polutnik
Babson College

David L. Prychitko
State University of New York, Oswego

Salim Rashid
*University of Illinois,
Urbana-Champaign*

Margaret A. Ray
Mary Washington College

Geoffrey Renshaw
University of Warwick

John Ridpath
York University

Greg Rose
Sacramento City College

B. Peter Rosendorff
University of Southern California

Robert J. Rossana
Wayne State University

Marina Rosser
James Madison University

Kartic C. Roy
University of Queensland

Daniel Rubenson
Southern Oregon State College

Jeffrey Rubin
Rutgers University

Robert S. Rycroft
Mary Washington College

Jonathan Sandy
University of San Diego

Gary Saxonhouse
University of Michigan

Edward Scahill
University of Scranton

James Byron Schlomach
Texas A&M University

Torsten Schmidt
University of New Hampshire

Thomas J. Shea
Springfield College

William J. Simeone
Providence College

Michael Smitka
Washington & Lee University

Ronald Soligo
Rice University

John L. Solow
University of Iowa

Clifford Sowell
Berea College

Michael Spagat
Brown University

David Spencer
Brigham Young University

Sarah L. Stafford
College of William and Mary

J. R. Stanfield
Colorado State University

Ann B. Sternlicht
University of Richmond

Richard Stevenson
Liverpool University

James Stodder
Rensselaer Polytechnic Institute

Leslie S. Stratton
University of Arizona

Robert Stuart
Rutgers University

Dave Surdam
Loyola University, Chicago

James Swoffard
University of South Alabama

Bette Lewis Tokar
Holy Family College

Paul Turner
University of Leeds

Lee J. Vanscyoc
University of Wisconsin, Oshkosh

Gerald R. Visgilio
Connecticut College

Manhar Vyas
University of Pittsburgh

Shaianne T.O. Warner
Ithaca College

William V. Weber
Eastern Illinois University

Akila Weerapana
Wellesley College

Karl Wesolowski
Salem State College

Joseph Wesson
State University of New York, Potsdam

Geoff Whittam
University of Glasgow

Kenneth P. Wickman
State University of New York, Cortland

Catherine Winnett
University of Bath

Jennifer P. Wissink
Cornell University

Simon Wren-Lewis
University of Strathclyde

Peter R. Wyman
Spokane Falls Community College

Yung Y. Yang
California State University, Sacramento

Introduction to Economics

CHAPTER 1

The Central Idea

This is a true story. In the spring of 1996, a 19-year-old college sophomore, who had just finished taking introductory economics, was faced with a *choice*: to continue college for an additional two years or to devote full time to a job. The job was being a professional golfer on the Pro Tour—a job for which the sophomore was uniquely qualified, having won three U.S. amateur titles. Doing both college and the Pro Tour was not an option because time is *scarce*: With only 24 hours in the day, he simply did not have time to do both. For this sophomore, completing college had a great cost: not only the two years of college expenses, but also the forgone tournament winnings and advertising endorsements that a successful pro golf career would bring. The golfer—his name is Tiger Woods—made a choice. He became a pro. By the fall of 1996 he was selected Sportsman of the Year by *Sports Illustrated*. In 1997 he stunned the golfing world with a record-setting win of the venerable Masters Tournament, and with his second Masters victory in 2001, Woods became the first player to hold all major championships at the same time. By 2001 Tiger Woods had earned over $25 million in prizes, and much more in advertising.

Tiger Woods would not have had the same opportunity had he not been able to *interact with people*. Golf fans who enjoyed watching him play golf interacted with him: They paid to see him play. Executives who ran companies like Nike and American Express interacted with him: They paid him for his endorsement. And Tiger's family, teachers, and friends interacted with him: They conveyed basic skills, enhanced his confidence, and helped him remain cool under pressure. Tiger gained from these interactions with people—and the people gained, too.

This true story illustrates the idea that lies at the center of economics: that people make *purposeful choices* with *scarce* resources, and *interact* with other

economics: the study of how people deal with scarcity.

scarcity: the situation in which the quantity of resources is insufficient to meet all wants.

choice: a selection among alternative goods, services, or actions.

economic interaction: exchanges of goods and services between people.

market: an arrangement by which economic exchanges between people take place.

The choice was to continue college or join the pro tour. What would you have done?

people when they make these choices. More than anything else, **economics** is the study of how people deal with scarcity.

Scarcity is a situation in which people's resources are limited. People always face a scarcity of something—frequently, as in Tiger Woods' case, time. Scarcity implies that people must make a **choice** to forgo, or give up, one thing in favor of another: to work full-time or go to school, to take economics or biology this term, to work or stay at home with the children.

Economic interaction between people occurs every time they trade or exchange goods or services with each other. For example, a college student buys education services from a college in exchange for tuition. A teenager sells labor services to Taco Bell in exchange for cash. Within a family, one spouse may agree to cook every day in exchange for the other spouse's doing the dishes every day.

As these examples indicate, economic interactions can occur either within an *organization* or *group*, such as a family, or in a *market*. A **market** is simply an arrangement by which buyers and sellers can interact and exchange goods and services with each other. Examples of interactions in markets are the buying and selling of a college education and the buying and selling of the labor services of Taco Bell workers. There are many, many other markets, from the New York stock market to a local flea market.

The purpose of this book is to introduce you to the field of economics and to help you understand the economic challenges and opportunities you face as an individual in the economy. The goal is not to peek passively at economics but to learn to think like an economist.

The first step toward this goal is for you to get an intuitive feel for how pervasive scarcity, choice, and economic interaction are in the real world—and to learn some of the powerful implications of this basic fact of economic life. That is the purpose of this chapter.

Scarcity and Choice for Individuals

It is easy to find everyday examples of how people make purposeful choices when they are confronted with a scarcity of time or resources. A choice that may be on your mind when you study economics is how much time to spend on it versus other activities. If you spend all your time on economics, you may get 100 on the final exam, but that might mean you get a zero in biology. If you spend all your time on biology, then you may get 100 in biology and a zero in economics. Most people resolve the choice by *balancing* out their time to get a decent grade in both subjects.

ECONOMICS IN ACTION

Gains from Trade on the Internet

The Internet has created many new opportunities for gains from trade. Internet auction sites like eBay allow sellers a way to offer their goods for sale and buyers a way to make bids on sale items. The gains are similar to those of Maria and Adam as they trade sunglasses for hats. Hundreds of different types of sunglasses and baseball hats (and millions of other things) can be bought and sold on eBay—5,566 types of sunglasses and 913 types of baseball hats were for sale at last count.

If you—like Maria—want to sell a pair of sunglasses and buy a hat, you can simply go to *www.ebay.com*, offer a pair of sunglasses to sell, and search for the hat you would like to buy. The computer screen will show photos of some of the sunglasses and baseball hats offered.

Whereas many Internet-related businesses started in the mid-1990s have contracted or disappeared completely in the tech implosion of recent years, eBay has remained hugely successful—perhaps because it is so simple. It provides information and a means of communicating transactions—a sort of virtual flea market. Today there are nearly 50 million registered users, with millions of sales transacted in a single day.

How well do you think the simple example of Maria and Adam illustrates the real-world gains from trade by people using eBay to buy and sell things?

The founder (left) and the chief executive (right) of eBay offer new ways to gain from trade.

If you are premed, then biology will probably get more time. If you are interested in business, then more time on economics might be appropriate.

Now let us apply this basic principle to two fundamental economic problems: individual choices about what to *consume* and *produce*. For each type of economic problem, we first show how scarcity forces one to make a choice, then show how people gain from interacting with other people.

Consumer Decisions

Consider Maria, who is going for a hike in a park on a sunny day. Maria would love to wear a hat (baseball style with her school logo) and sunglasses on the hike, but she has brought neither with her. Maria has brought $20 with her, however, and there is a store in the park that is having a "two for one" sale. She can buy two hats for $20 or two pairs of sunglasses for $20. Her scarcity of funds causes her to make a choice. The $20 limit on her spending is an example of a *budget constraint*, because she is limited to spending no more than this amount. Her choice will depend on her tastes. Let us assume that when she is forced by scarcity to make a choice, she will choose the sunglasses. She would prefer to buy one hat and one pair of sunglasses, but that is not possible.

■ **Opportunity Cost.** Maria's decision is an example of an economic problem that all people face: A budget constraint forces them to make a choice between dif-

opportunity cost: the value of the next-best forgone alternative that was not chosen because something else was chosen.

ferent items that they want. Such choices create opportunity costs. The **opportunity cost** of a choice is the value of the forgone alternative that was not chosen. The opportunity cost of the hats is the loss from not being able to wear the sunglasses. An opportunity cost occurs every time there is a choice. For example, the opportunity cost of going to an 8 A.M. class rather than sleeping in is the sleep you lose when you get up early. The opportunity cost of Tiger Woods's staying in college was millions of dollars in prize money.

In many cases involving choice and scarcity, there are many more than two things to choose from. If you choose vanilla ice cream out of a list of many possible flavors, then the opportunity cost is the loss from not being able to consume the *next-best* flavor, perhaps strawberry. In general, when there are more than two items, the opportunity cost is the value of the next best alternative.

Now, suppose Maria is not the only hiker. Also in the park is Adam, who also has $20 to spend. Adam also loves both hats and sunglasses, but he likes hats more than sunglasses. When forced to make a choice, he buys the hats. His decision is shaped by scarcity just as Maria's is: Scarcity comes from the budget constraint; he must make a choice, and there is an opportunity cost for each choice.

gains from trade: improvements in income, production, or satisfaction owing to the exchange of goods or services.

■ **Gains from Trade: A Better Allocation.** Now suppose that Adam and Maria meet each other in the park. Let's consider the possibility of economic interaction between them. Maria has two pairs of sunglasses and Adam has two hats, so Maria and Adam can trade with each other. Maria can trade one of her pairs of sunglasses for one of Adam's hats, as shown in Figure 1.1. Through such a trade, both Maria and Adam can improve their situation. There are **gains from trade** because the trade reallocates goods between the two individuals in a way they both prefer. Trade occurs because Maria is willing to exchange one pair of sunglasses for one hat, and Adam is willing to exchange one hat for one pair of sunglasses. Because trade is mutually advantageous for both Maria and Adam, they will voluntarily engage in it if they are able to. In fact, if they do not gain from the trade, then neither will bother to make the trade.

This trade is an example of an economic interaction in which a reallocation of goods through trade makes both people better off. There is no change in the total quantity of goods produced. The number of hats and sunglasses has remained the same. Trade simply reallocates existing goods.

The trade between Maria and Adam is typical of many economic interactions we will study in this book. Thinking like an economist in this example means recognizing that a voluntary exchange of goods between people must make them better off. Many economic exchanges are like this, even though they are more complicated than the exchange of hats and sunglasses.

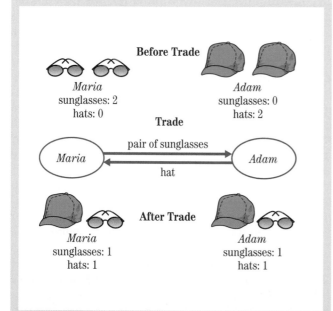

Figure 1.1
Gains from Trade Through a Better Allocation of Goods
Without trade, Maria has more pairs of sunglasses than she would like, and Adam has more hats than he would like. By trading a hat for a pair of sunglasses, they both gain.

Producer Decisions

Now consider two producers—Emily, a poet, and Johann, a printer. Both face scarcity and must make choices. Because of differences in training, abilities, or inclination, Emily is much better at writing poetry than Johann, but Johann is much better at printing greeting cards than Emily. Suppose that Emily and Johann cannot interact with each other (perhaps they live on different islands and cannot communicate).

If Emily writes poetry full time, she can produce 10 poems in a day; but if she wants to make and sell greeting cards with her poems in them, she must spend some time printing cards and thereby spend less time writing poems. However, Emily is not very good at printing cards; it takes her so much time to do so that if she prints one card, she has time to write only 1 poem rather than 10 poems during the day.

If Johann prints full time, he can produce 10 different greeting cards in a day. However, if he wants to sell greeting cards, he must write poems to put inside them. Johann is so poor at writing poems that if he writes only 1 poem a day, his production of greeting cards drops from 10 to 1 per day.

Following is a summary of the choices Emily and Johann face because of a scarcity of time and resources.

	Emily, the Poet		Johann, the Printer	
	Write Full Time	*Write and Print*	*Print Full Time*	*Write and Print*
Cards	0	1	10	1
Poems	10	1	0	1

If Emily and Johann cannot interact, then each can produce only 1 greeting card with a poem on the inside in a day. Alternatively, Emily could produce 10 poems without the cards and Johann could produce 10 cards without the poems, but then neither would earn anything. We therefore assume that when confronted with this choice, both Emily and Johann will each choose to produce 1 greeting card with a poem inside. In total, they produce 2 greeting cards.

■ **Gains from Trade: Greater Production.**   Now consider the possibility of economic interaction. Suppose that Emily and Johann can trade. Johann could sell his printing services to Emily, agreeing to print her poems on nice greeting cards. Then Emily could sell the greeting cards to people. Under this arrangement, Emily could spend all day writing poetry, and Johann could spend all day printing. In total, they could produce 10 different greeting cards together, expending the same time and effort it took to produce 2 greeting cards when they could not trade.

Note that in this example the interaction took place in a market: Johann sold his print jobs to Emily. Another approach would be for Emily and Johann to go into business together, forming a firm, Dickinson and Gutenberg Greetings, Inc. Then their economic interaction would occur within the firm, without buying or selling in the market.

Whether in a market or within a firm, the gains from trade in this example are huge. By trading, Emily and Johann can increase their production of greeting cards by five times, from 2 cards to 10 cards.

■ **Specialization, Division of Labor, and Comparative Advantage.**   This example illustrates another way in which economic interaction improves people's lives. Economic interaction allows for *specialization*: people concentrating on what they are good at. Emily specializes in poetry, and Johann specializes in printing. The specialization creates a division of labor. A **division of labor** occurs when some workers specialize in one task while others specialize in another task. They divide the overall production into parts, with some workers concentrating on one part (printing) and other workers concentrating on another part (writing).

division of labor: the division of production into various parts in which different groups of workers specialize.

comparative advantage: a situation in which a person or group can produce one good at a lower opportunity cost than another person or group.

The poetry/printing example of Emily and Johann also illustrates another economic concept, **comparative advantage.** In general, a person or group of people has a comparative advantage in producing one good relative to another good if that person or group can produce that good with comparatively less time, effort, or resources than another person or group can produce that good. For example, compared with Johann, Emily has a comparative advantage in writing relative to printing. And compared with Emily, Johann has a comparative advantage in printing relative to writing. As this example shows, production can be increased if people specialize in the skill in which they have a comparative advantage[1]—that is, if Emily specializes in writing and Johann in printing.

International Trade

international trade: the exchange of goods and services between people or firms in different nations.

Thus far, we have said nothing about where Emily and Johann live or work. They could reside in the same country, but they could also reside in different countries. Emily could live in the United States; Johann, in Germany. If this is so, when Emily purchases Johann's printing service, **international trade** will take place because the trade is between people in two different countries. Similarly, Maria could live in Detroit, Michigan, and Adam in Windsor, Ontario. If this is so, their trade will also be international.

The gains from international trade are thus of the same kind as the gains from trade within a country. By trading, people can better satisfy their preferences for goods (as in the case of Maria and Adam), or they can better utilize their comparative advantage (as in the case of Emily and Johann). In either situation, there is a gain to both participants from trade.

REVIEW

- All individuals face scarcity in one form or another. Scarcity forces people to make choices. When there is choice, there is also an opportunity cost of not doing one thing because another thing has been chosen.

- People benefit from economic interactions—trading goods and services— with other people.

- Gains from trade occur because goods and services can be allocated in ways that are more satisfactory to people.

- Gains from trade also occur because trade permits specialization through the division of labor. People should specialize in the production of goods in which they have a comparative advantage.

Scarcity and Choice for the Economy as a Whole

Just as individuals face scarcity and choice, so does the economy as a whole. The total amount of resources in an economy—workers, land, machinery, factories—is limited. Thus, the economy cannot produce all the health care, crime prevention, education, or entertainment that people want. A choice must be made. Let us first

---

1. Other examples are explored in the chapter "The Gains from International Trade," where you can see that comparative advantage can also occur when one person is absolutely better at both activities.

consider how to represent scarcity and choice in the whole economy and then consider alternative ways to make the choices.

Production Possibilities

Table 1.1
Production Possibilities

	Movies	Computers
A	0	25,000
B	100	24,000
C	200	22,000
D	300	18,000
E	400	13,000
F	500	0

production possibilities:
alternative combinations of production of various goods that are possible, given the economy's resources.

To simplify things, let us suppose that production in the economy can be divided into two broad categories. Suppose the economy can produce either computers (mainframes, PCs, hand calculators) or movies (thrillers, love stories, mysteries, musicals). The choice between computers and movies is symbolic of one of the most fundamental choices individuals in any society must face: how much to invest in order to produce more or better goods in the future versus how much to consume in the present. Computers help people produce more or better goods. Movies are a form of consumption. Other pairs of goods could also be used in our example. Another popular example is guns versus butter, representing defense goods versus nondefense goods.

With a scarcity of resources such as labor and capital, there is a choice between producing some goods, such as computers, versus other goods, such as movies. If the economy produces more of one, then it must produce less of the other. Table 1.1 gives an example of the alternative choices, or the **production possibilities,** for computers and movies. Observe that there are six different choices, some with more computers and fewer movies, others with fewer computers and more movies.

Table 1.1 tells us what happens as available resources in the economy are moved from movie production to computer production or vice versa. If resources move from producing movies to producing computers, then fewer movies are produced. For example, if all resources are used to produce computers, then 25,000 computers and zero movies can be produced, according to the table. If all resources are used to produce movies, then no computers can be produced. These are two extremes, of course. If 100 movies are produced, then we produce 24,000 computers rather than 25,000 computers. If 200 movies are produced, then computer production must fall to 22,000.

Increasing Opportunity Costs

The production possibilities in Table 1.1 illustrate the concept of opportunity cost for the economy as a whole. The opportunity cost of producing more movies is the value of the forgone computers. For example, the opportunity cost of producing 200 movies rather than 100 movies is 2,000 computers.

An important economic idea about opportunity costs is demonstrated in Table 1.1. Observe that movie production increases as we move down the table. As we move from row to row, movie production increases by the same number: 100 movies. The decline in computer production between the first and second rows—from 25,000 to 24,000 computers—is 1,000 computers. The decline between the second and third rows—from 24,000 to 22,000 computers—is 2,000 computers. Thus, the decline in computer production gets greater as we produce more movies. As we move from 400 movies to 500 movies, we lose 13,000 computers. In other words, the opportunity cost, in terms of computers, of producing more movies increases as we produce more movies. Each extra movie requires a loss of more and more computers. What we have just described is called **increasing opportunity costs,** with emphasis on the word *increasing*.

increasing opportunity cost:
a situation in which producing more of one good requires giving up an increasing amount of production of another good.

Why do opportunity costs increase? You can think about it in the following way. Some of the available resources are better suited for movie production than for computer production, and vice versa. Workers who are good at building computers might

Teaching Jobs and Graduate School Applications— Two Sides of the Same Coin

Dozens of new teachers join schools in Silicon Valley, California. Applications to MBA programs at Chicago and MIT soar. Do these two seemingly unrelated events have anything in common? Actually, they do. Behind them we find the same economic phenomenon at work: opportunity costs.

For years, California and other parts of the United States have experienced teacher shortages. During the economic boom of the 1990s, college graduates who might have been interested in teaching had better-paying alternatives in the private sector. In 2000, a teaching job in Silicon Valley paid an average salary of $50,000, while a job in the computer industry paid an average of $80,000, not counting possible gains from stock options—at least a $30,000 differential.

At the same time, college graduates who were considering advancing their education faced a similar decision: "Should I get an MBA and improve my career and future salaries, or should I accept an immediate, high-paying job at a start-up or consulting firm?"

As the recession hit the United States in 2001, many workers were laid off, and others saw their salaries reduced. The U.S. unemployment rate grew from 4.7 percent in January 2001 to 5.6 percent in January 2002, and in Santa Clara county—the heart of Silicon Valley—the increase in the unemployment rate was more dramatic: from 1.7 percent to 7.7 percent. Hewlett-Packard, for example, laid off 6,000 workers—almost 7 percent of its work force—while one of its spinoffs, Agilent, reduced salaries 10 percent for all its 48,000 employees in 2001.

With lower salaries and fewer jobs in the private sector, the opportunity cost of teaching and studying fell. Business schools reported a barrage of applications, with increases between 50 and 100 percent over the previous year. School districts witnessed a sharp decrease in the number of vacancies available, with many new teachers willing to undergo months of training and substantial pay cuts relative to their old high-tech jobs.

Think of the options you will be facing when you graduate. Given the jobs and salaries currently available, what career do you think you would like to pursue? What would your opportunity cost be?

not be so good at acting, for example, or moviemaking may require an area with a dry, sunny climate. As more and more resources go into making movies, we are forced to take resources that are much better at computer making and use them for moviemaking. Thus, more and more computer production must be lost to increase the production of movies by the same amount. Adding specialized computer designers to a movie cast would be very costly in terms of lost computers, and it might add little to movie production.

The Production Possibilities Curve

Figure 1.2 is a graphical representation of the production possibilities in Table 1.1 that nicely illustrates increasing opportunity costs. We put movies on the horizontal axis and computers on the vertical axis of the figure. Each pair of numbers in a row of the table becomes a point on the graph. For example, point *A* on the graph is from row A of the table. Point *B* is from row B, and so on.

When we connect the points in Figure 1.2, we obtain the **production possibilities curve.** It shows the maximum number of computers that can be produced for each quantity of movies produced. Note that the curve in Figure 1.2 slopes downward and is bowed out from the origin. That the curve is bowed out indicates that the opportunity cost of producing movies increases as more movies are produced. As resources move from computer making to moviemaking, each additional movie means a greater loss of computer production.

production possibilities curve: a curve showing the maximum combinations of production of two goods that are possible, given the economy's resources.

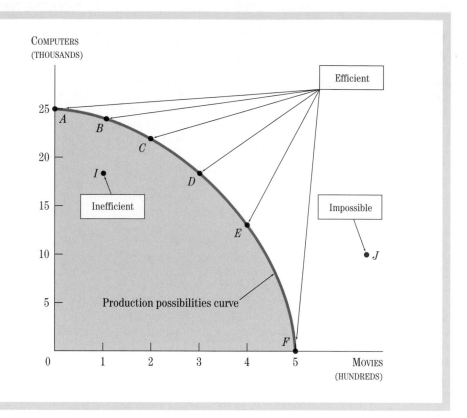

Figure 1.2
The Production Possibilities Curve
Each point on the curve shows the maximum amount of computers that can be produced when a given amount of movies is produced. The points with letters are the same as those in Table 1.1 and are connected by smooth lines. Points in the shaded area inside the curve are inefficient. Points outside the curve are impossible. For the efficient points on the curve, the more movies that are produced, the fewer computers are produced. The curve is bowed out because of increasing opportunity costs.

■ **Inefficient, Efficient, or Impossible?** The production possibilities curve shows the effects of scarcity and choice in the economy as a whole. Three situations can be distinguished in Figure 1.2, depending on whether production is in the shaded area, on the curve, or outside the curve.

First, imagine production at point *I*. This point, with 100 movies and 18,000 computers, is inside the curve. But the production possibilities curve tells us that it is possible with the same amount of resources to produce more computers, more movies, or both. For some reason, the economy is not working well at point *I*. For example, instead of using movie film, people may be taking still photos and then sticking them together with tape to make the movie. Points inside the curve, like point *I*, are *inefficient* because the economy could produce a larger number of movies, as at point *D*, or a larger number of computers, as at point *B*. Points inside the production possibilities curve are possible, but they are inefficient.

Second, consider points on the production possibilities curve. These points are *efficient*. They represent the maximum amount that can be produced with available resources. The only way to raise production of one good is to lower production of the other good. Thus, points on the curve show a *tradeoff* between one good and another.

Third, consider points to the right and above the production possibilities curve, like point *J* in Figure 1.2. These points are *impossible*. The economy does not have the resources to produce those quantities.

■ **Shifts in the Production Possibilities Curve.** The production possibilities curve is not immovable. It can *shift* out or in. For example, the curve is shown to shift out in Figure 1.3. More resources—more workers, for example—shift the production possibilities curve out. A technological innovation that allowed one to edit movies

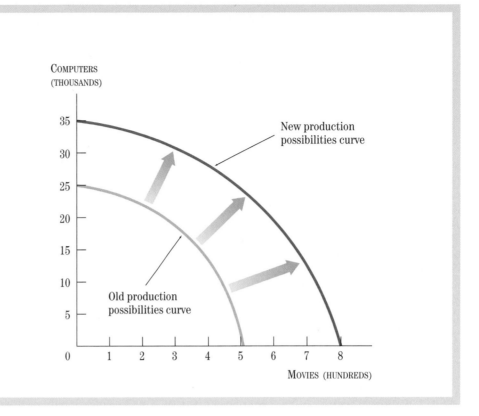

**Figure 1.3
Shifts in the Production
Possibilities Curve**
The production possibilities
curve shifts out as the economy
grows. The maximum amounts
of movies and computers
that can be produced increase.
Improvements in technology,
more machines, or more labor
permit the economy to produce
more.

faster would also shift the curve outward. So would more cameras, lights, and studios. When the production possibilities curve shifts out, the economy grows because more goods and services can be produced. The production possibilities curve need not shift outward by the same amount in all directions. There can be more movement up than to the right, for example.

As the production possibilities curve shifts out, impossibilities are converted into possibilities. Some of what was impossible for the U.S. economy in 1970 is possible now. Some of what is impossible now will be possible in 2020. Hence, the economists' notion of possibilities is a temporary one. When we say that a certain combination of computers and movies is impossible, we do not mean "forever impossible," we only mean "currently impossible."

■ **Scarcity, Choice, and Economic Progress.**   However, the conversion of impossibilities into possibilities is also an economic problem of choice and scarcity: If we invest less now—in machines, in education, in children, in technology—and consume more now, then we will have less available in the future. If we take computers and movies as symbolic of investment and consumption, then choosing more investment will result in a larger outward shift of the production possibilities curve, as illustrated in Figure 1.4. More investment enables the economy to produce more in the future.

The production possibilities curve represents a *tradeoff*, but it does not mean that some people win only if others lose. First, it is not necessary for someone to lose in order for the production possibilities curve to shift out. When the curve shifts out, the production of both items increases. Although some people may fare better than others as the production possibilities curve is pushed out, no one necessarily loses.

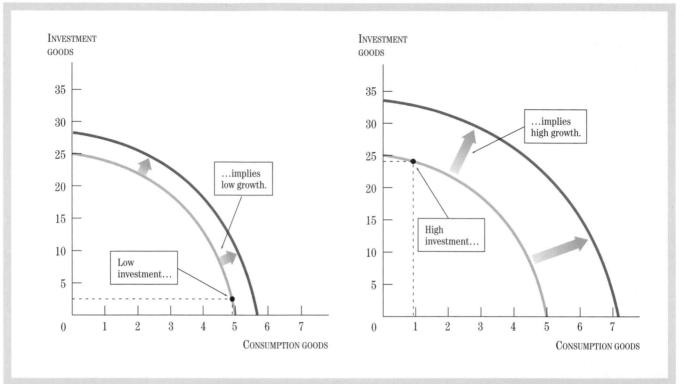

**Figure 1.4
Shifts in the Production
Possibilities Curve Depend
on Choices**

On the left, few resources are devoted to investment for the future; hence, the production possibilities curve shifts only a little over time. On the right, more resources are devoted to investment and less to consumption; hence, the production possibilities curve shifts out by a larger amount over time.

In principle, everyone can gain. Second, if the economy is at an inefficient point (like point *I* in Figure 1.2), then production of both goods can be increased with no trade-off. In general, therefore, the economy is more like a win-win situation, where everyone can achieve a gain.

REVIEW

- The production possibilities curve represents the choices open to a whole economy when it is confronted by a scarcity of resources. As more of one item is produced, less of another item must be produced. The opportunity cost of producing more of one item is the reduced production of another item.

- The production possibilities curve is bowed out because of increasing opportunity costs.

- Points inside the curve are inefficient. Points on the curve are efficient. Points outside the curve are impossible.

- The production possibilities curve shifts out as resources increase.

- Outward shifts of the production possibilities curve or moves from inefficient to efficient points are the reasons why the economy is not a zero-sum game, despite the existence of scarcity and choice.

Market Economies and the Price System

The production possibilities curve enables us to discuss key questions about the economy.

Three Questions

There are three essential questions or problems that every economy must find a way to solve, whether it is a small island economy or a large economy like the United States.

- *What* is to be produced: movies, computers, guns, butter, greeting cards, Rollerblades, health care, or something else? In other words, where on the production possibilities curve should an economy be?

- *How* are these goods to be produced? In other words, how can an economy use the available resources so that it is not at an inefficient point inside the production possibilities curve?

- *For whom* are the goods to be produced? We know from the hat/sunglasses example that the allocation of goods in an economy affects people's well-being. An economy in which Maria could not trade her sunglasses for a hat would not work as well as one in which such trades and reallocations are possible. Moreover, an economy in which some people get everything and others get virtually nothing is also not working well.

The Three Fundamental Economic Questions
Any economic system has to answer three questions: What goods and services should be produced—cars, televisions, or something else? How should these goods or services be produced—in what type of factory, and with how much equipment and labor? And for whom should these goods be produced?

What?

How?

For Whom?

market economy: an economy characterized by freely determined prices and the free exchange of goods and services in markets.

command economy: an economy in which the government determines prices and production; also called a centrally planned economy.

Broadly speaking, the **market economy** and the **command economy** are two alternative approaches to these questions. In a market economy, most decisions about what, how, and for whom to produce are made by individual consumers, firms, governments, and other organizations interacting in markets. In a command, or centrally planned, economy, most decisions about what, how, and for whom to produce are made by those who control the government, which, through a central plan, commands and controls what people do.

Centrally planned economies are much less common today than they were in the mid-twentieth century, when nearly half the world's population lived in centrally planned economies, including the countries of Eastern Europe, the Soviet Union, and China.

In recent years, the people of these countries have been trying to convert their command economies into market economies. After many decades, they became disillusioned with the way in which their command economies were working. By comparison, the market economies in Western Europe, the United States, and Japan worked much better: These economies were more productive and offered greater quality and more variety of goods and services to consumers.

Key Elements of a Market Economy

Let us consider some of the key features of a market economy.

freely determined price: a price that is determined by the individuals and firms interacting in markets.

■ **Freely Determined Prices.**   In a market economy, most prices—such as the price of computers—are freely determined by individuals and firms interacting in markets. These **freely determined prices** are an essential characteristic of a market economy. In a command economy, most prices are set by government, and this leads to inefficiencies in the economy. For example, in the Soviet Union, the price of bread was set so low that farmers fed bread to the cows. Feeding bread to livestock is an enormous waste of resources. Livestock could eat plain grain. By feeding the cows bread, farmers added the cost of the labor to bake the bread and the fuel to heat the bread ovens to the cost of livestock feed. This is inefficient, like point I in Figure 1.2.

In practice, not all prices in market economies are freely determined. For example, some cities control the price of rental apartments. We will look at these exceptions later. But the vast majority of prices are free to vary.

property rights: rights over the use, sale, and proceeds from a good or resource.

■ **Property Rights and Incentives.**   Property rights are another key element of a market economy. **Property rights** give individuals the legal authority to keep or sell property, whether land or other resources. Property rights are needed for a market economy because they give people the ability to buy and sell goods. Without property rights, people could take whatever they wanted without paying. People would have to devote time and resources to protecting their earnings or goods.

incentive: a device that motivates people to take action, usually so as to increase economic efficiency.

Moreover, by giving people the rights to the earnings from their work, as well as letting them suffer some of the consequences or losses from their mistakes, property rights provide **incentives.** For example, if an inventor could not get the property rights to an invention, then the incentive to produce the invention would be low or even nonexistent. Hence there would be few inventions, and we would all be worse off. If there were no property rights, people would not have incentives to specialize and reap the gains from the division of labor. Any extra earnings from specialization could be taken away.

■ **Freedom to Trade at Home and Abroad.**   Economic interaction is a way to improve economic outcomes, as the examples in this chapter indicate. Allowing

Economic interactions can take place in a marketplace, between two friends, on the Internet, or even on the radio, as this article attests. All you need is someone who wants to sell something and someone else who wants to buy. Tradio helps potential buyers and sellers learn about each other in a virtual market, realizing gains from trade that would not be possible without the exchange of information. Even though radio stations do not charge buyers and sellers, you will notice that tradio is not just a public service. Tradio is very low-cost programming that attracts a large audience and many paid ads from local businesses—a win-win situation for individual buyers and sellers, radio stations, and local businesses. Gains from trade in action!

Who Needs eBay? For Towns Across U.S., Tradio Is Real Deal

By Reid J. Epstein
Staff Reporter of
THE WALL STREET JOURNAL

GLASGOW, Mont.—It was a little after nine one recent morning, and local residents were already on the line to Lori Mason's radio show.

One caller wanted to unload a riding lawnmower ($500). Another tried to sell an irrigation pump ($100), and four offered up washing machines, including one that "leaks a little bit" ($10). Others still were looking to buy eight bales of straw, fresh dill and a large dog house.

When one young woman phoned in to put her '79 GMC pickup on the block, the 54-year-old Ms. Mason not only recognized her voice but urged her to loosen up.

"Oh, sorry," said the caller, 23-year-old day-care provider Jamie Seyfert. "We're willing to trade for guns, jet skis or anything fun."

This is the sound of "tradio" (pronounced TRADE-ee-o), a kind of on-air swap meet that has been a fixture of small-town stations from Florida to Alaska for decades. Far from being rendered obsolete by the Internet, many tradio shows are doing surprisingly well these days. They are the top moneymakers for some stations, often commanding a premium from local advertisers. And the format may be pushing into bigger markets. In April, WCCO in Minneapolis introduced "The WCCO Great Garage Sale" and saw its ratings jump 29% in the time slot.

Three-Stoplight Town

Here in Glasgow, a three-stoplight railroad town of 3,253 people on the lonely plains of northeastern Montana, the half-hour show is simulcast three mornings a week from the second-floor studio of locally owned stations KLTZ and KLAN. Virtually everyone in town, from the mayor to the editor of the weekly paper, has bought or sold something on the show.

Here's how it works: Callers announce they're selling something—a gas heater that "would be good in your garage, your huntin' shack or whatever," a "very large collection of Fiestaware dishes in all the new colors" or some "very friendly young goats"—and leave their phone number. Anyone interested calls the seller, and the transaction is negotiated face-to-face.

Internet Connection

While it may sound archaic in the age of eBay, the tradio format seems to be benefiting from the buzz generated by the popular Web auction site. Some tradio shows are using the Internet to their advantage—allowing listeners to submit items for sale via e-mail and posting items called into the show on their Web sites.

The tradio format first took hold in the early 1950s when powerful nation-wide radio networks cut back on programming. To fill the void, small-town stations began broadcasting obituaries, birthdays and anniversaries. An appliance-store owner in Seguin is believed by many in the industry to have started the first tradio show. He began buying air time to read notices of items for sale that customers had posted on a bulletin board inside his store.

In small towns that don't have daily newspapers—the closest daily to Glasgow is the *Herald* in Williston, N.D., 144 miles away—tradio takes the place of classifieds and, perhaps more important, gossip. When Ms. Mason heard a caller say he was selling his $100 irrigation pump, she exclaimed, "You're on the new water line!" and quizzed him about the difference that had made in his water supply.

Another big attraction is the price. A classified ad in the weekly *Glasgow Courier* costs $5.25 per column inch, while calls to "Tradio" are free. And eBay, which exacts a sliding fee based on the price of the item sold, also requires a hookup to the Internet.

Alicia Sibley, a 24-year-old hay farmer, is a regular listener to the Glasgow show. She was driving her tractor a few weeks ago when she heard a caller offering to sell a 6-foot freezer. She phoned the seller—who had bought the freezer to stock up on frozen foods for fear of a catastrophe at the turn of the millennium—and made a deal for $200. "It's a real nice one, too," Ms. Sibley said. "I saved around $200."

people to interact freely is thus another necessary ingredient of a market economy. Freedom to trade can be extended beyond national borders to other economies.

International trade increases the opportunities to gain from trade. This is especially important in small countries, where it is impossible to produce everything. But the gains from exchange and comparative advantage also exist for larger countries.

■ **A Role for Government.**   Just because prices are freely determined and people are free to trade in a market economy does not mean that there is no role for government. For example, in virtually all market economies, the government provides defense and police protection. The government also helps establish property rights. But how far beyond that should it go? Should the government also address the "for whom" question by providing a safety net—a mechanism to deal with the individuals in the economy who are poor, who go bankrupt, who remain unemployed? Most would say yes, but what should the government's role be? Economics provides an analytical framework to answer such questions. In certain circumstances—called **market failure**—the market economy does not provide good enough answers to the "what, how, and for whom" questions, and the government has a role to play in improving on the market. However, the government, even in the case of market failure, may do worse than the market, in which case economists say there is **government failure.**

market failure: any situation in which the market does not lead to an efficient economic outcome and in which there is a potential role for government.

government failure: a situation in which the government makes things worse than the market, even though there may be market failure.

■ **The Role of Private Organizations.**   It is an interesting feature of market economies that many economic interactions between people take place in organizations—firms, families, charitable organizations—rather than in markets. Some economic interactions that take place in organizations could take place in the market. In some circumstances, the same type of interaction takes place in a firm and in a market simultaneously. For example, many large firms employ lawyers as part of their permanent staff. Other firms simply purchase the services of such lawyers in the market; if the firm wants to sue someone or is being sued by someone, it hires an outside lawyer to represent it.

Economic interactions in firms differ from those in the market. Staff lawyers inside large firms are usually paid annual salaries that do not depend directly on the number of hours worked or their success in the lawsuits. In contrast, outside lawyers are paid an hourly fee and a contingency fee based on the number of hours worked and how successful they are.

Incentives within an organization are as important as incentives in markets. If the lawyers on a firm's legal staff get to keep some of the damages the firm wins in a lawsuit, they will have more incentive to do a good job. Some firms even try to create marketlike competition between departments or workers in order to give more incentives.

Why do some economic interactions occur in markets and others in organizations? Ronald Coase of the University of Chicago won the Nobel Prize for showing that organizations such as firms are created to reduce market *transaction costs*, the costs of buying and selling, which include finding a buyer or a seller and reaching agreement on a price. When market transaction costs are high, we see more transactions taking place within organizations. For example, a firm might have a legal staff rather than outside lawyers because searching for a good lawyer every time there is a lawsuit is too costly. In a crisis, a good lawyer may not be available.

The Price System

The previous discussion indicates that in market economies, freely determined prices are essential for determining what is produced, how, and for whom. For this reason, a market economy is said to use *the price system* to solve these problems. In this section, we show that prices do a surprising amount of work: (1) Prices serve as *signals* about what should be produced and consumed when there are changes in tastes or changes in technology, (2) prices provide *incentives* to people to alter their production or consumption, and (3) prices affect the *distribution of income*, or who gets what in the economy.

Let's use an example. Suppose that there is a sudden new trend for college students to ride bicycles more and drive cars less. How do prices help people in the economy decide what to do in response to this new trend?

■ **Signals.** First, consider how the information about the change in tastes is signaled to the producers of bicycles and cars. As students buy more bicycles, the price of bicycles rises. A higher price will signal that it is more profitable for firms to produce more bicycles. In addition, some bicycle components, like lightweight metal, will also increase in price. Increased lightweight metal prices signal that production of lightweight metal should increase. As the price of metal rises, wages for metalworkers may increase. Thus, prices are a signal all the way from the consumer to the metalworkers that more bicycles should be produced. This is what is meant by the expression "prices are a signal."

It is important to note that no single individual knows the information that is transmitted by prices. Any economy is characterized by limited information, where people cannot know the exact reasons why prices for certain goods rise or fall. Hence, it is rather amazing that prices can signal this information.

■ **Incentives.** Now let's use this example to consider how prices provide incentives. A higher price for bicycles will increase the incentives for firms to produce bicycles. Because they receive more for each bicycle, they produce more. If there is a large price increase that is not merely temporary, new firms may enter the bicycle business. In contrast, the reduced prices for cars signal to car producers that production should decrease.

■ **Distribution.** How do prices affect the distribution of income? On the one hand, workers who find the production of the good they make increasing because of the higher demand for bicycles will earn more. On the other hand, income will be reduced for those who make cars or who have to pay more for bicycles. Local delivery services that use bicycles will see their costs increase.

REVIEW

- The market economy and the command economy are two alternative systems for addressing the questions any economy must face: what to produce, how to produce, and for whom to produce.

- A market economy is characterized by several key elements, such as freely determined prices, property rights, and freedom to trade at home and abroad.

- For a market economy to work well, markets should be competitive and the government should play a role.

- Prices are signals, they provide incentives, and they affect the distribution of income.

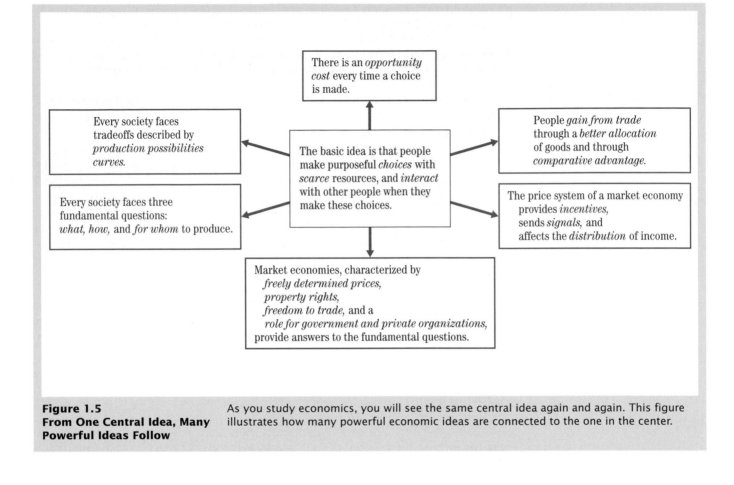

Figure 1.5
From One Central Idea, Many
Powerful Ideas Follow

As you study economics, you will see the same central idea again and again. This figure illustrates how many powerful economic ideas are connected to the one in the center.

Conclusion

One basic idea lies at the center of economics: People make purposeful choices with scarce resources, and interact with other people when they make these choices.

This introductory chapter illustrates this idea, starting with Tiger Woods' decision to leave school and continuing with simple examples of people making choices about what to consume or produce.

From this central idea, many other powerful ideas follow, as summarized visually in Figure 1.5. There is an *opportunity cost* every time a choice is made. People *gain from trade*, both through a *better allocation* of goods and through *comparative advantage*. Every society faces tradeoffs described by *production possibilities curves*. Every society faces three fundamental questions: *what, how,* and *for whom* to produce. Market economies—characterized by *freely determined prices, property rights, freedom to trade,* and *a role for both government and private organizations*—give an answer to these three questions. The price system of a market economy works by providing *incentives,* sending *signals,* and affecting the *distribution* of income.

You will see this central idea again and again as you study economics.

KEY POINTS

1. Everyone faces a scarcity of something, usually time or resources.

2. Scarcity leads to choice, and choice leads to opportunity costs.

3. Trade leads to gains because it allows goods and services to be reallocated in a way that improves people's well-being.

4. Trade also leads to gains because it permits people to specialize in what they are relatively good at.

5. The production possibilities curve summarizes the tradeoffs in the whole economy due to scarcity. Economic production is efficient if the economy is on the production possibilities curve.

6. The three basic questions that any economy must face are what, how, and for whom production should take place.

7. A well-functioning market system involves freely determined prices, property rights, freedom to trade, and a role for government and private organizations.

8. If prices are set at the wrong levels by government, waste and inefficiency—such as feeding bread to livestock—will result.

9. Prices transmit signals, provide incentives, and affect the distribution of income.

KEY TERMS

economics
scarcity
choice
economic interaction
market
opportunity cost

gains from trade
division of labor
comparative advantage
international trade
production possibilities

increasing opportunity cost
production possibilities curve
market economy
command economy

freely determined prices
property rights
incentives
market failure
government failure

QUESTIONS FOR REVIEW

1. How do scarcity, choice, and economic interaction fit into the basic idea at the center of economics?

2. Why does scarcity imply a choice among alternatives?

3. Why does choice create opportunity costs?

4. What is the difference between economic interaction in markets and in organizations?

5. Why is there a gain from trade even if total production of goods and services does not change?

6. How can specialization lead to a gain from trade?

7. What is the principle of increasing opportunity costs?

8. What are the key ingredients of a market economy?

9. What are the three basic questions that any economic system must address?

10. What are the three roles of prices?

PROBLEMS

1. Suppose that you are president of the student government, and you have $10,000 for guest speakers for the year. Spike Lee costs $10,000 per appearance. Former economic advisers to the government charge $1,000 per lecture. Hence, you cannot have both Spike Lee and the former economic advisers. Explain the economic

problem of choice and scarcity in this case. What issues would you consider in arriving at a decision?

2. Compare the opportunity cost of one more year of school versus working for one year for (1) a high school graduate, (2) a college graduate, and (3) a medical school graduate.

3. Allison will graduate from high school next June. She has ranked her three possible postgraduation plans in the following order: (1) work for two years at a consulting job in her home town paying $20,000 per year, (2) attend a local community college for two years, spending $5,000 per year on tuition and expenses, and (3) travel around the world tutoring a rock star's child for pay of $5,000 per year. What is the opportunity cost of her choice?

4. Suppose you have two salt shakers and a friend of yours has two pepper shakers. Explain how you can both gain from trade. Is this a gain from trade through *better allocation* or *greater production*? Suppose now that your friend lives in another country, whose government does not allow trade between your countries. Who would lose as a result of this trade barrier?

5. Suppose Tina and Julia can produce jars of salsa and computer-designed advertisements in the following combinations in a given week:

Tina		Julia	
Salsa	*Ads*	*Salsa*	*Ads*
50	0	25	0
40	1	20	1
30	2	15	2
20	3	10	3
10	4	5	4
0	5	0	5

a. If Tina and Julia are each currently producing 2 advertisements per week, how many jars of salsa are they producing? What is the total production of salsa and advertisements between them?

b. Is there a possibility for increasing production? Why or why not?

c. Suppose Julia completely specializes in producing advertisements and Tina completely specializes in producing salsa. What will be the total production of advertisements and salsa?

6. Suppose you must divide your time between studying for your math final and writing a final paper for your English class. The fraction of time you spend studying math and its relation to your grade in the two classes is given in the table in the next column.

Fraction of Time Spent on Math	Math Grade	English Grade
0	0	97
20	45	92
40	65	85
60	75	70
80	82	50
100	88	0

a. Draw a tradeoff curve for the math grade versus the English grade.

b. What is the opportunity cost of increasing the time spent on math from 80 to 100 percent? What is the opportunity cost of increasing the time spent on math from 60 to 80 percent?

c. Are there increasing opportunity costs from spending more time on math? Explain.

d. What can you do to get a 92 in both subjects? Explain.

7. A small country produces only two goods, cars and computers. Given its limited resources, this country has the following production possibilities:

Cars	Computers
0	200
25	180
50	130
75	70
100	0

a. Draw the production possibilities curve.

b. Suppose car production uses mainly machines and computer production uses mainly labor. Show what happens to the curve when the number of machines increases but labor remains unchanged.

8. After World War II and until the 1980s, the Japanese economy grew very rapidly, and its citizens now enjoy a high standard of living. How would you explain the fast Japanese growth in terms of tradeoffs and decisions made by individuals and societies?

9. Tracy tells Huey that he can improve his economics grades without sacrificing fun activities or grades in other courses. Can you imagine ways in which this might be possible? What does that imply about the initial situation?

If Huey is taking just two courses and he can improve his economics grade without hurting his math grade, how could you represent this situation graphically?

10. Compare two countries. In one country, the government sets prices and never adjusts them. In the other country, the government adjusts prices daily, endeavoring to

allocate resources to consumers to satisfy their tastes. Is either of these a market economy? Why or why not?

11. Suppose decreased production of oil in the Middle East causes the price of oil to rise all over the world. Explain how this change in the price signals information to U.S. producers, provides incentives to U.S. producers, and affects the distribution of income.

12. "When you look at the economies in the United States, Europe, or Japan, you see most of the ingredients of a market economy. For example, consider bicycles. Prices in the bicycle market are free to vary; people have property rights to the bicycles they buy; many people sell bicycles; many bicycles sold in the United States, Europe, and Japan come from other countries; the government regulates bicycle use (no bicycles on the freeways, for example); and bicycle production takes place within firms with many workers." Replace bicycles with another good or service of your choosing in this quotation and comment on whether the quotation is still true.

CHAPTER 2

Observing and Explaining the Economy

Mark McClellan is a lot like Tiger Woods. He trained long and hard before he became a professional, and he now excels in his field.

But Mark is not an expert at driving and putting golf balls. Rather, he is an expert at observing and explaining economic trends in the biggest industry in America.

After college, Mark went on to earn a Ph.D. in economics. He also went to medical school, completed an internship and residency in a hospital, and became a practicing medical doctor. Why would an economist become a doctor? Because the biggest industry in America is not automobiles, oil, or construction—but health care. Mark concluded that to observe and explain the health-care industry, he needed to be an expert in economics as well as medicine. And all of the training has paid off. As a health-care economist, Mark has demonstrated, among other things, that doctors sometimes provide treatments of little actual value to their patients and that it is the fear of malpractice suits that motivates doctors to do so. His economic expertise and insights on health-care policy have earned him a place, first as one of the three members of President Bush's Council of Economic Advisers, and now as Commissioner of the Food and Drug Administration.

The purpose of this chapter is to give you a broad overview of economics by looking at the kinds of things economists such as Mark McClellan actually do. Economics is a way of thinking. It entails accurately *describing* economic events, *explaining* why the events occur, *predicting* under what circumstances such events might take place in the future, and *recommending* appropriate courses of action. To make use of economics, you will want to learn to do the describing, the explaining, and even the predicting and recommending yourself—that is, to reason and think like an economist. By making use of economics in this way, you can better understand the economic challenges and opportunities you face, and thereby make improvements in your own life or the lives of those around you.

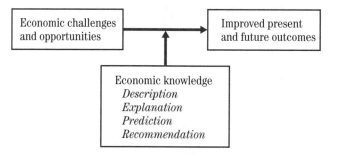

Just as physicists try to explain the existence of black holes in outer space or biologists try to explain why dinosaurs became extinct, economists try to explain puzzling observations and facts about the economy. Many observations come from everyday life. Are there some economic observations—from your own experience, from recent news stories, or from your history or political science courses—that you find puzzling? Some of your questions might be like these:

- Why is college tuition so high?
- Why have the wages of college graduates increased much more rapidly than the wages of high school dropouts since the 1970s?
- Why are there 17 different types of Colgate toothpaste now, while there were only two types 30 years ago?
- Why is the average income of people in the United States about 35 times higher than that of people in China?
- Why is unemployment much higher in Europe than in the United States?
- Why did health-care spending slow down compared to the rest of the U.S. economy in the 1990s?
- Why has the price of health care increased more than most other prices?

All these questions are based on observations about the economy. Some, like the questions about college tuition, are fairly obvious and are based on casual observation. But in order to answer such questions, economists, like physicists or biologists, need to systematically document and quantify their observations and look for patterns. If we can establish the date when dinosaurs became extinct, then we may be able to test our hunch that a cataclysmic event such as an asteroid hitting the earth caused their extinction. To illustrate how economists document and quantify their observations, let us briefly focus on the last two of the preceding questions, the ones concerning health care and the economy. This will also give us an opportunity to introduce some key indicators used to measure the economy.

Health-Care Spending in America

Health-care spending and prices are more than a curiosity. The more a society spends on health care, the less it can spend on other things, as we know from the production possibilities curve of Chapter 1. Concerns about health-care spending have led to major proposals for changing the way health care is provided and paid for in the United States. Health care *is* a major political issue. People who are dissatisfied with their own health care want the right to sue their health-care providers. Debates about how to slow rising spending on Medicare—a government health-care program for the elderly—raged during the 2000 presidential and congressional elections, and, more recently, debates over drug-benefit measures have taken center stage. But let's focus on our first observation and question.

How has health-care spending changed relative to the rest of the economy? To determine this, we need a measure of health-care spending and a measure of the size of the overall economy.

> **Observation 1:** Health-care spending slowed compared to the rest of the U.S. economy in the 1990s.

Spending as a Share of GDP

gross domestic product (GDP): a measure of the value of all the goods and services newly produced in an economy during a specified period of time.

The most comprehensive available measure of the size of an economy is the **gross domestic product (GDP).** For the United States, GDP is the total value of all products made in the United States during a specified period of time, such as a year. GDP includes all newly made goods, such as cars, trucks, shoes, airplanes, houses, and telephones; it also includes services, such as education, rock concerts, and health care. To measure the total value of all products made in the economy, economists add up the dollars that people spend on the products.

How large is GDP in the United States? In 2001, it was $10,082 billion, or about $10.1 trillion. We can compute GDP for any year. The question about health-care spending and the size of the economy requires that we look at the U.S. economy since 1990. In 1990, GDP was $5,803 billion. Column (1) of Table 2.1 provides a history of GDP since 1990.

Graphs are frequently a more helpful way to present data like those shown in Table 2.1. Figure 2.1 plots the data on GDP from column (1) of Table 2.1. The vertical axis is measured in billions of dollars; the horizontal axis is measured in years. For example, the point at the extreme lower left in Figure 2.1 represents GDP of $5,803 billion (on the vertical axis) in the year 1990 (on the horizontal axis). The points are connected by a line, which helps us visualize the steady growth of GDP during this period.

Now let us consider health-care spending, which includes payments for hospital services, lab tests, nursing homes, visits to the doctor or dentist, drugs, hearing aids, and eyeglasses. If we add up all spending on health care, we get $1,027 billion in 2001. This amount is about three times as large as the entire automobile industry, including cars, trucks, and parts. Health care is the biggest industry in the United States.

Health-care spending since 1990 is listed in column (2) of Table 2.1 and is plotted in Figure 2.2. Figures 2.1 and 2.2 show that both GDP and health-care spending have grown since 1990. One way to assess the growth of health-care spending compared to spending on all goods and services is to look at health-care spending as a share, or

Table 2.1
GDP and Health-Care Spending, 1990–2001

Year	(1) GDP	(2) Health-Care Spending	(3) Health-Care Share of GDP (percent)
1990	5,803	541	9.3
1991	5,986	591	9.9
1992	6,319	653	10.3
1993	6,642	701	10.6
1994	7,054	737	10.4
1995	7,401	781	10.6
1996	7,813	814	10.4
1997	8,318	855	10.3
1998	8,782	899	10.2
1999	9,274	937	10.1
2000	9,825	992	10.1
2001	10,082	1,027	10.6

Note: GDP and health-care spending are measured in billions of dollars.
Source: The source of all data in this case study is the U.S. Department of Commerce national income and product accounts.

100 times column 2 divided by column 1

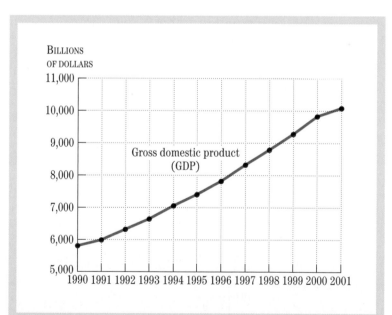

Figure 2.1
Gross Domestic Product (GDP) in the United States, 1990–2001
GDP is the total dollar value of newly produced goods and services. It can be measured by adding up what people spend on everything, from health care to cars. For each year from 1990 to 2001, GDP is plotted; the line connects all the points.

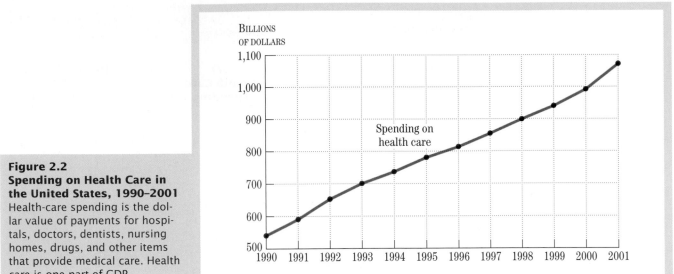

Figure 2.2
Spending on Health Care in the United States, 1990–2001
Health-care spending is the dollar value of payments for hospitals, doctors, dentists, nursing homes, drugs, and other items that provide medical care. Health care is one part of GDP.

percentage, of GDP. For example, in 2000, health-care spending was $992 billion, and GDP was $9,825 billion. Thus, the share (in percentage terms) of GDP going to health care was:

$$\frac{\text{Health-care spending}}{\text{GDP}} \times 100 = \frac{\text{health-care spending}}{\text{as a share of GDP}}$$

$$\frac{992}{9,825} \times 100 = 10.1 \text{ percent}$$

Observation 2: The price of health care has risen compared with the price of other goods and services in the economy.

Column (3) of Table 2.1 gives the results of this calculation for all years from 1990 to 2001. Again, it is helpful to plot the shares, as in Figure 2.3. Observe how health-care spending rose as a percentage of GDP—or relative to the size of the economy—in the early 1990s and then began to slow down in the mid-1990s. We have now quantified the observation about rising health-care spending. Now let us go on to

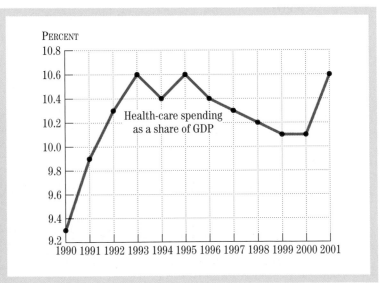

Figure 2.3
Health-Care Spending as a Share of GDP
Each point on the graph is the ratio of spending on health care from Figure 2.2 to GDP from Figure 2.1, expressed as a percentage. For example, in 1998, health-care spending was $899 billion and GDP was $8,782 billion. The ratio is 899/8,782 = .102, or 10.2 percent.

consider the second question about health care and see whether the price of health care has risen compared with the price of other goods and services in the economy.

The Relative Price

relative price: the price of a particular good compared to the price of other things.

To see whether the price of health care has increased more or less rapidly than other things, we look at the relative price of health care. The **relative price** is a measure of health-care prices compared with the average prices of all goods and services, computed by dividing the health-care price by the average price of all goods and services:

$$\text{Relative price of health care} = \frac{\text{health-care price}}{\text{average price of all goods and services}}$$

The relative price of health care is shown in Table 2.2 and plotted in Figure 2.4. Observe that the relative price of health care has risen since 1990. In other words, the price of health care has increased relative to the average of all other prices.

Correlations Between Economic Variables

economic variable: any economic measure that can vary over a range of values.

So far, we have focused on two economic variables to quantify our observations about health care in the United States. These variables are (1) health-care spending's share of GDP and (2) the relative price of health care. An **economic variable** is any economic measure that can vary over a range of values. Are these two economic variables correlated? Are there interesting patterns?

Figure 2.5 is useful for determining whether the relative price of health care and health care's share of GDP have been correlated. Each point in the figure corresponds to a relative price and a health-care share taken from Table 2.2 and from the last column of Table 2.1. The relative price is on the vertical axis, and health care as a share of GDP is on the horizontal axis.

Table 2.2
Relative Price of Health Care

Year	Relative Health-Care Price
1990	0.879
1991	0.898
1992	0.928
1993	0.961
1994	0.981
1995	0.998
1996	1.000
1997	1.003
1998	1.016
1999	1.022
2000	1.031
2001	1.044

Note: The relative price is a ratio of the price of health care to the average price of all goods and services. The ratio is set to 1 in 1996. This year is arbitrary: Using another year would not change the patterns of the relative prices.

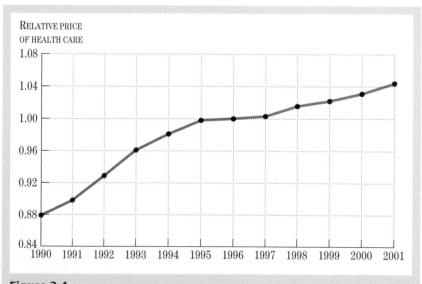

Figure 2.4
Relative Price of Health Care
Health-care prices have risen more rapidly than other prices in the 1990s. Hence, the relative price of health care has increased; the increase was especially rapid in the early 1990s.

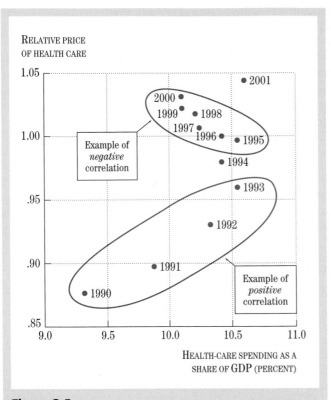

RELATIVE PRICE
OF HEALTH CARE

Figure 2.5
Relative Price of Health Care versus Health-Care Spending Share
The figure plots pairs of points: the relative price of health care on the vertical axis and health-care spending as a share of GDP on the horizontal axis. The observations come from Table 2.2 and the last column of Table 2.1.

The points in Figure 2.5 trace out some patterns. As the relative price of health care increased from 1990 to 1993, so did spending on health care as a share of GDP. Two variables are *correlated* if they tend to move up or down at the same time. There is a *positive correlation* if the two variables move in the same direction: When one goes up, the other goes up. Health-care spending as a share of GDP and the relative price of health care were positively correlated from 1990 to 1993.

Two variables are negatively correlated if they tend to move in opposite directions. From 1995 to 2000, a higher relative price of health care was associated with lower spending shares; thus, there was a *negative correlation* during those years.

■ **Correlation versus Causation.** Just because there is a correlation between two variables does not mean that one caused the other. There is a difference between *causation* and *correlation*. *Correlation* means that one event is usually observed to occur along with another. For example, high readings on a thermometer occur when it is hot outside. *Causation* means that one event brings about another event. But correlation does not imply causation. For example, the high reading on the thermometer does not cause the hot weather, even though the high reading and the hot weather are correlated. In this example, we know that the causation is the other way around: Hot weather causes the reading on the thermometer to be high.

More to the point for economics, if you looked only at the correlation in Figure 2.5 from 1990 to 1993, you might be tempted to say that the higher price of health care caused health-care spending to rise. But that correlation does not permit us to make such a conclusion about causation. We need to know more about the effects of the price of health care on health-care spending and about what determines the price before we can make statements about causality. In fact, since 1995, spending on health care has fallen as a share of GDP as the relative price rose, so one would have been proven wrong if one had argued that there was a positive causation.

■ **The Lack of Controlled Experiments in Economics.** In many sciences—certainly psychology, medicine, and biology—investigators perform **controlled experiments** to determine whether one event causes another event. An example of a controlled experiment is the clinical trial of new drugs. New drugs are tested by trying them out on two groups of individuals. One group gets the drug; the other group gets a placebo (a pill without the drug). If the experiment results in a significantly greater number of people being cured among the group taking the drug than among the control group not taking the drug, investigators conclude that the drug causes the cure.

Unfortunately, such controlled experiments are rare in economics. In the case of health-care prices and health-care spending, we cannot go back and repeat the years from 1990 to 2001 with a different health-care price and see what happens. True, we could look at other countries' experience, or we could look at the experience of different states within the United States. Economists use such comparisons to help

controlled experiments: empirical tests of theories in a controlled setting in which particular effects can be isolated.

determine causation. For example, we could look at one state in which the price of medical care increased and one in which it did not. We could then look at the health-care spending in each state to see if higher prices caused health-care spending to increase. But, unfortunately, no two countries or states are alike in all respects. Thus, attempting to control for other factors is not as easy as in the case of clinical trials.

In recent years, economists have adapted some methods of experimental science and have begun to conduct economic experiments in laboratory settings that are similar to the real world. The experiments can be repeated, and various effects can be controlled for. **Experimental economics** is a growing area of economics. The findings of experimental economics have affected economists' understanding of how the economy works. Experiments in economics also provide an excellent way to *learn* how the economy works, much as experiments in science courses can help one learn about gravity or the structure of plant cells. But because it is difficult to replicate real-world settings exactly in such experiments, they have not yet been applied as widely as the clinical or laboratory experiments in other sciences.

experimental economics: a branch of economics that uses laboratory experiments to analyze economic behavior.

■ **Faulty Data.** Economic data are not always accurate. People sometimes do not understand the survey questions, are too busy to fill them out carefully, or do not have the correct information. Hospitals reporting data on health-care prices, for example, may not take into account changes in the quality of health care. When people purchase medical care, the quality of the service provided can vary widely over time and from doctor to doctor.

If the quality of health care is improving, then the higher relative prices we have observed might partly reflect better service rather than an increase in the price of the same service. The actual increase in the price of health care might have been less rapid if we measured the improved quality, such as reduced chances of serious stroke or depression because of better drugs.

REVIEW

- Economists endeavor to explain facts and observations about the economy, but it is not always easy to establish what the facts are. To establish patterns, it is sometimes necessary to carefully organize information and present it in tables or graphs.

- GDP is a measure of all the goods and services produced in a country during a period of time.

- Correlation does not imply causation. Because controlled experiments are rare in economics, establishing causation is more difficult in economics than in other sciences.

- Recent advances in experimental economics are improving this situation.

- Economic observations are not always accurate. For example, the quality of a service such as medical care can be difficult to measure.

The Circular Flow Diagram: People Interacting in Markets

Behind the health-care and GDP observations in the figures and tables we've just examined are real people who purchase and produce health care and other services and goods in the economy. Any explanation of spending trends must be based on the choices these people make and how they interact with each other. In order to

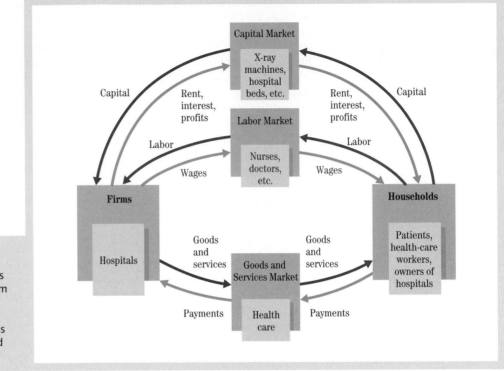

**Figure 2.6
A Circular Flow Diagram**
This diagram shows how funds flow through the economy from households to firms and back again. Buying and selling take place in the goods and services markets, the labor market, and the capital market.

circular flow diagram: a diagram illustrating the flow of funds through the economy as people buy and sell in markets.

organize our thinking about who these people are and how they interact in the economy, a diagram is helpful. It is called the **circular flow diagram** and is shown in Figure 2.6. The circular flow diagram shows how funds flow through the economy as people buy and sell things. Notice the arrows pointing in a circular pattern (that's how the diagram gets its name). To understand how the diagram works, we need to discuss the boxes that the arrows point into and out of.

When using a circular flow diagram, economists place the things that people buy and sell into three groups: (1) *goods and services*, such as flu shots or medical physicals; (2) *labor*, such as the work of nurses and doctors; and (3) *capital*, such as the x-ray machines or the hospital beds that are needed to provide health care. In general, the term *capital* refers to the equipment and structures used to produce goods and services. Corresponding to each of these three groups is a market in which items in the group are bought and sold: (1) *the goods and services market*, (2) *the labor market*, and (3) *the capital market*. These three markets are shown by the blue boxes in the middle part of Figure 2.6, with the yellow boxes giving examples from the health-care industry.

Now consider the *households* and the *firms* in the circular flow diagram. A household is an individual or group of individuals occupying a set of living quarters. For example, a household could be a group of college graduates sharing an apartment, a divorced person living alone, a family with four children, or a single retiree. A firm is a producer of goods and services. For example, a firm in the health-care industry could be a local hospital or a large health maintenance organization. Of course, there are many other types of producers in the economy: General Motors produces cars, the University of Texas produces educational services, the U.S. government produces defense services, and so on. The circular flow diagram puts all producers into the "firm" category.

The households and firms are shown in the blue boxes on the right and left, respectively, of the circular flow diagram, with the yellow boxes again giving examples from the health-care industry. The households are shown doing three things in the circular flow diagram:

- Households buy goods and services; for example, an older person gets a flu shot at the doctor's office.

- Households sell their labor services to firms in the labor market; for example, a nurse works for an HMO and receives wages in return.

- Households supply capital to firms in the capital market; for example, a young couple may rent out the first floor of their house as a doctor's office and receive rent in return. Households also supply capital by owning shares in firms (and receiving part of the profits) or making loans to firms (and receiving interest).

Note that in each of these cases, firms are on the other side of the market from households. Thus the firms are also shown doing three things: They sell goods and services to households, they buy labor services from households, and they buy capital from households.

The arrows in the circular flow diagram show the results of all this buying and selling. The counterclockwise (red) arrows show the movement of goods and services, labor, and capital. The clockwise (green) arrows show the flow of funds used to pay for these items: payments for goods and services, wages for labor, and rent, interest, and profit for capital. Funds flow through the economy from households to firms and back again.

The circular flow diagram is a useful visual device for keeping track of the people in the economy and the markets in which they interact. If we are going to understand the workings of any part of the economy—including health care—we must think about these households and firms as they interact in the markets. That is where economic theory or models come into play.

REVIEW
- The circular flow diagram is useful for showing how households and firms interact in markets and how funds flow through the economy.

Economic Models

economic model: an explanation of how the economy or part of the economy works.

In order to explain economic facts and observations, one needs an economic theory, or a *model*. An **economic model** is an explanation of how the economy or a part of the economy works. In practice, most economists use the terms *theory* and *model* interchangeably, although sometimes the term *theory* suggests a general explanation and the term *model* suggests a more specific explanation. The term *law* is also typically used interchangeably with the terms *model* and *theory* in economics.

What Are Economic Models?

Economic models are always abstractions, or simplifications, of the real world. They take very complicated phenomena, such as the behavior of people, firms, and governments, and simplify them, in much the same way as a model of a building used by architects is an abstraction, or simplification, of the actual building. Some models can be very detailed; others are just broad abstractions. Be sure to remember that the model and the phenomenon being explained by the model are different.

Do not be critical of economic models just because they are simplifications. In every science, models are simplifications of reality. Models are successful if they explain reality reasonably well. In fact, if they were not simplifications, they would be hard to use effectively. Economic models differ from those in the physical sciences because they endeavor to explain human behavior, which is complex and often unpredictable. It is for this reason that the brilliant physicist Max Planck said that economics was harder than physics.

Economic models can be described with words, with numerical tables, with graphs, or with algebra. To use economics, it is important to be able to work with these different descriptions. Figures 2.7 and 2.8 show how models can be illustrated with graphs. By looking at graphs, we can see quickly whether the model has an inverse or a direct relationship. If a model says that one variable varies inversely with the other, this means that if the first variable rises, then the second falls. If a model says that one variable varies directly with another, this means that if one variable rises, the other also rises. In economics, the expression "is positively related to" is frequently used in place of the phrase "varies directly with," which is more common in other sciences. Similarly, the expression "is negatively related to" is frequently used in place of "varies inversely with."

positively related: a situation in which an increase in one variable is associated with an increase in another variable; also called *directly related.*

negatively related: a situation in which an increase in one variable is associated with a decrease in another variable; also called *inversely related.*

In Figure 2.7, two variables—perhaps a relative price variable and a spending variable—are shown to be **positively related.** In other words, when variable 1 increases from *A* to *B*, variable 2 increases from *C* to *D* by the specific amount given by the curve. Likewise, when variable 1 decreases from *B* to *A*, variable 2 decreases from *D* to *C*. In Figure 2.8, a model with two variables that are **negatively related** is shown. Here, when variable 1 increases from *A* to *B*, variable 2 decreases from *D* to *C*. Likewise, when variable 1 decreases from *B* to *A*, variable 2 increases from *C* to *D*.

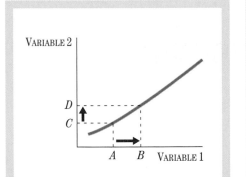

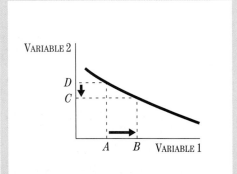

Figure 2.7
A Model with Two Positively Related Variables
The upward-sloping line shows how the variables are related. When one variable increases from *A* to *B*, the other variable increases from *C* to *D*. If one variable declines from *B* to *A*, the other variable declines from *D* to *C*. We say that variable 1 is positively related to variable 2, or that variable 1 varies directly with variable 2.

Figure 2.8
A Model with Two Negatively Related Variables
When one variable increases from *A* to *B*, the other variable decreases from *D* to *C*. Likewise, when one variable decreases from *B* to *A*, the other variable increases from *C* to *D*. We say variable 1 is negatively related to variable 2, or that variable 1 varies inversely with variable 2.

Models have *constants* as well as variables. The constants in the models in Figures 2.7 and 2.8 are the positions and shapes of the curves.

As you study economic models in this book, you will begin to see that they have a common approach to human behavior. Economic models describe how people deal with scarcity, or with situations where they would like to have more, or do more, than their resources will allow. Scarcity requires that people *choose* between one thing and another. For example, in developing a model of health-care spending, an economist would examine how people with a limited amount of income would choose between more health care and less of something else. Or the economist might examine how a health-maintenance organization would decide whether to hire more nurses and fewer doctors in producing a given amount of health care in the community. In modeling the behavior of consumers and firms, economists assume that people make purposeful choices to improve their well-being when confronting such scarcity. More than anything else, the problem of scarcity provides a broad and common core to the field of economics.

■ **An Example: A Model with Two Variables.**   Figure 2.9 shows a model describing how doctors employed in a health maintenance organization provide physical examinations. The model states that the more doctors who are employed at the HMO, the more physical exams can be given. The model is represented in four different ways: (1) with words, (2) with a numerical table, (3) with a graph, and (4) with algebra.

On the lower right of Figure 2.9, we have the verbal description: more doctors, more physical exams, but additional doctors increase the number of exams by smaller amounts, presumably because the diagnostic facilities at the HMO are limited; for example, there are only so many rooms available for physical exams.

On the upper left, we have a table with numbers showing how the number of examinations depends on the number of doctors. Exactly how many examinations are given by each number of doctors is shown in the table. Clearly this table is much more specific than the verbal description. Be sure to distinguish between the meaning of a table that presents a model (like the table in Figure 2.9) and a table that presents data (like Table 2.1). They look similar, but one is a model of the real world and the other represents observations about the real world.

On the upper right, we have a curve showing the relationship between doctors and physical examinations. The curve shows how many exams each number of doctors can perform. The points on the curve are plotted from the information in the table. The vertical axis has the number of examinations; the horizontal axis has the number of doctors. The points are connected with a line to help visualize the curve.

Finally, in the lower left we show the doctor-examination relationship in algebraic form. In this case, the number of exams is equal to the square root of the number of doctors times 20. If we use the symbol y for the number of exams and x for the number of doctors, the model looks a lot like the equations in an algebra course.

All four ways of representing models have advantages and disadvantages. The advantage of the verbal representation is that we usually communicate with people in words, and if we want our economic models to have any use, we need to communicate with people who have not studied economics. However, the verbal representation is not as precise as the other three. In addition to verbal analysis, in this book we will focus on tabular and graphical representations rather than on algebraic descriptions.

■ **Prediction and the *Ceteris Paribus* Assumption.**   Prediction is one of the most important uses of models. For example, using the model in Figure 2.8, we can predict that if variable 1 rises from A to B, then variable 2 will fall from D to C. Using the model for physical exams at an HMO, we might predict that having more doctors

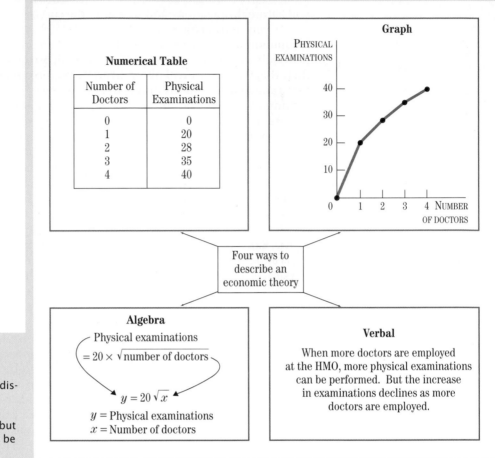

Figure 2.9
Economic Models in Four Ways
Each way has advantages and disadvantages; this book focuses mostly on verbal descriptions, graphs, and numerical tables, but occasionally some algebra will be used to help explain things.

at the HMO will increase the number of physicals that can be given. Economists use models to predict variables ranging from GDP next year to the price of medical care in the year 2007.

In order to use models for prediction, economists use the assumption of ***ceteris paribus,*** which means "all other things equal." For example, the prediction that variable 2 will fall from *D* to *C* assumes that the curve in Figure 2.8 does not shift: The position of the curve when variable 1 is at *A* is *equal* to the position of the curve when variable 1 is at *B*. If other things were not equal—if the curve shifted—then we could not predict that variable 2 would fall from *D* to *C* when variable 1 rose from *A* to *B*. Similarly, predicting that more doctors can produce more physical exams assumes that there is no power outage that would cause the diagnostic equipment to stop operating.

ceteris paribus: "all other things being equal"; refers to holding all other variables constant or keeping all other things the same when one variable is changed.

Microeconomic Models versus Macroeconomic Models

There are two main branches of economics: microeconomics and macroeconomics; thus, there are both microeconomic and macroeconomic models.

microeconomics: the branch of economics that examines individual decision-making at firms and households and the way they interact in specific industries and markets.

Microeconomics studies the behavior of individual firms and households or specific markets like the health-care market or the college graduate market. It looks at variables such as the price of a college education or the reason for increased wages of college graduates. Microeconomic models explain why the price of gasoline varies from station to station and why there are discount airfares.

macroeconomics: the branch of economics that examines the workings and problems of the economy as a whole—GDP growth and unemployment.

Macroeconomics focuses on the whole economy—the whole national economy or even the whole world economy. It tries to explain the changes in GDP over time rather than the changes in a part of GDP like health-care spending. It looks at questions such as what causes the GDP to grow and why many more workers are unemployed in Europe than in the United States.

The Use of Existing Models

Because economics has been around for a long time, there are many existing models that can be applied to explain observations or make predictions that are useful to decision-makers. Much of what economists do in practice, whether in government or business or universities, is use models that are already in existence.

The models are used in many different types of applications, from determining the effects of discrimination in the workplace to evaluating the gains from lower health-care prices. Frequently the models are applied in new and clever ways.

The Development of New Models

Like models in other sciences, economic models change and new models are developed. Many of the models in this book are very different from the models in books published 40 years ago. New economic models evolve because some new observations cannot be explained by existing models.

The process of the development of new models or theories in economics proceeds much like that in any other science. First one develops a *hypothesis*, or a hunch, to explain a puzzling observation. Then one tests the hypothesis by seeing if its predictions of other observations are good. If the hypothesis passes this test, then it becomes accepted. In practice, however, this is at best a rough description of the process of scientific discovery in economics. Existing models are constantly being re-examined and tested. Some economists specialize in testing models; others specialize in developing them. There is an ongoing process of creating and testing of models in economics.

REVIEW

- Economists use economic models to explain economic observations. Economic models are similar to models in other sciences. They are abstractions, or simplifications, of reality, and they have variables and constants. But economic models are different from models in the physical sciences because they must deal with human behavior. Models can be represented verbally, with numerical tables, with graphs, and with algebra.

- New economic models are developed in part because existing models cannot explain facts or observations.

The Impact of Economics on Public Policy

Ever since the birth of economics as a field—around 1776, when Adam Smith published the *Wealth of Nations*—economists have been concerned about and motivated by a desire to improve the economic policy of governments. In fact, economics

mixed economy: a market economy in which the government plays a very large role.

positive economics: economic analysis that explains what happens in the economy and why, without making recommendations about economic policy.

normative economics: economic analysis that makes recommendations about economic policy.

Council of Economic Advisers: a three-member group of economists appointed by the president of the United States to analyze the economy and make recommendations about economic policy.

was originally called *political economy*. Much of the *Wealth of Nations* is about what the government should or should not do to affect the domestic and international economy.

Adam Smith argued for a system of *laissez faire*—little government control—where the role of the government is mainly to promote competition, provide for national defense, and reduce restrictions on the exchange of goods and services. Karl Marx, in contrast, argued in the nineteenth century against a laissez-faire approach. Marx's ideas led to a view that the government should essentially own and control all production. The centrally planned economies that arose in the Soviet Union, Eastern Europe, and China in the twentieth century can be traced to Marx's ideas. Today the debate about the role of government continues. Most countries have rejected the command economy and have moved toward market economies. But in many modern market economies, the government plays a large role, and for this reason such economies are sometimes called **mixed economies.** How great should the role of government be in a market economy? Should the government provide health-care services? Should it try to break up large firms?

Positive versus Normative Economics

In debating the role of government in the economy, economists distinguish between positive and normative economics. **Positive economics** is about what is; **normative economics** is about what should be. For example, positive economics endeavors to explain why health-care spending slowed down in the mid-1990s. Normative economics aims to develop and recommend policies that might prevent health-care spending from rising rapidly in the future. In general, normative economics is concerned with making recommendations about what the government should do—whether it should control the price of electricity or health care, for example. Economists who advise governments spend much of their time doing normative economics. In the United States, the president's **Council of Economic Advisers** has legal responsibility for advising the president about which economic policies are good and which are bad.

Positive economics can also be used to explain *why* governments do what they do. For example, why did the U.S. government control airfares and then stop? Why were tax rates cut in the 1980s, increased in the 1990s, then cut again in the 2000s? Positive analysis of government policy requires a mixture of both political science and economic science, with a focus on what motivates voters and the politicians they elect.

Economists Yellen and Hubbard
Janet Yellen served as the chair of the president's Council of Economic Advisers (CEA) from 1997 to 1999; Glenn Hubbard serves as the current chair of the CEA.

Economics as a Science versus a Partisan Policy Tool

Although economics, like any other science, is based on facts and theories, it is not always used in a purely scientific way.

In political campaigns, economists put forth arguments in favor of one candidate, emphasizing the good side of their candidate and de-emphasizing the bad side. In a court of law, one economist may help a defendant—making the best case possible—and another economist may help the plaintiff—again, making the best case possible. In other words, economics is not always used objectively. A good reason to learn economics for yourself is to see through fallacious arguments.

But economics is not the only science that is used in these two entirely different modes. For example, there is currently a great controversy about the use of biology and chemistry to make estimates of the costs and benefits of different environmental policies. This is a politically controversial subject, and some on both sides of the controversy have been accused of using science in nonobjective ways.

Science or Persuasion?

In a recent court case, a grocery store chain, Lucky Stores, was sued for discriminating against female workers. The case illustrates how economics can be used in a partisan as well as a scientific way.

Economists were called as expert witnesses for both sides. Labor economist John Pencavel testified for the plaintiffs, the women who brought the suit. He found that women at Lucky earned between 76 and 82 percent of what Lucky's male workers earned. Pencavel found that women were regularly placed in jobs that paid less than jobs given male coworkers, although there was no significant difference between them in terms of education and experience. There was little difference in the wages of the male and female workers within each type of job, but some jobs paid more than others, and women happened to be assigned to the lower-paying jobs.

Joan Haworth, another labor economist, was an expert witness for the defendant, Lucky Stores. She reported survey evidence showing that Lucky's assignment of women and men to different jobs reflected differences in the work preferences of men and women. Thus, Lucky justified its job assignments by arguing that there was a gender difference in attitudes toward work. Lucky argued that its employment policies were based on observed differences in the career aspirations of male and female employees. For example, one manager at Lucky testified that women were more interested in cash register work and men were more interested in floor work.

After weighing the facts and economic arguments, the judge decided the case in favor of the plaintiffs.

You be the judge. Would you have been persuaded by the economic argument used by Lucky stores or by the defendants?

Although male and female employees received equal pay for equal work, the judge concluded that Lucky's employment policies involved discrimination. The judge wrote: "The court finds defendant's explanation that the statistical disparities between men and women at Lucky are caused by differences in the work interests of men and women to be unpersuasive."

The decision is a landmark because of the economic analysis that showed that discrimination could exist even if men and women were being paid the same wage for equal work. Of course, not all sex discrimination cases are decided in favor of the plaintiffs. But whoever wins a given case, economics is almost always a key consideration in the judge's decision.

Economics Is Not the Only Factor in Policy Issues

Although economics can be very useful in policy decisions, it is frequently not the only factor. For example, national security sometimes calls for a recommendation on a policy issue different from one based on a purely economic point of view. Although most economists recommend free exchange of goods between countries, the U.S. government restricted exports of high-technology goods such as computers during the cold war because defense specialists worried that the technology could help the military in the Soviet Union, and this was viewed as more important than the economic argument. There are still heavy restrictions on trade in nuclear fuels for fear of the proliferation of nuclear weapons.

Disagreement Between Economists

Watching economists debate issues on television or reading their opinions in a newspaper or magazine certainly gives the impression that they rarely agree. There are major controversies in economics, and we will examine them in this book. But when people survey economists' beliefs, they find a surprising amount of agreement.

Why, then, the popular impression of disagreement? Because there are many economists, and one can always find some economist with a different viewpoint. When people sue other people in court and economics is an issue, it is always possible to find economists who will testify for each side, even if 99 percent of economists would agree with one side. Similarly, television interviews or news shows want to give both sides of public policy issues. Thus, even if 99 percent of economists agree with one side, it is possible to find at least one on the other side.

Economists are human beings with varying moral beliefs and different backgrounds and political views that are frequently unrelated to economic models. For example, an economist who is very concerned about the importation of drugs into the United States might appear to be more willing to condone a restriction on coffee exports from Brazil and other coffee-exporting countries, which might give Colombia a higher price for its coffee to offset a loss in revenue from cocaine. Another economist, who felt less strongly about drug imports, might argue strongly against such a restriction on coffee. But if they were asked about restrictions on trade in the abstract, both economists would probably argue for government policies that prevent them.

REVIEW
- Economic theory can be used to make better economic decisions. Improving government policy decisions has long been a purpose of economics.

- The most basic economic policy questions concern the general role of government in a market economy.

Conclusion: A Reader's Guide

In Chapter 1, we explored the central idea of economics: scarcity, choice, and economic interaction. In this chapter, we discussed how economists observe economic phenomena and use economic models to explain these phenomena. It is now time to move on and learn more about the models and application of the central idea. As you study economic models in the following chapters, it will be useful to keep three points in mind. They are implied by the ideas raised in this chapter.

First, *economics—more than other subjects—requires a mixture of verbal and quantitative skills.* Frequently, those who come to economics with a good background in physical science and mathematics find the mix of formal models with more informal verbal descriptions of markets and institutions unusual and perhaps a little difficult. If you are one of these people, you might wish for a more cut-and-dried, or mathematical, approach.

In contrast, those who are good at history or philosophy may find the emphasis on formal models and graphs difficult and might even prefer a more historical approach that looked more at watershed events and famous individuals and less at formal models of how many individuals behave. If you are one of these people, you might wish that economic models were less abstract.

In reality, however, economics is a mixture of formal modeling, historical analysis, and philosophy. If you are very good at math and you think the symbols and graphs of elementary economics are too simple, think of Max Planck's comment about economics and focus on the complexity of the economic phenomena that these simple models and graphs are explaining. Then when you are asked an open-ended question about government policy that does not have a simple yes or no answer, you will not be caught off guard. Or if your advantage is in history or philosophy, you should spend more time honing your skills at using models and graphs. Then when you are asked to solve a cut-and-dried economic problem with an exact answer requiring graphical analysis, you will not be caught off guard.

Second, *economics is about more than the stock market*. When your friends or relatives hear that you are taking economics, they may ask you for advice about what stock to buy. Economists' friends and relatives are always asking them for such advice. But economics alone offers no predictions about the success of particular companies. Rather, economics gives you some tools you can use to obtain information about companies and to analyze them yourself—perhaps eventually to become an investment adviser.

Economics will also help you answer questions about whether to invest in the stock market or in a bank or how many stocks to buy. But the scope of economics is much, much broader than the stock market or banks, as the questions at the start of the chapter indicate. In fact, the scope of economics is even wider than these examples. Economists use their models, or theories, to study environmental pollution, crime, discrimination, and who should have the right to sue whom.

Third, and perhaps most important, *the study of economics is an intellectually fascinating adventure in its own right*. Yes, economics is highly relevant, and it affects people's lives. But once you learn how economic models work, you will find that they are actually fun to use. And they would be just as much fun if they were not so relevant. Every now and then, just after you have learned about a new economic model, put the book down and think of the economic model independent of its message or relevance to society—try to enjoy it the way you would a good movie. In this way, too, you will be learning to think like an economist.

HEY POINTS

1. Economics is a way of thinking that requires observation (describing economic events), building and using economic models to explain economic events and predict future events, and recommending courses of action for government—and business—based on these observations and models.

2. Economic models are abstractions, or simplifications, of reality and attempt to explain human behavior as expressed by economic measures.

3. Economic models, like models in other sciences, can be described with words, with tables, with graphs, or with mathematics. All four ways are important and complement one another.

4. The circular flow diagram shows the major players in the economy and how they interact in markets.

5. A plot showing that two variables are correlated during a period of time does not mean that one causes the other.

6. Faulty data and the lack of controlled experiments sometimes make economic observations difficult to interpret.

7. Sometimes new facts require that economists develop new models.

8. Decisions about the role of government in areas from airfares to health care are influenced by economic analysis.

9. Improving economic policy has been a goal of economists since the time of Adam Smith.

KEY TERMS

gross domestic product (GDP)
relative price
economic variable
controlled experiments

experimental economics
circular flow diagram
economic model
positively related
negatively related

ceteris paribus
microeconomics
macroeconomics
mixed economy

positive economics
normative economics
Council of Economic Advisers

QUESTIONS FOR REVIEW

1. Why do economists need to document and quantify observations about the economy?
2. What is the most comprehensive available measure of the size of an economy?
3. What is meant by a relative price?
4. Why doesn't correlation imply causation?
5. What do the arrows in the circular flow diagram indicate?
6. How do economic models differ from the economic phenomena they explain?
7. Why are controlled experiments rare in economics?
8. What is the difference between macroeconomics and microeconomics?
9. What is the difference between positive and normative economics?
10. How do economists use the *ceteris paribus* assumption?

PROBLEMS

1. Which of the following items are microeconomic, and which are macroeconomic?
   a. The number of people with jobs in the United States
   b. A tax on sport utility vehicles
   c. Prices of sunglasses
   d. GDP
2. Identify whether the following policy statements are positive or normative. Explain.
   a. "The price of Internet stocks is too high."
   b. "The government should control the price of health care."
   c. "Increases in consumer spending improved the economy last year."
   d. "The government should break up Microsoft."
3. Interpret the data on spending on clothing in the table in the next column by filling in the blanks.
   a. What has happened to clothing spending as a share of GDP over this 30-year period?
   b. What has happened to the relative price of clothing over this period, and how could it be related to the clothing spending share?

c. Draw a graph showing the relationship between clothing spending as a share of GDP and the relative price of clothing.

Year	GDP (billions of dollars)	Spending on Clothing	Clothing Spending as a Share of GDP (%)	Relative Clothing Price
1970	1,039.7	47.8		1.88
1980	2,795.6		3.84	1.43
1990		204.1	3.52	1.17
2000	9,872.9	319.1		0.89

4. Draw a diagram like Figure 2.6 for the market for air travel and give examples of capital, labor, and firms in that market. Show that there is a complete circular flow of funds and goods in the economy as a whole.
5. Why is it typical for economists to make the *ceteris paribus* assumption when making predictions?
6. Consider an economic model of web page production. Show how to represent this model graphically, algebraically, and verbally, as in Figure 2.9.

Number of Programmers	Web Pages
0	0
1	10
4	20
9	30
16	40

7. What is the difference between the price of a good and its relative price? Which information is more useful if you are interested in analyzing the change in spending on that good?
8. Indicate whether you expect positive or negative correlation for the following pairs of variables. What is required in order to show causation?
   a. Sunrise and crowing roosters
   b. Price of theater tickets and number of theatergoers
   c. Purchases of candy and purchases of Valentine's Day cards

Reading, Understanding, and Creating Graphs

Whether you follow the stock market, the health care market, or the whole economy, graphs are needed to understand what is going on. That is why the financial pages of newspapers contain so many graphs. Knowing how to read, understand, and even create your own graphs is part of learning to "think like an economist." Graphs help us see correlations, or patterns in economic observations. Graphs are also useful for understanding economic models. They help us see how variables in the model behave. They help us describe assumptions about what firms and consumers do.

Computer software to create graphs is now widely available. A graphing program with many examples is provided with the software that accompanies this text. To understand how helpful graphs can be, you might want to create a few of your own graphs using the time-series data in the "Explore" section of the software. Here we provide an overview of basic graphing techniques.

Visualizing Observations with Graphs

Most economic graphs are drawn in two dimensions, like the surface of this page, and are constructed using a **Cartesian coordinate system.** The idea of Cartesian coordinates is that pairs of observations on variables can be represented in a plane by designating one axis for one variable and the other axis for the other variable. Each point, or coordinate, on the plane corresponds to a pair of observations.

Time-Series Graphs

In many instances, we want to see how a variable changes over time. Consider the federal debt held by the public—all the outstanding borrowing of the federal government that has not yet been paid back. Table 2A.1 shows observations of the U.S. federal debt. The observations are for every 10 years. The observations in Table 2A.1 are graphed in Figure 2A.1. The graph in Figure 2A.1 is called a **time-series graph** because it plots a series— that is, several values of the variable—over time.

Observe the scales on the horizontal and vertical axes in Figure 2A.1. The six years are put on the horizontal axis, spread evenly from the year 1950 to the year 2010. The last year is a forecast. For the vertical axis, one needs to decide on a scale. The range of variation for the debt in Table 2A.1 is very wide—from a minimum of $219 billion to a maximum of $3,464 billion. Thus, the range on the vertical axis—from $0 to $4,000 billion in Figure 2A.1—must be wide enough to contain all these points.

Now observe how each pair of points from Table 2A.1 is plotted in Figure 2A.1. The point for the pair of observations for the year 1950 and the debt of $219 billion is found by going over to 1950 on the horizontal axis, then going up to $219 billion and putting a dot there. The

Year	Debt (billions of dollars)
1950	219
1960	237
1970	283
1980	709
1990	2,410
2000	3,464
2010	941

Table 2A.1
U.S. Federal Government Debt

Source: *Budget of the U.S. Government, Fiscal Year 2001*: Analysis of the President's Budgetary Proposal for the Fiscal Year 2001, Congressional Budget Office, April 2000.

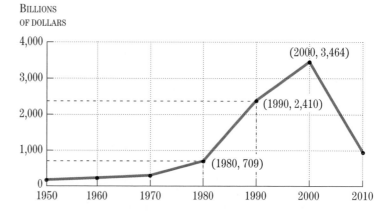

Figure 2A.1
U.S. Federal Debt
Each point corresponds to a pair of observations—the year and the debt—from Table 2A.1.

Figure 2A.2
Stretching the Debt Story in Two Ways
The points in both graphs are identical to those in Figure 2A.1, but by stretching or shrinking the scales the problem can be made to look either less dramatic or more dramatic.

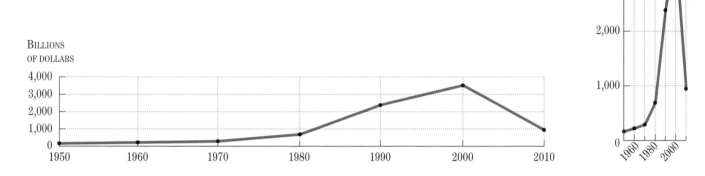

point for 1960 and $237 billion and all the other points are found in the same way. In order to better visualize the points, they can be connected with lines. These lines are not part of the observations; they are only a convenience to help in eyeballing the observations. The points for 1980, 1990, and 2000 are labeled with the pairs of observations corresponding to Table 2A.1, but in general there is no need to put in such labels.

One could choose scales different from those in Figure 2A.1, and if you plotted your own graph from Table 2A.1 without looking at Figure 2A.1, your scales would probably be different. The scales determine how much movement there is in a time-series graph. For example, Figure 2A.2 shows two ways to stretch the scales to make the increase and decrease in the debt look more or less dramatic. So as not to be fooled by graphs, therefore, it is important to look at the scales and think about what they mean.

As an alternative to time-series graphs with dots connected by a line, the observations can be shown on a bar graph, as in Figure 2A.3. Some people prefer the visual look of a bar graph, but, as is clear from a comparison of Figures 2A.1 and 2A.3, they provide the same information.

The debt as a percentage of GDP is given in Table 2A.2 and graphed in Figure 2A.4. Note that this figure makes the debt look very different from the way it looks in the first one. As a percentage of GDP, the debt fell from the end of World War II (when it was very large because of the war debt) until around 1980. It increased during the 1980s, but started to decline again in the 1990s.

Sometimes the data to be graphed have no observations close to 0, in which case including 0 on the vertical axis would leave some wasted space at the bottom of the graph. To eliminate this space and have more room to see the graph itself, we can start the range near the minimum value and end it near the maximum value. This is done in Figure 2A.5, where the debt as a percentage of GDP is shown *up to 1980*. Note, however, that cutting off the bottom of the scale could be misleading to people who do not look at the axis. In particular, 0 percent is no longer at the point where the horizontal and vertical axes intersect. To warn people about the missing part of the scale, a little cut is sometimes put on the axis, as is done in Figure 2A.5, but you have to look carefully at the scale.

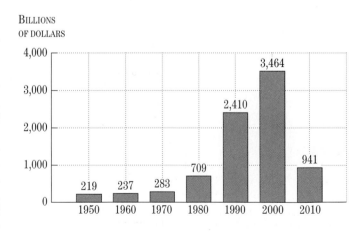

Figure 2A.3
U.S. Federal Debt in Bars
The observations are identical to those in Figure 2A.1.

Table 2A.2
U.S. Federal Debt as a Percentage of GDP

Year	Debt (percent of GDP)
1950	82.5
1960	46.8
1970	28.7
1980	26.8
1990	44.2
2000	36.1
2010	6.3

Source: U.S. Department of Commerce and Table 2A.1.

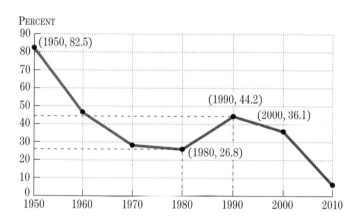

Figure 2A.4
U.S. Federal Debt as a Percentage of GDP
Each point corresponds to a pair of observations from Table 2A.2.

Time-Series Graphs Showing Two or More Variables

So far, we have shown how a graph can be used to show observations on one variable over time. What if we want to see how two or more variables change over time together? Suppose, for example, we want to look at how observations on debt as a percentage of GDP compare with the interest rate the government must pay on its debt. (The interest rate for 2010 is, of course, a forecast.) The two variables are shown in Table 2A.3.

The two sets of observations can easily be placed on the same time-series graph. In other words, we can plot the observations on the debt percentage and connect the dots and then plot the interest rate observations and connect the dots. If the scales of measurement of the two variables are much different, then it may be hard to see both, however. For example, the interest rate ranges between 1 and 12 percent; it would not be very visible

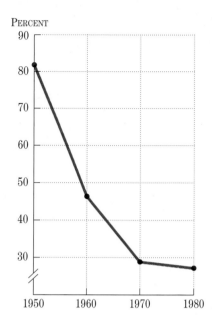

Figure 2A.5
A Look at Debt as a Percentage of GDP from 1950 to 1980
(*Note:* To alert the reader that the bottom part of the axis is not shown, a break point is sometimes used, as shown here.)

on a graph going all the way from 0 to 100 percent, a range that is fine for the debt percentage. In this situation, a **dual scale** can be used, as shown in Figure 2A.6. One scale is put on the left-hand vertical axis, and the other scale is put on the right-hand vertical axis. With a dual-scale diagram, it is very important to be aware of the two scales. In Figure 2A.6 we emphasize the different axes by the color line segment at the top of each vertical axis. The color line segment corresponds to the color of the curve plotted using that scale.

Table 2A.3
Interest Rate and Federal Debt as a Percentage of GDP

Year	Debt (percent of GDP)	Interest Rate (percent)
1950	82.5	1.2
1960	46.8	2.9
1970	28.7	6.5
1980	26.8	11.5
1990	44.2	7.5
2000	36.1	5.5
2010	6.3	4.8

Source: Federal Reserve Board and Table 2A.2.

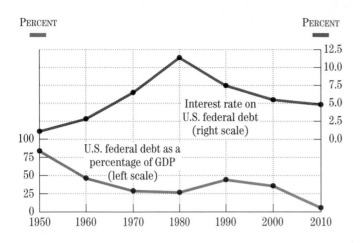

Figure 2A.6
Comparing Two Time Series with a Dual Scale
When two variables have different scales, a dual scale is useful. Here the interest rate and the debt as a percentage of GDP are plotted from Table 2A.3.

Scatter Plots

Finally, two variables can be usefully compared with a **scatter plot.** The Cartesian coordinate method is used, as in the time-series graph; however, we do not put the year on one of the axes. Instead, the horizontal axis is used for one of the variables and the vertical axis for the other variable. We do this for the debt percentage and the interest rate in Figure 2A.7. The interest rate is on the vertical axis, and the debt percentage is on the horizontal axis.

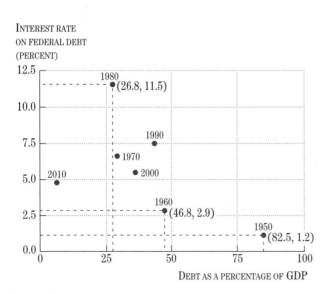

Figure 2A.7
Scatter Plot
Interest rate and debt as a percentage of GDP are shown.

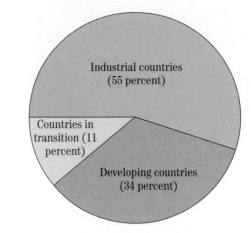

Figure 2A.8
Pie Chart Showing the Shares of the World's GDP
The pie chart shows how the world's GDP is divided up into that produced by (1) the industrial countries, such as the United States, Germany, and Japan; (2) the developing countries, such as India, China, and Nigeria; and (3) countries in transition from communism to capitalism, such as Russia and Poland.

For example, the point at the upper left is 26.8 percent for the debt as a percentage of GDP and 11.5 percent for the interest rate.

Pie Charts

Time-series graphs, bar graphs, and scatter plots are not the only visual ways to observe economic data. For example, the *pie chart* in Figure 2A.8 is useful for comparing percentage shares for a small number of different groups or a small number of time periods. In this example, the pie chart is a visual representation of how the industrial countries produce more than half of the world's GDP, while the developing countries produce 34 percent and the former communist countries in Eastern Europe and the former Soviet Union, now in transition toward market economies, produce about 11 percent.

Visualizing Models with Graphs

Graphs can also represent models. Like graphs showing observations, graphs showing models are usually restricted to curves in two dimensions.

Slopes of Curves

Does a curve slope up or down? How steep is it? These questions are important in economics, as in other sciences. The **slope** of a curve tells us how much the variable on the vertical axis changes when we change the variable on the horizontal axis by one unit.

The slope is computed as follows:

$$\text{Slope} = \frac{\text{change in variable on vertical axis}}{\text{change in variable on horizontal axis}}$$

In most algebra courses, the vertical axis is usually called the y-axis and the horizontal axis is called the x-axis. Thus, the slope is sometime described as

$$\text{Slope} = \frac{\text{change in } y}{\text{change in } x} = \frac{\Delta y}{\Delta x}$$

where the Greek letter Δ (delta) means "change in." In other words, the slope is the ratio of the "rise" (vertical change) to the "run" (horizontal change).

Figure 2A.9 shows how to compute the slope. In this case, the slope declines as the variable on the x-axis increases.

Observe that *the steeper the curve, the larger the slope*. When the curve gets very flat, the slope gets close to zero. Curves can either be upward-sloping or downward-sloping. If the curve slopes up from left to right, as in Figure 2A.9, it has a **positive slope,** and we say that the two variables are positively related. If the curve slopes down from left to right, it has a **negative slope,** and we say that the two variables are negatively related. Figure 2A.10 shows a case where the slope is negative. When x increases by 1 unit ($\Delta x = 1$), y declines by 2 units ($\Delta y = -2$). Thus, the slope equals -2; it is negative. Observe how the curve slopes down from left to right.

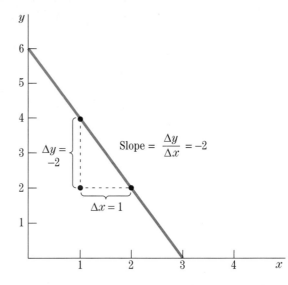

Figure 2A.10
A Relationship with a Negative Slope
Here the slope is negative: $(\Delta y)/(\Delta x) = -2$. As x increases, y falls. The line slopes down from left to right. In this case, y and x are inversely, or negatively, related.

If the curve is a straight line, then the slope is a constant. Curves that are straight lines—as in Figure 2A.10—are called **linear.** But economic relationships do not need to be linear, as the example in Figure 2A.9 makes clear. Figure 2A.11 shows six different examples of curves and indicates how they are described.

Graphs of Models with More than Two Variables

In most cases, economic models involve more than two variables. For example, the number of physical examinations could depend on the number of nurses as well as the number of doctors. Or the amount of lemonade demanded might depend on the weather as well as on the price.

Economists have devised several methods for representing models with more than two variables with two-dimensional graphs. Suppose, for example, that the relationship between y and x in Figure 2A.10 depends on a third variable z. For a given value of x, larger values of z lead to larger values of y. This example is graphed in Figure 2A.12. As in Figure 2A.10, when x increases, y falls. This is a **movement along the curve.** But what if z changes? We represent this as a **shift of the curve.** An increase in z shifts the curve up; a decrease in z shifts the curve down.

Thus, by distinguishing between shifts of and movements along a curve, economists represent models with more than two variables in only two dimensions. Only two variables (x and y) are shown explicitly on the graph,

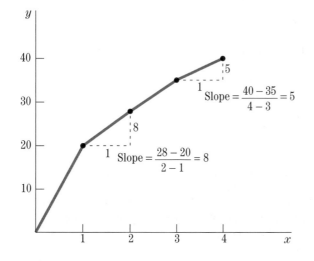

Figure 2A.9
Measuring the Slope
The slope between two points is given by the change along the vertical axis divided by the change along the horizontal axis. In this example, the slope declines as x increases. Since the curve slopes up from left to right, it has a positive slope.

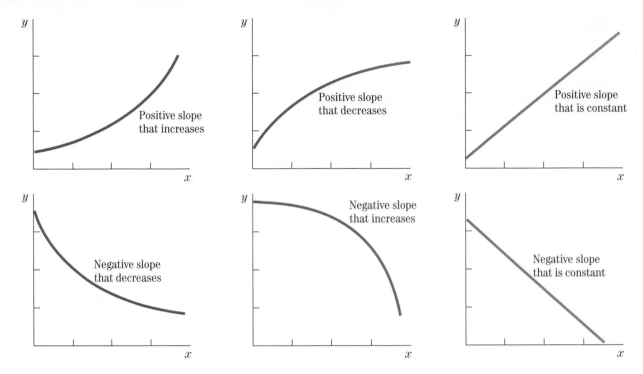

Figure 2A.11
Six Types of Relationships
In the top row, the variables are positively related. In the bottom row, they are negatively related.

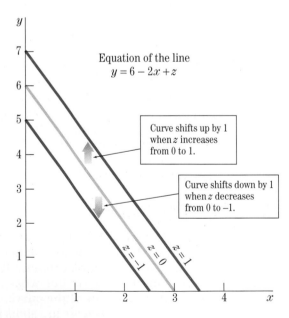

Figure 2A.12
A Third Variable Shifts the Curve
In order to represent models with three variables (x, y, and z) on a two-dimensional graph, economists distinguish between movements along the curve (when x and y change, holding z unchanged) and shifts of the curve (when z changes).

and when the third (z) is fixed, changes in x and y are movements along the curve. When z changes, the curve shifts. The distinction between "movements along" and "shifts of" curves comes up many times in economics.

Key Terms and Definitions

Cartesian coordinate system: a graphing system in which ordered pairs of numbers are represented on a plane by the distances from a point to two perpendicular lines, called axes.

time-series graph: a graph that plots a variable over time, usually with time on the horizontal axis.

dual scale: a graph that uses time on the horizontal axis and different scales on the left and right vertical axes to compare the movements of two variables over time.

scatter plot: a graph in which points in a Cartesian coordinate system represent the values of two variables.

slope: a characteristic of a curve that is defined as the change in the variable on the vertical axis divided by the change in the variable on the horizontal axis.

positive slope: a slope of a curve that is greater than zero, representing a positive or direct relationship between two variables.

negative slope: a slope of a curve that is less than zero, representing a negative or inverse relationship between two variables.

linear: a situation in which a curve is straight, with a constant slope.

movement along the curve: a situation in which a change in the variable on one axis causes a change in the variable on the other axis, but the position of the curve is maintained.

shift of the curve: a change in the position of a curve, usually caused by a change in a variable not represented on either axis.

Questions for Review

1. What is the difference between a scatter plot and a time-series graph?

2. Why are dual scales sometimes necessary?

3. What is the advantage of graphs over verbal representations of models?

4. What does a curve with a negative slope look like?

5. What is the difference between a shift in a curve and a movement along a curve?

Problems

1. The table at the right presents data on the debt and the debt to GDP ratio predicted by the Congressional Budget Office for the United States for each year through 2010.
   a. Construct a time-series plot of the ratio of government debt to GDP.
   b. Construct a time-series plot of the debt.
   c. Construct a scatter plot of the debt ratio and the debt.

Year	Debt	Debt to GDP Ratio
2000	3,464	36.1
2001	3,287	32.7
2002	3,100	29.5
2003	2,903	26.5
2004	2,690	23.5
2005	2,465	20.7
2006	2,204	17.7
2007	1,907	14.7
2008	1,587	11.7
2009	1,236	8.7
2010	941	6.3

Source: An Analysis of the President's Budgetary Proposals for Fiscal Year 2001, Congressional Budget Office, April 2000.

2. The following table presents data on U.S. turkey production and prices.

Year	Turkey Production (billions of pounds)	Price per Pound
1985	3.7	49.1
1986	4.1	47.1
1987	4.9	34.8
1988	5.1	38.6
1989	5.5	40.9
1990	6.0	39.4

Source: Statistical Abstract of the United States, 1993.

a. Construct a time-series plot of turkey production in the United States.
b. Construct a time-series plot of the price of turkey per pound.
c. Construct a scatter plot of turkey production and turkey prices.

3. The following table shows the number of physical examinations given by doctors at an HMO with three different-size clinics: small, medium, and large. The larger the clinic, the more patients the doctors can handle.

Exams per Small Clinic	Exams per Medium Clinic	Exams per Large Clinic	Number of Doctors
0	0	0	0
20	30	35	1
28	42	49	2
35	53	62	3
40	60	70	4

a. Show the relationship between doctors and physical exams given with *three* curves, where the number of doctors is on the horizontal axis and the number of examinations is on the vertical axis.
b. Describe how the three relationships compare with one another.
c. Is a change in the number of doctors a shift of or a movement along the curve?
d. Is a change in the size of the clinic a shift of or a movement along the curve?

CHAPTER 3

The Supply and Demand Model

It's pretty much the same thing every March. Four college basketball teams win a place in the top round of the national tournament, the Final Four.

Each college lets students at the college buy a limited number of tickets for about $100 a seat. Then, when the students get to the city where the Final Four is being played, they find people on the street willing to pay huge amounts of money for those tickets—as much as $1,000. And it is always tempting to sell the tickets and watch the game on TV. Some, of course, do sell. But how are these prices on the street market determined? How are prices in general determined? What causes the price of health care to rise? What causes the price of computers to fall? What determines the price at which people buy or sell gasoline, electronic goods, printing services, or foreign currencies? The purpose of this chapter is to show how to find the answers to such questions.

To do so, we need to construct a model—a simplified description of how a market works. The model economists use to explain how prices are determined in a market is called the *supply and demand model*. This model describes how particular markets—such as the health-care market or the computer market—work. It consists of three elements: *demand*, describing the behavior of consumers in the market; *supply*, describing the behavior of firms in the market; and *market equilibrium*, connecting supply and demand and describing how consumers and firms interact in the market.

Economists like to compare the supply and demand model to a pair of scissors. Demand is one blade of the scissors. Supply is the other. Either blade alone is incomplete and virtually useless; but when the two blades of a pair of scissors are connected to form the scissors, they become an amazingly useful, yet simple, tool. So it is with the supply and demand model.

In this chapter, we first describe each of the three elements of the model. We then show how to use the model to answer a host of questions about price determination in a market economy.

Demand

demand: a relationship between **price** and **quantity demanded.**

price: the amount of money or other goods that one must pay to obtain a particular good.

quantity demanded: the quantity of a good that people want to buy at a given price during a specific time period.

Table 3.1
Demand Schedule for Bicycles (millions of bicycles per year)

Price	Quantity Demanded
$140	18
$160	14
$180	11
$200	9
$220	7
$240	5
$260	3
$280	2
$300	1

demand schedule: a tabular presentation of demand showing the price and quantity demanded for a particular good, all else being equal.

law of demand: the tendency for the quantity demanded of a good in a market to decline as its price rises.

To an economist, the term *demand*—whether the demand for health care or the demand for computers—has a very specific meaning. **Demand** is a relationship between two economic variables: (1) *the price of a particular good* and (2) *the quantity of the good consumers are willing to buy at that price during a specific time period*, all other things being equal. For short, we call the first variable the **price** and the second variable the **quantity demanded.** The phrase *all other things being equal*, or *ceteris paribus*, is appended to the definition of demand because the quantity consumers are willing to buy depends on many other things besides the price of the good; we want to hold these other things constant, or equal, while we examine the relationship between price and quantity demanded.

Demand can be represented with a numerical table or a graph. In either case, demand describes how much of a good consumers will purchase at each price. Consider the demand for bicycles in the United States. An example of the demand for bicycles is shown in Table 3.1. Several prices for a typical bicycle are listed in the first column of the table, ranging from $140 to $300. Of course, there are many kinds of bicycles—mountain bikes, racing bikes, children's bikes, and inexpensive one-speed bikes with cruiser brakes—so you need to think about the price of an average, or typical, bike.

Listed in the second column of Table 3.1 is the quantity demanded (in millions of bicycles) each year in the United States at the price in the first column. This is the total demand in the bicycle market. For example, at a price of $180 per bicycle, consumers would buy 11 million bicycles. That is, the quantity demanded would be 11 million bicycles each year in the United States, according to Table 3.1.

Observe that as the price rises, the quantity demanded by consumers goes down. If the price goes up from $180 to $200 per bicycle, for example, the quantity demanded goes down from 11 million to 9 million bicycles. On the other hand, if the price goes down, the quantity demanded goes up. If the price falls from $180 to $160, for example, the quantity demanded rises from 11 million to 14 million bicycles.

The relationship between price and quantity demanded in Table 3.1 is called a **demand schedule.** This relationship is an example of the law of demand. The **law of demand** says that the higher the price, the lower the quantity demanded in the market; and the lower the price, the higher the quantity demanded in the market. In other words, the law of demand says that the price and the quantity demanded are negatively related, all other things being equal.

The Demand Curve

Figure 3.1 represents demand graphically. It is a graph with the price of the good on the vertical axis and the quantity demanded of the good on the horizontal axis. It shows the demand for bicycles given in Table 3.1. Each of the nine rows in Table 3.1

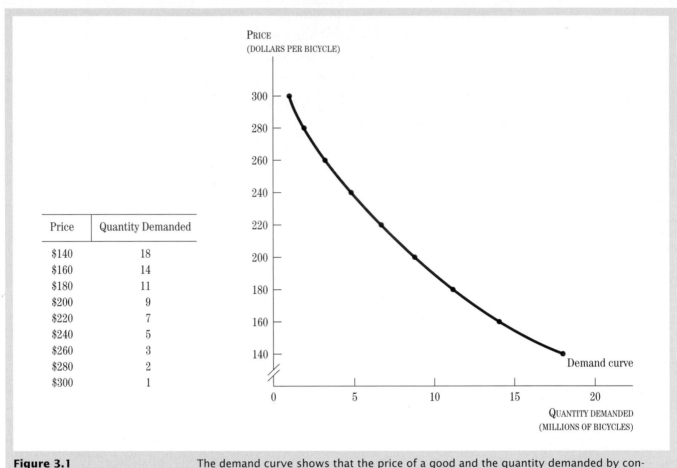

Price	Quantity Demanded
$140	18
$160	14
$180	11
$200	9
$220	7
$240	5
$260	3
$280	2
$300	1

Figure 3.1
The Demand Curve

The demand curve shows that the price of a good and the quantity demanded by consumers are negatively related. The curve slopes down. For each price, the demand curve gives the quantity demanded, or the quantity that consumers are willing to buy at that price. The points along the demand curve for bicycles shown here are the same as the pairs of numbers in Table 3.1.

demand curve: a graph of demand showing the downward-sloping relationship between price and quantity demanded.

corresponds to one of the nine points in Figure 3.1. For example, the point at the lower right part of the graph corresponds to the first row of the table, when the price is $140 and the quantity demanded is 18 million bicycles. The resulting curve showing all the combinations of price and quantity demanded is the **demand curve.** It slopes downward from left to right because the quantity demanded is negatively related to the price. To remember that the *d*emand curve slopes *d*ownward, think of the *d* in *demand.*

Why does the demand curve slope downward? The demand curve tells us the quantity demanded by all consumers. Consumers must make choices with scarce resources. They must choose between bicycles and other goods. If the price of bicycles falls, then some consumers who previously found the price of bicycles too high may decide to buy a bicycle. The lower price of bicycles gives them an incentive to buy bicycles rather than other goods. It is important to remember that when economists draw a demand curve, they hold constant the price of other goods: running shoes, in-line skates, motor scooters, etc. When the price of bicycles falls, bicycles become more attractive to people in comparison with these other goods. As a result, the quantity demanded rises when the price falls. Conversely, when the price of bicycles rises, some people may decide to buy in-line skates or motor scooters instead of bicycles. As a result, the quantity demanded declines when the price rises.

Shifts in Demand

Now price is not the only thing that affects the quantity of a good that people buy. The weather, people's concerns about the environment, or the availability of bike lanes on roads can influence people's decisions to purchase bicycles, for example. The quantity of bicycles bought might increase if a climate change brought on an extended period of dry weather. Because people would enjoy riding their bicycles more in dry weather, more bicycles would be purchased at any given price. Or perhaps a health trend might lead people to get exercise by riding bicycles rather than driving their cars. This would also lead to more purchases of bicycles.

The demand curve is drawn assuming that all other things are equal, except the price of the good. A change in any one of these other things, previously assumed to be equal, will shift the demand curve. An increase in demand shifts the demand curve to the right. A decrease in demand shifts the demand curve to the left. This is illustrated in Figure 3.2. The lightly shaded curve labeled "old demand curve" is the same as the demand curve in Figure 3.1. The arrow shows how this curve has shifted to the right to the more darkly shaded curve labeled "new demand curve." Thus, Figure 3.2 shows the demand curve for bicycles shifting to the right. When the

Figure 3.2
A Shift in the Demand Curve
The demand curve shows how the quantity demanded of a good is related to the price of the good, all other things being equal. A change in one of these other things—the weather or people's tastes, for example—will shift the demand curve, as shown in the graph. In this case, the demand for bicycles increases; the demand curve for bicycles shifts to the right.

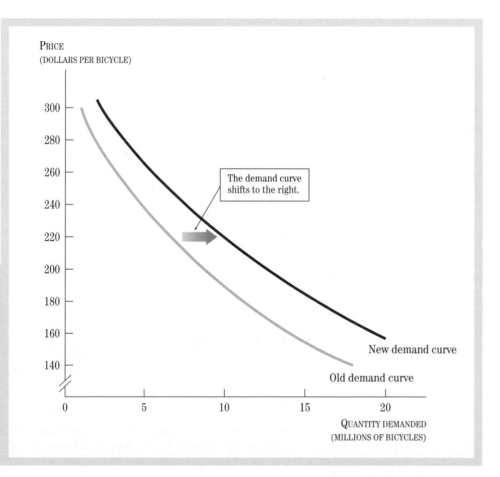

demand curve shifts to the right, more bicycles are purchased than before at any given price. For example, before the shift in demand, a $200 price led to 9 million bicycles purchased. But when the demand curve shifts to the right because of drier weather, that same price leads to 13 million bicycles purchased. The demand curve would shift to the left if a climate change to wetter weather reduced people's purchases of bicycles at any given price.

There are many reasons the demand curve may shift. Most of them can be attributed to one of several sources: *consumers' preferences, consumers' information, consumers' incomes, the number of consumers in the market, consumers' expectations of future prices*, and *the price of related goods*. Let us briefly consider each source of shifts in demand.

■ **Consumers' Preferences.** In general, a change in people's tastes or preferences for a product compared to other products will change the amount of the product they purchase at any given price. The physical fitness craze leading to an increase in the demand for bicycles is an example. Other examples of changes in preferences that cause shifts in demand for other goods and services include an increase in the demand for over-the-counter cold remedies when the weather turns wet and chilly in the winter, a decrease in the demand for taxis on sunny days, and an increase in the demand for travel on subways because of declining concerns about crime.

■ **Consumers' Information.** A change in information relating to a product can also cause the demand curve to shift. For example, when people learned about the dangers of smoking, the demand for cigarettes declined. Similarly, information about the effects of cholesterol may have reduced the demand for beef and increased the demand for chicken. The demand curve for chicken shifted to the right. The demand curve for beef shifted to the left.

■ **Consumers' Incomes.** If people's incomes change, then their purchases of goods usually change. An increase in income increases the demand for most goods. For example, higher incomes increase the demand for eating out, for cars, for movies. A decline in income reduces the demand for these goods. Goods for which demand increases when income rises and decreases when income falls are called **normal goods** by economists.

However, the demand for some goods—such as one-speed bicycles or day-old bread—may decline when income increases. Such goods are called **inferior goods** by economists. The demand for inferior goods declines when people's income increases because they can afford more attractive goods, such as fresh bread or 15-speed bicycles. But whether goods are normal or inferior, the demand for them usually shifts when consumers' incomes change.

normal good: a good for which demand increases when income rises and decreases when income falls.

inferior good: a good for which demand decreases when income rises and increases when income falls.

■ **Number of Consumers in the Market.** Demand is a relationship between price and the quantity demanded by *all* consumers in the market. If the number of consumers increases, then demand will increase. If the number of consumers falls, then demand will decrease. For example, the number of teenagers in the U.S. population expanded sharply in the late 1990s. This increased the demand for *Seventeen* magazine, for Rollerblades, for Clearasil, and for other goods that teenagers tend to buy. As the number of older people in the population increases, the demand for nursing homes rises.

■ **Consumers' Expectations of the Future Price.** If people expect the price of a good to increase, they will want to buy it before the price increases. Conversely, if people expect the price to decline, they will purchase less and wait for the decline.

Substitutes and Complements
Butter and margarine are examples of substitutes; they have similar characteristics. For example, margarine can be substituted for butter on toast. A rise in the price of butter will increase *the demand for margarine. Hot dogs and hot dog buns are examples of complements; they tend to be consumed together. A rise in the price of hot dogs will* decrease *the demand for hot dog buns.*

One sees this effect of expectations of future price changes often. "We'd better buy before the price goes up" is a common reason for purchasing items during a clearance sale. Or, "Let's put off buying that bicycle until the postholiday sales."

In general, it is difficult to forecast the future, but sometimes consumers know quite a bit about whether the price of a good will rise or fall, and they react accordingly. Thus, demand increases if people expect the *future* price of the good to rise. And demand decreases if people expect the *future* price of the good to fall.

■ **Prices of Closely Related Goods.** A sharp decrease in the price of motor scooters or Rollerblades will decrease the demand for bicycles. Why? Because buying these related goods becomes relatively more attractive than buying bicycles. Motor scooters and Rollerblades are examples of substitutes for bicycles. A **substitute** is a good that provides some of the same uses or enjoyment as another good. Butter and margarine are substitutes. In general, the demand for a good will increase if the price of a substitute for the good rises, and the demand for a good will decrease if the price of a substitute falls.

substitute: a good that has many of the same characteristics as and can be used in place of another good.

On the other hand, a sharp increase in the cost of bicycle helmets—another good closely related to bicycles—will decrease the demand for bicycles, especially if there is a law that requires that bicycle riders, but not Rollerbladers, wear helmets. A bicycle helmet is an example of a good that is a complement to a bicycle. In general, a **complement** is a good that tends to be consumed together with another good. Coffee and sugar are complements. The demand for a good (sugar) increases if the price of a complement (coffee) decreases, and the demand for a good (sugar) decreases if the price of a complement (coffee) increases.

complement: a good that is usually consumed or used together with another good.

Movements Along versus Shifts of the Demand Curve

We have shown that the demand curve can shift, and we have given many possible reasons for such shifts. In using demand curves, it is very important to distinguish *shifts* of the demand curve from *movements along* the demand curve. This distinction is illustrated in Figure 3.3.

A *movement along* the demand curve occurs when the quantity demanded changes as a result of a *change in the price of the good*. For example, if the price of bicycles rises, causing the quantity demanded by consumers to fall, then there is a

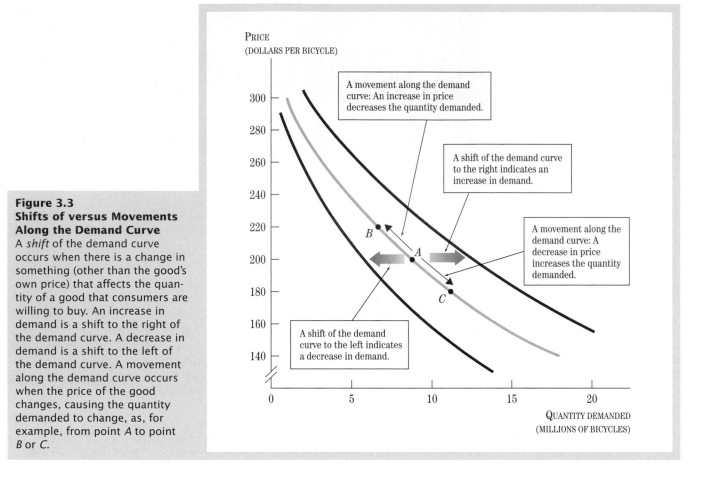

Figure 3.3
Shifts of versus Movements Along the Demand Curve
A *shift* of the demand curve occurs when there is a change in something (other than the good's own price) that affects the quantity of a good that consumers are willing to buy. An increase in demand is a shift to the right of the demand curve. A decrease in demand is a shift to the left of the demand curve. A movement along the demand curve occurs when the price of the good changes, causing the quantity demanded to change, as, for example, from point *A* to point *B* or *C*.

movement along the demand curve. A movement along the demand curve for bicycles occurs when the quantity demanded changes from point *A* to point *B* or from point *A* to point *C* in Figure 3.3. At point *A*, the price is $200 and the quantity demanded is 9 million. At point *B*, the price is $220 and the quantity demanded is 7 million. If the quantity changes because the price changes, economists say that there is a *change in the quantity demanded*.

A *shift* of the demand curve, on the other hand, occurs if there is a change due to *any source except the price*. When the demand curve shifts, economists say that there is a *change in demand*. Remember, the term *demand* refers to the entire curve or schedule relating price and quantity demanded, while the term *quantity demanded* refers to a single point on the demand curve. You should be able to tell whether any economic event causes (1) a change in demand or (2) a change in the quantity demanded; or, equivalently, (1) a shift in the demand curve or (2) a movement along the demand curve.

REVIEW ▪ Demand is a relationship between the price of a good and the quantity people will buy at each price, all other things being equal. The demand curve slopes down. The price and the quantity demanded are negatively related.

- When the price of a good changes, the quantity demanded changes and we have a movement along the demand curve.

- When something other than the price changes and affects demand, there is a shift in the demand curve, or, simply, a change in demand.

Supply

supply: a relationship between **price** and **quantity supplied.**

quantity supplied: the quantity of a good that firms are willing to sell at a given price.

Table 3.2
Supply Schedule for Bicycles (millions of bicycles per year)

Price	Quantity Supplied
$140	1
$160	4
$180	7
$200	9
$220	11
$240	13
$260	15
$280	16
$300	17

supply schedule: a tabular presentation of supply showing the price and quantity supplied of a particular good, all else being equal.

law of supply: the tendency for the quantity supplied of a good in a market to increase as its price rises.

supply curve: a graph of supply showing the upward-sloping relationship between price and quantity supplied.

Whereas demand refers to the behavior of consumers, supply refers to the behavior of firms. The term *supply*—whether it is the supply of health care or the supply of computers—has a very specific meaning for economists. **Supply** is a relationship between two variables: (1) *the price of a particular good* and (2) *the quantity of the good firms are willing to sell at that price,* all other things being the same. For short, we call the first variable the **price** and the second variable the **quantity supplied.**

Supply can be represented with a numerical table or a graph. An example of the supply of bicycles is shown in Table 3.2. Listed in the first column of Table 3.2 is the price of bicycles; the range of prices is the same as for the demand schedule in Table 3.1. The second column lists the quantity supplied (in millions of bicycles) in the entire market by bicycle-producing firms at each price. For example, at a price of $180, the quantity supplied is 7 million bicycles. Observe that as the price increases, the quantity supplied increases, and that as the price decreases, the quantity supplied decreases. For example, if the price rises from $180 to $200, the quantity supplied increases from 7 to 9 million bicycles. The relationship between price and quantity supplied in Table 3.2 is a **supply schedule.** This relationship is an example of the law of supply. The **law of supply** says that the higher the price, the higher the quantity supplied, and the lower the price, the lower the quantity supplied. In other words, the law of supply says that the price and the quantity supplied are positively related.

The Supply Curve

We can represent the supply schedule in Table 3.2 graphically by plotting the price and quantity supplied on a graph, as shown in Figure 3.4. The scales of each axis in Figure 3.4 are exactly the same as those in Figure 3.1, except that Figure 3.4 shows the quantity supplied, whereas Figure 3.1 shows the quantity demanded. Each pair of numbers in Table 3.2 is plotted as a point in Figure 3.4. The resulting curve showing all the combinations of prices and quantities supplied is the **supply curve.** Note that the curve slopes upward: $280 represents a high price, and there the quantity supplied is high—16 million bicycles. If the price is down at $160 a bicycle, then firms are willing to sell only 4 million bicycles.

Why does the supply curve slope upward? Imagine yourself running a firm that produces and sells bicycles. If the price of the bicycles goes up, from $180 to $280, then you can earn $100 more for each bicycle you produce and sell. Given your production costs, if you earn more from each bicycle, you will have a greater incentive to produce and sell more bicycles. If producing more bicycles increases the costs of producing each bicycle, perhaps because you must pay the bike assembly workers a higher wage for working overtime, the higher price will give you the incentive to incur these costs. Other bicycle firms will be thinking the same way. Thus, firms are willing to sell more bicycles as the price rises. Conversely, the incentive for firms to

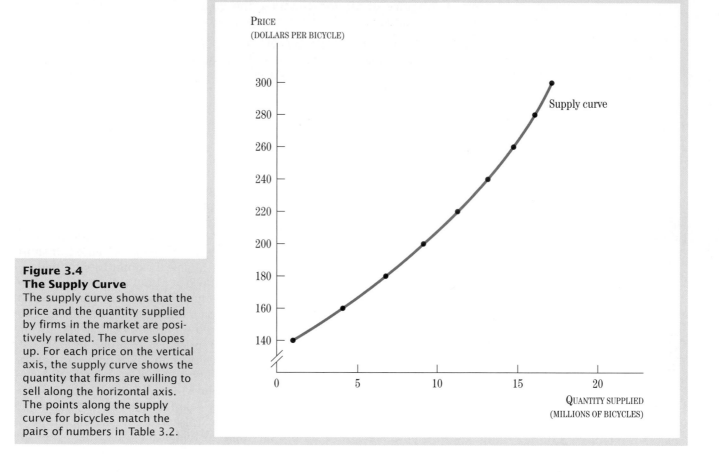

Figure 3.4
The Supply Curve
The supply curve shows that the price and the quantity supplied by firms in the market are positively related. The curve slopes up. For each price on the vertical axis, the supply curve shows the quantity that firms are willing to sell along the horizontal axis. The points along the supply curve for bicycles match the pairs of numbers in Table 3.2.

sell bicycles will decline as the price falls. Basically, that is why there is a positive relationship between price and quantity supplied.

Shifts in Supply

The supply curve is drawn on the assumption that all other things are equal, except the price of the good. If any one of these other things changes, then the supply curve shifts. For example, suppose a new machine is invented that makes it less costly for firms to produce bicycles; then firms would have more incentive at any given price to produce and sell more bicycles. Supply would increase; the supply curve would shift to the right.

Figure 3.5 shows how the supply curve for bicycles would shift to the right because of a new cost-reducing machine. The supply curve would shift to the left if there were a decrease in supply. Supply would decrease, for example, if bicycle-producing firms suddenly found that their existing machines became too hot and had to be oiled with an expensive lubricant each time a bicycle was produced. This would raise costs, lower supply, and shift the supply curve to the left.

Many things can cause the supply curve to shift. Most of these can be categorized by the source of the change in supply: *technology, the price of goods used in production, the number of firms in the market, expectations of future prices,* and

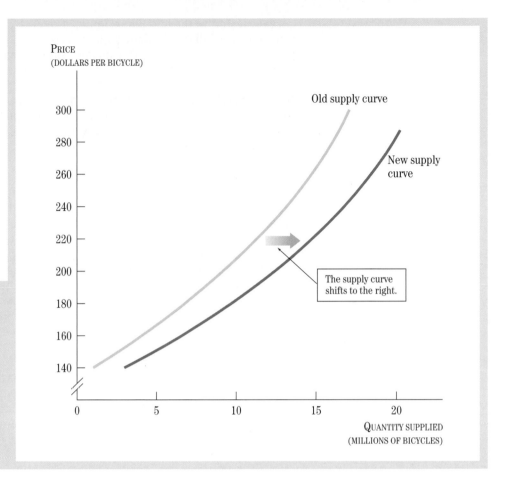

Figure 3.5
A Shift in the Supply Curve
The supply curve is a relation-ship between the quantity sup-plied of a good and the price of the good, all other things being equal. A change in one of these other things (other than the good's price) will shift the supply curve, as shown in the graph. In this case, the supply of bicycles increases; the supply curve for bicycles shifts to the right.

government taxes, subsidies, and regulations. Let us briefly consider the sources of shifts in supply.

■ **Technology.**   Anything that changes the amount a firm can produce with a given amount of inputs to production can be considered a change in technology. Because of new discoveries and ideas for improving production, technology usually gets better over time. Better bicycle-making machinery is an example. Another example is the rapid improvement in the technology for producing computers. These technological improvements increase supply and shift the supply curve to the right.

Droughts, earthquakes, and terrorists' bombing of factories also affect the amount that can be produced with given inputs. A drought that reduces the amount of wheat that can be produced on a farm in the Midwest and a freeze that reduces the number of oranges yielded by trees in Florida orchards are examples. Because such events change the amount that can be produced with a given amount of inputs, they are similar to changes in technology, though these examples reduce rather than increase supply. In these cases, the supply curve shifts to the left.

■ **The Price of Goods Used in Production.**   If the prices of the inputs to production—raw materials, labor, and capital—increase, then it becomes more costly to produce goods, and firms will produce less at any given price; the supply curve will shift to the left. For example, if the price of fertilizer rises, then the cost of growing corn will rise, and the supply of corn will decrease. On the other hand, if the price of an input, such as fertilizer, falls, supply increases and the supply curve shifts to the right.

■ **The Number of Firms in the Market.**   Remember that the supply curve refers to *all* the firms producing the product—all the corn farmers, for example. If the number of firms increases, then more goods will be produced at each price; supply increases, and the supply curve shifts to the right. For example, as more firms entered the overnight package delivery service in the 1980s and 1990s, the supply of this service increased.

A decline in the number of firms would shift the supply curve to the left. For example, the number of drive-in movie theaters has declined sharply over the last 30 years; hence the supply curve has shifted to the left.

■ **Expectations of Future Prices.**   If firms expect the price of the good they produce to rise in the future, then they will hold off selling at least part of their production until the price rises. For example, farmers in the United States who anticipate an increase in wheat prices because of political turbulence in Russia may decide to store more wheat in silos and sell it later, after the price rises. Thus, expectations of *future* price increases tend to reduce supply. Conversely, expectations of *future* price decreases tend to increase supply.

■ **Government Taxes, Subsidies, and Regulations.**   The government has the ability to affect the supply of particular goods produced by firms. For example, the government imposes taxes on firms to pay for such government services as education, police, and national defense. These taxes increase firms' costs and reduce supply. The supply curve shifts to the left when a tax on what firms sell in the market increases.

The government also makes payments—subsidies—to firms to encourage the firms to produce certain goods. Many farms now receive subsidies to produce certain food products. Such subsidies have the opposite effect of taxes on supply. An increase in subsidies reduces firms' costs and increases the supply.

Governments also regulate firms. In some cases, such regulations can change the firms' costs of production and thereby affect supply. For example, when the government requires that firms install safety features on their products, the cost of producing the products rises, and thus supply declines.

Movements Along versus Shifts of the Supply Curve

Figure 3.6 compares *shifts* of the supply curve with *movements along* the supply curve. A *movement along* the supply curve occurs when a change in price causes a change in the quantity supplied. Economists then say that there is a *change in the quantity supplied*, as, for example, when the quantity supplied changes from point *D* to point *F* or from point *D* to point *E* in Figure 3.6.

A *shift* of the supply curve occurs if there is a change due to *any source except the price*. When the supply curve shifts, economists say that there is a *change in supply*. The term *supply* refers to the entire supply curve. The term *quantity supplied* refers to a point on the supply curve. As we will soon see, it is important to be able to tell whether a change in something causes (1) a change in supply or (2) a change in the quantity supplied; or, equivalently, (1) a shift in the supply curve or (2) a movement along the supply curve.

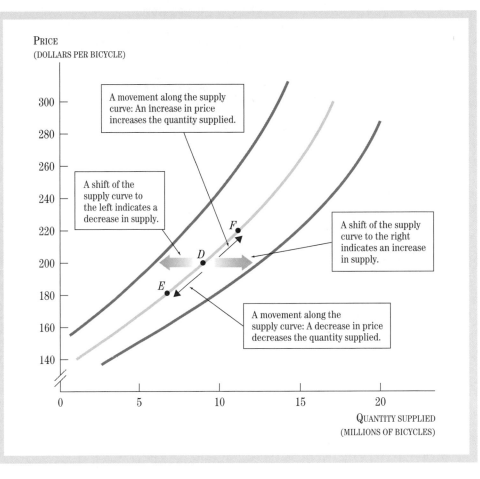

Figure 3.6
Shifts of versus Movements Along the Supply Curve
A *shift* of the supply curve occurs when there is a change in something (other than the price) that affects the amount of a good that firms are willing to supply. An increase in supply is a shift to the right of the supply curve. A decrease in supply is a shift to the left of the supply curve. A movement along the supply curve occurs when the price of the good changes, caus ing the quantity supplied by firms to change—for example, from point *D* to point *E* or *F*.

REVIEW
- Supply is a positive relationship between the price of a good and the quantity supplied of the good by firms. The supply curve slopes upward because higher prices give firms more incentive to produce and sell more.

- When the quantity supplied changes because of a change in price, we have a movement along the supply curve. Other factors—such as technology, the number of firms, and expectations—affect supply. When these determinants change, the supply curve shifts.

Market Equilibrium: Combining Supply and Demand

Thus far, as summarized in Figure 3.7, we have examined consumers' demand for goods in a market and firms' supply of goods in a market. Now we put supply and demand together to complete the supply and demand model. When consumers buy goods and firms sell goods, they interact in a market, and a price is determined. Recall that a market does not need to be located at one place; the U.S. bicycle market

SUPPLY

Supply describes firms.

The supply curve looks like this:

Price

S

QUANTITY SUPPLIED

DEMAND

Demand describes consumers.

The demand curve looks like this:

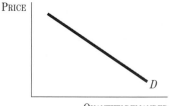

Price

D

QUANTITY DEMANDED

Law of Supply

| Price and quantity supplied are positively related. |

Law of Demand

| Price and quantity demanded are negatively related. |

Movements along supply curve occur

when price rises and quantity supplied rises
or
when price falls and quantity supplied falls.

Movements along demand curve occur

when price rises and quantity demanded falls
or
when price falls and quantity demanded rises.

Shifts in supply are due to:

Technology (new inventions)

Number of firms in market

Price of goods used in production (inputs such as fertilizer, labor)

Expectations of future prices (firms will sell less now if prices are expected to rise; for example, farmers may store goods to sell next year)

Government taxes, subsidies, regulations (commodity taxes, agricultural subsidies, safety regulations)

Shifts in demand are due to:

Preferences (nice weather or fitness craze changes tastes)

Number of consumers in market

Consumers' information (about cholesterol or smoking, for example)

Consumers' income (normal goods versus inferior goods)

Expectations of future prices (consumers will buy more now if prices are expected to rise in the future)

Price of related goods (both substitutes, like butter and margarine, and complements, like coffee and sugar)

**Figure 3.7
Overview of Supply and
Demand**

consists of all the bicycle firms that sell bicycles and all the consumers who buy bicycles.

Although it may sound amazing, no single person or firm determines the price in the market. Instead, the market determines the price. As buyers and sellers interact, prices may go up for a while and then go down. Alfred Marshall, the economist who did the most to develop the supply and demand model in the late nineteenth century, called this process the "higgling and bargaining" of the market. The assumption underlying the supply and demand model is that, in the give and take of the marketplace, prices adjust until they settle down at a level where the quantity supplied by firms equals the quantity demanded by consumers. Let's see how.

Determination of the Market Price

To determine the market price, we combine the demand relationship between the price and the quantity demanded with the supply relationship between the price and the quantity supplied. We can do this using either a table or a diagram. First consider Table 3.3, which combines the demand schedule from Table 3.1 with the supply schedule from Table 3.2. The price is in the first column, the quantity demanded by consumers is in the second column, and the quantity supplied by firms is in the third column. Observe that the quantity consumers are willing to buy is shown to decline with the price, while the quantity firms are willing to sell is shown to increase with the price. In order to determine the price in the market, consider each of the prices in Table 3.3.

shortage (excess demand): the situation in which quantity demanded is greater than quantity supplied.

■ **Finding the Market Price.**   Pick a price in Table 3.3, any price. Suppose the price you choose is $160. Then the quantity demanded by consumers (14 million bicycles) is greater than the quantity supplied by firms (4 million bicycles). In other words, there is a shortage of 14 − 4 = 10 million bicycles. A **shortage,** or **excess demand,** is a situation in which the quantity demanded is greater than the quantity supplied. With a shortage of bicycles, the price will quickly rise above $160; firms will charge higher prices, and consumers who are willing to pay more than $160 for a bicycle will pay higher prices to firms. Thus, $160 cannot last as the market price. Observe that as the price rises above $160, the quantity demanded falls and the quantity supplied rises. Thus, as the price rises, the shortage begins to decrease. If you choose any price below $200, the same thing will happen: There will be a shortage, and the price will rise. The shortage disappears only when the price rises to $200, as shown in Table 3.3.

Now pick a price above $200. Suppose you pick $260. Then the quantity demanded by consumers (3 million bicycles) is less than the quantity supplied by firms (15 million bicycles). In other words, there is a surplus of 12 million bicycles. A **surplus,** or **excess supply,** is a situation in which the quantity supplied is greater than the quantity demanded. With a surplus of bicycles, the price will fall: Firms that are willing to sell bicycles for less than $260 will offer to sell to consumers at lower prices. Thus, $260 cannot be the market price either. Observe that as the price falls below $260, the quantity demanded rises and the quantity supplied falls. Thus, the surplus decreases. If you choose any price above $200, the same thing will happen: There will

surplus (excess supply):   the situation in which quantity supplied is greater than quantity demanded.

Table 3.3
Finding the Market Equilibrium

Price	Quantity Demanded	Quantity Supplied	Shortage, Surplus, or Equilibrium	Price Rises or Falls
$140	18	1	Shortage = 17	Price rises
$160	14	4	Shortage = 10	Price rises
$180	11	7	Shortage = 4	Price rises
$200	9	9	Equilibrium	No change
$220	7	11	Surplus = 4	Price falls
$240	5	13	Surplus = 8	Price falls
$260	3	15	Surplus = 12	Price falls
$280	2	16	Surplus = 14	Price falls
$300	1	17	Surplus = 16	Price falls

Quantity supplied equals quantity demanded. →

be a surplus, and the price will fall. The surplus disappears only when the price falls to $200.

Thus, we have shown that for any price below $200, there is a shortage, and the price rises; while for any price above $200, there is a surplus, and the price falls. What if the market price is $200? Then the quantity supplied equals the quantity demanded; there is neither a shortage nor a surplus, and there is no reason for the price to rise or fall. This price of $200 is therefore the most likely market price. It is called the **equilibrium price** because at this price the quantity supplied equals the quantity demanded, and there is no tendency for the price to change. There is no other price for which quantity supplied equals quantity demanded. If you look at all the other prices, you will see that there is either a shortage or a surplus, and thus there is a tendency for the price to either rise or fall.

equilibrium price: the price at which quantity supplied equals quantity demanded.

The quantity bought and sold at the equilibrium price is 9 million bicycles. This is the **equilibrium quantity.** When the price equals the equilibrium price and the quantity bought and sold equals the equilibrium quantity, we say that there is a **market equilibrium.**

equilibrium quantity: the quantity traded at the equilibrium price.

Our discussion of the determination of the equilibrium price shows how the market price coordinates the buying and selling decisions of many firms and consumers. We see that the price serves a *rationing function.* That is, the price alleviates shortages: A higher price reduces the quantity demanded or increases the quantity supplied when necessary to eliminate a shortage. Similarly, a lower price increases the quantity demanded or decreases the quantity supplied when there is a surplus. Thus, both shortages and surpluses are eliminated by the forces of supply and demand.

market equilibrium: the situation in which the price is equal to the equilibrium price and the quantity traded equals the equilibrium quantity.

■ **Two Predictions.** By combining supply and demand, we have completed the supply and demand model. The model can be applied to many markets, not just the example of the bicycle market. One prediction of the supply and demand model is that *the price in the market will be the price for which the quantity supplied equals the quantity demanded.* Thus, the model provides an answer to the question of what determines the price in the market. Another prediction of the model is that *the quantity bought and sold in the market is the quantity for which the quantity supplied equals the quantity demanded.*

Finding the Equilibrium with a Supply and Demand Diagram

The equilibrium price and quantity in a market can also be found with the help of a graph. Figure 3.8 combines the demand curve from Figure 3.1 and the supply curve from Figure 3.4 in the same diagram. Observe that the downward-sloping demand curve intersects the upward-sloping supply curve at a single point. At that point of intersection, the quantity supplied equals the quantity demanded. Hence, the *equilibrium price occurs at the intersection of the supply curve and the demand curve.* The equilibrium price of $200 is shown in Figure 3.8. At that price, the quantity demanded is 9 million bicycles, and the quantity supplied is 9 million bicycles. This is the equilibrium quantity.

If the price were lower than this equilibrium price, say $160, then the quantity demanded would be greater than the quantity supplied. There would be a shortage, and the price would begin to rise, as shown in the graph. On the other hand, if the price were above the equilibrium price, say $260, then there would be a surplus, as shown in the graph, and the price would begin to fall. Thus, the market price will tend to move toward the equilibrium price at the intersection of the supply curve and the demand curve. We can calculate exactly what the equilibrium price is on the graph by drawing a line over to the vertical axis. And we can calculate the equilibrium quantity by drawing a line down to the horizontal axis.

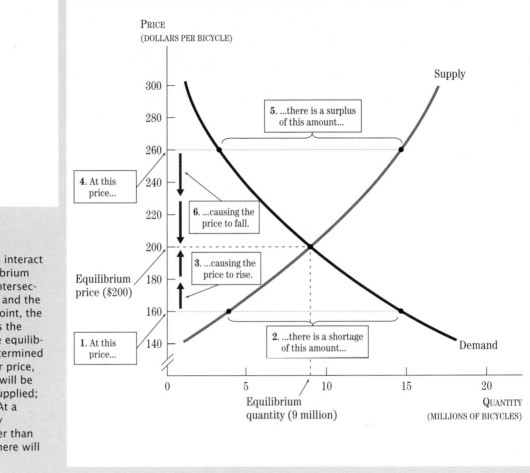

**Figure 3.8
Equilibrium Price and
Equilibrium Quantity**
When buyers and sellers interact in the market, the equilibrium price is at the point of intersection of the supply curve and the demand curve. At this point, the quantity supplied equals the quantity demanded. The equilibrium quantity is also determined at that point. At a higher price, the quantity demanded will be less than the quantity supplied; there will be a surplus. At a lower price, the quantity demanded will be greater than the quantity supplied; there will be a shortage.

A Change in the Market

In order to use the supply and demand model to explain or predict changes in prices, we need to consider what happens to the equilibrium price when there is a change in supply or demand. We first consider a change in demand and then a change in supply.

■ **Effects of a Change in Demand.**   Figure 3.9 shows the effects of a shift in the demand curve for bicycles. Suppose that a shift occurs because of a fitness craze that increases the demand for bicycles. The demand curve shifts to the right, as shown in graph (a) in Figure 3.9. The demand curve before the shift and the demand curve after the shift are labeled the "old demand curve" and the "new demand curve," respectively.

If you look at the graph, you can see that something must happen to the equilibrium price when the demand curve shifts. The equilibrium price is determined at the intersection of the supply curve and the demand curve. With the new demand curve, there is a new intersection and, therefore, a new equilibrium price. The equilibrium price is no longer $200 in Figure 3.9(a); it is up to $220 per bicycle. Thus, the supply and demand model predicts that the price in the market will rise if there is an

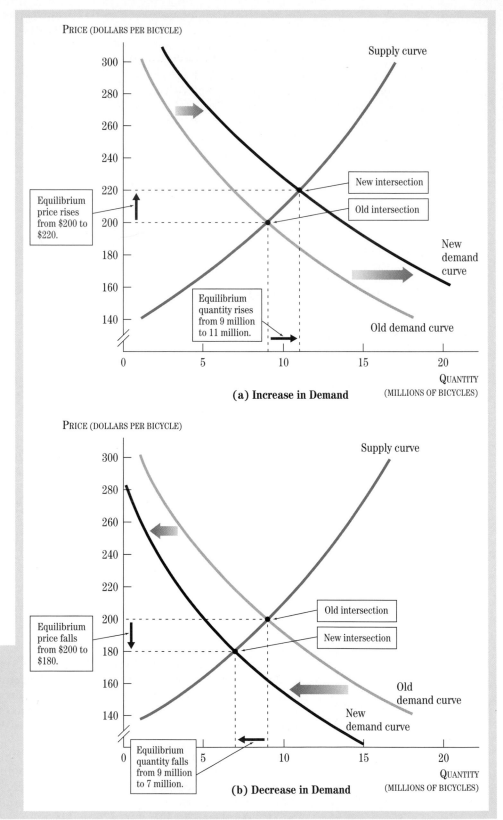

(a) Increase in Demand

(b) Decrease in Demand

Figure 3.9
Effects of a Shift in Demand
When demand increases, as in graph (a), the demand curve shifts to the right. The equilibrium price rises, and the equilibrium quantity also rises. When demand decreases, as in graph (b), the demand curve shifts to the left. The equilibrium price falls, and the equilibrium quantity also falls.

increase in demand. Note also that there is a change in the equilibrium quantity of bicycles. The quantity of bicycles sold and bought has increased from 9 million to 11 million. Thus, the equilibrium quantity has increased along with the equilibrium price. The supply and demand model predicts that an increase in demand will raise both the price and the quantity sold in the market.

We can use the same method to find out what happens if demand decreases, as shown in graph (b) in Figure 3.9. In this case, the demand curve shifts to the left. At the new intersection of the supply and demand curves, the equilibrium price is lower, and the quantity sold is also lower. Thus, the supply and demand model predicts that a decrease in demand will both lower the price and lower the quantity sold in the market.

Note in these examples that when the demand curve shifts, it leads to a movement along the supply curve. First, the demand curve shifts to the right or to the left. Then there is movement along the supply curve because the change in the price affects the quantity of bicycles firms will sell.

■ **Effects of a Change in Supply.**   Figure 3.10 shows what happens when there is a change in the market that shifts the supply curve. In graph (a) of Figure 3.10 we show the effect of an increase in supply, and in graph (b) we show the effect of a decrease in supply.

When the supply curve of bicycles shifts to the right, there is a new equilibrium price, which is lower than the old equilibrium price. In addition, the equilibrium quantity rises. Thus, the supply and demand model predicts that an increase in the supply of bicycles—perhaps because of better technology in bicycle production— will lower the price and raise the quantity of bicycles sold.

When the supply curve of bicycles shifts to the left, the equilibrium price rises, as shown in graph (b) of Figure 3.10, and the equilibrium quantity falls. Thus, the model predicts that anything that reduces supply will raise the price of bicycles and lower the quantity of bicycles produced.

Table 3.4 summarizes the results of this analysis of shifts in the supply and demand curves.

■ **When Both Curves Shift.**   The supply and demand model is easiest to use when something shifts either demand or supply but not both. However, in reality, it is possible for something or several different things to simultaneously shift both supply and demand. To predict whether the price or the quantity rises or falls in such cases, we need to know whether demand or supply shifts by a larger amount. Dealing with the possibility of simultaneous shifts in demand and supply curves is important in practice, as we show in the next section.

Table 3.4
Effects of Shifts in Demand and Supply Curves

Shift	Effect on Equilibrium Price	Effect on Equilibrium Quantity
Increase in demand	Up	Up
Decrease in demand	Down	Down
Increase in supply	Down	Up
Decrease in supply	Up	Down

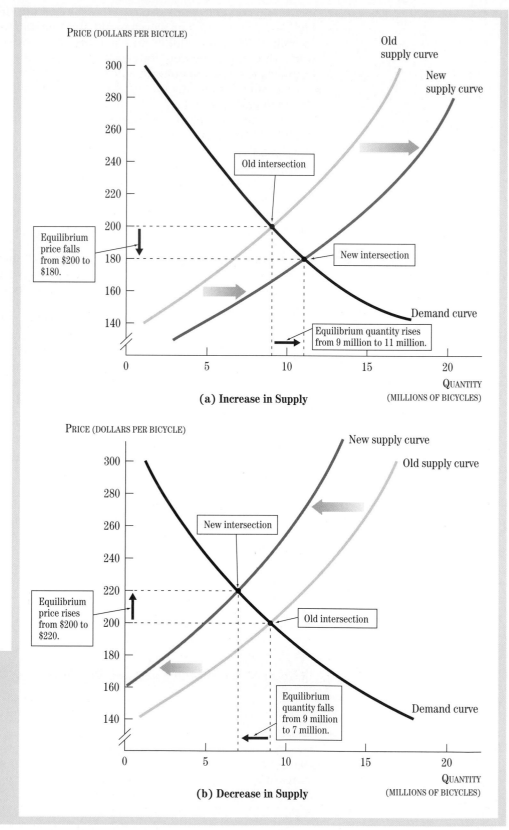

Figure 3.10
Effects of a Shift in Supply
When supply increases, as in graph (a), the supply curve shifts to the right; the equilibrium price falls, and the equilibrium quantity rises. When supply decreases, as in graph (b), the supply curve shifts to the left; the equilibrium price rises, and the equilibrium quantity falls.

REVIEW

- When firms and consumers interact in a market, a price is determined by the market.

- The supply and demand model predicts that the price is found at the intersection of the supply and demand curves. This price is called the equilibrium price.

- At this price, the quantity supplied equals the quantity demanded, and there is no tendency for the price to change.

- A shift in the demand curve or the supply curve will change the equilibrium price and the equilibrium quantity. By considering changes in supply or demand, the model can be used to explain or predict price changes.

Using the Supply and Demand Model

CASE STUDY

Economists use the supply and demand model both to explain past observations about prices and to predict what would happen to prices under different scenarios. The hypothetical example of the bicycle market has been useful for defining and explaining general features of the supply and demand model. But now we want to show how to apply the model in real-world situations. In real-world applications, economists have to decide exactly what goods are included in the market and the time period for the application. To illustrate the application of the supply and demand model, we look in detail at some actual events in a specific market—the peanut market in the United States.

Explaining and Predicting Peanut Prices

To apply the supply and demand model to the peanut market, we need to know a little about where peanuts are produced in the United States. Figure 3.11 shows that most peanuts are produced on farms in the Southeast. The biggest peanut-producing state is Georgia, which produces over 1.8 billion of the 4 billion pounds of peanuts produced in the United States.

Figure 3.12 shows a supply and demand model for peanuts. The model is an accurate description of the peanut market based on many observations over the years. You can see that the demand curve for peanuts is downward-sloping. In the diagram, prices range from $.20 a pound all the way to $1.80 a pound for raw shelled peanuts. As you can see, when the price for peanuts is high, the quantity demanded is low. The supply curve shows that at a higher price, farmers will want to produce more peanuts. The equilibrium price is shown to be $.60 a pound, and the equilibrium quantity about 4 billion pounds.

■ **A Big Drought in the Southeast.**   In 1990, there was a severe drought in the southeastern part of the United States, where most of the peanuts are grown. The drought meant that supply declined. Production dropped sharply in Georgia, Alabama, and Florida. In the supply and demand model, we would show that drought by a shift to the left in the supply curve for peanuts, as shown in Figure 3.13.

As you can see in Figure 3.13, the equilibrium price rises. In fact, the price of peanuts during the drought did rise from about $.60 a pound to about $1.25 a pound. Thus, the supply and demand model can explain the rise in the peanut price.

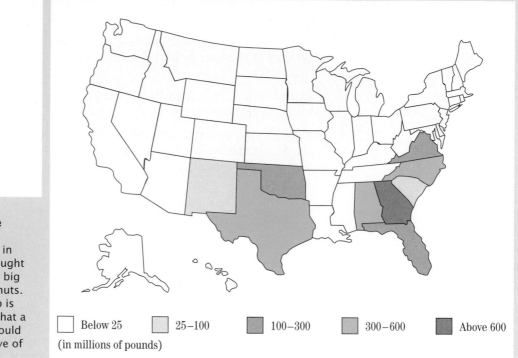

Figure 3.11
Peanut Production in the United States
Most peanuts are produced in the Southeast. Hence, a drought in the Southeast will have a big effect on the supply of peanuts. The information in this map is important for establishing that a drought in the Southeast would indeed shift the supply curve of peanuts to the left.

Below 25   25–100   100–300   300–600   Above 600
(in millions of pounds)

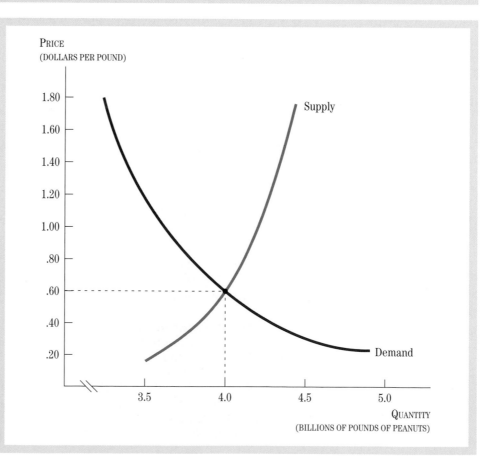

Figure 3.12
Supply and Demand for Peanuts
The quantity refers to the number of pounds produced in the United States. The price is the average price of raw peanuts in the United States.

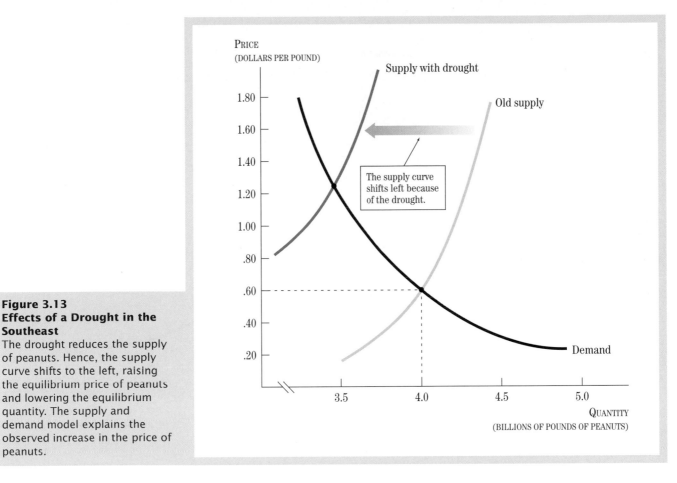

PRICE
(DOLLARS PER POUND)

Supply with drought

Old supply

The supply curve
shifts left because
of the drought.

Demand

QUANTITY
(BILLIONS OF POUNDS OF PEANUTS)

Figure 3.13
Effects of a Drought in the Southeast
The drought reduces the supply of peanuts. Hence, the supply curve shifts to the left, raising the equilibrium price of peanuts and lowering the equilibrium quantity. The supply and demand model explains the observed increase in the price of peanuts.

Quite understandably, this price rise forced some hard choices on people who consume a lot of peanuts. Poor people tend to eat more peanut butter than rich people, so the price change affected the distribution of income. Further, the school lunch program that provides meals for poor children in the United States had to stop buying peanut butter because it got so expensive.

Thus, the price performed its three roles. The higher price lowered the quantity demanded by providing incentives for people to choose some other food. It transmitted information about the effects of the drought in the Southeast all over the country. It also affected the distribution of income because people who buy peanuts and peanut butter had less to spend on other things.

■ **A Change in the Foreign Peanut Quota?**   Although the market responded to the drought as predicted, the higher price made life difficult for some consumers. Was there anything to be done? Could the supply and demand model help in deciding what to do? Could it predict what would happen under various courses of action?

Believe it or not, there is a law limiting the amount of peanuts imported into the United States. The limit is called a *quota*.

One simple way to lower the price would be to allow more foreign peanuts to come into the United States from Argentina, China, and other peanut-growing countries. In fact, the supply and demand model predicts that the price would fall if the quota were increased.

Allowing more foreign peanuts into the United States would shift the supply curve of peanuts to the right, as illustrated in Figure 3.14. That would lower the

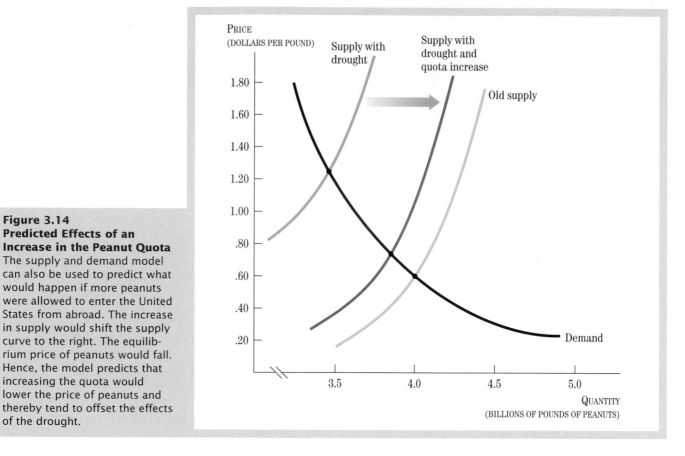

Figure 3.14
Predicted Effects of an Increase in the Peanut Quota
The supply and demand model can also be used to predict what would happen if more peanuts were allowed to enter the United States from abroad. The increase in supply would shift the supply curve to the right. The equilibrium price of peanuts would fall. Hence, the model predicts that increasing the quota would lower the price of peanuts and thereby tend to offset the effects of the drought.

equilibrium price. For a rightward shift of the size shown in the diagram, the price would go down to about $.75 a pound, which would help the peanut consumers who were being hurt by the drought.

However, that is not what happened in 1990. Economists who worked for the federal government used a supply and demand model just like the one in Figure 3.14 to analyze the situation and make a recommendation to increase the quota. But others—including the peanut growers and some members of Congress—claimed that there was no reason to increase the quota. They argued that the demand for peanuts had decreased after the drought and that an increase in the supply of foreign peanuts was unnecessary. One peanut growers' group was quoted as saying, "Demand for peanut butter and peanut products will be less this year because the [school lunch program] has drastically reduced its purchases of peanut products."[1] Such statements confuse shifts of the demand curve and movements along the demand curve. As shown in Figure 3.13, the drought led to a movement along the demand curve because higher peanut prices forced people to reduce the quantity demanded. But this was not a decline in demand. Rather, consumers reduced the quantity demanded because the price was so high.

These debates led to delays, and ultimately only a very small amount of peanuts was imported. Although the ultimate result may have been disappointing, the 1990 drought and peanut quota increase still provide an excellent case study of how the supply and demand model is used in practice.

---

1. *Peanuts*, U.S. International Trade Commission Publication 2369, March 1991, p. A-70.

The following *Chicago Tribune* news article (March 31, 1991) describes the peanut market after the drought described in our case study. Observe how the supply and demand model corroborates ① the size of the price increase and the reason for the price increase, ② the effects on the price of increasing peanut imports by 300 million pounds, and ③ the typical rationalization on the part of growers that there was no reason to increase the quota because "supply was sufficient," while not mentioning that it was the doubling of prices that brought the quantity demanded down to equal the lower quantity supplied.

Peanuts could sell for peanuts again

By John Schmeltzer

Peanut butter, that staple of the American school lunch menu that all but disappeared last fall when peanut prices soared, may soon make a comeback, industry leaders say.

In recent months, prices for shelled peanuts more than doubled on the wholesale level, to $1.25 a pound from 60 cents a pound—a move that prompted the Department of Agriculture to substitute cholesterol-rich cheese in the school lunch program for the cholesterol-free peanut butter.

Analysts said the peanut shortfall was caused by severe import restrictions and last year's drought in the Southeast.

Peanut butter, which had been selling in the grocery store for about $3 for a 28-ounce jar, quickly skyrocketed to more than $4.

"You can import pistols but not peanuts," said James Mack on Wednesday, referring to restrictions that all but set quotas for how many goobers each U.S. peanut farmer is allowed to produce each year. Mack is general

"You can import pistols but not peanuts."
—James Mack,
Peanut Butter and
Nut Processors Association

counsel for the Peanut Butter and Nut Processors Association.

But processors say they expect a decision in as little as two weeks by President Bush on a temporary lifting of import restrictions, which would allow as much as 300 million pounds of peanuts to be imported between now and July 31. The temporary relaxation has been recommended by the U.S. International Trade Commission.

Since the ITC recommendation last week, prices for shelled peanuts have fallen to about $1 a pound, according to Mack. He said if the ITC recommendation is adopted, prices will probably drop to about 75 cents a pound —still 25 percent higher than before last year's poor crop hit the market.

The ITC recommendation is being opposed by growers and congressional leaders, who maintain there is sufficient supply for the domestic market and say Mack's association only represents 30 percent of the producers, none of whom are the major manufacturers of brands such as Planters or Skippy.

Sen. Wyche Fowler Jr. (D-Ga.), in a letter signed by 11 other senators, argued that opening the door to increased imports could end up costing U.S. taxpayers because of price-support programs.

"We don't think the importation of peanuts is necessary," said Emery Murphy, assistant executive director of the Georgia Peanut Commission. "We're certain there will be adverse effects to the industry and the government."

The nut processors association has been joined in its efforts to lift the import ban by the Consumer Alert Advocate Fund, whose president, Barbara Keating, said slow action by the government already has cost consumers $553 million.

REVIEW
- The supply and demand model can be used in practical applications to explain price changes in many markets. It can also be used to predict what will happen to prices when certain actions—such as increasing a quota—are taken.

- In applying the model, economists consider shifts of the supply curve or the demand curve. In the case study of the drought, the supply curve for peanuts shifted.

Interference with Market Prices

Thus far, we have used the supply and demand model in situations in which the price is freely determined without government control. But many times throughout history, and around the world today, governments have attempted to control market prices. The usual reason is that government leaders have not been happy with the outcome of the market, or they were pressured by groups who would benefit from price controls.

price control: a government law or regulation that sets or limits the price to be charged for a particular good.

Price controls were used widely by the U.S. government during World War II and again in the early 1970s. Price controls now exist in certain housing markets, agriculture markets, and labor markets in the United States. What are the effects of this government interference in the market? The supply and demand model can help answer this question.

Price Ceilings and Price Floors

price ceiling: a government price control that sets the maximum allowable price for a good.

In general there are two broad types of government price controls. Controls can stipulate a **price ceiling,** or a maximum price at which a good can be bought and sold. For example, the United States government controlled oil prices in the early 1970s, stipulating that firms could not charge more than a stated maximum price of $5.25 per barrel of crude oil; the equilibrium price was well over $10 per barrel at this time. Some cities in the United States have price controls on rental apartments. Landlords are not permitted to charge a rent higher than the maximum stipulated by the **rent control** law in these cities. Price ceilings are imposed by governments because of complaints that the market price is too high. The purpose is to help the consumers who must pay the prices. For example, rent controls exist in order to help people who must pay rent. However, as we will see, price controls have harmful side effects that can end up hurting those consumers the law is apparently trying to help.

rent control: a government price control that sets the maximum allowable rent on a house or apartment.

price floor: a government price control that sets the minimum allowable price for a good.

Government price controls can also stipulate a **price floor,** or a minimum price. Price floors are imposed by governments in order to help the suppliers of goods and services. For example, the U.S. government requires that the price of sugar not fall below a certain amount in the United States. In the labor market, the U.S. government requires that firms pay workers a wage of at least a given level, called the **minimum wage.**

minimum wage: a wage per hour below which it is illegal to pay workers.

Shortages and Related Problems Resulting from Price Ceilings

If the government prevents firms from charging more than a certain amount for their products, then a shortage is likely to result, as illustrated in Figure 3.15. When the maximum price remains below the equilibrium price for the market, there is a persistent shortage; sellers are unwilling to supply as much as buyers want to buy. This is illustrated for the general case of any good in the top graph in Figure 3.15 and for the specific case of rent control in the bottom graph.

■ **Dealing with Persistent Shortages.** Because higher prices are not allowed, the shortage must be dealt with in other ways. Sometimes the government issues a limited amount of ration coupons to people to alleviate the shortage; this was done in World War II. The law required that people present these ration coupons at stores

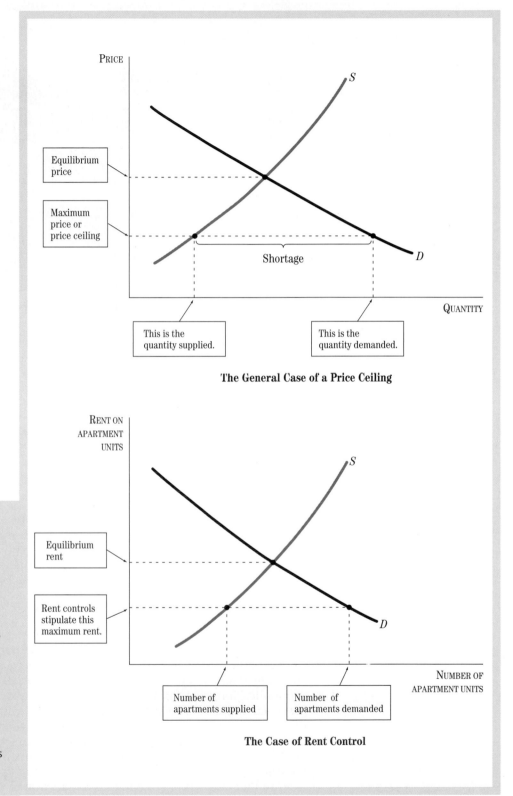

**Figure 3.15
Effects of a Maximum
Price Law**
The top diagram shows the general case when the government prevents the market price from rising above a particular maximum price, or sets a price ceiling below the equilibrium price. The lower diagram shows a particular example of a price ceiling, rent controls on apartment units. The supply and demand model predicts that there will be a shortage. The shortage occurs because the quantity supplied is less than consumers are willing to buy at that price. The shortage leads to rationing, black markets, or lower product quality.

PRICE

Equilibrium
price

Maximum
price or
price ceiling

Shortage

S

D

QUANTITY

This is the
quantity supplied.

This is the
quantity demanded.

The General Case of a Price Ceiling

RENT ON
APARTMENT
UNITS

Equilibrium
rent

Rent controls
stipulate this
maximum rent.

S

D

NUMBER OF
APARTMENT UNITS

Number of
apartments supplied

Number of
apartments demanded

The Case of Rent Control

What Do Price Ceilings on ATMs Do?

Automated teller machines are all over the place; there are about 230,000 in the United States. ATMs are very popular; they get used about 30 million times each day. When you withdraw cash from an ATM, you usually have to pay a surcharge or a fee—a *price*—unless you happen to have an account with the bank that operates the ATM. The average price for withdrawing cash from an ATM is about $1.40 in the United States.

But the price is much less in Santa Monica and San Francisco. In 1999 these two cities banned ATM fees. Using the terminology of economics, the cities placed a *price ceiling* of $0.00 on the price charged by banks to noncustomers who use ATMs. Although ATM services might seem like a more complicated product than peanuts, the supply and demand model is a good way to analyze the effect of a price ceiling on ATM fees.

Let's adapt the supply and demand model in Figure 3.15 to the case of ATMs. On the vertical axis of the supply and demand diagram in the top part of Figure 3.15, pencil in "price of an ATM transaction," and on the horizontal axis pencil in "quantity of ATM transactions." The "maximum price or price ceiling" is $0.00, and the equilibrium price is about $1.40, assuming that the equilibrium price is equal to the average price in the United States.

Now observe what the supply and demand model predicts about the effect of such a price ceiling: The quantity supplied will decline, and there will be a shortage of—an excess demand for—ATM services.

And that appears to be what happened: Two banks operating in Santa Monica—the Bank of America and Wells Fargo—closed their services to noncustomers when the ban was put in place (see the photograph). Hence, people who were willing to pay the fee were turned away—in effect, they felt a shortage of ATM services.

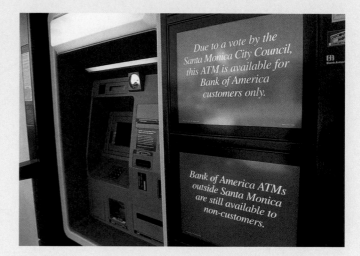

This ATM was closed to everyone except Bank of America customers; the quantity of ATMs supplied fell because of the price ceiling.

As the possibility of such bans spread through the country in 1999, many newspapers wrote editorials against them. Here is what the *New York Times* editorial said: People "need to recognize the banks do, after all, have a right to charge for their services. More important, efforts to ban the surcharge are apt to backfire and cause customers more harm than good." The San Francisco and Santa Monica bans have been suspended pending the outcome of a lawsuit.

What is the "more harm than good" that such a price ceiling on ATM services would cause? How does such a price ceiling differ from rent control? Will you vote for such a ban if the question comes to a vote in your city? Why do you think these cities put a ceiling on ATM prices and not clothing prices?

in order to buy goods. Thus, the total quantity demanded could not be greater than the amount of ration coupons. Alternatively, if there are no ration coupons, then the shortage might result in long waiting lines. In the past, in centrally planned economies, long lines for bread were frequently observed because of price controls on bread. Sometimes black markets develop, in which people buy and sell goods outside the watch of the government and charge whatever price they want. This typically happens in command economies. Black markets are also common in less-developed countries today when the governments in these countries impose price controls.

Another effect of price ceilings is a reduction in the quality of the good sold. By lowering the quality of the good, the producer can reduce the costs of producing it.

Low-quality housing frequently results from rent control. By lowering the quality of the apartments—perhaps being slow to paint the walls or repair the elevator—landlords make the apartments shoddy and unattractive.

■ **Making Things Worse.**   Although the stated purpose of price ceilings is to help people who have to pay high prices, the preceding examples indicate how they can make things worse. Issuing ration coupons raises difficult problems about who gets the coupons. In the case of a price ceiling on gasoline, for example, should the government give more coupons to those who commute by car than to those who do not? More generally, who is to decide who deserves the coupons? Rationing by waiting in line is also a poor outcome. People waiting in line could be doing more enjoyable or more useful things. Similarly, black markets, being illegal, encourage people to go outside the law; people thereby lose their rights to protection in the case of theft or fraud. Lowering the quality of the good is also a bad way to alleviate the problem of a high price. This simply eliminates the higher-quality good from production; consumers and producers lose.

Paradoxically, price ceilings frequently end up hurting those they try to help. Many people who benefit from controls, for example, are not poor at all. If rent controls reduce the supply of apartments, they make less housing available for everyone.

Surpluses and Related Problems Resulting from Price Floors

If the government imposes a price floor, then a surplus will occur, as shown in Figure 3.16. With the price above the equilibrium price, suppliers of goods and services want to sell more than people are willing to buy. Hence, there is a surplus. This is illustrated for the general case of any good in the top graph of Figure 3.16 and for the specific case of the minimum wage in the bottom graph.

How is this surplus dealt with in actual markets? In markets for farm products, the government usually has to buy the surplus and, perhaps, put it in storage; but buying farm products above the equilibrium price costs taxpayers money, and the higher price raises costs to consumers. For this reason, economists argue against price floors on agricultural goods. As an alternative, the government sometimes reduces the supply by telling firms to plant fewer acres or to destroy crops, or by restricting the amount that can come from abroad. In the United States, the federal government uses acreage restrictions in the case of wheat and other grains; it also uses import restrictions in the case of sugar. But government requirements that land be kept idle or crops destroyed are particularly repugnant to most people.

As we will see in more detail later in this book, the supply and demand model can also be applied to labor markets. In that case, the price is the price of labor, or the wage. What does the supply and demand model predict about the effects of a minimum wage? In the case of labor markets, a minimum wage can cause unemployment. If the equilibrium wage is below the minimum wage, then some workers would be willing to work for less than the minimum wage. But employers are not permitted to pay them less than the minimum wage. Therefore, there is an oversupply of workers at the minimum wage. The number of workers demanded is less than the number of workers willing to work; thus, the supply and demand model predicts that the minimum wage causes unemployment.

The minimum wage would have no effect if the equilibrium wage were above the minimum wage. The supply and demand model predicts that the minimum wage affects workers whose wages would be below the minimum. Thus, a minimum wage would be most likely to increase unemployment for teenage workers with very few skills if their wages would otherwise be below the minimum.

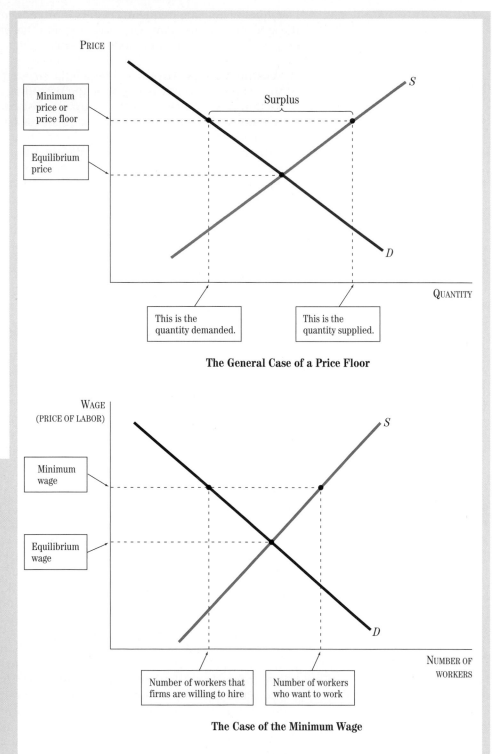

Figure 3.16
Effects of a Minimum Price Law
The top diagram shows the general case when the government prevents the market price from falling below a particular minimum price, or sets a price floor above the equilibrium price. The lower diagram shows a particular example when the price of labor—the wage—cannot fall below the minimum wage. The supply and demand model predicts that sellers are willing to sell a greater quantity than buyers are willing to buy at that price. Thus, there is a surplus of the good or, in the case of labor, unemployment for some of those who would be hired only at a lower wage.

PRICE

Minimum price or price floor

Surplus

S

Equilibrium price

D

This is the quantity demanded.

This is the quantity supplied.

QUANTITY

The General Case of a Price Floor

WAGE
(PRICE OF LABOR)

Minimum wage

S

Equilibrium wage

D

Number of workers that firms are willing to hire

Number of workers who want to work

NUMBER OF WORKERS

The Case of the Minimum Wage

> **REVIEW**
> - Price ceilings cause persistent shortages, which, in turn, cause rationing, black markets, and a reduced quality of goods and services.
> - Price floors cause persistent surpluses and unemployment, according to the supply and demand model. In the case of price floors on agricultural products, the surpluses are bought by the government and put in storage. In the case of the minimum wage, the surpluses mean more unemployment for those who can get jobs only at a wage below the minimum wage.

Elasticity of Demand and Supply

There is an elegant, but remarkably useful, economic concept called *elasticity* that economists use when they work with the supply and demand model. In economics, elasticity is a measure of how sensitive one variable is to another. In the case of the supply and demand model, elasticity measures how sensitive the quantity of a good that people demand, or that firms supply, is to the price of the good. Let us consider first demand and then supply.

Defining the Price Elasticity of Demand

The price elasticity of demand is a measure of the sensitivity of the *quantity demanded* of a good to the *price* of the good. "Price elasticity of demand" is sometimes shortened to "elasticity of demand," the "demand elasticity," or even simply "elasticity" when the meaning is clear from the context. The price elasticity of demand always refers to a particular demand curve or demand schedule, such as the world demand for oil or the U.S. demand for bicycles. For a particular demand curve, all other things besides the price of the good being equal, these relationships hold: As the price increases, the quantity demanded by consumers declines; as the price decreases, the quantity demanded by consumers increases. The price elasticity of demand is a measure of *how much* the quantity demanded changes when the price changes.

For example, when economists report that the price elasticity of demand for contact lenses is high, they mean that the quantity of contact lenses demanded by people changes by a large amount when the price changes. Or if they report that the price elasticity of demand for bread is low, they mean that the quantity of bread demanded changes by only a small amount when the price of bread changes.

price elasticity of demand: the percentage change in the quantity demanded of a good divided by the percentage change in the price of that good.

We can define the price elasticity of demand clearly with a formula: **Price elasticity of demand** is the percentage change in quantity demanded divided by the percentage change in the price. That is,

$$\text{Price elasticity of demand} = \frac{\text{percentage change in quantity demanded}}{\text{percentage change in the price}}$$

We emphasize that the price elasticity of demand refers to a particular demand curve; thus, the numerator of this formula is the percentage change in quantity demanded when the price changes by the percentage amount shown in the denominator. All the other factors that affect demand are held constant when we compute the price elasticity of demand.

For example, the price elasticity of demand for gasoline is about .2. Thus, if the price of gasoline increases by 10 percent, the quantity of gasoline demanded will fall by 2 percent (.2 × 10). The price elasticity of demand for alcoholic beverages is about

1.5; thus, if the price of alcoholic beverages rises by 10 percent, the quantity demanded will fall by 15 percent (1.5 × 10). As you can see from these examples, elasticity is a way to determine by *how much* the quantity demanded changes when the price changes.

Defining the Price Elasticity of Supply

Knowing how sensitive the quantity supplied is to a change in price is just as important as knowing how sensitive the quantity demanded is. The price elasticity of supply measures this sensitivity. "Price elasticity of supply" is sometimes shortened to "supply elasticity" or "elasticity of supply." Supply describes the behavior of firms that produce goods. A high price elasticity of supply means that firms raise their production by a large amount if the price increases. A low price elasticity of supply means that firms raise their production only a little if the price increases.

price elasticity of supply: the percentage change in quantity supplied divided by the percentage change in price.

The price elasticity of supply can be defined in much the same way as the price elasticity of demand. The **price elasticity of supply** is the percentage change in the quantity supplied divided by the percentage change in the price. That is,

$$\text{Price elasticity of supply} = \frac{\text{percentage change in quantity supplied}}{\text{percentage change in the price}}$$

The price elasticity of supply refers to a particular supply curve, such as the supply curve for peanuts. All other things that affect supply are held constant when we compute the price elasticity of supply. For example, suppose the price elasticity of supply for peanuts is .5. Then, if the price of peanuts rises by 10 percent, the quantity of peanuts supplied will increase by 5 percent (.5 × 10).

REVIEW

- The price elasticity of demand is a number that tells us how sensitive the quantity demanded is to the price. It is defined as the percentage change in the quantity demanded divided by the percentage change in the price.

- The price elasticity of supply is a number that tells us how sensitive the quantity supplied is to the price. It is defined as the percentage change in the quantity supplied divided by the percentage change in the price.

Conclusion

This chapter has shown how prices are determined in markets where buyers and sellers interact freely. The supply and demand model is used to describe how prices are determined in such markets. It is probably the most frequently used model in economics and has been in existence for over a hundred years in pretty much the same form as economists use it now. You will come to appreciate it more and more as you study economics.

A key feature of the model is that the price is found by the intersection of the supply and demand curves. To apply the model in practice, we need to look for factors that shift either the supply curve or the demand curve. In the most successful applications of the supply and demand model, the factors that affect supply and demand can be separated.

In later chapters we will see more about how the supply and demand model is implied by the central economic idea that people make purposeful choices with scarce resources and interact with other people as they make these choices. By doing so, we will be able to take a closer look at the three basic questions: what, how, and for whom to produce.

HEY POINTS

1. Demand is a negative relationship between the price of a good and the quantity demanded by consumers. It can be shown graphically by a downward-sloping demand curve.

2. A movement along the demand curve occurs when a higher price reduces the quantity demanded or a lower price increases the quantity demanded.

3. A shift of the demand curve occurs when something besides the price causes the quantity people are willing to buy to change.

4. Supply is a positive relationship between the price of a good and the quantity supplied by firms. It can be shown graphically by an upward-sloping supply curve.

5. A movement along the supply curve occurs when a higher price increases the quantity supplied or a lower price decreases the quantity supplied.

6. A shift of the supply curve occurs when something besides the price causes the quantity firms are willing to sell to change.

7. The equilibrium price and equilibrium quantity are determined by the intersection of the supply curve and the demand curve, where the quantity supplied equals the quantity demanded.

8. By shifting either the supply curve or the demand curve, observations on prices can be explained and predictions about prices can be made.

9. Price ceilings cause shortages, with the quantity supplied less than the quantity demanded. Shortages lead to rationing or black markets.

10. Price floors cause surpluses, with the quantity supplied greater than the quantity demanded.

11. Elasticity is a measure of the sensitivity of one economic variable to another. For example, the price elasticity of demand measures how much the quantity demanded changes when the price changes.

12. The price elasticity of supply is defined as the percentage change in the quantity supplied divided by the percentage change in the price.

HEY TERMS

demand	inferior good	supply curve	price ceiling
price	substitute	shortage (excess demand)	rent control
quantity demanded	complement	surplus (excess supply)	price floor
demand schedule	supply	equilibrium price	minimum wage
law of demand	quantity supplied	equilibrium quantity	price elasticity of demand
demand curve	supply schedule	market equilibrium	price elasticity of supply
normal good	law of supply	price control	

QUESTIONS FOR REVIEW

1. Why does the demand curve slope downward?

2. Why does the supply curve slope upward?

3. What is the difference between a shift in the demand curve and a movement along the demand curve?

4. What are four things that cause a demand curve to shift?

5. What are four things that cause a supply curve to shift?

6. What is the difference between a shift in the supply curve and a movement along the supply curve?

7. What are the equilibrium price and equilibrium quantity?

8. What happens to the equilibrium price if the supply curve shifts to the right and the demand curve does not shift?

9. What happens to the equilibrium price if the demand curve shifts to the right and the supply curve does not shift?

10. Do price ceilings cause shortages or surpluses? What about price floors? Explain.

11. If the price elasticity of demand for textbooks is 2 and the price of textbooks increases by 10 percent, by how much does the quantity demanded fall?

PROBLEMS

1. Consider the following supply and demand model of the world tea market (in billions of pounds).

Price per Pound	Quantity Supplied	Quantity Demanded
$.38	1,500	525
$.37	1,000	600
$.36	700	700
$.35	600	900
$.34	550	1,200

  a. Is there a shortage or a surplus when the price is $.38? What about $.34?

  b. What are the equilibrium price and the equilibrium quantity?

  c. Graph the supply curve and the demand curve.

  d. Show how the equilibrium price and quantity can be found on the graph.

  e. If there is a shortage or surplus at a price of $.38, calculate its size in billions of pounds and show it on the graph.

2. Consider the supply and demand model in problem 1. Suppose that there is a drought in Sri Lanka that reduces the supply of tea by 400 billion pounds at every price. Suppose demand does not change.

  a. Write down in a table the new supply schedule for tea.

  b. Find the new equilibrium price and the new equilibrium quantity. Explain how the market adjusts to the new equilibrium.

  c. Did the equilibrium quantity change by more or less than the change in supply?

  d. Graph the new supply curve along with the old supply curve and the demand curve.

  e. Show the change in the equilibrium price and the equilibrium quantity on the graph.

3. Use the supply and demand model to explain what happens to the equilibrium price and the equilibrium quantity for frozen yogurt in the following cases:

  a. There is a large expansion in the number of firms producing frozen yogurt.

  b. It is widely publicized in the press that frozen yogurt isn't as healthful as was previously thought.

  c. There is a sudden increase in the price of milk, which is used to produce frozen yogurt.

  d. Frozen yogurt suddenly becomes popular because a movie idol promotes it in television commercials.

4. For each of the following markets, indicate whether the stated change causes a shift in the supply curve, a shift in the demand curve, a movement along the supply curve, and/or a movement along the demand curve.

  a. The housing market: Consumers' incomes fall.

  b. The tea market: The price of sugar goes down.

  c. The coffee market: There is a freeze in Brazil that severely damages the coffee crop.

  d. The fast food market: The number of fast food restaurants in an area decreases.

5. Draw a supply and demand diagram to indicate the market for prescription drugs in the United States, with the equilibrium price and quantity labeled. Suppose the government imposes a strict ceiling on the price of prescription drugs sold in the United States. Show what happens in this market if the ceiling is less than the equilibrium price. How would the pharmaceutical firms that develop such drugs in their research laboratories respond?

6. Consider the market for automatic teller machine services in a city. The price is the fee for a cash withdrawal.

  a. Sketch the demand curve and the supply curve for ATM transactions.

  b. How is the equilibrium price determined?

  c. If the town council imposes a ban on ATM fees, equivalent to a price ceiling in this market, what happens to quantity supplied and quantity demanded?

  d. Economists frequently argue against price controls because of the incentives they give to suppliers. Explain why this interference in the market may provide bad incentives.

7. In 1991 the price of milk fell 30 percent. Senator Leahy of Vermont, a big milk-producing state, supported a law in the U.S. Congress to put a floor on the price. The floor was $13.09 per hundred pounds of milk. The market price was $11.47.
   a. Draw a supply and demand diagram. Explain the effects of the legislation. Would the legislation cause a surplus or a shortage?
   b. The dairy farmers supported the legislation, and consumer groups opposed it. Why?

8. Why is it necessary for people to stand in line for days before the sale of tickets to concerts by the most famous performers? Is the price mechanism working properly? Why are scalpers present on these occasions?

9. Assuming that either supply or demand, but not both, changes, indicate the direction and change in either supply or demand that must have occurred to produce the following:
   a. A decrease in the price and quantity of apples
   b. A decrease in the price of bananas with an increase in the quantity of bananas
   c. An increase in the price and quantity of cars
   d. An increase in the quantity of computers with a decrease in the price

10. Using the demand and supply diagrams (one for each market), show what short-run changes in price and quantity would be expected in the following markets if worries about air safety cause travelers to shy away from air travel. Each graph should contain the original and new demand and supply curves, and the original and new equilibrium prices and quantities. For each market, write one sentence explaining why each curve shifts or does not shift.
    a. The market for air travel
    b. The market for rail travel
    c. The market for hotel rooms in Hawaii

11. Determine which of the following four sentences use the terminology of the supply and demand model correctly.
    a. "The price of bicycles rose, and therefore the demand for bicycles went down."
    b. "The demand for bicycles increased, and therefore the price went up."
    c. "The price of bicycles fell, decreasing the supply of bicycles."
    d. "The supply of bicycles increased, and therefore the price of bicycles fell."

12. a. Suppose you find out that an increase in the price of first-class postage leads to an increase in the demand for overnight delivery service and a decrease in the demand for envelopes. For which good is postage a complement, and for which is it a substitute?
    b. Suppose someone told you that an increase in the price of gasoline caused a decrease in the demand for public transportation by train. Is this what you would predict? Why or why not?
    c. Suppose an economic forecasting group has determined that an increase in the price of orange juice has no effect on the demand for soft drinks. What can you conclude from this information?

13. Suppose a decrease in consumers' incomes causes a decrease in the demand for chicken and an increase in the demand for potatoes. Which good is inferior and which is normal? How will the equilibrium price and quantity change for each good?

14. a. Straight-line demand and supply curves can be represented by linear algebraic equations. Given the following algebraic expressions for supply and demand, calculate the equilibrium price and quantity by solving the two equations for P and Q.

    Supply: $Q = 5 + 2P$
    Demand: $Q = 9 - 2P$

    b. For the equations defined in part (a), show that when you substitute the equilibrium price into either the supply or the demand equation, you get the same equilibrium quantity.
    c. Suppose that the demand curve shifts as a result of an increase in consumers' incomes. The new demand equation is $Q = 13 - 2P$. Calculate the new equilibrium price and quantity.

15. Assume that the price elasticity of demand for peanuts is .12 and that this number does not change.
    a. Suppose that the price of peanuts rises by 50 percent; by what percentage does the quantity of peanuts demanded decrease? What if the price falls by 10 percent?
    b. Now suppose that the price of peanuts rises from $.60 to $1.25; by what percentage does the quantity demanded fall? If the quantity demanded was 4.0 billion pounds before this price increase, what is the quantity demanded (in billions of pounds) after the price increase?
    c. Compare your answers to part (b) with the change in the price and the change in the quantity in Figure 3.13.

Principles of Macroeconomics

CHAPTER 4

Macroeconomics: The Big Picture

An economic expansion is a period of continuous economic growth without a significant economic downturn. In 2001, the longest economic expansion in American history came to an end. The record-breaking expansion had begun in 1991; throughout the decade, unemployment was low and falling, as is often the case in an expansion, and spending by consumers and investors was very robust.

An economic downturn that ends an expansion is known as a recession. During 2001, unemployment increased, as it often does in a recession, and spending by consumers and business firms fell. While the tragic events of September 11 contributed substantially to the economy's going into recession, all indications were that the economic slowdown had begun almost six months earlier. Once the signs of recession were evident, the president, members of Congress, and the Federal Reserve expressed their concern and moved quickly to implement policies that they claimed would help the economy return to a period of expansion.

Recent economic data seem to indicate that the slowdown was short-lived: The longest economic expansion on record seems to have been followed by one of the shortest recessions on record. Why was the expansion so long? What caused the economy to go into recession? Why was the recession so short-lived? Did the policy responses put in place in 2001 help the economy out of the recession? These are the types of questions that the study of macroeconomics helps us answer.

Macroeconomics is the study of the *whole market economy.* Like other parts of economics, macroeconomics uses the central idea that people make purposeful decisions with scarce resources. However, instead of focusing on the workings of one market—whether the market for peanuts or the market for bicycles—macroeconomics focuses on the economy as a whole. Macroeconomics looks at the big picture: Economic growth, recessions, unemployment, and inflation are among its subject matter. You should accordingly put on your "big picture glasses" when you study macroeconomics.

Macroeconomics is important to you and your future. For example, you will have a much better chance of finding a desirable job after you graduate from college during a period of economic expansion than during a period of recession. Strong economic growth can help alleviate poverty, free up resources to clean up the environment, and lead to a brighter future for your generation. By studying macroeconomics, you can better understand the changes that are taking place in the economy, better understand the role of good economic policies in driving economic growth and reducing unemployment, and become a more informed and educated citizen.

This chapter summarizes the overall workings of the economy, highlighting key facts to remember. It also provides a brief preview of the macroeconomic theory designed to explain these facts. The theory will be developed in later chapters.

Real GDP over Time

real gross domestic product (real GDP): a measure of the value of all the goods and services newly produced in a country during some period of time, adjusted for changes in prices over time.

economic growth: an upward trend in real GDP, reflecting expansion in the economy over time.

economic fluctuations: swings in real GDP that lead to deviations of the economy from its long-term growth trend.

Gross domestic product (GDP) is the economic variable of most interest to macroeconomists. GDP is the total value of all goods and services produced in the economy during a specified period of time, usually a year or a quarter. The total value of goods and services can change either because the quantities of goods and services are changing or because their prices are changing. As a result, economists often prefer to use **real gross domestic product (real GDP)** as the measure of production; the adjective *real* means that we adjust the measure of production to account for changes in prices over time. Real GDP, also called *output* or *production,* is the most comprehensive measure of how well the economy is doing.

Figure 4.1 shows the changes in real GDP in recent years in the United States. When you look at real GDP over time, as in Figure 4.1, you notice two simultaneous patterns emerging. Over the long term, increases in real GDP demonstrate an upward trend, which economists call long-term **economic growth.** In the short term, there are **economic fluctuations**—more transient increases or decreases in real GDP. These short-term fluctuations in real GDP are also called *business cycles.* The difference between the long-term economic growth trend and the economic fluctuations can be better seen by drawing a relatively smooth line between the observations on real GDP. Such a smooth trend line is shown in Figure 4.1. Sometimes real GDP fluctuates above

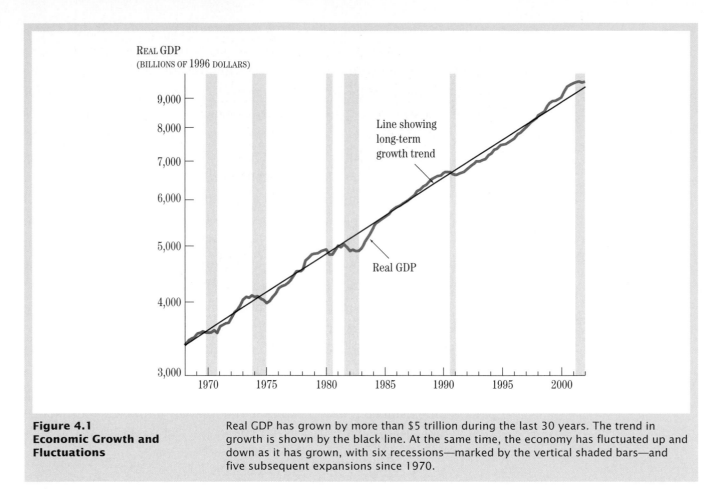

Figure 4.1
Economic Growth and
Fluctuations

Real GDP has grown by more than $5 trillion during the last 30 years. The trend in growth is shown by the black line. At the same time, the economy has fluctuated up and down as it has grown, with six recessions—marked by the vertical shaded bars—and five subsequent expansions since 1970.

the trend line, and sometimes it fluctuates below the trend line. In this section we look more closely at these two patterns: economic growth and economic fluctuations.

Economic Growth: The Relentless Uphill Climb

The large increase in real GDP shown in Figure 4.1 means that people in the United States now produce a much greater amount of goods and services each year than they did 30 years ago. Improvements in the economic well-being of individuals in any society cannot occur without such an increase in real GDP. To get a better measure of how individuals benefit from increases in real GDP, we consider average production per person, or *real GDP per capita*. Real GDP per capita is real GDP divided by the number of people in the economy. It is the total production of all food, clothes, cars, houses, CDs, concerts, education, computers, etc., per person. When real GDP per capita is increasing, then the well-being—or the standard of living—of individuals in the economy, at least on average, is improving.

How much economic growth has there been during the last 30 years in the United States? The annual *economic growth rate*—the percentage increase in real GDP each year—provides a good measure. On the average, for the last 30 years, the annual economic growth rate has been about 3 percent. This may not sound like much, but it means that real GDP has nearly tripled. The increase in production in the United States over the past 30 years is larger than what Japan and Germany together now produce. It is as if all the production of Japan and Germany—what is made by all the workers, machines, and technology in these countries—were annexed to the U.S. economy, as illustrated in Figure 4.2.

How much has real GDP *per capita* increased during this period? Because the U.S. population increased by about 100 million people during this period, the increase in real GDP per capita has been less dramatic than the increase in real GDP, but it is impressive nonetheless. The annual growth rate of real GDP per capita is the percentage increase in real GDP per capita each year. It has averaged about 1.7 percent per year. Again, this might not sound like much, but it has meant that real GDP per capita doubled from about $10,000 per person in the 1950s to about $20,000 per person in the 1990s. That extra $10,000 per person represents increased opportunities for travel, VCRs, housing, washing machines, aerobics classes, health care, antipollution devices for cars, and so on.

Over long spans of time, small differences in economic growth—even less than 1 percent per year—can transform societies. For example, economic growth in the southern states was only a fraction of a percent greater than in the North in the 100 years after the Civil War. Yet this enabled the South to rise from a real income per capita about half that of the North after the Civil War to one about the same as that of the North today. Economic growth is the reason that Italy has caught up with and even surpassed the United Kingdom in real GDP per capita; 100 years ago, Italy had a real GDP per capita about half that of the United Kingdom. Economic growth is also key to improvements in the less-developed countries in Africa, Asia, and Latin America. Because economic growth has been lagging in many of these countries, their real GDP per capita is considerably less than that of the United States.

Economic Fluctuations: Temporary Setbacks and Recoveries

Clearly, real GDP grows over time, but every now and then real GDP stops growing, falls, and then starts increasing rapidly again. These ups and downs in the economy—that is, economic fluctuations or business cycles—can be seen in Figure 4.1.

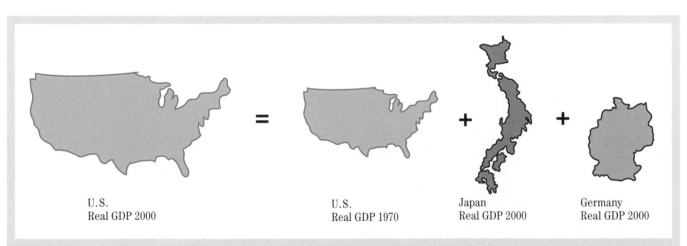

U.S.
Real GDP 2000

U.S.
Real GDP 1970

Japan
Real GDP 2000

Germany
Real GDP 2000

Figure 4.2 Visualizing Economic Growth   Over the last 30 years, production in the U.S. economy has increased by more than the total current production of the Japanese and German economies combined. It is as if the United States had annexed Germany and Japan.

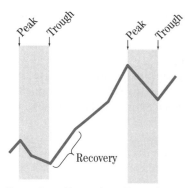

Recession Expansion Recession

recession: a decline in real GDP that lasts for at least six months.

peak: the highest point in real GDP before a recession.

trough: the lowest point of real GDP at the end of a recession.

expansion: the period between the trough of a recession and the next peak, consisting of a general rise in output and employment.

recovery: the early part of an economic expansion, immediately after the trough of the recession.

One of these business cycles, the one in the early 1990s, is blown up for closer examination in Figure 4.3. No two business cycles are alike. Certain phases are common to all business cycles, however. These common phases are shown in the diagram in the margin. When real GDP falls, economists say that there is a **recession;** a rule of thumb says that the fall in real GDP must last for a half year or more before the decline is considered a recession. The highest point before the start of a recession is called the **peak.** The lowest point at the end of a recession is called the **trough,** a term that may cause you to imagine water accumulating at the bottom of one of the dips.

The period between recessions—from the trough to the next peak—is called an **expansion,** as shown for a typical fluctuation in the margin. The early part of an expansion is usually called a **recovery** because the economy is just recovering from the recession.

The peaks and troughs of the six recessions since the late 1960s are shown by vertical bars in Figure 4.1. The shaded areas represent the recessions. The area between the shaded bars shows the expansions. The dates of all peaks and troughs back to 1920 are shown in Table 4.1. The average length of each business cycle from peak to peak is five years, but it is clear from Table 4.1 that business cycles are not regularly occurring ups and downs, like sunup and sundown. Recessions occur irregularly. There were only 12 months between the back-to-back recessions of the early 1980s, while 58 months of uninterrupted growth occurred between the 1973–1975 recession and the 1980 recession. The recession phases of business cycles also vary in duration and depth. The 1980 recession, for example, was not nearly as long or as deep as the 1973–1975 recession.

The 1990–1991 recession was one of the shortest recessions in U.S. history, and it was followed by the longest expansion in U.S. history. Before that recession, almost uninterrupted economic growth had occurred for most of the 1980s—from the trough of the previous recession in November 1982 to a peak in July 1990.

Economists debate whether economic policies were responsible for the expansions of the 1980s and 1990s. We will examine these debates in later chapters. Another debate is the cause of the recession that began in 1990. The first month of the recession occurred just after Iraq invaded Kuwait, causing a disruption in the oil fields and a jump in world oil prices. Some argue that this jump in oil prices was a factor in the recession.

Figure 4.3
The Phases of Business Cycles
Although no two business cycles are alike, they have common features, including the *peak, recession,* and *trough,* shown here for 1990–1991.

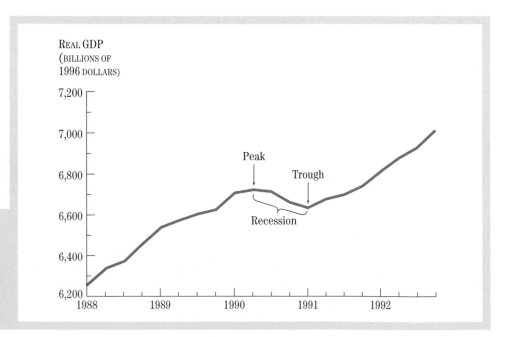

Table 4.1
Comparison of Recessions

Recession		Duration of Recession (months from peak to trough)	Decline in Real GDP (percent from peak to trough)	Duration of Next Expansion (months from trough to peak)
Peak	*Trough*			
Jan 1920–Jul 1921		18	8.7	22
May 1923–Jul 1924		14	4.1	27
Oct 1926–Nov 1927		13	2.0	21
Aug 1929–Mar 1933		43	32.6	50
May 1937–Jun 1938		13	18.2	80
Feb 1945–Oct 1945		8	11.0	37
Nov 1948–Oct 1949		11	1.5	45
Jul 1953–May 1954		10	3.2	39
Aug 1957–Apr 1958		8	3.3	24
Apr 1960–Feb 1961		10	1.2	106
Dec 1969–Nov 1970		11	1.0	36
Nov 1973–Mar 1975		16	4.9	58
Jan 1980–Jul 1980		6	2.5	12
Jul 1981–Nov 1982		16	3.0	92
Jul 1990–Mar 1991		8	1.4	120
Mar 2001–		13*		

*As of April 2002.

Source: National Bureau of Economic Research.

■ **A Recession's Aftermath.**   The economy usually takes several years to return to normal after a recession. Thus, a period of bad economic times always follows a recession while the economy recovers. Remember that economists define recessions as periods in which real GDP is declining, not as periods in which real GDP is down. Despite the technical definition, many people still associate the word *recession* with bad economic times. For example, although the 1990–1991 recession ended in March 1991, most people felt that the bad economic times extended well into 1992, and they were right. But, technically speaking, the recession was over in March 1991 when GDP began to grow again—well before the effects of an improving economy were felt by most people.

■ **Recessions versus Depressions.**   Recessions have been observed for as long as economists have tracked the economy. Some past recessions lasted so long and were so deep that they are called *depressions*. There is no formal definition of a depression. A depression is a huge recession.

Fortunately, we have not experienced a depression in the United States for a long time. Figure 4.4 shows the history of real GDP for about 100 years. The most noticeable decline in real GDP occurred in the 1929–1933 recession. Real GDP fell by 32.6 percent in this period. This decline in real GDP was so large that it was given its own designation by economists and historians—the *Great Depression*. The recessions of recent years have had much smaller declines.

Table 4.1 shows how much real GDP fell in each of the fifteen recessions since the 1920s. The 1920–1921 recession and the 1937–1938 recession were big enough to be classified as depressions, but both are small compared to the Great Depression. Real GDP also declined substantially after World War II, when war production declined.

Clearly, recent recessions have not been even remotely comparable in severity to the Great Depression or the other huge recessions of the 1920s and 1930s. The

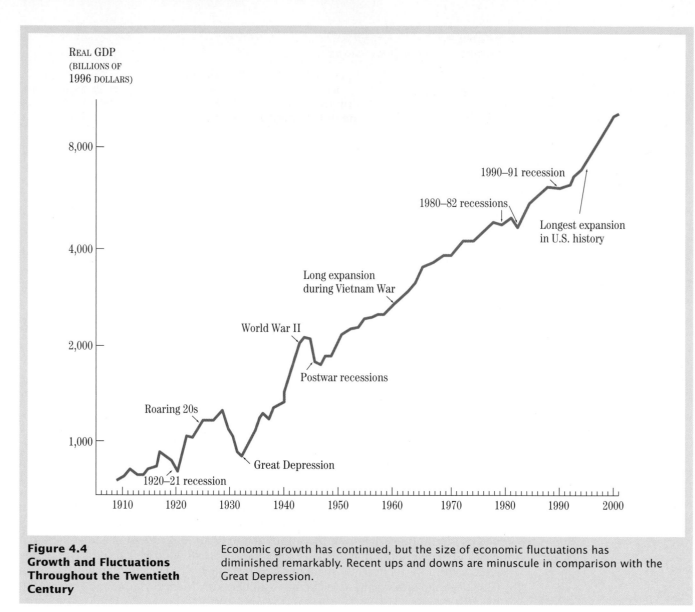

Figure 4.4
Growth and Fluctuations Throughout the Twentieth Century

Economic growth has continued, but the size of economic fluctuations has diminished remarkably. Recent ups and downs are minuscule in comparison with the Great Depression.

1990–1991 recession, for example, had only one-twentieth the decline in real GDP that occurred during the Great Depression. But because any recession rivets attention on people's hardship and suffering, there is always a tendency to view a current recession as worse than all previous recessions. Some commentators reporting on the 1990–1991 recession wondered whether it should be compared with the Great Depression. For example, in September 1992, Louis Uchitelle of the *New York Times* wrote, "Technically, the recession is over, but spiritually, it continues. . . . The question is, what to call these hard times. What has been happening in America since 1989 seems momentous enough to enter history as a major economic event of the 20th century."[1]

---

1. Louis Uchitelle, "Even Words Fail in This Economy," *New York Times*, September 8, 1992, p. C2.

REVIEW
- Economic growth and economic fluctuations occur simultaneously.

- Economic growth provides lasting improvements in the well-being of people. But recessions interrupt this growth.

- The Great Depression of the 1930s was a much larger downturn than recent recessions. It was about twenty times more severe than the 1990–1991 recession when measured by the decline in real GDP.

Unemployment, Inflation, and Interest Rates

As real GDP changes over time, so do other economic variables, such as unemployment, inflation, and interest rates. Looking at these other economic variables gives us a better understanding of the human story behind the changes in real GDP. They also provide additional information about the economy's performance—just as a person's pulse rate or cholesterol level gives information different from the body temperature. No one variable is sufficient.

Unemployment During Recessions

unemployment rate: the percentage of the labor force that is unemployed.

There are fluctuations in unemployment just as there are fluctuations in real GDP. The **unemployment rate** is the number of unemployed people as a percentage of the labor force; the labor force consists of those who are either working or looking for work. Every time the economy goes into a recession, the unemployment rate rises because people are laid off and new jobs are difficult to find. The individual stories behind the unemployment numbers frequently represent frustration and distress.

Figure 4.5 shows what happens to the unemployment rate as the economy goes through recessions and recoveries. The increase in the unemployment rate during a recession is eventually followed by a decline in unemployment during the recovery. Note, for example, how unemployment rose during the recessions of 1969–1970 and 1973–1975. Around the time of the 1990–1991 recession, the unemployment rate rose from 5.2 percent to 7.7 percent.

Figure 4.5
The Unemployment Rate
The number of unemployed workers as a percentage of the labor force—the unemployment rate—increases during recessions because people are laid off and it is difficult to find work. Sometimes the unemployment rate continues to increase for a while after the recession is over, as in 1971 and 1991. But eventually unemployment declines during the economic recovery.

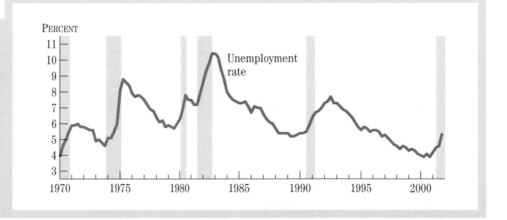

Figure 4.6 shows how high the unemployment rate got during the Great Depression. It rose to over 25 percent; one in four workers was out of work. Fortunately, recent increases in unemployment during recessions have been much smaller. The unemployment rate reached 10.4 percent in the early 1980s, the highest level since World War II.

Even though the most recent recession pales in comparison to the Great Depression, it still caused a lot of pain and hardship across the country. Figure 4.7 illustrates how rapidly unemployment rose, even in what most economists described as a mild recession. In the 12 months from the end of 2000 to the end of 2001, the unemployment rate increased by almost 2 percentage points. To put this number in more human terms, the number of unemployed workers across the country increased by about 2.5 million.

Inflation

inflation rate: the percentage increase in the overall price level over a given period of time, usually one year.

Just as output and unemployment have fluctuated over time, so has inflation. The **inflation rate** is the percentage increase in the average price of all goods and services from one year to the next. Figure 4.8 shows the inflation rate for the same 30-year period we have focused on in our examination of real GDP and unemployment. Clearly, a low and stable inflation rate has not been a feature of the United States during this period. There are several useful facts to note about the behavior of inflation.

First, inflation is closely correlated with the ups and downs in real GDP and employment: Inflation increased prior to every recession in the last 30 years and then subsided during and after every recession. We will want to explore whether this close correlation between the ups and downs in inflation and the ups and downs in the economy helps explain economic fluctuations.

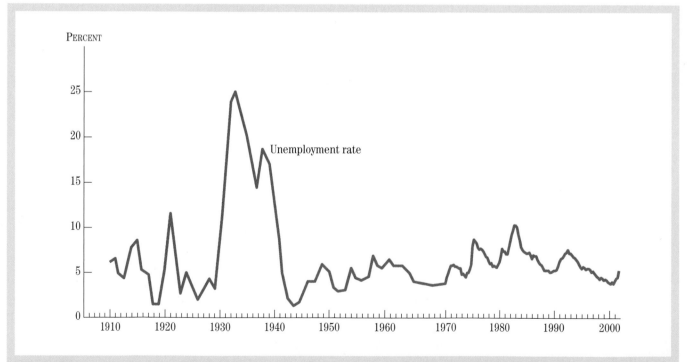

Figure 4.6
Unemployment During the Great Depression

The increase in unemployment in the United States during the Great Depression was huge compared with the increases in unemployment during more mild downturns in the economy. More than one in four workers were unemployed during the Great Depression.

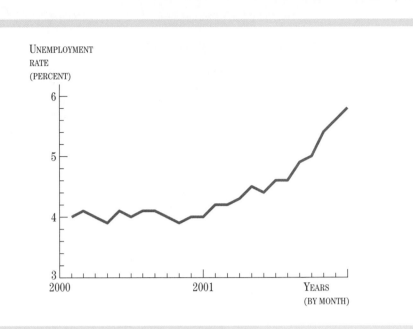

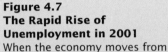

Figure 4.7
The Rapid Rise of
Unemployment in 2001
When the economy moves from
expansion into recession, unemployment can climb very rapidly
over a period of a few months, as
we saw at the end of the long
expansion in 2001.

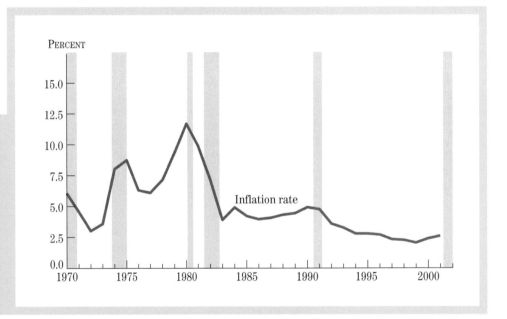

Figure 4.8
The Ups and Downs in
Inflation
Inflation has increased before
each recession and then declined
during and immediately after
each recession. In addition, a
longer-term upward trend in
inflation began in the mid-1960s
and, after several ups and
downs, reached a peak in 1980.
In 1981–1983, America had a
disinflation—a decline in the rate
of inflation.

Second, there are longer-term trends in inflation. For example, inflation rose
from a low point in the mid-1960s to a high point of double-digit inflation in 1980.
This period of persistently high inflation from the mid-1960s until 1980 is called the
Great Inflation. The Great Inflation ended in the early 1980s, when the inflation rate
declined substantially. Such a decline in inflation is called *disinflation.* (When inflation is negative and the average price level falls, economists call it *deflation*).

Third, judging by history, there is no reason to expect the inflation rate to be zero,
even on average. The inflation rate has averaged around 2 or 3 percent in the 1990s in
the United States.

Why does inflation increase before recessions? Why does inflation fall during and
after recessions? What caused the Great Inflation? Why is inflation not equal to zero

The Economic Impact of September 11

The tragic events of September 11, 2001, left a trail of human destruction that was hitherto almost unimaginable. In the days and months following September 11, people all over the United States tried to assess the human and economic toll of the events of that fateful day. The assessment that many macroeconomists were asked to make was to calculate the economic impact of the events of September 11. As the economist Paul Krugman, who is also a regular columnist for the *New York Times,* said in his Op-Ed column a few days after September 11, "It seems almost in bad taste to talk about dollars and cents after an act of mass murder. Nonetheless, we must ask about the economic aftershocks from Tuesday's horror." Macroeconomic theory can help us understand the long- and short-term economic impact of this and other such tragedies.

In the case of September 11, the most obvious short-term costs were the destruction of life and property in New York, Washington, D.C., and Pennsylvania; the disruption of financial markets, given that many large financial institutions were located in and around the World Trade Center; and the costs to airlines from disruptions in air travel in the days following the tragedy. However, the theory of economic fluctuations, presented in Chapters 10 and 11, tells us that spending shocks have feedback effects that aggravate the initial direct effects. In the case of New York, the disruption to the economy was substantially greater than the destruction of property and clean-up costs would indicate because of drastic cutbacks in tourism, which led to a sharp falloff in hotel stays, dining out in restaurants, and shopping for expensive goods in Manhattan. The lack of spending by consumers led firms in the hotel, restaurant, and retail industries to lay off thousands of workers. According to a study done by the New York City Chamber of Commerce in September 2001, the cost in terms of reduced economic activity was expected to be almost $40 billion, and the cost in terms of employment was expected to be almost 25,000 jobs. Financial markets were severely disrupted in the short run: They were closed for the remainder of the week, and when they opened the following week, the Dow Jones Industrial Average fell from 9605.5 to 8920.7, a decline of about 7 percent at the end of the first week of trading, the Dow had fallen to 8235.8, a decline of about 14 percent. The airline industry was hit hard: In the weeks following September 11, airlines announced plans to lay off tens of thousands of workers—20,000 apiece at American Airlines and United Airlines.

The theory of economic fluctuations states that when faced with an economic shock that reduces spending, policymakers can respond by putting into place specific measures designed not only to stop the fall in spending, but indeed to try to restore both confidence and spending by consumers and firms. The president promised $20 billion in federal aid to New York to help the city rebuild. As fears that one or more airlines would have to go into bankruptcy mounted, both Congress and the Senate sought to provide relief for the beleaguered airline industry by overwhelmingly approving a bill that provided $5 billion in federal funds and $10 billion in loan guarantees.

even in more normal times, when the economy is neither in recession nor in boom? What can economic policy do to keep inflation low and stable? These are some of the questions and policy issues about inflation addressed by macroeconomics.

Interest Rates

interest rate: the amount received per dollar loaned per year, usually expressed as a percentage (e.g., 6 percent) of the loan.

The **interest rate** is the amount that lenders charge when they lend money, expressed as a percentage of the amount loaned. For example, if you borrow $100 for a year from a friend and the interest rate on the loan is 6 percent, then at the end of the year you must pay your friend back $6 in interest in addition to the $100 you borrowed. The interest rate is another key economic variable that is related to the growth and change in real GDP over time.

■ **Different Types of Interest Rates and Their Behavior.** There are many different interest rates in the economy: The *mortgage interest rate* is the rate on loans to buy a house; the *savings deposit interest rate* is the rate people get on their

The response of monetary policymakers to the events of September 11 was equally swift: On September 17, the Federal Reserve cut interest rates from 3.5 percent to 3 percent, making it cheaper for firms and individuals to borrow money, and also announced its willingness to take steps to restore normalcy to financial markets. Help was not offered only by the government and the Federal Reserve; millions of people all over the United States contributed hundreds of millions of dollars to charities that helped the victims and their families make payments on their rent, school tuition, and health care, doing their part to keep the negative effects from deepening.

The theory of economic growth tells us that the long-term growth of an economy depends on its ability to produce goods and services, which in turn depends on the economy's stocks of labor, capital, and technology. While the destruction of life and property in New York and Washington, D.C., was substantial—"more than we can bear," in the words of Mayor Giuliani—the loss of labor and capital was small relative to the size of the entire U.S. population and the entire U.S. capital stock. In the same Op-Ed piece mentioned earlier, Paul Krugman speculated that the long-term effects would not be substantial: "Nobody has a dollar figure for the damage yet, but I would be surprised if the loss is more than 0.1 percent of U.S. wealth—comparable to the material effects of a major earthquake or hurricane." While such calculations may seem a little too cold-blooded at first glance, it is important that macroeconomists make such assessments so that we can develop a more complete understanding of the impacts of such tragedies, and also so that we can come up with appropriate policy responses to these events.

The prediction that the events of September 11 would not have a long-term effect seems to have been vindicated by a reassessment of the situation six months later. In the weeks following September 11, the financial markets seemed to stabilize and then recover: by November 9 the Dow had reached the level it was at on September 10, and it ended the year almost 6 percent higher, at 10,178.7. GDP grew rapidly in the fourth quarter of 2001: It increased at a rate of 1.4 percent, signaling a possible return to the sustained positive growth rates experienced during the long expansion. Finally, the unemployment rate seemed to stabilize and then improve as well—after increasing from 5 percent to 5.8 percent over the last four months of 2001, it came back down to 5.4 percent in the first two months of 2002.

savings deposits at banks; the *Treasury bill rate* is the interest rate the government pays when it borrows money from people for a year or less; the *federal funds rate* is the interest rate banks charge each other on very short-term loans. Interest rates influence people's economic behavior. When interest rates rise, for example, it is more expensive to borrow funds to buy a house or a car, so many people postpone such purchases.

Figure 4.9 shows the behavior of a typical interest rate, the federal funds rate, during the last 30 years. First, note how closely the ups and downs in the interest rate are correlated with the ups and downs in the economy. Interest rates rise before each recession and then decline during and after each recession. Second, note that, as with the inflation rate, there are longer-term trends in the interest rate. The interest rate rose from the mid-1960s until the 1980s. Each fluctuation in interest rates during this period brought forth a higher peak in interest rates. Then, in the 1980s, the interest rate began a downward trend; each peak was lower than the previous peak. By the early 1990s, interest rates had returned to the levels of the early 1970s.

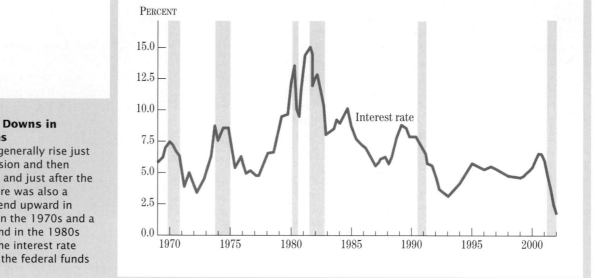

Figure 4.9
The Ups and Downs in Interest Rates
Interest rates generally rise just before a recession and then decline during and just after the recession. There was also a longer-term trend upward in interest rates in the 1970s and a downward trend in the 1980s and 1990s. (The interest rate shown here is the federal funds interest rate.)

■ The Concept of the Real Interest Rate.

As we will see, the trends and fluctuations in interest rates are intimately connected with the trends and fluctuations in inflation and real GDP. In fact, the long-term rise in interest rates in the 1960s and 1970s was partly due to the rise in the rate of inflation. When inflation rises, people who lend money will be paid back in funds that are worth less because the average price of goods rises more quickly. To compensate for this decline in the value of funds, lenders require a higher interest rate. For example, if the inflation rate is 20 percent and you lend someone $100 for a year at 6 percent, then you get back $106 at the end of the year. However, the *average* price of the goods you can buy with your $106 is now 20 percent higher. Thus, your 6 percent gain in interest has been offset by a 20 percent loss. It is as if you receive *negative* 14 percent interest: 6 percent interest less 20 percent inflation. The difference between the stated interest rate and the inflation rate is thus a better measure of the real interest rate. Economists define the **real interest rate** as the interest rate less the inflation rate people expect. The term **nominal interest rate** is used to refer to the interest rate on a loan, making no adjustment for inflation. For example, the real interest rate is 2 percent if the nominal interest rate is 5 percent and inflation is expected to be 3 percent (5 − 3 = 2). To keep the real interest rate from changing by a large amount as inflation rises, the nominal interest rate has to increase with inflation. Thus, the concept of the real interest rate helps us understand why inflation and interest rates have moved together. We will make much more use of the real interest rate in later chapters.

real interest rate: the interest rate minus the expected rate of inflation; it adjusts the nominal interest rate for inflation.

nominal interest rate: the interest rate uncorrected for inflation.

REVIEW

- The unemployment rate rises during recessions and falls during recoveries.
- Inflation and interest rates rise prior to recessions and then fall during and just after recessions.
- There was a long-term increase in interest rates and inflation in the 1970s. Interest rates and inflation were lower in the 1990s.

Macroeconomic Theory and Policy

Because strong economic growth raises the living standards of people in an economy, and because increases in unemployment during recessions cause hardship, two goals of economic policy are to raise long-term growth and to reduce the size of short-term economic fluctuations. However, the facts—summarized above—about economic growth and fluctuations do not give economists a basis for making recommendations about economic policy. Before one can be confident about recommending a policy, one needs a coherent theory to explain the facts.

Macroeconomic theory is divided into two branches. *Economic growth theory* aims to explain the long-term upward rise of real GDP over time. *Economic fluctuations theory* tries to explain the short-term fluctuations in real GDP. Economic growth theory and economic fluctuations theory combine to form *macroeconomic theory*, which explains why the economy both grows and fluctuates over time.

The Theory of Long-Term Economic Growth

Economic growth theory starts by distinguishing the longer-term economic growth trend from the short-term fluctuations in the economy. This is not as easy as it may seem because the long-term growth trend itself may change.

It will be useful to give a name to the upward trend line in real GDP shown in Figure 4.1. We will call it **potential GDP.** Potential GDP represents the long-run tendency of the economy to grow. Real GDP fluctuates around potential GDP. No one knows exactly where potential GDP lies and exactly what its growth rate is, but any trend line that has the same long-term increase as real GDP and intersects real GDP in several places is probably a good estimate.

Note that potential GDP as defined here and as used by most macroeconomists is not the maximum amount of real GDP. As Figure 4.1 shows, sometimes real GDP goes above potential GDP. Thus, potential GDP is more like the average or normal level of real GDP.

Economic growth theory postulates that the potential GDP of an economy is given by its **aggregate supply.** *Aggregate* means total. Aggregate supply is all goods and services produced by all the firms in the economy using the available labor, capital, and technology. **Labor** is the total number of hours workers are available to work in producing real GDP. **Capital** is the total number of factories, cultivated plots of land, machines, computers, and other tools available for the workers to use to produce real GDP. **Technology** is all the available know-how—from organizational schemes to improved telecommunications to better computer programming skills—that workers and firms can use when they produce real GDP. Labor, capital, and technology jointly determine aggregate supply.

■ **The Production Function.** We can summarize the relationship between the three determinants and the aggregate supply of real GDP as

Real GDP = F(labor, capital, technology)

which we say in words as "real GDP is a function, F, of labor, capital, and technology." The function F means that there is some general relationship between these variables. For this relationship, we assume that higher capital, higher labor, and higher technology all mean higher real GDP; and lower capital, lower labor, and lower

potential GDP: the economy's long-term growth trend for real GDP, determined by the available supply of capital, labor, and technology. Real GDP fluctuates above and below potential GDP.

aggregate supply: the total value of all goods and services produced in the economy by the available supply of capital, labor, and technology (also called potential GDP).

labor: the number of hours people work in producing goods and services.

capital: the factories, improvements to cultivated land, machinery and other tools, equipment, and structures used to produce goods and services.

technology: anything that raises the amount of output that can be produced with a given amount of labor and capital.

Aggregate Supply and the Production Function
The theory of economic growth is based on the production function, which is a model of how labor, capital,
and technology jointly determine the aggregate supply of output in the economy. Here the workers at the
*automobile plant are part of the economy's **labor** (left), the tools that the workers are using to assemble the*
*cars are the economy's **capital** (middle), and computer programming skills are part of the economy's **tech-***
*nology** (right), which raises the value of output for a given amount of labor and capital.*

production function: the relationship that describes output as
a function of labor, capital, and
technology.

technology all mean less real GDP. We call this relationship the **production function**
because it tells us how much production (real GDP) of goods and services can be
obtained from a certain amount of labor, capital, and technology inputs. A higher
long-term economic growth rate for the economy requires a higher growth rate for
one or more of these three determinants. A lower long-term economic growth rate
may be due to a slower growth rate for one or more of these three determinants.

The production function applies to the entire economy, but we also have production functions for individual firms in the economy. For example, consider the production of cars. The car factory and the machines in the factory are the capital. The workers
who work in the factory are the labor. The assembly-line production method is the technology. The cars coming out of the factory are the output. The production function for
the economy as a whole has real GDP as output, not just cars, and all available labor,
capital, and technology as inputs, not just those producing cars.

The Role of Government Policy

Most governments have been interested in finding ways to increase economic
growth. Economic policies that aim to increase long-term economic growth are
sometimes called *supply-side policies* because they concentrate on increasing the
growth of potential GDP, which is the aggregate supply of the economy.

■ **Fiscal Policy.** Our preview of growth theory already tells us where policies to
increase growth should focus: on increasing the available supply of labor, capital,
and technology. The growth rate of capital depends on how much businesses invest
in new capital each year. The amount that businesses choose to invest depends in
part on the incentives they have to invest. We will see that the incentive to invest
depends on the amount of taxing, spending, and borrowing by government. Hence,
government policy can affect the incentive to invest and thereby stimulate long-term
economic growth. Government policy concerning taxing, spending, and borrowing
is called *fiscal policy.*

Labor supply also depends on incentives. In the case of labor, it is the incentive
for firms to hire workers, for people to work harder or longer, for workers who are not

in the labor force to come into the labor force, or for people to retire later in life. Again, government policy toward taxing, spending, and borrowing affects these incentives.

Finally, technology growth can also be affected by government policy if the government gives incentives for researchers to invent new technologies or provides funds for education so that workers can improve their skills and know-how.

■ **Monetary Policy.** Keeping inflation low and stable is another part of government policy to stimulate long-term economic growth. We will see that the government has an important role to play in determining the inflation rate, especially over the long term, because the inflation rate in the long term depends on the growth rate of the money supply, which can be controlled by the government. Government policy concerning the money supply and the control of inflation is called *monetary policy.* The institution of government assigned to conduct monetary policy is the central bank. In the United States the central bank is the Federal Reserve System.

Why should low and stable inflation be part of an economic growth policy? An examination of inflation and economic growth in a number of countries indicates that inflation is negatively correlated with long-term economic growth. The reason for this negative correlation over the long term may be that inflation raises uncertainty and thereby reduces incentives to invest in capital or improve technology. The theory of economic growth tells us that lower capital growth and lower technological growth reduce economic growth.

The Theory of Economic Fluctuations

Our review of the performance of the economy showed some of the hardships that come from economic fluctuations, especially the recessions and unemployment. Can government economic policy improve economic performance by reducing the size of the fluctuations? To answer these questions, we need a theory to interpret the facts of economic fluctuations.

■ **Aggregate Demand and Economic Fluctuations.** The theory of economic fluctuations emphasizes fluctuations in the demand for goods and services as the reason for the ups and downs in the economy. Because the focus is on the sum of the demand for all goods and services in the economy—not just the demand for peanuts or bicycles—we use the term *aggregate demand.* More precisely, **aggregate demand** is the sum of the demands from the four groups that contribute to demand in the whole economy: consumers, business firms, government, and foreigners.

aggregate demand: the total demand for goods and services by consumers, businesses, government, and foreigners.

According to this theory, the declines in real GDP below potential GDP during recessions are caused by declines in aggregate demand, and the increases in real GDP above potential GDP are caused by increases in aggregate demand. For example, the decrease in real GDP in the 1990–1991 recession may have been due to a decline in government demand. In fact, government military spending did decline sharply. Or the recession may have been due to a decline in demand by consumers as they learned about Iraq's invasion of Kuwait in August 1990, saw oil and gasoline prices rise, and worried about the threat of war.

Thus, a key assumption of the theory of economic fluctuations is that real GDP fluctuates around potential GDP. Why is this a good assumption? How do we know that the fluctuations in the economy are not due solely to fluctuations in potential GDP, that is, in the economy's aggregate supply? The rationale for the assumption is that most of the determinants of potential GDP usually change rather smoothly. Clearly, population grows relatively smoothly. We do not have a sudden drop in the U.S. population every few years, nor is there a huge migration of people from the United States during recessions. The same is true with factories and equipment in the economy. Unless there is a major war at home, we do not suddenly lose equipment or factories in the economy on a massive scale. Even disasters such as the 1992 hurricane in Florida, the 1994 earthquake in California, or the tragic events of September 11, although devastating for those hit, take only a tiny fraction out of the potential GDP of the entire U.S. economy. Finally, technological know-how does not suddenly decline; we do not suddenly forget how to produce things. The steady upward movement of potential GDP thus represents gradual accumulations—growth of population, growth of capital, and growth of technology. However, although many economists place more emphasis on the role of aggregate demand in short-run economic fluctuations than on fluctuations in potential GDP, it is too extreme to insist that there are absolutely no fluctuations in potential GDP.

The Role of Macroeconomic Policy

Macroeconomic policy can have substantial effects on economic fluctuations. Many governments would like to implement policies that either help to avoid recessions or minimize the impact of recessions when they do occur. Monetary policymakers typically prefer to implement policies that minimize fluctuations in GDP. Policies used to influence economic fluctuations are sometimes called *demand-side policies* because they aim to influence aggregate demand in the economy.

■ **Fiscal Policy.**   On the fiscal side, the primary tools that the government uses to influence demand are government purchases and taxes. If the economy shows signs of entering a recession, the government can try to increase demand by implementing tax cuts and/or spending increases. A good example was the tax cuts implemented by Congress in 2001 when the economy was showing signs of sliding into recession. Often these policies are intended to mitigate the negative impact on aggregate demand of other factors, such as a fall in consumer or investor confidence or a fall in our exports because of a recession in one of the countries that is among our major trading partners.

■ **Monetary Policy.**   To keep inflation low and stable, the Federal Reserve will also implement policies that influence demand. The primary tools that the Federal Reserve uses to influence demand are changes in interest rates. If there are signs that inflation is on the rise because aggregate demand is growing faster than potential output, the Federal Reserve may step in and raise interest rates, which will slow down spending, as you will soon learn in Chapter 6. In addition to keeping inflation low and stable, the Federal Reserve is also concerned with minimizing the adverse impact of recessions. When the economy goes into recession, the Federal Reserve will try to increase demand by lowering interest rates. A good example of this type of behavior was seen in 2001 when the Federal Reserve lowered interest rates eleven times—going from an interest rate of 6 percent to an interest rate of 1.75 percent.

REVIEW
- Economic growth theory concentrates on explaining the long-term upward path of the economy.

- Economic growth depends on three factors: the growth of capital, labor, and technology.

- Government policy can influence long-term economic growth by affecting these three factors. To raise long-term economic growth, government fiscal policies can provide incentives for investment in capital, for research and development of new technologies, for education, and for increased labor supply. A monetary policy of low and stable inflation can also have a positive effect on economic growth.

- Economic fluctuations theory assumes that fluctuations in GDP are due to fluctuations in aggregate demand.

- Monetary policy and fiscal policy can reduce the fluctuations in real GDP. Finding good policies is a major task of macroeconomics.

Conclusion

This chapter started with a brief review of the facts of economic growth and fluctuations. The key facts are that economic growth provides impressive gains in the well-being of individuals over the long term, that economic growth is temporarily interrupted by recessions, that unemployment rises in recessions, and that inflation and interest rates rise before recessions and decline during and after recessions. These are the facts on which macroeconomic theory is based and about which macroeconomic policy is concerned. Remembering these facts helps you understand theory and make judgments about government policy.

After showing how we measure real GDP and inflation in Chapter 5, we then go on to look at explanations for the facts and proposals for macroeconomic policies.

KEY POINTS

1. Macroeconomics is concerned with economic growth and fluctuations in the whole economy.

2. The U.S. economy and many other economies have grown dramatically in recent years.

3. Economists agree that economic growth occurs because of increases in labor, capital, and technological know-how.

4. Economic policies that provide incentives to increase capital and resources devoted to improving technology can raise productivity growth.

5. Economic fluctuations consist of recessions (when real GDP falls and unemployment increases) followed by recoveries (when real GDP rises rapidly and unemployment falls).

6. Recent recessions have been much less severe than the Great Depression of the 1930s, when real GDP fell by over 30 percent.

7. The unemployment rate is well above zero even when the economy is booming.

8. The most popular theory of economic fluctuations is that they occur because of fluctuations in aggregate demand.

9. Macroeconomic policies include monetary and fiscal policies that are aimed at keeping business cycles small and inflation low.

10. Economic growth theory and economic fluctuations theory combine to form macroeconomic theory, which explains why the economy grows and fluctuates over time.

KEY TERMS

real gross domestic product (real GDP)

economic growth

economic fluctuations

recession

peak

trough

expansion

recovery

unemployment rate

inflation rate

interest rate

real interest rate

nominal interest rate

potential GDP

aggregate supply

labor

capital

technology

production function

aggregate demand

QUESTIONS FOR REVIEW

1. What is the difference between economic growth and economic fluctuations?

2. Why do bad economic times continue after recessions end?

3. Why does unemployment rise in recessions?

4. How many recessions have there been since the Great Depression?

5. How do the 1990–1991 recession and the 2001 recession compare?

6. What are the two broad branches of macroeconomic theory?

7. What are the three determinants of economic growth?

8. What is potential GDP?

9. What is aggregate demand?

10. What is the difference between monetary policy and fiscal policy?

PROBLEMS

1. The graph on the opposite page shows a business cycle that occurred in the United States in the 1970s. Draw in potential GDP and show the peak, recession, trough, and recovery phases of this business cycle in the 1990s shown in Figure 4.3.

2. Suppose the U.S. economy is currently at the trough of a business cycle. What is the relationship between real and potential GDP? Is it likely that real GDP will stay in this relative position for a long period of time (say, 10 years)? Explain briefly.

3. Using the data from Canada and Britain shown in the table in the opposite column, plot the unemployment rate on the vertical axis.

Rate of Unemployment (percent)

Year	Canada	Britain
1990	7.7	6.9
1991	9.8	8.8
1992	10.6	10.1
1993	10.8	10.5
1994	9.5	9.6
1995	8.6	8.7
1996	8.8	8.1
1997	8.4	7.0
1998	7.7	6.3
1999	7.0	6.0
2000	6.1	5.5

How do unemployment rates compare with the U.S. rate shown in Figure 4.5?

4. Compare Figure 4.5, showing unemployment, with Figure 4.8, showing the inflation rate for the same period in the United States. Describe how unemployment and inflation are correlated over the long term and over the short term.

5. Suppose that you had savings deposited in an account at an interest rate of 5 percent and your father told you that he earned 10 percent interest 20 years ago. Which of you was getting the better return? Is that all the information you need? Suppose that the inflation rate in the United States was 12 percent 20 years ago and is 3 percent now. Does this information change your answer? Be sure to use the concept of the real interest rate in your answer.

6. Suppose you have $1,000, which you can put in two different types of accounts at a bank. One account pays interest of 8 percent per year; the other pays interest at 2 percent per year plus the rate of inflation. Calculate the real return you will receive after 1 year if the inflation rate is 5 percent. Which account will you choose if you expect the rate of inflation to be 8 percent? Why?

Problem 1

The Business Cycle Surrounding the 1974–75 Recession

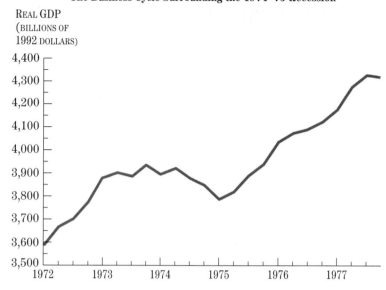

7. Suppose people start retiring at a later age because of improved medical technology. How will this affect the economy's potential GDP? Why might the government want to encourage later retirement?

8. What factors can cause fluctuations in aggregate demand? Are these the same as the determinants of potential GDP? Why do economists think that changes in aggregate demand are the primary cause of short-term economic fluctuations?

9. What determines potential GDP? What factors could cause the growth rate of potential GDP to slow down? What economic policies can the government use to affect potential GDP?

10. The table in the opposite column shows the amount of output that can be produced using different combinations of labor and capital in a hypothetical economy with a given type of technology. For example, 650 units of output are produced when 200 units of labor and 100 units of capital are combined. This table is an example of a production function.

a. Hold capital constant at 100 while you increase labor. What happens to output?

b. Now hold labor constant at 100 and raise the level of capital. What happens to the output?

c. Finally, what happens when you raise labor and capital by the same amount?

			Labor		
	50	**100**	**150**	**200**	**250**
50	200	324	432	528	618
100	246	400	532	650	760
150	278	452	600	734	858
200	304	492	654	800	936
250	324	526	700	856	1,000

(Capital is labeled vertically along the left side of the table.)

The Miracle of Compound Growth

Compound growth explains why small differences in the annual economic growth rate make such huge differences in real GDP over time. Here we explain this compounding effect, show how to compute growth rates, and discuss alternative ways to plot growing variables over time.

How Compound Growth Works

Compound growth works just like compound interest on a savings account. Compound interest is defined as the "interest on the interest" you earned in earlier periods. For example, suppose you have a savings account in a bank that pays 6 percent per year in interest. That is, if you put $100 in the account, then after one year you will get $100 times .06, or $6 in interest. If you leave the original $100 plus the $6—that is, $106—in the bank for a second year, then at the end of the second year you will get $106 times .06, or $6.36 in interest. The $.36 is the "interest on the interest," that is, $6 times .06.

At the end of the second year, you have $100 + $6 + $6.36 = $112.36. If you leave that in the bank for a third year, you will get $6.74 in interest, of which $.74 is "interest on the interest" earned in the first two years. Note how the "interest on the interest" rises from $.36 in the second year to $.74 in the third year. Following the same calculations, the "interest on the interest" in the fourth year would be $1.15. After 13 years, the "interest on the interest" is greater than the $6 interest on the original $100! As a result of this compound interest, the size of your account grows rapidly. At the end of 20 years, it is $320.71; after 40 years, your $100 has grown to $1,028.57.

Compound growth applies the idea of compound interest to the economy. Consider, for example, a country in which real GDP is $100 billion and the growth rate is 6 percent per year. After one year, real GDP would increase by $100 billion times .06, or by $6 billion. Real GDP rises from $100 billion to $106 billion. In the second year, real GDP increases by $106 billion times .06, or by $6.36 billion. Real GDP rises from $106 billion to $112.36 billion. Table 4A.1 shows how, continuing this way, real GDP grows, rounding to the nearest $.1 billion.

Thus, in one person's lifetime, real GDP would increase by about 60 times.

Exponential Effects

A convenient way to compute these changes is to multiply the initial level by 1.06 year after year. For example,

Table 4A.1
Example of Compound Growth

	Real GDP (billions)		Real GDP (billions)
Year 0	$100.0	Year 20	$ 320.7
Year 1	$106.0	Year 30	$ 574.3
Year 2	$112.4	Year 40	$1,028.6
Year 3	$119.1	Year 50	$1,842.0
Year 4	$126.2	Year 60	$3,298.8
Year 5	$133.3	Year 70	$5,907.6
Year 10	$179.1		

the level of real GDP after one year is $100 billion times .06 plus $100 billion, or $100 billion times 1.06. After two years, it is $106 billion times 1.06, or $100 billion times $(1.06)^2$. Thus, for n years, we have

$$\text{(Initial level)} \times (1.06)^n = \text{level at end of } n \text{ years}$$

where the initial level could be $100 in a bank, the $100 billion level of real GDP, or anything else. For example, real GDP at the end of 70 years in the table shown earlier is $100 billion times $(1.06)^n$ = $100 billion times 59.076 = $5,907.6 billion, with $n = 70$. Here the growth rate (or the interest rate) is 6 percent. In general, we have:

$$\text{(Initial level)} \times (1 + g)^n = \text{level at end of } n \text{ years}$$

where g is the annual growth rate, stated as a decimal: that is, 6 percent is .06. If you have a hand calculator with a key that does y^x, it is fairly easy to make these calculations, and if you try it you will see the power of compound growth. The term *exponential growth* is sometimes used because the number of years (n) appears as an exponent in the above expression.

When economists refer to average annual growth over time, they include this compounding effect. The growth rate is found by solving for g. That is, the growth rate, stated as a decimal fraction, between some initial level and a level n years later is given by

$$g = \left(\frac{\text{level at end of } n \text{ years}}{\text{initial level}}\right)^{1/n} - 1$$

For example, the average annual growth rate from year 0 to year 20 in the table is

$$g = \left(\frac{320.7}{100}\right)^{1/20} - 1$$

$$= (1.06) - 1$$

$$= .06$$

or 6 percent. Again, if your calculator has a key for y^x, you can make these calculations easily.

To get the annual growth rate for one year, you simply divide the level in the second year by the level in the first year and subtract 1 to get the growth rate.

Rule of 72

You can also find how long it takes something to increase by a certain percentage. For example, to calculate how many years it takes something that grows at rate g to dou-

ble, you solve $(1 + g)^n = 2$ for n. The answer is approximately $n = .72/g$. In other words, if you divide 72 by the growth rate in percent, you get the number of years it takes to double the amount. This is called the *rule of 72*. If your bank account pays 7.2 percent interest, it will double in 10 years.

Plotting Growing Variables

You may have noticed that some time-series charts have vertical scales that shrink as the economic variable being plotted gets bigger. Look, for example, at the scale in Figures 4.1 and 4.4 for real GDP. This type of scale, which is called a *ratio scale* (or sometimes a *proportional scale* or *logarithmic scale*), is used by financial analysts and

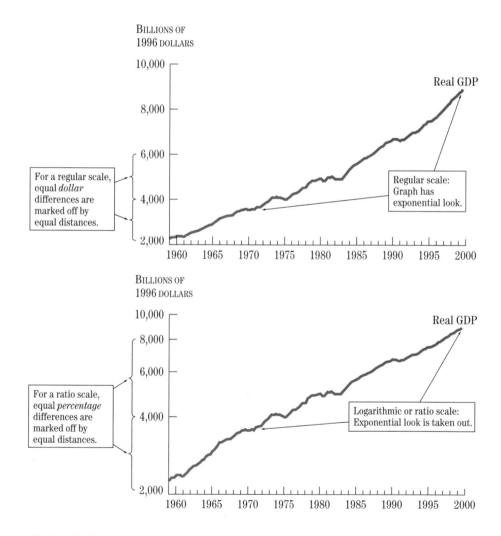

Figure 4A.1
Comparison of Two Different Scales: "Regular" versus "Ratio"

economists to present variables that grow over time. The purpose of a ratio scale is to make equal percentage changes in the variable have the same vertical distance.

If you plot a variable that grows at a constant rate on a ratio scale, it looks like a straight line, even though it would look as if it were exploding on a standard scale. To show what ratio scales do, real GDP for the past 40 years is plotted in Figure 4A.1 using a regular scale and a ratio scale. Note how the fluctuations in real GDP in the 1960s look smaller on a regular scale compared with the ratio scale, and how the ratio scale tends to take out the exponential look. This difference is one reason to look carefully at the scales of graphs. (The reason that ratio scales are sometimes called logarithmic scales is that plotting the logarithm of a variable is the same as plotting the variable on a ratio scale.)

Key Points

1. Compound growth is analogous to compound interest. Rather than applying the interest rate to the interest from earlier periods, one applies the growth rate to the growth from the previous period.

2. With compound growth, seemingly small differences in growth rates result in huge differences in real GDP.

3. When you see a diagram with the scale shrunk for the higher values, it is a logarithmic or ratio scale.

4. A ratio or logarithmic scale is more useful than a regular scale when a variable is growing over time.

Key Term and Definition

compound growth: applying the growth rate to growth from the previous period; analogous to compound interest.

Questions for Review

1. What is the rule of 72?

2. What is a ratio scale?

Problems

1. Suppose that the annual rate of growth of GDP per capita is 2 percent. How much will real GDP per capita increase in 10 years? How much will it increase in 50 years? Answer the same questions for a growth rate of 1 percent.

2. Plot the data for the example economy in the table in this appendix on a graph at ten-year intervals from year 20 to year 60 on a *regular* scale. Now create a new graph with a *ratio* scale by first marking off 300, 600, 1,200, 2,400, and 4,800 at equal distances on the vertical axis. Plot the same data on this graph. Compare the two graphs.

CHAPTER 5

Measuring the Production, Income, and Spending of Nations

On January 30, 2002, the Bureau of Economic Analysis (BEA), which releases the official government statistics on real GDP, announced

in a press release that "real gross domestic product—the output of goods and services produced by labor and property located in the United States—increased at an annual rate of 0.2 percent in the fourth quarter of 2001." Exactly four weeks later, the BEA issued the following news release announcing the revision of the GDP figure released on January 30: "Real gross domestic product—the output of goods and services produced by labor and property located in the United States—increased at an annual rate of 1.4 percent in the fourth quarter of 2001." The difference between the two estimates was more than 1 percentage point of GDP, the equivalent of almost $100 billion! This example illustrates the complexity of measuring economic variables like real GDP and also shows the importance of having reliable data, because the appropriate policy measures for an economy that has close to zero growth may be very different from the policies for an economy that is showing signs of returning to robust growth. In fact, top officials at the White House (including the president) find these data so important that they make sure they get them the night before they are released to the public.

Measuring the economy in a timely and accurate manner is also essential for people in financial markets and other lines of business. Bond and stock traders in New York, Tokyo, London, and everywhere else keep their eyes glued to their computer terminals when a new government statistic measuring the course of the economy is about to be released. By buying or selling quickly in response to the new information, they can make millions or avoid losing millions.

To economists, economic measurement is interesting in its own right, involving clever solutions to intriguing problems. One of the first Nobel Prizes in economics was given to Simon Kuznets for solving some of these measurement problems. Economics students cannot help but learn a little about how the economy works when they study how to measure it, just as geology students cannot help but learn a little about earthquakes when they study how the Richter scale measures them.

In this chapter, we examine how economists measure a nation's production, income, and spending. We stated in Chapter 4 that real gross domestic product (real GDP) is the most comprehensive measure we have of a country's production. But before we can measure real GDP, we must show how to measure GDP itself. In the process of describing the measurement of GDP, we will observe several key relationships and interpret what these relationships mean. We will focus on examples from the United States, but the same ideas apply to any country.

Measuring GDP

To use GDP as a measure of production, we must be precise about *what* is included in production, *where* production takes place, and *when* production takes place.

A Precise Definition of GDP

GDP is a measure of the value of all the final goods and services newly produced in a country during some period of time. Let us dissect this definition to determine what is in GDP and what is not, as well as where and when GDP is produced.

- *What?* Only *newly produced* goods and services are included. That 10-year-old baby carriage sold in a garage sale is not in this year's GDP; it was included in GDP 10 years ago, when it was produced. Both *goods*—such as automobiles and new houses—and *services*—such as bus rides or a college education—are included in GDP.

- *Where?* Only goods and services produced *within the borders* of a country are included in GDP. Goods produced by Americans working in another country are not part of U.S. GDP; they are part of the other country's GDP. Goods and services produced by foreigners working in the United States are part of U.S. GDP.

- *When?* Only goods and services produced *during some specified period* of time are included in GDP. We always need to specify the period during which we are measuring GDP. For example, U.S. GDP in 2001 is the production during 2001. Production during a year is 365 times larger than production for a typical day.

Rounded off to the nearest billion, GDP, or total production, was $10,208 billion in the United States in 2001. Rounded off to the nearest trillion, GDP was $10 trillion. That is an average production of about $27 billion worth of goods and services a day for each of the 365 days during the year.

■ **Prices Determine the Importance of Goods and Services in GDP.**   GDP is a single number, but it measures the production of many different things, from apples to oranges, from car insurance to life insurance, from audio CDs to cassette tapes. How can we add up such different products? Is a CD more important than a tape? Each good is given a weight when we compute GDP, and that weight is its *price*. If the price of a CD is greater than that of a tape, then the CD will count more in GDP.

To see this, imagine that production consists entirely of CDs and tapes. If a CD costs $15 and a tape costs $5, then producing three CDs will add $45 to GDP, and producing seven tapes will add $35 to GDP. Thus, producing three CDs plus seven tapes adds $80 to GDP, as shown in Table 5.1.

Although this method of weighting by price might not appeal to you personally—you might like tapes more than CDs—it is hard to imagine anything more workable. In a market system, prices tend to reflect the cost and value of the goods and services produced. One of the great problems of measuring GDP in centrally planned economies such as the Soviet Union was that the price of goods was set by the government; thus, the weight given each item may have had little to do with its cost or value to individuals. Without market prices, measuring GDP in the Soviet Union was difficult.

■ **Intermediate Goods versus Final Goods.**   When measuring GDP, it is important not to count the same item more than once. Consider bicycle tires. When you buy a $150 bicycle, the tires are considered part of the bicycle. Suppose the tires are worth $20. It would be a mistake to count both the $20 value of the tires and the $150 value of the bicycle, for a total value of $170. That would count the tires twice, which is called double counting. When a tire is part of a new bicycle, it is an example of an **intermediate good.** Intermediate goods are part of **final goods,** which by definition are goods that undergo no further processing—in this case, the bicycle. *To avoid double counting, we never count intermediate goods; only final goods are part of the GDP.* If in a few years you buy a new $25 bicycle tire, then the tire will be a final good.

intermediate good: a good that undergoes further processing before it is sold to consumers.

final good: a new good that undergoes no further processing before it is sold to consumers.

■ **Three Ways to Measure GDP.**   Economists measure GDP in three ways. All three give the same answer, but they refer to conceptually different activities in the economy and provide different ways to think about GDP. All three are reported in the national income and product accounts, the official U.S. government tabulation of GDP put together by economists and statisticians at the Department of Commerce.

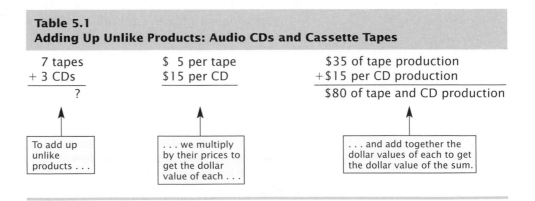

Table 5.1
Adding Up Unlike Products: Audio CDs and Cassette Tapes

7 tapes + 3 CDs ——— ?	$ 5 per tape $15 per CD ————	$35 of tape production +$15 per CD production ———————————— $80 of tape and CD production

To add up unlike products . . .

. . . we multiply by their prices to get the dollar value of each . . .

. . . and add together the dollar values of each to get the dollar value of the sum.

Table 5.2
Components of Spending in 2001 (billions of dollars)

Gross domestic product (GDP)	$10,208
Consumption	7,064
Investment	1,634
Government purchases	1,840
Net exports	−330

Source: U.S. Department of Commerce.

The first way measures the total amount that people *spend* on goods and services made in America. This is the *spending* approach. The second way measures the total income that is earned by all the workers and businesses that produce American goods and services. This is the *income* approach. In this approach, your income is a measure of what you produce. The third way measures the total of all the goods and services as they are *produced,* or as they are shipped out of the factory. This is the *production* approach. Note that each of the approaches considers the whole economy, and thus we frequently refer to them as aggregate spending, aggregate income, and aggregate production, where the word *aggregate* means total. Let us consider each of the three approaches in turn.

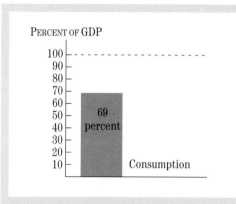

PERCENT OF GDP

69 percent

Consumption

Figure 5.1
Consumption as a Share of GDP
Consumption is 69 percent of GDP in the United States.

The Spending Approach

Typically, total spending in the economy is divided into four components: *consumption, investment, government purchases,* and *net exports,* which equal exports minus imports. Each of the four components corresponds closely to one of four groups into which the economy is divided: consumers, businesses, governments, and foreigners. Before considering each component, look at Table 5.2, which shows how the $10,208 billion of GDP in the United States in 2001 was divided into the four categories.

consumption: purchases of final goods and services by individuals.

■ **Consumption.** The first component, **consumption,** is purchases of final goods and services by individuals. Government statisticians who collect the data in most countries survey department stores, discount stores, car dealers, and other sellers to see how much consumers purchase each year ($7,064 billion in 2001, as given in Table 5.2). They count anything purchased by consumers as consumption. Consumption does not include spending by business or government. Consumer purchases may be big-ticket items such as a new convertible, an operation to remove a cancerous tumor, a new stereo, a weekend vacation, or college tuition, or smaller-ticket items such as an oil change, a medical checkup, a bus ride, or a driver's education class. Consumption is a whopping 69 percent of GDP in the United States (see Figure 5.1).

investment: purchases of final goods by firms plus purchases of newly produced residences by households.

■ **Investment.** The second component, **investment,** consists of purchases of final goods by business firms and of newly produced residences by housholds. When a business such as a pizza delivery firm buys a new car, economists consider that purchase as part of investment rather than as consumption. The firm uses the car to make deliveries, which contributes to its production of delivered pizzas. Included in investment are all the new machines, new factories, and other tools used to produce goods and services. Purchases of intermediate goods that go directly into a manufactured product—such as a tire on a bicycle—are not counted as investment. These items are part of the finished product—the bicycle, in this case—purchased by consumers. We do not want to count such items twice.

The new machines, factories, and other tools that are part of investment in any year are sometimes called *business fixed investment;* this amounted to $1,246 billion in 2001. There are two other items that government statisticians include as part of investment: inventory investment and residential investment.

Inventory investment is defined as the change in *inventories,* which are the goods on store shelves, on showroom floors, or in warehouses that have not yet been sold or assembled into a final form for sale. For example, cars on the lot of a car dealer are part of inventories. When inventory investment is positive, then inventories are rising. When inventory investment is negative, then inventories are falling. For example, if a car dealer has an inventory of 20 cars on September 30, gets 15 new cars shipped from the factory during the month of October, and sells no cars during the month, then the dealer's inventory will be 35 cars on October 31. Inventory investment is positive 15 cars, and inventory rises from 20 cars to 35 cars. If 22 cars are then sold during the month of November and there are no shipments from the factory, the dealer's inventory will be 13 cars on November 30. Inventory investment is negative 22 cars, and inventory decreases from 35 cars to 13 cars.

Why is inventory investment included as a spending item when we compute GDP? The reason is that we want a measure of production. Consider the car example again. Car production rises by one car when a complete Jeep rolls out of the factory. But the Jeep is not usually instantaneously purchased by a consumer. First, the Jeep is shipped to a Jeep dealer, where it is put on the lot. If the government statisticians look at what consumers purchase, they will not count the Jeep because it has not been purchased yet. But if inventory investment is counted as part of investment spending, then the Jeep will get counted. That is why we include inventory investment in spending.

What happens when a consumer purchases the Jeep? Consumption will rise because the purchases of Jeeps have risen, and the car dealer's inventory goes down by one car. Thus, inventory investment is negative one car. Adding one Jeep consumed to negative one Jeep of inventory investment gives zero, which is just what we want because there is no change in production.

In 2001, inventory investment throughout the economy was −$58 billion. Some firms added inventories, but others subtracted a greater amount. Inventory investment tends to fluctuate up and down and therefore plays a big role in the business cycle.

The other part of investment that is not business fixed investment is *residential investment,* the purchase of new houses and apartment buildings. About $446 billion worth of housing and apartments were constructed in 2001. Although much of this was purchased by consumers rather than businesses, it is included in investment because it produces services: shelter and, in some cases, a place to relax and enjoy life.

Combining the three parts of investment, we find that investment was $1,634 billion in 1999: $1,246 billion of business fixed investment, $446 billion of residential investment, and −$58 billion of inventory investment. Investment was about 16 percent of GDP in 2001 (see Figure 5.2).

Note the special way the term *investment* is used in this discussion. To an economist, investment means the purchase of new factories, houses, or equipment. In everyday language, however, investment usually refers to an individual's putting away some funds for the future,

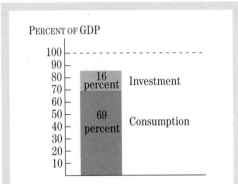

Figure 5.2
Investment and Consumption as a Share of GDP
Investment is a much smaller share of GDP than is consumption.

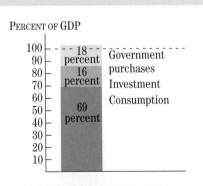

Figure 5.3
Government Purchases, Investment, and Consumption as a Share of GDP
Government purchases as a share of GDP are greater than investment and less than consumption. When the stacked bar goes above the 100 percent line, there are negative net exports (a trade deficit), as shown here. If the stacked bar stops below the 100 percent line, there is a trade surplus.

Distinguishing Between Stocks and Flows

The distinction between *stocks* and *flows* is one of the most useful concepts in economics. For example, it helps businesses understand the important difference between inventories and inventory investment (the change in inventories). The amount of inventories at a firm *at a particular date* is a *stock,* while the change in inventories *during a particular period* between two dates is a *flow.* To remember the distinction, notice that the expression "to take stock" means adding up all the inventories on the shelves. If a car dealer has 35 cars on the lot at the close of business on October 31, we say the stock of inventory is 35 cars. If the stock increases to 40 cars by the close of business on November 30, then the flow of inventory investment is 5 cars during the month of November.

The economist's distinction between stocks and flows can be illustrated by picturing water flowing into and out of a lake—for example, the Colorado River flowing into and out of Lake Powell behind Glen Canyon Dam. When more water flows in than flows out, the stock of water in Lake Powell rises. Similarly, a positive flow of inventory investment raises the stock of inventory at a firm. And just as the stock of water falls when more water flows out than flows in, negative inventory investment lowers the stock of inventory.

The distinction between stocks and flows is useful in other economic applications as well. The factories in America on December 31, 2003, are a stock. The number of factories built during 2003 is a flow. The funds in your checking account are a stock. The deposit you made last week is a flow.

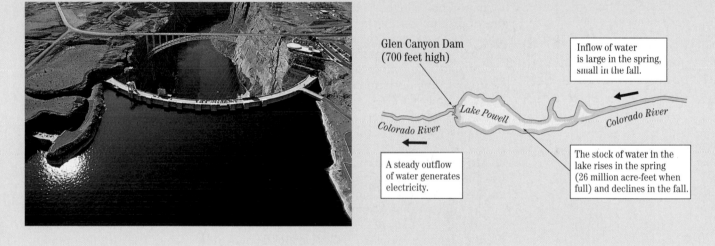

Glen Canyon Dam (700 feet high)

Inflow of water is large in the spring, small in the fall.

Lake Powell

Colorado River

Colorado River

A steady outflow of water generates electricity.

The stock of water in the lake rises in the spring (26 million acre-feet when full) and declines in the fall.

perhaps in the stock market, such as "I'll invest in the stock market." Be sure to stay aware of this distinction.

government purchases: purchases by federal, state, and local governments of new goods and services.

■ **Government Purchases.** The third component of spending, **government purchases,** is spending by federal, state, and local governments on new goods and services. Most U.S. government purchases are for the military. At the state and local level, education, roads, and police dominate government purchases. Government purchases of goods and services were equal to $1,840 billion in 2001 (see Figure 5.3).

Not all government outlays are included in government purchases. A government welfare payment or retirement payment to an individual is not a purchase of a good or service; it is a *transfer payment* of income from the government to an individual. Transfer payments do not represent new production of anything, unlike the purchase of a weapon or a new road or a new building. Because GDP measures the production of new goods and services, government outlays on transfer payments like social security, unemployment compensation, and welfare payments are excluded. Only purchases are counted because only these items represent something produced. Government *outlays* are purchases plus transfer payments.

113

net exports: the value of exports minus the value of imports.

exports: the total value of the goods and services that people in one country sell to people in other countries.

imports: the total value of the goods and services that people in one country buy from people in other countries.

trade balance: the value of exports minus the value of imports.

■ **Net Exports.**   The final spending component is **net exports,** the difference between exports and imports. American **exports** are what Americans sell to foreigners, whether pharmaceuticals, computers, grain, or a vacation in Florida. American **imports** are what Americans buy from foreigners, whether cars, VCRs, shirts, or a vacation in France. Net exports are defined as exports minus imports. Net exports are a measure of how much more we sell to foreigners than we buy from foreigners. Another term for net exports is the **trade balance.** If net exports are positive, we have a trade surplus. If net exports are negative, we have a trade deficit. By these calculations, the United States had a trade deficit in 2001: $1,050 billion in exports and $1,380 billion in imports. Hence, net exports were a negative $330 billion, and appear in Table 5.2 as −$330 billion.

Why are net exports added in when computing GDP by the spending approach? There are two reasons. First, we included foreign goods in consumption and investment spending. For example, an imported Toyota purchased at a car dealer in the United States is included in consumption even though it is not produced in the United States. To measure what is produced in the United States, that Toyota must be deducted. Thus, imports must be subtracted to get a measure of total production in the economy. The second reason is that the exports Americans sell abroad are produced in the United States, but they are not counted in consumption or investment or government purchases in the United States. Thus, exports need to be added in to get a measure of production. Because, by definition, net exports are exports minus imports, adding net exports to spending is the same as adding in exports and subtracting out imports. Adding net exports to total spending kills two birds with one stone.

In 2001, the United States imported more than it exported, so the sum of consumption plus investment plus government purchases overstated what was produced in America. The sum of these three items exceeds GDP, as shown in Figure 5.3. In other words, GDP was $330 billion less than the sum of consumption plus investment plus government purchases.

■ **Algebraic Summary.**   The notion that we can measure production by adding up consumption, investment, government purchases, and net exports is important enough to herald with some algebra.

Let the symbol C stand for consumption, I for investment, G for government spending, and X for net exports. Let Y stand for GDP because we use G for government purchases. We will use these symbols many times again. The idea that production equals spending can then be written as

> This is a key equation stating that production equals spending.

$$Y = C + I + G + X$$

This equation states, using algebraic symbols, that production, Y, equals spending: consumption, C, plus investment, I, plus government purchases, G, plus net exports, X (meaning exports minus imports). In 1999 the values of these items (in billions of dollars) were

$$10{,}208 = 7{,}064 + 1{,}634 + 1{,}840 + (-330)$$

This simple algebraic relationship plays a key role in later chapters.

The Income Approach

The income that people earn producing GDP in a country provides another measure of GDP. To see why, first consider a simple example of a single business firm.

Suppose you start a driver's education business. Your production and sales of driver's education services in your first year is $50,000; this is the amount you are paid in total by 500 people for the $100 service. To produce these services, you pay two driving teachers $20,000 each, or a total of $40,000, which is your total cost because the students use their own cars. Your profits are defined as the difference between sales and costs, or $50,000 − $40,000 = $10,000. Now, if you add the total amount of income earned in the production of your driver's education service—the amount earned by two teachers plus the profits you earn—you get $20,000 + $20,000 + $10,000. This sum of incomes is exactly equal to $50,000, which is the same as the amount produced. Thus, by adding up the income of the people who produce the output of the firm, you get a measure of the output. The same idea is true for the country as a whole, which consists of many such businesses and workers.

To show how this works, we look at each of the income items in Table 5.3. We first describe each of these items and then show that when we add the items up we get GDP.

■ Labor Income.   Economists classify wages, salaries, and fringe benefits paid to workers as **labor income,** or payments to people for their labor. *Wages* refers to payments to workers paid by the hour; *salaries* refers to payments to workers paid by the month or year; and *fringe benefits* refers to retirement, health, and other benefits paid by firms on behalf of workers. As shown in Table 5.3, labor income was $6,010 billion in 2001.

labor income: the sum of wages, salaries, and fringe benefits paid to workers.

■ Capital Income.   Economists classify profits, rental payments, and interest payments as **capital income.** *Profits* include the profits of large corporations like General Motors or Exxon and also the income of small businesses and farms. The royalties an independent screenwriter receives from selling a movie script are also part of profits. *Rental payments* are income to persons who own buildings and rent them out. The rents they receive from their tenants are rental payments. *Interest payments* are income received from lending to business firms. Interest payments are included in capital income because they represent part of the income generated by the firms' production. Because many individuals pay interest (on mortgages, car loans, etc.) as well as receive interest (on deposits at a bank, etc.), interest payments are defined as the difference between receipts and payments. Table 5.3 shows that capital income was $2,208 billion in 2001, much less than labor income. Capital income is about 37 percent of labor income.

capital income: the sum of profits, rental payments, and interest payments.

■ Depreciation.   **Depreciation** is the amount by which factories and machines wear out each year. A remarkably large part of the investment that is part of GDP each year goes to replace worn-out factories and machines. Businesses need to replace depreciated equipment with investment in new equipment just to maintain productive capacity—the number of factories and machines available for use.

depreciation: the decrease in an asset's value over time; for capital, it is the amount by which physical capital wears out over a given period of time.

Table 5.3
Aggregate Income and GDP in 2001 (billions of dollars)

Aggregate income	
Labor income (wages, salaries, fringe benefits)	$6,010
Capital income (profits, interest, rents)	2,208
Depreciation	1,351
Indirect business taxes	794
Net income of foreigners	5
Statistical discrepancy	−160
Equals GDP	10,208

Source: U.S. Department of Commerce.

The difference between investment, the purchases of final goods by firms, and depreciation is called *net investment,* a measure of how much new investment there is each year after depreciation is subtracted. Net investment was $283 billion ($1,634 billion − $1,351 billion) in 2001. Sometimes the $1,634 billion of investment, including depreciation, is called *gross investment.* The reason for the term *gross* in gross domestic product is that it includes gross investment, not just net investment.

When profits and the other parts of capital income are reported to the government statisticians, depreciation has been subtracted out. But depreciation must be included as part of GDP because the new equipment that replaces old equipment must be produced by someone. Thus, when we use the income approach, it is necessary to add in depreciation if we are to have a measure of GDP.

■ **Indirect Business Taxes.** *Indirect business taxes* consist mainly of sales taxes sent directly by businesses to the government. For example, the price of gasoline at the pump includes a tax that people who buy gasoline pay as part of the price and that the gasoline station sends to the government. When we tabulate total production by adding up the value of what people spend, we use the prices businesses

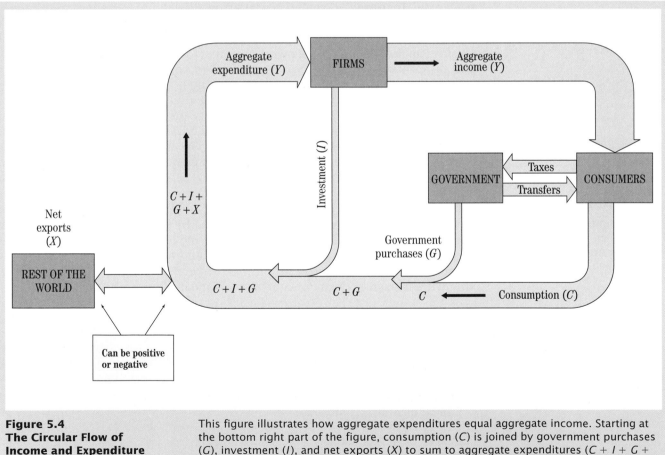

**Figure 5.4
The Circular Flow of
Income and Expenditure**

This figure illustrates how aggregate expenditures equal aggregate income. Starting at the bottom right part of the figure, consumption (C) is joined by government purchases (G), investment (I), and net exports (X) to sum to aggregate expenditures (C + I + G + X) on the left. At the top of the figure, this aggregate spending is received by firms that produce the goods, and they pay out aggregate income (Y) to households in the form of wages and salaries as well as rents, interest, and profits. The government takes in taxes and makes transfer payments and government purchases.

charge for a specific good—such as gasoline. That price includes the sales tax that is sent to the government, but, like depreciation, the sales tax is not included in firms' profits. Thus, capital income does not include the sales taxes paid by businesses to the government. But those taxes are part of the income generated in producing GDP. We therefore must add sales taxes to capital and labor income.

■ **Net Income of Foreigners.** Foreigners produce part of the GDP in the United States. However, their income is not included in labor income or capital income. For example, the salary of a Canadian hockey player who plays for the Pittsburgh Penguins and keeps his official residence as Canada would not be included in U.S. labor income. But that income represents payment for services produced in the United States and so is part of U.S. GDP. We must add such income payments to foreigners for production in the United States because that production is part of GDP. Moreover, some of U.S. labor and capital income is earned producing GDP in other countries, and to get a measure of income generated in producing U.S. GDP, we must subtract that out. For example, the salary of a U.S. baseball player who plays for the Toronto Blue Jays and keeps his official residence as the United States represents payment for services produced in Canada and so is not part of U.S. GDP. We must exclude such income payments for production in other countries. To account for both of these effects, we must add *net* income earned by foreigners in the United States—that is, the income earned by foreigners in the United States less what Americans earned abroad—to get GDP. In 2001, Americans earned less abroad ($335 billion) than foreigners earned in the United States ($340 billion); hence, in 2001, *net* income of foreigners was $5 billion, as shown in Table 5.3.

Table 5.3 shows the effects of adding up these five items. The sum is close but not quite equal to GDP. The discrepancy reflects errors made in collecting data on income or spending. This discrepancy has a formal name: the *statistical discrepancy.* In percentage terms the amount is small, less than 1 percent of GDP, considering the different ways the data on income and spending are collected. If we add in the statistical discrepancy, then we have a measure of *aggregate income* that equals GDP. From now on we can use the same symbol (Y) to refer to GDP and to aggregate income, because GDP and aggregate income amount to the same thing.

The circular flow diagram in Figure 5.4 illustrates the link between aggregate income and aggregate spending. People earn income from producing goods and services, and they spend this income (Y) to buy goods and services (C, I, G, and X).

The Production Approach

The third measure of GDP adds up the production of each firm or industry in the economy. In order to make this method work, we must avoid the "double counting" problem discussed earlier. For example, if you try to compute GDP by adding new automobiles to new steel to new tires, you will count the steel and the tires that go into producing the new automobiles twice. Thus, when we measure GDP by production, it is necessary to count only the **value added** by each manufacturer. Value added is the value of a firm's production less the value of the intermediate goods used in production. In other words, it is the value the firm adds to the intermediate inputs to get the final output. An automobile manufacturer buys steel, tires, and other inputs and adds value by assembling the car. When we measure GDP by production, we count only the value added at each level of production. Figure 5.5 shows how adding up the value added for each firm involved in producing a cup of espresso in the economy will automatically avoid double counting and give a measure of the final value of the cup of espresso when it is purchased at a coffeehouse or cafe. The same is true for the economy as a whole.

value added: the value of the firm's production minus the value of the intermediate goods used in production.

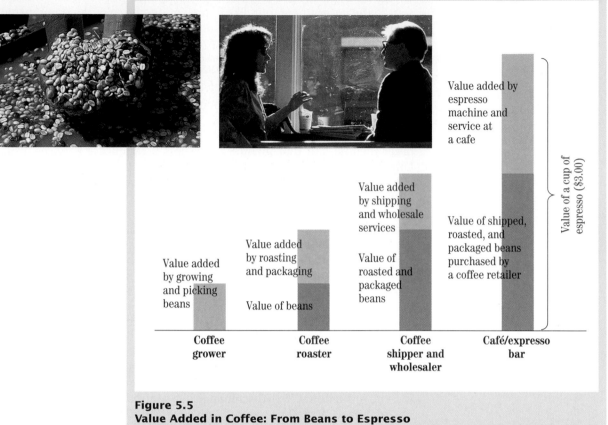

Figure 5.5
Value Added in Coffee: From Beans to Espresso
By adding up the value added at each stage of production, from coffee bean growing to espresso making, we get a measure of the value of a cup of espresso. Double counting is avoided. Using the same procedure for the whole economy permits us to compute GDP by adding up production.

REVIEW
- Adding up all the spending—consumption, investment, government purchases, and net exports—in the U.S. economy gives a measure of total production—gross domestic product (GDP). Inventory investment is treated as part of investment spending to ensure that we get a measure of production. Net exports are added to ensure that imported goods that are part of consumption are not counted as U.S. production and that U.S. exports are counted as U.S. production.

- The sum of labor income, capital income, depreciation, sales taxes, and net income paid to foreigners gives another way to measure GDP.

- GDP can also be measured by adding up production, but with this method we must be careful not to double count. By adding up only the value added by each firm or industry, we automatically prevent double counting. Value added is the difference between a firm's sales and its payments for intermediate inputs to production.

Savings

Another important macroeconomic measure is the total amount of saving undertaken by an economy. The **total amount of saving** is a measure of the amount of
resources that the country has available for investment, either in its own country or
abroad. Countries with a high level of saving have a greater ability to undertake
investment projects than countries with low levels of saving. It is important to keep
in mind, however, that a country with a low level of saving can increase investment
substantially if people and firms in other nations are willing to lend or invest their
own savings to that country. The U.S. economy in the latter part of the 1990s was able
to sustain a high level of investment even when their saving was low. In this section,
we will define the concept of national saving and show how it is calculated.

Individual Saving

For an individual, saving is defined as income less taxes and consumption. If you
earn $25,000 in income during the year and pay taxes of $5,000 while spending
$18,000 on consumption—food, rent, movies—by definition your saving for the year
is $2,000 ($25,000 − $5,000 − $18,000). But if you instead spend $23,000 on food,
rent, and movies for the year, then your saving is −$3,000; you will either have to take
$3,000 out of the bank or borrow $3,000.

National Saving

For a country, saving is defined in a similar manner: by subtracting from a country's
economy what is consumed. **National saving** is the sum of all saving in the economy.
It is defined as income less consumption and government purchases. That is,

National saving = income − consumption − government purchases

Using the symbol S for national saving and the symbols already introduced for
income (Y), consumption (C), and government purchases (G), we define national
saving as

Algebraic definition of national saving	→

$$S = Y - C - G$$

Using the numbers from Table 5.2, national saving in 2001 was $1,304 billion
($10,208 billion − $7,064 billion − $1,840 billion).

The major component of national saving is private saving: the sum of all savings
by individuals in the economy. Some people save a lot, some do not save at all, and
some are *dissaving*—that is, they have negative saving. For example, when people
retire, they usually consume a lot more than their income—they are dissaving. When
people are middle-aged, their income is usually greater than their consumption—
they are saving. Most young people either save very little or, if they are able to borrow,
dissave. We define private saving as

Private saving $= Y - C - T$

For a country, however, there is also a government, and so we need to include
government saving in our calculation of national saving. What do we mean by saving
by the government? Most government purchases (about 85 percent) are on services
that are like consumption—park services, police services, social services, and

national defense services. The difference between the government's receipts from taxes and the government's expenditures, the budget surplus, is called government saving. When the surplus is negative, there is a budget deficit—the government is dissaving. We define government saving as

$$\text{Government saving} = T - G$$

Combining private and government saving, we see that

$$\text{Private saving} + \text{government saving} = (Y - C - T) + (T - G) = (Y - C - G)$$
$$\text{Private saving} + \text{government saving} = \text{national savings}$$

REVIEW
- For an individual, saving equals income minus consumption. For the United States, national saving is defined as income minus consumption minus government purchases. Government purchases are subtracted because many of them provide consumptionlike services.

Measuring Real GDP

Economists use GDP to assess how the economy is changing over time. For example, they might want to know how rapidly the production of goods and services has grown and what that implies about economic growth in the future. However, the dollar value of the goods and services in GDP is determined by the price of these goods and services. Thus, an increase in the prices of all goods and services will make measured GDP grow, even if there is no real increase in the amount of production in the economy. Suppose, for example, that the prices of all goods in the economy double and that the number of items produced of every good remains the same. Then the dollar value of these items will double even though physical production does not change. A $10,000 car will become a $20,000 car, a $10 CD will become a $20 CD, and so on. Thus, GDP will double as well. Clearly, GDP is not useful for comparing production at different dates when there are increases in all prices. Although the example of doubling all prices is extreme, we do know from Chapter 4 that there is a tendency for prices on the average to rise over time—a tendency that we have called inflation. Thus, when there is inflation, GDP becomes an unreliable measure of the changes in production over time.

real gross domestic product (real GDP): a measure of the value of all the goods and services newly produced in a country during some period of time, adjusted for changes in prices over time. (Ch. 4)

nominal GDP: gross domestic product without any correction for inflation; the same as GDP; the value of all goods and services newly produced in a country during some period of time, usually a year.

Adjusting GDP for Inflation

Real GDP is a measure of production that corrects for inflation. To emphasize the difference between GDP and real GDP, we will define **nominal GDP** as what has previously been referred to as GDP.

■ **Computing Real GDP Growth Between Two Years.** To see how real GDP is calculated, consider an example. Suppose that total production consists entirely of the production of audio CDs and cassette tapes and that we want to compare this total production in two different years: 2001 and 2002.

	2001		**2002**	
	Price	*Quantity*	*Price*	*Quantity*
CDs	$15	1,000	$20	1,200
Tapes	$ 5	2,000	$10	2,200

Notice that the number of CDs produced increases by 20 percent and the number of tapes produced increases by 10 percent from 2001 to 2002. Notice also that the price of CDs is greater than the price of tapes, but both increase between the two years because of inflation. Nominal GDP is equal to the dollar amount spent on CDs plus the dollar amount spent on tapes, or $25,000 in 2001 and $46,000 in 2002, a substantial 84 percent increase.

Nominal GDP in 2001 = $15 × 1,000 + $5 × 2,000 = $25,000

Nominal GDP in 2002 = $20 × 1,200 + $10 × 2,200 = $46,000

Clearly, nominal GDP is not a good measure of the increase in production: Nominal GDP increases by 84 percent, a much greater increase than the increase in either CD production (20 percent) or tape production (10 percent). Thus, failing to correct for inflation gives a misleading estimate.

To calculate real GDP, we must use the *same* price for both years and, thereby, adjust for inflation. That is, the number of CDs and tapes produced in the two years must be evaluated at the same prices. For example, production could be calculated in both years using 2001 prices. That is,

Using 2001 prices, production in 2001 = $15 × 1,000 + $5 × 2,000 = $25,000

Using 2001 prices, production in 2002 = $15 × 1,200 + $5 × 2,200 = $29,000

Keeping prices constant at 2001 levels, we see that the increase in production is from $25,000 in 2001 to $29,000 in 2002, an increase of 16 percent.

However, production can also be calculated in both years using 2002 prices. That is,

Using 2002 prices, production in 2001 = $20 × 1,000 + $10 × 2,000 = $40,000

Using 2002 prices, production in 2002 = $20 × 1,200 + $10 × 2,200 = $46,000

Keeping prices constant at 2002 levels, we see that the increase in production is from $40,000 in 2001 to $46,000 in 2002, an increase of 15 percent.

Observe that the percentage increase in production varies slightly (16 percent versus 15 percent) depending on whether 2001 or 2002 prices are used. Such differences are inevitable, because there is no reason to prefer the prices in one year to those of another year when controlling for inflation. Economists arrive at a single percentage by simply *averaging* the two percentages.[1] In this example, they would conclude that the *increase in real GDP from 2001 to 2002 is 15.5 percent,* the average of 16 percent and 15 percent.

This 15.5 percent increase in real GDP is much less than the 84 percent increase in nominal GDP and much closer to the actual increase in the number of CDs and tapes produced. By adjusting for inflation in this way, real GDP gives a better picture of the increase in actual production in the economy.

---

1. A "geometric" average is used. The geometric average of two numbers is the square root of the product of the two numbers.

■ **A Year-to-Year Chain.**   This example shows how the growth rate of real GDP between the two years 2001 and 2002 is calculated in the case of two goods. The same approach is used for any other two years and more than two goods. To correct for inflation across more than two years, economists simply do a series of these two-year corrections and then "chain" them together. Each year is a link in the chain. For example, if the growth rate from 2002 to 2003 is 13.5 percent, then chaining this together with the 15.5 percent from 2001 to 2002 would imply an average annual growth rate of 14.5 percent for the two years from 2001 to 2003. That is,

By chaining other years together, link by link, the chain can be made as long as we want.

■ **From the 1996 Base Year to Other Years.**   To obtain real GDP in any one year, we start with a *base year* and then use the growth rates to compute GDP in another year. The base year is a year in which real GDP is set equal to nominal GDP. Currently, 1996 is the base year for government statistical calculations of GDP in the United States. Thus, real GDP in 1996 and nominal GDP in 1996 are the same: $7,813 billion.

To get real GDP in other years, economists start with the base year and use the real GDP growth rates to find GDP in any other year. Consider 1997. The growth rate of real GDP in 1997—calculated using the methods just described for the entire economy—was 4.5 percent. Thus, real GDP in 1997 was $8,165 billion, or 4.5 percent greater than $7,813 billion. The $8,165 billion is 1997 real GDP measured in 1996 dollars. To emphasize that this number is calculated by chaining years together with growth rates, government statisticians say that real GDP is measured in "chained 1996 dollars."

■ **Real GDP versus Nominal GDP over Time.**   Figure 5.6 compares real and nominal GDP during the 1990s. Observe that for the 1996 base year, real GDP and nominal GDP are equal. However, by 1998, real GDP reached about $8.5 trillion, whereas nominal GDP was at $8.8 trillion. Thus, just as in the example, real GDP increased less than nominal GDP. For the years prior to 1996, real GDP is more than nominal GDP because 1996 prices were higher than prices in earlier years. From Figure 5.6 we can see that nominal GDP would give a very misleading picture of the U.S. economy.

The GDP Deflator

Nominal GDP grows faster than real GDP because of inflation. The greater the difference between nominal GDP growth and real GDP growth, the greater is the inflation. If there were a deflation, with prices falling, then nominal GDP would increase less than real GDP. Hence, a by-product of computing real GDP is a measure of the rate of inflation.

More precisely, if we divide nominal GDP by real GDP, we get the **GDP deflator,** a measure of the **price level,** which is the level of all the prices of the items in real GDP. That is,

$$\text{GDP deflator} = \frac{\text{nominal GDP}}{\text{real GDP}}$$

Here the GDP deflator is defined so that its value in the base year, such as 1996, is 1.00. (Sometimes it is scaled to equal 100 in the base year by multiplying by 100.)

GDP deflator: nominal GDP divided by real GDP; it measures the level of prices of goods and services included in real GDP relative to a given base year.

price level: the average level of prices in the economy.

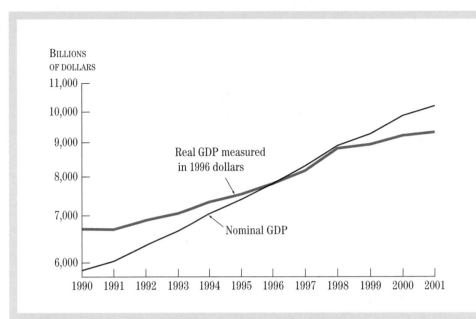

BILLIONS
OF DOLLARS

Figure 5.6
Real GDP versus Nominal GDP
Real GDP increases less than nominal GDP because real GDP takes out the effect of rising prices. The chart shows real GDP for the 1996 base year, when real GDP and nominal GDP are equal. Nominal GDP is below real GDP in earlier years because prices were generally lower before 1996.

The reason for the term *deflator* is that to get real GDP, we can deflate nominal GDP by dividing it by the GDP deflator. That is,

$$\text{Real GDP} = \frac{\text{nominal GDP}}{\text{GDP deflator}}$$

The percentage change in the GDP deflator from one year to the next is a measure of the rate of inflation.

Alternative Inflation Measures

consumer price index (CPI): a price index equal to the current price of a fixed market basket of consumer goods and services relative to a base year.

There are other measures of inflation. A frequently cited one is based on the **consumer price index (CPI)**, which is the price of a fixed collection—a "market basket"—of consumer goods and services in a given year divided by the price of the same collection in some base year. For example, if the market basket consists of one CD and two tapes, then the CPI for 2002 compared with the base year 2001 in the previous example would be

$$\frac{\$20 \times 1 + \$10 \times 2}{\$15 \times 1 + \$5 \times 2} = \frac{40}{25} = 1.60$$

The CPI inflation rate is the percent change in the CPI; it measures how fast the prices of the items in the basket increase in price.

The use of a fixed collection of goods and services in the CPI is one of the reasons economists think the CPI overstates inflation. When the price of goods rises, the

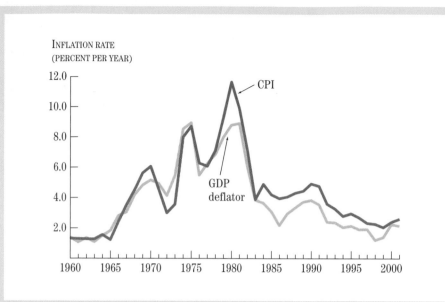

Figure 5.7
Comparison of Measures of Inflation
Measuring inflation with either the CPI or the GDP deflator shows the rise in inflation in the 1960s and 1970s and the lower inflation in the 1980s and early 1990s. The CPI is more volatile: It bounces around more. (The inflation rate is based on yearly percent changes in the stated variable.)

quantity demanded should decline; when the price falls, the quantity demanded should rise. Thus, by not allowing the quantities to change when the price changes, the CPI puts too much weight on items with rising prices and too little weight on items with declining prices. The result is an overstatement of inflation.

During the 1990s, a group of economists appointed by the U.S. Senate and chaired by Michael Boskin of Stanford University found that the government, by adjusting expenditures according to this overstated CPI, was spending billions of dollars more than it would with a correct CPI. Hence, getting the economic statistics right makes a big difference.

Figure 5.7 shows how measures of inflation using the GDP deflator and the CPI compare. The general inflation movements are similar. The CPI is more volatile, however.

Yet another measure of inflation is the producer price index (PPI), which measures the prices of raw materials and intermediate goods as well as the prices of final goods sold by producers. Prices of raw materials—oil, wheat, copper—are sometimes watched carefully because they give early warning signs of increases in inflation.

REVIEW
- Real GDP corrects nominal GDP for inflation. Real GDP measures the production of goods and services in the dollars of a given base year, such as 1996.

- Real GDP is a better measure of changes in the physical amount of production in the economy than is nominal GDP.

> • The GDP deflator is a measure of the price level in the economy. It is defined as the ratio of nominal GDP to real GDP. The percentage change in the GDP deflator from year to year is a measure of the inflation rate.

Shortcomings of the GDP Measure

Although GDP is the best measure of overall production we have, it is deficient in several ways. First, there are revisions to GDP that can change the assessment of the economy. Second, GDP omits some production. Third, the production of goods and services is only part of what affects the quality of life.

Revisions in GDP

Government statisticians obtain data on GDP from surveys of stores and businesses, and even from income tax data from the Internal Revenue Service. Not all of these data are collected quickly. Data on sales at stores and large firms come in within a month; exports and imports take several months. Some income tax data are reported only once a year. Information about small firms comes in even more slowly.

For this reason, the statistics on GDP are frequently revised as new data come in. For those who use the GDP data to make decisions, either in business or in government, faulty data on GDP, which are apparent only when the data are revised, can lead to mistakes. Revisions of GDP are inevitable and occur in all countries.

Omissions from GDP

Most of the production that is omitted from GDP either does not occur in a formal market or is difficult for government statisticians to measure. Examples are work done in the home, illegal commerce, and quality improvements in goods.

■ **Home Work and Production.**   Much of the production that people do at home—making dinner or a sweater, changing the car oil or a baby's diapers, cutting the grass or the kids' hair—is productive activity, but it is not included in GDP because the transactions are not recorded in markets where statisticians measure spending. Such production would be included in GDP if people hired and paid someone else to do any of these things.

Note that some home production is included in GDP. If you run a mail order or telemarketing business out of your home and pay taxes on your income, then this production is likely to be counted in GDP.

■ **Leisure Activity.**   Much leisure activity is not included in GDP even though it may be enjoyable. Going to the beach or hiking in the mountains more often and working less might be something you decide to do as your income increases. If people start taking Friday afternoons off, GDP will go down but the level of well-being may increase. The consumption of leisure is omitted from GDP unless it involves a purchase in the market, such as a ticket to a movie or a ballgame.

■ **The Underground Economy.** A large amount of production is not counted in GDP because it is purposely hidden from the view of the government. Illegal activity—growing marijuana in the California coastal range, selling pharmaceuticals not yet approved by the Food and Drug Administration—is excluded from GDP because no one wants to report this activity to the government. People who get cash payments—perhaps in the form of tips at hotels or restaurants—may not report them in order to avoid taxes, and these are not counted either. If people do not report interest on a loan to a friend or relative, this is also omitted from GDP.

The sum of all the missing items is referred to as the *underground economy*. Estimates of the size of the underground economy are understandably uncertain. They range from about 10 percent of GDP in the United States to about 25 percent in Italy to over 40 percent in Peru.

The underground economy makes GDP a less useful measure of the size of an economy, and we should be aware of it when we use GDP. But the underground economy does not render GDP a useless measure. It is unlikely that the underground economy grows much more or much less rapidly than the rest of the economy. Changes in laws can increase or decrease the incentives to produce outside the legal market economy, but these are unlikely to be large enough to change the estimated growth rates of GDP by much.

■ **Quality Improvements.** Our measure of GDP sometimes misses improvements in the quality of goods and services. For example, a new model car may be more comfortable and absorb shocks better than the old model, but if the price is the same, it will not lead to an increase in GDP.

Other Measures of Well-Being

Even if real GDP did include the underground economy and all the improvements in goods and services, it would not serve as the only measure of well-being. There are many other important aspects of the well-being of individuals: a long and healthy life expectancy; a clean environment; a small chance of war, crime, or the death of a child. The production of goods and services in a country can affect these other things, and indeed be affected by them, but it is not a measure of them.

Consider what has happened to some other measures of well-being as real GDP per capita has grown. Life expectancy in the United States has increased from about 69 years in the 1950s to 76 years in the 1990s. This compares with a life expectancy of only 47 years in the early part of the last century. Infant mortality has also declined, from about 2.6 infant deaths per 100 live births in the mid-1950s to 0.9 in the mid-1990s. In the early part of the last century, infant mortality in the United States was 10 deaths for every 100 live births. The fraction of women who die in childbirth has also declined. So by some of these important measures, the quality of life has improved along with real GDP per capita.

But there are still serious problems and room for gains; as death rates from car accidents, heart disease, and stroke have decreased, death rates among young people from AIDS, suicide, and murder have been rising. Also of serious concern is the increasing percentage of children who live in poverty. Thus, the impressive gain in real GDP per capita has been correlated with both gains and losses in other measures of well-being.

A clean and safe environment is also a factor in the quality of life. But GDP itself does not provide an indication of whether pollution or many of the other measures of the quality of life are improving or getting worse.

Near the end of every month, stories about the latest GDP measurement for the United States appear in most newspapers around the country (and on web pages seen around the world). The stories are a response to the release of GDP data by economic statisticians at the U.S. Department of Commerce, where the national income and product accounts are tabulated.

The following story appeared in the online version of the *Wall Street Journal* on April 26, 2002. The discussion of GDP in this chapter should give you the information you need to understand the article and to judge whether the headline, the reporter's interpretation of the GDP data, and the public official's comments make sense. It reports strong GDP growth for the economy, as reflected in its headline and general tone.

There are several points to keep in mind when reading news stories about GDP.

First, the measures of GDP are reported for each of the four quarters of the year. There is a news story each month because the data are revised twice. In the first

month after the end of the quarter, the first estimate of GDP is given; that is what is reported in the following article. In the second and third months, the estimates are revised as new data about the economy are obtained. Sometimes you have to read carefully to know whether what you are reading is a first-time report or a revision.

Second, the GDP measure for a quarter of a year represents the aggregate production during the quarter, but the amount of production is stated at an *annual rate* to make the magnitude comparable to that of the annual GDP measure.

Third, the GDP measures for each quarter are *seasonally adjusted*. There is always more production in some seasons of the year than in other seasons, and these differences have little to do with where the economy is going. For example, in the fourth quarter (October–December), there is usually more production in anticipation of the holidays. Seasonal adjustments try to take out these fluctuations so that they do not show up in the reported measures of GDP.

Economy Surged 5.8% in 1st Quarter As Businesses Slowed Inventory Cuts

A WALL STREET JOURNAL ONLINE NEWS ROUNDUP Updated April 26, 2002 12:51 p.m. EDT

The U.S. economy grew at a sizzling 5.8% annual rate in the first quarter, rocketing back after last year's recession and the terrorist attacks.

After limping through the last six quarters, gross domestic product—the broadest measure of the economy's health—posted its strongest showing since the final quarter of 1999, the Commerce Department reported Friday. The figures reinforced the view that the country not only emerged from a recession that began in March 2001 but that the downturn will probably go down as the mildest in history.

The economy's first-quarter rebound is especially remarkable given that GDP shrank at a 1.3% rate in the third quarter of 2001. The economy grew at a 1.7% rate in the fourth quarter. "Growth is back!" said Ken Mayland, president of ClearView Economic. "This economy is getting back on a good growth track, which down the road will mean good things for the restoration of jobs and companies' profits."

[Refers to growth rate of real GDP]

Economists' predictions of first-quarter GDP varied widely, according to a survey by Thomson Global Markets. On average the forecast was for a 5% rise, but predictions ranged from 3.5% to 6%. The jump in GDP was driven largely by businesses easing off on paring inventory. Businesses also slowed their cuts to spending, and consumer spending—a key component of economic growth—remained healthy. Business inventories fell just $36.2 billion in last quarter after falling a record $119.3 billion in the fourth. The change added 3.1 percentage points to GDP.

Friday's report also showed that businesses began shedding their reluctance to spend. Business investment, which has been dropping for more than a year, fell once again. But the 5.7% reduction was much milder than the 13.8% plunge in the fourth quarter. And spending on equipment and software declined by only 0.5% after sharper drops in previous quarters.

Consumer spending, which accounts for two-thirds of overall economic growth, rose at a 3.5% annual pace in the first quarter, down from the strong 6.1% pace in the fourth quarter. Fourth-quarter spending had been driven largely by temporary financing promotions from auto makers.

[Explanation for why consumer spending increased]

Spending on durable goods in the first quarter, which includes autos, fell by 8%. That was offset by an 8.4% gain in spending for nondurable goods such as clothing and food, as well as a 3.8% rise in spending for services. Home purchases jumped 15.7%.

REVIEW
- Real GDP per capita is not without its shortcomings as an indicator of well-being in a society. Certain items are omitted—home production, leisure, the underground economy, and some quality improvements.
- There are other indicators of the quality of life, including vital statistics on mortality and the environment, that can be affected by GDP per capita but that are conceptually distinct and independently useful.

Conclusion

In this chapter, we have shown how to measure the size of an economy in terms of its GDP. In the process, we have explained that income, spending, and production in a country are all equal and that GDP can be adjusted to make comparisons over time.

In conclusion, it is important to recall that aggregate income (or production or spending), the subject of our study, tells us much about the quality of life of the people in a country, but it does not tell us everything. As the economist-philosopher John Stuart Mill said in his *Principles of Political Economy*, first published in 1848: "All know that it is one thing to be rich, another to be enlightened, brave or humane . . . those things, indeed, are all indirectly connected, and react upon one another."[2]

KEY POINTS

1. U.S. gross domestic product (GDP) is the total production of new goods and services in the United States during a particular period.

2. GDP can be measured by adding all spending on new goods and services in the United States. Changes in inventories and net exports must be added to spending.

3. GDP can also be measured by adding labor income, capital income, depreciation, sales taxes, and net income of foreigners. Except for a small statistical discrepancy, the income approach gives us the same answer as the spending approach.

4. Value added is a measure of a firm's production. Value added is defined as the difference between the value of the production sold and the cost of inputs to production. GDP can be measured by adding the value added of all firms in the economy.

5. National saving in the United States is defined as income less consumption less government purchases.

6. Real GDP is a measure of production adjusted for inflation. It is the best overall measure of changes in the production of goods and services over time.

7. GDP is not without its shortcomings. It does not include production in the underground economy or much work done in the home. And it is only one of many measures of well-being.

---

2. John Stuart Mill, *Principles of Political Economy* (New York: Bookseller, 1965), pp. 1–2.

KEY TERMS

intermediate good	net exports	capital income	price level
final good	exports	value added	consumer price index
consumption	imports	national saving	(CPI)
investment	trade balance	nominal GDP	
government purchases	labor income	GDP deflator	

QUESTIONS FOR REVIEW

1. Why do we add up total spending in order to compute GDP when GDP is supposed to be a measure of production?

2. Approximately what were the percentages of consumption, investment, government purchases, and net exports in GDP in the United States?

3. Why is the sum of all income equal to GDP?

4. What is national saving?

5. What is the significance of value added, and how does one measure it for a single item?

6. Why does national saving equal the sum of private and government saving?

7. Why are increases in nominal GDP not a good measure of economic growth?

8. Why is the production of meals in the home not included in GDP? Should it be?

9. Why is the purchase of a used car not included in GDP? Should it be?

10. Why do we add inventory investment to spending when computing GDP?

PROBLEMS

1. Determine whether each of the following would be included in GDP, and explain why or why not.
   a. You buy a used CD from a friend.
   b. You buy a new CD at a music shop.
   c. You cook your own dinner.
   d. You hire someone to cook your dinner.

2. Determine whether each of the following is consumption, investment, or neither. Explain your answer.
   a. A landscaping company buys a new four-wheel-drive vehicle to carry bushes and flowers.
   b. A doctor buys a new four-wheel-drive vehicle to use on vacation.
   c. A family puts a new kitchen in their house.
   d. The campus bookstore increases its inventory of text-books.
   e. You buy toothpaste at the drugstore.
   f. The state government of Alaska buys four-wheel-drive vehicles for its game wardens.

3. Suppose that the Internet increases the size of the economy.
   a. How will this affect the accuracy of GDP as a measure of production?
   b. State two ways in which the Internet affects GDP as a measure of well-being.

4. In market economies, prices reflect the value people place on goods and services, and therefore it makes sense to use them as weights when calculating GDP. In centrally planned economies, however, prices are controlled by the government instead of by the market. Examine the following data for a centrally planned economy that subsequently frees prices:

Good	Quantity	Controlled Price	Market Price
Electricity	1,000	$ 2	$10
Gasoline	500	$20	$15

   a. Calculate GDP under the controlled prices and under market prices, assuming the quantities do not change. Did governmentally set prices mean an under- or overvaluation of production on the whole?
   b. How do people value each good in relation to the previously controlled prices?

5. Look at two scenarios for monthly inventories and sales for a company producing cereal, shown on the next page. In both scenarios, the company's sales are the same.
   a. Calculate the inventory investment during each month and the resulting stock of inventory at the beginning of the following month for both scenarios.
   b. Does maintaining constant production lead to greater or lesser fluctuations in the stock of inventory? Explain.

SCENARIO A

Month	Start-of-the-Month Inventory Stock	Production	Sales	Inventory Investment
Jan.	50	50	45	
Feb.		50	55	
Mar.		50	80	
Apr.		50	50	
May		50	40	

SCENARIO B

Month	Start-of-the-Month Inventory Stock	Production	Sales	Inventory Investment
Jan.	50	45	45	
Feb.		55	55	
Mar.		80	80	
Apr.		50	50	
May		40	40	

6. Given the information in the table below for three consecutive years in the U.S. economy, calculate the missing data.

7. Suppose there are only the following three goods in the economy.

Year	Good	Price	Quantity
2001	Tomatoes	$2.50	1,000
	Squash	$1.25	500
	Telephones	$100	10
2002	Tomatoes	$3.50	800
	Squash	$2.25	400
	Telephones	$100	14

a. Calculate nominal GDP for 2001 and 2002.
b. Calculate the percentage change in GDP from 2001 to 2002 using 2001 prices and using 2002 prices.
c. Calculate the percentage change in real GDP from 2001 to 2002 using your answers from (b).
d. What is the GDP deflator for 2002 if it equals 1.0 in 2001?

8. Use the following data for a South Dakota wheat farm.

Revenue	$1,000
Costs	
Wages and salaries	$700
Rent on land	$50
Rental fee for tractor	$100
Seed, fertilizer	$100
Pesticides, irrigation	$50

a. Calculate the value added by this farm.
b. Profits are revenue minus costs. Capital income consists of profits, rents, and interest. Show that value added equals capital income plus labor income paid by the farm.
c. Suppose that, because of flooding in Kansas, wheat prices increase suddenly and revenues rise to $1,100, but prices of intermediate inputs do not change. What happens to value added and profits in this case?

Problem 6

Year	Nominal GDP (in billions of U.S. dollars)	Real GDP (in billions of 1996 dollars)	GDP Deflator (1996 = 100)	Inflation (percent change in GDP deflator)	Real GDP per Capita (in 1996 dollars)	Population (in millions)
1996	7,813		100.0	1.8		249.9
1997		8,165		1.7		252.7
1998			102.86		33,344	255.4

9. In 1991, national saving in Japan was 154 trillon yen. If the government had a 5 trillion yen surplus, how much was saving by consumers and businesses in Japan? What if the government instead had a 5 trillion yen deficit?

10. Suppose the data in the following table describe the economic activity in a country for 2002. Given these data, calculate the following:
    a. Inventory investment
    b. Net exports
    c. Gross domestic product
    d. Statistical discrepancy
    e. National saving

    Verify that national saving equals investment plus net exports.

Component of Spending	Value in Billions of Dollars
Consumption	140
Business fixed and residential investment	27
Inventory stock at the end of 2001	10
Inventory stock at the end of 2002	5
Depreciation	12
Government outlays	80
Government purchases	65
Total government tax receipts	60
Exports	21
Imports	17
Labor income	126
Capital income	70
Net income of foreigners	5
Sales taxes	28

6

The Spending Allocation Model

In 1994, economists working on the president's Council of Economic Advisors predicted that the administration's plan to reduce the share of government purchases in GDP would increase the share of investment in GDP. Their reasoning was that a reduction in the share of government purchases would lead to lower interest rates in the economy, which in turn would raise investment because "lower interest rates . . . are the way that the market accomplishes expenditure switching . . . away . . . from government purchases toward investment."[1]

The subsequent behavior of the economy confirms that the president's economic advisers were correct. Between 1994 and 1998, the share of investment in real GDP *increased* from 15 to 18 percent as the share of government purchases in real GDP *decreased* from 19 to 17 percent. How were the economic advisors able to make such a prediction? What type of economic model would predict that lowering the share of government purchases in GDP would result in lower interest rates, and, in turn, that lower interest rates would raise the share of investment purchases in GDP?

In this chapter, we will develop such an economic model, which we will call the *spending allocation model*, to determine how GDP is allocated among the major components of spending: consumption, investment, government purchases, and net exports. Because each share of spending must compete for the scarce resources in GDP, an increase in the share of one of the components will lead to a reduction in the share of another component. Our model shows that interest rates are a key factor that both influences and is influenced by

---

1. *Economic Report of the President*, 1994, p. 83.

spending. By explaining how interest rates are determined, our model helps us predict, just as the president's economic advisors predicted, how much of GDP goes to each of the four components: consumption, investment, government purchases, and net exports.

The spending allocation model has some very useful applications. We can use it not only to understand the macroeconomic implications of the reduction in government purchases in the early 1990s, but also to understand why the share of investment in GDP fell during the 1980s. However, when you read the description of the spending allocation model, keep in mind that this model applies more to the long run than to the short run. Therefore, it is most useful in thinking about economic developments that occur over a period of years instead of months. For example, the Council of Economic Advisors was very careful to note that the positive impact of the reduction of the share of government purchases on the share of investment would take several years to materialize.

The Spending Shares

We know that GDP is divided into four components: consumption, investment, government purchases, and net exports. Symbolically,

$$Y = C + I + G + X$$

where Y equals GDP, C equals consumption, I equals investment, G equals government purchases, and X equals net exports. This equation is the starting point for determining how large a share of GDP is allocated to each spending component.

Defining the Spending Shares

consumption share: the proportion of GDP that is used for consumption; equals consumption divided by GDP, or C/Y.

investment share: the proportion of GDP that is used for investment; equals investment divided by GDP, or I/Y. Sometimes called investment rate.

net exports share: the proportion of GDP that is equal to net exports; equals net exports divided by GDP, or X/Y.

government purchases share: the proportion of GDP that is used for government purchases; equals government purchases divided by GDP, or G/Y.

The **consumption share** of GDP is the proportion of GDP that is used for consumption. The consumption share of GDP is defined as consumption (C) divided by GDP, or C/Y. For example, if $C = \$6$ trillion and $Y = \$10$ trillion, then the consumption share is $C/Y = 0.6$, or 60 percent. We can define the other shares of GDP analogously: I/Y is the **investment share,** X/Y is the **net exports share,** and G/Y is the **government purchases share.** Sometimes the investment share is called the *investment rate.*

We can establish a simple relationship between the shares of spending in GDP by taking the equation $Y = C + I + G + X$ and dividing both sides by Y. This simple division gives us a relationship that says that the sum of the shares of spending in GDP must equal 1. Writing that algebraically yields

$$1 = \frac{C}{Y} + \frac{I}{Y} + \frac{G}{Y} + \frac{X}{Y}$$

If we use the shares that existed in 2001 (see Table 5.2), we get

$$1 = \frac{7,064}{10,208} + \frac{1,634}{10,208} + \frac{1,840}{10,208} + \frac{(-330)}{10,208}$$

$$= .6920 + .1601 + .1802 + (-.0323)$$

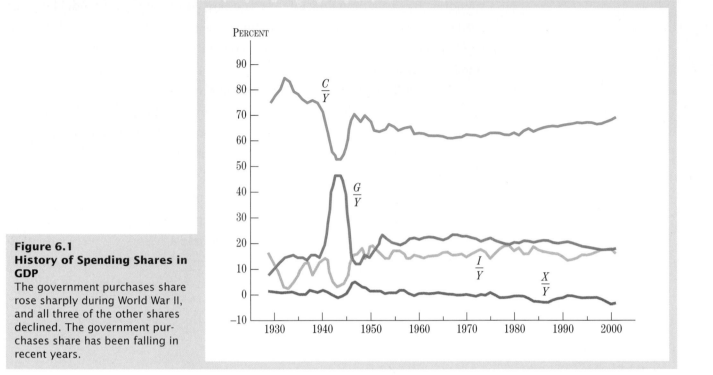

Figure 6.1
History of Spending Shares in GDP
The government purchases share rose sharply during World War II, and all three of the other shares declined. The government purchases share has been falling in recent years.

In other words, consumption accounted for 69.20 percent of GDP; investment for 16.01 percent of GDP; government purchases for 18.02 percent of GDP; and net exports, in deficit at negative $330 billion, for about negative 3.23 percent of GDP. In this example, the sum of the four shares on the right equals 1, or, in percentage terms, 100 percent. And, of course, this must be true for any year. The negative share for net exports occurs because Americans imported more than they exported in 2001.

Figure 6.1 shows the four shares of spending in GDP for the last 70 years in the United States. A huge temporary fluctuation in the shares of spending in GDP occurred in World War II, when government spending on the military rose sharply. Government purchases reached 50 percent of GDP, and the other three shares declined.

Clearly, the movements in government spending as a share of GDP are a factor in determining the share of investment in GDP. Since World War II, the shares have been much steadier, but starting in the late 1980s the government purchases share has gone down and the consumption and investment shares have gone up. The net exports share has been negative for the last 25 years, as the United States has run trade deficits. (Recall that when net exports are negative, there is a trade deficit.)

If One Share Goes Up, Another Must Go Down

The shares of spending equation demonstrates a simple but important point: A change in one of the shares implies a change in one or more of the other shares. That the shares must sum to 1 means that an increase in any of the shares must entail a reduction in one of the other shares. For example, an increase in the share of spending going to government purchases must result in a decrease in the share going to one or more of the other components of spending. Similarly, a decrease in the government purchases share must result in an increase in some other share, such as the investment share. One cannot have an increase in government purchases as a share of GDP (going from, say, 19 percent to 25 percent) without a decline in the share of either consumption or investment or net exports.

What determines how the shares of GDP are allocated? What is the mechanism through which a change in one share—such as the government share of GDP—brings about a change in one of the other shares? Does the investment share change? Or do the consumption and net exports shares change? To answer these questions, we need to consider the interest rate, which plays an important role in relating changes in one share to changes in another.

REVIEW
- Defining spending components as shares of GDP is a convenient way to describe how spending is allocated.

- Simple arithmetic tells us that the sum of all the shares of spending in GDP must equal 1.

- Thus, an increase in the share of GDP going to government purchases, for example, must be accompanied by a reduction in one or more of the other three shares—consumption, investment, or net exports.

The Effect of Interest Rates on Spending Shares

In this section, we show that the interest rate affects the three shares of spending by the private sector: consumption, investment, and net exports. Each private spending component competes for a share of GDP along with government purchases, and the interest rate is a key factor in determining how the spending is allocated.

Consumption

The consumption share of GDP depends on people's decisions to consume, which are like any other choice with scarce resources, as defined in Chapter 1. If people raise their consumption relative to their income, then the consumption share of GDP will increase. Conversely, if people lower their consumption relative to their income, then the consumption share of GDP will decrease.

■ **Consumption and the Interest Rate.**   Keep in mind that people's decisions to consume more or less of their income today has implications for their consumption decisions tomorrow. Individuals who consume *more* today save *less,* and therefore have less to consume tomorrow. On the other hand, individuals who consume *less* today save *more,* and therefore have more to consume tomorrow. A person's choice between consuming today and consuming tomorrow depends on a relative price, just like any other economic decision. This relative price is the price of consumption today relative to the price of consumption tomorrow.

Changes in the interest rate will change the relative price. For instance, a higher interest rate will raise the price of consumption today relative to that of consumption tomorrow. Why? If the interest rate is higher, then any saving will deliver more funds in the future, which can then be used for future consumption (a larger home or more

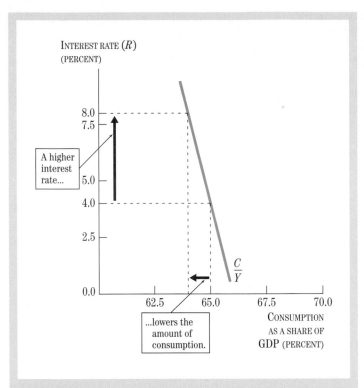

INTEREST RATE (R)
(PERCENT)

A higher interest rate...

...lowers the amount of consumption.

$\frac{C}{Y}$

CONSUMPTION
AS A SHARE OF
GDP (PERCENT)

Figure 6.2
The Consumption Share and the Interest Rate
A higher interest rate lowers the amount of consumption relative to GDP. A higher interest rate discourages consumption and encourages saving.

college education, for example). Therefore, a higher interest rate, by raising the price of today's consumption, will result in lower consumption today. Conversely, a lower interest rate will reduce the price of consumption today relative to that of consumption tomorrow and bring about higher consumption today.

We can better illustrate this link between the interest rate and consumption with a numerical example. Suppose the interest rate increases from 2 percent to 6 percent. At an interest rate of 2 percent, putting $100 into a bank account will enable an individual to have $102 at the end of a year. However, at an interest rate of 6 percent, the same individual will be able to get $106 in a year by putting $100 in a bank account today. The increase in the interest rate from 2 percent to 6 percent raises the price of consuming $100 worth of goods today by $4. Even though this may seem like a small amount, keep in mind that small differences in interest rates can add up when you consider saving large sums of money to finance a college education or for retirement. So a higher interest rate gives people more incentive to consume less and save for the future, whereas a lower interest rate gives people more incentive to consume today instead of saving for the future. We can therefore conclude that consumption is negatively related to the interest rate.

What is true for individuals on average will also be true for the economy as a whole. Figure 6.2 shows how the consumption share is negatively related to the interest rate. For this example, when the interest rate is 4 percent, the share of consumption in GDP will be about 65 percent. If the interest rate increases to 8 percent, then the share declines to 64 percent. Alternatively, if the interest rate declines, the consumption share increases.

■ **Movements Along versus Shifts of the Consumption Share Line.** Observe that the relationship between the interest rate and consumption as a share of GDP in Figure 6.2 looks like a demand curve. Like a demand curve, it is downward-sloping. And like a demand curve, it shows the quantity consumers are willing to consume at each interest rate. The interest rate is like a price: A higher price—that is, a higher interest rate—reduces the amount of goods and services people will consume, and a lower price—that is, a lower interest rate—increases the amount they will consume. When an increase in the interest rate leads to a decline in consumption, we see a *movement along* the consumption share line, as shown in Figure 6.2.

As with a demand curve, it is important to distinguish such movements along the consumption share line from *shifts of* the consumption share line. The interest rate is not the only thing that affects consumption as a share of GDP. When a factor other than the interest rate changes the consumption share of GDP, there is a shift in the consumption share line in Figure 6.2. For example, an increase in taxes on consumption—such as a national sales tax—would reduce the quantity of goods people would consume relative to their income. In other words, an increase in taxes on consumption would shift the consumption share line in Figure 6.2 to the left: Less

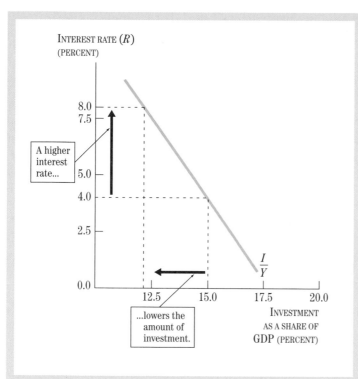

INTEREST RATE (R)
(PERCENT)

8.0
7.5

A higher
interest
rate...

5.0

4.0

2.5

0.0

12.5   15.0   17.5   20.0

$\frac{I}{Y}$

INVESTMENT
AS A SHARE OF
GDP (PERCENT)

...lowers the
amount of
investment.

Figure 6.3
The Investment Share and the Interest Rate
A higher interest rate lowers the share of investment. The sensitivity of investment to the interest rate is greater than that of consumption to the interest rate, as shown in Figure 6.2.

would be consumed relative to GDP at every interest rate. Conversely, a decrease in taxes on consumption would shift the consumption share line in Figure 6.2 to the right.

Investment

A similar relationship exists for investment and the interest rate. Figure 6.3 shows that there is a negative relationship between the interest rate and the investment share. For this example, when the interest rate rises from 4 percent to 8 percent, the investment share decreases from 15 percent to 12 percent. Economists have observed that investment is more sensitive to interest rates than consumption is. Therefore, the line for I/Y in Figure 6.3 is less steep than the line for C/Y in Figure 6.2.

Why does this negative relationship exist in the case of investment? When businesses decide to invest, they frequently have to borrow the funds to buy new machines and equipment or to build a new factory. Higher interest rates raise the cost of borrowing. Investment projects that would be undertaken at lower interest rates may be postponed or cancelled when interest rates rise because higher costs of borrowing discourage borrowing. Less borrowing means that fewer purchases of new equipment will be undertaken and fewer new factories built. On the other hand, when interest rates fall, the cost of borrowing falls as well, thus encouraging firms to purchase more equipment and build new factories. Note that this relationship holds even if firms use their own funds to finance their investment projects. Higher interest rates increase the opportunity cost of using their own funds for investment: Firms are tempted to leave their money in the bank earning a higher interest rate, instead of putting those funds into investment projects.

Recall that investment also includes the purchases of new houses. Most people need to take out loans (mortgages) to purchase houses. When the interest rate on mortgages rises, people purchase fewer or smaller houses; when the interest rate falls, people purchase more or larger houses.

The negative relationship between investment as a share of GDP and the interest rate has been observed in the economy for many years, and it makes sense: A higher interest rate discourages investment, and a lower interest rate encourages investment.

Observe that the relationship between the investment share of GDP and the interest rate in Figure 6.3 looks like a demand curve. It is downward-sloping. The interest rate is like the price: A higher interest rate decreases the amount of investment firms will do, and a lower interest rate increases the amount of investment firms will do.

Other factors besides the interest rate also affect investment; when these factors change, the investment share line

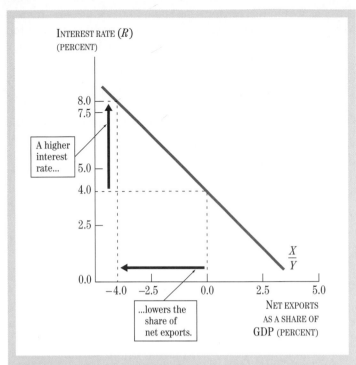

Figure 6.4
The Net Exports Share and the Interest Rate
A higher interest rate lowers the share of net exports because it tends to raise the exchange rate. The higher exchange rate lowers exports and raises imports, thereby lowering net exports. When net exports are negative, there is a trade deficit. When net exports are positive, there is a trade surplus.

in Figure 6.3 will *shift.* For example, an investment tax credit, which lowers a firm's taxes if the firm buys new equipment, would increase the amount that firms would invest at each interest rate. An investment tax credit would shift the investment share line in Figure 6.3 to the right: The investment that firms are willing to do as a share of GDP at a given interest rate would rise. A change in firms' expectations of the future could also shift the investment share line; if firms feel that new computing or telecommunications equipment will lower their costs in the future, they will purchase the equipment, thereby increasing their investment at a given interest rate; the investment share line will shift to the right. Conversely, pessimism on the part of firms about the benefits of investment could shift the line to the left.

Net Exports

Net exports are also negatively related to the interest rate. As you can see in Figure 6.4, a negative relationship exists that is much like the relationship of consumption and investment to the interest rate. For this example, when the interest rate goes up from 4 percent to 8 percent, net exports go from zero to about −4 percent of GDP. Remember that when net exports are negative, there is a trade deficit.

The story behind this relationship is somewhat more involved than that for investment or for consumption. However, you may find the story more interesting because it includes the role of the foreign *exchange rate*—the price of foreign currency in terms of the domestic currency—in determining exports and imports, as well as the relationship between the interest rate and the exchange rate. In any case, it is important to grasp the key features. The story has three parts.

■ **The Interest Rate and the Exchange Rate.**   Let us start with the relationship between the interest rate and the **exchange rate**. International investors must decide whether to put their funds in assets denominated in dollars—such as an account at a U.S. bank in New York City—or in assets denominated in foreign currencies—such as an account at a Japanese bank in Tokyo. If interest rates rise in the United States, then international investors will put more funds in dollar-denominated assets. They can earn more by doing so. For example, suppose the interest rate paid on U.S. dollar deposits in New York rises and there is no change in the interest rate in Japan. Then international investors will shift their funds from Tokyo to New York in order to take advantage of the higher interest rate. As funds are shifted to the United States, the demand for dollars begins to increase. This increased demand puts upward pressure on the dollar exchange rate. The exchange rate will rise, which means that more foreign currency will be exchanged for one dollar in the foreign exchange market. In other words, the higher interest rate causes a higher level of the dollar exchange rate. For example, an increase in the interest rate in the United States might cause the dollar to increase from 100 yen per dollar to 120 yen per dollar. Conversely, a lower interest rate in the United States brings about a lower exchange rate for the dollar.

exchange rate: the price of one currency in terms of another in the foreign exchange market. We express the exchange rate as the number of units of foreign currency that can be purchased with one unit of domestic currency.

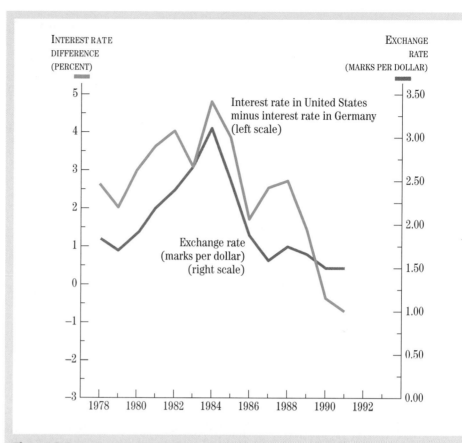

Figure 6.5
The Interest Rate and the Exchange Rate
The green line is the interest rate on U.S. Treasury bonds relative to the interest rate on German bonds (the difference between the two interest rates). As the U.S. interest rate rose compared to that in Germany, the value of the dollar rose relative to the German mark. The same type of relationship holds true for other currencies.

Thus, the interest rate and the exchange rate are positively related. Such a relationship is confirmed by observing interest rates and exchange rates in the market over several years. When the interest rate increases compared to interest rates abroad, the exchange rate rises. For example, Figure 6.5 shows that a large rise in the U.S. dollar relative to the German mark occurred in the mid-1980s when the U.S. interest rate rose sharply compared to the German interest rate.

■ **The Exchange Rate and Net Exports.** A higher dollar exchange rate brought about by a higher interest rate will tend to make goods imported into the United States more attractive because it makes these foreign goods cheaper. For example, the dollar exchange rate against the yen was relatively high, about 150 yen per dollar, in 1998 and comparatively low, 100 yen per dollar, in 1999. In 1998, when the exchange rate between the dollar and the yen was 150 yen per dollar, one could buy a kimono costing 15,000 yen for $100 (15,000/150). This was much cheaper than in 1999, when the exchange rate was 100 yen per dollar and the kimono cost $150 (15,000/100). Thus, a higher exchange rate increases the quantity demanded of imported goods.

In addition, the higher exchange rate makes U.S. exports less attractive because it makes American goods more expensive. For example, a $20,000 Jeep Cherokee cost 3 million yen in Japan in 1998 and only 2 million yen in 1999 because the dollar was higher in 1998. Thus, the exchange rate affects exports.

We have shown that a higher exchange rate means more imports and fewer exports. Since net exports are the difference between exports and imports, a higher exchange rate must mean that net exports are going down. Conversely, a lower exchange rate must mean that net exports are going up. To arrive at this result, we used a combination of some simple arithmetic that emphasizes net exports as the difference between exports and imports as well as an economic rationale that says both exports and imports should depend on the exchange rate.

■ **Combining the Two Relationships.**   Let us combine the two relationships. One relates the interest rate to the exchange rate, and the other relates the exchange rate to net exports. Combining the two, we get the following relationship between the interest rate and net exports:

Interest Rate		Exchange Rate		Net Exports
up	⟶	up	⟶	down
down	⟶	down	⟶	up

If the interest rate goes up, then the exchange rate goes up and net exports go down. Thus, a higher interest rate reduces net exports. The link is the exchange rate, which is increased by the higher interest rate and which, in turn, makes net exports fall. Of course, all of this works in reverse, too. If the interest rate goes down, then the exchange rate goes down and net exports go up. Thus, a lower interest rate increases net exports, because a lower interest rate means a lower exchange rate for the dollar, which stimulates U.S. exports and discourages imports.

By combining the relationships between the interest rate, the exchange rate, exports, and imports, we have derived the relationship between net exports as a share of GDP and the interest rate shown in Figure 6.4. Like the consumption share line and the investment share line, the net export share line in the figure looks like a demand curve. It is downward-sloping. Changes in the interest rate lead to movements along the net export line in Figure 6.4. Changes in other factors—such as a shift in foreign demand for U.S. products—may cause the line to shift.

Putting the Three Shares Together

We have shown that the consumption, investment, and net exports shares are all negatively related to the interest rate. The three diagrams—Figures 6.2, 6.3, and 6.4—summarize this key idea. Our next task is to determine the interest rate and, thereby, a particular value for each share. To determine the interest rate, we will require that the sum of these three shares equals what is left over after the government takes its share. This will ensure that all shares sum to 1.

REVIEW
- Consumption, investment, and net exports are negatively related to the interest rate.

- Higher interest rates raise the price of consumption this year relative to next year. This means that fewer goods will be consumed this year.

- Business firms invest less when interest rates rise because higher interest rates raise borrowing costs.

- Higher interest rates raise the exchange rate and thereby discourage exports and encourage imports, leading to a decline in net exports.

- Other factors besides the interest rate may affect consumption, investment, and net exports. When one of these factors changes, the relationship between the interest rate and consumption, investment, or net exports shifts.

Determining the Equilibrium Interest Rate

Because the interest rate affects each of the three shares (consumption, investment, and net exports), it also affects the *sum* of the three shares. This is shown by the downward-sloping line in diagram (d) of Figure 6.6. In diagram (d), an increase in the interest rate reduces the sum of the three shares of GDP.

Adding the Nongovernment Shares Graphically

Note carefully how Figure 6.6 is put together and how the downward-sloping line in diagram (d) is derived. We have taken the graphs from Figures 6.2, 6.3, and 6.4 and assembled them horizontally in diagrams (a), (b), and (c) of Figure 6.6. The downward-sloping red line in diagram (d) is the sum of the three downward-sloping lines in diagrams (a), (b), and (c). It is the nongovernment share of GDP, or NG/Y, where $NG = C + I + X$ and, as usual, Y is GDP. For example, when the interest rate is 4 percent, the line in diagram (d) shows that the nongovernment share—the sum of investment, consumption, and net exports as a share of GDP—is 80 percent; this is the sum of 65 percent for the consumption share, 15 percent for the investment

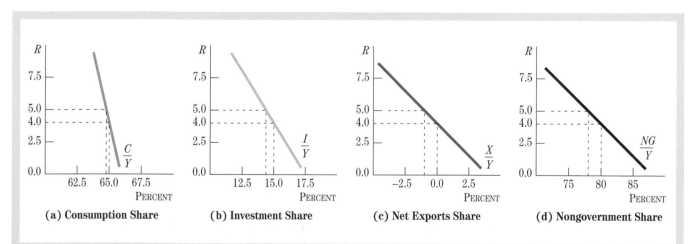

Figure 6.6
Summing Up Consumption, Investment, and Net Exports Shares

Diagrams (a), (b), and (c) are reproductions of Figures 6.2, 6.3, and 6.4. For each interest rate, the three shares are added together to get the sum of shares shown in diagram (d). For example, when the interest rate is 4 percent, we get 65 percent for consumption share, 15 percent for investment share, and 0 percent for net exports, summing to 80 percent. The sum of the three nongovernment shares (NG/Y) is negatively related to the interest rate (R).

share, and zero percent for the net exports share. Similarly, the other points in diagram (d) are obtained by adding up the three shares at other interest rate levels. For example, at an interest rate of 5 percent, we see that the sum of the share of consumption, investment, and net exports is down to about 78 percent.

The Share of GDP Available for Nongovernment Use

To determine the interest rate, we must consider the fourth share: government. The government share determines how much is available for nongovernment use, that is, for either consumption, investment, or net exports. For example, if the government share is 22 percent of GDP, then the sum of the consumption share, the investment share, and the net export share must equal 78 percent.

What brings this equality about? In a market economy, the government does not stipulate that consumption, investment, and net exports must equal 78 percent, or any other share of GDP. Instead, prices—in this case, the interest rate—adjust to provide individual consumers or firms with the incentive to make the necessary adjustments. Recall from Chapter 1 that the price in a market serves as both a signal and an incentive to individuals. In a market economy as a whole, the interest rate adjusts to ensure equality between (1) the sum of the investment, consumption, and net exports shares, and (2) the share of GDP available for investment, consumption, and net exports.

The Government's Share of GDP

We have determined that the interest rate has a negative effect on the consumption, investment, and net exports shares of GDP. What about the impact of interest rates on government purchases? We will assume that government purchases do not depend on the interest rate; instead, they are likely to be affected by the decisions made by elected representatives on behalf of the voters who elected them to office. So the share of government purchases will not be affected by fluctuations in interest rates.

Putting all these relationships together, we can conclude that the sum of the consumption, investment, and net exports shares must equal the share of GDP available after the government takes its share. In mathematical terms, we can describe this relationship as

$$\frac{NG}{Y} = 1 - \frac{G}{Y}$$

If consumption, investment, or net exports increases, then the nongovernment share will begin to rise above the share of GDP available after the government takes its share. This rise in spending will cause the interest rate in the economy to increase and bring consumption, investment, net exports, or all three back down so that the nongovernmental share once again equals the available share left by the government.

Finding the Equilibrium Interest Rate Graphically

Figure 6.7 illustrates how the interest rate brings about this equality. Look first at diagram (d). In diagram (d), the share of GDP available for nongovernment use is indicated by the vertical line. Since the government share of spending is assumed to depend not on the interest rate, but rather on public decisions made by voters and politicians, the share of GDP available for nongovernment use is represented by a vertical line. In the case where government purchases are 22 percent of GDP, the vertical line is at 78 percent, as shown in Figure 6.7(d). If the government share were larger, we would draw the vertical line further to the left, showing that the share available for nongovernment use was smaller.

The sum of the three nongovernment shares is shown by the downward-sloping line in Figure 6.7(d). This is the same line we derived in Figure 6.6(d). At the intersection of this downward-sloping line and the vertical line, the sum of investment, consumption, and net exports is equal to the share that is available for nongovernment use. For example, when the share available is 78 percent, we see in diagram (d) of Figure 6.7 that the point of intersection occurs when the interest rate is 5 percent. This is the **equilibrium interest rate,** the interest rate that makes the sum of the consumption, investment, and net export shares equal to the share of GDP available. It is also the interest rate for which the sum of all shares of GDP equals 1.

Once we determine the equilibrium interest rate, we can find the investment, consumption, and net exports shares. Each of these shares depends on the interest rate, as shown in diagrams (a), (b), and (c) of Figure 6.7. To determine each of the shares, simply draw a line across the three diagrams at the equilibrium interest rate. Then in diagram (a) we find the consumption share, in diagram (b) the investment share, and in diagram (c) the net exports share.

> **equilibrium interest rate:** the interest rate that equates the sum of the consumption, investment, and net export shares to the share of GDP available for nongovernment use.

■ **Analogy with Supply and Demand.**   Observe that the intersection of the two lines in diagram (d) of Figure 6.7 is much like the intersection of a demand curve and a supply curve, as shown in the margin. The red downward-sloping line—showing how the sum of investment, consumption, and net exports is negatively related to the interest rate—looks just like a demand curve. The blue vertical line—showing the share of GDP available for consumption, investment, and net exports—looks like a vertical supply curve. The intersection of the two curves determines the equilibrium price—in this case, the equilibrium interest rate in the economy as a whole. In the next section, we show how shifts in one or both of these two curves lead to a new

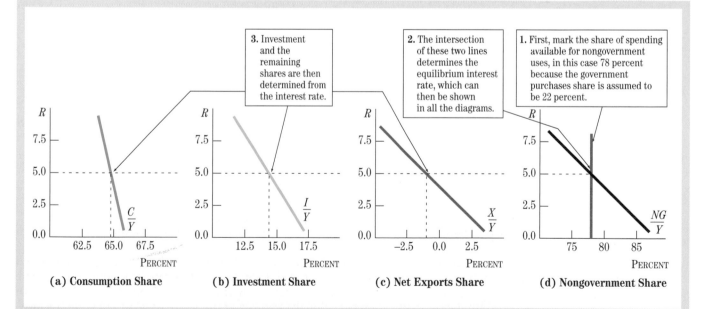

Figure 6.7
Determining the Equilibrium Interest Rate and the Shares of Spending

In this case, government purchases are assumed to be 22 percent of GDP. Mark the implied share available for nongovernment uses, 78 percent, in diagram (d). The equilibrium interest rate is determined at the intersection of the two lines in diagram (d). Given this interest rate, we can compute the consumption, investment, and net exports shares of spending in GDP using diagrams (a), (b), and (c).

equilibrium interest rate, much as shifts in supply and demand curves lead to a new equilibrium price.

■ **The Real Interest Rate in the Long Run.** Having determined the equilibrium interest rate, it is important to mention once more that our analysis applies to the *long run*—perhaps three years or more—rather than to short-run economic fluctuations. It takes time for consumers and firms to completely respond to a change in interest rates.

Moreover, the interest rate in the analysis refers to the *real* interest rate, which, as defined in Chapter 4, is the interest rate on loans adjusted for inflation. The real interest rate is defined as the nominal interest rate less the expected inflation rate. If the inflation rate is low, there is little difference between the real interest rate and the nominal interest rate; but if inflation is high, there is a big difference, and the real interest rate is a much better measure of the incentives affecting consumers and firms. An interest rate of 50 percent would seem high but would actually be quite low—2 percent in real terms—if people expected inflation to be 48 percent.

Broadly speaking, the analysis in this section shows that the real interest rate in the long run is determined by balancing people's demands for consumption, investment, and net exports with the available supply of goods and services in the economy.

REVIEW
- The sum of the consumption, investment, and net exports shares of GDP is negatively related to the interest rate because each of the individual components is negatively related to the interest rate.

- The equilibrium interest rate is determined by the condition that the sum of the three nongovernment shares of GDP equals the share available to the private sector. Using the equilibrium interest rate, we can then find each of the nongovernment shares.

CASE STUDY

Shifts in Government Purchases and Consumption

Now let us show how the spending allocation model is used to predict the effects of actual changes in the economy. We focus on two shifts: a shift in government purchases and a shift in consumption. Thus, this case study has two separate parts.

A Shift in the Share of Government Purchases

What happens when government purchases increase or decrease as a share of GDP? We know as a matter of arithmetic that some other share must move in a direction opposite to that of the government share.

Suppose that the government share of GDP decreases by 2 percent, as happened in the 1990s as a result of a decrease in defense spending and other budget cuts. The effects of this change are shown in Figure 6.8. If government purchases as a share of GDP decrease by 2 percent, then we know that the share of GDP available for nongovernment use must *increase* by 2 percent. Thus, in diagram (d) of Figure 6.8, we shift the vertical line marking the available share to the right by 2 percentage points. As Figure 6.8(d) shows, there is now a new intersection of the two lines and a new, lower equilibrium interest rate. The decrease in the interest rate is the market mech-

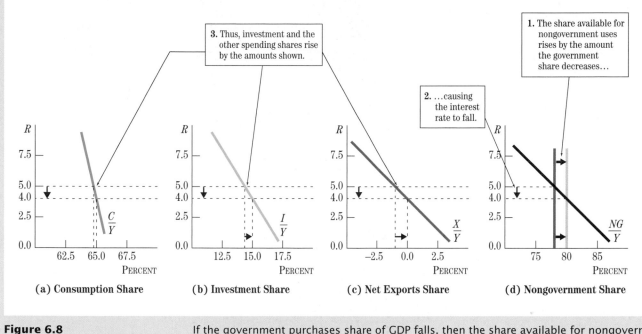

Figure 6.8
A Decrease in the Share of Government Purchases

If the government purchases share of GDP falls, then the share available for nongovernment uses must rise by the same amount. This causes a fall in interest rates, which increases consumption, investment, and net exports as a share of GDP.

anism that brings about an increase in consumption plus investment plus net exports as a share of GDP.

Diagram (d) of Figure 6.8, for example, shows that the new interest rate is 4 percent rather than 5 percent. That is, the interest rate has decreased by 1 percentage point.

To see the effect on consumption, investment, and net exports, we draw a horizontal line at 4 percent interest, as shown in Figure 6.8, and read off the implied shares. According to the diagram, the share of consumption increases, the share of investment increases, and the share of net exports increases. Thus, we have a prediction about consumption, investment, and net exports.

Table 6.1 shows how the analysis explains the effects of a reduction in government purchases in the 1990s. The government purchases share was reduced by 2.2 percent between 1989 and 1997, much as in Figure 6.8. During the same period, all of the other shares increased as a result of the decline in the interest rate. Although the precise magnitudes may not be exactly the same, the model explains the direction of movement very well.

The same process would work in reverse if we increased government purchases as a share of GDP. In Figure 6.8, the interest rates would have to rise. To find out the

Table 6.1
Change in Spending Shares: 1989–1997 (percent)

Consumption share	+1.0
Investment share	+0.8
Net export share	+0.4
Government purchases share	**−2.2**

A *big shift in the government purchases share* is assumed to cause the changes in the other shares in this case study.

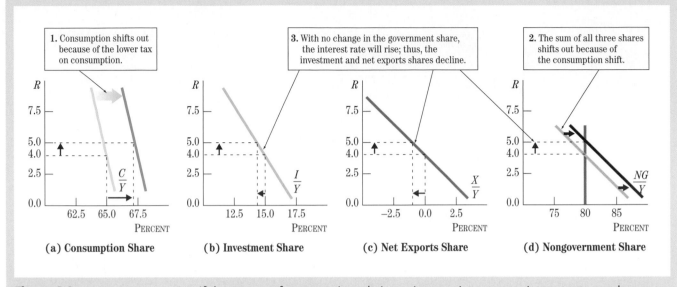

**Figure 6.9
A Shift in the Share of
Consumption**

If the amount of consumption relative to income rises at every interest rate—perhaps because of a tax change that reduces the tax on consumption—the interest rate will rise. Both investment and net exports decline.

effect on the other components of spending, we would draw a horizontal line at a higher interest rate. That would show us that investment, net exports, and consumption would fall as a share of GDP.

Sometimes a decline in investment due to an increase in government purchases is called **crowding out** because investment is "crowded out" by the government purchases. Thus, we have shown that an increase in government purchases as a share of GDP causes a crowding out of investment in the long run. However, because net exports and consumption also fall, the crowding out of investment is not as large as it would otherwise be.

crowding out: the decline in private investment owing to an increase in government purchases.

A Shift in Consumption

The second application of the model involves an increase in the amount people want to consume at every interest rate. This might occur because of an increase in people's wealth, which encourages them to consume more, relative to their income.

The impact of such a shift in the share of consumption is analyzed in Figure 6.9. The relationship between the interest rate and the consumption share shifts out in diagram (a); this causes the sum of investment, consumption, and net export shares to shift out, as shown by the shift in the line in diagram (d).

**Table 6.2
Change in Spending Shares: 1979–1989 (percent)**

Consumption share	**+3.3**
Investment share	−3.1
Net export share	−0.5
Government purchases share	+0.3

A *big shift in the consumption share* is assumed to cause changes in the other shares in this case study.

The result is an increase in the equilibrium interest rate and a decline in the share of investment. However, because the share of net exports also declines, the impact on the share of investment is much less than if net exports had not changed. The action of foreigners reduces substantially the effect of the increased consumption on capital formation.

The overall prediction of the effects of such a shift are very close to what has happened in the United States during the 1980s, as shown in Table 6.2. As the consumption share rose, the investment share and the net exports share fell. (The government purchases share was nearly unchanged.) According to most estimates, the real interest rate was higher in the 1980s than in the 1970s. Thus, the theory of investment put forth in this chapter explains the long-term trends in the shares of spending and interest rates under the assumption that there was a shift in the share of consumption.

REVIEW
- The impact on capital accumulation of a change in government spending can be analyzed by looking at what happens to the interest rate and each component of GDP.

- An increase in the government spending share reduces the share available for nongovernment use by exactly the same amount. This means that interest rates must rise. The rise in interest rates causes investment, consumption, and net exports to fall.

- An upward shift in the share of consumption causes the investment and net export shares to fall and interest rates to rise.

The National Saving Rate

In Chapter 5, we defined national saving (S) as GDP minus consumption minus government purchases, or

$$S = Y - C - G$$

national saving rate: the proportion of GDP that is saved, neither consumed nor spent on government purchases; equals national saving (S) divided by GDP, or S/Y.

The ratio of national saving to GDP, or S/Y, is the **national saving rate.** For example, in 2001, national saving was $1,304 billion and GDP was $10,208 billion, so the national saving rate was $1,304/10,208 = .128$ or 12.8 percent. The spending allocation model has implications for the national saving rate. If we divide each term in the definition of national saving by Y, we can write the national saving rate as 1 minus the shares of consumption and government purchases in GDP. That is,

$$\frac{\text{National}}{\text{saving rate}} = 1 - \frac{\text{consumption}}{\text{share}} - \frac{\text{government}}{\text{purchases share}}$$

or

$$\frac{S}{Y} = 1 - \frac{C}{Y} - \frac{G}{Y}$$

This equation tells us that a change in the economy will affect the national saving rate through its effect on the consumption share and the government purchases share.

Note also that the equations tell us that the national saving rate depends on the interest rate. In particular, the national saving rate is positively related to the interest

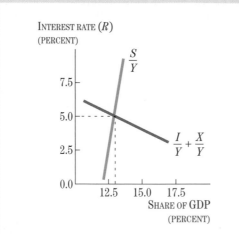

Figure 6.10
Determining the Interest Rate Using the Saving Rate Relationship
The saving rate (green line) depends positively on the interest rate. The sum (purple line) of the investment share and the net export share depends negatively on the interest rate. The equilibrium interest rate is determined at the point where national saving equals investment plus net exports, or the intersection of the two lines.

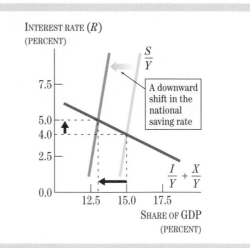

Figure 6.11
The Effect of a Downward Shift in the Saving Rate
The effect is the same as the shift upward in the consumption share illustrated in Figure 6.9. The lower national saving rate raises interest rates and lowers the investment share and the net exports share.

rate because the consumption share is negatively related to the interest rate. In other words, when the interest rate rises, the consumption share falls, implying that the saving rate rises.

Since

$$\frac{C}{Y} + \frac{I}{Y} + \frac{G}{Y} + \frac{X}{Y} = 1$$

we can use the above definition of the national saving rate to write

$$\frac{S}{Y} = \frac{I}{Y} + \frac{X}{Y}$$

or, in other words, the national saving rate equals the investment share plus the net exports share. Both sides of this equation depend on the interest rate, as shown in Figure 6.10. The upward-sloping line in Figure 6.10 shows the national saving rate. An increase in the interest rate causes the saving rate to rise. The downward-sloping line shows the sum of I/Y and X/Y; this sum is negatively related to the interest rate because both the investment share I/Y and the net export share X/Y are negatively related to the interest rate.

At the intersection of the two lines in Figure 6.10, the national saving rate equals the investment share plus the net exports share. The intersection determines the equilibrium interest rate. The interest rate is exactly the same as that in Figure 6.7, which is based on exactly the same relationships.

Now let us look at the same shift in consumption share considered in the previous section, but with a focus on saving. An upward shift in the consumption share is equivalent to a downward shift in the saving rate. Thus, we shift the interest rate–saving rate relationship to the left in Figure 6.11, representing a downshift in the national saving rate. As shown in the figure, this leads to a higher interest rate and lower shares for investment and net exports. Hence the predictions are the same as those of the previous analysis in Figure 6.9.

Conclusion

In this chapter, we have developed a model that determines the equilibrium interest rate and explains how the shares of spending are allocated in the whole economy. The model can be used to analyze the impact of a change in government purchases or a shift in consumption or saving.

The model has introduced an important macroeconomic factor to consider when assessing the appropriate size of government. Private investment is affected by the size of government in the economy. Private investment is greater when government purchases are less.

On the other hand, government spending is needed to provide the roads, education, and legal system that help produce economic growth. But even when government spending does these good things, it reduces the share of GDP available for private investment. To the extent that consumption and net exports also shrink as government purchases increase, the effect on private investment is smaller.

Thus, there is a need for balance between government purchases and private investment. The mix will ultimately be determined in the political debate. This chapter provides some economic analysis, which is useful in that debate.

KEY POINTS

1. Over the long term, consumption, investment, net exports, and government purchases compete for a share of GDP.

2. The four spending shares must sum to 1.

3. Higher interest rates raise the price of consumption and lead to a reduction of consumption as a share of GDP.

4. Higher interest rates also reduce investment.

5. Higher interest rates lower the share of net exports by causing the exchange rate to rise, which reduces exports and raises imports.

6. The equilibrium interest rate is found by equating the sum of the consumption, investment, and net exports shares to the share of GDP available for nongovernment use.

7. A decrease in the share of government purchases will lead to an increase in all the other shares of spending.

8. An increase in the share of government purchases crowds out the investment share in GDP by raising interest rates. Consumption and net export shares also fall, crowding out the investment less severely.

KEY TERMS

consumption share	net exports share	exchange rate	crowding out
investment share	government purchases share	equilibrium interest rate	national saving rate

QUESTIONS FOR REVIEW

1. Why does an increase in the government share in GDP require a decrease in some other share?

2. What is the relationship between consumption and interest rates?

3. Why does investment fall when interest rates rise?

4. Why is there a relationship between the exchange rate and the interest rate?

5. How does the relationship between net exports and the exchange rate tie into the negative relationship between interest rates and net exports?

6. What determines the equilibrium interest rate?

7. What is crowding out?

8. In what sense does the theory in this chapter apply to the long run rather than to short-run economic fluctuations?

PROBLEMS

1. Suppose $C = 700$, $I = 200$, $G = 100$, and $X = 0$.
   a. What is GDP? Calculate each component's share of GDP.
   b. Suppose government spending increases to 150 and GDP does not change. What is government spending's share of GDP now? What is the new nongovernment share?
   c. Without doing any calculations, explain in general terms what happens to C/Y, X/Y, and I/Y after the government spending increase in (b). Describe the mechanism by which each of these changes happens.

2. Using the diagram at the bottom of the page, find the equilibrium interest rate when the government share is 20 percent. What is the investment share? Show what happens to all the variables if there is an upward shift in the investment relation because of a new tax policy that encourages investment.

3. Describe the long-run impact of a decline in defense spending by 1 percent of GDP on interest rates and on consumption, investment, and net exports as a share of GDP. Consider two different cases:
   a. No other changes in policy accompany the defense cut.
   b. The funds saved from the defense cut are used to increase government expenditures on roads and bridges.

4. a. As government's share in GDP decreases, the non-government share increases. Depict this in a diagram. What happens to interest rates?
   b. As interest rates fall, what change is there in the exchange rate? What happens to net exports in this case? Does this match your earlier picture?
   c. Suppose net exports are very sensitive to changes in interest rates. Does that mean a relatively big or a relatively small change in net exports?

5. Many people believe that the U.S. saving rate is too low. Suppose all private citizens save at a higher rate. Show what happens in this case in the saving and investment diagram, where the S/Y curve shifts. Now show the same situation in the C/Y, I/Y, and X/Y diagrams. Which curve shifts? If government's share in GDP doesn't change, then what must happen to interest rates? Explain how this affects X/Y.

Problem 2

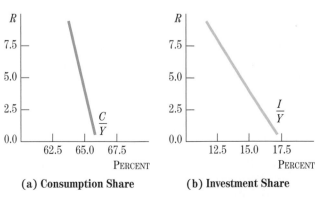

(a) Consumption Share

(b) Investment Share

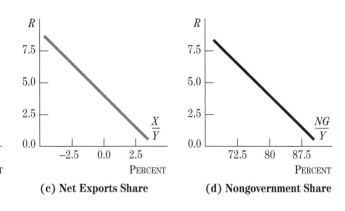

(c) Net Exports Share

(d) Nongovernment Share

6. Draw two sets of diagrams like Figure 6.7 to depict two situations. In one set, draw investment and net exports as very sensitive to interest rates—that is, the I/Y and X/Y curves are very flat. In the other set, draw investment and net exports as insensitive to interest rates—that is, the I/Y and X/Y curves are nearly vertical. For the same increase in government's share in GDP, in which set of diagrams will interest rates rise more? Why?

7. The Tax Reform Act of 1986 eliminated the investment tax credit, thus increasing investment costs. Assuming that the government share of GDP is fixed, what effect should this have had on the interest rate and the shares of consumption and net exports in GDP?

8. Suppose that there is a leftward shift in the C/Y line due to higher consumption taxes, but at the same time, the government increases its share of GDP to maintain the same interest rates. Describe graphically how this affects each of the shares of GDP. If the investment share is the only thing that affects growth in this system, what will happen to growth as a result of this government policy?

9. Suppose the following equations describe the relationship between shares of spending in GDP (Y) and the interest rate (R), measured in decimal fractions (that is, $R = .05$ means that the interest rate is 5 percent).

$$\frac{C}{Y} = .7 - .2(R - .05)$$

$$\frac{I}{Y} = .2 - .8(R - .05)$$

$$\frac{X}{Y} = 0 - .95(R - .05)$$

$$\frac{G}{Y} = .2$$

   a. Use algebra to determine the values of the interest rate and the shares of spending in GDP.
   b. Do the calculations again for a government share of 17 percent rather than 20 percent (that is, $G/Y = .17$).

10. Graph the relationships defined in problem 9a to scale in a four-part diagram like Figure 6.6. Use the diagram to analyze each of the following situations:
   a. Suppose there is an increase in the foreign demand for U.S. goods that changes the coefficient in the net exports share equation from 0 to .05. What happens to the interest rate and the consumption, investment, net exports, and government purchases shares in the United States?
   b. Determine how an increase in taxes that reduces the coefficient in the consumption share equation from .7 to .68 would affect the interest rate and the consumption, investment, net exports, and government purchases shares.
   c. Suppose firms are willing to invest 30 percent rather than 20 percent of GDP at an interest rate of 5 percent. How would this affect the interest rate and the shares of spending in GDP?

11. Derive and draw the national saving rate—interest rate relation (as in Figure 6.10) from the information on consumption, government spending, and net exports used in problem 9. In the same graph, draw investment plus net exports as a share of GDP. Determine the equilibrium level of saving and the interest rate using this graph.

CHAPTER 7

Unemployment and Employment

Jennifer, a 21-year-old college senior, was worried about her prospects of finding a job after graduating from college in 2002 because she had learned that in the previous year, the unemployment rate for young women in her age group was 9 percent. However, Jennifer was somewhat comforted by the thought that among female college graduates like herself, the unemployment rate was only 2.3 percent. Jennifer was also interested in living and working in Spain for a few years to fully develop the Spanish language skills she had acquired in college. However, she had learned that the unemployment rate for young female workers in Spain was 42 percent, almost five times that in the United States. She was particularly puzzled by this high unemployment rate because she had read that the Spanish economy was doing well, unlike the U.S. economy, which she knew was in recession.

Unemployment is the macroeconomic variable that affects people most personally. When the economy is booming and unemployment is low, it is easier for individuals to find jobs that are satisfying to them and that also pay well. In contrast, when the economy is in recession and unemployment is high, jobs are harder to find, and people will settle for jobs that do not closely match their skills and don't pay very much money. However, as Jennifer's story illustrates, unemployment rates often fluctuate for reasons that are unrelated to the state of the economy. Unemployment rates can, and do, vary among groups of individuals of different gender, age, race, and education. They also vary dramatically across countries, even to the extent that economies that are in recession may have lower unemployment rates than economies that are booming.

Why do unemployment rates differ so much among countries? Is it because of differences in education levels? Is it because of differences in attitudes toward work? Or is it because of differences in the economic policies implemented by the different countries' governments? This chapter will examine the nature and causes of unemployment and teach you how to use a simple model that can answer these questions and more. When you study the concepts in this chapter, keep in mind that unemployment has painful economic consequences. For those who experience it, there are the obvious hardships of income loss, loss of self-esteem, and an increasing toll on family life, along with the failure of young people who live in a world of persistent unemployment to acquire job skills that will help them become productive citizens in the future. Beyond these individual and family hardships, there are macroeconomic consequences of unemployment as well. When more workers are unemployed, the production of goods and services is less than it would be if more of those workers were employed. In other words, the economy is underutilizing its productive resources. It is essential for aspiring macroeconomists to learn more about unemployment and how to reduce it.

Unemployment and Other Labor Market Indicators

In this section, we show how unemployment is defined and measured, and we discuss the various causes of unemployment.

Cyclical, Frictional, and Structural Unemployment

natural unemployment rate: the unemployment rate that exists when there is neither a recession nor a boom and real GDP is equal to potential GDP.

cyclical unemployment: unemployment due to a recession, when the rate of unemployment is above the natural rate of unemployment.

frictional unemployment: unemployment arising from normal turnover in the labor market, such as when people change occupations or locations, or are new entrants.

structural unemployment: unemployment due to structural problems such as poor skills, longer-term changes in demand, or insufficient work incentives.

Recall from Chapter 4 that the unemployment rate rises when the economy goes into a recession and falls when the economy expands. For example, as shown in Figure 7.1, the unemployment rate fell in the 1980s as the economy expanded rapidly and then rose when the economy went into a recession in 1990 and 1991. Then the unemployment rate declined in the 1990s expansion.

Economists use the term **natural unemployment rate** to refer to the unemployment rate that exists when the economy is not in a recession or a boom and real GDP is equal to potential GDP. The increase in unemployment above the natural rate during recessions is called **cyclical unemployment** because it is related to the short-term cyclical fluctuations in the economy. For example, the increase in the unemployment rate from 2001 to 2002 was cyclical. The natural unemployment rate is caused by a combination of **frictional unemployment** and **structural unemployment.** Frictional unemployment occurs when new workers enter the labor force and must look for work, or when workers change jobs for one reason or another and need some time to find another job. Most frictional unemployment is short-lived. In contrast, some workers are unemployed for a long time, six months or more; they may have trouble finding work because they have insufficient skills or because their skills are no longer in demand as a result of a technological change or a shift in people's tastes toward new products. Such unemployment is called structural

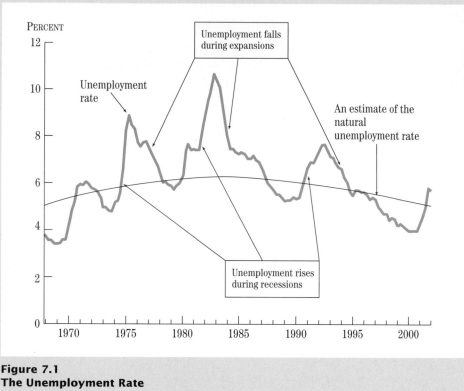

Figure 7.1
The Unemployment Rate
The unemployment rate fluctuates around the natural unemployment rate, rising during recessions and falling when the economy grows rapidly during expansions.

unemployment. The amount of frictional unemployment and structural unemployment in the economy is not constant, so the natural unemployment rate changes over time. But such changes are gradual and are not related to short-term economic fluctuations.

An estimate of the natural unemployment rate is shown in Figure 7.1. The natural rate of unemployment increased in the 1970s. One possible reason for the increase was the influx of young baby boom workers into the labor force in the 1970s. Young people tend to have higher unemployment rates than older people. The natural unemployment rate is now declining again as the labor force ages. It is important to remember that the natural unemployment rate is not a constant and that economists do not know its value precisely.

When economists use the term *natural* unemployment rate, they do not mean to say that this is "okay" or "just fine," as when your doctor tells you that having a higher temperature in the evening than in the morning is "natural." They simply mean that whenever the operation of the overall macroeconomy is close to normal in the sense that real GDP is near potential GDP, the unemployment rate hovers around this natural rate.

How Is Unemployment Measured?

To understand what the data on unemployment mean, one must understand how unemployment is measured. Each month, the U.S. Census Bureau surveys a sample

Current Population Survey: a monthly survey of a sample of U.S. households done by the U.S. Census Bureau; it measures employment, unemployment, the labor force, and other characteristics of the U.S. population.

labor force: all those who are either employed or unemployed.

working-age population: persons over 16 years of age who are not in an institution such as a jail or hospital.

of about 60,000 households in the United States. This survey is called the **Current Population Survey.** By asking the people in the survey a number of questions, the Census Bureau determines whether each person 16 years of age or over is employed or unemployed. The **labor force** consists of all people 16 years of age and over who are either employed or unemployed.

■ **Who Is Employed and Who Is Unemployed?** To be counted as unemployed, a person must be looking for work, but not have a job. To be counted as employed, a person must have a job, either a job outside the home—as in the case of a teaching job at a high school or a welding job at a factory—or a *paid* job inside the home—as in the case of a freelance editor or a telemarketer who works for pay at home. A person who has an *unpaid* job at home—for example, caring for children or working on the house—is not counted as employed. If a person is not counted as either unemployed or employed, then the person is not in the labor force. For example, a person who is working at home without pay and who is not looking for a paid job is considered not in the labor force.

Figure 7.2 illustrates the definitions of employment, unemployment, and the labor force. Using January 2002 as an example, it shows that out of a **working-age population** of 212.8 million, there were 133.4 million employed and 7.9 million unemployed; the remaining 71.5 million were of working age but were not in the labor force.

■ **The Labor Force and Discouraged Workers.** It is difficult to judge who should be counted as being in the labor force and who should not be counted. For example, consider two retired people. One decided to retire at age 65 and is now enjoying retirement in Florida. The other was laid off from a job at age 55 and, after looking for a job for two years, got discouraged and stopped looking, feeling forced into retirement. You may feel that the second person, but not the first, should be counted as unemployed. However, according to the official statistics, neither is unemployed; they are not in the labor force because they are not looking for work. In general, workers, such as the second retired worker, who have left the labor force after not being able to find a job are called *discouraged workers.*

Defining and measuring the labor force is the most difficult part of measuring the amount of unemployment. A recent change in the way the questions in the Current Population Survey were phrased revealed that many women who were working at home without pay were actually looking for a paid job; as a result of the change in the question, these women are now counted as unemployed rather than as out of the labor force.

■ **Part-Time Work.** A person is counted as employed in the Current Population Survey if he or she has worked at all during the week of the survey. Thus, part-time workers are counted as employed. The official definition of a *part-time worker* is one who works between 1 and 34 hours per week. About 11 percent of U.S. workers are employed part time.

There is a big difference between the percentage of men who work part time and the percentage of women who work part time. About 20 percent of women work part time, while only about 7 percent of men work part time. Women give personal choice rather than unavailability of full-time jobs as a reason for part-time work more frequently than men do. About 29 percent of employed women who have children under 6 work part time.

Because of part-time work, the average number of hours of work per worker each week is about 34 hours, less than the typical 40 hours a week.

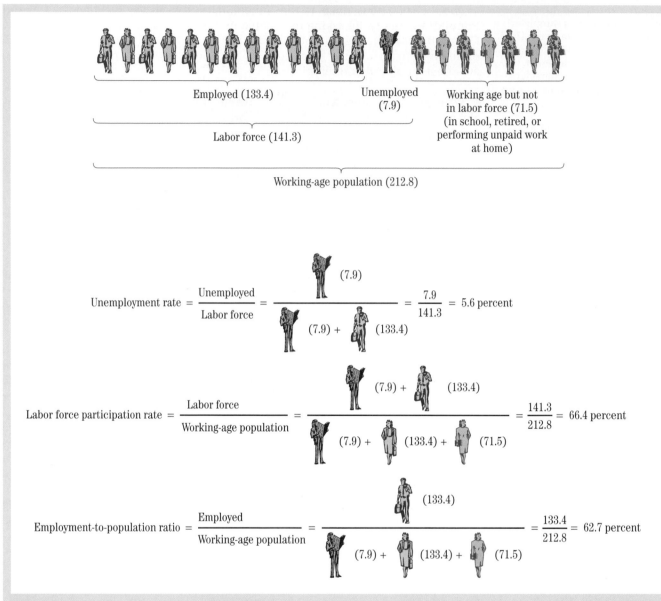

Figure 7.2
How to Find Labor Market Indicators

As shown at the top of this diagram, the working-age (16 years of age and over) population is divided into three groups: employed, unemployed, and not in the labor force. Three key labor market indicators are then computed from these categories. For example, the unemployment rate is the number of people unemployed divided by the number of people in the labor force. (The numbers in parentheses are in millions and are the statistics for January 2002.)

unemployment rate: the percentage of the labor force that is unemployed. (Ch. 4)

labor force participation rate: the ratio (usually expressed as a percentage) of people in the labor force to the working-age population.

Comparing Three Key Indicators

Now let us examine the three key indicators of conditions in the labor market. These are

1. The *unemployment rate,* the percentage of the labor force that is unemployed

2. The **labor force participation rate,** the ratio of people in the labor force to the working-age population

3. The **employment-to-population ratio,** the ratio of employed workers to the working-age population

Figure 7.2 gives an example of how each indicator is calculated. Both the unemployment rate and the labor force participation rate depend on the labor force, and therefore have the same measurement difficulties that the labor force does. Only the employment-to-population ratio does not depend on the labor force.

The labor force participation rate and the employment-to-population ratio have both had important longer-term upward trends. For example, the employment-to-population ratio has increased in the last 25 years from about 57 percent in 1976 to about 63 percent in 2002. The employment-to-population ratio is almost as high now as it has been at any previous time in U.S. history. In this sense, the U.S. economy is creating more jobs now than at any other time in its history. How does one explain this?

The rising percentage of women who are employed is a major factor, as shown in Figure 7.3. This increase is mainly due to more women entering the labor force, a trend that has been going on since the 1950s. In the early 1950s, about 32 percent of women were in the labor force, but now about 60 percent are. Possible explanations for this trend include reduced discrimination, increased opportunities and pay for women, the favorable experience of many women working for pay during World War II, and the women's movement, which emphasized the attractiveness of paid work outside the home.

Aggregate Hours of Labor Input

As we have seen, some people work part time. Others work full time; some work overtime. For these reasons, the number of people employed is not a good measure of the labor input to production in the economy. For example, consider two typists who both work half time; one works 4 hours in the morning, and the other works 4 hours in the afternoon, both 5 days a week. Together they work as much as one full-time typist; to say that the labor input of these two typists is twice as much as the labor input of one full-time typist would be an obvious mistake. Rather, their combined labor input is the same as that of one full-time typist: 40 hours a week.

**Figure 7.3
Employment-to-Population
Ratio for Men, Women, and
Everyone**
The percentage of working-age
women who are employed has
increased steadily since the 1950s.
The percentage of working-age
men who are employed
declined until the late 1970s,
when it leveled off and started
increasing.

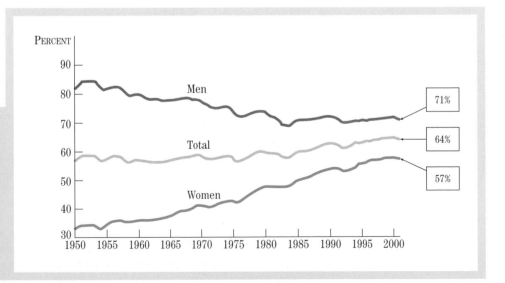

aggregate hours: the total number of hours worked by all workers in the economy in a given period of time.

This example shows why economists consider the number of hours people work rather than the number of people who work when they measure labor input to production, whether it is typists at a firm or workers in the whole economy. Thus, the most comprehensive measure of labor input to the production of real GDP is the total number of hours worked by all workers, or **aggregate hours.** The number of aggregate hours of labor input depends on the number of hours of work for each person and the number of people working.

The growth of aggregate labor hours in the United States is slowing down. It grew by about 1.7 percent per year in the 1970s and 1980s and is expected to grow by about 1.2 percent per year in the next ten years. The main reason for this slowdown is that the growth of the working-age population is slowing down.

REVIEW

- The unemployment rate in the United States fluctuates cyclically. The unemployment rate in the absence of cyclical increases or decreases is called the natural unemployment rate.

- Unemployment and employment in the United States are measured by the Current Population Survey.

- To be counted as unemployed, you have to be looking for work.

- The employment-to-population ratio has risen in the 1980s and 1990s. More women have been entering the labor force since the early 1950s.

- Aggregate hours is the most comprehensive measure of labor input.

The Nature of Unemployment

Having examined the aggregate data, let us now look at the circumstances of people who are unemployed. There are many reasons for people to become unemployed, and people's experiences with unemployment vary widely.

Reasons People Are Unemployed

We can divide up the many reasons people become unemployed into four broad categories. People are unemployed because they have either lost their previous job (*job losers*), quit their previous job (*job leavers*), entered the labor force to look for work for the first time (*new entrants*), or re-entered the labor force after being out of it for a while (*re-entrants*). Figure 7.4 shows how the 5.5 percent unemployment rate in January 2002 was divided into four categories.

■ **Job Losers.** Among the people who lost their jobs in a typical recent year was a vice president of a large bank in Chicago. When the vice president's financial services marketing department was eliminated, she lost her job. After three months of unemployment, which were spent searching for work and waiting for responses to her letters and telephone calls, the former vice president took a freelance job, using her banking expertise to advise clients. Within a year, she was making three times her former salary.

The vice president's unemployment experience, although surely trying for her at the time, had a happy ending. In fact, you might say that the labor market worked pretty well. At least judging by her salary, she is more productive in her new job. Although one job was destroyed, another one—better, in this case—was created.

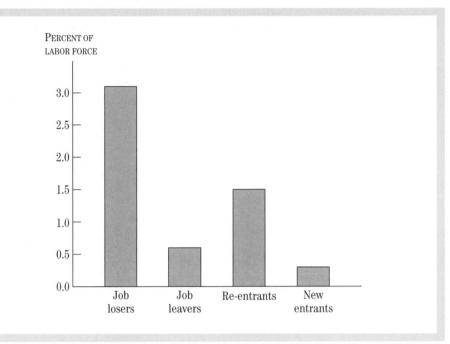

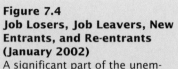

Figure 7.4
Job Losers, Job Leavers, New Entrants, and Re-entrants (January 2002)
A significant part of the unemployment rate consists of people who lost their jobs. The rest consists of people who left their jobs to look for another job or who have just entered or re-entered the labor force.

This transition from one job to another is part of the dynamism of any free market economy. The economist Joseph Schumpeter called this dynamism *creative destruction,* referring to the loss of whole business firms as well as jobs when new ideas and techniques replace the old. Creative destruction means that something better is created as something else is destroyed. In this case, a better job was created when another job was destroyed. On average, about 5 percent of jobs are destroyed each year by plant closings, bankruptcies, or downsizing of firms. In 2000, that amounted to about 7 million jobs destroyed. On balance, for an economy with growing employment, more jobs are created than are destroyed. For example, in January 2000, enough jobs were created that on balance, employment increased by nearly 400,000 jobs. But unemployment, at least part of it, is a by-product of these changes.

Many people who lose their jobs are not as lucky as the woman in our story. Among the unemployed in recent years were middle-aged workers let go by "dot-com" firms after several years of employment. Finding a comparable job was difficult for such workers because most other such firms were also in financial difficulties, laying off workers instead of hiring them. The loss of such a job not only has disastrous effects on income, but can also have psychological effects. It may mean that a worker's children cannot go to college, or that the worker must sell his or her house. Unemployment compensation provides some relief—perhaps about $200 a week until it runs out. In many cases, though, this is well below what these workers were earning. Until they find a new job, they are obviously part of the millions of unemployed. Some may wait until a comparable job comes along; others may accept a lower-paying job. For example, one laid-off software programmer took a job as a lab instructor for one-fourth the pay.

People may lose their jobs even when the economy is not in a recession. On average, about half of all unemployed workers are unemployed because they lost their jobs for one reason or another.

Each month—usually on the first Friday of the month—the U.S. Department of Labor releases information about employment and unemployment in the previous month. The following is excerpted from the news release issued by the Bureau of Labor Statistics. You should be able to find the terms discussed in this article in the text.

Note that the unemployment rate rose from 5.7 percent in March 2002 to 6.0 percent in April 2002. How does this compare with the unemployment rate in 1991 or in 1982? (See Figure 7.1.)

Employment Situation Summary

http://www.bls.gov/cps/

THE EMPLOYMENT SITUATION: APRIL 2002

The unemployment rate rose to 6.0 percent in April, and payroll employment was little changed (+43,000), the Bureau of Labor Statistics of the U.S. Department of Labor reported today. Employment rose in the services industry but fell in construction. Job losses in manufacturing continued to moderate.

Unemployment (Household Survey Data)

Shows the increase in the unemployment rate during the recession

In April, the number of unemployed persons rose by 483,000 to 8.6 million, after seasonal adjustment. The unemployment rate increased by 0.3 percentage point to 6.0 percent. Since its recent low of 3.9 percent in October 2000, the jobless rate has increased by 2.1 percentage points, and the number of unemployed persons has risen by 3.1 million.

Illustrates how unemployment rates vary by race and gender

The unemployment rate for adult women rose by 0.4 percentage point over the month, and the rate for adult men edged up. Both rates were 5.4 percent in April. The jobless rate for whites increased by 0.3 percentage point to 5.3 percent. The jobless rates of the other major worker groups—teenagers (16.8 percent), blacks (11.2 percent), and Hispanics (7.9 percent)—showed little change in April.

Total Employment and the Labor Force (Household Survey Data)

Over the month, the civilian labor force rose by 565,000 to 142.6 million, after seasonal adjustment. The labor force participation rate also increased over the month to 66.8 percent. With the exception of a few large monthly fluctuations, the participation rate has held close to its current level since last spring. Both the level of employment (134.0 million) and the employment-population ratio (62.8 percent) were little changed in April.

About 7.3 million persons (not seasonally adjusted) held more than one job in April. These multiple jobholders represented 5.4 percent of the total employed—the same proportion as a year earlier.

Persons Not in the Labor Force (Household Survey Data)

About 1.4 million persons (not seasonally adjusted) were marginally attached to the labor force in April, up from 1.1 million a year earlier. These individuals reported that they wanted and were available for work and had looked for a job sometime in the prior 12 months. They were not counted as unemployed, however, because they had not actively searched for work in the 4 weeks preceding the survey. The number of discouraged workers was 317,000 in April, little changed from a year earlier. Discouraged workers, a subset of the marginally attached, were not currently looking for work specifically because they believed no jobs were available for them.

Reasons People Are Unemployed
People are unemployed for different reasons: some lost their job and are looking for another job (left), others quit their previous job and are still looking for a new job (middle), and still others just entered or re-entered the labor force and are unemployed while looking for work (right).

job vacancies: positions that firms are trying to fill, but for which they have yet to find suitable workers.

The economy is always in a state of flux, with some firms going out of business or shrinking and other firms starting up or expanding. Tastes change, new discoveries are made, and competition improves productivity and changes the relative fortune of firms and workers.

Job vacancies are the jobs firms are trying to fill. Job vacancies and unemployment exist simultaneously. Unfortunately, many job vacancies require different skills from those of unemployed workers, are in another part of the country, or are at lower wages than these workers' former salaries. Workers skilled at one job may be unemployed while firms cannot find workers with other skills.

The number of unemployed workers who have lost their jobs increases during recessions. It is more difficult to find a new job in a recession, when fewer firms are hiring.

■ **Job Leavers.** On average, American workers change jobs every three or four years. Many of these job changes occur when people are young: Young workers are finding out what they are good at or what they enjoy or are rapidly accumulating skills that give them greater opportunities. A small part of unemployment—less than one-fourth—consists of people who quit their previous job to look for another job. While they are looking for work, they are counted as unemployed.

There is very little increase in unemployment due to quits in recessions. Why? Two opposing forces net out to produce little change. In a recession, when unemployment is high, fewer workers quit their jobs because they fear being unemployed for a long period of time. This reduces quit unemployment; however, the lower number of job vacancies makes finding a job more difficult and raises unemployment.

■ **New Entrants and Re-entrants.** Figure 7.4 also shows that a large number of the unemployed workers have just entered the work force. If you do not have a job lined up before you graduate, there is a good chance that you will be unemployed for a period of time while you look for work following graduation. In fact, there is a huge increase in unemployment each June as millions of students enter the labor force for the first time. This is called *seasonal unemployment* because it occurs each graduation "season." In contrast, unemployment is relatively low around the holiday season, when many businesses hire extra employees. Government statisticians smooth

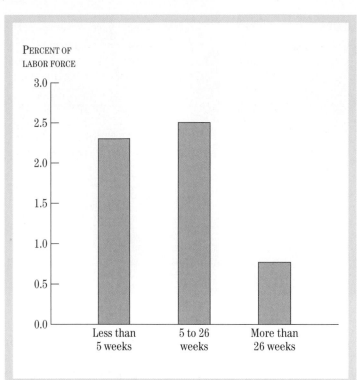

Figure 7.5
Unemployment by Duration (April 2002)
The overall unemployment rate was 6.0 percent in April 2002. A small fraction of this unemployment was long term—more than 26 weeks. Long-term unemployment increases during recessions.

out this seasonal unemployment to help them see other trends in unemployment, so the newspaper reports on the unemployment rate rarely mention this phenomenon.

Some unemployed workers are re-entering the labor force. For example, a young person may decide to go back to school and then re-enter the labor force afterward. Others might choose to drop out of the labor force for several years to take care of small children at home—a job that is not counted in the unemployment statistics.

Some new entrants to the labor force find it very difficult to find a job. They remain unemployed for long periods of time. In fact, although the hardships of people who lose their jobs are severe, the hardships for many young people who seem to be endlessly looking for work are also severe.

The Duration of Unemployment

The hardships associated with unemployment depend on its duration. Figure 7.5 shows how the unemployment rate divides up according to how long the unemployed workers have been unemployed. A significant fraction of unemployment is very short term. A market economy with millions of people exercising free choice could not possibly function without some very short term unemployment as people changed jobs or looked for new opportunities.

About one-eighth of unemployed workers are unemployed for more than six months—the truly long-term unemployed. Although the number of short-term unemployed does not vary much over the business cycle, the number of long-term unemployed increases dramatically in recessions.

Table 7.1
Unemployment Rates for Different Demographic Groups (percent of labor force for each group)

| | Unemployment Rates | |
	1991	*2000*
All persons	6.9	4.0
All females	6.5	4.1
All males	7.2	3.9
All Whites	6.1	3.5
All Blacks	12.5	7.6
All Hispanics	10.1	5.7
All females, 19 years and older	5.7	3.6
All males, 19 years and older	6.4	3.3
All teens, 16–19	19.0	12.6
Black male teens, 16–19	36.3	24.0
Black female teens, 16–19	36.0	23.8

Source: U.S. Department of Labor.

Unemployment for Different Groups

Regardless of how one interprets the numbers, certain groups of workers experience very long spells of unemployment and suffer great hardships as a result of the difficulty they have in finding work. Table 7.1 shows the unemployment rates for several different demographic groups in the United States in two time periods: 1991, when the economy was in recession, and early 2000, when the economy was much stronger.

Unemployment is lowest for adult men and women. But unemployment is very high for teenagers. To some extent this is due to more frequent job changes and the period of time required to find work after graduating from school. But many teenagers who are looking for work have dropped out of school and therefore are unskilled and have little or no experience. Their unemployment rates are extremely high, especially those for young minorities. The unemployment rate for black teenagers is over 20 percent. Thus, even when there is good news about the overall unemployment rate, the news may remain bleak for those with low skills and little experience. The overall unemployment rate does not capture the long-term hardships experienced by certain groups.

REVIEW

- People become unemployed when they lose their job, quit their job, or decide to enter or re-enter the labor force to look for a job. In a market economy, job loss occurs simultaneously with job creation.

- Quitting a job is the least likely reason for people to be unemployed. Losing a job and looking for work after some time out of the labor force are more likely reasons to be unemployed.

- Many unemployed people have been unemployed for a very short period of time. This frictional unemployment is probably not very harmful and is a necessary part of any market economy.

- On average, about one-eighth of unemployed people have been unemployed for six months or more. Long-term unemployment increases dramatically in recessions.

- Teenagers and minorities in the United States have very high unemployment rates, even in boom years.

Explaining Unemployment and Employment Trends

A good explanation of unemployment and employment trends is the supply and demand model of Chapter 3.

Labor Demand and Labor Supply

labor demand curve: a downward-sloping relationship showing the quantity of labor firms are willing to hire at each wage.

labor supply curve: the relationship showing the quantity of labor workers are willing to supply at each wage.

Figure 7.6 shows a labor demand curve and a labor supply curve. On the vertical axis is the price of labor (wage), and on the horizontal axis is the quantity of labor supplied or demanded. In a labor market, the **labor demand curve** describes the behavior of firms, indicating how much labor they would demand at a given wage. The **labor supply curve** describes the behavior of workers, showing how much labor they would supply at a given wage. The *wage*, usually measured in dollars per hour of work, is the price of labor. To explain employment in the whole economy, it is best to

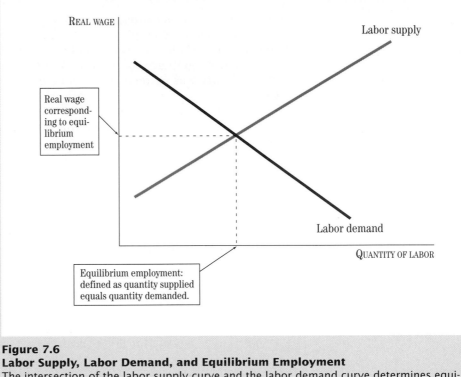

Figure 7.6
Labor Supply, Labor Demand, and Equilibrium Employment
The intersection of the labor supply curve and the labor demand curve determines equilibrium employment and the real wage.

real wage: the wage or price of labor adjusted for inflation; in contrast, the nominal wage has not been adjusted for inflation.

think of the wage relative to the average price of goods. In other words, the wage on the vertical axis is the **real wage,** which we define as

$$\text{Real wage} = \frac{\text{wage}}{\text{price level}}$$

Firms consider the wages they must pay their workers in comparison with the price of the product they sell. The workers consider the wage in comparison with the price of goods they buy. Thus, in the whole economy, it is the real wage that affects the quantity of labor supplied and demanded.

The labor demand curve slopes downward because the higher the real wage, the less labor firms demand. A lower real wage gives firms an incentive to hire more workers.

The labor supply curve slopes upward, showing that the higher the wage, the more labor workers are willing to supply. A higher real wage gives workers more incentive to work or to work longer hours.

As in any market, we would predict that the amount of labor traded—the number of workers employed—should be at the intersection of the labor demand curve and the labor supply curve, as shown in Figure 7.6. The intersection also determines the equilibrium real wage that brings the quantity supplied into equality with the quantity demanded.

Explaining Employment Trends

Our review of employment trends in the United States in recent decades showed that the employment-to-population ratio has been increasing. The labor supply and demand analysis provides an explanation for this increase.

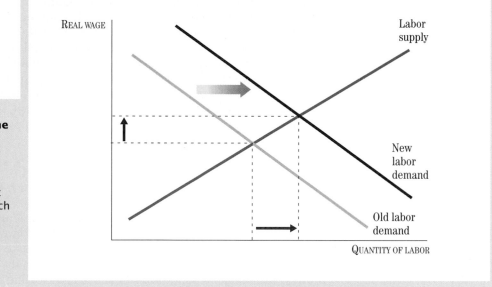

Figure 7.7
Explaining the Increase in the Employment-to-Population Ratio
One explanation for the rise in the employment-to-population ratio in recent decades is a shift in the labor demand curve, which would raise both the real wage and employment. For this purpose, interpret the horizontal axis as employment relative to the population.

Throughout the post–World War II period, real wages have been rising. Thus, we have a combination of an increased real wage and an increased proportion of the population working. This pattern is consistent with a shift in the labor demand curve and movement along the labor supply curve, as shown in Figure 7.7.

As described by the upward-sloping supply curve, the higher wages could be attracting more people into the work force. In fact, as wages have increased, there has been an especially large increase in the percentage of women in the work force. But what could have caused this movement along the supply curve? And why should it have been especially strong for women?

One possibility is that the growth of the service industries—medical, legal, retail trade, telecommunications, transportation—caused an especially large increase in the demand for labor. Economists have found that the labor supply of women is more sensitive to changes in the wage than the labor supply of men is. Thus, the increase in labor demand in service industries could explain the especially large rise in the employment-to-population ratio for women as well as the increase in the real wage.

Although labor supply and demand analysis can explain this phenomenon, other factors also may have played a role, such as laws prohibiting discrimination and the women's movement. The point here is to show that the supply and demand model fits the facts.

Many other employment trends can be explained by labor supply and labor demand analysis. The reduction in the labor force participation of older men because of earlier retirement, for example, can be explained by the increased retirement pay from private pensions and from social security, through which the government supports the elderly. Higher retirement payments make retirement more attractive compared to work and thus reduce labor supply.

Why Is the Unemployment Rate Always Greater Than Zero?

Despite its usefulness in explaining employment trends, the supply and demand model must be modified if it is to explain unemployment. Having read about unemployment in this chapter, do you see something wrong with the picture in

Figure 7.6? It seems inconsistent with the discussion of unemployment. With the quantity of labor supplied equal to the quantity of labor demanded, as in Figure 7.6, there seems to be no unemployment. The intersection of the supply and demand curves seems to predict a market situation that is contrary to the facts. Hence, in order to use the basic supply and demand analysis to explain why unemployment is greater than zero in the real world, we need to modify the story.

Economists have developed two different explanations that adapt the standard labor supply and demand analysis to account for unemployment. Though quite different, the explanations are complementary. In fact, it is essential for us to use both simultaneously if we are to understand unemployment. We will refer to the two explanations as **job rationing** and **job search.**

job rationing: a reason for unemployment in which the quantity of labor supplied is greater than the quantity demanded because the real wage is too high.

job search: a reason for unemployment in which uncertainty in the labor market and workers' limited information requires people to spend time searching for a job.

■ **Job Rationing.** The job-rationing story has two parts. One is an assumption that *the wage is higher than what would equate the quantity supplied with the quantity demanded.* There are several reasons why this might be the case, but first consider the consequences for the labor supply and demand diagram. Figure 7.8 shows the same labor supply and demand curves as Figure 7.6. However, in Figure 7.8, the wage is higher than the wage that would equate the quantity of labor supplied with the quantity of labor demanded. At this wage, the number of workers demanded by firms is smaller than the number of workers willing to supply their labor.

The other part of the job-rationing story tells us how to determine the number of workers who are unemployed. This part of the story assumes that the number of workers employed equals the number of workers demanded by business firms. When the wage is too high, firms hire a smaller number of workers, and workers supply whatever the firms demand. Figure 7.8 shows the resulting amount of employment at the given wage as point *A* on the labor demand curve. With employment equal to the number of workers demanded, we see that the number of workers willing to supply their labor is greater than the number of workers employed; the excess supply therefore results in unemployment. In the diagram, the amount of unemployment is measured in the horizontal direction.

Figure 7.8
Excess Supply of Labor and Unemployment
The supply and demand curves are exactly as in Figure 7.6. Here, however, the real wage is too high to bring the quantity supplied into equality with the quantity demanded. The number of workers employed is given by point *A* on the demand curve, where the real wage is above the equilibrium wage. At this higher real wage, the quantity supplied is greater than the quantity demanded—a situation we can think of as unemployment.

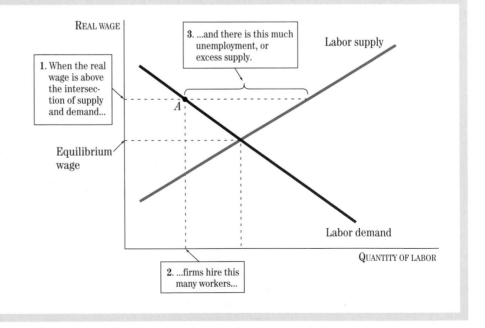

This is a situation in which workers would be willing to take a job at the wage that firms are paying, but there are not enough job offers at that wage. In effect, the available jobs are rationed—for example, by a first-come-first-served rule or by seniority. It is as if, when enough workers have been hired, the firms close their hiring offices, and the remaining workers stay unemployed. If the wage were lower, then the firms would hire more workers, but the wage is not lower.

In most markets, a situation of excess supply brings about a reduction in the price—in this case, the wage. Thus, if this explanation of unemployment is to work in practice, there has to be a force at work that prevents the wage from falling. If the theory is to be helpful in explaining unemployment, then the force has to be permanently at work, not just in a recession. Why doesn't the wage fall when there is an excess supply of workers?

There are three explanations why the wage might be always too high to bring the quantity of labor demanded into balance with the quantity of labor supplied.

minimum wage: a wage per hour below which it is illegal to pay workers. (Ch. 3)

1. *Minimum wages.* Most countries have a legal *minimum wage,* or lowest possible wage, that employers can pay their employees. In the United States, in 2000 the minimum wage was $5.15 per hour and legislation had been proposed to raise it to around $6.00. A minimum wage can cause unemployment to be higher than it otherwise would be, as shown on the diagram in Figure 7.8: Employers would move down and to the right along their labor demand curve and hire more workers if the wage were lower.

    One of the reasons teenage unemployment is high (as shown in Table 7.1) may be related to the minimum wage. Because many teenagers are unskilled, the wage firms would be willing to pay them is low. A minimum wage, therefore, may price them out of the market and cause them to be unemployed.

insider: a person who already works for a firm and has some influence over wage and hiring policy.

outsider: someone who is not working for a particular firm, making it difficult for him or her to get a job with that firm even though he or she is willing to work for a lower wage.

2. *Insiders versus outsiders.* Sometimes groups of workers—**insiders,** who have jobs—can prevent the wage from declining. If these workers have developed skills unique to the job, or if there is legislation preventing their firing without significant legal costs, then they have some power to keep wages up. Labor unions may help them keep the wage higher than it would otherwise be. One consequence of the higher wage is to prevent the firm from hiring unemployed workers—the **outsiders**—who would be willing to work at a lower wage. This is a common explanation for the very high unemployment in Europe, and the theory has been developed and applied to Europe by Swedish economist Assar Lindbeck and British economist Dennis Snower.

efficiency wage: a wage, higher than that which would equate quantity supplied and quantity demanded, set by employers in order to increase worker efficiency—for example, by decreasing shirking by workers.

3. *Efficiency wages.* Firms may choose to pay workers an **efficiency wage**—an extra amount to encourage them to be more efficient. There are many reasons why workers' efficiency or productivity might increase with the wage. Turnover will be lower with a higher wage because there is less reason for workers to look for another job: They are unlikely to find a position paying more than their current wage. Lower turnover means lower training costs. Moreover, workers might not shirk as much with a higher wage. This is particularly important to the firm when jobs are difficult to monitor. With efficiency wages, workers who are working are paid more than the wage that equates the quantity supplied with the quantity demanded. When workers are paid efficiency wages, unemployment will be greater than zero.

■ **Job Search.**   We now turn to the second explanation that modifies the standard labor supply and demand analysis. The labor market is constantly in a state of flux, with jobs being created and destroyed and people moving from one job to another. The demand for one type of work falls, and the demand for another type of work increases. Labor supply curves also shift.

In other words, the labor market is never truly in the state of rest conveyed by the fixed supply and demand curves in Figure 7.6. But how can we change the picture? Imagine labor demand and labor supply curves that constantly bounce around. The demand for labor, the supply of labor, and the wage will be different every period. Figure 7.6 will be in perpetual motion. Mathematicians use the adjective *stochastic* to describe this constant bouncing around. Economists apply the term *stochastic* to models of the labor market that are in perpetual motion. Rather than a fixed equilibrium of quantity and a fixed wage, there is a *stochastic equilibrium*. This stochastic equilibrium in the labor market is a way to characterize the constant job creation and job destruction that exist in the economy. People enter the work force, move from one job to another, lose their jobs, or drop out of the labor force. Wages change, inducing people to enter or re-enter the market. Figure 7.9 is a schematic representation of the flows of workers into and out of the labor market.

In a stochastic equilibrium, at any point in time people will be searching for a job. Many who do so will be unemployed for some time. They lost their job, quit their job, or came back to the job market after an absence from work. One of the reasons they remain unemployed for a while is that they find it to their advantage not to accept the first job that comes along. Rather, they wait for a possibly higher-paying job. While they wait, they are unemployed.

■ **Policies to Reduce the Natural Unemployment Rate.** Both the job-rationing model and the job-search model have implications for how public policy

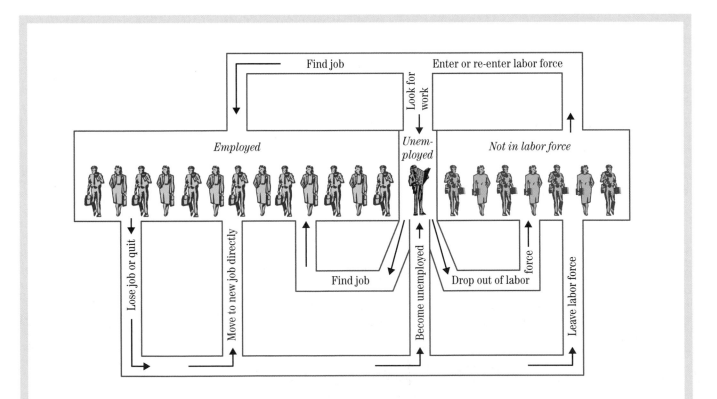

Figure 7.9
Labor Market Flows

The labor market is constantly in a state of flux, as people lose jobs, quit jobs, find jobs, and get in and out of the labor force. Most people pass through the unemployment box for a short period, but among the unemployed, some have not held jobs for a long time.

can reduce the natural rate of unemployment. We already mentioned how a very high minimum wage can increase unemployment. Conversely, a lower minimum wage for young workers could reduce unemployment. And if information about jobs is increased through job-placement centers or improved communication about the labor market, we would expect unemployment from job search to go down.

Unemployment compensation, paid to workers who have been laid off from their job, also affects job search. Unemployment compensation enables workers to spend more time looking for a job or to hold out for a higher-paying job. But in the United States, unemployment compensation does not last forever. In normal times it runs out after 26 weeks, and the evidence shows that many people stop searching and take a job just when their unemployment compensation runs out. Clearly, unemployment compensation not only helps mitigate the hardships associated with unemployment but allows people more time to search. But as a by-product, unemployment compensation increases unemployment.

REVIEW

- The supply and demand for labor is the starting point for explaining long-term employment trends. The intersection of supply and demand curves determines the amount of employment, and shifts in demand can explain why the employment-to-population ratio has increased.

- But the basic supply and demand theory needs to be modified to account for unemployment. Economists use two approaches, job rationing and job search, to explain why unemployment occurs.

- Job rationing occurs when the wage is too high. Unemployment can be interpreted as the difference between the quantity supplied and the quantity demanded at that high wage. Wages can be too high because of minimum-wage laws, insiders, or efficiency wages.

- Job search is another reason for unemployment. It takes time to find a job, and people have an incentive to wait for a good job.

CASE STUDY

Unemployment Among Young People Around the World

Unemployment rates for teenagers and young adults are generally much higher than for older workers because younger workers are less skilled and tend to change jobs more frequently.

But national unemployment rates vary greatly around the world. For example, Figure 7.10 shows the unemployment rate for young men and women in their early 20s in the United States and three other countries: Australia, France, and Spain. Observe that unemployment rates are higher for both men and women in Australia, and significantly higher in France and Spain, than in the United States. The United States has had lower unemployment rates for most demographic groups than many countries in the last 20 years, though the reverse was true in the 1960s and 1970s.

There is perhaps no more important macroeconomic problem than these high unemployment rates among young people. What factors cause the differences among the countries? Will the differences persist? Will Europe's unemployment problem improve? Will the United States unemployment rate increase?

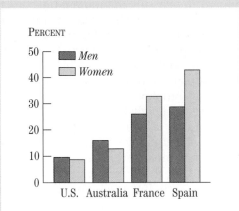

Figure 7.10
Unemployment Rates for Young Adults (ages 20–24)
Large, persistent differences are seen among different countries.

We can begin by ruling out the explanation that the differences are due to cyclical factors such as recessions. The differences in unemployment have persisted for many years through various ups and downs in the overall economy. Hence, the differences must reflect differences in the natural unemployment rate rather than cyclical differences in the countries.

Now, let's see whether the supply and demand model, augmented by rationing and job search, can explain the unemployment differences in Figure 7.10. According to the model, there are several possible explanations.

Differences in Unemployment Compensation for Young Adults

The story of job search tells us that a policy of more generous government compensation of unemployed workers leads to higher unemployment rates because unemployed workers can spend more time searching.

In fact, unemployment compensation for young adults is much greater in Australia and Spain than it is in the United States—amounting to only 10 percent of the average wage in the United States and as high as 40 percent in Australia and Spain. (Comparable data for France are not available.) Thus this explanation of unemployment from job search theory appears to fit the facts.

Differences in Lifestyles

Suppose that for cultural or religious reasons it was more acceptable in some countries than in others for young adults to live with their parents. With basic needs met for food and shelter, unemployed young people in these cultures might have less incentive to take any available job. Therefore, unemployment rates for young adults would tend to be higher in these countries.

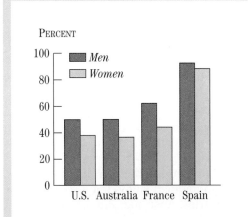

Figure 7.11
Percentage of 20–24-year-olds Still Living with Parents
Observe the close similarity with the unemployment rates for these countries in Figure 7.10.

Figure 7.11 shows the percentage of young adults living with their parents in the four countries in our case study. Observe from the graph that there is a strong correlation between this percentage and unemployment rates. Spain, which has the highest percentage of 20–24-year-olds living with their parents, has the highest unemployment rate in the case study. The United States is at the opposite end of the scale: lower unemployment and a lower percentage of young adults living at home.

The job search theory again appears to be consistent with the data, but we need to worry about a reverse effect: It is possible that more young people live with their parents *because* they are unemployed.

Differences in the Minimum Wage

The supply and demand model predicts that higher minimum wage laws would raise unemployment for younger people with low skills whose market wage was below the minimum. Minimum wages do differ across countries. Do they explain part of the differences in the unemployment rates for young people?

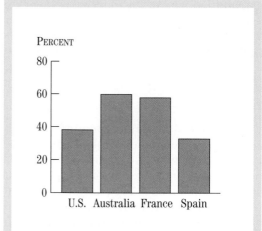

Figure 7.12
Minimum Wage as a Percentage of Average Wage
The minimum is lower in the United States than in France or Australia, but lowest in Spain.

Figure 7.12 shows the minimum wage as a percentage of the average wage in each of the four countries in our case study. The United States has a lower minimum wage than Australia and France, which suggests that this might be a reason for the lower unemployment rate in the United States.

Note that Spain also has a low minimum wage, even though it has the highest unemployment rates of the four countries. What could cause this apparent contradiction to the theory? One possibility is that the tradition of young adults living at home is so strong in Spain that it offsets the effect of the low minimum wage. In fact, lifestyle combined with the low minimum wage is a reasonable explanation for Spain's unemployment rates.

Differences in Taxes

Finally, let us consider differences in tax rates on wage income in the different countries. A higher tax rate on wages shifts the labor demand curve down, as shown in Figure 7.13, as firms find it more expensive to hire workers. Employment declines and unemployment increases.

Figure 7.14 gives the tax rates on wages for the four countries in the case study. The tax rate includes all forms of taxes on wages. Once again the theory that high taxes on labor can reduce labor demand and increase unemployment appears to be supported when one compares

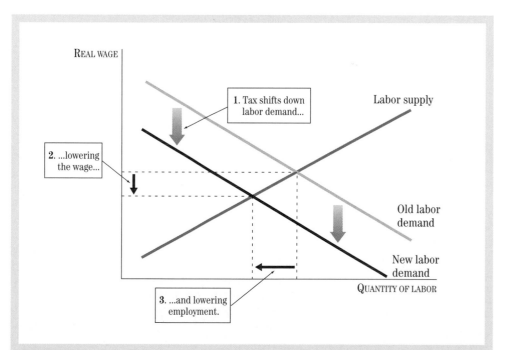

Figure 7.13
Effects of a Tax on Wages
A tax on labor lowers the labor demand curve by the amount of the tax because employers must pay more for workers. The new equilibrium has a lower wage and less employment.

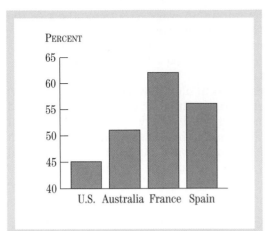

Figure 7.14
Tax Rates on Wages
The U.S. has a lower tax rate on wage income than the other three countries in the case.

the United States, Australia, and France. And while the tax rates are higher in Spain than in Australia and the United States, they are lower than in France, meaning that some other factor, such as lifestyle differences, is needed to fully explain the very high unemployment in Spain compared to France.

Policy Implication and Forecast

In sum, the labor supply and demand model augmented with job rationing and job search provides a pretty good explanation for the international differences in unemployment rates. According to this analysis, the economic policies that would reduce unemployment among young adults in Europe include: allowing a lower minimum wage for young workers, reducing unemployment compensation, and reducing taxes (or even subsidizing employment). None of these policies would be implemented without cost to the workers, the firms that employ them, or the politicians who propose these policies. Therefore, we can predict that differences in unemployment rates in these countries will persist.

REVIEW

- Unemployment rates differ greatly across countries.

- At least in the case of young adults, the unemployment differences appear to be due to differences in unemployment compensation, lifestyle, minimum wages, and taxes.

- These explanations show the practical usefulness of the supply and demand model in understanding many, if not all, of the unemployment differences between countries.

Conclusion

Our analysis of employment and unemployment has put the spotlight on two different roles of labor. In one role, labor is simply an input to the production of real GDP. We showed that the amount of aggregate hours of all workers is the most comprehensive measure of labor input.

In its other role, labor is the people doing the work. The study of labor in this role looks at the problems people face when they lose their job, decide to enter the labor force, or take a part-time job. It also looks at the effects of minimum wages and unemployment compensation on unemployment, at the serious problems that high rates of unemployment seem to cause, and at the reasons why more women have entered the labor force in the past several decades.

KEY POINTS

1. Unemployment data are collected in the monthly Current Population Survey.

2. A person is unemployed if he or she is old enough to work and is looking for work, but does not have a job.

3. Unemployment is never zero in a market economy.

4. The employment-to-population ratio has risen in the United States during recent decades, and the average number of hours each worker works has declined.

5. Aggregate hours of work by all workers is the most comprehensive measure of labor input to production of real GDP.

6. People are unemployed for four reasons: They have lost their job, they have quit their job, they have entered the labor force for the first time, or they have re-entered the labor force.

7. The labor supply and demand model can be used to explain trends in employment in the economy.

8. Unemployment can be explained by both job rationing, in which the wage is too high to equate supply and demand, and job search, in which unemployed people look for work.

9. Economic policies, such as exemptions for teenagers from the minimum-wage laws, time limits on unemployment compensation, or the provision of information about job openings to reduce job search time, can reduce the natural unemployment rate.

KEY TERMS

natural unemployment rate
cyclical unemployment
frictional unemployment
structural unemployment
Current Population Survey
labor force

working-age population
labor force participation rate
employment-to-population ratio

aggregate hours
job vacancies
labor demand curve
labor supply curve
real wage

job rationing
job search
insider
outsider
efficiency wage

QUESTIONS FOR REVIEW

1. How do economists define unemployment, and how do they measure how many people are unemployed?

2. How is the working-age population defined?

3. What is the definition of the labor force?

4. What has happened to the employment-to-population ratio for men and women since the 1950s?

5. What is the difference between frictional and structural unemployment?

6. Why isn't the unemployment rate equal to zero?

7. What fraction of unemployment is due to job loss, job quits, and new entrants and re-entrants?

8. What is the difference between unemployment due to job rationing and unemployment due to job search?

9. What three economic policies would reduce the natural rate of unemployment?

PROBLEMS

1. Which of the following people would be unemployed according to official statistics? Which ones would *you* define as unemployed? Why?
   a. A person who is home painting the house while seeking a permanent position as an electrician
   b. A full-time student
   c. A recent graduate who is looking for a job
   d. A parent who decides to stay home taking care of children full-time
   e. A worker who quits his job because he thinks the pay is insufficient
   f. A teenager who gets discouraged looking for work and stops looking

2. The table at the top of the next page shows the demand for and supply of skilled labor at different hourly wages.

Demand for Labor		Supply of Labor	
Wage/Hour	*Quantity*	*Wage/Hour*	*Quantity*
$12	75	$12	47
14	68	14	54
16	61	16	61
18	54	18	68
20	47	20	75
22	40	22	82

a. Draw the supply and demand curves for labor.
b. What are the wage and quantity of labor at equilibrium?
c. Suppose a law is passed forbidding employers to pay wages less than $20 per hour. What will the new quantity of labor in the market be? Who gains and who loses from this law?

3. a. Suppose the government decides to eliminate the minimum wage. What is likely to happen to the wages of unskilled workers in an area where the cost of living is very low? What is likely to happen to the wages of highly skilled computer programmers? Will this change in government policy reduce unemployment? Why or why not?
   b. Now suppose instead that the government changes unemployment benefits so that they end after two weeks. What is likely to happen to the unemployment rate? Will this change in government policy lead to an increase in labor productivity? Why or why not?

4. Job search and advertising are now on the Internet. Using e-mail, job applicants can submit résumés to prospective employers. One popular web site of this kind is www.hotjobs.com.
   a. How should this service affect the unemployment rate?
   b. Suppose everybody in the working-age population has access to hotjobs.com. Would you expect unemployment to be eliminated? Explain.

5. Suppose you own and run a bicycle repair shop with several employees. You decide to use your facilities at home to manage your business rather than hang around the bike shop while you do the books. You are surprised to discover that the productivity of your business falls. What happened? If you decide to keep your office at home, what will you have to do to increase the productivity of your business back to its previous level? If this same phenomenon is true of all businesses, then why may there be job rationing?

6. Use a supply and demand diagram to show the possible reduction in teenage unemployment from a lower minimum "training" wage for workers under 20 years of age. For what reasons might older unskilled workers complain about such a policy?

7. Use the theories of job rationing and job search to try to explain why the natural rate of unemployment in the United States is below that in France. What can the French government do to try to remedy this situation? Might these remedies be politically unpopular?

8. Suppose that the unemployment rate is 4 percent.
   a. If the working-age population is 205 million and the total labor force is 135 million, how many people are unemployed?
   b. What is the labor force participation rate?
   c. What is the employment-to-population ratio?

9. What effect would a decline in part-time employment have on average weekly hours per worker in the United States? If the employment-to-population ratio increases, what will happen to total hours of work in the United States?

10. Show that employment in the economy is equal to the working-age population times the labor force participation rate times (1 minus the unemployment rate) when both rates are measured as fractions. Use this equation to fill in the table below, which gives historical data for the United States. Calculate the 1950 employment-to-population ratio and compare it with the figures given in Figure 7.2. If the employment-to-population ratio for January 2000 were the same as in 1950, what would total employment be in January 2000?

Problem 10

Year	Total Employment (millions)	Unemployment Rate (percent)	Labor Force Participation Rate (percent)	Working-Age Population (millions)
1950		5.2	59.7	106.2
1960	67.6	5.4	60.0	
1970	80.8		61.0	139.2

Source: U.S. Department of Labor.

11. The total employment in the economy is equal to the working-age population times (1 minus the unemployment rate) times the labor force participation rate.
    a. Using the data, fill in the table below, showing how many employed people there were in the United States at the turn of each decade.
    b. Suppose the projection for the working-age population in the year 2020 for the United States is 255 million. If the unemployment rate and the labor force participation rate are the same in 2020 as they are in 1990, how much employment will there be?
    c. Using the same projection of 255 million for working-age population in 2020, calculate employment with an unemployment rate of 6 percent and a labor force participation rate of 60 percent. Do the same for a labor force participation rate of 70 percent. Which of these estimates do you think is more realistic? Why?

12. The age distribution of the population changes over time—in the United States, better health care and smaller family size in recent years means that there are increasingly larger proportions of people over age 16. At the same time, there is likely to be a decline in the labor force participation rate as baby boomers retire. Using the same method as in the previous question, calculate total employment and the employment-to-population ratio based on the scenario in the table below.
    a. Describe what happens to total employment and the employment-to-population ratio in this scenario.
    b. Is it possible that labor force participation falls so much that total employment falls? How low would the labor force participation rate have to be in 2010 for total employment to be lower than in 1990?

Problem 11

Year	Total Employment (millions)	Unemployment Rate (percent)	Labor Force Participation Rate (percent)	Working-Age Population (millions)
1970		4.8	61.0	139.2
1980		7.0	63.8	169.3
1990		5.4	66.6	189.7

Source: U.S. Department of Labor.

Problem 12

Year	Unemployment Rate (percent)	Labor Force Participation Rate (percent)	Working-Age Population (millions)	Total Employment (millions)	Employment-to-Population Ratio
1990	5.5	66.4	188		
2000	5.5	64.0	208		
2010	5.5	62.0	230		

Source: U.S. Department of Labor.

8

Productivity and Economic Growth

For most of human history, there was no economic growth. True, vast quantities of wealth were amassed by kings and queens through

conquest and exploitation; coliseums, pyramids, and great walls were constructed by millions of slaves; and great works of art were produced by talented individuals of all continents. But output per hour of work—the productive power of labor that determines the well-being of most people—grew hardly at all for thousands of years. Except for the ruling classes, people lived in extreme poverty.

This situation changed dramatically around the eighteenth century. Figure 8.1 shows the growth rates of *output per hour of work,* or **productivity,** for different periods during the last 300 years. Observe that there was almost no growth in output per hour of work for most of the 1700s, much as in the thousands of years before. Then, in the late 1700s and early 1800s—the period historians call the Industrial Revolution—economic growth began to pick up. Growth accelerated in the early 1800s and then rose to historically unprecedented levels in the twentieth century.

The increase in economic growth during the last 200 years has taken the average person's income in the advanced countries to a level never dreamed of in antiquity, except by the richest emperors and empresses.

Why did the growth of real GDP per hour of work begin to increase and then take off in the eighteenth century? The purpose of this chapter is to develop a theory of economic growth that helps answer this and many other questions. The theory of economic growth tells us that increases in labor can increase the

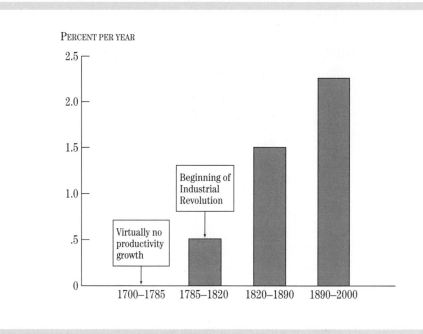

Figure 8.1
Productivity Growth During the Past 300 Years
Productivity is defined as output per hour of work. Productivity *growth* is defined as the percentage increase in productivity from one year to the next. The bars indicate the average productivity growth during the years stated.

productivity: output per hour of work.

growth of real GDP but not the growth of real GDP per hour of work. To explain the growth of productivity, we must focus on the two other factors: capital and technology. Capital raises real GDP per hour of work by giving workers more tools and equipment to work with. Increasing the investment share of GDP will increase the growth of capital. However, as we will show in this chapter, capital alone is not sufficient to achieve the growth we have seen over the past 200 years. Technology—the knowledge and methods that underlie the production process—must also have played a big role.

Understanding the role of technology enables economists to better evaluate the advantages and disadvantages of various economic policies to improve economic growth. For example, should economic policies designed to stimulate economic growth focus more on capital or more on technology? Perhaps the most promising feature of the recent U.S. economy is an increase in productivity growth that began in the mid-1990s after nearly 25 years of relatively slow productivity growth. The right economic policies regarding technology might go a long way toward maintaining or even increasing this productivity growth rate.

Labor and Capital Without Technology

To prove that technology must have played a key role in the economic growth of the past two centuries, we consider a theory of economic growth that omits technology. We start with a simplified theory in which real GDP depends only on labor. That is, the amount of output in the economy can be described by the production function $Y = F(L)$, where Y is real GDP and L is labor input. When labor input increases, real GDP increases.

The proof that technology must have been a quantitatively important influence on economic growth goes as follows: First, we show that the theory with labor alone is too limited to explain growth. Second, we add capital and show that, although the theory begins to look promising, it still fails to explain growth. The implication is that we need technology in order to grow.

The theory without capital is actually very close to the economic theory used by Thomas Robert Malthus to make pessimistic predictions about economic growth in his famous *Essay on the Principle of Population,* published in 1798. Let's see why the predictions were so pessimistic.

Labor Alone

First, consider the production of a single good. Imagine workers on a one-acre vineyard planting, maintaining, and harvesting grapes, and suppose that the only input that can be varied is labor. With more workers, the vineyard can produce more goods, but, according to the simple story that output depends only on labor, the vineyard cannot increase capital because there is no capital. For example, the vineyard cannot buy wagons or wheelbarrows to haul fertilizer around. The only way the vineyard can increase output is by hiring more workers to haul the fertilizer.

Now, suppose all this is true for the economy as a whole. The firms in the economy can produce more output by hiring more workers, but they cannot increase capital. The situation is shown for the entire economy in Figure 8.2. On the vertical axis is output. On the horizontal axis is labor input. The curve shows that more labor can produce more output. The curve is a graphical plot of the aggregate production function $Y = F(L)$ for the whole economy.

diminishing returns: a situation in which successive increases in the use of an input, holding other inputs constant, will eventually cause a decline in the additional production derived from one more unit of that input.

■ **Diminishing Returns to Labor.** The slope of the curve in Figure 8.2 is important. The flattening out of the curve shows that there are **diminishing returns** to labor: The greater the number of workers used in producing output, the less the additional output that comes from each additional worker. Why? Consider production of a single good again, such as grapes at the vineyard. Increasing employment at the one-acre vineyard from one to two workers raises production more than increasing employment from 1,001 to 1,002 workers. A second worker could take charge of irrigation or inspect the vines for insects while the first worker harvested grapes. But with 1,001 workers on the vineyard, the 1,002nd worker could find little to do to raise production. Diminishing returns to labor exist because labor is the only input to production that we are changing. As more workers are employed on the same one-acre plot, the contribution that each additional worker makes goes down. Adding one worker when only one worker is employed can increase production by a large amount. But adding one worker when there are already 1,001 on the one-acre plot cannot add as much! For the same reasons, diminishing returns to labor exist for the whole economy.

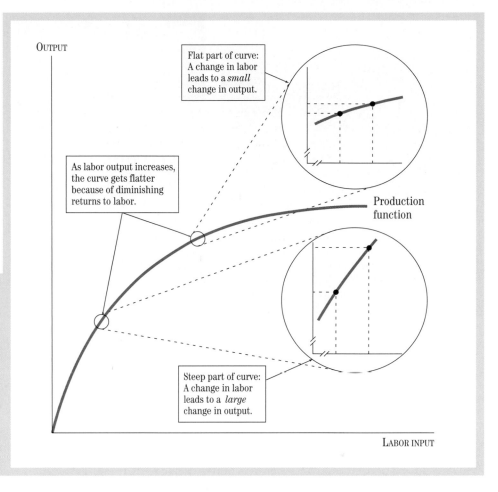

Figure 8.2
A Theory in Which Only Changes in Labor Can Change Output
The curve shows the production function $Y = F(L)$, where Y is output and L is labor input (hours of work). In this theory, capital and technology are out of the picture. With more labor working on a fixed supply of land, there are diminishing returns, as shown by the curvature of the production function.

When early economists, such as Malthus, wrote about economics in the late eighteenth and early nineteenth century, agriculture was a large part of the economy, employing more than 75 percent of all workers, compared with about 2 percent in the United States today. Farm product and gross domestic product were almost the same thing. Hence, agricultural examples such as the preceding one were very fitting. Although the amount of farmland could be increased somewhat by clearing more forests, the number of acres of land available for producing farm goods was limited, especially in England, where many early economists lived. It was not so unrealistic for them to think of labor as the only input to production that could be increased. Moreover, they saw only small improvements in farming methods in Europe for thousands of years, so they can be excused for underestimating the effects of capital and technology on output when they developed their economic theories.

Real GDP per worker was just beginning to grow rapidly as Malthus wrote (see Figure 8.1). As this growth continued, it gradually became clear that his dismal predictions that real GDP will gravitate toward the subsistence level of output were not coming true in England or in the other countries about which he wrote. The population was expanding, rather than stabilizing. Hence, Malthus turned out to be wrong.

To be sure, starvation has not disappeared from the planet. Population growth in the underdeveloped parts of the world has frequently faced limited food supplies, resulting in situations like those depicted by Malthus. But since the problems of less-developed countries have occurred alongside a remarkable fiftyfold increase in living

The Capital Stock, Before and After Net Investment
Left: *Start with an existing capital stock—the buildings in Chicago many years ago.*
Middle: *Add net investment—new construction, less depreciated buildings—each year, for many years.*
Right: *The result is a larger capital stock—the buildings in Chicago today.*
These pictures illustrate the equation below. Does the larger capital stock lead to more output?

standards in the advanced countries, history suggests that there are non-Malthusian explanations for the persistent poverty observed in many less-developed countries.

Labor and Capital Alone

Now let us add capital to the growth theory. The total amount of capital in the economy increases each year by the amount of net investment during the year. More precisely,

$$\text{Capital at the end of this year} = \text{net investment during this year} + \text{capital at the end of last year}$$

> Recall that net investment is equal to gross investment less depreciation (p. 116). Depreciation is the amount of capital that wears out each year.

For example, if $10,000 billion is the value of all capital in the economy at the end of last year, then $100 billion of net investment during this year would raise the capital stock to $10,100 billion by the end of this year. This is a 1 percent increase in the capital stock.

With capital as an input to production, the production function becomes $Y = F(L, K)$, where K stands for capital. Output can be increased by using more capital, even if the amount of labor is not increased. Consider the vineyard example again. If a wheelbarrow is bought to haul the fertilizer around the vineyard, the vineyard can produce more grapes with the same number of workers. More capital at the vineyard increases output. The same is true for the economy as a whole. By increasing the amount of capital in the economy, more real GDP can be produced with the same number of workers.

Figure 8.3 illustrates how more capital raises output. The axes are the same as those in Figure 8.2, and the curve again shows that more output can be produced by more labor. But, in addition, Figure 8.3 shows that if we add capital to the econ-

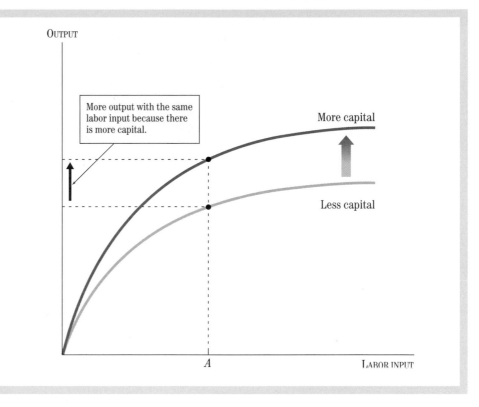

Oᴜᴛᴘᴜᴛ

More output with the same labor input because there is more capital.

More capital

Less capital

A Lᴀʙᴏʀ ɪɴᴘᴜᴛ

Figure 8.3
Capital Becomes a Factor of Production
The axes are just like those in Figure 8.2, but now if more capital is added to production, more output can be produced with the same labor input. For example, when labor input is at point *A*, more output can be produced with more capital.

omy—by investing a certain amount each year—the relationship between output and labor shifts up: More capital provides more output at any level of labor input. To see this, pick a point on the horizontal axis, say point *A,* to designate a certain amount of labor input. Then draw a vertical line up from this point, such as the dashed line shown. The vertical distance between the curve marked "less capital" and the curve marked "more capital" shows that additional capital raises production.

■ **Diminishing Returns to Capital.**   However, the addition of capital to the theory does not solve everything. If labor has diminishing returns, why would not capital? Figure 8.4 shows that there are *diminishing returns to capital* too. Each additional amount of capital—another wheelbarrow or another hoe—results in a smaller addition to output. Hence, the gaps between the several production functions in Figure 8.4 get smaller and smaller as more capital is added. As more capital is added, there is less ability to increase output per worker. Compare adding one wheelbarrow to the vineyard when there is already one with adding one wheelbarrow when there are already fifty. Clearly, the fifty-first wheelbarrow would increase farm output by only a minuscule amount, certainly much less than the second wheelbarrow. With a one-acre vineyard, there would not even be much room for the fifty-first wheelbarrow!

Diminishing returns to capital also occur for the economy as a whole. Thus, adding more capital per worker cannot raise real GDP per worker above some limit, and even getting close to that limit will require an enormous amount of capital. Investment would have to be such a large share of GDP that there would be little left for anything else. Thus, even with capital, the model yields a very pessimistic conclusion—not as devastating as Malthus's prediction, but not nearly as optimistic as the

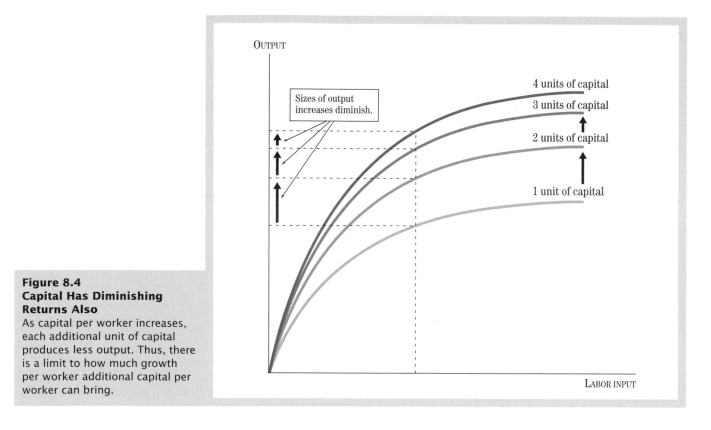

Figure 8.4
Capital Has Diminishing Returns Also
As capital per worker increases, each additional unit of capital produces less output. Thus, there is a limit to how much growth per worker additional capital per worker can bring.

fiftyfold (and still counting) gain in productivity that we have observed. Eventually, growth in output per hour of work would stop.

Thus, labor and capital alone cannot explain the phenomenal growth in either farm output or real GDP during the last 200 years.

REVIEW

- An economic growth theory with labor alone cannot account for the sustained increase in real GDP per hour of work that began in the late 1700s and continues today. Under such a theory, production would remain at subsistence levels.

- Adding capital to the theory can explain why real GDP can remain far above subsistence levels indefinitely, even with the population growing at a steady rate. However, it cannot explain the sustained *increases* in real GDP per hour of work that we have observed.

Technology: The Engine of Growth

We have seen that growth driven by increases in capital and labor, while important, is not sustainable. Diminishing returns imply that the additional output obtained by increasing these inputs becomes smaller and smaller, eventually leading to no further economic growth. In order for output to grow over the very long run, we need

Examples of Changes in Technology That Increased Output
Replacing horse-drawn tractors (on the left) with steam-powered tractors (in the center) is an example of a change in technology that increased output per worker. Another example is the introduction of computer technology for maintenance scheduling or ordering spare tractor parts on the Internet. What other advances in technology have increased farm output?

not just to add *more* inputs, but also to get more output from *existing* inputs. Technology is what enables us to get more output from a given quantity of inputs.

What Is Technology?

technology: anything that raises the amount of output that can be produced with a given amount of labor and capital.

Technology is very difficult to define, envision, and measure. A broad definition of **technology** is that it is anything that raises the amount of output that can be produced with a given amount of inputs (labor and capital). In essence, technology is the stock of knowledge or ideas that exist in an economy: the ideas that help produce goods and services such as baby food, wine, laser light shows, and satellite television; the ideas that help save lives, such as penicillin, vaccines, and heart transplants; and the ideas that help us travel all over the world and beyond, such as the jetliner and the space shuttle.

When we add technology to capital and labor, we have the modern theory of economic growth. The theory can be summarized by the now familiar aggregate production function

$$Y = F(L, K, T)$$

technological change: improvement in technology over time.

where T stands for technology. Increases in technology will therefore increase output. Such increases in technology are termed technological progress. Since technology is usually increasing over time, we sometimes use the term **technological change** instead of technological progress.

invention: a discovery of new knowledge.

innovation: application of new knowledge in a way that creates new products or significantly changes old ones.

■ **Invention, Innovation, and Diffusion.** Technological change occurs when new ideas are developed into new products that increase production, such as the steel plow, the harvester, the combine, the automobile, radar, the telephone, the computer, the airplane, lasers, and fiber optic cable. Economists distinguish between an **invention,** which is the discovery of new knowledge or a new principle, such as electricity, and **innovation,** in which the new knowledge is brought into application

diffusion: the spreading of an innovation throughout the economy.

with a new product, such as the electric light bulb. Economists also distinguish between the innovation itself and the **diffusion** of the innovation throughout the economy, a process that involves advertising, marketing, and spreading the innovation to new uses, such as the use of the electric light bulb to create night shifts in factories.

Thus, technology is much more than scientific knowledge. The discovery of DNA did not improve technology until it was applied to genetic engineering. The knowledge of mathematics made possible the invention and development of computers in the 1940s, a technology that has obviously improved productivity. Technology depends in part on scientific knowledge, and many people feel that science will become more and more important in future technological change.

The sewing machine is a good illustration of invention, innovation, and diffusion. In 1847, "17 machines capable of mechanically forming a stitch had been invented," according to Ross Thompson, an economic historian. But only one of these, Elias Howe's sewing machine, developed into a commercially successful innovation. A Boston machinist turned entrepreneur, Howe tried to sell his invention. As he did so, he and others found out how to modify the invention to make it more useful and attractive to potential buyers. Soon the invention turned into a popular innovation that was used widely. Wide diffusion of the innovation occurred as others produced household versions of the sewing machine, like the one marketed by the Singer Company. This story also illustrates that innovation and diffusion usually require the work of an entrepreneur who recognizes the potential of the invention.

■ **Organization and Specialization.** Technology also includes the way firms are organized. Better organization schemes can mean a smaller bureaucracy and more output per hour of work without the addition of capital. More efficient organization can improve the flow of information within a firm and thereby affect labor productivity. Better incentive programs that encourage workers to communicate their ideas to management, for example, increase productivity.

Henry Ford's idea of the assembly line greatly increased the productivity of workers. The assembly line enabled the car to come to the worker rather than having the worker go to the car. Thus, each worker could specialize in a certain type of activity; through specialization, productivity increased. The assembly line alone is estimated to have reduced the time it took a group of workers to produce a car from $12\frac{1}{2}$ hours to $\frac{1}{2}$ hour. Productivity increased, and so did wages.

New technology can affect how labor and capital are used at a firm. Economists distinguish between *labor-saving* and *capital-saving* technological change. *Labor-saving technological change* means that fewer workers are needed to produce the same amount of output; *capital-saving technological change* means that fewer machines are needed to produce the same amount of output. An example of a labor-saving technological change would be a steam-powered tractor replacing a horse-drawn plow, and later gasoline power replacing steam power, enabling the same worker to plow many more acres. An example of a capital-saving technological change is the night shift. Adding two crews of workers—one working in a steel mill from 4 P.M. to midnight and another working from midnight to 8 A.M.—makes the same steel-making furnaces three times as productive as when the working hours are only from 8 A.M. to 4 P.M.

Specialization of workers at a firm adds to productivity. Adam Smith emphasized the importance of specialization in his *Wealth of Nations;* his phrase *division of labor* refers to the way a manufacturing task could be divided up among a group of workers, each of whom would specialize in a part of the job.

Because specialization permits workers to repeat the same task many times, their productivity increases, as in the old adage "practice makes perfect." Each time

learning by doing: a situation in which workers become more proficient by doing a particular task many times.

the task is repeated, the worker becomes more proficient—a phenomenon economists call **learning by doing.** The common-sense principle of learning by doing is that the more one does something, the more one learns about how to do it. For example, as the number of airplanes produced of a particular type—say a DC-10—increases, the workers become more and more skilled at producing that type of airplane. Careful studies of aircraft production have shown that productivity increases by 20 percent for each 100 percent increase in output of a particular type of plane. This relationship between learning and the amount of production is commonly called the "learning curve." Learning is a type of technological progress.

■ **Human Capital.** Many firms provide training courses for workers to increase their skills and their productivity. *On-the-job training* is a catchall term for any education, training, or skills a worker receives while at work.

Most workers receive much of their education and training before they begin working, whether in grade school, high school, college, or professional schools. Because increases in education and training can raise workers' productivity, such increases are considered another source of technological change.

human capital: a person's accumulated knowledge and skills.

The education and training of workers, called **human capital** by economists, is similar to physical capital—factories and equipment. In order to accumulate human capital—to become more educated or better trained—people must devote time and resources, much as a firm must devote resources to investment if physical capital is to increase.

The decision to invest in human capital is influenced by considerations similar to those that motivate a firm to invest in physical capital: the cost of the investment versus the expected return. For example, investing in a college education may require that one borrow the money for tuition; if the interest rate on the loan rises, then people will be less likely to invest in a college education. Thus, investment in education may be negatively related to the interest rate, much as physical investment is. This is one reason why, in order to encourage more education and thereby increase economic growth and productivity, the U.S. government provides low-interest loans to college students, making an investment in college more attractive. We will return to the government's role in education as part of its broader policy to increase economic growth later in the chapter.

The Production of Technology: The Invention Factory

Technology is sometimes discovered by chance by a lone inventor and sometimes by trial and error by an individual worker. A secretary who experiments with several different filing systems to reduce search time or with different locations for the computer, the printer, the telephone, and the photocopier is engaged in improving technology around the office. Frequently, technological progress is a continuous process in which a small adjustment here and a small adjustment there add up to major improvements over time.

But more and more technological change is the result of huge expenditures of research and development funds by industry and government. Thomas Edison's "invention factory" in Menlo Park, New Jersey, was one of the first examples of a large industrial laboratory devoted to the production of technology. It in turn influenced the development of many other labs, such as the David Sarnoff research lab of RCA. Merck & Co., a drug company, spends nearly $1 billion per year on research and development for the production of new technology.

Edison's Menlo Park laboratory had about 25 technicians working in three or four different buildings. In the six years from 1876 to 1882, the laboratory invented the light bulb, the phonograph, the telephone transmitter, and electrical generators.

Two Invention Factories: Past and Present
The amount of technology produced at Thomas Edison's invention factory (left) or at the research lab of a modern biotechnology firm like Cetus (right) can be explained by the laws of supply and demand. But how is technology different from most other goods? If one person uses more technology, is there just as much available for others to use?

Each of these inventions turned out to be a successful innovation that was diffused widely. For each innovation, a *patent* was granted by the federal government. A patent indicates that the invention is original and gives the inventor the exclusive right to use it until the patent expires. In order to obtain a patent on the rights to an invention, an inventor must apply to the Patent and Trademark Office of the federal government. Patents give inventors an inducement to invent. The number of patents granted is an indicator of how much technological progress is going on. Edison obtained patents at a pace of about 67 a year at his lab.

Edison's invention factory required both labor and capital input, much like factories producing other commodities. The workers in such laboratories are highly skilled, with knowledge obtained through formal schooling or on-the-job training—human capital. A highly trained work force is an important prerequisite to the production of technology.

The supply of technology—the output of Edison's invention factory, for example—depends on the cost of producing the new technology, which must include the great risk that little or nothing will be invented, and the benefits from the new technology: how much Edison can charge for the rights to use his techniques for making light bulbs. Often inventive activity has changed as a result of shifts in the economy that change the costs and benefits. For example, increases in textile workers' wages stimulated the invention of textile machines, because such machines yielded greater profits by enabling the production of more output with fewer workers.

Special Features of the Technology Market

When viewed as a commodity that can be produced, technology has two special qualities that affect how much will be produced. The first is *nonrivalry*. This means that one person's use of the technology does not reduce the amount that another person can use. If one university uses the same book-filing system as another university, that does not reduce the quality of the first university's system. In contrast, most goods are rivals in consumption: If you drink a bottle of Coke, there is one fewer bottle of Coke around for other people to drink.

The second feature of technology is *nonexcludability*. This means that the inventor or the owner of the technology cannot exclude other people from using it. For example, the system software for Apple computers shows a series of logos and pull-down menus that can be moved around the screen with a mouse. The idea could easily be adapted for use in other software programs by other companies. In fact, the Windows program

Table 8.1
Classification of Goods and Services According to Rivalry and Excludability

	Rival	Nonrival
Excludable	Pencil CD player with headphones	Movie theater The opera
Nonexcludable	Swing in a public park Book in a public library	Fireworks on the Fourth of July Network television

of Microsoft has features similar to those of the Apple software, but, according to the court that ruled on Apple's complaint that Microsoft was illegally copying, the features were not so similar that Microsoft could not use them. Examples of rival, nonrival, excludable, and nonexcludable goods are given in Table 8.1.

As the example of Apple and Microsoft shows, the legal system and the enforcement of *intellectual property laws* determine in part the degree of nonexcludability. Intellectual property laws provide for trademarks and copyrights as well as patents. These laws help inventors exclude others from using their inventions without compensation. But it is impossible to exclude others from using much technology.

Thus, technology may *spill over* from one activity to another. If your economics teacher invents a new way to teach economics on a computer, it might spill over to your chemistry teacher, who sees how the technology can be applied to a different subject. Sometimes spillovers occur because research personnel move from one firm to another. Henry Ford knew Thomas Edison and was stimulated to experiment on internal combustion engines by Edison. Hence, Edison's research spilled over to another industry, but Edison would have found it very difficult to get compensation from Henry Ford even if he had wanted to.

Because inventors cannot be fully compensated for the benefits their ideas provide to others, they may produce too little technology. The private incentives to invent are less than the gain to society from the inventions. If the incentives were higher—say through government subsidies to research and development—more inventions might be produced. Thus, there is a potential role for government in providing funds for research and development, both in industry and at universities. Before we consider this role, we must examine how to measure technological change in the economy as a whole.

REVIEW

- Technological change has a very broad definition. It is anything that increases production for a given level of labor and capital. Technological change has been an essential ingredient in the increase in the growth of real GDP per hour of work in the last 200 years.

- Technology can be improved by the education and training of workers—investment in human capital. Technology can also be improved through inventions produced in "invention factories" or industrial research laboratories, as well as by trial and error. In any case, the level of technology is determined by market forces.

- But technology exhibits nonrivalry in consumption and a high degree of nonexcludability. These are precisely the conditions in which there will be an underproduction of technology.

Measuring Technology

Both technology and capital cause productivity—real GDP per hour of work—to grow. Is it possible to determine how much productivity growth has been due to technology, as distinct from capital? Surprisingly, the answer is yes. A significant modern development in economics is the discovery and application of a technique to measure how important capital and technology each are for productivity growth in the economy. Robert Solow of MIT made the pioneering contribution and won the Nobel Prize for his innovation. In 1957 he published a paper that contained a simple mathematical formula. It is this formula—called the **growth accounting formula**—that enables economists to estimate the relative contributions of capital and technology.

growth accounting formula: an equation that states that the growth rate of productivity equals capital's share of income times the growth rate of capital per hour of work plus the growth rate of technology.

The Formula and Its Coefficient

The growth accounting formula is remarkably simple. It can be written as follows:

$$\text{Growth rate of productivity} = \frac{1}{3}\left(\begin{array}{c}\text{growth rate of capital} \\ \text{per hour of work}\end{array}\right) + \begin{array}{c}\text{growth rate} \\ \text{of technology}\end{array}$$

The two ingredients in the growth of productivity—the growth of *capital* and the growth of *technology*—are apparent in the formula. The growth accounting formula allows us to measure the importance of these two ingredients.

The growth accounting formula can be derived from the aggregate production function. The box on the next page contains a brief graphical explanation of the derivation.

It is important to know why the growth rate of capital per hour of work is multiplied by a coefficient that is less than one, or only 1/3 in the above formula. The simplest reason is that economists view the production function for the economy as one in which output rises by only 1/3 of the percentage by which capital increases. For example, a vineyard owner can estimate by what percent grape output will rise if the workers have more wheelbarrows to work with. If the number of wheelbarrows at the vineyard is increased by 100 percent and if the 1/3 coefficient applies to the vineyard, then grape production per hour of work will increase by 33 percent. In other words, this is a property of the grape production function. Statistical studies suggest that the 1/3 coefficient seems to apply to the production function for the economy as a whole.

Another reason for the 1/3 coefficient on capital growth relies on the basic principle of economics that inputs to production receive income according to their contribution to production. If you look back at Table 5.3, you will find that capital income (including depreciation) totaled $3,559 billion, which is about 1/3 of aggregate income ($10,208 billion). This provides statistical support for the 1/3 coefficient.

We should not give the impression, however, that economists know the coefficient on capital growth in the growth accounting formula with much precision. There is uncertainty about its size. It could be 1/4 or even 5/12. In any case, the growth accounting formula is a helpful rule of thumb to assist policymakers in deciding what emphasis to place on capital versus technology when developing programs to stimulate economic growth.

Using the Formula

Here is how the formula works. The growth rates of productivity and capital per hour of work are readily determined from available data sources in most countries. Using the formula, we can express the growth rate of technology as shown on page 190.

A Formula Goes to Washington

In 1957, when Robert Solow first published the growth accounting formula, it was of course a new idea. He therefore had to explain it in very simple terms if it was to have any impact. He presented the idea graphically, and it caught on quickly. By the early 1960s, he was being called to Washington to apply the ideas at President Kennedy's Council of Economic Advisers. The graphical approach is still used today. Here is how it works:

The growth accounting formula divides the growth of productivity into two sources: the growth of capital per hour of work and the growth of technological change. The figure on the left below explains this dissection graphically through the familiar distinction between the shifts of and movements along the curves. The figure shows the relationship between productivity (Y/L) and capital per hour of work (K/L). More capital per hour leads to more output per hour, as shown by the purple curves in the figure. Technological change shifts the purple curve up because, by definition, technological change is anything that raises productivity for a given level of capital per hour of work.

The purple curves in the figure are much like a production function, except that productivity (Y/L), rather than output (Y), is what is being explained. Hence, we call each purple curve in the figure a *productivity curve*. The production function and the productivity curve are perfectly compatible with each other, but one focuses on output and the other on output per hour of work. Actual productivity increases in the economy are due to a combination of *movements along* the productivity

curve, because of more capital per hour, and *shifts of* the productivity curve, because of technological change. The purpose of the growth accounting formula is to determine how much of the increase is due to movement along the curve and how much is due to a shift. This is illustrated by two observations on productivity and capital per hour in two different years (year 1 and year 2). Observe how the increase in productivity from year 1 to year 2 is due partly to an upward shift of the productivity curve and partly to a movement along the curve.

This graphical approach can be applied in practice, as shown in the graph on the lower right. This graph focuses on the upper portion of three U.S. productivity curves corresponding to the three years 1955, 1975, and 1995 (the lower portions have been cut away for better visibility).

Observe on the vertical axis that productivity increased by a smaller percentage from 1975 to 1995 than it did from 1955 to 1975. Observe also that the curve shifted up by a much smaller amount from 1975 to 1995 than it did from 1955 to 1975. In fact, the decline in productivity growth from the earlier to the later period was almost entirely due to a smaller shift in the curve rather than to a smaller percentage increase in capital per hour of work. Once again, the role of technology is significant.

The case study later in this chapter shows that there has been an increase in productivity growth since 1995. Can you guess what it has mostly been due to?

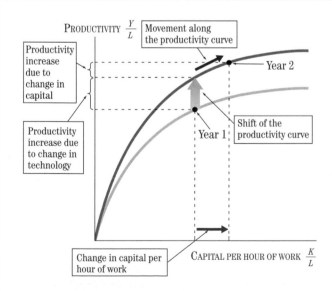

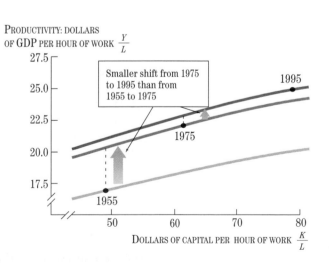

$$\begin{array}{c} \text{Growth rate} \\ \text{of technology} \end{array} = \begin{array}{c} \text{growth rate of} \\ \text{productivity} \end{array} - \frac{1}{3}\left(\begin{array}{c} \text{growth rate of capital} \\ \text{per hour of work} \end{array}\right)$$

Thus, the growth rate of technology can be determined by subtracting 1/3 times the growth rate of capital per hour of work from the growth rate of real GDP per hour of work.

Consider an example. Suppose the growth rate of real GDP per hour of work is 2 percent per year. Suppose also that the growth rate of capital per hour of work is 3 percent per year. Then the growth rate of technology must be 1 percent per year: $2 - (1/3 \times 3) = 1$. Thus, one-half of the growth of productivity is due to technological change and one-half to growth of capital per hour of work.

REVIEW

- The growth accounting formula shows explicitly how productivity growth depends on the growth of capital per hour of work and on the growth of technology.

- Using the growth accounting formula along with data on productivity and capital, one can calculate the contribution of technology to economic growth.

CASE STUDY

Growth Accounting in Practice

Let us now examine what the growth accounting formula tells us about the importance of technology for economic growth.

The 1970s Productivity Growth Slowdown

Table 8.2 shows productivity growth in the United States for three different periods. It also shows the amount of this productivity growth that is due to the growth of capital and the growth of technology. The table was computed using the growth accounting formula.

If you compare the first two rows of the table, you can see that productivity growth slowed down in the 1970s, from 2.5 percent per year to only 1.2 percent per year. This slowdown was a major concern of policymakers during this period. At first, policymakers were slow to recognize it. When statisticians at the Bureau of Labor Statistics first reported the slowdown in the mid-1970s, many people thought that it was probably temporary and that productivity growth would soon rebound. Instead, productivity continued to grow slowly for nearly 20 years.

What was the reason for the slowdown? The growth accounting formula helps answer the question. According to the formula, both the growth of capital and the growth of technology slowed down. But the slowdown in the growth of technology was larger. Technology growth fell by .8 percentage point from the 1956–1975 period to the 1976–1995 period while capital growth fell by .5 percentage point. This suggested that a greater focus on policies to stimulate technological change and education would be appropriate.

The 1990s Rebound and the New Economy

After remaining low for nearly a generation, productivity growth finally started to pick up again in the mid-1990s. The last row of Table 8.2 shows this rebound in pro-

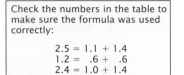

Check the numbers in the table to make sure the formula was used correctly:

2.5 = 1.1 + 1.4
1.2 = .6 + .6
2.4 = 1.0 + 1.4

So they check.

Table 8.2
Accounting for the 1970s Productivity Slowdown and the 1990s Productivity Rebound

Period	(1) Productivity Growth	(2) 1/3 Capital per Hour of Work	(3) Technology Growth
1956–1975	2.5	1.1	1.4
1976–1995	1.2	.6	.6
1996–1999	2.4	1.0	1.4

Source: Bureau of Labor Statistics, and Stephen Oliner and Daniel Sichel, "The Resurgence of Growth in the Late 1990s: Is Information Technology the Story?", Federal Reserve Board, 2000.

ductivity growth. In the second half of the 1990s productivity growth rose to 2.4 percent—almost what it was before the slowdown. Was capital or technology the main reason for the rebound? According to the growth accounting formula, technology growth surged from 1996 to 1999, contributing twice as much as capital.

This increase in productivity growth and the important role of technology in the 1990s led people to call the U.S. economy the **new economy,** a term used to convey the idea that new technology—especially information technology such as faster computers, wireless phones, and the Internet—has enabled workers to be more productive, thereby raising productivity growth. That this technology growth is a big factor in the rebound is consistent with the term *the new economy.* But whatever one calls it, the higher productivity growth has already had an impact, from higher wage growth to more resources for both the public and private sectors to spend. See the box "Reading the News About the Productivity Growth Rebound" for some press reaction to this rebound in productivity.

new economy: a term used to describe the period of high productivity growth, attributed largely to better computer and information technology

Demise of the Soviet Union

Table 8.3 shows the application of the growth accounting formula to the former Soviet Union. It shows the high rates of productivity growth in the Soviet Union in the 1970s and the early 1980s. During that time many Americans were still worried about the Soviet Union overtaking the United States, recalling former Soviet Premier Nikita Khrushchev's highly publicized statement "We will bury you."

Table 8.3
Growth Accounting in the Former Soviet Union

Period	(1) Productivity Growth	(2) 1/3 Capital per Hour of Work	(3) Technology Growth
1971–1975	4.5	3.0	1.5
1976–1980	3.3	3.9	−.6
1981–1985	2.7	3.5	−.8

Source: A Study of the Soviet Economy, International Monetary Fund, The World Bank, Organization for Economic Cooperation and Development, and European Bank for Reconstruction and Development, 1999. Reprinted by permission.

This article appeared in the *Financial Times* on February 13, 2002. It summarizes some data on the recent rapid productivity growth in the United States and emphasizes the importance of productivity growth for economic growth and higher living standards in the long run. The authors also identify the source of productivity growth: business investment spending by firms seeking to cut costs and increase their efficiency.

As you read the article, keep in mind that the 3.5 percent increase in productivity in the fourth quarter of 2001 is part of a sustained increase in productivity growth that began in 1995. The resurgence in productivity seems to have been strong enough even to withstand the onset of a recession after 10 years of growth.

Confounding the sceptics: Accelerating productivity is ushering in a period of solid US economic growth, argue John Lipsky and Jim Glassma

By Jim Glassma and John Lipsky

The striking news that US productivity increased at an annual rate of 3.5 per cent in the final quarter of 2001 will surely change the debate on the US economic and financial outlook. We now know that productivity grew by close to 2 per cent for last year as a whole. To put this result in perspective, remember that productivity fell in every previous US recession of the past 50 years.

Moreover, **productivity growth** will accelerate as the economy recovers, as is typical for this stage of the business cycle. Until the past decade, the expert consensus held that trend US **productivity growth** was no higher than 1–1.25 per cent a year. With productivity advancing at a faster pace than that even through a recession, what will the pessimists and sceptics, who declared the 1990s boom was little more than a new economy mirage, say now? The speed of productivity growth is critical to justifying our bullish assessment of US economic prospects. Productivity gains help to achieve stronger output growth and lower inflation. They will also underpin the value of US financial assets and the dollar. Moreover, optimism about productivity trends will encourage the Federal Reserve to adopt a patient attitude regarding the need for interest rate increases later this year.

[Benefits of productivity growth]

The practical importance of strong underlying productivity growth will be visible in the coming profits rebound. Still-to-be-published figures of the National Income Accounts will probably show that aggregate corporate profits turned the corner in last year's fourth quarter. This momentum shift has not yet been reflected clearly in analysts' estimates, which tend to focus on year-on-year earnings comparisons.

Faster productivity growth typically has been associated with faster income growth as well. Productivity surged between 1995 and 2000 at an average annual rate of about 2.6 per cent, spurred by a historic rise in business capital spending. At the same time, gross domestic product growth averaged about 4.1 per cent a year. Profits grew rapidly, reaching the highest share of GDP in three decades. Annual wage growth nonetheless averaged 2.1 per cent when adjusted for inflation, up from 0.6 per cent in the previous five-year period.

This performance was far more favourable than expert opinion had considered possible. A chorus of academics and analysts claimed the results were a statistical illusion caused by the internet mania; reality would be restored once the inevitable cyclical downturn arrived.

[The surge in productivity in the 1990s]

Closer consideration of the data has significantly undermined the curmudgeons' position, however. In particular, it turns out that only about 30 per cent of high-technology spending by businesses during 1995–2000 was accounted for by the communications and manufacturing sectors. The balance went to the service sector. One implication is that a significant portion of high-tech investment was used for cost reduction rather than for building excess new capacity, such as broadband networks.

[Sources of productivity growth]

The end-of-investment story is incomplete, too. In fact, US business capital spending remains impressively large. It is true that such spending has fallen by about Dollars 100bn, or about 1 per cent of GDP, since mid-2000—the sharpest drop for any 18-month period of the past 50 years. However, business spending on equipment and software still accounted for nearly 9 per cent of 2001 GDP, the fourth highest annual share in the past 50 years.

As profits improve, and businesses regain confidence, investment spending will rise. Based on forward-looking figures, we believe that business capital spending may begin to grow by this year's second quarter, much sooner than consensus expectations.

But as the table shows, most of that growth was due to increases in capital per worker and not to technological change. Such high rates of capital growth could not be maintained without a severe burden on the people. Eventually, the Soviet citizens complained about the high share of their output going to investment. They wanted the consumer goods that were being most visibly obtained in the market economies. One could have predicted problems and perhaps even the demise of the Soviet Union from an examination of the sources of growth.

REVIEW

- The productivity growth slowdown in the United States in the 1970s seems to have been due to a slowdown in both technology growth and capital growth, but technology played a larger role.

- Technology also played a larger role than capital in the 1990s rebound in productivity growth.

- Applying the growth accounting formula to the former Soviet Union reveals that there was a serious problem of technological progress.

Technology Policy

The growth accounting formula tells us that if economic policy is to help maintain the higher productivity growth that began in the mid-1990s in the United States, it must provide incentives for, or remove disincentives to, technological progress. What policies might improve technological progress?

Policy to Encourage Investment in Human Capital

One policy is to improve education. A more highly trained work force is more productive. Better-educated workers are more able to make technological improvements. In other words, human capital can improve the production of technology. Hence, educational reform (higher standards, incentives for good teaching) and more funding would be ways to increase technological change. Some studies have shown that the U.S. educational system is falling behind other countries, especially in mathematics and science in the K–12 schools; hence, additional support seems warranted in order to increase economic growth.

Policy to Encourage Research and Innovation

Today, the United States and other advanced countries spend huge quantities on *research and development (R&D)*. Some of the research supports pure science, but much of it is applied research in engineering and medical technology. About 2.6 percent of U.S. GDP goes to research and development. The government provides much of its R&D funds through research grants and contracts to private firms and universities through the National Science Foundation and the National Institutes of Health and through its own research labs. But private firms are the users of most of the research funds.

The United States spends less on research and development as a share of GDP than other countries, but more in total. Total spending on research rather than spending as a share of GDP is a better measure of the usefulness of the spending if the benefits spill over to the whole economy.

During the cold war, much of U.S. research and development spending went for national defense. What should happen to those research dollars now that the cold war is over and overall defense spending has come down? Some argue that more civilian research should be supported. For many years the Defense Advanced Research Projects Agency (DARPA) funded research on computer networks and artificial intelligence. In 1993, the *D* in DARPA was dropped, signaling the new focus on civilian research.

Increased government support for research and development regardless of industry can be achieved through tax credits. A *tax credit for research* allows firms to deduct a certain fraction of their research expenditures from their taxes in order to reduce their tax bill. This increases the incentive to engage in research and development. Another way to increase the incentive for inventors and innovators is to give them a more certain claim to the property rights from their inventions. The government has a role here in defining and enforcing property rights through patent laws, trademarks, and copyrights.

Technology Embodied in New Capital

Although we have emphasized that capital and technology have two distinct effects on the growth rate of productivity, it is not always possible to separate them in practice. In order to take advantage of a new technology, it may be necessary to invest in new capital. Consider the Thompson Bagel Machine, invented by Dan Thompson, which can automatically roll and shape bagels. Before the machine was invented, bakers rolled and shaped the bagels by hand. According to Dan Thompson, who in 1993 was running the Thompson Bagel Machine Manufacturing Corporation, headquartered in Los Angeles, "You used to have two guys handshaping and boiling and baking who could turn out maybe 120 bagels an hour. With the machine and now the new ovens, I have one baker putting out 400 bagels an hour."[1] That is a productivity increase of over 500 percent! But the new technology is inseparable from the capital. In order to take advantage of the technology, bagel producers have to buy the machine and the new ovens to go with it.

Economists call this *embodied technological change* because it is embodied in the capital. An example of *disembodied technological change* would be the discovery of a new way to forecast the demand for bagels at the shop each morning so that fewer people would be disappointed on popular days and fewer bagels would be wasted on slack days. Taking advantage of this technology might not require any new capital.

The relationship between capital and technology has implications for technology policies. For example, policies that provide incentives for firms to invest might indirectly improve technology as they encourage investment in new, more productive equipment.

Is Government Intervention Appropriate?

Any time there is a question about whether government should intervene in the economy, such as with the technology policies just discussed, the operation of the private market should be examined carefully. For example, we noted that incentives for technology production may be too low without government intervention. Certainly some of the research a business firm undertakes can be kept secret from others. In such cases, the firm may have sufficient incentive to do the research. But many research results are hard to keep secret. In that case, there is a role for government intervention in subsidizing the research. In general, policies to increase economic growth should be given the test for whether government intervention in the

---

1. *The New York Times*, April 25, 1993.

economy is necessary: Is the private market providing the right incentives? If not, can the government do better without a large risk of government failure? If the answers are "no" and "yes," respectively, then government intervention is appropriate.

REVIEW
- Policy proposals to increase productivity growth by providing incentives to increase technology include educational reform, tax credits for research, increased funding for research, moving government support toward areas that have significant spillovers, and improving intellectual property laws to better define the property rights of inventors and extend them globally.

- Many technologies are embodied in new capital. Hence, policies to stimulate capital formation could also increase technology.

Conclusion: Where Does Potential GDP Go from Here?

When we first examined the growth of the economy over time in Chapter 4, we noted the longer-term trend in real GDP. The long-run trend was called potential GDP. The growth of potential GDP depends on three factors: labor, capital, and technology, which we studied in this chapter.

To conclude our discussion of economic growth, let us see how economists combine forecasts of labor growth, capital growth, and technology growth to project potential GDP growth in the future. In March 2002, the Congressional Budget Office (CBO) forecast potential GDP growth of 3.1 percent per year from 2002 to 2012. The growth rate of potential GDP is the sum of the growth rate of total hours of work plus the growth rate of output per hour of work, or the productivity growth rate. The assumptions that underlie this forecast are a growth rate of total hours of .8 percent per year and a productivity growth rate of 2.3 percent per year.

A growth rate of 3.1 percent per year for potential GDP is quite reasonable, but the CBO warned that uncertainty about the roles of technology and capital makes such a projection particularly uncertain in the future.

After discussing the monetary system in Chapter 9, we will turn to the study of fluctuations of real GDP around potential GDP.

HEY POINTS

1. The productivity growth rate—the percentage increase in output per hour of work—determines the economic well-being of people in the long run.

2. Malthus's pessimistic growth prediction was wrong because it omitted the effects of capital and, more importantly, technology.

3. Technology, along with labor and capital, determines economic growth. Technological progress explains much of the productivity growth wave that started in the late 1700s and enabled developed countries to get rich.

4. Technology as defined by economists is much broader than "high-tech" products or inventions. Technology includes such things as better organizational structure for a firm and better education for workers as well as innovations like fiber optic cables.

5. As a commodity, technology has the special features of nonexcludability and nonrivalry.
6. Patent laws attempt to make technology more excludable and thereby increase the incentives to invest.
7. The growth accounting formula is itself a great invention that has enabled economists to better understand the role of technology in the economy.
8. Technology policy has the goal of offsetting disincentives to invest and innovate that exist in the private market.
9. Government support for education and research is a key part of a modern technology policy.

KEY TERMS

productivity
diminishing returns
technology
technological change
invention
innovation
diffusion
learning by doing
human capital
growth accounting formula
new economy

QUESTIONS FOR REVIEW

1. Why did Malthus's predictions turn out to be wrong for England?
2. What is the essential difference between economic growth in the last 200 years and in the 2,000 years before that?
3. Why are economists so sure that technology played a big role in economic growth during the last 200 years?
4. Why does technology include different ways to organize a business firm?
5. How is technology produced?
6. What is the importance of nonrivalry and nonexcludability for technology?
7. Of what practical use is the growth accounting formula?
8. What is wrong with a growth policy that focuses on capital formation but not on technology?
9. What do intellectual property rights have to do with economic growth?
10. What is the rationale for government intervention in the production of technology?

PROBLEMS

1. The following table shows how output (shaded) depends on capital and labor. Using the table, draw the production function $Y = F(L)$ when the capital stock (K) is 50 and when it is 100. What do you observe? Now draw the same curve when the capital stock is 150 and 200. Do you observe any difference in the resulting increase in output?

Capital \ Labor	*50*	*100*	*150*	*200*	*250*
50	200	324	432	528	618
100	246	400	532	650	760
150	278	452	600	734	858
200	304	492	654	800	936
250	324	526	700	856	1,000

2. Consider a country in which capital per hour of work from 1950 to 1973 grew by 3 percent per year and output per hour of work grew by about 3 percent per year. Suppose that from 1973 to 1991, capital per hour of work did not grow at all and output per hour of work grew by about 1 percent per year. How much of the slowdown in productivity (output per hour of work) growth was due to technological change? Explain. (Assume that the coefficient on capital in the growth accounting formula is 1/3.)
3. According to the spending allocation model in Chapter 6, a decrease in government spending results in, among other things, an increase in investment in the long run. Suppose the capital stock is $1 trillion and a fall in government spending causes a $50 billion rise in investment. Determine the effect of the change in government purchases on long-run output growth, using the growth accounting formula. (Assume that the coefficient on capital in the growth accounting formula is 1/3.)

4. The former Soviet Union had high rates of economic growth, especially in the 1950s and 1960s, but could not maintain them. Why? What does this tell us about the limitations of capital and of government?

5. **a.** Suppose that a country has no growth in technology, and that capital and labor hours are growing at the same rate. What is the growth rate of real GDP per hour of work? Explain.

   b. Suppose that capital in the country described in part (a) continues to grow at its previous rate, technology growth is still zero, but growth in labor hours falls to half its previous rate. What happens to growth in real GDP per hour of work?

6. If we incorrectly estimate the share of capital in income, it can affect our estimation of how large technological growth has been. Rework problem 2 assuming that capital's share is 1/4. Explain intuitively the difference in the importance of technology.

7. Identify each of the following as either a capital-saving or a labor-saving technological change:

   a. A gas station installs gasoline pumps that can be activated by a customer with a credit card.

   b. A university upgrades its phone system to include voicemail.

   c. A university reorganizes its departments in order to cut back on administrative costs.

8. Write a short memo explaining what government can do to increase economic growth in light of technology's special qualities.

9. Which of the following types of government spending are likely to help economic growth? Why?

   a. Military spending on advertising for recruits

   b. Military spending on laser research

   c. Funding for a nationwide computer network

   d. Subsidies for a national opera company

   e. Extra funding for educational programs

10. Many U.S. companies in the software, music, and movie industries have been asking the Chinese government to better enforce intellectual property rights. Discuss the impact of this enforcement on

    a. Chinese firms

    b. American firms

    c. Chinese consumers

Deriving the Growth Accounting Formula

The growth accounting formula states that

$$\begin{pmatrix}\text{Growth rate of} \\ \text{productivity}\end{pmatrix} = \frac{1}{3}\begin{pmatrix}\text{growth rate} \\ \text{of capital} \\ \text{per hour} \\ \text{of work}\end{pmatrix} + \begin{pmatrix}\text{growth rate} \\ \text{of technology}\end{pmatrix}$$

To derive the formula, we start with the relationship between productivity (Y/L) and capital per hour of work (K/L) shown in Figure 8A.1. Because of diminishing returns to capital, the line is curved: As capital per hour of work increases, the increased productivity that comes from the additional capital per hour diminishes.

The curve in Figure 8A.1 is called a **productivity curve;** it can be represented in symbols as $(Y/L) = f(K/L)$, or productivity is a function of capital per hour of work.

An upward shift in the productivity function due to an increase in technological change is shown in Figure 8A.2. For example, with capital per hour constant at point A in the figure, more technology leads to more productivity.

Productivity increases in the economy are due to a combination of *movements along* the productivity curve because of more capital per hour, and of *shifts* of the productivity curve, because of technological change. The

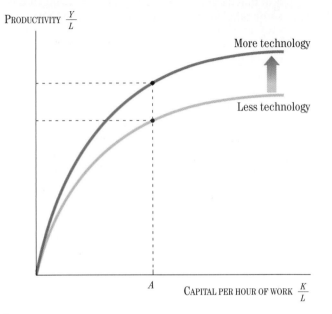

Figure 8A.2
A Shift in the Productivity Curve Due to Technology
An increase in technology permits an increase in productivity even if there is no change in capital per hour of work. For example, if capital per hour of work stays at A, productivity increases when the productivity curve shifts up.

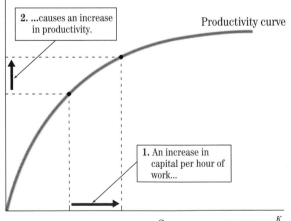

Figure 8A.1
Productivity Curve
Productivity, or output per hour of work, is shown to increase with the amount of capital that workers have, as measured by capital per hour of work. The productivity curve gets flatter as output per hour of work increases because of diminishing returns to capital.

growth accounting formula is derived by translating the *movements along* and the *shifts into* two algebraic terms.

In Figure 8A.3, productivity and capital per hour in two different years (year 1 and year 2) are shown. These could be 2002 and 2003 or any other two years. In this example, the growth rate of productivity is given by the increase in productivity (C minus A) divided by the initial level of productivity (A), or $(C - A)/A$. (The definition of the growth rate of a variable is the change divided by the initial level.)

Observe in Figure 8A.3 how the increase in productivity can be divided into the part due to higher capital per hour of work (C minus B) and the part due to technology (B minus A). Thus, we have

$$\underbrace{(C - A)/A}_{\substack{\text{Growth rate of} \\ \text{productivity}}} = \underbrace{(C - B)/A}_{\substack{\text{term related to} \\ \text{capital per hour}}} + \underbrace{(B - A)/A}_{\substack{\text{growth rate} \\ \text{of technology}}}$$

which is already close to the growth accounting formula.

To finish the derivation, we need to examine the first term on the right. How does this term relate to capital per

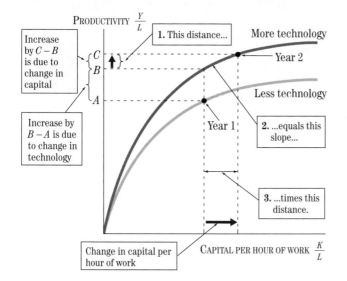

PRODUCTIVITY $\frac{Y}{L}$

Increase by $C - B$ is due to change in capital

1. This distance...

More technology

Year 2

Less technology

Increase by $B - A$ is due to change in technology

Year 1

2. ...equals this slope...

3. ...times this distance.

Change in capital per hour of work

CAPITAL PER HOUR OF WORK $\frac{K}{L}$

Figure 8A.3
Growth Accounting with Capital per Hour and Technology Increasing
Here a shift in the productivity curve and a movement along the productivity curve due to more capital per hour of work are combined. Productivity increases. The part of the increase due to capital and the part due to technological change are shown in the diagram.

hour of work? The numbered boxes in Figure 8A.3 show that $C - B$ equals the *change* in capital per hour of work $\Delta(K/L)$ times the *slope* of the productivity curve. (The slope times the change along the horizontal axis gives the changes along the vertical axis.) Let the symbol r be the slope, which measures how much additional capital increases output. Thus, $(C - B)/A$ is given by

$$\frac{\Delta(K/L)r}{Y/L} = \frac{\Delta(K/L)}{(K/L)}r(K/Y)$$

The expression on the right is obtained by multiplying the numerator and the denominator of the expression on the left by (K/Y). You might want to check the multiplication on your own. Now the term on the right is simply the growth rate of capital per hour times $r(K/Y)$. The amount of income paid to capital is r times K if capital is paid according to how much additional capital increases output. Aggregate income is given by Y. Thus, the term $r(K/Y)$ is the share of capital income in aggregate income. This share is approximately ⅓. Thus, the expression $(C - B)/A$ is the growth rate of capital per hour of work times ⅓. Thus, the growth accounting formula is derived.

Key Points

1. The productivity curve describes how more capital per hour of work increases productivity, or output per hour of work.

2. The productivity curve shifts up if there is an increase in technology.

3. The growth accounting formula is derived by dividing an increase in productivity into (1) a shift in the productivity curve due to more technology and (2) a movement along the productivity curve due to more capital per worker.

Key Term and Definition

productivity curve: a relationship stating the output per hour of work for each amount of capital per hour of work in the economy.

Questions for Review

1. What is the difference between the productivity curve and the production function?

2. What is the difference between a shift of the productivity curve and a movement along the curve?

3. Why does the share of capital income in total income appear in the growth accounting formula?

Problems

1. Consider the following relation between productivity and capital per hour for the economy.

Capital per Hour of Work (*K/L*)	Output per Hour of Work (*Y/L*)
$20	$40
$40	$80
$60	$110
$80	$130
$100	$140

   a. Plot the productivity curve.
   b. Suppose that in year 1, $K/L = 40$ and $Y/L = 80$, but in year 2, $K/L = 60$ and $Y/L = 110$. How much has technology contributed to the increase in productivity between the two years?
   c. Suppose that between year 2 and year 3, the productivity curve shifts up by $20 at each level of capital per hour of work. If $K/L = 80$ and $Y/L = 150$ in year 3, how many dollars did capital contribute to productivity growth between year 2 and year 3? How much was the contribution as a fraction of the growth rate of capital per worker?

2. Suppose the production function $Y = f(K, L)$ is such that Y equals the square root of the product (K times L). Plot the production function with Y on the vertical axis and L on the horizontal axis for the case where $K = 100$. Plot the productivity curve with Y/L on the vertical axis and K/L on the horizontal axis.

CHAPTER 9

Money and Inflation

In 1896, William Jennings Bryan won the Democratic Party's nomination for president of the United States with the most riveting speech on an economic topic in American history. The speech was all about money. In a booming voice, he rallied the delegates at the national convention against a policy—called the *gold standard*—in which money was linked to the supply of gold. He roared, "We will answer their demands for a gold standard by saying to them: You shall not press down upon the brow of labor this crown of thorns. You shall not crucify mankind upon a cross of gold."

Bryan was against the gold standard because he wanted silver to be part of the monetary standard too. That way, both silver and gold could be made into coins. Bryan knew that if silver as well as gold was coined, there would be more money, and that more money would cause more inflation. He thought inflation would be a good thing. Bryan was right that more money would cause more inflation, but he lost the election. The voters apparently did not view inflation as a good thing. Instead of Bryan, they elected William McKinley, who supported the gold standard.

The purpose of this chapter is to examine the role of money in the economy. We first define money and show that commercial banks play a key role in providing money in a modern economy. We then examine how central banks—such as the Fed (the Federal Reserve) in the United States or the ECB (European Central Bank) in Europe—can control the supply of money. We also show why *excessive increases in the supply of money cause inflation*—a very important macroeconomic principle that was behind not only the 1896 election in the United States, but also many other political successes and failures around the world in the more than 100 years since then.

What Is Money?

money: that part of a person's wealth that can be readily used for transactions; money also serves as a store of value and a unit of account.

In a broad sense, money performs three functions in the economy: It can serve as a medium of exchange, a unit of account, and a store of value. More details about the three functions are given below. Economists emphasize the medium of exchange dimension in defining money. They define **money** as the part of a person's wealth that can be readily used for transactions, such as buying a sandwich or a bicycle. This definition differs from the more typical usage, in which the term is used to describe someone's wealth or income—as when we say that "she makes a lot of money" or "he has a lot of money." To an economist, money does not include what a person earns in a year or the total assets that she has, but it does include the portion of that person's wealth—such as the notes and coins in her purse—that can be easily used for transactions.

Three Functions of Money

medium of exchange: something that is generally accepted as a means of payment.

■ **Medium of Exchange.**   Money serves as a **medium of exchange** in that it is an item that people are willing to accept as payment for what they are selling because they in turn can use it to pay for something else they want. For example, in ancient times, people received coins for their agricultural produce, such as grain, and then used these coins to buy clothing.

The use of coins was a great technological improvement over *barter,* in which goods are exchanged only for other goods. Under a barter system, there is no single medium of exchange. Thus, under a barter system, if you make shoes and want to buy apples, you have to find an apple seller who needs new shoes. The disadvantage of a barter system is that it requires a rare *coincidence of wants* in which the person who wants to consume what you want to sell (shoes, for example) has exactly what you want to consume (apples, for example).

store of value: something that will allow purchasing power to be carried from one period to the next.

■ **Store of Value.**   Money also serves as a **store of value** from one period to another. For example, in ancient times, people could sell their produce in September for gold coins and then use the coins to buy staples in January. In other words, they could store their purchasing power from one season to another.

Coins are not the only thing that can serve as a store of value. For example, rice and corn can also be stored from one season to the next; therefore, they can also serve as a store of value. But if you are not a farmer with a large storage bin, coins are much more likely to be used as money.

unit of account: a standard unit in which prices can be quoted and values of goods can be compared.

■ **Unit of Account.**   Money also serves a third function: providing a **unit of account.** The prices of goods are usually stated in units of money. For example, prices of shoes or apples in ancient Greece were stated in a certain number of tetradrachmas because people using these coins were familiar with that unit. Originally, units of money were determined by the weight of the metal. The British pound, for example, was originally a pound of silver. That terminology stuck even though, as we will see, modern money is unrelated to silver or any other metal.

To better understand the difference between the unit of account and the medium of exchange, it is helpful to find examples where they are based on different monies. For example, when inflation got very high in Argentina in the early 1990s, the prices of many goods were quoted in U.S. dollars rather than Argentine pesos, but people usually exchanged pesos when they bought or sold goods. Thus, the U.S.

dollar was the unit of account, while the medium of exchange was still the peso. But such cases are the exception; the unit of account and the medium of exchange are usually the same money.

Commodity Money

Many items have been used for money throughout history. Salt, cattle, furs, tobacco, shells, and arrowheads have been used as money. Traces of their former use can still be found in our vocabulary. The word *salary* comes from the Latin word for salt, and the word *pecuniary* comes from the Latin word for cattle. In World War II prisoner of war camps, cigarettes were used for money. On the island of Yap in the Pacific Ocean, huge stones weighing several tons were used for money.

Throughout history, the most common form of money has been metallic coins, usually gold, silver, or bronze. Gold coins were used as early as the seventh century B.C. in Lydia (now western Turkey). The Chinese were issuing bronze coins with a hole in the middle in the fifth century B.C., and in the fourth century the Greeks issued silver coins called tetradrachmas that had the goddess Athena on one side and her sacred animal, the owl, on the other. All these examples of money are commodities and are therefore called *commodity money*. Metals proved to be the most common form of commodity money because they could be divided easily into smaller units, are very durable, and could be carried around.

When gold, silver, and other commodities were used as money, changes in the supply of these commodities would change their price relative to all other goods. An increase in the supply of gold, all else equal, would increase the number of gold coins that people were willing to pay in order to purchase other goods and services. In other words, the price of all other goods in the economy would rise relative to gold. Such an increase in the price of all goods in the economy is called inflation, as you

Stone Money of Yap Island, Micronesia

Silver Coins of Ancient Greece

may recall from the definitions of key economic concepts given in Chapter 5. Thus, increases in the supply of gold or any other commodity used as money would cause inflation. Whenever there were huge gold discoveries, the price of gold fell and there were increases in inflation in countries that used gold as money. Thus, inflation was determined largely by the supply of precious metals. This relationship between the supply of money and inflation, which seems so clear in the case of commodity money, has persisted into modern times, even though there are now many other forms of money.

From Coins to Paper Money to Deposits

Although coins and other commodity monies are improvements over barter, there are more efficient forms of money. Starting in the late eighteenth and early nineteenth centuries, *paper money* began to be used widely and supplemented or replaced coins as a form of money. Although there are a few examples of paper money being used earlier, it was at this time that it became generally recognized that paper money was easier to use and could save greatly on the use of precious metals.

Originally, the amount of paper currency was linked by law or convention to the supply of commodities. One reason for this link was the recognition that more money would cause inflation and that limiting the amount of paper money to the amount of some commodity like gold would limit the amount of paper money. Irving Fisher of Yale University, perhaps the most prolific and influential American economist of the early twentieth century, argued for linking paper money to commodities for precisely this reason. Many countries of the world linked their paper money to gold in the nineteenth and early twenteeth centuries. They were on a *gold standard,* which meant that the price of gold in terms of paper money was fixed by the government. The government fixed the price by agreeing to buy and sell gold at that price. Today the United States and other countries have severed all links between their money and gold. They are no longer on the gold standard and apparently have no intention of returning. Governments now supply virtually all the coin and paper money—the two together are called **currency.**

currency: money in its physical form: coin and paper money.

Although paper money was much easier to make and to use than coins, it too has been surpassed by a more efficient form of money. Today many people have **checking deposits,** at banks or other financial institutions. These are deposits of funds on which an individual can write a check to make payment for goods and services. The deposits serve as money because people can write checks on them. For example, when a student pays $100 for books with a check, the student's checking deposit at the bank goes down by $100 and the bookstore's checking deposit at the bank goes up by $100. Checking deposits are used in much the same way as when a student pays with a $100 bill, which is then placed in the store's cash register. The student's holding of money goes down by $100, and the store's goes up by $100. Deposits are used by many people as a partial replacement for coin or paper money. Writing checks to pay for goods has become more common than using currency.

checking deposit: an account at a financial institution on which checks can be written; also called checkable deposit.

Measures of the Money Supply

money supply: the sum of currency (coin and paper money) and deposits.

Today economists define the **money supply** as the sum of currency (coin and paper money) and deposits. But there are differences of opinion about what types of deposits should be included.

The narrowest measure of the money supply is called *M1.* The M1 measure consists mainly of currency plus checking deposits (travelers checks are also part of M1 but constitute less than 1 percent of total M1). The items in M1 have a great degree of

Table 9.1	
Measures of Money in the United States, January 2002 (billions of dollars)	
Currency	586
M1: Currency plus checking deposits	1,182
M2: M1 plus time deposits, savings deposits, and other deposits on which check writing is limited or not allowed	5,474

Source: Federal Reserve Board.

liquidity, which means that they can be quickly and easily used to purchase goods and services.

Many things that people would consider money, however, are not included in M1. For example, if you had no cash but you wanted to buy a birthday gift for a relative, you could withdraw cash from your savings deposit. A *savings deposit* is a deposit that pays interest and from which funds can normally be easily withdrawn at any time. In other words, a savings deposit is also liquid, but not quite as liquid as a checking deposit. Similarly, *time deposits*—which require the depositor to keep the money at the bank for a certain amount of time or else lose interest—are not as liquid as checking deposits, but it is possible to withdraw funds from them. Economists have created a broader measure of the money supply, called *M2*, that includes all that is in M1 plus savings deposits, time deposits, and certain accounts on which check writing is very limited. Still broader concepts of the money supply can be defined, but M1 and M2 are the most important ones. Table 9.1 shows the total amounts of different definitions of the money supply for the whole U.S. economy in May 2002.

Only about one-half of the M1 definition of the money supply is currency, and only about one-tenth of the M2 definition is currency. There is disagreement among economists as to whether the more narrowly defined M1 or the more broadly defined M2 or something else is the best definition of the money supply. There is probably no best definition for all times and all purposes. For simplicity, in the rest of this chapter we make no distinction between the Ms but simply refer to the money supply, *M,* as currency plus deposits.

REVIEW
- Commodity money—usually gold, silver, or bronze coins—originally served as the main type of money in most societies. Increases in the supply of these commodities would reduce their price relative to all other commodities and thereby cause inflation.

- Later, paper currency and deposits at banks became forms of money.

- There are three roles for money—as a medium of exchange, as a store of value, and as a unit of account.

The Fed, the Banks, and the Link from Reserves to Deposits

We have seen that increases in the supply of commodity money such as gold would increase inflation. So would the excessive printing of paper money (currency) by governments. But in today's world, money consists of both currency and deposits.

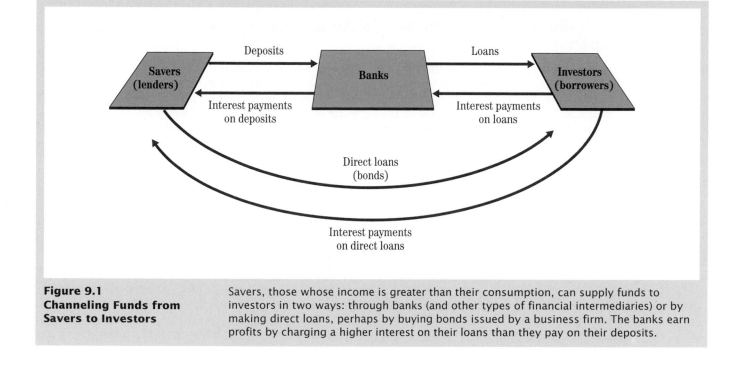

Figure 9.1
Channeling Funds from
Savers to Investors

Savers, those whose income is greater than their consumption, can supply funds to investors in two ways: through banks (and other types of financial intermediaries) or by making direct loans, perhaps by buying bonds issued by a business firm. The banks earn profits by charging a higher interest on their loans than they pay on their deposits.

Federal Reserve System (the Fed): the central bank of the United States, which oversees the creation of money in the United States.

bank: a firm that channels funds from savers to investors by accepting deposits and making loans.

Nevertheless, it is possible for governments—usually through a central bank—to to control the supply of money. In the United States, the central bank is the **Federal Reserve System,** nicknamed the "Fed." To understand how the Fed can control the supply of money, we must first look at how the Fed can control the amount of deposits at banks.

A **bank**—such as FleetBoston or Chase Manhattan—is a firm that channels funds from savers to investors by accepting deposits and making loans. Figure 9.1 illustrates this function of banks. Banks are a type of *financial intermediary* because they "intermediate" between savers and investors. Other examples of financial intermediaries are credit unions and savings and loan institutions. Banks are sometimes called *commercial banks* because many of their loans are to business firms engaged in commerce. Banks accept deposits from people who have funds and who want to earn interest and then lend the funds to other individuals who want to borrow and who are willing to pay interest. A bank earns profits by charging a higher interest rate to the borrowers than it pays to the depositors.

The Fed

The *central bank* of a country serves as a bank to other banks. In other words, commercial banks deposit funds at the central bank, and the central bank in turn makes loans to other commercial banks. We will see that the deposits of the commercial banks at the central bank are very important for controlling the money supply.

The Fed was established as the central bank for the United States in 1913 and now has over 25,000 employees spread all over the country.

■ **Board of Governors.**   At the core of the Fed is the *Federal Reserve Board,* or Board of Governors, consisting of seven people appointed to nonrenewable

The Second (?) Most Powerful Person in America: Alan Greenspan

Alan Greenspan was appointed to the Board of Governors of the Federal Reserve System in August of 1987, to fill an unexpired term. He is scheduled to serve on the Board of Governors until 2006. Dr. Greenspan has served as chairman of the Board of Governors ever since his initial appointment in 1987. The general public believes that Chairman Greenspan is the person most responsible for the long economic expansion of the 1990s, and his public reputation is unrivaled among policymakers. A good example of Alan Greenspan's lofty standing was the title chosen by Bob Woodward for Greenspan's biography: *Maestro*.

What then is the background of this man, considered by many to be the second (and by some the first!) most powerful man in America? According to the information provided by the Federal Reserve, Alan Greenspan was born on March 6, 1926, in New York City. He received a B.S. in economics (summa cum laude) in 1948, an M.A. in economics in 1950, and a Ph.D. in economics in 1977, all from New York University. It is interesting to note that Dr. Greenspan, unlike many academic economists, received his Ph.D. somewhat late in his career. In between his master's

degree and his doctoral degree, Dr. Greenspan was chairman and president of Townsend-Greenspan & Co., Inc., an economic consulting firm in New York City. He used the experience he gained from his study of the economy, in particular through his understanding of economic forecasting, to serve as chairman of the President's Council of Economic Advisers under President Ford. He also served a stint from 1981 to 1983 as chairman of the National Commission on Social Security Reform. Prior to joining the Fed, Dr. Greenspan acquired a wide variety of policy experience by serving as a member of President Reagan's Economic Policy Advisory Board, a senior adviser to the Brookings Panel on Economic Activity, and a consultant to the Congressional Budget Office.

So now you have a glimpse of what it takes to become the second most powerful person in America: a doctorate in economics, a thorough understanding of the economy, a wide background in policy, and the respect of everyone who comes into contact with you. A tall order indeed, but you can be comforted by the thought that introductory macroeconomics is the first step toward that goal.

One of the duties of the United States Federal Reserve Chairman is to present monetary policy reports to Congress. On March 7, 2002, Federal Reserve Chairman Alan Greenspan testified before the U.S. Senate Banking, Housing and Urban Affairs Committee about the economic recovery, essentially declaring the recession over.

fourteen-year terms by the president of the United States and confirmed by the Senate. The Federal Reserve Board is located in Washington, D.C.

One of the governors is appointed by the president as chairman of the board; this appointment also requires Senate confirmation and can be renewed for additional terms. Alan Greenspan was appointed chairman by President Reagan in 1987 and reappointed by President Bush in 1991 and by President Clinton in 1996 and again in 2000.

■ **The District Federal Reserve Banks.** The Federal Reserve System includes not only the Federal Reserve Board in Washington but also twelve Federal Reserve Banks in different districts around the country (see Figure 9.2).

The term *Fed* refers to the whole Federal Reserve System, including the Board of Governors in Washington and the twelve district banks. Each district bank is headed by a president, who is chosen by commercial bankers and other people in the district and approved by the Board of Governors.

■ **The Federal Open Market Committee (FOMC).** The Fed makes decisions about the supply of money through a committee called the **Federal Open Market Committee (FOMC).** The members of the FOMC are the seven governors and the twelve district bank presidents, but only five of the presidents vote at any one time. Thus, there are twelve voting members of the FOMC at any one time. The FOMC meets in Washington about eight times a year to decide how to implement monetary

Federal Open Market Committee (FOMC): the committee, consisting of the seven members of the Board of Governors and the twelve presidents of the Fed district banks, that meets about eight times per year and makes decisions about the supply of money; only five of the presidents vote at any one time.

policy. Figure 9.3 shows the relationship between the FOMC, the Board of Governors, and the district banks.

Even though the chair of the Fed has only one of the twelve votes on the FOMC, the position has considerably more power than this one vote might indicate. The chair also has executive authority over the operations of the whole Federal Reserve, sets the agenda at FOMC meetings, and represents the Fed in testimony before Congress. When journalists in the popular press write about the Fed, they usually talk as if the chair has almost complete power over Fed decisions. Some view the chair of the Fed as the second most powerful person in America, after the president of the United States.

Now that we have described the Fed, let us examine the operation of banks and how they, along with the Fed, create money.

The Banks

A commercial bank accepts deposits from individuals and makes loans to others. To understand how a bank functions, it is necessary to look at its balance sheet, which shows these deposits and loans. Table 9.2 is an example of a balance sheet for a bank, called BankOne.

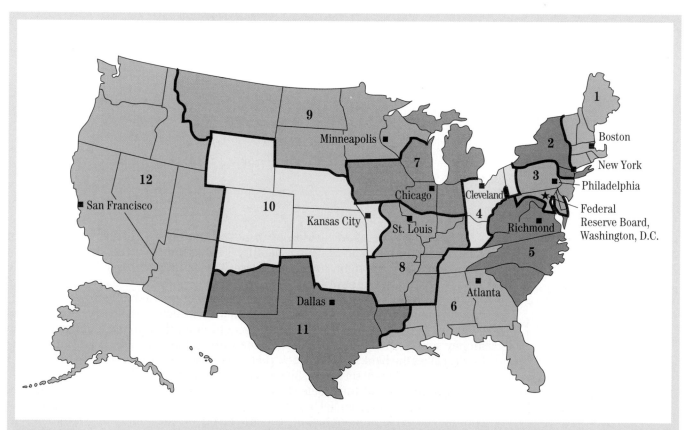

**Figure 9.2
The Twelve Districts of
the Fed**

The country is divided into twelve districts, each with a district Federal Reserve Bank. Each district bank is headed by a president, who sits on the FOMC. Alaska and Hawaii are in District 12.

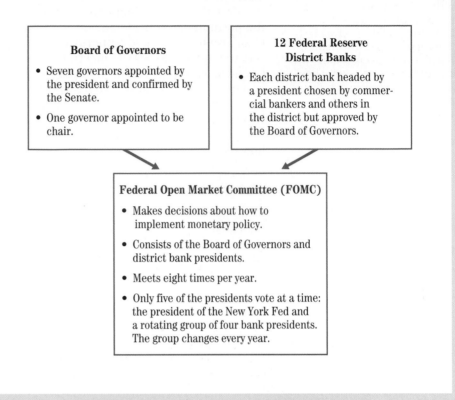

Figure 9.3
The Structure of the Fed
Decisions about monetary policy are made by the FOMC, which consists of the Fed governors and district Fed presidents.

asset: something of value owned by a person or a firm.

liability: something of value that a person or firm owes to someone else.

reserves: deposits that commercial banks hold at the Fed.

The different items are divided into *assets* and *liabilities*. An **asset** is something of value owned by a person or firm. A **liability** is something of value that a person or a firm owes, such as a debt, to someone else. Thus a bank's assets are anything the bank owns and any sum owed to the bank by someone else. A bank's liabilities are anything the bank owes to someone else. People's *deposits* at banks are the main liability of banks, as shown in Table 9.2. Certain assets, such as the bank's building and furniture, are not shown in this balance sheet because they do not change when the money supply changes. Also, when a bank starts up, the owners must put in some funds, called the bank's capital stock, that can be used in case the bank needs cash in an emergency. This asset is not shown in this balance sheet either.

Consider each of the assets shown in the balance sheet in Table 9.2. **Reserves** are deposits that commercial banks hold at the Fed, much as people hold deposits at commercial banks. Remember, the Fed is the bank for the commercial banks. Just as you can hold a deposit at a commercial bank, a commercial bank can hold a deposit at the Fed. Reserves are simply a name for these deposits by commercial banks at the Fed.

Table 9.2
Balance Sheet of BankOne (millions of dollars)

Assets		Liabilities	
Loans	70	Deposits	100
Bonds	20		
Reserves	10		

This is the initial situation. The ratio of reserves to deposits is .1.

required reserve ratio: the fraction of a bank's deposits that it is required to hold at the Fed.

Under U.S. law, a commercial bank is required to hold reserves at the Fed equal to a fraction of the deposits people hold at the commercial bank; this fraction is called the **required reserve ratio.** Banks may in fact choose to hold a greater fraction of their deposits in the form of reserves at the Fed than they are required to. In reality, then, the ratio of reserves to deposits, known as the *reserve ratio,* may differ from the required reserve ratio: It can be larger, but it cannot be smaller. In the following example, we will assume that banks do not exercise this option, so that the reserve ratio is equal to the required reserve ratio. We will also assume that the required reserve ratio is 10 percent, which is very close to what it really is in the United States.

The two other assets of the bank are loans and bonds. *Loans* are made by banks to individuals or firms for a period of time; the banks earn interest on these loans. *Bonds* are promises of a firm or government to pay back a certain amount after a number of years. Bonds are issued by the U.S. government and by large corporations. Banks sometimes buy and hold such bonds, as BankOne has done in Table 9.2.

The Link from Reserves to Deposits

Because deposits at banks are a form of money, the Fed must be able to control the total amount of these deposits if it is to control the money supply. The link between the deposits at banks and the reserves at the Fed provides the key mechanism by which the Fed can exert control over the amount of deposits at the commercial banks. To see this, we first look at some examples to show how this link between reserves and deposits works in the whole economy. To make the story simpler for now, we assume that everyone uses deposits rather than currency for their money. (We will take up currency again in the next section.)

■ **A Formula Linking Reserves to Deposits.** To see how the Fed can change the amount of deposits in the economy, let us assume that the Fed increases the amount of reserves that banks hold at the Fed. The Fed can cause such an increase in reserves simply by buying something from a bank and paying for it by increasing that bank's reserves at the Fed. The Fed usually buys government bonds when it wants to increase reserves because banks have a lot of bonds.

On any given day, the Fed buys and sells billions of dollars of government bonds. When the Fed buys government bonds, it has to pay for them with something. It pays for them with bank reserves—the deposits banks have with the Fed. For example, if the Fed wants to buy bonds held by Citibank, it says, "We want $1 billion worth of bonds, and we will pay for them by increasing Citibank's account with us by $1 billion." This is an electronic transaction. Citibank's deposits at the Fed (reserves) have increased by $1 billion, and the Fed gets the bonds. They have exchanged bank reserves for the bonds. The buying or selling bonds by the Federal Reserve is called an **open market operation.**

open market operation: the buying or selling of bonds by the central bank.

So let's assume that the Fed buys $10 million of government bonds from BankOne and pays for the bonds by increasing BankOne's reserves by $10 million. Thus reserves rise at banks in the economy. Now, with the reserve ratio the same (in this example equal to .1) for each bank in the economy, there is a formula linking reserves and deposits for the whole economy. It is given by

$$\text{Reserves} = (\text{reserve ratio}) \times \text{deposits}$$

where reserves and deposits refer to the amounts in the whole economy. If we divide both sides of this expression by the reserve ratio, we get

$$\text{Deposits} = \left(\frac{1}{\text{reserve ratio}}\right) \times \text{reserves}$$

Thus, any increase in reserves is multiplied by the inverse of the reserve ratio to get the increase in deposits. For example, if the $10 million change in reserves is multiplied by $(1/.1) = 10$, we get $100 million change in deposits.

One could have started the example by assuming that the Fed bought $10 million in government bonds from some person other than a bank. That person would deposit the check from the Fed in a bank, and in the end, the answer would be exactly the same: A $10 million increase in reserves leads to a $100 million increase in deposits.

One could also analyze the effects of a decrease in reserves using the same formula linking reserves and deposits. A decrease in reserves occurs when the Fed sells bonds. For example, a decrease in reserves of $10 million would lead to a decrease in deposits of $100 million.

■ **Bank-by-Bank Deposit Expansion.** Now let's look at the details of what is going on in the banks. In our example, when the Fed buys bonds, BankOne's holdings of bonds decline by $10 million, from $20 million to $10 million, and BankOne's reserves at the Fed increase by $10 million, from $10 million to $20 million. The balance sheet would then look like Table 9.3, a change from Table 9.2. The key point is that there are now $10 million more reserves in the economy than before the Fed purchased the government bonds from BankOne. The reserves are held by BankOne, but they will not be held for long.

Recall that banks hold reserves equal to a certain fraction of their deposits, a fraction called the reserve ratio, which in this example we are assuming is 10 percent. But now, after the Fed's actions, BankOne has 20 percent of its deposits as reserves, or more than the required 10 percent. Because the reserves do not pay any interest, while loans and bonds do, the bank will have incentive to reduce its reserves and make more loans or buy more bonds.

Table 9.3
Balance Sheet of BankOne after Reserves Increase (millions of dollars)

Assets		Liabilities	
Loans	70	Deposits	100
Bonds	10		
Reserves	20		

Note the effect of the Fed's purchase of bonds: Compared with Table 9.2, bonds are lower and reserves are higher in Table 9.3. The ratio of reserves to deposits is .2.

Table 9.4
Balance Sheet of BankOne after It Makes Loans

Assets		Liabilities	
Loans	80	Deposits	100
Bonds	10		
Reserves	10		

> By making more loans, the bank reduces the ratio of reserves to deposits back to .1.

Suppose BankOne decreases its reserves by making more loans; with the reserve ratio of .1, the bank can loan $10 million. Suppose the bank loans $10 million to UNO, a small oil company, which uses the funds to buy an oil tanker from DOS, a shipbuilding firm. UNO pays DOS with a check from BankOne, and DOS deposits the check in its checking account at its own bank, BankTwo. Now BankTwo must ask BankOne for payment; BankOne will make the payment by lowering its reserve account at the Fed and increasing BankTwo's reserve account at the Fed by $10 million. BankOne's balance sheet at the end of these transactions is shown in Table 9.4.

Hence, after BankOne makes the loan and transfers its reserves to BankTwo, its reserves are back to 10 percent of its deposits. This is the end of the story for BankOne, but not for the economy as a whole because BankTwo now has $10 million more in reserves, and this is going to affect BankTwo's decisions. Let us see how.

Now BankTwo finds itself with $10 million in additional deposits and $10 million in additional reserves at the Fed. (Remember that deposits are a liability to BankTwo and the reserves are an asset; thus, assets and liabilities each have risen by $10 million.) However, BankTwo needs to hold only $1 million in reserves for the additional $10 million in deposits. Thus, BankTwo will want to make more loans until its reserves equal 10 percent of its deposits. It will lend out to other people an amount equal to 90 percent of the $10 million, or $9 million. In Table 9.5, the increase in

Table 9.5
Deposit Expansion (millions of dollars)

	Deposits	Loans	Reserves
BankTwo	10.00	9.00	1.000
BankThree	9.00	8.10	0.900
BankFour	8.10	7.29	0.810
BankFive	7.29	6.56	0.729
BankSix	6.56	5.90	0.656
BankSeven	5.90	5.31	0.590
BankEight	5.31	4.78	0.531
BankNine	4.78	4.30	0.430
BankTen	4.30	3.87	0.387
.	.	.	.
.	.	.	.
.	.	.	.
Final Sum	100.00	90.00	10.000

> The numbers in each column get smaller and smaller; if we add up the numbers for all the banks, even those beyond BankTen, we get the sum at the bottom.

deposits, loans, and reserves at BankTwo is shown in the first row. This is the end of the story for BankTwo, but not for the economy as a whole.

The people who get loans from BankTwo will use these loans to pay others. Thus, the funds will probably end up in yet another bank, called BankThree. Then, BankThree will find itself with $9 million in additional deposits and $9 million in additional reserves. BankThree will then lend 90 percent of the $9 million, or $8.1 million, as shown in the second row of Table 9.5. This process will continue from bank to bank. We begin to see that the initial increase in reserves is leading to a much bigger expansion of deposits. The whole process is shown in Table 9.5. Each row shows what happens at one of the banks. The sums of the columns show the change for the whole economy. If we sum the columns through the end of the process, we will see that deposits, and thus the money supply, increase by $100 million as a result of the $10 million increase in reserves. The increase in deposits is 10 times the actual increase in reserves—exactly what the formula predicted! In reality, the whole process takes a short period of time (days rather than weeks) because banks adjust their loans and reserves very quickly.

REVIEW
- Banks serve two important functions: They help channel funds from savers to investors, and their deposits can be used as money.
- Commercial banks hold deposits, called reserves, at the Fed.
- The Fed increases reserves by buying bonds and reduces reserves by selling bonds.
- The deposits at banks expand by a multiple of any increase in reserves. Thus, there is a link between reserves and deposits in the overall economy.

How the Fed Controls the Money Supply: Currency plus Deposits

We have now seen how the Fed can, through an increase in reserves, increase the amount of deposits or, through a decrease in reserves, reduce the amount of deposits. But the money supply includes currency as well as deposits. So let us now add currency to the story. With currency in the picture, there are now three things to keep track of: deposits, reserves, and currency. We will find it useful to introduce some shorthand notation to keep track of all three.

The Money Supply *(M)* and Bank Reserves *(BR)*

The supply of money is currency plus deposits. That is,

Money supply = currency + deposits

If we let CU stand for currency and D stand for deposits, then

$$M = CU + D$$

or, in words, the money supply equals currency plus deposits.

We already know that commercial banks hold a fraction of their deposits at the Fed. Let BR represent the reserves the commercial banks hold at the Fed, and let rr be the reserve ratio. Then the relationship between reserves and deposits described in the previous section can be written using symbols as

$$BR = rrD$$

or, in words, bank reserves equal the reserve ratio (rr) times deposits (D). For example, if banks are required to hold 10 percent of their deposits as reserves at the Fed, then $rr = .1$. Remember, reserves, held at the central bank by the commercial banks, are just like any other deposit, such as a checking deposit. For example, Chase Manhattan, a commercial bank headquartered in New York City, holds a large amount of reserves at the Fed.

Currency versus Deposits

Although currency and deposits are both part of the money supply, they have different characteristics. For some purposes, people prefer currency to checking deposits, and vice versa. These preferences determine how much currency and checking deposits there are in the economy. If you want to hold more currency in your wallet because you find it is more convenient than a checking deposit, you just go to the bank and reduce your checking deposit and carry around more currency. If you are worried about crime and do not want to have much currency in your wallet, then you go to the bank and deposit a larger amount in your checking account. Thus, people decide on the amount of currency versus deposits in the economy. In Japan, where crime is less prevalent than in many other countries, people use much more currency compared to checking accounts than in other countries. Even Japanese business executives who earn the equivalent of $120,000 a year frequently are paid monthly with the equivalent of $10,000 in cash.

In order to determine the amount of currency versus deposits in the economy as a whole, we assume that people want to hold currency equal to a certain fraction of their deposits. More precisely, we assume that there is a ratio called the **currency to deposit ratio** that at any time describes how much currency people want to hold compared to their deposits. If people are happy holding an amount of currency equal to 40 percent of their deposits, then the currency to deposit ratio is .4. If deposits equal $700 billion and the currency to deposit ratio is .4, then currency would equal $280 billion and the money supply would equal $980 billion. Different individuals will have different tastes, but on the average, there will be an overall ratio of currency to deposits in the economy. That ratio depends on people's behavior, on custom, and, as already mentioned, on security in the community.

The ratio also depends on technology; for example, credit cards have reduced the currency to deposit ratio. Note, however, that credit cards are not money any more than a driver's license used for identification when cashing a check is money. Credit cards make more use of checking deposits relative to currency because people usually pay their credit card bills with a check.

At any given point in time, we can take the currency to deposit ratio as a fairly stable number. If the currency to deposit ratio is k, then we can write

$$\text{Currency} = (\text{currency to deposit ratio}) \times \text{deposits}$$
$$= k \times \text{deposits}$$

Using the symbols we have already introduced, we can write this as

$$CU = kD$$

We now use this expression along with the previous two expressions for the money supply (M) and bank reserves (BR) to show how the Fed can control the money supply.

currency to deposit ratio: the proportion of currency that people in the economy want to hold relative to their deposits; it equals currency divided by deposits.

The Money Multiplier

We saw that the Fed can change the amount of bank reserves by buying and selling bonds. We also saw that when the Fed increases reserves, deposits expand. If currency held by people is equal to k times deposits, then currency will increase when deposits increase. Thus, by buying and selling bonds, the Fed can affect the supply of currency. The Fed can therefore control both currency and reserves. The sum of currency plus reserves is called the **monetary base** by economists. That is,

Monetary base = currency + reserves

Because the Fed can control both currency and reserves, it can control the monetary base. If we let MB stand for the monetary base, then

$$MB = CU + BR$$

Table 9.6 shows the size of the monetary base in the U.S. economy in January 2002.

We now want to derive a link between the monetary base MB and the money supply M. That link can be used by the Fed to control the money supply. To derive the link, we will use some algebra and equations just like those the people at the Fed use. We can use the equation showing that the money supply equals currency plus deposits and the equation showing that currency is a certain fraction of deposits to get a relationship between the money supply and deposits. That is, substitute $CU = kD$ into the equation $M = CU + D$ to get $M = kD + D$, or

$$M = (k + 1)D$$

There is also the relationship that exists between bank reserves and deposits, $BR = rrD$, which together with $CU = kD$ can be substituted into the equation $MB = CU + BR$ to get $MB = kD + rrD$, or

$$MB = (k + rr)D$$

Now, to find the link between MB and M, divide M by MB and cancel out D to get

$$\frac{M}{MB} = \frac{(k + 1)}{(k + rr)} \Rightarrow M = \frac{(k + 1)}{(k + rr)}MB$$

We call this ratio, $(k + 1)/(k + rr)$, the money multiplier. For example, if the reserve ratio rr is .1 and the currency to deposit ratio k is .2, then the money multiplier is $(.2 + 1)/(.2 + .1) = 1.2/.3 = 4$. An increase in the monetary base MB of $100 million would increase the money supply M by $400 million. This large increase is the reason for the term *multiplier*. In general, the **money multiplier** is the number you multiply the monetary base by to get the money supply.

To see how the money multiplier works in practice, suppose the Fed buys bonds so as to increase the monetary base by $1 billion; according to the money multiplier, the money supply in the economy should increase by $4 billion. The actual increase in the money supply occurs through a bank-by-bank process just like that shown in Table 9.5, with currency now changing as well. With currency in the story, the total effect on the money supply of a change in the monetary base is smaller than in Table 9.5 because people do not put all their money in banks. This reduces the amount of deposit expansion. Note that if $k = 0$, the case without currency, the money multiplier is $(1/rr)$, just as in the formula relating deposits to reserves in the previous section. That is, with $k = 0$ and $CU = 0$ we have that deposits equal $1/r$ times reserves. With $rr = .1$, the money multiplier is 10. Thus, an increase in the monetary base of $10 million will increase money by $100 million, as in the previous section.

More important than the fact that the multiplier is greater than 1 is that it provides a link between the monetary base and the money supply in the economy. As

monetary base: currency plus reserves; the monetary base can be tightly controlled by the Fed.

Follow the economic logic behind the algebra. The first equation links the *money supply* to deposits. The second equation links the *monetary base* to deposits. Thus the money supply and the monetary base must be linked together, as indicated by the third equation showing the money multiplier.

---

money multiplier: the multiple by which the money supply changes as a result of a change in the monetary base.

Table 9.6
The Monetary Base for the United States, January 2002 (billions of dollars)

Currency	586
Reserves	55
Monetary Base	641

Source: Federal Reserve Board.

long as the currency to deposit ratio and the reserve ratio do not change, the Fed can control the money supply by adjusting the monetary base.

REVIEW
- The monetary base is the sum of currency plus bank reserves. The Fed can change the money supply—currency plus deposits—by adjusting the monetary base. A change in the monetary base changes the money supply by a multiple of the increase in the monetary base. The multiple is called the money multiplier.

- The money multiplier depends on the reserve ratio and the currency to deposit ratio.

Money Growth and Inflation

Early in this chapter, in the section "Commodity Money," we showed that when gold, silver, or other commodities were the primary form of money, then increases in the supply of money would cause inflation. Even though paper currency and deposits are now the main forms of money, the same principle holds today. That is, *all other things being equal,* an increase in the supply of money will cause inflation. In this section we examine this principle by looking at two important episodes of inflation during the twentieth century. Before we do so, we introduce a famous equation that can help us test the principle that an increase in the supply of money eventually causes inflation.

Consider first a simple example. Suppose that all of your transactions are in a video game arcade with food-vending machines and video game machines. You will need money in your pocket to carry out your transactions each day. If you use the vending and video game machines ten times a day, you will need ten times more money in your pocket than if you use the machines once a day. Hence, ten times more transactions means ten times more money. If the prices for vending machine items and minutes on a video game machine double, then you will need twice as much money for each day's activities, assuming that the higher price does not cure your habit. Hence, whether the value of transactions increases because the number of items purchased increases or because the price of each item increases, the amount of money used for transactions will rise.

What is true for you and the machines is true for the whole population and the whole economy. For the whole economy, real GDP is like the number of transactions with the machines, and the GDP deflator (a measure of the average price in the economy) is like the average price of the vending and game machines. Just as the amount of money you use for transactions in the game arcade is related to the number of transactions and the price of each transaction, so too is the supply of money in the economy related to real GDP and the GDP deflator.

quantity equation of money: the equation relating the price level and real GDP to the quantity of money and the velocity of money: The quantity of money times its velocity equals the price level times real GDP.

The Quantity Equation of Money

This relationship between money, real GDP, and the GDP deflator can be summarized by the **quantity equation of money,** which is written (as shown on page 216)

$$\text{Money supply} \times \text{velocity} = \text{GDP deflator} \times \text{real GDP}$$

or

$$MV = PY$$

where V is velocity, P is the GDP deflator, and Y is real GDP. For example, if the money supply was $1,000 billion, real GDP was $8,000, and the GDP deflator was 1.1, then a value of 8.8 for velocity would satisfy the quantity equation ($1,000 \times 8.8 = 1.1 \times 8,000$).

velocity: a measure of how frequently money is turned over in the economy.

The term **velocity** measures how frequently money is turned over. It is the number of times a dollar is used on average to make purchases. To see this, suppose an automatic teller machine (ATM) is installed in the room with the vending machines and video games from the preceding example. Each morning you get cash from the ATM for your morning games, and each day at midday an employee takes the cash from the vending and game machines and restokes the ATM. You then replenish your cash from the ATM to pay for your afternoon use of the games and vending machines; you now need to carry only half as much currency in your pocket as before they installed the ATM, when you had to bring enough cash to last all day. From your perspective, therefore, the velocity of money doubles. Money turns over twice as fast. As this example shows, velocity in the economy depends on technology and, in particular, on how efficient we are at using money.

Now, let's use the quantity equation to show how an increase in the money supply is related to inflation. If you look carefully at the quantity equation of money, you can see that if velocity and real GDP are not affected by a change in money, then an increase in the money supply will increase the GDP deflator (the average level of prices in the economy). A higher percentage increase in money—that is, *higher money growth*—will lead to a higher percentage increase in prices—that is, *higher inflation*. Thus the quantity equation of money shows that higher rates of money growth lead to higher inflation, just as in the case of commodity money early in the chapter.

A restatement of the quantity equation using growth rates leads to a convenient relationship between money growth, inflation, real GDP growth, and velocity growth. In particular,

$$\text{Money growth} + \text{velocity growth} = \text{inflation} + \text{real GDP growth}$$

For example, if the money supply growth is 5 percent per year, velocity growth is 0 percent per year, and real GDP growth is 3 percent per year, then this equation says that inflation is 2 percent per year. (This growth rate form of the quantity equation follows directly from the quantity equation itself; in general, the rate of growth of a product of two terms is approximately equal to the sum of the growth rates of the two terms. Thus, the growth rate of M times V equals the growth rate of M plus the growth rate of V, and the growth rate of P times Y equals the growth rate of P plus the growth rate of Y.)

The quantity equation tells us that along a long-run economic growth path in which real GDP growth is equal to potential GDP growth, an increase in money growth by a certain number of percentage points will result in the long run in an increase in inflation of the same number of percentage points unless there is a change in velocity growth. Thus, higher money growth will lead to higher inflation in the long run. If velocity growth remains at zero, as in the previous example, and real GDP growth remains at 3 percent per year, then an increase in money growth by 10 percentage points, from 5 to 15 percent, will increase inflation by 10 percentage points, from 2 to 12 percent.

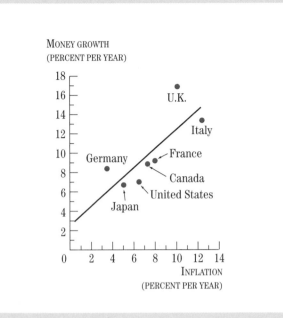

MONEY GROWTH
(PERCENT PER YEAR)

Figure 9.4
The Relation Between Money Growth and Inflation
As the data for these several countries show, higher
money growth is associated with higher inflation. The data
pertain to the period 1973–1991, when inflation differed
greatly among the countries.

Evidence

What evidence do we have that higher money growth leads
to more inflation? The quantity equation tells us that we
should look for evidence during periods when changes in
real GDP and velocity were small compared to changes in
money growth and inflation. During such periods the
change in money growth and inflation will be the domi-
nant terms in the quantity equation.

■ **Worldwide Inflation in the 1970s and 1980s.**
Figure 9.4 shows such a period: the years from 1973 to
1991, when many economies had big inflations, some
much bigger than others. Money growth is plotted on the
vertical axis, and inflation on the horizontal axis. In Figure
9.4, each point represents a country. For countries with
higher money growth, inflation was higher. Hence, the
quantity equation works well during this period. During
the 1990s, inflation has been low in all these countries, so
there has not been enough of a difference to test how well
the equation works.

■ **Hyperinflations.**   Another, more dramatic type of
evidence showing that high money growth can cause inflation is hyperinflation. A hyperinflation is simply a period of
very high inflation. The inflation in Germany in 1923 is one
of the most famous examples of a hyperinflation. Inflation
rose to over 100 percent per week. The German government had incurred huge expenses during World War I, and

*100,000,000,000,000 German
Mark Reichsbank Note, 1923*

Hyperinflation and Too Much Money
*So much money was printed during the period of
German hyperinflation that it became cheaper to
burn several million German marks to cook
breakfast—as this woman was doing in 1923—
than to buy kindling wood with the nearly
worthless money.*

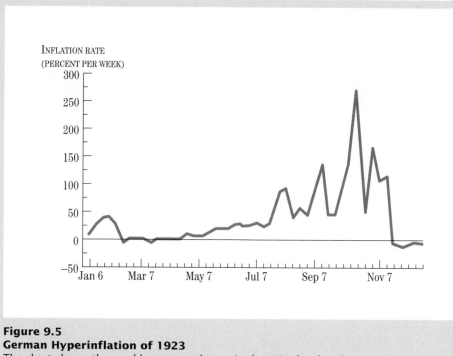

INFLATION RATE
(PERCENT PER WEEK)

Figure 9.5
German Hyperinflation of 1923
The chart shows the weekly percent change in the price level in Germany in 1923.
Inflation rose to truly astronomical levels for several months.

huge demands for war reparations from the victors in World War I compounded the problem. Because the government could not raise enough taxes to pay its expenses, it started printing huge amounts of money, which caused the hyperinflation of 1923. Figure 9.5 shows the *weekly* increase in German prices. Shop owners closed their shops at lunchtime to change the prices. Workers were paid twice weekly. People would rush to the stores and buy everything they needed for the next few days. Firms also set up barter systems with their workers, exchanging consumer goods directly for labor.

As just stated, the hyperinflation was initially caused by the huge increase in money growth. However, once it started, everyone tried to get rid of cash as soon as possible, accelerating the inflationary process. Also, by the time the government received its tax revenue, it was not worth much because prices had risen sharply. So the government had to print even more money. In the last months of hyperinflation, more than 30 paper mills worked at full capacity to deliver paper currency. One hundred fifty printing firms had 2,000 presses running 24 hours a day to print German marks, and they could not keep up with the need for new notes. On November 15, 1923, an economic reform stabilized the inflation rate. By then, the German prices were 100 billion times higher than they had been before the hyperinflation.

The German hyperinflation of 1923 was not a unique historical episode, and hyperinflation is not necessarily linked to war. There was hyperinflation in Brazil in the 1980s and in Argentina in the early 1990s. In the mid-1990s, high inflation in Russia was also caused by the creation of too much money. Money growth is the cause of all hyperinflations.

REVIEW
- The quantity equation of money says that the money supply times velocity equals real GDP times the GDP deflator.

- Higher rates of money growth will eventually lead to higher inflation.

- Evidence of the relation between money growth and inflation is found in the 1970s and 1980s in the United States and other large economies, as well as in hyperinflation in Germany in the 1920s and in Brazil, Argentina, and Russia more recently.

Conclusion

Money has fascinated economists for centuries. The famous quantity equation introduced in this chapter predates Adam Smith and was used by the economist-philosopher David Hume in the eighteenth century. Adam Smith placed money second only to the division of labor in the first chapters of the *Wealth of Nations*.

Although the role of money appears mysterious and has caused some great debates in economics and politics, the ideas presented in this chapter are not controversial. The three functions of money, the deposit expansion process, the money multiplier, the technical ability of the central bank to control the monetary base, and the fact that money is the cause of inflation in the long run are things many economists now agree on.

Many of the controversies about money pertain to the short-run fluctuations in the economy and revolve around the effects the Fed has on real GDP in the short run. After considering the reasons why real GDP may depart from potential GDP in the short run in Chapters 10 and 11, we will return to the effects the Fed has on short-run fluctuations in the economy.

KEY POINTS

1. Money has three roles: a medium of exchange, a store of value, and a unit of account.

2. Commodity money, ranging from salt to gold coins, has been used in place of barter for many centuries. Now paper money and deposits are also part of money.

3. Commercial banks are financial intermediaries; their deposits are part of the money supply.

4. Commercial banks hold reserves at the central bank.

5. The central bank changes reserves by buying and selling bonds.

6. The monetary base is currency plus reserves.

7. The central bank can control the monetary base by buying and selling bonds.

8. The money multiplier tells us how much the money supply changes when the monetary base changes.

9. The central bank in the United States is the Federal Reserve System (the Fed).

10. When stated in terms of growth rates, the quantity equation of money describes the relationship between money growth, real GDP growth, and inflation.

11. Higher money growth eventually leads to higher inflation.

KEY TERMS

money

medium of exchange

store of value

unit of account

currency

checking deposit

money supply

Federal Reserve System (the Fed)

bank

Federal Open Market Committee (FOMC)

asset

liability

reserves

required reserve ratio

open market operation

currency to deposit ratio

monetary base

money multiplier

quantity equation of money

velocity

QUESTIONS FOR REVIEW

1. What are the differences between the medium of exchange, store of value, and unit of account roles of money?

2. What are some examples of commodity money?

3. Why is it that currency is a part of money but that an expensive purse to put the currency in is not?

4. What is a bank?

5. What is the Fed, and how is the FOMC organized?

6. What happens to bank reserves when the Fed buys bonds?

7. What happens to the monetary base when the Fed buys bonds?

8. What is the money multiplier, and why does it depend on the required reserve ratio?

9. Why does higher money growth cause inflation?

10. What is the quantity equation of money?

PROBLEMS

1. Which of the following are money, and which are not?
   a. A credit card
   b. A dollar bill
   c. A check in your checkbook
   d. Funds in a checking account

2. State whether each of the following statements is true or false. Explain your answers in one or two sentences.
   a. The smaller the reserve ratio at banks, the larger the money multiplier.
   b. The Federal Reserve reduces reserves by buying government bonds.
   c. The same money is always used as both a unit of account and a medium of exchange at any one time in any one country.
   d. When commodity money is the only type of money, a decrease in the price of the commodity serving as money is inflation.

3. Credit cards are not included in the money supply, but currency and deposits at banks are included. Explain why credit cards are excluded. (*Hint:* Credit cards are a form of identification that allows you to borrow.)

4. Suppose the Fed buys a government bond for $10,000 from Chase bank.
   a. For simplicity, suppose that $k = 0$: People hold no currency. If the required reserve ratio is 10 percent, how much of this initial $10,000 will Chase bank lend out?
   b. Suppose the process of lending and depositing continues through the banking system until there is nothing left to lend. At that point, how much is the total increase in deposits created by the initial $10,000?
   c. How will the total increase in deposits change from part (b) if $k > 0$? Why?

5. Suppose that before the invention of the automatic teller machine, people held currency equal to 20 percent of their bank deposits. If the required reserve ratio is 20 percent, what is the money multiplier? Now suppose that after the invention of the ATM, people hold only 10 percent of the value of their deposits in currency. What is the money multiplier now? Explain how the change in the money multiplier occurs.

6. Suppose the Fed buys government bonds and the monetary base rises by $1 billion. If the required reserve ratio is .10 and the currency to deposit ratio is .5, by how much will the money supply change?

7. Assume that required reserves are 7 percent of deposits and that people hold no currency—all money is held in the form of checking deposits.

   a. Suppose that the Federal Reserve purchases $30,000 worth of government bonds from Ellen (a private citizen), and that Ellen deposits all of the proceeds from the sale into her checking account at Z Bank. Construct a balance sheet, with assets on the left and liabilities on the right, to show how Ellen's deposit creates new assets and liabilities for Z Bank.

   b. How much of this new deposit can Z Bank lend out? Assume that it lends this amount to George, who then deposits the entire amount into his account at Y Bank. Show this on Y Bank's balance sheet.

   c. Suppose George uses the loan to build an addition to his house. His contractor, Joe, deposits the money in his account at X Bank. How much is this deposit? How much in new excess reserves is created when he makes this new deposit?

   d. The process of lending and relending creates money throughout the banking system. As a result of Ellen's deposit, how much money, in the form of deposits, has been created so far?

   e. If this process resulting from Ellen's deposit continues forever, how much money will be created?

8. Consider the following table:

Year	Quantity of Money (billions of $)	Velocity	Real GDP (billions of $)	GDP Deflator
1997	1,066	7.78	8,165	
1998	1,078	8.13	8,516	
1999	1,101	8.40	8,859	

   a. Fill in the missing data, using the quantity equation of money.

   b. Why might velocity change in this way?

   c. Calculate the inflation rate for 1998 and 1999.

   d. If money growth had been 5 percent per year in 1998 and 1999, what would inflation have been, assuming real GDP and velocity as in the table?

PART THREE

Economic Fluctuations and Macroeconomic Policy

CHAPTER 10

The Nature and Causes of Economic Fluctuations

In the early part of 2001, the record economic expansion that began all the way back in 1991 came to an end. A sharp fall in U.S. stock markets, particularly in the technology sector; falling consumer confidence; decisions by firms to cut back on investment spending; rapid increases in interest rates by the Federal Reserve in the year 2000; and rising oil prices are all possible explanations for the economic slowdown. The slowdown was considerably worsened by the tragic events of September 11 and the subsequent fall in spending and output. By 2002, however, the economy was starting to show strong signs of recovery, encouraged perhaps by the actions of the government to cut taxes and the Federal Reserve to lower interest rates, along with robust consumer spending on big-ticket items such as automobiles and houses.

In this section, we take a closer look at economic fluctuations of the type that we saw in 2001 and 2002, as well as other episodes in U.S. history, which have very different features. The goal is to improve our understanding of economic fluctuations, which are defined as departures of the economy from its long-term growth trend. These departures include recessions, which are periods in which GDP declines sharply, moving the economy below its long-term trend, as well as booms, in which GDP in the economy rises rapidly and goes above its long-term trend. Examples of recessions include the most recent slowdown of 2001, the sharp recession that hit the U.S. economy in the early 1980s, and the recessions that devastated the economies of Malaysia, Indonesia, and Korea in the late 1990s. Examples of booms include the long growth period between 1991 and 2001, in which the U.S. economy grew for over 120 consecutive months!

Studying economic fluctuations is vital because recessions bring unemployment and hardship to many people. While the importance of economic growth cannot be overstated, fluctuations around the growth trend are also vital for the livelihood of millions of people. John Maynard Keynes said it best in his book *A Tract on Monetary Reform:* "But this *long run* is a misleading guide to current affairs. *In the long run* we are all dead. Economists set themselves too easy, too useless a task if in tempestuous seasons they can only tell us that when the storm is long past the ocean is flat again." In less eloquent terms, the study of fluctuations is vital to understanding macroeconomics.

Economic fluctuations have been common for at least 200 years, but recessions have changed over time. One notable difference is that they have diminished in frequency and severity in the United States and many other countries, especially over the past two decades. A key purpose of studying economic fluctuations is to explain why this weakening of recessions has occurred and to determine whether economic policies are responsible for this trend.

Only one economic fluctuation occurred in the United States in the 1990s. As shown in the magnified portion of Figure 10.1, real GDP was clearly above potential GDP in early 1990, but in mid-1990, real GDP began to fall. As the recession took hold, real GDP fell below potential GDP and continued to fall through the first quarter of 1991, when it reached its lowest point. A recovery then started that brought real GDP back to potential GDP by 1994. For the rest of the 1990s, the U.S. economy grew more smoothly. In fact, the expansion that began in 1991 did not end until ten years later.

Economic fluctuations occur simultaneously with long-term growth, as shown by the longer history in Figure 10.1. Real GDP has fluctuated around what might otherwise have been a steady upward-moving trend. Although no two economic fluctuations are alike—some are long, some are short; some are deep, some are shallow—they do have common features. Perhaps the most important one is that after a departure of real GDP from potential GDP, the economy eventually returns to a more normal long-run growth path.

In this chapter, we look at the first steps the economy takes as it moves away from potential GDP. In other words, we examine the initial, or short-run, increase or decrease of real GDP above or below potential GDP. We will show that the first steps of real

"We figure it was HERE when the recession officially began."

GDP away from potential GDP are caused by changes in aggregate demand. Aggregate demand is the total amount that consumers, businesses, government, and foreigners are willing to spend on all goods and services in the economy. In contrast, the growth of potential GDP is caused by increases in the available supply of inputs to production: labor, capital, and technology.

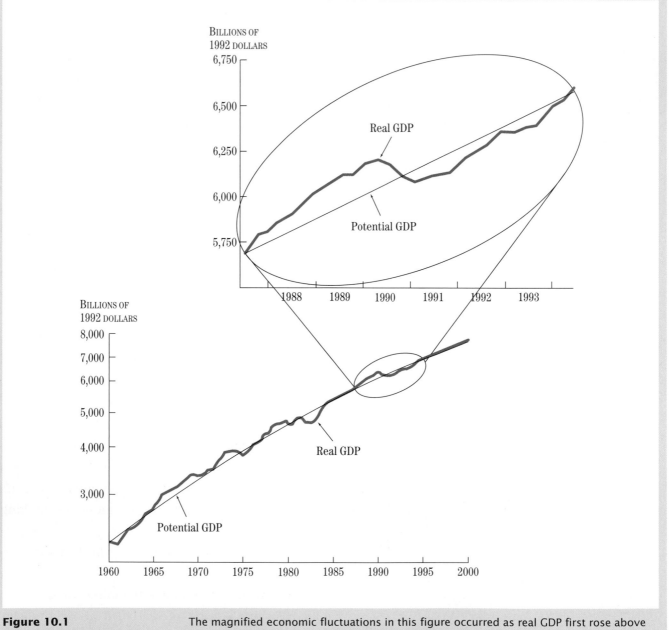

Figure 10.1
Narrowing the Focus on
Economic Fluctuations

The magnified economic fluctuations in this figure occurred as real GDP first rose above potential GDP and then fell below potential GDP as the economy went into a recession in 1990. For the remainder of the 1990s, the economy grew smoothly.

Changes in Aggregate Demand Lead to Changes in Production

Figure 10.2 illustrates the essential idea used to explain economic fluctuations: that increases or decreases in real GDP to levels above or below potential GDP occur largely because of increases or decreases in aggregate demand in the economy. Changes in aggregate demand occur when consumers, business firms, government, or foreigners expand or cut back their spending. Potential GDP in three years is represented by points *a*, *b*, and *c* in Figure 10.2. These three values of potential GDP are part of the longer-term steady increase in potential GDP over time due to increases in the supply of labor and capital and improvements in technology. Potential GDP represents what firms would want to produce in "normal times," when the economy is neither in a recession nor in a boom. In normal times, real GDP is equal to potential GDP. Years 1 and 2 in Figure 10.2 are assumed to be normal years. However, year 3 is not a normal year. Point *d* in the left panel of the figure shows a recession because real GDP has declined from point *b*. Real GDP is below potential GDP at point *d*. Firms produce less and lay off workers. Unemployment rises. Eventually—this part

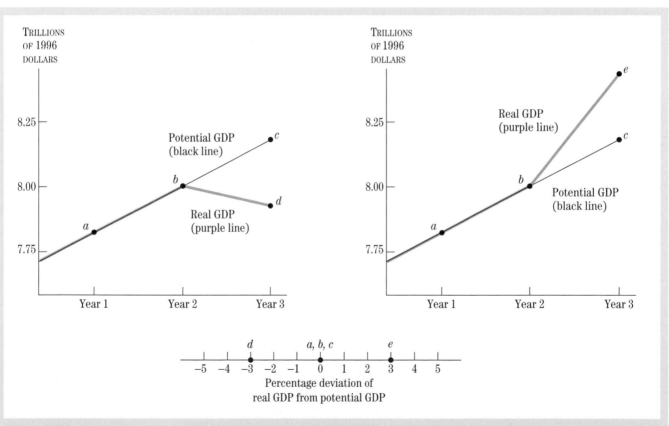

Figure 10.2
The First Step of an
Economic Fluctuation

Potential GDP is shown by the black upward-sloping line in both diagrams. Points *a*, *b*, and *c* represent three different levels of potential GDP in three years. A downward departure of real GDP (shown in purple) from potential GDP is illustrated by point *d* on the left. Since real GDP falls, this is a recession. An upward departure of real GDP from potential GDP is illustrated by point *e* on the right. The departures are explained by changes in aggregate demand. The line at the bottom shows the percent deviation of real GDP from potential GDP.

of the story comes in later chapters—if demand stays low, firms begin to cut their prices, and real GDP moves back toward potential GDP. Thus, in recessions, changes in aggregate demand cause fluctuations in real GDP.

Point *e* in the right panel represents another departure of real GDP from potential GDP. In this case, real GDP rises above potential GDP. Firms produce more in response to the increase in aggregate demand; they employ more workers, and unemployment declines. Eventually—again this part of the story comes in later chapters—if demand for their product stays high, firms raise their prices, and real GDP goes back down toward potential GDP.

Economists frequently measure the departures of real GDP from potential GDP in percentages rather than in dollar amounts. For example, if potential GDP is $8.0 trillion and real GDP is $8.4 trillion, then the percentage departure of real GDP from potential GDP is 5 percent: $(8.4 − 8.0)/8.0 = .05$. If real GDP were $7.6 trillion and potential GDP remained at $8.0 trillion, then the percentage departure would be −5 percent: $(7.6 − 8.0)/8.0 = −.05$. Percentages make it easier to compare economic fluctuations in different countries that have different sizes of real GDP. At the bottom of the two panels in Figure 10.2 is a horizontal line representing the size of the fluctuations in real GDP around potential GDP in year 1, year 2, and year 3. Points *d* and *e* in Figure 10.2 represent the first steps of an economic fluctuation.

Production and Demand at Individual Firms

Why do firms produce more—bringing real GDP above *potential GDP*—when the demand for their products rises? Why do firms produce less—bringing real GDP below potential GDP—when the demand for their products falls? These questions have probably occupied more of economists' time than any other question in macro-economics. Although more work still needs to be done, substantial improvements in economists' understanding of the issues have been made in the last 20 years.

■ The Unemployment Rate and the Deviations of Real GDP from Potential GDP. First consider some simple facts about how firms operate. In normal times, when real GDP is equal to potential GDP, most firms operate with some excess capacity so that they can expand production without major bottlenecks. Small retail service businesses from taxi companies to dry cleaners can usually increase production when customer demand increases. Another taxi is added to a busy route and one of the drivers is asked to work overtime. One of the dry cleaning employees who has been working part time is happy to work full time. The same is true for large manufacturing firms. When asked what percent of capacity their production is in normal times, manufacturing firms typically answer about 80 percent. Thus, firms normally have room to expand production: Capacity utilization sometimes goes up to 90 percent or higher. If firms need more labor in order to expand production, they can ask workers to work overtime, call workers back from previous layoffs, or hire additional workers. *The unemployment rate drops below the natural unemployment rate when real GDP rises above potential GDP.*

In recessions, when demand declines, these same firms clearly have the capability to reduce production, and they do. In recessions, capacity utilization goes down to 70 percent or lower. Firms ask workers to stop working overtime, they move some workers to part time, or they lay off some workers. Some firms institute hiring freezes to make sure the personnel office does not keep hiring workers. *The unemployment rate rises above the natural unemployment rate when real GDP falls below potential GDP.* For example, the unemployment rate rose to more than 7 percent when the 1990–1991 recession brought real GDP below potential GDP. The relationship between the unemployment rate and the movements of real GDP relative to potential GDP is illustrated in the margin.

potential GDP: the economy's long-term growth trend for real GDP determined by the available supply of capital, labor, and technology. Real GDP fluctuates above and below potential GDP. (Ch. 4)

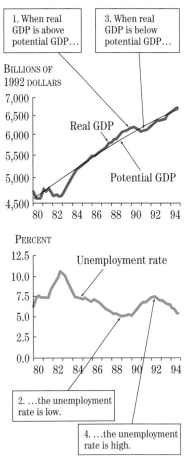

1. When real GDP is above potential GDP...

3. When real GDP is below potential GDP...

BILLIONS OF 1992 DOLLARS

Real GDP

Potential GDP

7,000
6,500
6,000
5,500
5,000
4,500

80 82 84 86 88 90 92 94

PERCENT

Unemployment rate

12.5
10.0
7.5
5.0
2.5
0.0

80 82 84 86 88 90 92 94

2. ...the unemployment rate is low.

4. ...the unemployment rate is high.

Production Decisions By Actual Firms
Individual firms—Mayflower moving services being just one example—raise production during booms when the demand for their goods or services rises, and lower production during recessions when the demand for their goods or services declines. These decisions by individual firms lead to fluctuations of real GDP above or below potential GDP.

■ Real-Life Examples of How Firms Respond to Demand.

Consider a typical service firm at the start of the 1990–1991 recession. Mayflower, the moving company named after the ship that moved the Pilgrims, found the demand for its moving and storage services growing rapidly in the boom of the late 1980s. The company expanded production by moving more households and, as a result, increased its employment from 6,800 workers in 1987 to 11,400 in 1989. In 1990, as the recession took hold, demand for Mayflower's services began to fall. The company reduced production—moved fewer households—and employment fell from 11,400 in 1989 to 10,900 in 1990, a decline of about 5 percent.

Consider the example of a construction firm at about the same time. As is typical in recessions, construction was hit hard in the 1990–1991 recession. Trammell Crow, the real estate construction company based in Dallas, Texas, found the demand for its construction services falling off dramatically in 1990. Hence, the firm produced fewer of these services. It built fewer shopping malls and convention centers. Total square feet under construction by Trammell Crow fell from 44 million in 1989 to 27 million in 1990. Employment at Trammell Crow also fell from the year 1989 to 1990. Employment had expanded rapidly during the 1988–1989 boom. Thus, Trammell Crow is another example showing how fluctuations in demand cause a change in production.

Could Economic Fluctuations Also Be Due to Changes in Potential GDP?

> Recall from Chapter 4 that *potential GDP* depends on the economy's *aggregate supply*, which is determined by the available *capital, labor,* and *technology*. A drought or a flood would reduce supply.

real business cycle theory:
a theory of macroeconomics that stresses that shifts in potential GDP are a primary cause of fluctuations in real GDP; the shifts in potential GDP are usually assumed to be caused by changes in technology.

Our discussion thus far of the production decisions of individual firms has shown why it is natural to identify fluctuations in real GDP with fluctuations in aggregate demand. To be sure, economic fluctuations also occur because of changes in potential GDP. For example, when agriculture was a much larger fraction of real GDP, droughts and floods had more noticeable effects on real GDP. Although agriculture is currently a very small fraction of total production, the possibility that increases or decreases in potential GDP may still play a large role in economic fluctuations is a topic currently being examined by economists. Economic theories that emphasize changes in potential GDP as a source of economic fluctuations are called **real business cycle theories.** Most frequently, changes in technology are assumed to be the reason for changes in potential GDP in real business cycle theories.

The factors that underlie potential GDP growth—population, capital, technological know-how—tend to evolve relatively smoothly. Population growth, for example, is much steadier than real GDP growth. We do not have a drop in the population every few years and a sudden spurt the next year. Slowdowns in population growth occur gradually over time as birthrates and death rates change. Similarly, although individual factories or machines may be lost in a hurricane or flood, such losses do not happen in such a massive way across the whole country that they would show up as a recession or a boom in the whole economy. Thus, the amount of capital changes slowly over time. Even technological change does not seem capable of explaining most fluctuations. It is true that some inventions and innovations raise productivity substantially in certain sectors of the economy over short periods of time. The impact on the whole economy is more spread out and gradual, however. Moreover,

In the aftermath of the tragic events of September 11, 2001, economists were called upon to analyze the potential effects on the U.S. economy. At the time, there were fears that the attacks could drive the economy into a longer recession, although many economists speculated that the effect would not be as long-lasting as had been feared. The following article, published almost a year after the attacks, summarizes the impact of the tragedy on the economy. It concludes that while certain sectors, such as the airline industry, are still feeling the impacts of the attack, for most companies the bad news has come in the form of other negative events, such as the accounting scandals of 2002.

A Year After Sept. 11, Attacks' Economic Impact Lingers, but Effect is Disparate

By ADAM GELLER, AP Business Writer

NEW YORK—A year ago, planted in front of televisions, numbed by endless images of the World Trade Center's destruction, consumers froze—and briefly forgot to consume. Investors stopped investing, and dumped stock. Travelers stopped traveling, at least by plane. Scores of companies slashed thousands of jobs, and economists warned that the combined effects could snowball.

But a year after terrorists attacked the trade center, the Pentagon—and by extension, the economy—the impact has not proven to be nearly as deep or as lasting as was feared. The economic consequences of Sept. 11 still linger, certainly. But the toll has proved disparate, inflicting the heaviest damage on sectors such as travel and tourism while leaving others unscathed. And it turns out events before and after have played a far larger role in shaping the economy than the attacks.

"I would say the impact has been less than we had initially thought in terms of economic contraction," said Gus Faucher, a senior economist with Economy.com, a research firm in West Chester, Pa. "It's a contributing factor to the weak economy, but it's not the primary factor."

Sizing up the impact of the attacks is complicated because the economy was already in a recession before last September. In the months since, it has been buffeted by other crises, including the collapse of Enron and a host of other corporate scandals, severe problems in the telecommunications industry, and the drop-off in the stock market. "Economically, the stock market setback may have had more of an impact than the terrorist attacks because it shaved some $7 trillion from our wealth,' said Sung Won Sohn, an economist with Wells Fargo and Co.

Some of the expectations that shaped economic forecasts immediately after the attacks, particularly fears of a long war in Afghanistan with heavy American casualties, did not come to pass, said Ross DeVol, director of regional studies for the Millken Institute in Santa Barbara, Calif. The think tank early this year estimated the attacks would result in the elimination of 1.6 million jobs nationwide. But DeVol says now the number will probably be 1.2 million or less, most concentrated in industries like air travel and tourism, or in New York City.

The uneven impact means that assessments of the damage vary by vantage point. "The attacks certainly accelerated the action," said Terry Mercer, a technical illustrator for Boeing Corp., who's been unable to find work since the aerospace giant eliminated his job and 5,000 others from its Wichita, Kan., operations. "But everybody's feeling was that it (some cuts) was going to be coming anyway. We didn't have a lot of work even before the attacks."

The landscape looks very different to home builder Bob Simmons of McLean, Va., who said he was prepared for the worst last fall—but never had time to stop and wait for it. "For me, it's almost like a recap of last August except we have about 10 percent more sales," said Simmons, who builds homes in the suburbs of Washington, D.C.

Economists say the healthy housing market shows how a variety of factors helped mitigate the damage of Sept. 11. Consumers, told one of the best things they could for their nation was to shop, did just that. Record low interest rates kept families buying homes, and refinancing mortgages put cash in their pockets for other purchases. Detroit's zero-percent financing for new cars late last year captured consumers' attention. Government spending pumped additional money into the economy. "Who knows what the psychology was, but (the attack) was not as big a blow as we were expecting," said Economy.com's Faucher. "People still went out to dinner, they still went out to the mall to buy things and things just held up better than expected."

> September 11 was one of the many negative factors affecting the economy in 2001/2002.

> Even in bad times, some sectors continue to flourish.

people do not suddenly forget how to use a technology. There do not seem to be sudden decreases in technological know-how. For these reasons, potential GDP usually tends to grow relatively smoothly over time, compared to the fluctuations in aggregate demand.

REVIEW

- Economic fluctuations are largely a result of fluctuations in aggregate demand.

- When aggregate demand decreases, firms produce less; real GDP falls below potential GDP. Unemployment rises. When aggregate demand increases, firms first produce more; real GDP rises above potential GDP. Firms also hire more workers, and the unemployment rate falls.

- Short-run fluctuations in potential GDP also occur, but in reality most of the larger fluctuations in real GDP seem to be due to fluctuations of real GDP around a more steadily growing potential GDP.

Forecasting Real GDP

To illustrate how we use the idea that changes in aggregate demand lead to short-run fluctuations in real GDP, we will focus on an important macroeconomic task: short-term economic forecasting of real GDP about one year ahead. To *forecast* real GDP, economic forecasters divide aggregate demand into its four key components: consumption, investment, government purchases, and net exports. Remember that real GDP can be measured by adding together the four types of spending: what people *consume,* what firms *invest,* what *governments purchase,* and what *foreigners purchase* net of what they sell in the United States. In symbols, we have

$$Y = C + I + G + X$$

In other words, real GDP (Y) is the sum of consumption (C), investment (I), government purchases (G), and net exports (X).

A Forecast for Next Year

Suppose that it is December 2004 and a forecast of real GDP (Y) is being prepared for the year 2005. Using the preceding equation, a reasonable way to proceed would be to forecast consumption for the next year, then forecast investment, then forecast government purchases, and, finally, forecast net exports. When forecasting each item, the forecaster would consider a range of issues: Consumer confidence might affect consumption; business confidence might be a factor in investment; the mood of the country might be a factor in government purchases; and developments in foreign countries might affect the forecast for net exports. In any case, adding these four spending items together would give a forecast for real GDP for the year 2005. For example, one economist may forecast that $C =$ \$7,000 billion, $I =$ \$900 billion, $X =$ \$100 billion, and $G =$ \$2,000 billion. Then that economist's forecast for real GDP is \$10,000 billion. Forecasts are typically expressed as growth rates of real GDP from one year to the next. If real GDP in 2004 is \$9,700, then the forecast would be for 3.1 percent growth for the year 2005.

Economics in Action

The Blue Chip Consensus Forecast

Short-term forecasting of real GDP—usually one year ahead—has become a major industry employing thousands of economists, statisticians, and computer programmers. Each month the *Blue Chip Economic Indicators* tabulates the forecasts of the top forecasters. A list of 54 different forecasters is given below. The average of all these forecasters is called the Blue Chip Consensus. If a government forecast differs much from this forecast, it is frequently criticized.

Consider, for example, the forecast for real GDP growth in the United States in 2001. The consensus forecast—the average of the economists surveyed in 2000 by the Blue Chip service—for 2001 was that U.S. GDP growth would be 3.4 percent, and that the chances of a recession were very small.

What did growth turn out to be in 2001? It turned out to be 1.2 percent. This growth rate was much smaller than the forecast, and the size of the error was also greater than the average expected error. What was the reason for the error? The forecasters were obviously unable to predict all the external trauma that the U.S. economy would go through in 2001.

Blue Chip Forecasters

Banc of America Corp.
Bank One
Bear Stearns & Co., Inc.
ClearView Economics
Comerica
Conference Board
Credit Suisse First Boston
DaimlerChrysler AG
Daiwa Institute of Research America
Deutsche Banc Alex Brown
DRI-WEFA
DuPont
Eaton Corporation
Econoclast
Eggert Economic Enterprises, Inc.
Evans, Carroll & Associates
Fannie Mae
Federal Express Corp.

Ford Motor Company
General Motors Corporation
Genetski.com
Georgia State University
Goldman Sachs & Co.
Huntington National Bank
Inforum—Univ. of Maryland
JPMorgan Chase
Kellner Economic Advisers
LaSalle National Bank
Loomis, Sayles & Company
Macroeconomic Advisers, LLC
Merrill Lynch
Moody's Investors Service
Morgan Stanley
Mortgage Bankers Assn. of America
Motorola, Inc.
Naroff Economic Advisors

National Assn. of Home Builders
National Association of Realtors
National City Corporation
Nomura Securities
Northern Trust Company
Perna Associates
Prudential Financial
Prudential Securities, Inc.
SOM Economics, Inc.
Standard & Poor's Corp.
Swiss Re
Turning Points (Micrometrics)
U.S. Chamber of Commerce
U.S. Trust Co.
UCLA Business Forecasting Proj.
Wachovia Securities
Wayne Hummer Investments LLC
Wells Capital Management

Impact of a Change in Government Purchases

The preceding forecast is prepared by making one's best assumption about what is likely for government purchases and the other three components of spending. Another type of forecast—called a *conditional forecast*—describes what real GDP will be under alternative assumptions about the components of spending. For example, in the year 2004, the president of the United States might want an estimate of the effect of a proposal to change government purchases on the economy in 2005. A conditional forecast would be a forecast of real GDP conditional on this change in government purchases. A conditional forecast for real GDP can be made using similar methods. Let's see how.

Suppose the proposal is to cut federal government purchases by $100 billion in real terms in one year. What is the effect of such a change in government purchases on aggregate demand in the short run? If the government demands $100 billion less, then firms will produce $100 billion less. A forecast conditional on a $100 billion spending cut would be $100 billion less for real GDP, or $9,900 billion. Again, we just add up $7,000 billion, $900 billion, $100 billion, and now $1,900 billion. Real GDP growth for the year is now forecast to be about 2.1 percent, conditional on the policy proposal.

The forecast is based on the equation $Y = C + I + G + X$ and the idea that changes in aggregate demand cause real GDP fluctuations. Although simple, it is specific and substantive. According to this method of forecasting, changes in aggregate demand are responsible for most of the short-run ups and downs in the economy. It is this explanation that most economic forecasters use when they forecast real GDP for one year ahead.

REVIEW

- The four components of spending can be added to make a forecast for real GDP. Making such a forecast is an important application of macroeconomics.

- Forecasts may be conditional on a particular event, such as a change in government purchases or a change in taxes.

The Response of Consumption to Income

In the forecasting example, we assumed that none of the other components—neither consumption, investment, nor net exports—change in response to the decline in government purchases. For example, consumption (C) was unchanged at $7,000 billion when we altered G in our conditional forecast. But these components of spending are likely to change. Thus, something important is missing from the procedure for forecasting real GDP. To improve the forecast, we must describe how the components of aggregate demand—consumption, investment, or net exports—might change in response to other developments in the economy. We will eventually consider the response of consumption, investment, and net exports to many factors, including interest rates, exchange rates, and income. However, bringing all these factors into consideration at once is complicated, and we must start with a *simplifying assumption.* Here the simplifying assumption is that consumption is the only component of expenditures that responds to income, and that income is the only influence on consumption. Consumption is a good place to begin because it is by far the largest component. Before we finish developing a complete theory of economic fluctuations, we will consider the other components and the other influences. Let us begin by examining why consumption may be affected by income.

The Consumption Function

consumption function: the positive relationship between consumption and income.

The **consumption function** describes how consumption depends on income. The notion of a consumption function originated with John Maynard Keynes, who wrote about it during the 1930s. Research on the consumption function has been intense ever since. For each individual, the consumption function says that the more income one has, the more one consumes. For the national economy as a whole, it says that the more income Americans have, the more Americans consume. For the world economy as a whole, it says that the more income there is in the world, the more the people in the world consume. Table 10.1 gives a simple example of how consumption depends on income in the United States economy.

Table 10.1
An Example of the
Consumption Function
(billions of dollars)

Consumption	Income
1,600	1,000
2,200	2,000
2,800	3,000
3,400	4,000
4,000	5,000
4,600	6,000
5,200	7,000
5,800	8,000
6,400	9,000
7,000	10,000
7,600	11,000
8,200	12,000
8,800	13,000
9,400	14,000

marginal propensity to consume (MPC): the slope of the consumption function, showing the change in consumption that is due to a given change in income.

As you can see from the table, as income increases from 1,000 to 2,000, consumption increases as well, from 1,600 to 2,200, and as income increases from 3,000 to 4,000, consumption increases from 2,800 to 3,400. More income means more consumption, but the consumption function also tells us *how much* consumption increases when income increases. Each change in income of 1,000 causes an increase in consumption of 600. The changes in consumption are smaller than the changes in income. Notice that, in this example, at very low levels of income, consumption is greater than income. If consumption were greater than income for a particular individual, that individual would have to borrow. At higher levels of income, when consumption is less than income, the individual would be able to save.

The consumption function is supposed to describe the behavior of individuals because the economy is made up of individuals. Consequently, it summarizes the behavior of all people in the economy with respect to consumption. The simple consumption function is not meant to be the complete explanation of consumption. Recall that it is based on a simplifying assumption.

■ **The Marginal Propensity to Consume.** A concept related to the consumption function is the **marginal propensity to consume,** or **MPC** for short. The marginal propensity to consume measures how much consumption changes for a given change in income. The term *marginal* refers to the additional amount of consumption that is due to a change in income. The term *propensity* refers to the inclination to consume. By definition,

$$\text{Marginal Propensity to Consume (MPC)} = \frac{\text{change in consumption}}{\text{change in income}}$$

What is the MPC for the consumption function in Table 10.1? Observe that the change in consumption from row to row is 600. The change in income from row to row is 1,000; thus the MPC = 600/1,000 = .6. Although this is only a simple example, it turns out that the MPC for the U.S. economy is around that magnitude.

Figure 10.3
The Consumption Function
For the economy as a whole, more income leads to more consumption, as shown by the example of an upward-sloping consumption function in the figure. This represents the sum of all the individuals in the economy, many of whom consume more when their income rises. The graph is based on the numbers in Table 10.1.

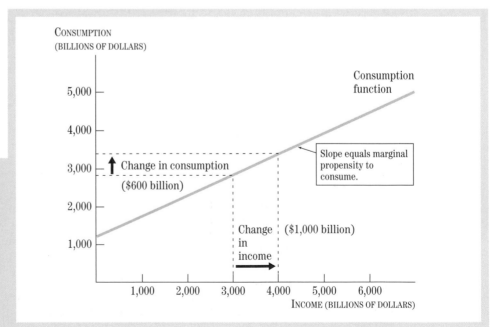

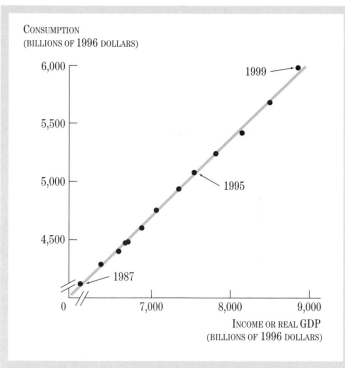

Figure 10.4
Consumption versus Aggregate Income
The graph shows the close relationship between consumption and aggregate income, or real GDP, in the U.S. economy. The points fall close to the straight line drawn in the diagram.

Figure 10.3 graphs the consumption function by putting income on the horizontal axis and consumption on the vertical axis. We get the upward-sloping line by plotting the pairs of observations on consumption and income in Table 10.1 and connecting them with a line. This line, which demonstrates that consumption rises with income, is the consumption function. Its slope is equal to the MPC. For this example, the MPC = .6. The graph shows that at low levels of income, consumption is greater than income, but at high levels of income, consumption is less than income.

■ **Which Measure of Income?**   The consumption function is a straight-line relationship between consumption and income. Income in the relationship is sometimes measured by *aggregate income* (Y), which is also equal to real GDP, and sometimes by disposable income. *Disposable income* is the income that households receive in wages, dividends, and interest payments plus transfers they may get from the government minus any taxes they pay to the government. Disposable income is the preferred measure of income when one is interested in household consumption because this is what households have available to spend. But the consumption function for the whole economy for aggregate income and that for disposable income look similar because aggregate income and disposable income fluctuate and grow together. In the United States and most other countries, taxes and transfers are nearly proportional to aggregate income.

For the rest of this chapter, we will use aggregate income, or real GDP, as the measure of income in the consumption function. We put real GDP, or income (we drop the word *aggregate* in aggregate income), on the horizontal axis of the consumption function diagram, because real GDP and income are always equal. Figure 10.4 shows the actual relationship between consumption and income, or real GDP. Note, however, that when we consider an explicit change in taxes, we must take into account the difference between disposable income and income.

What about Interest Rates and Other Influences on Consumption?

Other factors besides income affect consumption. For example, you may recall from Chapter 6 that people's consumption is affected by the interest rate. Also, people's wealth—including their savings in a bank and their house—may affect their consumption. A person with a large amount of savings in a bank might consume a considerable amount even if the person's income in any one year is very low. Why have we not brought the interest rate or wealth into the picture here?

The answer is simple. To keep the analysis manageable at the start, we are putting the interest rate and other influences aside. We eventually return to consider the effects of interest rates and other factors on consumption. But during economic fluctuations, the effects of changes in income on consumption are most important, and we focus on these now.

REVIEW

- The consumption function describes the response of consumption to changes in income. The elementary consumption function ignores the effects of interest rates and wealth on consumption.

- The marginal propensity to consume (MPC) tells us *how much* consumption changes in response to a change in income.

- For the economy as a whole, the consumption function can be expressed in terms of aggregate income or disposable income. Aggregate income is always equal to real GDP.

Finding Real GDP When Consumption and Income Move Together

Now let us use the consumption function to get a better prediction of what happens to real GDP in the short run when government purchases change. In other words, we want to improve the conditional forecast of real GDP when there is a change in government purchases by taking the consumption function into account. Again, as in the earlier example of forecasting, let us assume that government spending will decline by $100 billion next year. Our goal is to find out what happens to real GDP in the short run.

Our first attempt at forecasting said that a reduction in government spending is going to reduce real GDP. But now we see that something else must happen, because consumption depends on income, and real GDP is equal to income. A reduction in government spending will reduce income. The consumption function tells us that a reduction in income must reduce consumption, which further reduces GDP.

Here is the chain of logic in brief:

1. A cut in government spending reduces real GDP.

2. Real GDP = income; thus income is reduced.

3. Consumption depends on income; thus consumption is reduced.

4. A reduction in consumption further reduces real GDP.

In sum, consumption will decline when we reduce government spending.

For example, when the government reduces defense spending, the firms that produce the defense goods find demand falling and produce less. Some of the defense workers are going to either work fewer hours a week or be laid off. Therefore, they will receive a reduced income or no income at all. In addition, the profits at the defense firms will decline; thus, the income of the owners of the firms will decline. With less income, the workers and the owners will spend less; that is, their consumption will decline. This is the connection between government spending and consumption that we are concerned about: The change in government purchases reduces defense workers' income, which results in less consumption.

Consider a specific case study. This type of logic was applied by economists to estimate the impact of closing Fort Ord, the military base near Monterey Bay in California, on the Monterey economy. When the estimates were made, the base employed 3,000 civilians and 14,000 military personnel. Payroll was $558 million. Thus, closing the base would reduce incomes by as much as $558 million as these workers were laid off or retired. Although some workers might quickly find jobs elsewhere, there would be a decline in income that would result in a reduction in

Making *Time*'s Top 100

John Maynard Keynes was chosen by *Time* magazine as one of the 100 most influential people in the twentieth century. Keynes was the inventor of the marginal propensity to consume and of the broader idea emphasized in this chapter that a decline in aggregate demand could bring the economy below its potential.

Keynes was always active in bringing economics into practice. He gained notoriety in his thirties for a best-selling book called *The Economic Consequences of the Peace,* written in only two months during the summer of 1919. Keynes was an economic adviser to the British government, and he accompanied the prime minister to the Versailles peace conference in 1919 at the end of World War I. At that peace conference, the victors demanded heavy reparations from Germany, harming the German economy and thereby helping Hitler in his rise to power. In his 1919 book, Keynes predicted serious harm from the stiff reparations and ridiculed the heads of government at the conference, including his own prime minister, Lloyd George, and the American president, Woodrow Wilson.

Keynes's most influential book, however, was *The General Theory of Employment, Interest and Money.* He wrote it in the midst of the Great Depression, providing an explanation for a worldwide tragedy that prevailing economic theory—with its microeconomic emphasis—hardly addressed. Much of the *General Theory* is difficult to read unless you are an economist, because as Keynes put it, his book is chiefly addressed to "my fellow economists." But Keynes's well-developed writing skills emerge in some of the less technical passages, especially those on speculation and expectations in financial markets. Keynes's ideas, such as the marginal propensity to consume and the importance of aggregate demand, spread rapidly and had a lasting influence: Referring to these ideas as the "Keynesian revolution" is no exaggeration.

Keynes appeared on the cover of *Time* magazine in 1965, when the influence of his economics was at its peak in Washington. However, in the 1970s, when inflation was rising and economic growth was slowing, Keynes's theory was criticized because it did not deal with inflation and with long-run economic growth. Moreover, by emphasizing aggregate demand so much,

Keynes's theory suggested to some policymakers that increases in government spending could increase real GDP almost without limit, regardless of supply constraints.

Keynes's *Tract on Monetary Reform,* written in 1923, focused more on inflation than did the *General Theory.* His earlier writings suggest that, if he had lived longer, he might have explained the high inflation of the 1970s as effectively as he explained the Great Depression of the 1930s.

JOHN MAYNARD KEYNES, 1883–1946

Born: Cambridge, England, 1883

Education: Cambridge University, graduated 1906

Jobs: India Office, London, 1906–1909
Cambridge University, 1909–1915
British Treasury, 1915–1919
Cambridge University, 1919–1946

Major Publications: *The Economic Consequences of the Peace,* 1919; *A Tract on Monetary Reform,* 1923; *A Treatise on Money,* 1930; *The General Theory of Employment, Interest and Money,* 1936

consumption by those workers. Using an MPC of .6, consumption would decline by $335 million (.6 times 558) if income was reduced by $558 million. This would tend to throw others in the Monterey area out of work as spending in retail and service stores declined. This would further reduce consumption, and so on. Although this case study refers to a small region of the entire country, the same logic applies to the economy as a whole.

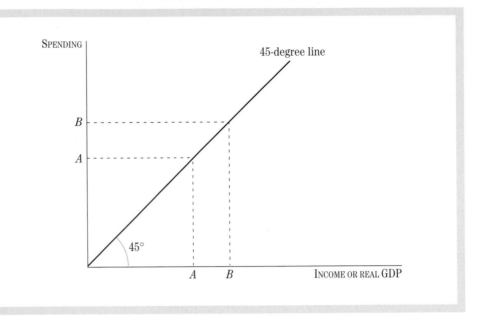

Figure 10.5
The 45-Degree Line
This simple line is a graphical representation of the income equals spending identity. The pairs of points on the 45-degree line have the same level of spending and income. For example, the level of spending at *A* is the same dollar amount as the level of income at *A*. Moreover, because income equals real GDP, we can put either income or real GDP on the horizontal axis.

The 45-Degree Line

We can use a convenient graph to calculate how much income and consumption change in the whole economy and thereby find out what happens to real GDP. In Figure 10.5 there is a line that shows graphically that income in the economy is equal to spending. That is, income (Y) equals spending ($C + I + G + X$). In Figure 10.5, income is on the horizontal axis and spending is on the vertical axis. All the points where spending equals income are on the upward-sloping line in Figure 10.5. The line has a slope of 1, or an angle of 45 degrees with the horizontal axis, because the distances from any point on the line to the horizontal axis and the vertical axis are equal. Along that line—which is called the **45-degree line**—spending and income are equal.

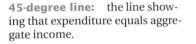

45-degree line: the line showing that expenditure equals aggregate income.

The Expenditure Line

expenditure line: the relation between the sum of the four components of spending ($C + I + G + X$) and aggregate income.

Figure 10.6 shows another relationship called the **expenditure line.** As in Figure 10.5, income or real GDP is on the horizontal axis, and spending is on the vertical axis. The top line in Figure 10.6 is the expenditure line. It is called the expenditure line because it shows how expenditure, or spending, depends on income. The four components that make up the expenditure line are consumption, investment, government purchases, and net exports. However, the expenditure line shows how these four components depend on income. It is this dependency of spending on income that is the defining characteristic of the expenditure line. Here is how the expenditure line is derived.

The consumption function is shown as the lowest line in Figure 10.6. It is simply the consumption function from Figure 10.3, which says that the higher income is, the more people want to consume. The next line above the consumption function in Figure 10.6 is parallel to the consumption function. This line represents the addition of investment to consumption at each level of income. It says that investment is so many billions of dollars in the U.S. economy, and the distance between the lines is this amount of investment. For example, if investment equals $800 billion, the distance between the consumption function and this next line is $800 billion.

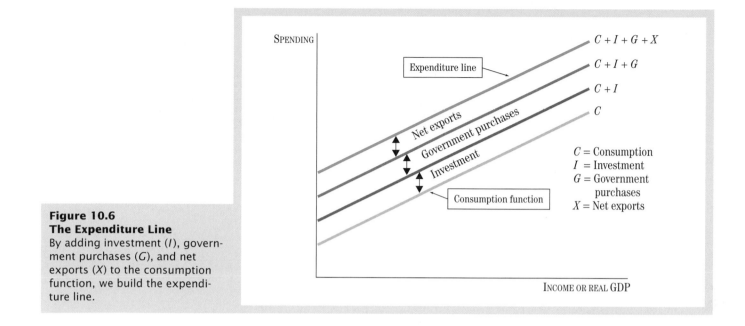

Figure 10.6
The Expenditure Line
By adding investment (*I*), government purchases (*G*), and net exports (*X*) to the consumption function, we build the expenditure line.

The reason the line is parallel to the consumption line is that we are starting our explanation by saying that investment does not depend on income. This simplifying assumption means that investment is a constant number, and the distance between the lines is the same regardless of income. We just add the same amount at each point.

The next line in Figure 10.6 adds in a constant level of government purchases. This line is also parallel to the other lines because the increase at every level of income is the same. The distance between the lines represents a fixed level of government purchases, say $1,600 billion, at every level of income.

Finally, to get the top line in Figure 10.6, we add in net exports. For simplicity, we assume that net exports do not depend on income, an assumption that we will change soon. Thus, the top line is parallel to all the other lines. The top line is the sum of $C + I + G + X$. It is the expenditure line. The most important thing to remember about the expenditure line is that it shows how the sum of the four components depends on income.

Before we can use the expenditure line, we must know what determines its slope and what causes it to shift.

■ **The Slope of the Expenditure Line.**   Observe in Figure 10.6 that the expenditure line is parallel to the consumption function. Therefore, the slope of the expenditure line is the same as the slope of the consumption function. We already know that the slope of the consumption function is the MPC. Hence, the slope of the expenditure line is also equal to the MPC.

Because the MPC is less than 1, the aggregate expenditure line is flatter (the slope is smaller) than the 45-degree line, which has a slope of exactly 1. This fact will soon be used to find real GDP.

■ **Shifts in the Expenditure Line.**   The expenditure line can shift for several reasons. Consider first what happens to the expenditure line if government purchases fall because of a cut in defense spending. As shown in Figure 10.7, the expenditure line shifts downward in a parallel fashion. The expenditure line is simply the sum $C + I + G + X$. Because G is less at all income levels, the line shifts down. The expenditure

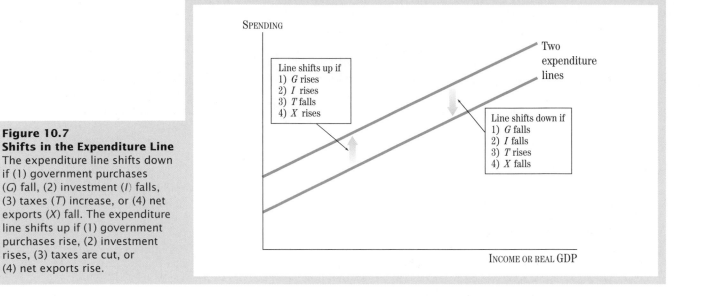

Figure 10.7
Shifts in the Expenditure Line
The expenditure line shifts down if (1) government purchases (*G*) fall, (2) investment (*I*) falls, (3) taxes (*T*) increase, or (4) net exports (*X*) fall. The expenditure line shifts up if (1) government purchases rise, (2) investment rises, (3) taxes are cut, or (4) net exports rise.

line is lowered because the distance between the consumption function and the other lines declines (see Figure 10.6). The reverse of this, an increase in government purchases, will cause the expenditure line to shift up.

What happens to the expenditure line if investment falls? Investment, remember, is the gap between the first and second lines in Figure 10.6. If investment declines (as might happen if businesses become pessimistic about the future and invest less), then the expenditure line shifts downward. With less investment, the gap between the lines shrinks. The reverse of this, an increase in investment, will cause the expenditure line to shift up, as shown in Figure 10.7.

A change in net exports, perhaps because of a change in the demand for U.S. exports to other countries, will also shift the expenditure line. A downward shift in net exports lowers the expenditure line, and an upward shift in net exports raises the expenditure line.

Finally, the expenditure line can also be shifted by changes in taxes. At any given level of income, an increase in taxes means that people have less to spend, and this will cause people to consume less. Hence, the expenditure line shifts down when taxes rise. The reverse of this, a cut in taxes, causes the expenditure line to shift up. We will use the symbol *T* to refer to taxes. For example, if *T* = $1,500 billion, then people pay and the government receives $1,500 billion in taxes.

Determining Real GDP Through Spending Balance

Having derived the expenditure line and the 45-degree line, we can combine the two to find real GDP. Figure 10.8 shows the expenditure line and the 45-degree line combined in one diagram. Observe that the two lines intersect. They must intersect because they have different slopes. Real GDP is found at the point of intersection of these two lines. Why?

Income and spending are always equal, and the 45-degree line is drawn to represent this equality. Therefore, at any point on the 45-degree line, income equals spending. Moreover, income and spending must be on the expenditure line, because only at points on that line do people consume according to the consumption function.

If both relationships hold—that is, income and spending are the same (we are on the 45-degree line) and people's consumption is described by the consumption function (we are on the expenditure line)—then logically we must be at the intersection of these two lines. We call that point of intersection **spending balance.** The level of income determined by that point is just the right level to cause people to purchase an amount of consumption that—when added to investment, government purchases, and net exports—gives exactly the same level of income. We would not have spending balance at either a higher or a lower level of income. The diagram in Figure 10.8 showing that the 45-degree line and the expenditure line cross is sometimes called the "Keynesian Cross" after John Maynard Keynes.

Table 10.2 provides an alternative way to determine spending balance. It uses a numerical tabulation of the consumption function rather than graphs. Total expenditure is obtained by adding the four columns on the right of Table 10.2. Consumption is shown to depend on income according to the same consumption function as in Table 10.1. Observe that there is only one row where income equals total expenditure. That row is where spending balance occurs. The row is shaded and corresponds to the point of intersection of the 45-degree line and the expenditure line in Figure 10.8.

Because the point of spending balance is at the intersection of two lines, we can think of it as an equilibrium, much as the intersection of a demand curve and a supply curve for wheat is an equilibrium. Because real GDP is not necessarily equal to potential GDP at this intersection, however, there is a sense in which the equilibrium is temporary; eventually real GDP will move back to potential GDP, as we will show in later chapters.

The point of spending balance is also an equilibrium in the sense that economic forces cause real GDP to be at that intersection. To see this, consider Table 10.2. As we noted, the shaded row corresponds to the intersection of the 45-degree line and the expenditure line: Income or real GDP equals expenditure. Suppose that income or real GDP were less than expenditure, as in one of the rows above the shaded row in Table 10.2. This would not be an equilibrium because firms would not be producing enough goods and services (real GDP) to satisfy people's expenditure on goods and

Figure 10.8
Spending Balance
Spending balance occurs when two relations are satisfied simultaneously: (1) income equals spending, and (2) spending equals consumption, which is a function of income, plus investment plus government purchases plus net exports. Only one level of income gives spending balance. That level of income is determined by the intersection of the 45-degree line and the expenditure line.

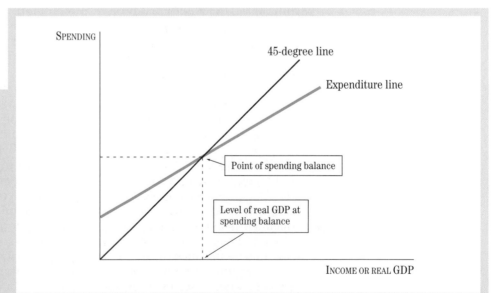

Table 10.2
A Numerical Example of Spending Balance (billions of dollars)

Income or Real GDP	Total Expenditure	Consumption	Investment	Government Purchases	Net Exports
6,000	7,600	4,600	900	2,000	100
7,000	8,200	5,200	900	2,000	100
8,000	8,800	5,800	900	2,000	100
9,000	9,400	6,400	900	2,000	100
10,000	10,000	7,000	900	2,000	100
11,000	10,600	7,600	900	2,000	100
12,000	11,200	8,200	900	2,000	100
13,000	11,800	8,800	900	2,000	100
14,000	12,400	9,400	900	2,000	100

services. Firms would increase their production, and real GDP would rise until it equaled expenditure. Similarly, if real GDP were greater than expenditure, as in one of the rows below the shaded row in Table 10.2, firms would be producing more than people would be buying. Hence, firms would reduce their production and real GDP would fall until it equaled expenditure.

A Better Forecast of Real GDP

Now let us return to forecasting real GDP using these new tools. Recall the example of making a forecast of real GDP for the year 2005 (from the vantage point of December 2004), conditional on a proposed decline in government purchases of $100 billion. Our new tools will enable us to take into account the effect of this decline on consumption, which we ignored in the simple forecast.

Figure 10.9 shows two expenditure lines. The top expenditure line is without the change in government purchases. In this case, G = $2,000 billion, C = $7,000 billion, I = $900 billion, and X = $100 billion, yielding income, or real GDP, of $10,000 billion. For the conditional forecast, we assume that G is cut by $100 billion, to $1,900 billion. In Figure 10.9, that causes the expenditure line to shift down to the "new" line. Observe that the expenditure line shifts down by $100 billion—a parallel shift. This new expenditure line cuts the 45-degree line at a lower point.

Logic tells us that the economy will now operate at a different point of spending balance, where the expenditure line and the 45-degree line now intersect. Thus we move from one intersection to a new intersection as a result of the decline in the expenditure line. The new point of spending balance is at a lower level of GDP.

We now have a prediction that real GDP will fall if government spending declines. Observe in Figure 10.9 that the decline in real GDP is larger than the $100 billion decline in government purchases and, therefore, larger than the $100 billion decline in real GDP in the simple forecast. The reason is that in addition to the decrease in government purchases, consumption has fallen because income has declined. The initial $100 billion is *multiplied* to create a larger than $100 billion change in real GDP because of the induced change in consumption. This multiplier phenomenon, which makes the change in real GDP larger than the change in government purchases, is called the *Keynesian multiplier* and applies to increases as well as to decreases in government purchases. In Figure 10.9, the multiplier looks quite large; the horizontal arrow is at least twice as large as the vertical arrow. It is certainly large enough to influence the administration's decision to reduce government

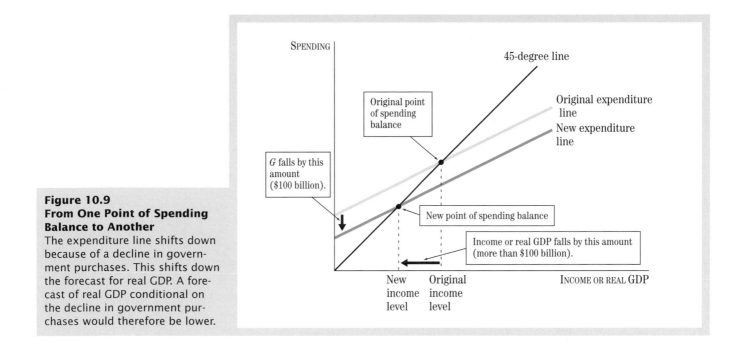

Figure 10.9
From One Point of Spending Balance to Another
The expenditure line shifts down because of a decline in government purchases. This shifts down the forecast for real GDP. A forecast of real GDP conditional on the decline in government purchases would therefore be lower.

purchases. The example and the application illustrate that it is not just for fun that we have derived the expenditure line. It is an essential tool of the practicing macroeconomist.

REVIEW
- Spending balance occurs when the identity $Y = C + I + G + X$ and the consumption function relating C to Y hold simultaneously.

- Spending balance can be shown on a graph with the 45-degree line and the expenditure line. The intersection of the two lines determines a level of income, or real GDP, that gives spending balance.

- A shift in the expenditure line brings about a new level of spending balance.

Spending Balance and Departures of Real GDP from Potential GDP

We have shown how to compute a level of real GDP for the purpose of making short-term forecasts. This level of real GDP is determined by aggregate demand—consumption, investment, government purchases, and net exports. It is not necessarily equal to potential GDP, which depends on the supply of labor, capital, and technology. Thus, we can have real GDP departing from potential GDP, as it does in recessions and booms. Let's now show this graphically.

Stepping Away from Potential GDP

Figure 10.10 illustrates how the departures of real GDP from potential GDP can be explained by shifts in the expenditure line. The left panel of the figure shows three

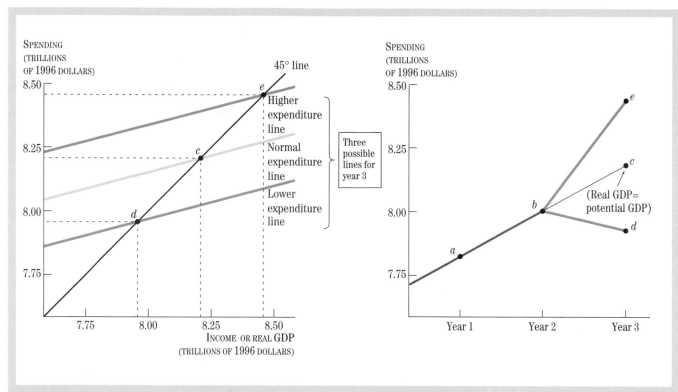

Figure 10.10
Spending Balance and
Departures of Real GDP
from Potential GDP

This figure shows how the levels of real GDP found through spending balance can explain the first steps of a recession or boom. The left panel shows spending balance for three expenditure curves; one (*c*) gives real GDP equal to potential GDP, a second (*e*) gives real GDP above potential GDP, and a third (*d*) gives real GDP below potential GDP. As shown in the right panel, two of these entail departures of real GDP from potential GDP.

different expenditure lines. Each line corresponds to a different level of government purchases or a different level of net exports or investment. The right panel of Figure 10.10—which is much like Figure 10.2—shows real GDP and potential GDP during a three-year period. There is a close connection between the left and right panels of Figure 10.10. The vertical axes are identical, and the points *c*, *d*, and *e* represent the same level of spending in both panels.

Observe how the three expenditure lines intersect the 45-degree line at three different levels of real GDP. Let us suppose that the middle expenditure line intersects the 45-degree line at a level of real GDP that is the same as potential GDP in year 3. This is point *c*. The lower expenditure line represents a recession; real GDP at the intersection of this expenditure line and the 45-degree line (point *d*) is at a level below potential GDP and also below the level of real GDP in year 2. Thus, real GDP would decline from year 2 to year 3 with this expenditure line. On the other hand, the higher expenditure line corresponds to the case in which real GDP is above potential GDP in year 3.

By referring to these values of real GDP as the *first* steps, we are emphasizing that they are not the end of the story. We will see that there are forces in the economy that tend to bring real GDP back toward potential GDP. This calculation of real GDP gives only the short-run impact of changes in government spending, investment, net exports, or taxes.

REVIEW

- Shifts in the expenditure line can explain the departures of real GDP from potential GDP.

- When the expenditure line shifts down, real GDP declines, and, if it was previously equal to potential GDP, it will fall below potential GDP. Upward shifts in the expenditure line will bring real GDP above potential GDP.

- The expenditure line can shift for many reasons. Changes in taxes, government purchases, investment, and net exports will cause the expenditure line to shift.

Conclusion

With this chapter, we have begun to develop a theory of economic fluctuations. We have shown how economists explain departures of real GDP from potential GDP, using the idea that these fluctuations are due to changes in aggregate demand. A recession occurs when aggregate demand falls, bringing real GDP below potential GDP. We used this explanation to make short-term forecasts of real GDP. The expenditure line—showing how the demand for consumption, investment, and net exports depends on income—and the 45-degree line are key parts of the forecasting process. However, our analysis thus far has made several simplifying assumptions. For example, we assumed that the only thing people's consumption decisions respond to is a change in income.

In the next chapter, we show that consumption as well as investment and net exports responds to interest rates and inflation. The responses to interest rates and inflation will explain why real GDP returns to potential GDP in the long run.

HEY POINTS

1. Economic fluctuations are temporary deviations of real GDP from potential GDP.

2. Employment and unemployment fluctuate with real GDP. Unemployment increases in recessions and decreases in booms.

3. The fluctuations in real GDP and potential GDP are mainly due to fluctuations in aggregate demand.

4. The idea that fluctuations in real GDP are mainly due to aggregate demand is used to find real GDP when making a short-term forecast.

5. Real GDP can be predicted on the basis of forecasts of consumption, investment, net exports, and government purchases. But these items depend on income and, thus, on the forecast of real GDP itself.

6. The consumption function describes how consumption responds to income.

7. The expenditure line is built up from the consumption function.

8. The 45-degree line tells us that expenditures equal income.

9. Combining the expenditure line and the 45-degree line in a diagram enables us to determine the level of income or real GDP.

10. The level of real GDP that gives spending balance changes when government spending changes. Real GDP will decline in the short run when government purchases are cut.

KEY TERMS

real business cycle theory
consumption function

marginal propensity to consume (MPC)

45-degree line
expenditure line

spending balance

QUESTIONS FOR REVIEW

1. Why do theories of economic fluctuations focus on aggregate demand rather than potential GDP as the main source of short-run economic fluctuations?

2. Why do theories of economic growth focus on potential GDP (with its three determinants) rather than aggregate demand as the main source of economic growth?

3. Why does the unemployment rate rise when real GDP falls below potential GDP?

4. What is the normal rate of capacity utilization in manufacturing firms? What is the significance of this normal rate for explaining economic fluctuations?

5. What is a forecast?

6. What accounting identity does the 45-degree line represent?

7. Why does the expenditure line have a slope less than 1?

8. Why do economic forecasters have to take into account the consumption function?

9. Why is real GDP given by the intersection of the 45-degree line and the expenditure line?

PROBLEMS

1. In the early part of 2001, the U.S. economy was hit by a sudden plunge in stock markets, accompanied by a slowdown in consumer and investor spending. Explain why these events would move real GDP below potential GDP.

2. Suppose the information in the following table describes the economic situation in the United States at the end of 2004.

Year	Real GDP (billions of 2004 dollars)	Potential GDP (billions of 2004 dollars)
2002	9,613	9,613
2003	9,854	9,854
2004	10,100	10,100
2005 (optimistic forecast)	10,600	10,353
2005 (pessimistic forecast)	9,900	10,353

a. Graph real GDP over time, placing the year on the horizontal axis. Calculate the growth rate of real GDP between 2003 and 2004.

b. The optimistic forecast for the year 2005 is based on the possibility that businesses are optimistic about the economy. What will the growth rate of real GDP be if the optimistic forecast turns out to be true?

c. The pessimistic forecast is based on the possibility that businesses will be pessimistic about the economy. What will the growth rate of real GDP be if this forecast is correct?

d. What is the deviation (in terms of dollars and as a percentage) of real GDP from potential GDP in 2005 if the optimistic forecast is correct? What is the deviation (in terms of dollars and as a percentage) from potential GDP in 2005 if the pessimistic forecast is correct?

3. The following table shows the relationship between income and consumption in an economy.

Income (Y) (in billions of dollars)	Consumption (C) (in billions of dollars)
0	5
10	11
20	17
30	23
40	29
50	35
60	41
70	47
80	53
90	59
100	65

Assume that investment (I) is $5 billion, government purchases (G) are $4 billion, and net exports (X) are $2 billion.

a. What is the numerical value of the marginal propensity to consume?

b. Construct a table that is analogous to text Table 10.2 for this economy. What is the level of income at the point of spending balance?

c. For this level of income, calculate national saving. Is national saving equal to investment plus net exports?

d. Sketch a diagram with a 45-degree line and an expenditure curve that describes the preceding relationships. Show graphically what happens to income when the government lowers taxes.

4. Describe what happens to the expenditure line in each of the following cases.
   a. Government spending on airport safety rises.
   b. The Koreans decide to spend $10 billion on aircraft built in the United States.
   c. Firms become very optimistic about the future.
   d. A law is enacted requiring that the government pay $10,000 to anyone who builds a new house.

5. Sketch a diagram with a 45-degree line and an expenditure line that describes macroeconomic spending balance. What factors determine how steep the expenditure line is? What macroeconomic relationship is described by the 45-degree line? Show on the diagram what will happen to the level of income if there is a rise in government purchases. Does U.S. income increase by more or by less than the upward shift in government purchases? Explain.

6. Suppose that business executives are very optimistic, and they raise their investment spending. What happens to the expenditure line? How will this affect real GDP? Sketch a diagram to demonstrate your answer.

7. Suppose that American goods suddenly become unpopular in Europe. What happens to net exports? How will this shift the expenditure line? What happens to real GDP? Demonstrate this in a diagram.

8. Suppose government purchases will increase by $100 billion, and a forecasting firm predicts that real GDP will rise in the short run by $100 billion as a result. Would you say that that forecast is accurate? Why? If you were running a business and you subscribed to that forecasting service, what questions would you ask about the forecast?

Deriving the Formula for the Keynesian Multiplier and the Forward-Looking Consumption Model

The Keynesian Multiplier

Here we derive a formula for the **Keynesian multiplier,** which gives the *short-run* impact on real GDP of things such as cuts in military purchases or a new federal program for construction of roads and bridges. We show how the multiplier depends on the marginal propensity to consume and on the marginal propensity to import.

A Graphical Review

Figure 10A.1 is a diagram like the one derived in Chapter 10, with income or real GDP on the horizontal axis and spending on the vertical axis. The 45-degree line equates spending and income. There are two expenditure lines in

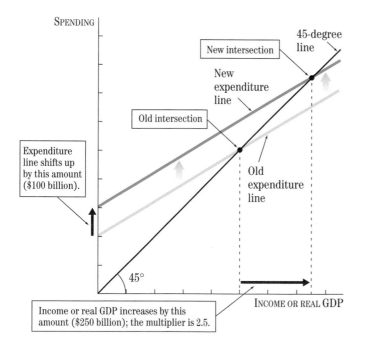

SPENDING

New intersection

45-degree line

New expenditure line

Old intersection

Expenditure line shifts up by this amount ($100 billion).

Old expenditure line

45°

INCOME OR REAL GDP

Income or real GDP increases by this amount ($250 billion); the multiplier is 2.5.

Figure 10A.1
Graphical Calculation of the Multiplier
An upward shift in the expenditure line raises real GDP in the short run by a multiple of the shift in the expenditure line. The multiplier can be found graphically. It is the ratio of the length of the black horizontal arrow to the length of the black vertical arrow.

Figure 10A.1. The "new" expenditure line is $100 billion higher than the "old" expenditure line, representing an upward shift due to an increase in government purchases, for example. Both expenditure lines show that expenditure in the economy—the sum of consumption plus investment plus government purchases plus net exports, or $C + I + G + X$—rises with income. We assume that the marginal propensity to consume (MPC) is equal to .6. Thus, the slope of both expenditure lines is .6.

Note that the "new" expenditure line intersects the 45-degree line at a different point from the "old" expenditure line. At this new intersection, the level of income, or real GDP, is higher than at the old intersection. On the horizontal axis, the black arrow pointing to the right shows this shift to a higher level of real GDP. Look carefully at the diagram to note the *size* of the change in real GDP along the horizontal axis and compare it with the change in the expenditure line. Observe that the horizontal change is *larger* than the vertical change. This is due to the multiplier. In fact, the term *multiplier* is used because the change in real GDP is a multiple of the shift in the aggregate expenditure line.

The multiplier is the ratio of the change in real GDP to the shift in the expenditure line, regardless of the reason for the shift in the expenditure line (whether it is due to a change in government purchases, a change in taxes, a change in investment, or a change in foreign demand). Thus, the multiplier is equal to the ratio of the length of the arrow along the horizontal axis to the length of the arrow along the vertical axis in Figure 10A.1. You can find the multiplier by measuring these lengths. If you do so, you will find that for the expenditure line with a slope of .6 in Figure 10A.1, the multiplier is 2.5.

The multiplier applies to anything that shifts the expenditure line. For example, an increase in government purchases of $100 billion would shift the expenditure line up by $100 billion. This would increase real GDP by $250 billion if the multiplier for government purchases is 2.5.

The Algebraic Derivation

We now want to derive a formula for the multiplier using algebra. Let us focus first on the case where the MPC is .6. To be specific, let us suppose that the particular reason for a change in the aggregate expenditure line is an increase in government purchases. Then the multiplier is the ratio of the change in real GDP to the change in government purchases.

The identity that income or real GDP (Y) equals consumption (C) plus investment (I) plus government purchases (G) plus net exports (X) can be written algebraically as

$$Y = C + I + G + X$$

To find the multiplier, we want to determine the impact of a *change* in government purchases on real GDP. That is, we want to find the change in Y that occurs when G changes. Any change in Y must come either directly from a change in G or indirectly from a change in C, I, or X, according to the preceding identity. Denote the change in any of these items by the Greek letter Δ. Then we can write the identity in terms of changes:

$$\Delta Y = \Delta C + \Delta I + \Delta G + \Delta X$$

That is, the *change* in real GDP is equal to the *change* in consumption plus the *change* in investment plus the *change* in government purchases plus the *change* in net exports. Now consider each of the four terms on the right.

The change in government purchases (ΔG) equals $100 billion. For convenience, to make things simple, we continue to assume that there is no change in investment or in net exports. In other words, we assume that neither responds to changes in income. Expressed in symbols, $\Delta I = 0$ and $\Delta X = 0$.

But we cannot assume that $\Delta C = 0$. The *consumption function* tells us that consumption changes when income changes. The consumption function we use for the algebraic calculation has an MPC of .6. Using algebra, we write $\Delta C = .6\Delta Y$. That is, the change in consumption equals .6 times the change in income; for example, if the change in income $\Delta Y = \$10$ billion, then the change in consumption $\Delta C = \$6$ billion if the MPC is .6.

Now let us take our ingredients:

1. $\Delta Y = \Delta C + \Delta I + \Delta G + \Delta X$.

2. The changes in investment and net exports are zero ($\Delta I = \Delta X = 0$).

3. The change in consumption is .6 times the change in income ($\Delta C = .6\Delta Y$).

Replacing ΔI with zero and ΔX with zero removes ΔI and ΔX from the right-hand side of the identity. Replacing ΔC with $.6\Delta Y$ in the same identity results in

$$\Delta Y = .6\Delta Y + \Delta G$$

Note that the term ΔY appears on both sides of this equation. Gathering terms in ΔY on the left-hand side of the equation gives

$$(1 - .6)\Delta Y = \Delta G$$

Dividing both sides by ΔG and by $(1 - .6)$ results in

$$\Delta Y/\Delta G = 1/(1 - .6)$$
$$= 1/.4$$
$$= 2.5$$

Thus, the change in income, or real GDP, that occurs when government purchases change, according to this calculation, is 2.5 times the change in government purchases. That is, $\Delta Y = 2.5\Delta G$. The number 2.5 is the multiplier. The algebraic calculation agrees with the graphical calculation.

You can perform this same calculation for *any value* of the marginal propensity to consume (MPC), not just .6. To see this, note that the change in consumption equals the MPC times the change in income, where the MPC is any number. Using the same approach as in the case of MPC = .6, we obtain a *formula for the multiplier*, which is

$$\frac{\Delta Y}{\Delta G} = \frac{1}{(1 - \text{MPC})}$$

The derivation of this formula is summarized in Table 10A.1.

Table 10A.1
Derivation of a Formula for the Keynesian Multiplier

Start with the identity

$$Y = C + I + G + X$$

and convert it to change form:

$$\Delta Y = \Delta C + \Delta I + \Delta G + \Delta X$$

Substitute $\Delta I = 0$, $\Delta X = 0$, and

$$\Delta C = \text{MPC} \times \Delta Y$$

into the change form of the identity to get

$$\Delta Y = \text{MPC} \times \Delta Y + \Delta G$$

Gather terms involving ΔY to get

$$(1 - \text{MPC}) \times \Delta Y = \Delta G$$

Divide both sides by ΔG and by $1 - \text{MPC}$ to get

$$\frac{\Delta Y}{\Delta G} = \frac{1}{1 - \text{MPC}}$$

Following the Multiplier Through the Economy To get a more complete understanding of the formula for the multiplier, it is useful to examine what happens as a change in government purchases winds its way through the economy.

Assume that the government increases its military purchases, perhaps to build a new missile defense system. In this example, the government increases purchases of electronic and aerospace equipment at defense firms. The immediate impact of the change in government purchases is an increase in the production of this equipment. With an increase in demand, defense firms produce more, and real GDP rises. The initial increase in real GDP from an increase in government purchases of $100 billion is that same $100 billion. If the government is purchasing more equipment, the production of equipment increases. We call this initial increase in real GDP the *first-round* effect, which includes only the initial change in government purchases.

The first round is not the end of the story. A further increase in real GDP occurs when the workers employed in making the equipment start working more hours and new workers are hired. As a result, the workers' income rises, and the profits made by the manufacturers increase. With both wage income and profit income rising, income in the economy as a whole rises by $100 billion. According to the consumption function, people will consume more. How much more? The consumption function tells us that .6 times the change in income, or $60 billion, will be the additional increase in consumption by the workers and owners of the defense firms. Real GDP rises by $60 billion, the increased production of the goods the workers and owners consume. This $60 billion increase in real GDP is the *second-round* effect. It is hard for anyone to know what the workers in the defense industry or the owners of the defense firms will start purchasing; presumably it will be an array of goods: clothes, VCRs, movies, and restaurant meals. But with an MPC of .6, we do know that they will purchase $60 billion more of these goods. The increase in production spreads throughout the economy. After this second round, real GDP has increased by $160 billion, the sum of $100 billion on the first round and $60 billion on the second round. This is shown in the first and second rows of Table 10A.2.

The story continues. The workers who make the clothes, VCRs, and other goods and services for which there is $60 billion more in spending also have an increase in their income. Either they are no longer unemployed or they work more hours. Similarly, the profits of the owners of those firms increase. As a result, they consume more. How much more? According to the consumption function, .6 times the increase in their income.

Table 10A.2
A Numerical Illustration of the Multiplier at Work
(billions of dollars)

Round	Change in Real GDP	Cumulative Change in Real GDP
First round	100.000	100.000
Second round	60.000	160.000
Third round	36.000	196.000
Fourth round	21.600	217.600
Fifth round	12.960	230.560
.	.	.
.	.	.
.	.	.
After an infinite number of rounds	0.000	250.000

The increase in income outside of defense production was $60 billion, so the increase in consumption must now be .6 times that, or a $36 billion increase. This increase is the *third-round* effect. As the increase permeates the economy, it is impossible to say what particular goods will increase in production, but we know that total production continues to increase. After three rounds, real GDP has increased by $196 billion, as shown in the third row of Table 10A.2.

The increase does not stop there. Another $36 billion more in consumption means that there is $36 billion more in income for people somewhere in the economy. This increases consumption further, by .6 times the $36 billion, or $21.6 billion. According to the column on the right of Table 10A.2, the cumulative effect on real GDP is now up to $217.6 billion after four rounds. Observe that each new entry in the first column is added to the previous total to get the cumulative effect on real GDP.

The story is now getting repetitive. We multiply .6 times $21.6 billion to get $12.96 billion. The total effect on real GDP is now $230.56 billion at the fifth round. In fact, we are already almost at $250 billion. If we kept on going for more and more rounds, we would get closer and closer to the $250 billion amount obtained from the graphs and the formula for the multiplier.

What If Net Exports Depend on Income? Thus far, we have made the simplifying assumption that net exports do not respond to income. When net exports do respond to income, the formula for the multiplier is a bit different. We now incorporate this response into our analysis.

We first need to consider how net exports respond to income. Recall that net exports are exports minus imports. To examine the effect of income, on net exports, we look first at exports and then at imports.

Exports are goods and services that we sell to other countries—aircraft, pharmaceuticals, telephones. Do U.S. exports depend on income in the United States? No, not much. If Americans earn a little more or a little less, the demand for U.S. exports is not going to increase or decrease. What is likely to make the demand for U.S. exports increase or decrease is a change in income abroad—changes in income in Japan, Europe, or Latin America will affect demand for U.S. exports. U.S. exports will not be affected even if the United States has a recession. Of course, if Japan or Europe has a recession, that is another story. In any case, we conclude that U.S. exports are unresponsive to the changes in U.S. income.

Imports are goods and services that people in the United States purchase from abroad—automobiles, sweaters, vacations. Does the amount purchased of these goods and services change when our incomes change? Yes, because imports are part of consumption. Just as we argued that consumption responds to income, so must imports respond to income. Higher income will lead to higher consumption of both goods purchased in the United States and goods purchased abroad. That reasoning leads us to hypothesize that imports are positively related to income. The hypothesis turns out to be accurate when we look at observations on income and imports.

The **marginal propensity to import (MPI)** is the amount that imports change when income changes. Suppose the MPI is .2. The MPI is smaller than the MPC because most of the goods we consume when income rises are not imported.

If exports are unrelated to income and imports are positively related to income, then net exports—exports less imports—must be negatively related to income. Algebraically, we have

$$\Delta X = -\text{MPI} \times \Delta Y$$

Using this expression for ΔX, we can now follow the same algebraic steps we followed earlier to derive a formula for the multiplier. The multiplier now depends on the MPI along with the MPC. The derivation is summarized in Table 10A.3. The formula for the multiplier is

$$\frac{\Delta Y}{\Delta G} = \frac{1}{1 - \text{MPC} + \text{MPI}}$$

For example, if MPC = .6 and MPI = .2, the multiplier is 1.7.

Table 10A.3
Derivation of a Formula for the Keynesian Multiplier with Both the MPC and the MPI

Start with

$$\Delta Y = \Delta C + \Delta I + \Delta G + \Delta X$$

Assume that

$$\Delta I = 0$$

and that

$$\Delta C = \text{MPC} \times \Delta Y$$

and that

$$\Delta X = -\text{MPI} \times \Delta Y$$

Putting the above expressions together, we get

$$\Delta Y = (\text{MPC} \times \Delta Y) + \Delta G - (\text{MPI} \times \Delta Y)$$

and solving for the change in Y, we get

$$\frac{\Delta Y}{\Delta G} = \frac{1}{1 - \text{MPC} + \text{MPI}}$$

The Forward-Looking Consumption Model

Although the consumption function introduced in Chapter 10 gives a good prediction of people's behavior in many situations, it sometimes works very poorly. For example, the marginal propensity to consume (MPC) turned out to be very small when taxes were cut in 1975; people saved almost the entire increase in disposable income that resulted from the tax cut. However, the MPC turned out to be very large for the tax cuts in 1982, only seven years later; people saved very little of the increase in disposable income in that case. The forward-looking consumption model was designed to explain such changes in the MPC.

The **forward-looking consumption model** assumes that people anticipate their future income when making consumption decisions. The forward-looking consumption model was developed independently and in different ways by two Nobel Prize–winning economists, Milton Friedman and Franco Modigliani. Friedman's version is called the **permanent income model,** and Modigliani's version is called the **life-cycle model.** Both models improved on the idea that consumption depends only on current income.

Forward-Looking People

The forward-looking model starts with the idea that people attempt to look ahead to the future. They do not simply consider their current income. For example, if a young medical doctor decides to take a year off from a high-paying suburban medical practice to do community service at little or no pay, that doctor's income will fall below the poverty line for a year. But the doctor is unlikely to cut consumption to a fraction of the poverty level of income. Even if the doctor were young enough to have little savings, borrowing would be a way to keep consumption high and even buy an occasional luxury item. The doctor is basing consumption decisions on expected income for several years in the future—making an assessment of a more permanent income, or a life-cycle income—not just for one year.

There are many other examples. Farmers in poor rural areas of Asia try to save something in good years so that they will be able to maintain their consumption in bad years. They try not to consume a fixed fraction of their income. In many cases, the saving is in storable farm goods like rice.

As these examples indicate, instead of allowing their consumption to vary with their income, which may be quite erratic, most people engage in **consumption smoothing** from year to year. Once people estimate their future income prospects, they try to maintain their consumption around the same level from year to year. If their income temporarily falls, they do not cut their consumption by much; *the marginal propensity to consume (MPC) is very small—maybe about .05—in the case of a temporary change in income*. But if they find out that their income will increase permanently, they will increase their consumption a lot; *the MPC is very large—maybe .95—in the case of a permanent change in income*. For example, if a new fertilizer doubles the rice yield of a rice farmer's land permanently, we can expect that the farmer's consumption of other goods will about double because of higher permanent income.

The difference between the forward-looking consumption model and the simple consumption function where consumption depends only on current income is illustrated in Figure 10A.2. In the right panel of Figure 10A.2, income is expected to follow a typical life-cycle pattern: lower when young, higher when middle-aged, and very low when retired. However, consumption does not follow these ups and downs; it is flat. The left panel shows the opposite extreme: the standard consumption function with a fixed MPC. In this case, people consume a lot when they are middle-aged but consume very little when they are young or old.

Occasionally, some people are prevented from completely smoothing their income because they have a **liquidity constraint;** that is, they cannot get a loan, and so they cannot consume more than their income. Such liquidity constraints do not appear to be important enough

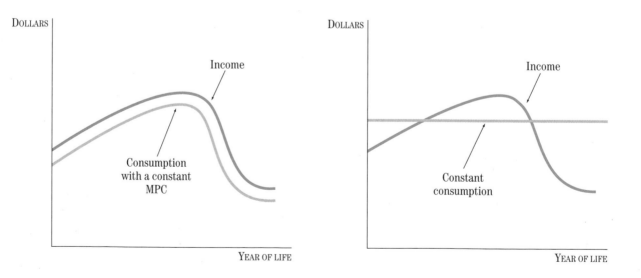

Figure 10A.2
Two Extreme Forms of Consumption Behavior
The right panel shows the future outlook of a young person or family described by the forward-looking model of consumption. The left panel shows the outlook of a young family with a constant MPC. The path of income is the same in both cases.

in the economy as a whole to negate the forward-looking model completely. Of course, not all people try to smooth their income; some people like to go on binges, spending everything, even if the binge is followed by a long lull.

Tests and Applications of the Forward-Looking Model

Observations on consumption and income for the economy as a whole indicate that the forward-looking model significantly improves our understanding of observed changes in the MPC. For example, economists have demonstrated that the measured MPC for the economy as a whole is lower for the temporary changes in income that occur during recessions and booms than for the more permanent increases in income that occur as potential GDP grows over time. Studies of thousands of individual families over time show that the individual MPC for temporary changes in income is about one-third of the MPC for permanent changes in income.

Permanent versus Temporary Tax Cuts   The forward-looking model is also the most promising explanation for the low MPC during the tax cut of 1975. That tax cut was explicitly temporary—a one-time tax rebate, good for only one year. In contrast, the tax cut in the early 1980s was explicitly permanent and was expected to apply for many years into the future. The MPC was large in this case.

With a permanent tax cut, the MPC is high, so there is a big impact on real GDP. For a temporary tax cut, the MPC is low, so there is only a small impact on GDP. In estimating the effects of various tax proposals on the economy, economic forecasters try to take these changes in the MPC into account.

Anticipating Future Tax Cuts or Increases   The forward-looking model changes our estimate of the impact of changes in taxes that are expected to occur in the future. For example, if people are certain of tax cuts in the future, they may begin to increase their consumption right away, before the tax decreases. In this case, the MPC is technically huge, because consumption increases with little or no observed change in current income. Conversely, people may reduce their consumption in anticipation of a tax increase.

It is difficult to know how large these effects are because we do not observe people's expectations of the future. Estimates based on the assumption that people forecast the future no better and no worse than economic forecasters—this is the *rational expectations assumption*—suggest that the effects are large and significant.

In situations where the expectations effects are obvious, we do see an impact. For example, in December 1992, after the 1992 presidential election, when a tax increase became more likely, there was evidence that many people who could do so shifted their reported income for tax purposes from 1993 to 1992. But whether people held back their consumption in anticipation of future tax increases is difficult to say. In any case, because people's behavior is affected by their expectations of the future, attempts to estimate the impact of a policy proposal like a change in taxes need to take these expectations into account.

Key Points

1. The multiplier can be found with graphs and with algebra. The algebraic approach results in a convenient formula.

2. The formula for the multiplier is $1/(1 - \text{MPC})$ when net exports do not depend on income.

3. If net exports are negatively related to income, then the formula for the multiplier is $1/(1 - \text{MPC} + \text{MPI})$.

4. The forward-looking consumption model explains why the MPC is low in some cases and high in others. It helps economists deal with the uncertainty in the multiplier.

5. The forward-looking consumption model also implies that anticipated changes in taxes affect consumption and are a further reason for uncertainty about the MPC. Although such effects have been observed, it is difficult to estimate their size in advance.

6. The rational expectations assumption, which suggests that people forecast the future no better and no worse than economic forecasters, is one basis for making such estimates. With this assumption, the effects of anticipated tax changes on consumption are quite high.

Key Terms and Definitions

Keynesian multiplier: the ratio of the change in real GDP to the shift in the expenditure line; the formula is $1/(1 - \text{MPC})$, where MPC is the marginal propensity to consume.

marginal propensity to import (MPI): the change in imports because of a given change in income.

forward-looking consumption model: a model that explains consumer behavior by assuming that people anticipate future income when deciding on consumption spending today.

permanent income model: a type of forward-looking consumption model that assumes that people distinguish between temporary changes in their income and permanent changes in their income; the permanent changes have a larger effect on consumption.

life-cycle model: a type of forward-looking consumption model that assumes that people base their consumption decisions on their expected lifetime income rather than on their current income.

consumption smoothing: the idea that, although their incomes fluctuate, people try to stabilize consumption spending from year to year.

liquidity constraint: the situation in which people cannot borrow to smooth their consumption spending when their income is low.

Questions for Review

1. Why is the size of the multiplier positively related to the MPC?

2. Why is the size of the multiplier negatively related to the marginal propensity to import?

3. Why do imports but not exports depend on income?

4. How does the forward-looking consumption model differ from the consumption function with a fixed MPC?

5. Why is the MPC for a temporary tax cut less than the MPC for a permanent tax cut? Are there examples that prove the point?

6. What is consumption smoothing?

7. Why do changes in future taxes that are anticipated in advance affect consumption?

Problems

1. Are the following statements true or false? Show using algebra.
   a. The multiplier is greater than 1 and rises if the marginal propensity to consume rises.
   b. The multiplier for an economy in which net exports respond to income is smaller than the multiplier for an economy in which net exports do not respond to income.

2. Suppose that the marginal propensity to consume in a closed economy (with no net exports) is estimated to be .6, but there is a 10 percent margin of error on either side. In other words, the MPC could be anywhere between .54 and .66. In what range will the multiplier lie? Quantify the range of impacts on real GDP of a $100 million increase in *G*. Do the same when the margin of error is 20 percent on either side of .6.

3. The following table shows real GDP and imports (in billions of dollars) for an economy.

Real GDP or Income	Imports
2,000	400
3,000	500
4,000	600
5,000	700
6,000	800
7,000	900

Suppose that exports are equal to $700 billion.
   a. Construct a graph showing how imports depend on income.
   b. Construct a graph showing how net exports depend on income.
   c. If the level of real GDP that occurs at spending balance is $6,000 billion, will there be a trade surplus or deficit? What type of policy regarding government purchases would bring the trade deficit or trade surplus closer to zero?
   d. If the marginal propensity to consume is .6, what is the size of the multiplier?

4. The following numerical example shows how an economy's consumption and net exports depend on income.

Real GDP or Income	Consumption	Net Exports
100	80	30
200	160	20
300	240	10
400	320	0
500	400	−10
600	480	−20
700	560	−30

   a. Find the marginal propensity to consume, the marginal propensity to import, and the multiplier.
   b. Suppose that *I* = 60 and *G* = 50, and taxes are zero. Find the total expenditure for each level of income listed in the table. What is the level of real GDP, consumption, and net exports at which spending balance occurs?
   c. Suppose that government purchases rise by 10. What happens to real GDP?

5. a. Suppose Joe spends every additional dollar of income that he receives. What is Joe's marginal propensity to consume? What does his consumption function look like?
   b. Suppose that Jane spends half of each additional dollar of income that she receives. What is the slope of Jane's consumption function?
   c. What differences in Joe's and Jane's incomes or jobs might explain the differences in their MPCs?

6. Each month, a certain fraction of employees pay is withheld and sent to the government as part of what is owed for personal income taxes. If the taxes owed for the year are less than the amount withheld, then a refund is sent early in the following year. Otherwise, additional taxes must be paid by April 15. In 1992, the amount of income tax *withheld* was lowered by about $10 billion to increase consumption and real GDP and thereby speed recovery from the 1990–1991 recession. However, the amount of taxes owed was not changed. Discuss why the impact of this 1992 change would be smaller than that of a cut in taxes of $10 billion during 1992.

CHAPTER 11

The Economic Fluctuations Model

The president of the United States is undeniably a very powerful person. But how much power does the president have to help the U.S. economy if it goes into a recession? Will a cut in taxes or an increase in spending end the recession earlier or speed up the recovery? Do such fiscal actions have to be well timed to be successful? Could a long delay in getting the needed legislation through Congress actually hurt the economy? What if the president simply stood by, watching while the Fed cut interest rates and underlying economic forces halted the decline in real GDP? How long would such a process take—one year? Five years?

To answer these important questions, we need a model of economic fluctuations—a simplified description of how the economy adjusts over time when it moves away from potential GDP, as in a recession.

The purpose of this chapter is to present, in graphical form, an economic fluctuations model. Economic fluctuations models are used to make decisions about monetary policy at the Fed and at other central banks all over the world. Private business analysts use the ideas to track the economy and predict central bank decisions.

This model is much newer than the supply and demand model, which has been around for over 100 years. It combines Keynes's idea, developed 50 years ago, that aggregate demand causes the departure of real GDP from potential GDP with newer ideas, developed in the 1980s and 1990s, about how expectations and inflation adjust over time.

Though newer, the economic fluctuations model is analogous to the supply and demand model (Chapter 3). Just as we presented the supply and demand model in a graph consisting of three elements:

- A *demand curve*

- A *supply curve*

- An *equilibrium* at the intersection of the two curves

we present the economic fluctuations model in a graph consisting of three elements:

- An *aggregate demand* (AD) *curve*

- An *inflation adjustment* (IA) *line*

- An *equilibrium* at the intersection of the curve and the line

We use the economic fluctuations model to explain fluctuations in real GDP and inflation in much the same way that we used supply and demand curves to explain quantity and price in the peanut or other microeconomic markets. In the microeconomic supply and demand model, the intersection of the *demand curve* and the *supply curve* gives us a prediction of price and quantity. In the economic fluctuations model, the intersection of the *aggregate demand* (AD) *curve* and the *inflation adjustment (IA) line* gives us a prediction of real GDP and inflation.

We will start our construction of the economic fluctuations model by deriving the aggregate demand curve and then the inflation adjustment line. We will then show how their intersection determines real GDP and inflation.

The Aggregate Demand Curve

aggregate demand (AD) curve: a line showing a negative relationship between inflation and the aggregate quantity of goods and services demanded at that inflation rate.

The **aggregate demand (AD) curve** is a relationship between two economic variables: real GDP and the inflation rate. Real GDP is usually measured as the percentage deviation from potential GDP, and the inflation rate is usually measured as the annual percentage change in the overall price level from year to year. Figure 11.1 shows an aggregate demand curve for the United States. Observe that inflation is measured on the vertical axis, that real GDP is measured on the horizontal axis, and that we have drawn a vertical dashed line to mark the point where real GDP equals potential GDP. The aggregate demand curve shows different combinations of real GDP and inflation. It is downward-sloping from left to right because real GDP is negatively related to inflation along the curve. The term *aggregate demand* is used because we interpret the movements of real GDP away from potential GDP as being due to fluctuations in the sum (aggregate) of the demand for consumption, investment, net exports, and government purchases.

Why does the aggregate demand curve slope downward? We will answer this question and derive the curve in three stages. First, we show that there is a negative

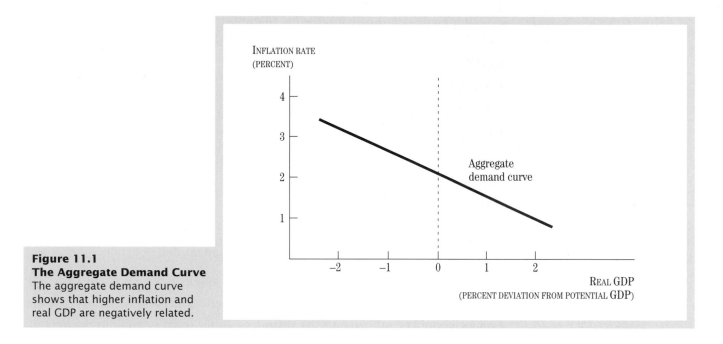

Figure 11.1
The Aggregate Demand Curve
The aggregate demand curve shows that higher inflation and real GDP are negatively related.

relationship between the real interest rate and real GDP. Second, we show that there is a positive relationship between inflation and the real interest rate. Third, we show that these two relationships imply that there is a negative relationship between real GDP and inflation, and that that relationship is the aggregate demand curve. The following schematic chart shows how the three stages fit together.

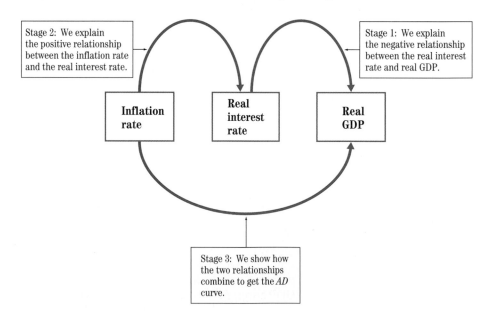

Interest Rates and Real GDP

Consumption, investment, and net exports are each negatively related to the interest rate. Combining these components helps provide an explanation of the negative relationship between real GDP and the interest rate. Keep in mind that the real interest rate is a better measure of the effects of interest rates on investment, consumption, and net exports because it corrects for inflation. Recall from Chapter 4 that the real interest rate equals the stated, or nominal, interest rate minus the inflation rate. The negative effect of the real interest rate on consumption, investment, and net exports is no different from that discussed in Chapter 6. If you have already studied that chapter, the next few pages will serve as review.

REAL INTEREST RATE

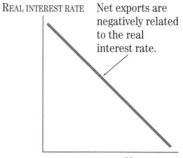

Investment is negatively related to the real interest rate.

INVESTMENT

■ **Investment.** Investment is the component of expenditure that is probably most sensitive to the real interest rate. Recall that part of investment is the purchase of new equipment or a new factory by a business firm. Many firms must borrow funds to pay for such investments. Higher real interest rates make such borrowing more costly. The additional profits the firm might expect to earn from purchasing a photocopier or a truck are more likely to be lower than the interest costs on the loan if the real interest rate is high. Hence, businesses that are thinking about buying a new machine and need to borrow funds will be less inclined to purchase such an investment good if real interest rates are higher, and so higher real interest rates reduce investment spending by businesses. Also, remember that part of investment is the purchase of new houses. Most people need to take out a mortgage in order to buy a house. Like any loan, the mortgage has an interest rate, and higher interest rates make mortgages more costly. Hence, with higher real interest rates, fewer people take out mortgages and buy new houses. Spending for new housing declines.

The same reasoning works to show why lower real interest rates will increase investment spending: Lower real interest rates reduce the cost of borrowing and make investment more attractive to firms and households.

To summarize, both business investment and housing investment decline when the real interest rate rises, and they increase when the real interest rate falls. At any time there are some firms or households deciding whether to buy a new machine or a new house, and they are going to be less inclined to buy such things when the interest rate is higher.

REAL INTEREST RATE

Net exports are negatively related to the real interest rate.

NET EXPORTS

■ **Net Exports.** The negative relationship between net exports and the real interest rate requires a somewhat more involved explanation than the relationship between the real interest rate and investment. The relationship exists because higher real interest rates in the United States tend to lead to a higher dollar exchange rate and, in turn, a higher exchange rate reduces net exports.

A higher real interest rate in the United States compared with other countries increases the demand for U.S. dollar bank accounts and other assets that pay interest. That increased demand bids up the price of dollars; hence, the exchange rate—the price of dollars—rises. Now, with a higher exchange rate, net exports will be lower because U.S.-produced exports become more expensive to foreigners, who must pay a higher price for dollars, and imported foreign goods become cheaper for Americans, who can get more foreign goods for higher-priced dollars. With exports falling and imports rising, net exports—exports less imports—must fall. In sum, higher real interest rates reduce net exports.

The same reasoning works for lower real interest rates as well. If the real interest rate falls in the United States, then U.S. dollar bank accounts are less attractive compared with bank accounts in other currencies, such as those of Germany or Japan. This bids down the price of dollars, and the exchange rate falls. Now, with a lower exchange rate, net exports will be higher because U.S.-produced exports are less expensive to foreigners and imported foreign goods are more expensive for Americans. With exports rising and imports falling, net exports must rise. Thus, lower real interest rates increase net exports.

To summarize, there is a negative relationship between the interest rate and the net exports that works through the exchange rate, as shown on the next page.

Interest Rate		Value of the Domestic Currency		Net Exports
up	→	up	→	down
down	→	down	→	up

If the interest rate goes up, then the value of the domestic currency goes up, causing net exports to go down. If the interest rate goes down, then the value of the domestic currency goes down, causing net exports to go up.

■ **Consumption.**   We have shown that two of the components of expenditure—investment and net exports—are sensitive to the real interest rate. What about consumption?

Although consumption is probably less sensitive to the real interest rate than the other components, there is some evidence that higher real interest rates encourage people to save a larger fraction of their income. Higher real interest rates encourage people to save because they earn more on their savings. Because more saving means less consumption, this implies that consumption is negatively related to the interest rate. However, most economists feel that the effect of interest rates on consumption is much less than on investment and net exports.

■ **The Overall Effect.**   To summarize the discussion thus far, investment, net exports, and consumption are all negatively related to the real interest rate. The overall effect of a change in real interest rates on real GDP can now be assessed.

Figure 11.2 shows the 45-degree line and two different expenditure lines corresponding to two different interest rates. Higher interest rates shift the expenditure line down because a higher interest rate lowers investment, net exports, and consumption, which are all part of expenditure.

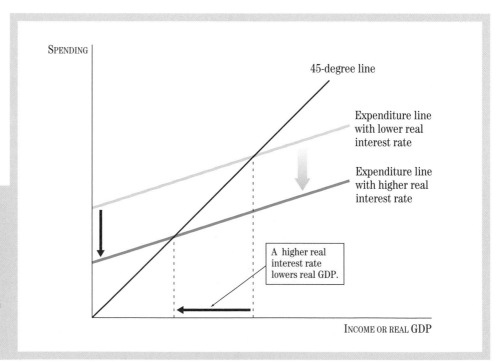

Figure 11.2
The Interest Rate, Spending Balance, and Real GDP
A higher real interest rate shifts the expenditure line down because consumption, investment, and net exports depend negatively on the real interest rate. Thus, real GDP declines with a higher real interest rate. Conversely, a lower real interest rate raises real GDP.

<table>
<tr><td>

**Finished with Stage 1:
Real GDP is negatively
related to the real interest
rate.**

Why?

• Consumption (*C*) is negatively related to the *real interest rate.*

• Investment (*I*) is negatively related to the *real interest rate.*

• Net exports (*X*) are negatively related to the *real interest rate.*

</td></tr>
</table>

Observe how the downward shift of the expenditure line leads to a new point of spending balance. The intersection of the expenditure line with the 45-degree line occurs at a lower level of real GDP. Note that real GDP is lower not only because the higher real interest rate lowers investment, net exports, and consumption, but also because a decline in income will lower consumption further. Real GDP declines by the amount shown on the horizontal axis, which is larger than the downward shift in the expenditure line. *Thus, an increase in the real interest rate lowers real GDP.*

What about a decline in the real interest rate? A lower real interest rate will raise the expenditure line. In that case, when the expenditure line shifts up, the point of spending balance at the intersection with the 45-degree line will be at a higher level of real GDP. *Thus, a decrease in the real interest rate raises real GDP.*

In sum, we have shown that there is a negative relationship between the real interest rate and real GDP.

Interest Rates and Inflation

Now that we have seen why interest rates affect real GDP, let us proceed to the second stage in our analysis. We want to show why a rise in inflation will increase the real interest rate and thereby lower real GDP, or why a decline in inflation will decrease the real interest rate and thereby raise real GDP.

■ **Central Bank Interest Rate Policy.**   The easiest way to see why the real interest rate rises when the inflation rate increases is to examine the behavior of the Fed. The Fed and central banks in other countries typically follow policies in which they respond to an increase in the inflation rate by raising the nominal interest rate. By far the most widely followed and analyzed decision by the Fed is its nominal interest rate decision.

Why do central banks raise the nominal interest rate when they think the inflation rate is rising? The inflation rate is ultimately the responsibility of the Fed, and the goal of controlling inflation requires that the central bank raise the nominal interest rate so that the real interest rate rises when the inflation rate rises. If the central bank raises the real interest rate successfully, then the higher real interest rate will reduce investment, consumption, and net exports. The reduced demand will then reduce inflationary pressures and bring inflation back down again.

The goal of controlling inflation also requires that the central bank lower the real interest rate when inflation falls. Suppose that the inflation rate starts to fall. If the central bank lowers the nominal interest rate so that the real interest rate falls, then the lower real interest rate will increase investment, consumption, and net exports. The increase in demand will put upward pressure on inflation.

Table 11.1 illustrates these actions of the Fed using a hypothetical example. For each inflation rate, a nominal interest rate decision by the Fed is shown. For example, when inflation is 2 percent, the nominal interest rate decision is 4 percent. When inflation rises to 4 percent, the nominal interest rate decision by the Fed is 7 percent. Thus, when inflation rises, the central bank raises the nominal interest rate, and when inflation falls, the central bank lowers the nominal interest rate.

Note that the nominal interest rate rises more than inflation rises in Table 11.1. The reason is that for an increase in the nominal interest rate to reduce demand, the real interest rate must rise because investment, consumption, and net exports depend negatively on the real interest rate, as described in the previous section. The nominal interest rate has to rise by more than the inflation rate in order for the real interest rate to rise and demand to decline. If, instead, the nominal interest rate rose by less than the increase in the inflation rate, then the real interest rate would not rise; rather, it would fall. The behavior of the central bank illustrated in the third column of Table 11.1 is called a **monetary policy rule** because it describes the systematic response of the real interest rate to inflation as decided by the central bank.

monetary policy rule: a description of how much the interest rate or other instruments of monetary policy respond to inflation or other measures of the state of the economy.

■ **How the Fed Changes the Interest Rate.** Keep in mind that the central bank does not set interest rates by decree or by direct control. Governments sometimes do control the price of goods; for example, some city governments control the rents on apartments. The central bank does not apply such controls to the interest rate. Rather, it enters the market in which short-term interest rates are determined by the usual forces of supply and demand. In the United States, the short-term interest rate

Table 11.1
A Numerical Example of Central Bank Interest Rate Policy

(a) Inflation Rate	(b) Nominal Interest Rate Decision (made by the central bank)	Resulting Real Interest Rate (b) − (a)
0.0	1.0	1.0
1.0	2.5	1.5
2.0	4.0	2.0
3.0	5.5	2.5
4.0	7.0	3.0
5.0	8.5	3.5
6.0	10.0	4.0
7.0	11.5	4.5
8.0	13.0	5.0

federal funds rate: the interest rate on overnight loans between banks that the Federal Reserve influences by changing the supply of funds (bank reserves) in the market.

Actions the Fed takes: To reduce the federal funds rate, the Fed increases the supply of reserves by buying bonds. To cut the federal funds rate, the Fed decreases the supply of reserves by selling bonds. The buying and selling of bonds are called *open market operations.*

target inflation rate: the central bank's goal for the average rate of inflation over the long run.

the Fed focuses on is the interest rate on overnight loans between banks. This is called the **federal funds rate,** and the overnight loan market is called the federal funds market because reserves at the Fed are what are loaned or borrowed in this market. When the Fed wants to lower this interest rate, it supplies more reserves to this market. When it wants to raise the interest rate, it reduces reserves. Recall from Chapter 9 that the Fed can change the amount of reserves in the banking system through *open market operations*—that is, by buying and selling government bonds. If the Fed wants to increase reserves and thereby lower the federal funds rate, it buys government bonds. If the Fed wants to decrease reserves and thereby increase the federal funds rate, it sells government bonds.

■ **A Graph of the Response of the Interest Rate to Inflation.** Figure 11.3 represents the monetary policy rule graphically, using the information in Table 11.1. When the inflation rate rises, the nominal interest rate rises along the green upward-sloping line. When the inflation rate declines, the nominal interest rate declines. The nominal interest rate must rise by more than the inflation rate if the *real* interest rate is to rise when inflation rises; this requires that the slope of the monetary policy rule in Figure 11.3 be greater than 1. For example, if the slope is 1.5, then when the inflation rate increases by 1 percentage point, the interest rate rises by 1.5 percentage points, as in Table 11.1. In other words, the nominal interest rate rises by .5 percentage point *more* than the inflation rate rises, causing the *real* interest rate to rise by .5 percentage point. The resulting real interest rate decision of the Fed is indicated by the purple line: The real interest rate changes by .5 percentage point when the inflation rate changes by 1 percentage point. The real interest rate policy rule is shown in Figure 11.4.

Most central banks have a **target inflation rate,** the inflation rate that the central bank tries to maintain on average over the long run. Because of various shocks to the economy, the central bank cannot control the inflation rate perfectly; sometimes the inflation rate will rise above the target inflation rate, and sometimes the inflation rate will fall below the target inflation rate. By reacting to these movements in inflation according to a monetary policy rule—that is, by increasing the interest rate when

Figure 11.3
A Monetary Policy Rule
The monetary policy rule shows that the Fed raises the real interest rate when inflation rises and lowers the real interest rate when inflation falls. In order to accomplish this, the Fed has to move the nominal interest rate by more than 1 percentage point when there is a 1 percentage point change in the rate of inflation.

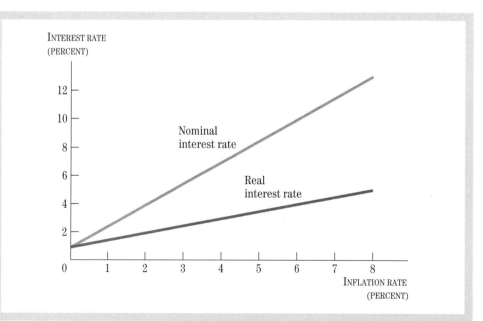

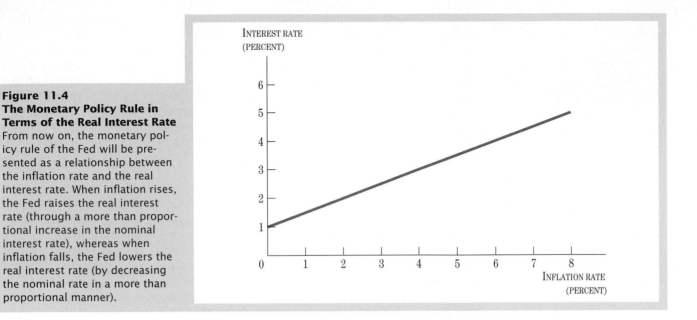

Figure 11.4
The Monetary Policy Rule in Terms of the Real Interest Rate
From now on, the monetary policy rule of the Fed will be presented as a relationship between the inflation rate and the real interest rate. When inflation rises, the Fed raises the real interest rate (through a more than proportional increase in the nominal interest rate), whereas when inflation falls, the Fed lowers the real interest rate (by decreasing the nominal rate in a more than proportional manner).

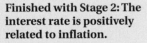

Finished with Stage 2: The interest rate is positively related to inflation.

The Fed and other central banks tend to

• Raise the real interest rate when inflation rises.

• Lower the real interest rate when inflation falls.

This is the *behavioral description* of the people at the Fed, much as a demand curve is a behavioral description of consumers.

This response is called a *monetary policy rule.*

inflation rises and cutting the interest rate when inflation falls—the central bank will cause the actual inflation rate to move back toward the target inflation rate over time. Some central banks, such as the Bank of England and the Reserve Bank of New Zealand, have explicit inflation targets. Other central banks, like the Fed, have implicit inflation targets that are not explicitly announced, but that can be assessed by observing central bank decisions over time. The target inflation rate for many central banks is about 2 percent. For the economy described in Figure 11.4, at the target inflation rate of 2 percent, the central bank sets real interest rates at 2 percent by choosing a nominal rate of 4 percent.

■ **A Good Simplifying Assumption.** The behavior of the central bank described in this section provides the easiest explanation of the response of interest rates to inflation, but it is not the only possible explanation. Economists have found that the general upward-sloping relationship in Figure 11.3, which we call the monetary policy rule, is common to many different types of monetary policies, including policies in which the central bank focuses on money growth. Although the position and shape of the monetary policy rule will differ for these different types of policies, the overall response of interest rates to inflation will be similar. Our reason for using this particular derivation is that it is the easiest to explain and describes the actual behavior of the Fed and other central banks.

Derivation of the Aggregate Demand Curve

Thus far, we have shown that the level of real GDP is negatively related to the real interest rate and that the real interest rate is positively related to the inflation rate through the central bank's policy rule. We now combine these two concepts to derive the aggregate demand curve—the inverse relationship between the inflation rate and real GDP.

The chain of reasoning that brings about the aggregate demand curve can be explained by considering what would happen if the inflation rate rose. First, the interest rate would rise because the Fed would raise the real interest rate in response to the higher inflation rate. Next, the higher real interest rate would mean less invest-

The following is a press release issued by the Federal Reserve on December 11, 2001, explaining its decision to lower the federal funds rate from 2 percent to 1.75 percent. This press release contains information that will subsequently appear in many newspapers around the world.

Notice how the Fed refers to the fact that inflation was falling and the role that that fall played in the Fed's decision to lower interest rates. Note also that the Fed is careful to refer to its decision as being to lower its "target for the federal funds rate." This reflects the fact that the Fed has no direct control over interest rates and can only influence rates toward a targeted value by buying and selling government bonds.

The Fed lowered the federal funds rate target as well as the discount rate. →

For immediate release

The Federal Open Market Committee decided today to lower its target for the federal funds rate by 25 basis points to 1¾ percent. In a related action, the Board of Governors approved a 25 basis point reduction in the discount rate to 1¼ percent.

The underlying reasons for the Fed's policy decision. →

Economic activity remains soft, with underlying inflation likely to edge lower from relatively modest levels. To be sure, weakness in demand shows signs of abating, but those signs are preliminary and tentative. The Committee continues to believe that, against the background of its long-run goals of price stability and sustainable economic growth and of the information currently available, the risks are weighted mainly toward conditions that may generate economic weakness in the foreseeable future.

Although the necessary reallocation of resources to enhance security may restrain advances in productivity for a time, the long-term prospects for productivity growth and the economy remain favorable and should become evident once the unusual forces restraining demand abate.

In taking the discount rate action, the Federal Reserve Board approved the requests submitted by the Boards of Directors of the Federal Reserve Banks of Boston, New York, Philadelphia, Chicago and San Francisco.

Finished with Stage 3: Real GDP is negatively related to inflation.

Suppose that *inflation increases:*

- The Fed will raise the real interest rate.
- The higher real interest rate will *decrease real GDP.*

Suppose that *inflation decreases:*

- The Fed will lower the real interest rate.
- The lower real interest rate will *increase real GDP.*

This negative relationship is the *AD* curve.

ment spending, a decline in net exports, and a decline in consumption. Lower investment spending would occur because investment would be made more costly by the high real interest rate. American goods would become more expensive, and foreign goods would become cheaper. Thus, net exports—exports minus imports—would decline.

The opposite chain of events would occur if there were a fall in inflation. First, the Fed would lower the real interest rate according to the monetary policy rule. The lower real interest rate, in turn, would cause investment, net exports, and consumption to rise. Hence, real GDP would rise.

In sum, we see that when the inflation rate rises, real GDP decreases, and when the inflation rate falls, real GDP increases. In other words, there is a negative relationship between inflation and real GDP. When we graph this relationship in a diagram with real GDP on the horizontal axis and inflation on the vertical axis, we get a downward-sloping curve like the one shown in Figure 11.1; this curve is the aggregate demand curve, which we have thus derived.

If you would like to go over the derivation again, seeing all the paragraphs together on the same page, a self-guided graphical overview is provided in Figure 11.5. If you read the explanatory boxes in numerical order, you will trace through the chain of events following an increase in inflation, including the Fed's real interest rate increase according to its policy rule and the decline in real GDP.

■ **Movements Along the Aggregate Demand Curve.** Thus far, we have explained why the aggregate demand curve has a negative slope—that is, why higher inflation means a lower real GDP. *A change in real GDP* due to a *change in inflation* is

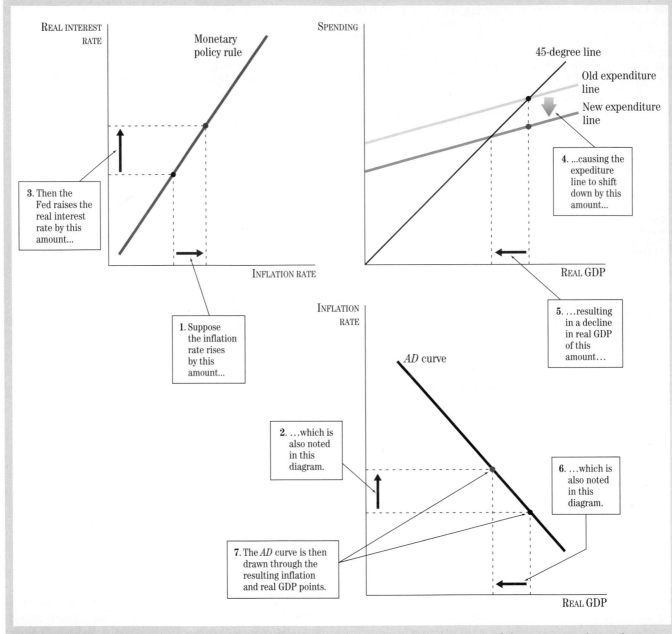

Figure 11.5
A Self-Guided Graphical Overview

Follow the numbers to see an overview of the derivation of the aggregate demand curve. The black dots represent the situation *before* we increase the inflation rate. The orange dots represent the situation *after* we increase the inflation rate. When inflation rises, the central bank raises the real interest rate, and this lowers real GDP. Hence, we have the aggregate demand curve.

thus a *movement along* the aggregate demand curve. Recall that in microeconomics, a similar movement along the demand curve occurs when a *change in the price* leads to a *change in quantity demanded*. When inflation rises, causing the Fed to raise the interest rate, and real GDP declines, there is a movement up and to the left along the aggregate demand curve. When inflation declines and the Fed lowers the interest rate, causing GDP to rise, there is a movement down and to the right along the aggregate demand curve.

■ **Shifts of the Aggregate Demand Curve.**   Now, the inflation rate is not the only thing that affects aggregate demand. Changes in government purchases, shifts in monetary policy, shifts in foreign demand for U.S. exports, changes in taxes, and changes in consumer confidence, among other things, affect aggregate demand. When any of these factors changes aggregate demand, we say there is a *shift* in the aggregate demand curve. Let us briefly consider some of those sources of shifts in the aggregate demand curve.

Government Purchases   Imagine that government purchases rise. We know from our analysis of spending balance in Chapter 10 that an increase in government purchases will increase real GDP in the short run. This increase in real GDP occurs at any inflation rate: at 2 percent, at 4 percent, or at any other level. Now, if real GDP increases at a given inflation rate, the aggregate demand curve will shift to the right. This is shown in Figure 11.6. The new aggregate demand curve will be parallel to the original aggregate demand curve because no matter what the inflation rate is in the economy, the shift in government purchases is going to have the same effect on real GDP. The same reasoning implies that a decline in government spending shifts the aggregate demand curve to the left.

Changes in the Target Inflation Rate   Suppose the Fed has an inflation target of 2 percent. Consider what happens when the Fed shifts its policy objectives. Suppose, for instance, that a new Fed chair becomes convinced that inflation should be higher, say 3 percent. In order to get inflation to rise, the Fed will immediately try to increase spending by lowering the real interest rate: The *AD* curve will shift to the right, as shown in Figure 11.7. In contrast, suppose that the new Fed chair wants to lower inflation, say to 1 percent. In order to get inflation to fall, the Fed will immediately try to lower spending by raising the real interest rate: The *AD* curve will shift to the left.

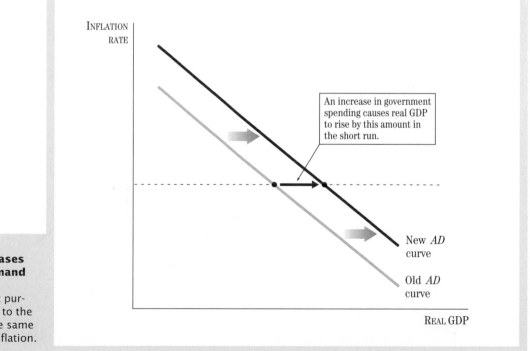

Figure 11.6
How Government Purchases Shift the Aggregate Demand Curve
An increase in government purchases shifts the *AD* curve to the right. Real GDP rises by the same amount at every level of inflation.

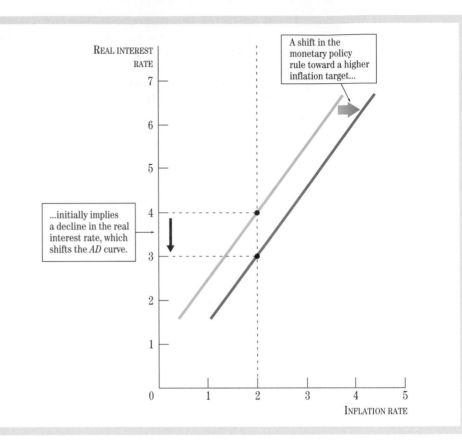

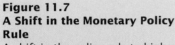

Figure 11.7
A Shift in the Monetary Policy Rule
A shift in the policy rule to higher inflation implies a decline in the real interest rate. The lower real interest rate increases real GDP in the short run. As a result, at a given inflation rate, the *AD* curve shifts to the right.

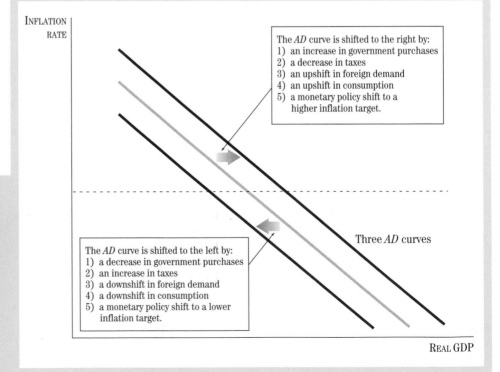

Figure 11.8
A List of Possible Shifts in the Aggregate Demand Curve
Many things shift the *AD* curve. An increase in government purchases shifts the *AD* curve to the right. A change in the monetary policy rule toward a higher inflation target shifts the *AD* curve to the right. A decline in government purchases and a change in the monetary policy rule toward a lower inflation target shift the curve to the left.

Other Changes Many other changes in the economy (other than a change in the inflation rate, which is a movement along the *AD* curve) will shift the *AD* curve. We considered many such possibilities in Chapter 10; their effects on the aggregate demand curve are listed in Figure 11.8. For example, an increase in the foreign demand for U.S. products will increase net exports, raise real GDP, and shift the aggregate demand curve to the right. A drop in consumer confidence that reduces the amount of consumption at every level of income will shift the aggregate demand curve to the left. Finally, an increase in taxes shifts the aggregate demand curve to the left, while a decrease in taxes shifts the aggregate demand curve to the right.

REVIEW

- The aggregate demand curve is an inverse relationship between inflation and real GDP.

- Investment, net exports, and consumption are negatively related to the real interest rate. Hence, real GDP falls when the real interest rate rises, and vice versa.

- When inflation increases, the central bank raises the real interest rate, and this lowers real GDP. Conversely, when inflation falls, the central bank lowers the real interest rate, and this raises real GDP. It does so by moving nominal interest rates by more than 1 percentage point when inflation changes by 1 percentage point. These are movements along the aggregate demand curve.

- The aggregate demand curve shifts to the right when the central bank changes its monetary policy rule toward more inflation and shifts to the left when the central bank changes its policy rule toward less inflation.

- Higher government purchases shift the aggregate demand curve to the right. Lower government purchases shift the aggregate demand curve to the left.

The Inflation Adjustment Line

inflation adjustment (IA) line: a flat line showing the level of inflation in the economy at a given point in time. It shifts up when real GDP is greater than potential GDP, and it shifts down when real GDP is less than potential GDP; it also shifts when expectations of inflation or raw materials prices change.

Having derived the aggregate demand curve and studied its properties, let us now look at the inflation adjustment line, the second element of the economic fluctuations model. The **inflation adjustment (*IA*) line** is a flat line showing the level of inflation in the economy at any point in time. Figure 11.9 shows an example of the inflation adjustment line in a diagram with inflation on the vertical axis and real GDP on the horizontal axis. For example, if the line touches 4 percent on the vertical axis, it tells us that inflation is 4 percent.

The inflation adjustment line describes the economic behavior of firms and workers setting prices and wages in the economy. There are several important features about the slope and position of the inflation adjustment line.

The Inflation Adjustment Line Is Flat

That the inflation adjustment line is flat indicates that firms and workers adjust their prices and wages in such a way that the inflation rate remains steady in the short run

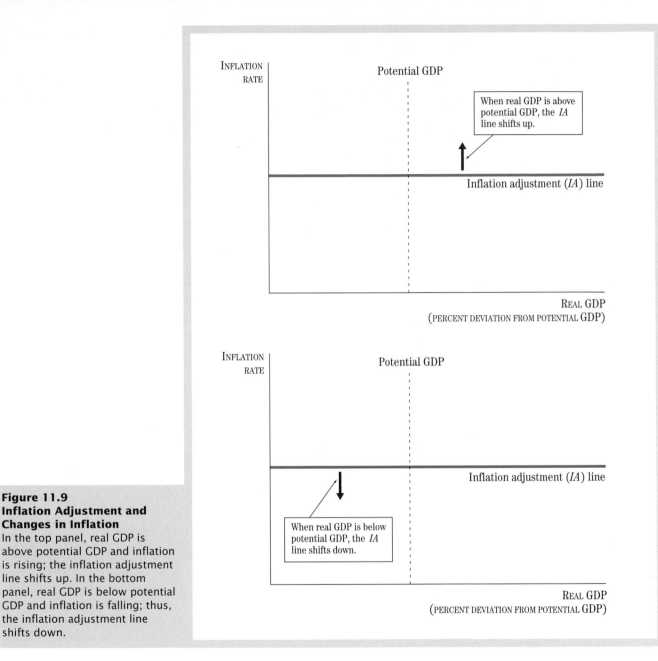

Figure 11.9
Inflation Adjustment and Changes in Inflation
In the top panel, real GDP is above potential GDP and inflation is rising; the inflation adjustment line shifts up. In the bottom panel, real GDP is below potential GDP and inflation is falling; thus, the inflation adjustment line shifts down.

as real GDP changes. Only over time does inflation change significantly and the line move. In the short run, inflation stays at 4 percent, or wherever the line happens to be when real GDP changes.

In interpreting the inflation adjustment line, it is helpful to remember that it is part of a *model* of the overall economy and is thus an approximation of reality. In fact, inflation does not remain *perfectly* steady, and the inflation adjustment line can have a small upward slope. But it is a good approximation to assume that the inflation adjustment line is flat.

There are two reasons why inflation does not change very much in the short run even if real GDP and the demand for firms' products changes: (1) expectations of continuing inflation and (2) staggered wage and price setting at different firms throughout the economy.

■ **Expectations of Continuing Inflation.** Expectations about the price and wage decisions of other firms throughout the economy influence a firm's price and wage decisions. For example, if the overall inflation rate in the economy has been hovering around 4 percent year after year, then a firm can expect that its competitor's prices will probably increase by about 4 percent per year, unless circumstances change. To keep prices near those of the competition, this firm will need to increase its price by about 4 percent each year. Thus, the inflation rate stays steady at 4 percent per year.

Wage adjustments are also influenced by expectations. If firms and workers expect that workers at other firms will be getting large wage increases, then meeting the competition will require similar large wage increases. A smaller wage increase would reduce the wage of the firm's workers relative to that received by other workers. Many firms base their wage decisions on the wages paid by other firms. If they see the wages at other firms rising, they will be more willing to increase wages.

Firms and workers also look to expectations of inflation when deciding on wage increases. In an economy with 4 percent inflation, wages will have to increase by 4 percent for workers just to keep up with the cost of living. Lower wage increases would result in a decline in workers' real wages.

■ **Staggered Price and Wage Setting.** Not all wages and prices are changed at the same time throughout the economy. Rather, price setting and wage setting are staggered over months and even years. For example, autoworkers might negotiate three-year wage contracts in 1993, 1996, 1999, etc. Dockworkers might negotiate three-year contracts in 1994, 1997, 2000, etc. Bus companies and train companies do not adjust their prices at the same time, even though they may compete for the same riders. On any given day, we can be sure that there is a wage or price adjustment somewhere in the economy, but the vast majority of wages and prices do not change.

Staggered price and wage setting slows down the adjustment of prices in the economy. When considering what wage increases are likely in the next year, firms and workers know about the most recent wage increases. For example, an agreement made by another firm to increase wages by 4 percent per year for three years into the future will affect the expectations of wages paid to competing workers in the future. This wage agreement will not change unless the firm is on the edge of bankruptcy, and perhaps not even then. Hence, workers and firms deciding on wage increases will tend to match the wage increases recently made at other firms. Thus, price and wage decisions made today are directly influenced by price and wage decisions made yesterday.

As with many things in life, when today's decisions are influenced by yesterday's decisions, inertia sets in. The staggering of the decisions makes it difficult to break the inertia. Unless there is a reason to make a change—such as a persistent decline in demand or a change in expectations of inflation—the price increases or wage increases continue from year to year. The flat inflation adjustment line describes this inertia.

The Inflation Adjustment Line Shifts Gradually When Real GDP Departs from Potential GDP

The inflation adjustment line does not always stay put; rather, it may shift up or down from year to year. If real GDP stays above potential GDP, then inflation starts to rise. Firms see that the demand for their products is remaining high, and they begin adjusting their prices. If the inflation rate is 4 percent, then the firms will have to raise their prices by more than 4 percent if they want their relative prices to increase. Hence, inflation starts to rise. The inflation adjustment line is shifted upward to illustrate this rise in inflation; it will keep shifting upward as long as real GDP is above potential GDP.

However, if real GDP is below potential GDP, then firms will see that the demand for their products is falling off, and they will adjust their prices. If inflation is 4 percent, the firms will raise their prices by less than 4 percent—perhaps by 2 percent—if they want the relative price of their goods to fall. Hence, inflation will fall. The inflation adjustment line is shifted down to illustrate this fall in inflation. Figure 11.9 shows the direction of these shifts.

If real GDP stays at potential GDP, neither to the left nor to the right of the vertical potential GDP line in Figure 11.9, then inflation remains unchanged. This steady inflation is represented by an unmoving inflation adjustment line year after year.

Changes in Expectations or Commodity Prices Shift the Inflation Adjustment Line

Even if real GDP is at potential GDP, some special events in the economy can cause the inflation adjustment line to shift up or down. One important example is *shifts in expectations* of inflation. If firms and workers expect inflation to rise, they are likely to raise wages and prices by a large amount to keep pace with the expected inflation. Thus, an increase in expectations of inflation will cause the inflation adjustment line to shift up to a higher inflation rate. And a decrease in expectations of inflation will cause the inflation adjustment line to shift down.

Another example is a change in commodity prices that affects firms' costs of production. For example, we will examine the effects on inflation of an oil price increase in Chapter 12. By raising firms' costs, such an oil price increase would lead firms to charge higher prices, and the inflation adjustment line would rise, at least temporarily.

Does the Inflation Adjustment Line Fit the Facts?

Are these assumptions about the inflation adjustment line accurate? Does inflation rise when real GDP is above potential GDP and fall when real GDP is below potential GDP? Figure 11.10 provides the relevant evidence. The points in the figure indicate the level of inflation and the percent deviation of real GDP from potential GDP for years when real GDP was more than 2 percent above or below potential GDP. (We use only deviations that are greater than 2 percent because it is difficult to measure the deviations with much better than 2 percent accuracy.) Up arrows indicate that inflation increased from the year before the labeled year. Down arrows indicate that inflation decreased. The length of the arrow is the size of the change.

Inflation usually declines when real GDP is less than—to the left of—potential GDP in Figure 11.10. The biggest decline in inflation occurred in 1982, when real GDP was far below potential GDP. When real GDP is greater than—to the right of—potential GDP, inflation is rising in the majority of cases. Figure 11.10 indicates that the theory of the inflation adjustment line shown in Figure 11.9 fits the facts very well. From 1993 to 1997, real GDP was very close to potential GDP, so inflation did not change much, and thus these years are not on the graph. In 1998 and 1999, real GDP rose above potential GDP, but inflation did not immediately start to rise. This led some commentators to think that the inflation adjustment relationship was changing, but by late 1999 and 2000 inflation rose as predicted by the theory.

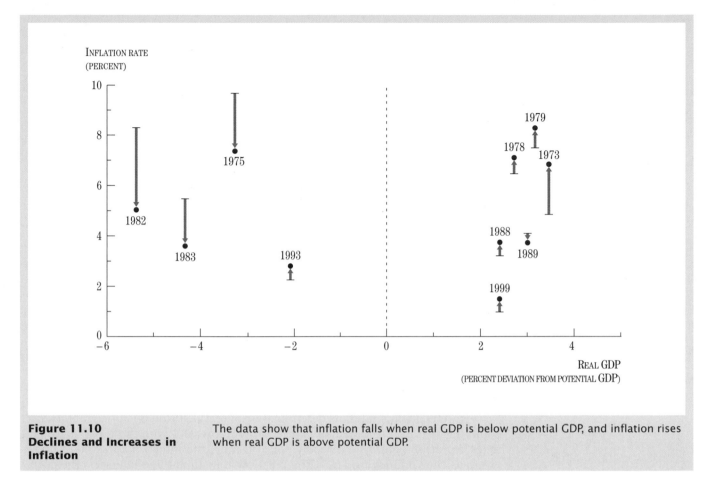

**Figure 11.10
Declines and Increases in
Inflation**

The data show that inflation falls when real GDP is below potential GDP, and inflation rises
when real GDP is above potential GDP.

REVIEW

- The inflation adjustment (*IA*) line, the second element of the economic
  fluctuations model, is a flat line showing the level of inflation in the economy at any point in time. The inflation adjustment line describes the economic behavior of firms and workers setting prices and wages in the
  economy.

- Firms do not change their prices instantaneously when the demand for
  their product changes. Thus, when aggregate demand changes and real
  GDP departs from potential GDP, the inflation rate does not immediately
  change; the inflation adjustment line does not shift in response to such
  changes in the short run.

- Staggered wage and price setting tends to slow down the adjustment of
  inflation in the economy as a whole.

- Over time, inflation does respond to departures of real GDP from potential
  GDP. This response can be described by upward and downward shifts in
  the inflation adjustment line over time.

Combining the Aggregate Demand Curve and the Inflation Adjustment Line

We have now derived two relationships—the aggregate demand curve and the inflation adjustment line—that describe real GDP and inflation in the economy as a whole. The two relationships can be combined to make predictions about real GDP and inflation.

Along the aggregate demand curve in Figure 11.1, real GDP and inflation are negatively related. This curve describes the behavior of firms and consumers as they respond to a higher real interest rate caused by the Fed's response to higher inflation. They respond by lowering consumption, investment, and net exports. This line presents a range of possible values of real GDP and inflation.

The inflation adjustment line in Figure 11.9, on the other hand, tells us what the inflation rate is at any point in time. Thus, we can use the inflation adjustment line to determine exactly what inflation rate applies to the aggregate demand curve. For example, if the inflation adjustment line tells us that the inflation rate for 2004 is 5 percent, then we can go right to the aggregate demand curve to determine what the level of real GDP will be at that 5 percent inflation rate. If the aggregate demand curve says that real GDP is 2 percent below potential GDP when inflation is 5 percent, then we predict that real GDP is 2 percent below potential GDP. The inflation adjustment line tells us the current location of inflation—and therefore real GDP—on the aggregate demand curve.

Figure 11.11 illustrates the determination of real GDP and inflation graphically. It combines the aggregate demand curve from Figure 11.1 with the inflation adjustment line from Figure 11.9. At any point in time, the inflation adjustment line is given, as shown in Figure 11.11. The inflation adjustment line intersects the aggregate demand curve at a single point. It is at this point of intersection that inflation and real GDP are determined. The intersection gives an *equilibrium* level of real GDP and inflation. At that point, we can look down to the horizontal axis of the diagram to determine the level of real GDP corresponding to that level of inflation. For example, the point of intersection in the left panel of Figure 11.11 might be when inflation is 5 percent and real GDP is 2 percent below potential GDP. The point of intersection in the right panel is at a lower inflation rate when real GDP is above potential GDP. The point of intersection in the middle panel of Figure 11.11 has real GDP equal to potential GDP.

As Figure 11.11 makes clear, the intersection of the inflation adjustment line and the aggregate demand curve may give values of real GDP that are either above or below potential GDP. But if real GDP is not equal to potential GDP, then the economy has not fully recovered from a recession, as on the left of Figure 11.11, or returned to potential GDP after being above it, as on the right. To describe dynamic movements of inflation and real GDP, we must consider how the inflation adjustment line and the aggregate demand curve shift over time. That is the subject of Chapter 12.

REVIEW

- In any year, the inflation adjustment line tells what the inflation rate is. Using the aggregate demand curve, we can then make a prediction about what real GDP is.

- The intersection of the aggregate demand curve and the inflation adjustment line gives a pair of observations on real GDP and inflation at any point in time.

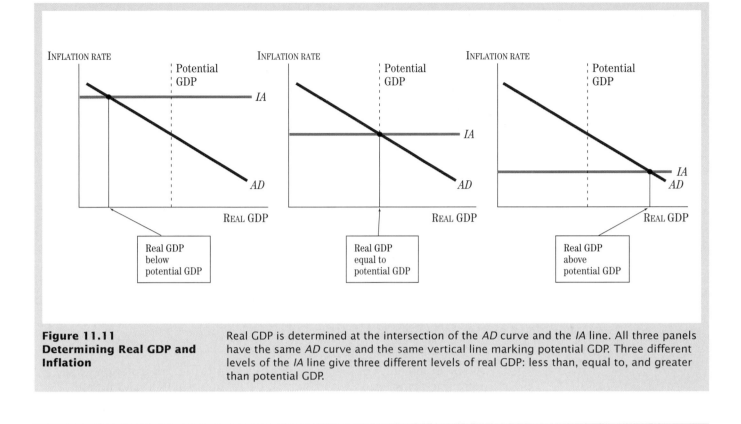

**Figure 11.11
Determining Real GDP and
Inflation**

Real GDP is determined at the intersection of the *AD* curve and the *IA* line. All three panels have the same *AD* curve and the same vertical line marking potential GDP. Three different levels of the *IA* line give three different levels of real GDP: less than, equal to, and greater than potential GDP.

Conclusion

With the essential elements of the economic fluctuations model—the aggregate demand curve, the inflation adjustment line, and their intersection—put together, we are now ready to use the model to explain the fluctuations of real GDP and inflation. In reviewing the model, it is useful to consider the scissors analogy mentioned in our discussion of the supply and demand model in Chapter 3.

The aggregate demand curve is like one blade of the scissors. The inflation adjustment line is the other blade. Either blade alone is insufficient to explain economic fluctuations. Either blade alone is an incomplete story. But when the two blades of the scissors are put together to form a pair of scissors, they become a practical tool to explain the ups and downs in the economy. And compared to the complexity and vastness of the whole economy with millions of firms and consumers, this particular pair of scissors is amazingly simple.

HEY POINTS

1. Along the aggregate demand curve, real GDP is negatively related to inflation.

2. Investment, net exports, and consumption depend negatively on the real interest rate. Hence, real GDP, which includes investment, net exports, and consumption, depends negatively on the real interest rate.

3. Central banks' actions to adjust the nominal interest rate to maintain low inflation result in a relationship between the real interest rate and

inflation. When inflation rises, the real interest rate rises. When inflation falls, the real interest rate falls.

4. The combined behavior of (1) the real interest rate response to inflation and (2) the private sector adjusting spending in response to the interest rate generates an inverse relationship between real GDP and inflation—the aggregate demand curve.

5. Movements along the aggregate demand curve occur when inflation rises, causing the real interest rate to rise and real GDP to fall. Such movements along the curve also occur when inflation falls, the interest rate declines, and real GDP rises.

6. The aggregate demand curve shifts for many reasons, including a change in government purchases and a change in monetary policy toward a higher inflation target.

7. When adjusting prices, firms respond slowly to changes in demand and take into account expectations of inflation. So do workers when wages are being adjusted. As a result, inflation tends to increase when real GDP is above potential GDP and tends to decrease when real GDP is below potential GDP.

8. The staggering of price and wage decisions tends to slow the adjustment of prices in the economy as a whole.

9. When combined with the aggregate demand curve, the inflation adjustment line provides us with a way to determine real GDP and inflation.

KEY TERMS

aggregate demand (*AD*) curve	monetary policy rule federal funds rate	target inflation rate	inflation adjustment (*IA*) line

QUESTIONS FOR REVIEW

1. Why are investment, net exports, and consumption inversely related to the real interest rate?

2. Why is real GDP inversely related to the real interest rate in the short run?

3. Why does the real interest rate rise when inflation begins to rise?

4. Why is real GDP inversely related to inflation in the short run? What is this relationship called?

5. What are examples of movements along the aggregate demand curve?

6. Why does a change in government purchases shift the aggregate demand curve to the right or left?

7. Why does a shift in monetary policy shift the aggregate demand curve to the right or left?

8. Why does inflation increase when real GDP is above potential GDP?

9. What is the significance of expectations of inflation for inflation adjustment?

10. Why does staggered price setting slow down price adjustment in the economy?

PROBLEMS

1. Compare and contrast the graphs used in the microeconomic supply and demand model with those used in the economic fluctuations model.

2. Which of the following statements are true, and which are false? Explain your answers in one or two sentences.
   a. An increase in the U.S. real interest rate will cause the dollar exchange rate to decline.
   b. The central bank typically raises the real interest rate when inflation rises.
   c. A higher real interest rate leads to greater net exports because the higher interest rate raises the value of the dollar.

3. Suppose that Japanese real interest rates are low relative to the rates in the United States, and the Fed decides to raise the real interest rate in order to counter an increase in the rate of inflation. What effect will this have on the dollar-yen exchange rate? Will U.S. net exports be higher or lower? Why?

4. Suppose the Fed is considering two different policy rules, shown in the following table. Graph the policy rules.

Inflation	Policy Rule 1 Interest Rate	Policy Rule 2 Interest Rate
0	1	3
2	3	5
4	5	7
6	7	9
8	9	11

If the Fed is currently following policy rule 1 and then shifts to policy rule 2, which way will the aggregate demand curve shift? What reasons might the Fed have for changing its policy? What effect will this have on real GDP in the short run?

5. Suppose you have the following information on the Fed's and the European Central Bank's (ECB) policy rules:

Fed real interest rate = 0.5 (inflation rate − 2)

ECB real interest rate = 0.2 (inflation rate − 2) + 1

   a. Graph these policy rules. If the inflation rate is 2 percent in both countries, what will be the real interest rate in each country?
   b. Some argue that Europe has a much lower tolerance for inflation than the United States. Can you tell—either from the diagram or from the equations—whether this is true?

6. The table at the top of the next column gives a numerical example of an aggregate demand curve.
   a. Sketch the curve in a graph.
   b. What is the average rate of inflation in the long run?
   c. Suppose that the central bank shifts policy so that the average rate of inflation in the long run is 2 percentage points higher than in (b). Sketch a new aggregate demand curve corresponding to the higher inflation rate.

Real GDP (percent deviation from potential GDP)	Inflation (percent per year)
3.0	1.0
2.0	1.5
1.0	2.0
0.0	3.0
−1.0	4.0
−2.0	6.0
−3.0	9.0

7. Suppose Japan's economy stagnates and the demand for U.S. exports is reduced.
   a. Assuming that U.S. imports of Japanese goods are unaffected, which way will the expenditure line shift?
   b. Will this cause a shift in the aggregate demand curve? Sketch the effects of this change in a diagram.

8. State which of the following changes causes a shift in the aggregate demand curve and which ones are a movement along it.
   a. A cut in government purchases
   b. A crash in the U.S. stock market
   c. A shift to lower inflation in the monetary policy rule
   d. Being thrifty becoming fashionable
   e. An increase in the European interest rate

9. Suppose you could use either a change in government purchases or a shift in monetary policy to increase real GDP in the short run. How would each policy affect investment in the short run? Why?

10. The following table gives a numerical example of an inflation adjustment line in the year 2004.

Real GDP (percent deviation from potential GDP)	Inflation (percent per year)
3.0	2.0
2.0	2.0
1.0	2.0
0.0	2.0
−1.0	2.0
−2.0	2.0
−3.0	2.0

   a. Sketch the line in a graph.
   b. If real GDP is above potential GDP in the year 2004, will the inflation adjustment line shift up or down in the year 2004? Explain.
   c. In the same graph as part (a), sketch in the aggregate demand curve given in problem 6. Find the equilibrium level of real GDP and inflation in the year 2004.
   d. Show what happens to the inflation adjustment line if there is a sudden increase in inflation expectations.

12

Using the Economic Fluctuations Model

The economic fluctuations model is one of the most powerful models in economics. Versions of this model are used in practice by business economists making forecasts for their clients, by regional economists in state capitals looking at the impact of changes in federal laws, by policy economists in Washington analyzing the effects of the president's economic policy proposals, and by international economists working at organizations like the International Monetary Fund trying to determine the effect of tax or spending changes in hundreds of countries around the world.

The purpose of this chapter is to show how to use this model. We use the model to determine the path the economy takes after a shift in aggregate demand, whether that shift is due to a big change in government purchases, a shift in monetary policy, or some other factor. We trace the path of real GDP from the time of its initial departure from potential GDP—as in a recession—to its recovery. We explain why a recovery occurs and how long it takes to occur. We then look at the effect of price shocks on the economy, and examine a case study that demonstrates how well the model works in practice in explaining the slowdown of the U.S. economy in 2001.

Keeping in mind that there is a similarity between *using* the supply and demand model and *using* the economic fluctuations model will help you learn the material in this chapter.

Changes in Government Purchases

We first use the economic fluctuations model to examine the forces leading to a return of real GDP to potential GDP. To do so, we focus on a particular example, a change in government purchases. In Chapter 10 we showed how a change in government purchases could push real GDP away from potential GDP in the short run. Now let's see the complete story.

Real GDP and Inflation over Time

Suppose the government cuts military purchases permanently. We want to examine the effects of this decrease in government purchases on the economy in the short run (about one year), the medium run (two to three years), and the long run (four to five years and beyond). The three lengths of time given in the parentheses are approximations; in reality, the times will not be exactly these lengths, but somewhat longer or shorter. We use the term *short run* to refer to the initial departure of real GDP from potential GDP, *medium run* to refer to the recovery period, and *long run* to refer to when real GDP is nearly back to potential GDP.

Figure 12.1 shows the aggregate demand curve and the inflation adjustment line on the same diagram. The intersection of the aggregate demand curve and the

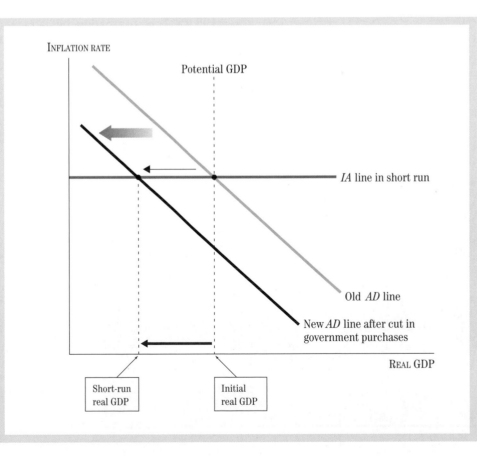

**Figure 12.1
Short-Run Effects of a
Reduction in Government
Purchases**
In the short run, the *IA* line does not move. Thus, in the short run, real GDP declines by the amount of the shift in the *AD* curve, as noted on the horizontal axis.

inflation adjustment line determines a level of inflation and real GDP. Let us assume that we began with real GDP equal to potential GDP. Thus, the initial intersection of the aggregate demand curve and the inflation adjustment line occurs at a level of real GDP equal to potential GDP.

Now, recall from Chapter 11 that a change in government purchases shifts the aggregate demand curve; in particular, a decline in government purchases shifts the aggregate demand curve to the left. Because the inflation adjustment line is flat, and because it does not move in the short run, a change in government purchases—shown by the shift from the "old" to the "new" aggregate demand curve in Figure 12.1—leads to a change in real GDP of the same amount as the shift in the aggregate demand curve. This is the short-run effect. The decrease in government purchases initially moves the aggregate demand curve to the left, and real GDP falls to the point indicated by the intersection of the inflation adjustment line and the new aggregate demand curve. At the new intersection, real GDP is below potential GDP.

As real GDP falls below potential GDP, employment falls because the decline in demand forces firms to cut back on production and lay off workers. The model predicts that unemployment rises, just as it does during actual declines in real GDP.

Now consider what happens over time. The tendency for inflation to adjust over time is represented by upward or downward shifts of the inflation adjustment line. Only in the short run does the inflation adjustment line stay put. What is likely to happen over time when real GDP is below potential GDP? Inflation should begin to decline, because firms will increase their prices by smaller amounts. We represent a decline in inflation by shifting the inflation adjustment line down, as shown in Figure 12.2. The initial impact of the change in government spending took us to a point we label *SR*, for short run, in Figure 12.2. At that point, real GDP is lower than potential GDP. Hence, inflation will fall and the inflation adjustment line shifts down, as shown in the diagram. There is now a new point of intersection; we label that point *MR*, for medium run.

Note that real GDP has started to recover. At the point labeled *MR* in the diagram, real GDP is still below potential GDP, but it is higher than at the low (*SR*) point in the downturn. The reason real GDP starts to rise is that the lower inflation rate causes the central bank to lower the real interest rate. The lower real interest rate increases investment spending and causes net exports to rise. As a result, real GDP rises, and as it does, firms start to call back workers who were laid off. As more workers are employed, unemployment begins to fall.

Because real GDP is still below potential GDP, there is still a tendency for inflation to fall. Thus, the inflation adjustment line continues to shift downward until real GDP returns to potential GDP. Figure 12.2 shows a third intersection at the point marked *LR*, for long run, where production has increased all the way back to potential GDP. At this point, real GDP has reached long-run equilibrium in the sense that real GDP equals potential GDP. With real GDP equal to potential GDP, the inflation adjustment line stops shifting down. Inflation is at a new lower level than before the decline in government purchases, but at the final point of intersection in the diagram, it is no longer falling. Thus, real GDP remains equal to potential GDP.

Note how successive downward shifts of the inflation adjustment line with intersections along the aggregate demand curve trace out values for real GDP and inflation as the economy first goes into recession and then recovers. In the short run, a decline in production comes about because of the decrease in government spending; that decline is followed by successive years of reversal as the economy recovers and real GDP returns to potential GDP. This behavior is shown in the sketch in the lower part of Figure 12.2. Thus, we have achieved one of the major goals of this chapter: showing how real GDP returns to potential GDP after an initial departure due to a shift in aggregate demand. In the case where the shift in aggregate demand is large enough to cause real GDP to decline as in a recession, then we have shown how recessions end and recoveries take the economy back to normal.

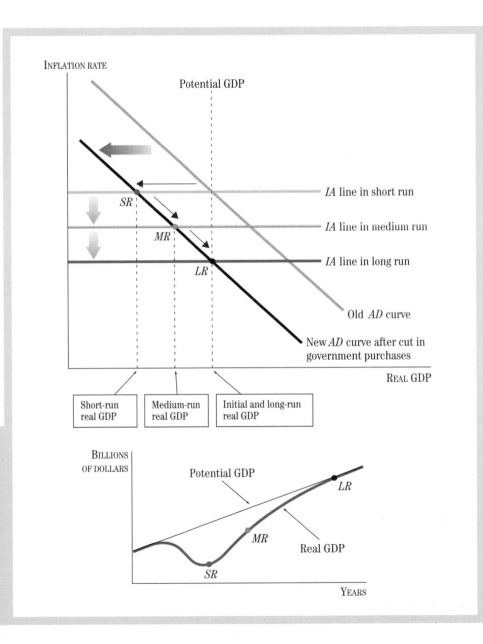

Figure 12.2
Dynamic Adjustment After a Reduction in Government Purchases
Initially, the reduction in government purchases shifts the *AD* curve to the left. This reduces real GDP to the point labeled *SR*, or the short run. Then the *IA* line begins to shift down because real GDP is less than potential GDP. The *IA* line keeps shifting down until real GDP is back to potential GDP.

Details on the Components of Spending

It is possible to give a more detailed report on what happens to consumption, net exports, and investment during this temporary departure from, and return to, potential GDP.

Let's focus first on the short run and then on the long run. Figure 12.3 summarizes how each component of real GDP changes in the short run and the long run. The arrows in the table indicate what happens compared with what would have happened in the absence of the change in government purchases. The path of the economy in the absence of the hypothetical change is called the *baseline*. The term *baseline* is commonly used in public policy discussions to refer to what would happen if a contemplated policy action were not taken; the arrows in the table tell whether a variable is up or down relative to the baseline. In this case, the baseline for real GDP is potential GDP. Thus, a downward-pointing arrow in the real GDP column means that real GDP is below potential GDP; the sideways arrows indicate that real GDP is equal to the baseline or potential GDP; an upward-pointing arrow would mean that real GDP is above potential GDP.

■ **Short Run.** The decline in government spending gets things started, lowering aggregate demand and the level of real GDP. With lower real GDP, income is down, and so people consume less, as explained by the consumption function in Chapter 10. In the short run, investment does not change because interest rates have not yet changed. However, net exports rise because the lower level of income in the United States means that people will import less from abroad. Recall that *net exports is defined as exports minus imports*. Thus, if imports fall, then net exports must rise.

These short-run effects are shown in the first row in the table. Real GDP and consumption are down *relative to the baseline*. Net exports are up *relative to the baseline*.

■ **Long Run.** Now consider the long run, approximately four to five years. By this time, real GDP has returned to potential GDP. Government spending is still lower than it was originally because we have assumed that this is a permanent decline in military spending. Because real GDP is equal to potential GDP, aggregate income in the economy—which equals real GDP—is back to normal. Because income is back to normal, the effects of income on consumption and net exports are just what they would have been in the absence of the change in government purchases.

What about interest rates and their effect on consumption, investment, and net exports? We know that real GDP is back to potential GDP, so the sum of consumption, investment, and net exports must be higher to make up for the decrease in government purchases. Thus, the real interest rate must remain lower, because investment, consumption, and net exports depend negatively on the real interest rate. With a lower real interest rate, more real GDP will go to investment, net exports, and consumption to make up for the decline in the amount of real GDP going to the government. The diagram in Figure 12.3 shows that consumption, investment, and net exports are higher in the long run. We would expect the consumption effects to be small, however, because consumption is not very sensitive to interest rates. Most of the long-run impact of the decline in government purchases is to raise investment and net exports.

To summarize, a decrease in government purchases has negative effects on the economy in the short run.

	Y	C	I	X	G
SR	↓	↓	↔	↑	↓
LR	↔	↑	↑	↑	↓

Figure 12.3
More Detailed Analysis of a Reduction in Government Purchases
The arrows in the diagram keep track of the changes in the major variables relative to the baseline.

Real GDP declines. Workers are laid off. Unemployment rises. In the long run, the economy is back to potential GDP, and consumption, investment, and net exports have gone up. Workers are called back, and unemployment declines to where it was before the recession. In the long run, the decrease in government purchases permits greater private investment and more net exports. The increase in investment benefits long-run economic growth, as we know from Chapter 6; hence, the path of potential GDP over time has risen, and now real GDP is growing more quickly, as shown in Figure 12.4.

Observe also that the rate of inflation is lower in the long run than it was before the temporary decline in real GDP. Inflation declined during the period when real GDP was lower than potential GDP, and it did not increase again. This lower inflation rate means that the Fed has implicitly allowed the *target* rate of inflation—the average level of inflation over the long run—to drift down. If the Fed wanted to keep the target rate of inflation from falling, it would have had to lower interest rates before the inflation rate started to fall. This decline in the interest rate would push the aggregate demand curve back to the right and thereby keep the inflation rate from falling. Such a cut in the interest rates by the Fed would be appropriate if it knows that the reduction in government spending was permanent and would therefore lower the real interest rate in the long run. For example, when government purchases were cut in the 1990s in an effort to reduce the federal budget deficit, economists in both the Bush and the Clinton administrations argued that the Fed should cut interest rates by an extra amount. They recognized that such action would cause the aggregate demand curve to shift to the right and prevent real GDP from declining in the short run while at the same time keeping the inflation rate from falling in the long run.

The Return to Potential GDP After a Boom

What if real GDP rises above potential GDP? Surprisingly, the adjustment of real GDP back to potential GDP can be explained using the same theory. For example, suppose an increase in real GDP above potential GDP is caused by an increase in government purchases for new highway construction. Starting from potential GDP, the aggregate demand curve would shift to the right. Real GDP would increase above potential GDP in the short run.

Figure 12.4
Increase in the Long-Term Growth After a Recession Caused by a Decrease in Government Purchases
The higher investment share of real GDP that results from the decline in government purchases leads to more capital and a higher growth of potential GDP. After the recession, real GDP will grow along, or fluctuate around, this higher growth path.

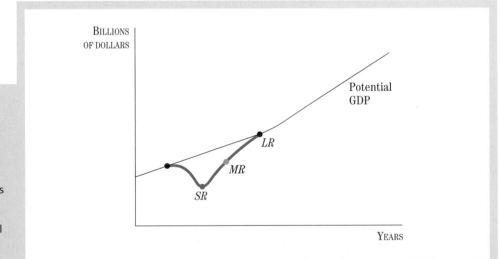

With real GDP above potential GDP, however, firms start to raise their prices more rapidly; inflation begins to rise. We would represent that as an upward shift in the inflation adjustment line. In the medium run, real GDP would still be above potential GDP, and inflation would continue to rise. Eventually, real GDP would go back to potential GDP and the boom would be over. Thus, we predict that real GDP goes back to potential GDP. However, in this case, because government purchases have risen, the new long-run equilibrium will have a higher interest rate, and the sum of consumption, investment, and net exports will be lower.

REVIEW

- Using the inflation adjustment line and the aggregate demand curve, we can now explain both the initial steps of real GDP away from potential GDP and the return to potential GDP.

- In the short run, a decline in government purchases shifts the aggregate demand curve to the left and causes real GDP to fall below potential GDP.

- In the medium run, when the interest rate starts to fall, real GDP begins to increase again. Investment and net exports start to rise and partly offset the decline in government purchases.

- In the long run, real GDP returns to potential GDP. Interest rates are lower, and consumption plus investment plus net exports have risen.

Changes in Monetary Policy

A large change in government spending is, of course, not the only thing that can temporarily push real GDP away from potential GDP. Changes in taxes, consumer confidence, or foreign demand can also cause recessions. But a particularly important factor is a change in monetary policy.

Consider, for example, a change in monetary policy that aims to lower the rate of inflation. Suppose that the inflation rate is 10 percent, as it was in the late 1970s, and a new head of the central bank is appointed who has the objective of reducing inflation. Suppose the aim is to reduce the inflation rate to 4 percent. In effect, the central bank changes the target inflation rate from 10 percent to 4 percent. A reduction in the inflation rate is called **disinflation. Deflation** means declining prices, or a negative inflation rate, which is different from a declining inflation rate. The aim of the policy in this example is disinflation, not deflation.

Figure 12.5 shows the short-run, medium-run, and long-run impact of such a shift in monetary policy. Recall from Chapter 11 (see Figures 11.7 and 11.8) that a change in monetary policy will shift the aggregate demand curve. A change in monetary policy toward higher inflation will shift the *AD* curve to the right, and a change in monetary policy toward lower inflation will shift the *AD* curve to the left. In this case, we are examining a change in monetary policy that aims to lower the inflation rate, so the change shifts the aggregate demand curve to the left. This occurs because the Fed raises interest rates to curtail demand and thereby lower inflationary pressures.

One effect of the increase in the interest rate is to lower investment. In addition, the higher interest rate causes the dollar to appreciate, and this tends to reduce net exports. Since inflation is slow to adjust, we do not move the inflation adjustment

disinflation: a reduction in the inflation rate.

deflation: a decrease in the overall price level, or a negative inflation rate.

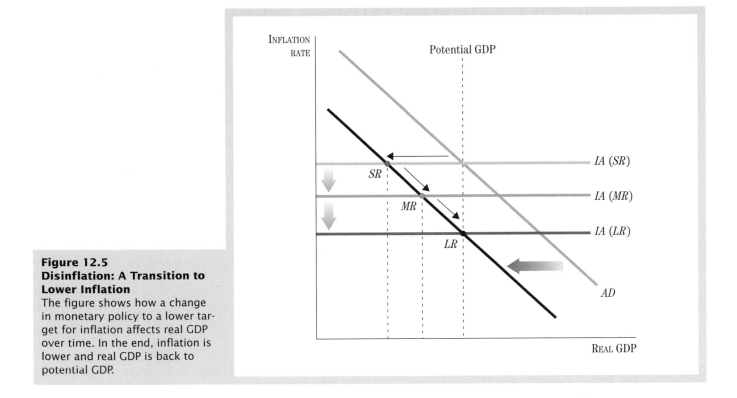

Figure 12.5
Disinflation: A Transition to Lower Inflation
The figure shows how a change in monetary policy to a lower target for inflation affects real GDP over time. In the end, inflation is lower and real GDP is back to potential GDP.

line yet. Thus, inflation remains at 10 percent in the short run. At this time, things seem very grim. The short-run effect of the change to a new monetary policy is to cause real GDP to fall below potential GDP. If the disinflation is large enough, this might mean a decline in real GDP, or a recession. If the disinflation is very small and gradual, then the decline in real GDP could result in a *temporary growth slowdown*. In a temporary growth slowdown, real GDP growth does not turn negative, as it does in a recession.

In any case, with real GDP below potential GDP, inflation will begin to decline. We show this in the diagram in Figure 12.5 by moving the inflation adjustment line down. The lower inflation adjustment line, labeled *MR* for medium run, intersects the aggregate demand curve at a higher level of real GDP. Thus, the economy has begun to recover. The recovery starts because as inflation comes down, the Fed begins to lower the interest rate. As the interest rate declines, investment and net exports begin to rise again, and we move back along the aggregate demand curve.

However, at this medium-run situation, real GDP is still below potential GDP, so the inflation rate continues to decline. We show this in the diagram by shifting the inflation adjustment line down again. To make a long story short, we show the inflation adjustment line shifting all the way down to where it intersects the aggregate demand curve at potential GDP. Thus, in the long-run equilibrium, the economy has fully recovered, and the inflation rate is at its new lower target. The long-run equilibrium has consumption, investment, and net exports back to normal.

The overall dynamic impacts of this change in monetary policy are very important. The initial impact of a monetary policy change is on real GDP. It is only later that the change shows up in inflation. Thus, there is a long lag in the effect of monetary policy on inflation.

Lower inflation is likely to make potential GDP grow faster, perhaps because there is less uncertainty and productivity rises faster. If this is so, the return of real GDP to potential GDP will mean that real GDP is higher, and the long-run benefits of the disinflation to people in the economy may be great over the years. But such changes in the growth of real GDP will appear small in the span of years during which a disinflation takes place and will not change the basic story that a reduction in the rate of inflation, unless it is very gradual, usually results in a recession.

The Volcker Disinflation

The scenario we just described is very similar to the disinflation in the United States in the early 1980s under Paul Volcker, the head of the Fed from 1979 to 1987. First, interest rates skyrocketed as the disinflation began. The federal funds rate went over 20 percent. By any measure, real GDP fell well below potential GDP in the early 1980s. Workers were laid off, the unemployment rate rose to 10.8 percent, investment declined, and net exports fell. Eventually, pricing decisions began to adjust and inflation began to come down. As inflation came down, the Fed began to lower the interest rate. The economy eventually recovered: In 1982, the recovery was under way, and by 1985, the economy had returned to near its potential. The good news was that inflation was down from over 10 percent to about 4 percent.

Reinflation

reinflation: an increase in the inflation rate caused by a change in monetary policy.

The opposite of disinflation might be called **reinflation,** an increase in the inflation rate caused by a shift in monetary policy. This could be analyzed with our theory simply by reversing the preceding process, starting with a change in monetary policy to a higher inflation rate target. This would cause the aggregate demand curve to shift right. Real GDP would rise above potential GDP, and unemployment would decline. But eventually inflation would rise and real GDP would return to potential.

Although it would be unusual for central bankers to explicitly admit they were raising the target inflation rate, there could be political pressures that would lead to less concern about inflation. In such a case, there would be an implicit rise in the target for inflation.

Reinflation is one way to interpret the increase in inflation in the United States and other countries in the 1970s. But there were other things going on at that time, including a quadrupling of oil prices as petroleum-exporting countries, many of which are located in the Middle East, banded together and formed a cartel. We consider oil price shocks in the next section.

REVIEW

- Disinflation is a reduction in inflation. It occurs when the central bank shifts monetary policy in the direction of a lower inflation target.

- According to the theory of economic fluctuations, disinflation has either a temporary slowing of real GDP growth or a recession as a by-product. A higher interest rate at the start of a disinflation lowers investment spending and net exports. This causes real GDP to fall below potential GDP. Eventually the economy recovers. Inflation comes down, and so does the interest rate.

- The large disinflation in the early 1980s in the United States was accompanied by a recession, as predicted by the theory.

Explaining the Recovery from the Great Depression

The Great Depression was the biggest economic downturn in American history. There is simply no parallel either before or since. As shown in the figure, from 1929 to 1933, real GDP declined 35 percent. Between 1933 and 1937, real GDP rose 33 percent; it then declined 5 percent in a recession in 1938. Real GDP increased by a spectacular 49 percent between 1938 and 1942. By 1942, real GDP had caught up with potential GDP, as estimated in the figure.

There is still much disagreement among economists about what caused the Great Depression—that is, what caused the initial departure of real GDP from potential GDP. In their monetary history of the United States, Milton Friedman and Anna Schwartz argue that it was caused by an error in monetary policy, which produced a massive leftward shift in the aggregate demand curve. Unfortunately, it took several years of continually declining real GDP, declining inflation, and even deflation before the errors in monetary policy were corrected.

Another explanation is that there was a downward shift in consumption and investment spending that lowered total expenditures. Peter Temin of MIT has argued that such a spending shift was a cause of the Great Depression.

But whatever the initial cause, there seems to be more consensus that monetary policy was eventually responsible for the recovery from the Great Depression. Interest rates (in real terms) fell precipitously in 1933 and remained low or negative throughout most of the second half of the 1930s. These low interest rates led to an increase in investment and net exports. Christina Romer of the University of California at Berkeley estimates that without the monetary response, "the U.S. economy in 1942 would have been 50 percent below its pre-Depression trend path, rather than back to its normal level." Could the recovery from the Great Depression have been associated with an increase in government purchases or a reduction in taxes? Evidently not. Romer shows that government purchases and tax policy were basically unchanged until 1941, when government spending increased sharply during World War II. By that time, the economy had already made up most of the Depression decline in real GDP relative to potential GDP.

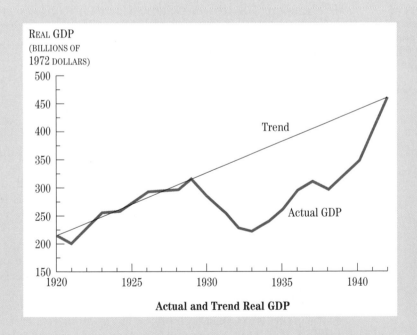

Actual and Trend Real GDP

Price Shocks

demand shock: a shift in one of the components of aggregate demand that leads to a shift in the aggregate demand curve.

Shifts in the aggregate demand curve are called **demand shocks.** The change in government purchases and the shift in monetary policy described in the previous two sections of this chapter are examples of demand shocks. However, shifts in the aggregate demand curve are not the only things that can push real GDP away from potential GDP. In particular, the inflation adjustment line can shift.

What Is a Price Shock?

price shock: a change in the price of a key commodity such as oil, usually because of a shortage, that causes a shift in the inflation adjustment line; also sometimes called a supply shock.

Shifts in the inflation adjustment line are called **price shocks.** A price shock usually occurs when a temporary shortage of a key commodity, or group of commodities, drives up prices by such a large amount that it has a noticeable effect on the rate of inflation. Oil price shocks have been common in the last 25 years. For example, oil prices rose sharply in 1974, in 1979, in 1990, and again in 2000. After such shocks, there have usually been declines in real GDP and increases in unemployment. Hence, such shocks appear to move real GDP significantly, though temporarily, away from potential GDP.

Price shocks are sometimes called *supply shocks* in an attempt to distinguish them from demand shocks due to changes in government spending or monetary policy. However, a shift in potential GDP—rather than a shift in the inflation adjustment line—is more appropriately called a supply shock. Shifts in potential GDP—such as a sudden spurt in productivity growth due to new inventions—can, of course, cause real GDP to fluctuate. Recall that *real business cycle theory* places great emphasis on shifts in potential GDP. Although a price shock might be accompanied by a shift in potential GDP, it need not be. Here we are looking at departures of real GDP from potential GDP and thus focusing on price shocks.

real business cycle theory: a theory of macroeconomics that stresses that shifts in potential GDP are a primary cause of fluctuations in real GDP; the shifts in potential GDP are usually assumed to be caused by changes in technology. (Ch. 10)

The Effect of Price Shocks

How does our theory of economic fluctuations allow us to predict the effect of price shocks? The impact of a price shock can be illustrated graphically, as shown in Figure 12.6. In the case of a large increase in oil prices, for example, the inflation adjustment line will shift up to a higher level of inflation. Why? Because a large increase in oil prices will at first lead to an increase in the price of everything that uses oil in production: heating homes, gasoline, airplane fuel, airfares, plastic toys, and many other things. The overall inflation rate is affected. When the inflation rate rises, the inflation adjustment line must shift up.

The immediate impact of the shock is to lower real GDP, as the intersection of the inflation adjustment line with the aggregate demand curve moves to the left. The reason this occurs is that the higher inflation rate causes the central bank to raise interest rates, reducing investment spending and net exports.

With real GDP below potential GDP, however, the reduction in spending will put pressure on firms to adjust their prices. The lower price increases being about a lower rate of inflation. Thus, in the period following the rise of inflation, we begin to see a reversal. Inflation starts to decline. As inflation falls, interest rates begin to decline, and the economy starts to recover again. The rate of inflation will return to where it was before the price shock.

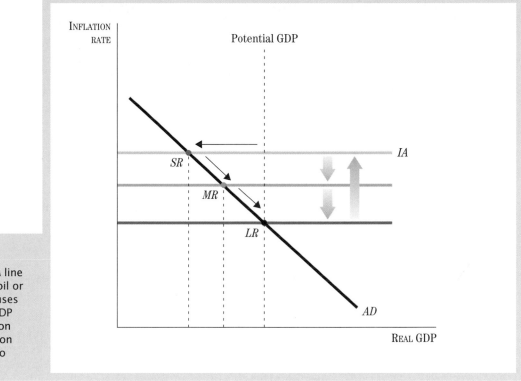

Figure 12.6
A Price Shock
Initially, inflation and the *IA* line rise because of a shock to oil or agricultural prices. This causes real GDP to fall. With real GDP below potential GDP, inflation begins to decline. As inflation declines, real GDP returns to potential GDP.

■ **Temporary Shifts in the Inflation Adjustment Line.**   In this analysis of the price shock, the central bank raises interest rates, and the resulting decline in real GDP exerts a countervailing force to reduce inflation. It is possible for some price shocks to have only a temporary effect on inflation. Such a temporary effect can be shown graphically as a rise followed by a quick fall in the inflation adjustment line. In such a situation—where the price shock would be expected to automatically reverse itself—it would be wise for the central bank to delay raising the interest rate. Then if the price shock has only a temporary effect on inflation, the decline in real GDP can be avoided. In reality, whenever there is a price shock, there is a great debate about whether it will have a temporary or a permanent effect on inflation. The debate is rarely settled until after the fact.

Price shocks can also occur when commodity prices fall. In this case there would be a *downward* shift in the inflation adjustment line—just the opposite as in the case of an increase in commodity prices—and this would cause real GDP to rise as the Fed lowered interest rates. For example, in 1986 there was a decline in oil prices. This resulted in a temporary decrease in inflation and a rise in real GDP—exactly what would be predicted by the theory of economic fluctuations.

■ **Stagflation.**   An important difference between price shocks and demand shocks is that in the case of a price shock, output declines while inflation rises. With demand shocks, inflation and output are positively related over the period of recession and recovery. The situation in which inflation is up and real GDP is down is called **stagflation.** As we have shown, price shocks can lead to stagflation.

stagflation: the situation in which high inflation and high unemployment occur simultaneously.

REVIEW
- A price shock is a large change in the price of some key commodity like oil. Such shocks can push real GDP below potential GDP.

- In the aftermath of a price shock, the interest rate rises. Eventually, with real GDP below potential GDP, inflation begins to come down, and the economy recovers.

The 2001 Recession

Let's see how the economic fluctuations model can explain actual fluctuations of the economy by studying the most recent slowdown of the U.S. economy in 2001, following 10 years of uninterrupted economic growth.

The Facts: Higher Inflation, then Recession, then Signs of a Recovery

The dating of U.S. recessions is formally done by a panel of economists at the National Bureau of Economic Research, who look at a wide variety of economic data. Toward the end of 2001, they determined that the U.S. economy had slid into recession in March of 2001. We will take a look at some important economic indicators in the period leading up to the recession, as well as in the aftermath of the recession.

This recession, like others, was preceded by a rise in real GDP above potential GDP, and by an increase in inflation. The behavior of real GDP in the late 1990s and the early 2000s is shown graphically in Figure 12.7. The graph of real GDP shows real GDP fluctuating around potential GDP. The lower graph shows inflation, measured as the percent change in the Consumer Price Index. Notice that in the years 1999 and 2000, when output was somewhat higher than potential output, inflation was showing signs of increasing. In 2001, in the aftermath of the recession, real GDP has fallen below potential GDP and inflation remains much lower.

Also important to our analysis of this case is the rise in the interest rate as fears of inflation increased before the recession. Once the recession began, interest rates fell sharply. Finally, as in all recessions, the unemployment rate rose as the recession hit the economy. These two variables are shown in Figure 12.8.

To summarize, Figure 12.7 shows that the economic fluctuations during the years from 1998 to 2002 can be viewed as a combination of two distinct periods: (1) a period when real GDP was above potential GDP and inflation was rising, and (2) a period when real GDP was below potential GDP and inflation was falling. The two periods are linked together. In the first period, interest rates were rising, while in the second period, interest rates were falling.

How Does the Economic Fluctuations Model Explain the Facts?

The best explanation of these economic fluctuations is achieved by combining a rightward shift of the *AD* curve with a subsequent leftward shift of the *AD* curve.

■ **Patching Together the Two Shifts.** To see how this works, look at the *AD-IA* diagram in Figure 12.9. It shows a shift in the *AD* curve to the right (the shifting arrow

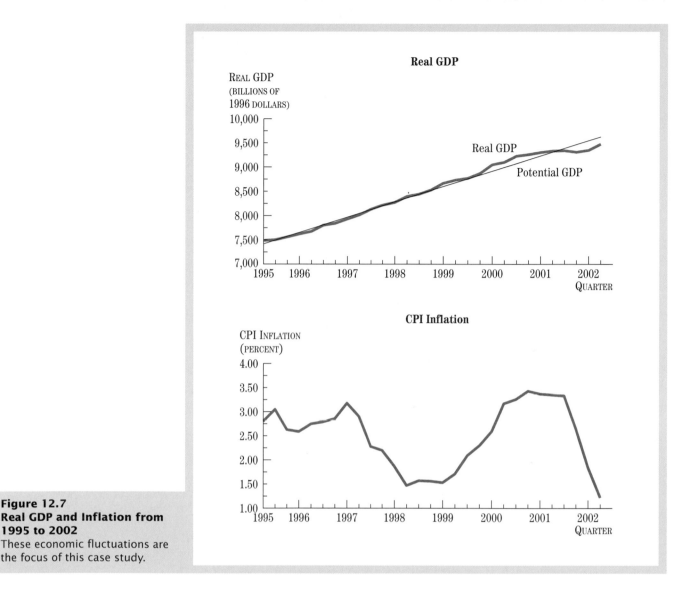

Figure 12.7
Real GDP and Inflation from 1995 to 2002
These economic fluctuations are the focus of this case study.

is labeled "1"). This shift first causes real GDP to rise above potential GDP, and then leads to rising inflation as the *IA* line shifts up gradually. Three intersections of the *AD* curve and the *IA* curve, labeled SR_1, MR_1, and LR_1, show this movement.

Figure 12.9 then shows a shift in the *AD* curve to the left (the shifting arrow is labeled "2"). This shift causes a recession, with real GDP falling below potential GDP, and leads to a reduction in inflation as the *IA* line shifts down gradually over time. Three intersections of the *IA* line and the *AD* curve during this period are labeled SR_2, MR_2, and LR_2. In sum, the movements in real GDP and inflation are represented by patching together two shifts of the *AD* curve.

The time-series sketches in the lower part of Figure 12.9 show the movement in real GDP and inflation that is traced out by the combination of these shifts. On the left, real GDP first rises above potential GDP, which is assumed to be growing over time, and then falls below potential GDP. If you compare these fluctuations in real

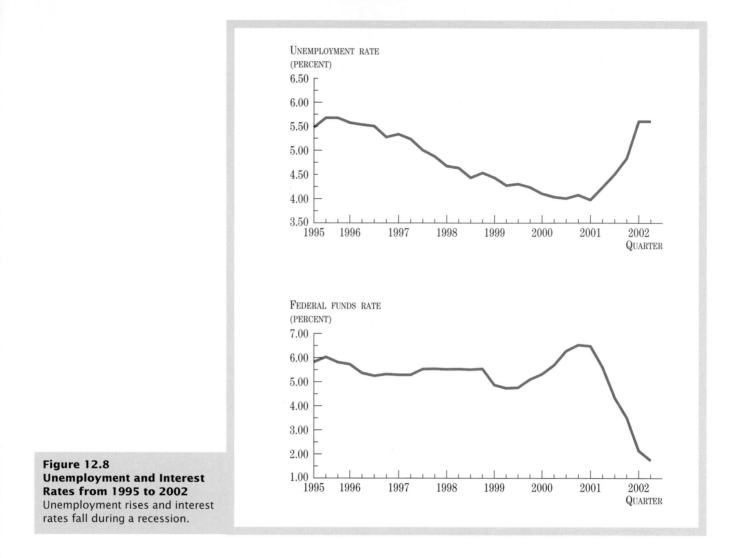

Figure 12.8
Unemployment and Interest Rates from 1995 to 2002
Unemployment rises and interest rates fall during a recession.

GDP with what actually happened, shown in Figure 12.7, you will see a close resemblance. The model seems to explain the actual data very well. The same close fit is seen for inflation. The movements in inflation implied by the model—a rise and then a fall—are very close to the movements in the data as shown in Figure 12.7.

■ **Why Did the *AD* Curve Shift Out Before the Recession?** Finding a single explanation for economic booms or recessions is almost always impossible. One potentially important explanatory variable for the boom in the latter part of the 1990s was the rapid rise in the stock market, particularly in technology stocks. The rising stock market led to both higher consumption, as stock-owning households spent some of their new-found wealth, and higher investment, as firms rushed to put out new products or to upgrade their technology infrastructure to take advantage of the Internet. These spending booms shifted the *AD* curve out and may even have pushed the economy above potential output. Note, however, that the new Internet technology could in fact increase potential output as well, as some of the "new economy" advocates were arguing. If, however, the increase in spending was substantial, or if the increase in potential output was not as substantial as some argued, the economy would see inflationary pressure starting to mount.

■ **Why Did the *AD* Curve Shift In During the Recession?**   What brought about the end of the long boom? Once the euphoria over some of the technology stocks died down, investors started to have doubts about the profitability of high-profile Internet companies, and started selling off these stocks. The Federal Reserve,

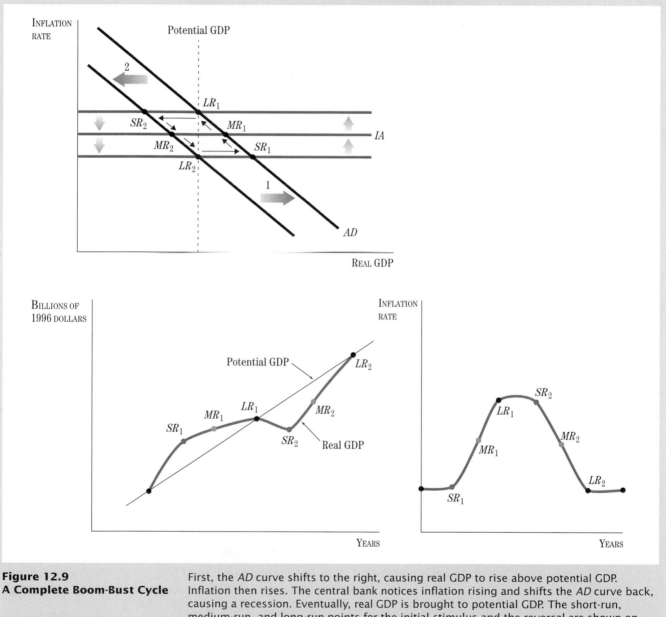

Figure 12.9
A Complete Boom-Bust Cycle

First, the *AD* curve shifts to the right, causing real GDP to rise above potential GDP. Inflation then rises. The central bank notices inflation rising and shifts the *AD* curve back, causing a recession. Eventually, real GDP is brought to potential GDP. The short-run, medium-run, and long-run points for the initial stimulus and the reversal are shown on both the upper and lower panels.

From Boom to Bust
Webvan, the online grocer, went bankrupt in 2001, as did many other Internet startups. The assets of Webvan were sold at a large auction in October 2001, signaling the abrupt end of a company whose prospects had seemed so bright only a year or so earlier.

concerned about higher inflation down the road, made a preemptive strike by raising interest rates, leading to a further slowdown in technology investment by firms. Once the stock market started to fall, consumer confidence soon followed, and the effects were tragically compounded by the events of September 11. These cutbacks in spending moved the *AD* curve to the left and moved the economy into recession.

■ **How Can We Get the *AD* Curve to Shift Out Again?**   Finally, what about the possibility of recovery? The fall in inflation will see the Fed lowering interest rates and moving the economy back toward potential. In the year 2001, the Fed lowered interest rates on eleven separate occasions! The government has also responded with tax cuts. Furthermore, the need for higher military expenditures has provided a short-run boost to spending. These will help move the *AD* curve to the right and move GDP back toward potential GDP again even faster.

A difference between macroeconomics and microeconomics is that in macroeconomics, identifying the reasons for the shifts of the curves is more difficult. Because macroeconomics is about the whole economy, the whole world economy, many different things can shift curves. Macroeconomics is therefore more controversial than microeconomics, and is likely to remain so.

REVIEW

- The economic fluctuations that occurred around the time of the 2001 recession included a period with real GDP above potential GDP followed by a period with real GDP below potential GDP. Inflation was rising in the first period and falling in the second period.

- These actual economic fluctuations can be explained by the model of economic fluctuations. Shifts in the *AD* curve cause real GDP to move away from potential GDP, followed by changes in inflation.

- The shifts in the *AD* curve could have been caused by lower consumer spending, lower investment spending, or by the pre-emptive actions of the Fed.

Conclusion

Using a diagram with the aggregate demand curve and the inflation adjustment line, we can explain not only the first steps toward recessions but also the recovery of the economy. The model works well in explaining actual economic fluctuations and is thus useful for analyzing macroeconomic policy, as we do in Chapters 13 and 14.

That the model implies that real GDP returns toward potential GDP in the long run is an attractive feature of the model because in reality all recessions have ended. Real GDP appears to fluctuate around potential GDP rather than getting stuck forever in a recession. The tendency for real GDP to return toward potential GDP allows us to use the theory of long-run growth when discussing long-run trends in the economy. As the economy fluctuates, potential GDP gradually increases over time.

KEY POINTS

1. To use the economic fluctuations model, you shift the aggregate demand curve and the inflation adjustment line.

2. Using the model is much like using the supply and demand model of microeconomics.

3. An increase in government purchases temporarily causes real GDP to rise, but eventually real GDP returns to potential GDP.

4. A decline in government purchases temporarily reduces real GDP, but over time the economy recovers.

5. Shifts in monetary policy, including explicit attempts to disinflate or reinflate, cause real GDP to depart from potential GDP temporarily. But eventually real GDP returns to potential GDP and only the inflation rate is changed.

6. Price shocks can cause recessions. A price shock that raises the inflation rate will cause the interest rate to rise and real GDP to fall.

7. If the Fed sets interest rates according to a monetary policy rule, then it will raise interest rates following a rise in inflation, and eventually inflation will come back down.

8. If a price shock is clearly temporary, then the Fed should not change the interest rate.

9. Shifts of the aggregate demand curve and the inflation adjustment line trace out actual observations fairly closely. Thus, the economic fluctuations model works well, but, like most models in economics and elsewhere, it is not perfect.

KEY TERMS

disinflation
deflation
reinflation
demand shock
price shock
stagflation

QUESTIONS FOR REVIEW

1. What causes the economy to recover after a recession?
2. What is the difference between the long-run and short-run effects of a change in government spending?
3. What is disinflation, and how does the central bank bring it about?
4. What is reinflation, and what impact does it have on real GDP in the short run and the long run?
5. What is a price shock, and why have price shocks frequently been followed by increases in unemployment?
6. What is the difference between a price shock and a supply shock?
7. Why do monetary policy errors lead to economic fluctuations?
8. In what way is the economic fluctuations model discussed in this chapter consistent with real-world observations?

PROBLEMS

1. Using the aggregate demand curve and the inflation adjustment line, describe what would happen to real GDP and inflation in the short run, in the medium run, and in the long run if there were a permanent increase in government spending on highway construction. Be sure to provide an economic explanation for your results.

2. Suppose there is a cut in government spending on defense. What would happen to consumption, investment, and net exports in the short run and in the long run? Explain your results, using a diagram with the aggregate demand curve and inflation adjustment line.

3. Suppose the central bank wants to return to the original inflation rate before the increase in government spending in problem 1. How can it achieve its objective? Describe the proposed change in policy and its short-run, medium-run, and long-run effects on real GDP and inflation.

4. Using the aggregate demand curve and the inflation adjustment line, show what happens if the central bank reinflates the economy. Suppose the target inflation rate is changed from 2 percent to 5 percent. What is the impact on the major components of spending in the short run and in the long run?

5. Suppose potential GDP is $5,000 billion. Use the following data to graph the aggregate demand curve with the percentage deviation of real GDP from potential GDP on the horizontal axis.

Inflation (percent)	Real GDP (billions of dollars)
5	4,800
4	4,900
3	5,000
2	5,100
1	5,200

a. Suppose the current inflation rate is 2 percent. Draw the inflation adjustment line. What is the current deviation of real GDP from potential GDP?
b. In the long run, what will the inflation rate be if there is no change in economic policy? Explain how this adjustment takes place.

6. For the data in problem 5, suppose that after the long-run adjustment back to potential, the Fed changes its policy rule so that the relationship between real GDP and inflation becomes the following:

Inflation (percent)	Real GDP (billions of dollars)
5	4,700
4	4,800
3	4,900
2	5,000
1	5,100

a. Draw the aggregate demand curve and compare it with the one in problem 5.
b. If the current inflation rate is 2 percent, what is the short-run deviation from potential GDP?
c. How will the inflation adjustment line adjust in the medium run and the long run? Explain how this adjustment takes place.

7. The economy begins at potential GDP with an inflation rate of 3 percent. Draw this situation with an aggregate demand curve and an inflation adjustment line. Suppose there is a price shock that pushes inflation up to 6 percent in the short run, but the effect on inflation is viewed as temporary by the Fed. It expects the inflation adjustment line to shift back down to 2 percent the next year, and in fact the inflation adjustment line does shift back down.
a. If the Fed follows its usual policy rule, where will real GDP be in the short run? How does the economy adjust back to potential?
b. Now suppose that since the Fed is sure that this inflationary shock is only temporary, it decides not to follow its typical policy rule, but instead maintains the interest rate at its previous level. What happens to real GDP? Why? What will the long-run adjustment be in this case? Do you agree with the Fed's handling of the situation?

8. Suppose that in 2003 the GDP deflator is 100, and in 2004 it is 105.
   a. Suppose that real GDP equals potential GDP in 2003 and 2004. What is the rate of inflation in 2004?
   b. Suppose instead that real GDP is below potential GDP in 2004. How is the adjustment back to potential made in this situation?

9. Suppose that there are two countries that are very similar except that one has a central bank with a higher target inflation rate. They have identical potential GDP and are both at their long-run equilibrium. Explain this situation by using two diagrams with an aggregate demand curve and an inflation adjustment line. Explain how these different equilibrium levels of inflation are possible. How do workers' and firms' expectations of inflation differ between the two countries?

10. Using the spending allocation model from Chapter 6, show the effect of a decrease in government spending as a share of GDP. Show that you get the same answer *in the long run* using the aggregate demand curve and the inflation adjustment line.

Fiscal Policy

Over the last few years, the budgetary situation of the federal government has resembled a roller coaster ride: first falling, then rising, only to fall again. These wild fluctuations from deficit to surplus to deficit again have not been the norm historically. In 1997, the U.S. government ran a budget deficit for the *twenty-eighth* year in a row. Further deficits were projected for 1998, 1999, 2000, and beyond. The political debate at that time centered around the consequences of running sustained budget deficits, concerns about how much debt was being accumulated, and how to trim spending and raise revenue to lower the budget deficit.

Then, seemingly overnight, there was a radical change. Unexpectedly, a budget surplus appeared in 1998. More surpluses appeared in 1999, and by the presidential election of 2000, forecasts called for budget surpluses as far as the eye could see. The political debate changed accordingly: Instead of discussing deficits and debt, the debate in the presidential election campaign centered around whether to use the surplus for tax cuts or for spending increases.

Just as the tax cuts were being passed by Congress, the budgetary situation took another turn, this time for the worse. The arrival of the U.S. recession in 2001 and the higher government expenditures associated with September 11 and the increased military buildup for the campaign in Afghanistan sent the budget projections into deficit mode again. There is considerable uncertainty at this time about what the budget situation will be for the next few years.

An understanding of the U.S. budget, the factors that caused it to switch from deficit to surplus and back to deficit again, and the projections for future budget deficits is vital if we are to improve our understanding of fiscal policy—spending and taxation decisions taken by the government. In this section, we will show how countercyclical fiscal policies (tax cuts and spending increases in recessions, tax hikes and spending cuts in booms) can help move the economy to potential output and minimize economic fluctuations. Expansionary fiscal policy may have played a significant role in cushioning the economy during the most recent recession, and as such fiscal policy remains a useful tool that policymakers have at their disposal.

We will begin this section by reviewing the U.S. budget and providing an explanation for the recent fluctuations. We will then move on to a discussion of the effectiveness and scope of fiscal policy in minimizing economic fluctuations.

The Government Budget

federal budget: a summary of the federal government's proposals for spending, taxes, and the deficit.

The **federal budget** is the major summary document describing fiscal policy in the United States. The budget includes not only the estimates of the surplus or deficit that get so much attention, but also proposals for taxes and spending. Let's look at how the federal budget in the United States is put together.

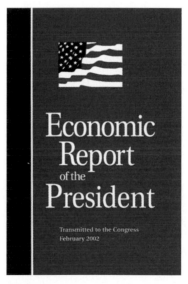

The CEA
The economic assumptions used for the federal budget are presented by the Council of Economic Advisers (CEA) in the Economic Report of the President.

balanced budget: a budget in which tax revenues equal spending.

budget surplus: the amount by which tax revenues exceed government spending.

budget deficit: the amount by which government spending exceeds tax revenues.

Setting the Annual Budget

In the United States, the president submits a new budget to Congress each year for the following fiscal year. The fiscal year runs from October to October. For example, *The Budget of the United States: Fiscal Year 2003* applied to spending and taxes from October 1, 2002, through September 30, 2003. It was submitted to Congress by the president in early 2002. The president typically devotes part of the State of the Union address to describing the budget and fiscal policy. Also at the start of each year, the *Economic Report of the President* is released, providing the economic forecasts underlying the budget, prepared by the Council of Economic Advisers (CEA). The Congressional Budget Office (CBO) makes its own economic forecasts. During the budget battles between President Clinton and Congress in the 1990s, one of the main points of dispute was a discrepancy between the economic forecasts of the CEA and the CBO.

In putting together the federal budget, the president proposes many specific spending programs that fit into an overall philosophy of what government should be doing. However, in any one year, most of the spending in the budget is determined by ongoing programs, which the president usually can do little to change. For example, payments of social security benefits to retired people are a large item in the budget, but the amount of spending on social security depends on how many eligible people there are. As more people retire, spending automatically goes up unless the social security law changes. Thus, in reality, the president can change only a small part of the budget each year.

■ **A Balanced Budget versus a Deficit or Surplus.** Taxes to pay for the spending programs are also included in the budget. As part of the budget, the president may propose an increase or a decrease in taxes. *Tax revenues* are the total dollar amount the government receives from taxpayers each year. When tax revenues are exactly equal to spending, there is a **balanced budget.** When tax revenues are greater than spending, there is a **budget surplus.** When spending is greater than tax revenues, there is a **budget deficit,** and the government must borrow to pay the difference.

Note the difference between **tax rate** and **tax revenues.** For the income tax, if the average tax rate is 20 percent and income is $3,000 billion, then tax revenues are $600 billion.

Budget Deficit	Budget Balance	Budget Surplus
Tax revenues < spending	Tax revenues = spending	Tax revenues > spending

■ **The Proposed Budget versus the Actual Budget.**   Keep in mind that the budget the president submits is only a *proposal*. The actual amounts of tax revenues and spending during the fiscal year are quite different from what is proposed. There are two main reasons for this difference.

First, Congress usually modifies the president's budget, adding some programs and deleting others. Congress deliberates on the specific items in the president's budget proposal for months before the fiscal year actually starts. After the president's budget has been debated and modified, it is passed by Congress. Only when the president signs the legislation is the budget enacted into law. Because of this congressional modification, the enacted budget is always different from the proposed budget.

Second, because of changes in the economy and other unanticipated events such as wars and natural disasters, the actual amounts of spending and taxes will be different from what is enacted. After the fiscal year has begun and the budget has been enacted, various *supplementals* are proposed and passed. A supplemental is a change in a spending program or a change in the tax law that affects the budget in the current fiscal year. In addition, recessions or booms always affect tax revenues and spending to some degree.

Figure 13.1 shows the difference between proposed tax revenues and expenditures for the fiscal year 2001 budget (submitted in January 2000) and the actual tax revenues and expenditures that occurred. Revenues were lower than forecast, and expenditures were higher than forecast. The weak economy was one reason why the difference was so large. The projected surplus turned out to be much smaller than anticipated.

Figure 13.1
The Shrinking Surplus
When the fiscal year 2001 budget was submitted to Congress in early 2000, a large surplus was forecast. By the time the fiscal year was over—almost two years later—there was a much smaller surplus. Tax revenues were sharply lower and spending was slightly higher than in the proposed budget.

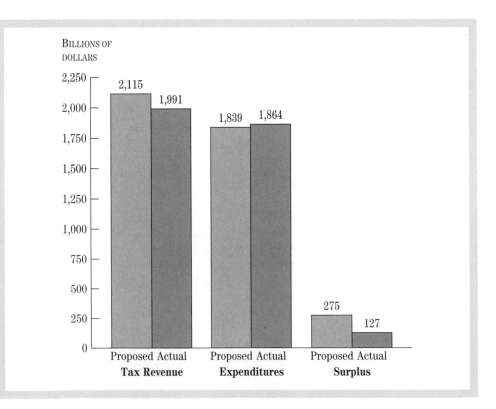

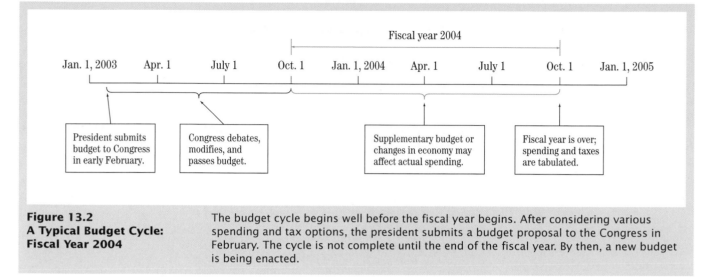

**Figure 13.2
A Typical Budget Cycle:
Fiscal Year 2004**

The budget cycle begins well before the fiscal year begins. After considering various spending and tax options, the president submits a budget proposal to the Congress in February. The cycle is not complete until the end of the fiscal year. By then, a new budget is being enacted.

Figure 13.2 shows how the fiscal year 2004 budget moved from a proposal in early 2003 to enactment in late 2003 to completion at the beginning of October 2004. The same *budget cycle* occurs every year. Because the whole cycle takes over two years, at any one time discussions about three budgets are taking place. For example, in September 2000, the budget for fiscal year 2000 was coming to a close, the budget for fiscal year 2001 was being considered by Congress, and the budget for fiscal year 2002 was being put together by the president's staff. The budget cycle does not always progress smoothly. In many years the president and Congress do not settle on a budget until well into the fiscal year.

A Look at the Federal Budget

Table 13.1 contains summary totals from the federal budget for fiscal year 2001. The full budget, which is over 2,000 pages long, provides much more detail.

**Table 13.1
FY 2001 Federal Tax Revenues and Expenditures** (billions of dollars)

Tax revenues	1,991	
Personal income		994
Corporate income		151
Payroll		694
Other		152
Expenditures	1,864	
Social security		433
Medicare		226
Defense		294
Interest		180
Other		731
Surplus	127	

Source: Economic Report of the President, 2002, Table B-80.

■ **The Surplus.** Table 13.1 shows that tax revenues were greater than expenditures, so there was a surplus. Budget deficits were common in the United States for many years. For every year from 1970 to 1997, there was a deficit. But 2001 was the fourth consecutive year of surplus. This consecutive run of surpluses is expected to end in 2002 in the aftermath of the recession.

■ **Taxes and Spending.** The tax revenues of $1,991 billion include *personal income taxes* paid by individuals on their total income, *corporate income taxes* paid by businesses on their profits, *sales taxes* paid on items such as gasoline and beer, and *payroll taxes*, a percentage of wages paid by workers and their employers that supports government programs such as social security. Sales taxes are the smallest of the four components of total revenue, and corporate tax revenues are only slightly larger. Payroll taxes provide a large amount of revenues, nearly as much as personal income tax revenues. Payroll taxes have grown rapidly as a share of federal government revenues in recent years, while the other types of taxes have fallen in relative importance.

Why Did All the Deficits Go Away in the Late 1990s?

During 1998, the Congressional Budget Office, the Council of Economic Advisers, and all private economic forecasters started to change their forecasts for the federal budget radically, from a long series of future deficits to a long series of future surpluses. And starting in 1998, the budget itself started moving from deficit to surplus. Why did the federal budget situation change so dramatically in 1998? Were tax rates suddenly increased? Did Congress eliminate the Department of Commerce and other government agencies as some politicians had proposed as cost-saving measures?

No. Although spending growth was curtailed somewhat, the main reason that the deficits went away was that tax revenues grew faster than anyone had anticipated, especially in the period from 1995 to 1998. Tax revenue grew in this period not because tax rates were increased (tax rates were increased in 1993), but because people's incomes grew very rapidly as the economy expanded.

The income growth was particularly rapid for rich people with high tax rates. The table below shows the share of income earned and taxes paid by high-income people—those with incomes of more than $200,000. Although such people are a very small percentage of the population, they pay a very large percentage of income taxes. Observe that from 1994 to 1998, the percentage of these high-income taxpayers rose rapidly, from 1.1 percent to 1.6 percent. The percentage of all income in the United States earned by this group also increased, from 15 percent to 22 percent. And—most important for the disappearance of the deficits—the share of taxes paid by this group rose from 30 percent to 40 percent. These data imply, of course, that there has been a rapid spreading apart of the income distribution, with the rich getting an increasing share of income. Since tax rates on the rich are higher than those on everyone else, tax revenues soared.

People with More than $200,000 in Income

	1994	1995	1996	1997	1998	1999	2000
Percentage of taxpayers	1.1	1.2	1.4	1.5	1.6	1.9	2.1
Percentage of U.S. income	15	16	18	20	22	24	26
Percentage of taxes paid	30	32	35	38	40	43	45

Source: Congressional Budget Office.

Why was there such a huge increase in the income of the rich? The stock market boomed in the 1990s. The gains from selling such stock are treated as income on which taxes must be paid. In addition, income and bonuses to people in start-up firms and to partners in law firms and financial firms grew rapidly, too. Whatever the reasons, this spreading of the income distribution underlies the switch from deficits to surpluses.

On the expenditure side of the budget, one must distinguish between *purchases* of goods and services (such as defense), *transfer payments* (such as social security and Medicare), and *interest payments*. Only purchases are included in the symbol G that we have been using in the text. Purchases represent *new* production, whether of computers, federal courthouses, or food for military troops. A surprisingly small fraction of the budget—less than 40 percent—is for the purchase of goods and services.

Interest payments are what the federal government pays every year on its debt. The government pays interest on its borrowings just like anyone else. In fiscal year 2001, interest payments amounted to $180 billion. Total interest payments equal the interest rate multiplied by the amount of government debt outstanding. For example, the interest rate on federal government debt averaged 5.2 percent in 1999, and total outstanding debt held by the public was about $3,320 billion ($180 billion in interest payments is approximately .054 times $3,320 billion).

The Federal Debt

federal debt: the total amount of outstanding loans owed by the federal government.

The **federal debt** is the total amount of outstanding loans that the federal government owes. If the government runs a surplus, the debt comes down by the amount of the surplus. If there is a deficit, the debt goes up by the amount of the deficit.

Consider an example involving thousands of dollars rather than trillions of dollars. Think of a student, Sam, who graduates from college with a $14,000 outstanding loan. In other words, he has a debt of $14,000. Suppose that the first year he works, his income is $30,000, but he spends $35,000. Sam's deficit for that year is $5,000, and his debt rises to $19,000. Assume that in his second year of work, he has income of $35,000 and spends $38,000; his deficit is $3,000, and his debt rises to $22,000. Each year his debt rises by the amount of his deficit. In the third year, Sam earns $40,000 and spends $33,000; he has a surplus of $7,000. This would reduce his debt to $15,000.

The laws of accounting that we apply to Sam also apply to Uncle Sam. The federal government's surplus of $236 billion in 2000 meant that the government paid back that amount of debt. As a result, the outstanding government debt decreased by $236 billion during 2000. Figure 13.3 shows the debt, deficit, and surpluses in the United States since 1950. Observe how the debt started to decline in 1998 when surpluses began.

■ **The Debt to GDP Ratio.** When looking at the debt and the deficit over time, it is important to consider the size of the economy. For example, a $3 trillion debt may not be much of a problem for an economy with a GDP of $10 trillion but could be overwhelming for an economy with a GDP of $1 trillion. An easy way to compare the debt to the size of the economy is to measure the debt as a percentage of GDP—the **debt to GDP ratio.** It is appropriate to consider the ratio of debt to nominal GDP rather than real GDP because the debt is stated in current dollars, just as nominal GDP is.

debt to GDP ratio: the total amount of outstanding loans the federal government owes divided by nominal GDP.

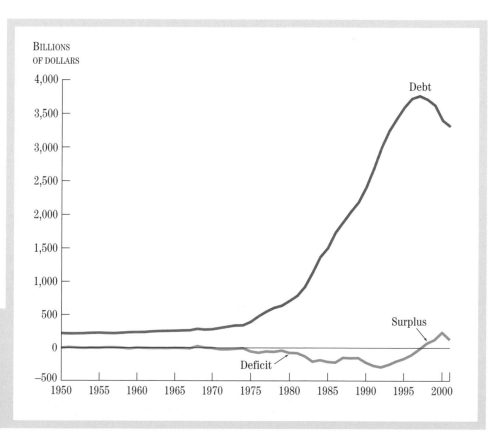

Figure 13.3
The Rise and Fall of Government Debt
When there is a deficit, the debt increases. When there is a surplus, the debt falls. The debt in 1950 was largely due to deficits during World War II.

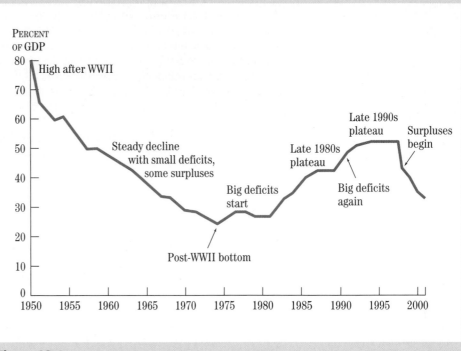

Figure 13.4
Debt as a Percentage of GDP
Relative to the size of GDP, the debt declined during the years after World War II. After rising for 20 years, the debt has been falling as a percentage of GDP since the late 1990s.

Figure 13.4 shows the behavior of the debt as a percentage of GDP in the United States since 1950. Note that the debt was a high percentage of GDP at the end of World War II because the U.S. government had borrowed large amounts to finance its military expenditures during the war. The debt to GDP ratio fell until the mid-1970s, when it began to increase again. The debt to GDP ratio is a good overall gauge of how a government is doing in managing its fiscal affairs.

State and Local Government Budgets

Much of the government spending and taxation in the United States occurs outside of the federal government, in state and local governments. Although fiscal policy usually refers to the plans of the federal government, it is the combined action of federal, state, and local governments that has an impact on the overall economy. For example, in the 1990–1991 recession, many states cut back on spending and raised taxes; both actions would tend to reduce real GDP in the short run, just as reduced spending and higher taxes at the federal level would. Taken as a whole, state and local governments are a large force in the economy. In 2001 state and local government expenditures were about two-thirds of federal government expenditures.

Most of the state and local government expenditures are for public schools, local police, fire services, and roads. Observe that state and local government *purchases* of goods and services are larger than federal government purchases, especially when national defense is excluded.

Unlike the federal government, the state and local governments have, on average, already been running deficits over the last year after a few years of surpluses.

REVIEW

- In the United States, the president submits a budget to Congress giving proposals for spending, for taxes, and for the deficit or surplus. The actual budget is different from the proposed budget because of congressional modifications and unforeseen events like unusually fast or slow economic growth.

- A budget surplus occurs when spending is less than tax revenues. Deficits occur when spending exceeds revenues.

- When a government or individual runs a deficit, the debt increases. Surpluses reduce the debt.

- It is appropriate to consider the debt in relation to the size of the economy by measuring it as a percentage of GDP.

- Federal government expenditures are larger than state or local government expenditures, but state and local government purchases are larger than federal government purchases.

Countercyclical Fiscal Policy

Government spending and taxes are called the *instruments* of fiscal policy. They are the variables that affect the economy. Now let's see how changes in the instruments of fiscal policy affect the size of economic fluctuations.

Impacts of the Instruments of Fiscal Policy

We first consider a change in government purchases and then go on to consider a change in taxes.

■ **Changes in Government Purchases.**   We know that if there is a change in government purchases, real GDP will initially change. If real GDP equaled potential GDP at the time of the change in government purchases, then real GDP would move away from potential GDP. Hence, a first lesson about fiscal policy is "do no harm." Erratic changes in government purchases can lead to fluctuations of real GDP away from potential GDP.

But suppose real GDP was already away from potential GDP. Then the change in government purchases could move real GDP closer to potential GDP. This is shown in Figure 13.5. In the top panel, real GDP starts out below potential GDP. An increase in government purchases shifts the aggregate demand curve to the right and moves real GDP back toward potential GDP. In the bottom panel, real GDP is above potential GDP, and a decrease in government purchases shifts the aggregate demand curve to the left, bringing real GDP back toward potential GDP. The important point is that a change in government purchases shifts the aggregate demand curve from wherever it happens to be at the time of the change.

Now, these effects of government purchases are short term. Eventually, prices will adjust; consumption, investment, and net exports will change; and real GDP will

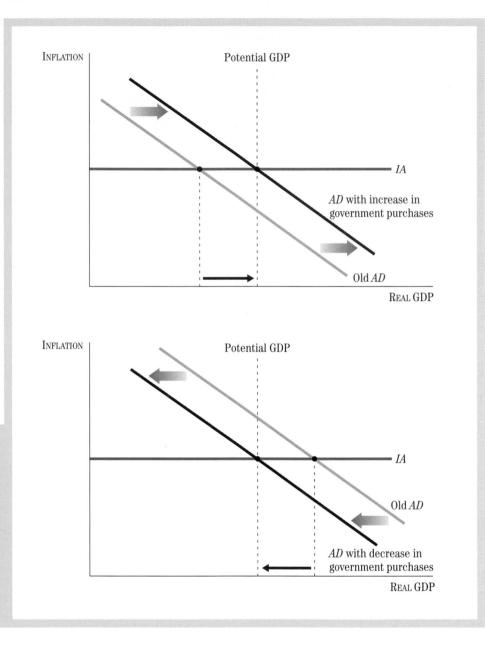

Figure 13.5
Effect of a Change in Government Purchases
If real GDP is below potential GDP, as in the top panel, an increase in government purchases, which shifts the *AD* curve to the right, will move real GDP toward potential GDP. If real GDP is above potential GDP, as in the bottom panel, a decrease in government purchases will move real GDP toward potential GDP. These are short-run effects.

return to potential GDP, regardless of the change in government purchases. Nevertheless, as we will see, the short-run impacts of government purchases provide fiscal policy with the potential power to reduce the size of economic fluctuations.

A decrease in government purchases for defense is one example of a leftward shift in the aggregate demand curve. An increase in government purchases on roads and bridges works in the opposite direction. Because the changes in government spending affect investment, in the long run they may affect potential GDP. But for now, we focus on how they can move the economy closer to potential GDP.

■ **Changes in Taxes.** A change in taxes also affects real GDP in the short run. At any given level of real GDP, people will consume less if there is a tax increase because

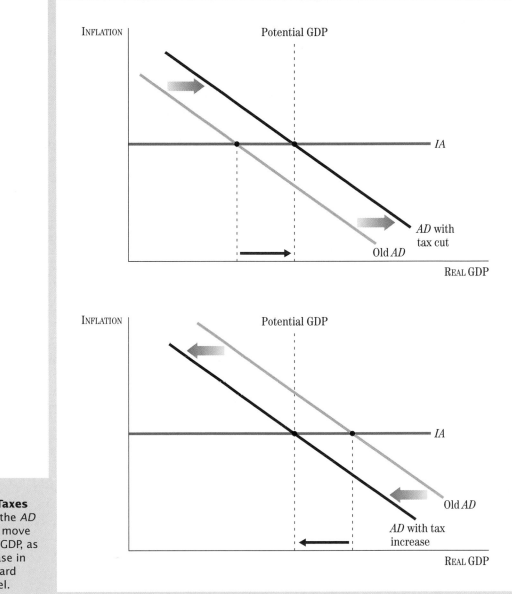

Figure 13.6
Effects of a Change in Taxes
A decrease in taxes shifts the *AD* curve to the right and can move real GDP toward potential GDP, as in the top panel. An increase in taxes moves real GDP toward potential in the lower panel.

they have less income to spend after taxes. They will consume more if there is a tax cut. In either case, the aggregate demand curve will shift. The top panel of Figure 13.6 shows how a tax cut will shift the aggregate demand curve to the right and push real GDP closer to potential GDP if it is below potential GDP. The bottom panel shows a tax increase reducing real GDP from a position above potential GDP. Again, these are short-term effects. Eventually prices will adjust and real GDP will return to potential GDP.

Both increases and decreases in taxes can also affect potential GDP. For example, if an increase in tax rates causes some people to work less, then the labor supply will not be as large and potential GDP will be lower. But here our focus is on the departures of real GDP from potential GDP.

Countercyclical Fiscal Policy

countercyclical policy: a policy designed to offset the fluctuations in the business cycle.

Because government spending and taxes affect real GDP in the short run, fiscal policy can, in principle, offset the impact of shocks that push real GDP away from potential GDP. Such use of fiscal policy is called **countercyclical policy,** because the cyclical movements in the economy are being "countered," or offset, by changes in government spending or taxes. Both booms and recessions can be countered, in principle. Recessions require cuts in taxes or increases in spending; booms require increases in taxes or cuts in spending.

Figure 13.7 shows what such a policy would ideally do. A possible recession in the year 2004 is shown, perhaps caused by a drop in foreign demand for U.S. products. Without any change in government purchases or taxes, the economy would eventually recover, as shown in the figure. But suppose that the government quickly cuts taxes or starts a road-building program. The hope is that this will raise real GDP, as shown in the figure, and hasten the return to potential GDP.

How would this work when prices are adjusting and the inflation rate is changing as well? Figure 13.8 provides the analysis. The recession is seen to be caused by the leftward shift in the aggregate demand curve. But the cut in taxes or increase in spending shifts the aggregate demand curve in the opposite direction. The aggregate demand curve shifts back to the right. If these countercyclical measures are timely enough and neither too small nor too large—both big ifs—then the recession may be small and short-lived. The example shows real GDP falling only slightly below potential GDP.

Figure 13.9 shows a less ideal case. Here government purchases are increased, but the response is too late. The increase occurs the year after the recession, during the recovery; it causes a boom, which could cause inflation to increase.

Disagreements about the usefulness of fiscal policy boil down to an assessment of whether Figure 13.7 or Figure 13.9 is more likely. Let's first consider some examples.

discretionary fiscal policy: changes in tax or spending policy requiring legislative or administrative action by the president or Congress.

■ **Discretionary Changes in the Instruments of Fiscal Policy.** Discretionary **fiscal policy** refers to specific changes in laws or administrative procedures, such as a change in an existing program to speed up spending, the creation of a new

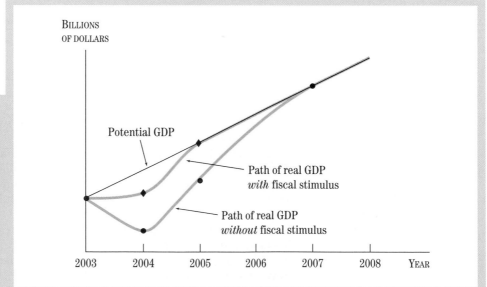

Figure 13.7
Effect of a Well-Timed Countercyclical Fiscal Policy
The figure shows a likely path of recovery from a recession caused by a decline in demand for U.S. products. A well-timed cut in taxes or increase in government purchases can reduce the size of the recession and bring real GDP back to potential GDP more quickly. The size of the economic fluctuation is smaller. The analysis is shown in Figure 13.8.

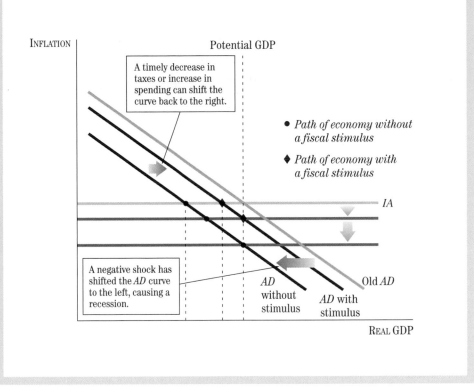

Figure 13.8
Analysis of a Well-Timed Countercyclical Fiscal Policy
A decline in demand—perhaps through a decrease in exports—shifts the *AD* curve to the left. Without a countercyclical fiscal policy, real GDP recovers back to potential GDP, but a timely cut in taxes or increase in government purchases can offset the drop in demand and bring real GDP back to potential GDP more quickly.

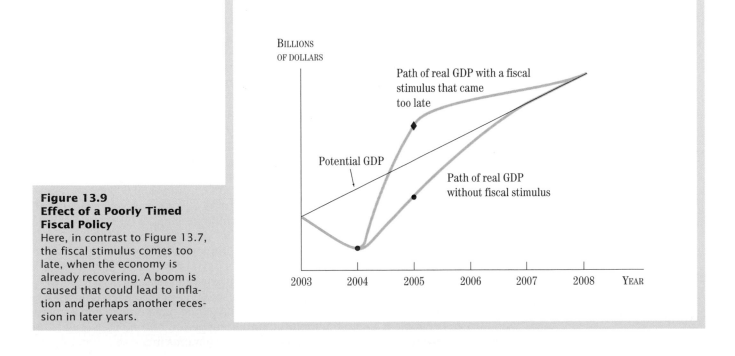

Figure 13.9
Effect of a Poorly Timed Fiscal Policy
Here, in contrast to Figure 13.7, the fiscal stimulus comes too late, when the economy is already recovering. A boom is caused that could lead to inflation and perhaps another recession in later years.

program (such as a new welfare program), or a change in the tax system (such as lower tax rates). These changes in the law are discretionary changes because they require action on the part of the Congress or the president.

One of the most significant post–World War II discretionary fiscal policy actions was the 1964 tax cut, proposed by President John F. Kennedy and enacted after his death when Lyndon Johnson was president. The early 1960s were a period when real GDP was below potential GDP, and this large discretionary tax cut was a factor in speeding the economic recovery. This cut in taxes also probably stimulated the growth of potential GDP and was therefore good for the long run.

Another example was the 1968 temporary income tax surcharge that raised tax rates by 10 percent. It was passed during the Vietnam War, when real GDP was above potential GDP, perhaps because the aim was to bring real GDP back toward potential GDP. However, in this case, the boom continued. The tax increase came long after the boom had started.

Another large discretionary fiscal policy action was the Reagan tax cut of the early 1980s, which lowered personal income tax rates by 25 percent. This tax cut helped the economy recover from the 1981–1982 recession. Like the Kennedy tax cut, this tax cut also probably raised the growth rate of potential GDP.

The most recent example of a discretionary fiscal policy is the Economic Growth and Tax Relief Reconciliation Act of 2001, enacted by Congress in June 2001. Among the sweeping changes in tax law introduced by this plan are lower income tax rates, more generous tax exemptions for married couples, and more generous tax exemptions for children. The first part of the plan was a $300 ($600 for couples) rebate check that the government mailed out to eligible taxpayers in the summer of 2001. The tax cut was helpful in raising spending during the recession, although the extent to which it helped is the source of some debate among economists, since many of the provisions are to be phased in over the next ten years instead of being effective immediately.

The impact of these examples of discretionary fiscal policy was neither as good as Figure 13.7 nor as bad as Figure 13.9. In none of these cases was the change in taxes speedy enough to offset a recession or a boom. The tax cuts came after the recessions, and the tax increase came after the boom. At best, the tax cuts speeded up the recovery.

■ **Automatic Changes in the Instruments of Fiscal Policy.** Discretionary actions by the government are not the only way in which taxes and spending can be changed. In fact, many of the very large changes in taxes and spending are automatic. Income tax revenues expand when people are making more and fall when people are making less. Thus, tax revenues respond automatically to the economy. Tax payments rise when the economy is in a boom and more people are working. Tax revenues fall when the economy is in a slump and unemployment rises.

These changes in tax revenues are even larger with a progressive income tax. With a *progressive tax* system, individual tax payments *rise* as a proportion of income as income increases. With a progressive tax, a person earning $100,000 per year pays proportionately more in taxes than a person earning $20,000 per year: Because of this progressive tax system, as people earn more, they pay a higher tax rate, and when they earn less, they pay a lower tax rate.

Parts of government spending also change automatically. Unemployment compensation, through which the government makes payments to individuals who are unemployed, rises during a recession. When unemployment rises, so do payments to unemployed workers. Social security payments also increase in a recession because people may retire earlier if job prospects are bad. Welfare payments rise in a recession because people who are unemployed for a long period of time may qualify for welfare. As poverty rates rise in recessions, welfare payments increase.

This article from the *New York Times* (August 23, 2001) discusses the factors that led to the end of a brief era of substantial budget surpluses in the United States. The article points out the two main culprits for the declining surplus—the economic slowdown and tax cuts (note that this article was published before September 11, 2001)—and shows how politically charged budget battles are likely to be. The article also discusses budget projections and how rapidly they change when the economy fluctuates. Finally, take note of how the article presents the absence of budget surpluses as an obstacle to discretionary fiscal policymaking.

Bush Projections Show Sharp Drop in Budget Surplus

By Richard W. Stevenson

Ending a brief but giddy era of fiscal plenty, the Bush administration released projections today showing that the federal budget surpluses outside the Social Security system will dwindle to almost nothing for the next several years. For the current fiscal year, the administration estimated, the government would run a surplus of about $600 million outside Social Security, an almost negligible amount in a $1.9 trillion budget and a $10 trillion economy. As recently as April, the White House projected a surplus of $122 billion in the non-Social Security system for the fiscal year, which ends on Sept. 30. Largely because of the tax cut passed by Congress this year and the economic slowdown, the surpluses outside Social Security will remain tiny for the next three or four years before beginning to grow again, the White House said. The government will continue to run substantial Social Security surpluses, the administration said, including $157 billion this year. But by agreement of the two parties, that money is off limits for spending or tax cuts and is reserved for reducing the national debt or shoring up the retirement system.

> **[Reasons for the dwindling surplus]**

The sharp turnabout comes just months after both parties were busily making plans for allocating what seemed to be an endless bounty from the prosperity of the late 1990's. It has set up a return to bitter budget battles and efforts by each party to turn the situation to its political advantage. White House officials sought to cast the news in the best possible light. They said that the country was still in sound financial condition and that an expected economic rebound should put enough money on the table over the next decade to deal with all the nation's priorities, especially if the tighter budget encourages Congress to pare wasteful or inefficient spending. Despite the economic slowdown, the surplus for this year, including Social Security, will still be the second largest on record. . . . The total surplus last year was $236.9 billion, a record.

Democrats responded that the administration had squandered the surplus by pushing through an irresponsibly large tax cut, putting the government into such a squeeze that not only Democratic initiatives but Mr. Bush's own agenda, including a big increase in military spending, would be impossible to carry out. "I believe President Bush's campaign promises are unraveling," said Senator Kent Conrad, Democrat of North Dakota, the chairman of the Senate Budget Committee. "He claimed we could afford his massive tax cut, a major defense buildup, more money for education, while paying down the debt and protecting Social Security and Medicare. He was wrong." . . . The new projections from the White House's Office of Management and Budget showed that the government would run a total budget surplus for the fiscal year ending Sept. 30 of $157.8 billion, of which $157.1 billion would come from Social Security. The surplus for next year, the administration projected, would be $173 billion, with $1 billion coming from outside Social Security. The total surplus in 2003 would be $195 billion, with $2 billion coming from outside Social Security. If those figures prove correct, it will mean that the government will spend nearly all of the surplus generated by part of the Medicare system, money that Democrats and most Republicans in Congress had also sought to put off limits. The Medicare surplus this year is about $30 billion.

> **[Forecast of future surpluses]**

The administration projected a gradual improvement in the fiscal outlook over the rest of the decade. The total surplus for the next decade should be $3.1 trillion, the White House said, compared with a projection of $5.6 trillion earlier this year, before the tax cut and the economic slowdown. It said the non-Social Security surplus for the next decade should be $575 billion, compared with a projection of $3.1 trillion at the beginning of the year. . . . The situation holds opportunity and peril for the administration and Republicans in Congress. To some degree, the administration's goal in pursuing the $1.35 trillion tax cut was to get as much of the surplus as possible out of Washington so that Congress could not spend it. Eliminating nearly all of the non-Social Security surplus limits the ability of Democrats—or Republicans for that matter—to propose big new spending programs. It also makes it easier for the administration to demand a reexamination of spending on programs that it opposes on policy grounds or judges to be ineffective. "The budget is tight, and that's exactly what we designed and exactly what we wanted," said Representative Jim Nussle, Republican of Iowa, the chairman of the House Budget Committee.

> **[Hence, the need for a "lockbox"?]**

automatic stabilizers: automatic tax and spending changes that occur over the course of the business cycle that tend to stabilize the fluctuations in real GDP.

These automatic tax and spending changes are called **automatic stabilizers** because they tend to stabilize the fluctuations of real GDP. How significant are these automatic stabilizers? Consider the 1990–1991 recession. Real GDP in 1989 was above potential GDP. But by late 1990 and 1991, real GDP was dropping below potential GDP. As this happened, government spending went up and taxes went down.

The magnitude of these effects was quite large. The difference between proposed and actual taxes and spending in the 1991 budget provides an estimate of the effect of the recession on taxes and spending. Tax revenue was $116 billion less than had been proposed before the recession. Thus, taxes were automatically reduced by this amount. However, spending was $91 billion more than had been proposed before the recession. Thus, spending rose by $91 billion in response to the recession. The combined effect of a $116 billion reduction in taxes and a $91 billion increase in spending was huge, and the timing was just about perfect. Since tax receipts went down in the recession and transfer payments went up, people's consumption was at a higher level than it would otherwise have been. These automatic changes in tax revenues and government spending tended to stabilize the economy and probably made the recession less severe than it would otherwise have been. These changes did not completely offset other factors, however, because there still was a recession.

The Discretion versus Rules Debate for Fiscal Policy

For many years economists have debated the usefulness of discretionary and automatic fiscal policy. Automatic fiscal policy is an example of a fiscal policy rule describing how the instruments of fiscal policy respond to the state of the economy. Thus, the debate is sometimes called the "discretion versus rules" debate.

The case for discretionary fiscal policy was made by President Kennedy's Council of Economic Advisers, which included Walter Heller and Nobel Prize–winning economist James Tobin. Proponents of discretionary fiscal policy argue that the automatic stabilizers will not be large enough or well-timed enough to bring the economy out of a recession quickly. Critics of discretionary policy, such as Milton Friedman, another Nobel Prize winner, emphasize that the effect of policy is uncertain and that there are long lags in the impact of policy. By the time spending increases and taxes are cut, a recession could be over; if so, the policy would only lead to an inflationary boom. Three types of lags are particularly problematic for discretionary fiscal policy: a *recognition lag,* the time between the need for the policy and the recognition of the need; an *implementation lag,* the time between the recognition of the need for the policy and its implementation; and an *impact lag,* the time between the implementation of the policy and its impact on real GDP.

Although lags and uncertainty continue to contribute to the discretion versus rules debate, other issues have also become central. Many economists feel that policy rules are desirable because of their stability and reliability. A fiscal policy rule emphasizing the automatic stabilizers might make government plans to reduce the deficit more believable. Countercyclical fiscal policy raises the deficit or reduces the surplus during recessions. With discretionary policy, there is no guarantee that the surplus will return or increase after the recession. With an automatic policy rule, there is an expectation that the deficit will decline after the recession is over.

Since the end of the 1980s, there have been few discretionary fiscal policy actions to counter recessions or booms in the United States or Europe. One reason discretionary actions did not occur was the high budget deficits and public concerns about the governments that had caused these deficits in the first place. The most significant discretionary fiscal policy of recent times, the tax cut enacted in June 2001, was facilitated by the large surpluses predicted for the economy, before the recession came along.

REVIEW	• Countercyclical fiscal policy is undertaken by governments to reduce economic fluctuations. The aim is to keep real GDP closer to potential GDP.
	• Two types of countercyclical fiscal policy are (1) discretionary policy, such as the Kennedy-Johnson tax cut, the 1968 tax surcharge, and the Reagan 1981 tax cut, and (2) automatic stabilizers, such as changes in unemployment payments, social security payments, and tax revenues due to changes in people's incomes.

The Structural versus the Cyclical Surplus

structural surplus: the level of the government budget surplus under the scenario where real GDP is equal to potential GDP; also called the full-employment surplus.

We noted earlier that taxes and spending change automatically in recessions and booms. These automatic changes affect the budget, so in order to analyze the budget, it is important to try to separate out these automatic effects. The *structural,* or *full-employment, surplus* was designed for this purpose. The **structural surplus** is what the surplus would be if real GDP equaled potential GDP.

Figure 13.10 introduces a graph to help explain the structural surplus. On the horizontal axis is real GDP. On the vertical axis is the budget surplus: tax revenues less expenditures. The budget is balanced when the surplus is zero, which is marked by a horizontal line in the diagram. The region below zero represents a situation in which taxes are less than spending and the government has a deficit. The region above zero is a situation in which the government budget has a surplus. On the horizontal axis, *A, B,* and *C* represent three different levels of real GDP.

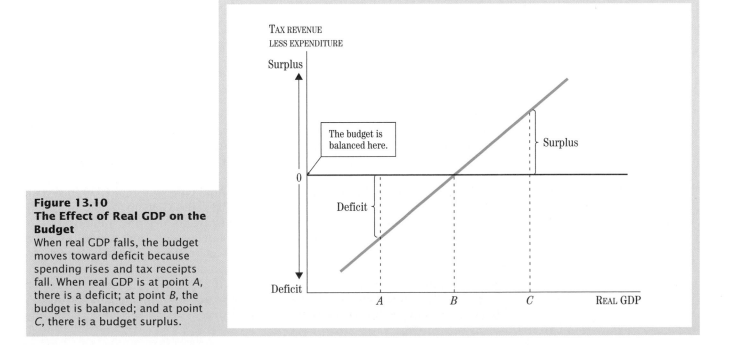

Figure 13.10
The Effect of Real GDP on the Budget
When real GDP falls, the budget moves toward deficit because spending rises and tax receipts fall. When real GDP is at point *A*, there is a deficit; at point *B*, the budget is balanced; and at point *C*, there is a budget surplus.

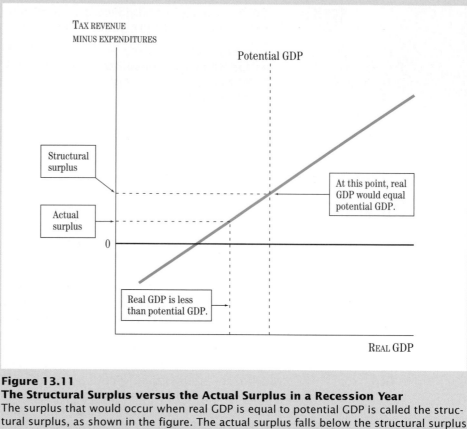

TAX REVENUE
MINUS EXPENDITURES

Potential GDP

Structural
surplus

At this point, real
GDP would equal
potential GDP.

Actual
surplus

0

Real GDP is less
than potential GDP.

REAL GDP

Figure 13.11
The Structural Surplus versus the Actual Surplus in a Recession Year
The surplus that would occur when real GDP is equal to potential GDP is called the structural surplus, as shown in the figure. The actual surplus falls below the structural surplus when real GDP falls below potential GDP. If there is a big recession, there could be an actual deficit even though there is a structural surplus.

The upward-sloping line in Figure 13.10 indicates that as real GDP rises, the budget surplus gets larger. Why? The automatic stabilizers are the reason. When real GDP rises, tax revenues rise and spending on transfer programs falls. Because the surplus is the difference between tax revenues and spending, the surplus gets larger. Conversely, when real GDP falls, tax receipts decline and spending on transfer programs increases, so the surplus falls. The upward-sloping line in Figure 13.10 pertains to a particular set of government programs and tax laws. A change in these programs or laws would *shift* the line. For example, a decrease in tax rates would shift the line down.

Figure 13.11, a similar diagram, shows potential GDP and real GDP in a year when real GDP is below potential GDP. Imagine raising real GDP up to potential GDP. We would predict that the surplus would go up, because tax receipts would rise as the economy grew and transfer payments would go down since there would be fewer people unemployed, fewer people retiring, and fewer people on welfare. As we move to the right in the diagram, the surplus gets larger. The structural surplus occurs when real GDP equals potential GDP.

The structural surplus provides a way to separate out cyclical changes in the budget caused by cyclical changes in the economy.

REVIEW
- Because tax revenues and spending fluctuate as the economy fluctuates, the surplus, or deficit, is cyclical. Deficits frequently arise or get bigger in recessions.
- The structural surplus adjusts the actual surplus for these cyclical changes in the economy.

Conclusion

Because the government is such a large player in the economy, its fiscal actions (spending, taxing, and borrowing) exert a powerful influence on real GDP and employment. Such actions can cause real GDP to depart from potential GDP and can alter the long-term growth rate of potential GDP.

A first principle of fiscal policy, therefore, is that government not take actions that would harm the economy. Avoiding erratic changes in fiscal policy and making sure that taxes are not increased during recessions are part of this first principle.

A second principle is that fiscal policy can be used to help smooth the fluctuations in the economy. Tax cuts and spending increases during recessions can help offset the declines in demand that cause recessions. Conversely, tax increases and spending cuts during booms can help offset the forces leading to inflation in the economy.

There is debate among economists about whether the government is capable of taking discretionary actions that will have these effects. Policy lags and uncertainty make discretionary fiscal policy difficult. There is little disagreement, however, about the importance of automatic stabilizers, under which tax and spending actions occur automatically without legislation. Automatic stabilizers cause the deficit to rise in recessions and fall during booms.

Another part of government policy that has powerful effects on the economy is monetary policy. We take up monetary policy in Chapter 14.

KEY POINTS

1. Fiscal policy consists of the government's plans for spending and taxes.

2. The government's budget is the primary document of fiscal policy. It gives the priorities for spending and taxes. In the United States, the president must submit a budget proposal to Congress.

3. The United States had large federal budget deficits from 1970 to 1997, and surpluses from 1998 to 2001.

4. Because Congress modifies the proposals and because of unanticipated events, the actual budget differs considerably from the proposed budget.

5. Changes in spending and taxes can move real GDP away from potential GDP in the short run. But in the long run, real GDP returns to potential GDP.

6. Discretionary changes in taxes and spending can be used to keep real GDP near potential GDP.

7. Lags and uncertainty make discretionary fiscal policy difficult.

8. Automatic stabilizers are an important part of fiscal policy. Tax revenues automatically decline in recessions. Transfer payments move in the reverse direction.

KEY TERMS

federal budget

balanced budget

budget surplus

budget deficit

federal debt

debt to GDP ratio

countercyclical policy

discretionary fiscal policy

automatic stabilizers

structural surplus

QUESTIONS FOR REVIEW

1. Why are actual expenditures and revenues always different from the president's proposals?

2. How is the government's debt affected by the government's budget surplus?

3. Why would a tax cut in a recession reduce the size of the recession?

4. Why might a proposal to cut taxes in a recession do little to mitigate the recession?

5. What is meant by the discretion versus rules debate?

6. What are automatic stabilizers, and how do they help mitigate economic fluctuations?

7. What is the difference between the structural surplus and the actual surplus?

8. What would happen to the actual surplus in a recession?

PROBLEMS

1. Suppose real GDP is less than potential GDP. Use a diagram with inflation on the vertical axis and real GDP on the horizontal axis to show the short-run, medium-run, and long-run effects of an increase in government purchases on the inflation rate and real GDP. Show how the aggregate demand curve and the inflation adjustment line shift over time.

2. Suppose you have the following data on projected and actual figures for the U.S. budget for 2004 (in billions of dollars).

	Projected Budget	Actual Budget
Taxes	2,200	2,100
Expenditures	2,100	2,200

a. What was the projected budget surplus or deficit? What was the actual budget surplus or deficit? Why might this happen?

b. If the government debt is $3,000 billion at the end of 2003, what is the debt at the end of 2004?

c. If GDP is $11,000 billion in 2004, what is the debt to GDP ratio? How does this compare to the debt to GDP ratio around 1990?

3. The Thai economy went into a recession in 1997 and 1998. Some people recommended reducing government spending in this situation. Was that good advice? Explain with a diagram.

4. Suppose the economy is currently $100 billion above potential GDP, and the government wants to pursue discretionary fiscal policy to cool off the economy. Show this situation using the aggregate demand curve. Indicate the effect on government purchases.

5. The federal budget deficit for the United States rose from about 3 percent of GDP in 1990 to about 5 percent of GDP in 1991.

a. Explain why at least part of this increase in the deficit was the result of the recession in 1991.

b. Suppose real GDP was equal to potential GDP in 1990 and below potential GDP in 1991. Sketch a diagram that shows the responsiveness of the deficit to GDP and show the structural surplus. Is it positive or negative?

c. Is it good or bad for the economy that the deficit increased as a result of the recession?

6. Examine the hypothetical budget data, shown at the top of the next page, for calendar years 1998–2001 (in billions of dollars).

Year	Budget Surplus	Government Debt as of January 1	GDP
1998	−150	1,000	4,000
1999	−100	1,150	4,200
2000	100		4,800
2001	200		5,400

    a. Fill in the missing values in the table.
    b. What is the percentage change in debt and GDP from 1998 to 1999?
    c. Calculate the debt to GDP ratio for each year. How does this ratio change over time? Why?

7. Suppose you get a summer job working in Congress and a recession begins while you are there. Write a memo to your boss, who is a member of Congress, on the pros and cons of a big highway building program to combat the recession.

8. Suppose the government surplus is 3 percent of real GDP, but economists say that the structural surplus is 2 percent.
    a. Is real GDP currently above or below potential GDP? Why? Draw the diagram showing this situation.
    b. In your diagram, show the situation when real GDP falls.

9. Suppose that real GDP has just fallen below potential GDP in a recession and the Council of Economic Advisers is trying to forecast the recovery from the recession. They are uncertain about whether Congress will pass the president's proposed tax cut right away or will delay a year. Trace out two possible scenarios with an *AD-IA* diagram that describes the uncertainty.

10. Suppose Congress is considering a balanced budget amendment to the Constitution that requires that the budget be balanced every fiscal year. Explain how this law could make the economy more unstable.

CHAPTER 14

Monetary Policy

I t was February 2002, and Alan Greenspan was testifying before Congress about the Fed's most recent *Monetary Policy Report to Congress.* In this report, Greenspan and the Fed reported that "last year was a difficult one for the economy of the United States. The slowdown in the growth of economic activity that had become apparent in late 2000 intensified in the first half of the year." However, they reiterated their belief that the Fed had helped minimize the adverse impacts of the developments of 2001 by acting quickly to cut interest rates. As they put it in their report, "The aggressive actions by the Federal Reserve to ease the stance of monetary policy in the first half of the year provided support to consumer spending and the housing sector." Furthermore, even though the Fed had, at least for the moment, stopped cutting interest rates, Greenspan outlined the stance of monetary policy in the months ahead: "However, reflecting a concern that growth could be weaker than the economy's potential for a time, the FOMC retained its assessment that the risks were tilted unacceptably toward economic weakness." In other words, the Fed believed that recession, not inflation, was the major threat at this point.

Notice, though, that Greenspan was testifying about his actions in the prior year. He clearly did not need to get permission from Congress to act; he was merely providing Congress with information about the Fed's policy decisions. What is the rationale for Congress giving Alan Greenspan and the Fed so much independence to set interest rates? Furthermore, notice that the Fed seemed to indicate that output had gone below potential output, thus making it more likely that the Fed would lower rates rather than raise them. But at what point would the Fed decide that the risks were no longer "tilted unacceptably toward economic weakness"? Would it then start raising rates again? Should we give one individual (Alan Greenspan), or one group of people (the FOMC) the power to decide what is acceptable and what is not?

The purpose of this chapter is to answer these and other monetary policy–related questions. We will first explain why central banks that are independent may bring about better economic performance. We will then examine the complexity of the decision facing the monetary policymaker who is given the independence to make policy decisions, and also consider some policy tools that such policymakers have at their disposal. Finally, we will look at how governments can choose to restrict their monetary policymakers' freedom by choosing to tie the value of their currency to that of another country's currency.

Why Are Central Banks Independent?

The most important feature of a central bank, whether it is the Fed, the Bank of Japan, or the European Central Bank, is the degree of independence from the government that the law gives it.

Fed officials are appointed to long terms that may span several different presidents; the four-year term of the chair of the Fed does not necessarily coincide with the term of any president. For example, Paul Volcker served through most of the Reagan years, even though he was appointed by President Carter. Alan Greenspan, originally appointed by President Reagan, served throughout the eight years of the Clinton presidency. Therefore, like Supreme Court justices in the United States, Fed officials develop an independence from governmental influence.

central bank independence: a description of the legal authority of central banks to make decisions on monetary policy with little interference by the government in power.

What is the rationale for **central bank independence?** The main rationale, as explained below, is that an independent central bank can prevent the government in power from using monetary policy in ways that appear beneficial in the short run but that can harm the economy in the long run.

William McChesney Martin 1951–1969   *Arthur Burns* 1969–1978   *G. William Miller* 1978–1979   *Paul Volcker* 1979–1987   *Alan Greenspan* 1987–

Fifty Years of Fed Chairs
There have been five chairs of the Federal Reserve Board during the past 50 years.

The "Gain Then Pain" Scenario

We showed in Chapter 12 that a shift in monetary policy toward a higher inflation target will temporarily raise real GDP above potential GDP, but that only inflation will be higher in the long run. Such a change in monetary policy would first entail a reduction in interest rates and would shift the aggregate demand (*AD*) curve to the right, as shown in Figure 14.1. Real GDP would rise along with investment, consumption, and net exports; unemployment would fall. In the short run, there would be no effect on inflation because of the slowness of firms to change their price decisions. The economic gain from the reduction in unemployment without an increase in inflation might help in a reelection, or it might enable the government to push legislation for new programs through the political system. The economic pain—higher inflation in the long run, also shown in Figure 14.1—would not be seen until after the election or after the legislation is passed.

Thus, there is a natural tendency toward higher inflation in the political system. If the government in power had complete control over the decisions of the central bank, it could take actions to make the economy look good in the short run for political purposes and not worry that it might look bad in the long run. Removing the central bank from the direct control of the government reduces this politically induced bias toward higher inflation because it is then more difficult for the government to get the central bank to take such actions.

■ **The Phillips Curve.**   Observe that during the period of time when the *IA* line is shifting up in the gain then pain scenario, real GDP is above potential GDP, and the inflation rate is higher than at the start of the scenario. For example, there is higher inflation and higher real GDP at the point labeled *MR* in Figure 14.1 than at the starting point. And during this period, the unemployment rate is lower because the unemployment rate falls when real GDP rises. In sum, during the period of time

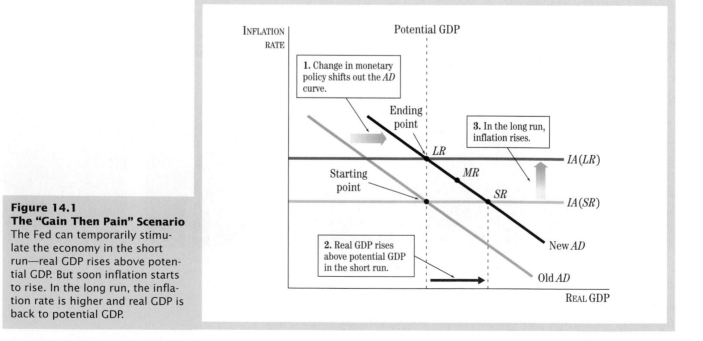

Figure 14.1
The "Gain Then Pain" Scenario
The Fed can temporarily stimulate the economy in the short run—real GDP rises above potential GDP. But soon inflation starts to rise. In the long run, the inflation rate is higher and real GDP is back to potential GDP.

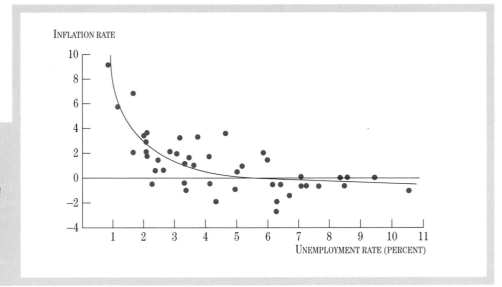

Figure 14.2
The Original Phillips Curve
A. W. Phillips first published this graph. Each point represents one year. The negatively sloped curve drawn through the scatter of points had enormous influence and led some to argue, mistakenly, that there was a long-run tradeoff between inflation and unemployment.

between the initial shift of the *AD* curve and the end of the scenario, the unemployment rate is *down* and the inflation rate is *up*. Thus, there is a negative correlation between unemployment and inflation.

In fact, a negative correlation between unemployment and inflation has been observed for many years in the real world, because of such shifts in the *AD* curve. This negative correlation between inflation and unemployment is called the *Phillips curve,* after A. W. Phillips, the economist who first showed that such correlations existed in British data from 1861–1957. A replica of the original Phillips curve is shown in Figure 14.2.

The Phillips curve was used in the 1960s and 1970s to justify a monetary policy that included higher inflation. People argued that higher inflation would lead to lower unemployment. In other words, they argued that there was a long-run tradeoff between inflation and unemployment.

How did they use the Phillips curve to support this view? Look at the Phillips curve in Figure 14.2. You might think that a monetary policy that aimed for higher inflation could lead to a lower unemployment rate in the long run. That is what the curve seems to suggest. But the theory in the *AD-IA* diagram, and, in particular, the gain then pain scenario, shows that there is no such tradeoff in the long run. If monetary policy raised inflation, eventually real GDP would return to potential GDP, the unemployment rate would return to the natural rate, and we would be left with only higher inflation, not lower unemployment.

It has become a basic principle of modern macroeconomics—implied by the *AD-IA* diagram—that there is no long-run tradeoff between inflation and unemployment. The facts are consistent with the principle: In the 1950s and early 1960s, inflation was low; in the late 1960s and 1970s, inflation was high, and in the 1980s and 1990s, inflation was low again. But the average unemployment rate in all these periods was roughly the same, around 5 or 6 percent. In particular, the higher inflation in the middle period did not result in lower unemployment. Any tendency for unemployment and inflation to be negatively correlated will disappear in the long run. This does not mean that there will be no short-run gain from a higher-inflation monetary policy. It does mean that there will be long-run pain.

Check your thinking about the implications of the gain then pain scenario for the relationship between unemployment and inflation.

In the short run, between the start and end of the scenario:

Inflation ↑
Real GDP > potential GDP
Unemployment rate <
            natural rate

So there is a negative correlation between inflation and unemployment, a Phillips curve.

In the long run:

Inflation ↑
Real GDP = potential GDP
Unemployment rate =
            natural rate

So there is no long-run tradeoff between inflation and unemployment.

political business cycle: a business cycle caused by politicians' use of economic policy to overstimulate the economy just before an election.

■ **The Political Business Cycle.** The **political business cycle** is the tendency of governments to use economic policy to cause real GDP to rise and unemployment to fall just before an election and then let the economy slow down right after the election. Many economic and political studies have shown that an incumbent's chances of being reelected are increased greatly if the economy is doing well. After the election, inflation may rise and cause a bust, but that would be long before the next election.

Research in the 1970s by William Nordhaus of Yale University uncovered some evidence of a political business cycle in the United States. For example, the strong economy before the 1972 election may have been due to a monetary policy change that pushed real GDP above potential GDP. On the other hand, the U.S. economy was in a recession just before the 1980 and 1992 elections—the exact opposite of a political business cycle. Thus, the evidence of a political business cycle in the United States is no longer strong. In any case, political business cycles are harmful to the economy. Preventing political business cycles is another reason for having a central bank that has some independence from the politicians that are in power.

■ **Time Inconsistency.** The temptation to use monetary policy for short-run gain despite the long-run pain is difficult for governments to resist. Even governments whose sole aim is to improve the well-being of the average citizen will say that they want low inflation but then stimulate the economy in order to lower unemployment, even though they are fully aware of the inflationary consequences down the road.

time inconsistency: the situation in which policymakers have the incentive to announce one economic policy but then change that policy after citizens have acted on the initial, stated policy.

This situation is known as **time inconsistency** because governments say they want low inflation but are later inconsistent by following policies that lead to higher inflation. They act like a teacher who tells the class that there will be an exam to get the students to study, but then, on the day of the exam, announces that the exam is canceled. The students are happy to miss the exam, and the teacher does not have to grade it. Everyone appears better off in the short run.

However, just as the teacher who cancels the exam will lose credibility with future classes, a central bank that tries the inconsistent policy will lose credibility. People will assume that the central bank will actually raise inflation even if it says it is aiming for low inflation.

Potential Disadvantages of Central Bank Independence

Central bank independence is no guarantee against monetary policy mistakes, however, and it could even lead to more mistakes. In principle, an independent central bank could cause more inflation than a central bank under the control of the government. For example, those in charge of the central bank could—after they are appointed—succumb to arguments that high inflation is not so harmful after all. Or, at the other extreme, those in charge of the central bank could become so focused on inflation that they are blinded to the effects of monetary policy on real GDP and employment and could either cause a recession or make an existing recession deeper or longer. Thus, a disadvantage of central bank independence is that it can be taken too far.

Whether independent or not, central banks need to be held *accountable* for their actions. If those in charge of the central bank do not perform their job well, it is appropriate that they not be reappointed. When the central bank of New Zealand was given greater independence in the 1980s, its accountability was formalized very explicitly: If the head of the central bank does not achieve low inflation goals agreed to in advance, the head is fired. But the central bank has independence in determining how to achieve these goals.

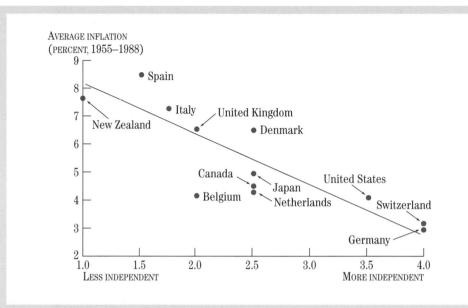

Figure 14.3
Central Bank Independence and Inflation
The scatter plot shows that the more independent a central bank is, the lower the average inflation rate. The independence of the central bank is calculated by studying the laws of each country, including the length of the term of office of the head of the central bank (a longer term means more independence) and restrictions on the central bank lending to the government.

Is there any evidence that independence has led to better inflation performance without any increase in the severity or frequency of recessions? If you look at Figure 14.3, you will see that central banks that have more independence have had lower inflation. This lower inflation has not been associated with more or longer recessions. Note that the graph shows New Zealand *before* the central bank was given more independence; since then, it has moved down and to the right, toward lower inflation.

REVIEW

- The gain then pain scenario shows that a central bank can lower unemployment below the natural unemployment rate in the short run, but by doing so it will raise inflation in the long run.

- The Phillips curve is a negative correlation between inflation and unemployment. However, there is no long-run tradeoff between inflation and unemployment.

- Central bank independence insulates the central bank from short-run political pressures to overstimulate the economy, which would ultimately raise inflation.

- Countries with more independent central banks have tended to have lower inflation than countries with less independent central banks.

Trying to Bring the Aggregate Demand Curve into Line in 2000

The previous section showed the inflationary harm caused by a monetary policy that intentionally pushes the aggregate demand curve to the right and raises real GDP above potential GDP. But even independent central bankers who have no intention of pursuing such an inflationary policy must still worry about shocks or unintentional shifts in the aggregate demand curve that would push real GDP away from potential GDP.

In fact, when the inflation rate is at the target inflation rate, monetary policy is a constant struggle to manage aggregate demand so as to keep real GDP near potential GDP, and thereby prevent inflation from veering away from its target. In this section, we illustrate this struggle with a case study of monetary policy in the United States in early 2000. It then appeared to the Fed that aggregate demand was too high and needed to be reduced with higher interest rates.

Aggregate Demand: Just Right, Too Hot, or Too Cold?

First consider Figure 14.4, which illustrates the problem monetary policy faces in trying to keep real GDP near to potential GDP. There are three graphs in Figure 14.4, each illustrating a different situation.

■ **The Goldilocks Economy: Just Right.** In the middle graph, the aggregate demand curve intersects the inflation adjustment line at the point where real GDP equals potential GDP and the inflation rate is equal to the target inflation rate. Because real GDP is equal to potential GDP, there is no tendency for inflation to rise or to fall. Thus, this graph represents an ideal point: The inflation rate is equal to the target inflation rate, and real GDP is equal to potential GDP. The aggregate demand curve is in the correct place, because it intersects the inflation adjustment line at the point where real GDP equals potential GDP *and* where the inflation rate equals the target inflation rate. Financial market analysts refer to this situation as a "Goldilocks economy": not too hot, not too cold, just right.

■ **A Misalignment: Aggregate Demand Is Too High.** In contrast to the middle panel in Figure 14.4, the other two panels represent misalignments of real GDP and potential GDP. In the right-hand panel, aggregate demand has increased too much—perhaps because of an expansionary shift in consumption, investment, or net exports. At this position, there are inflationary forces in place that will soon cause the inflation adjustment line to rise. Unlike the short-run position in Figure 14.1 (the gain then pain scenario, where the central bank has intentionally shifted monetary policy), the situation in the right-hand panel of Figure 14.4 is unintentional. The task of monetary policy is to try to prevent such misalignments, and to correct such misalignments once they occur.

How would the central bank correct this type of misalignment? It would raise the real interest rate above the level it would choose in the middle graph. The higher real interest rate would reduce aggregate demand and bring the *AD* curve back to a point where it intersected the inflation adjustment line at potential GDP. Financial market analysts would say that the Fed was trying to "cool off the economy" by raising the interest rate in this way.

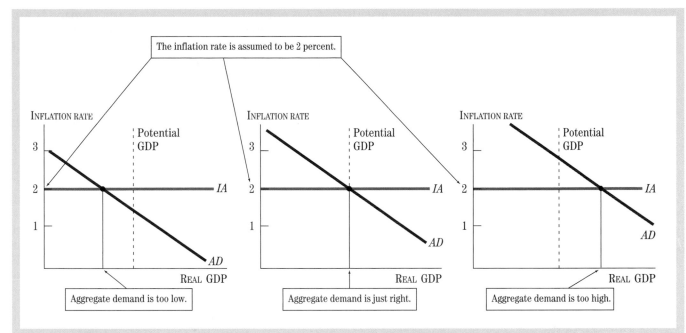

Figure 14.4
Aligning the Aggregate
Demand Curve

The aggregate demand curve is lined up correctly when real GDP equals potential GDP and the inflation rate is on target, as in the graph in the middle. Otherwise, aggregate demand is too high, and the Fed must raise the interest rate; or aggregate demand is too low, and the Fed must lower the interest rate.

■ **Another Type of Misalignment: Aggregate Demand Is Too Low.**   The left panel of Figure 14.4 represents the opposite, but no less undesirable, type of misalignment of real GDP and potential GDP. In this case, aggregate demand has gotten too low—perhaps because of a contractionary shift in consumption, investment, or net exports. With real GDP less than potential GDP, the inflation adjustment line will soon fall below the target inflation rate. Moreover, with real GDP below potential GDP, unemployment has increased. Monetary policy should try to prevent or correct this type of misalignment, too.

To correct such a misalignment, the central bank would lower the real interest rate below the level it would choose in the top right graph. The lower real interest rate would increase consumption, investment, and net exports and bring the *AD* curve back to the right.

Monetary Policy in Early 2000

For much of the economic expansion of the 1990s, the United States economy was much like the Goldilocks economy in the middle graph in Figure 14.4. The Fed had done a good job at estimating potential GDP and had managed to keep real GDP close to potential GDP during this period.

■ **"Rising Inflationary Pressure."**   However, by 1999, real GDP was clearly growing faster than potential GDP, and by early 2000 the Fed was convinced that real GDP was above potential GDP, a situation "that contains the seeds of rising inflationary and financial pressure," as the Fed put it in the February 2000 *Monetary Policy Report to Congress.*

The situation in early 2000 was exactly the one in the "Aggregate Demand Is Too High" graph of Figure 14.4. There had been no increase in inflation, but with real GDP above potential GDP, the Fed was concerned that inflation would rise. The Fed's analysis is the same as that contained in the *AD-IA* diagram, which is not surprising, since the type of model used by the economists at the Fed is essentially the same as the one in that diagram.

Why did the Fed think the aggregate demand curve had shifted? The main factor was the U.S. stock market. With stock prices having risen rapidly in 1998 and 1999, people were feeling wealthier, the Fed reasoned, and they would raise their consumption purchases, shifting up aggregate demand. Here is how Alan Greenspan put it in his congressional testimony: "Perhaps three to four cents out of every additional dollar of stock market wealth eventually is reflected in increased consumer purchases. The sharp rise in the amount of consumer outlays . . . has been consistent with this so-called wealth effect on household purchases."

Because of this shift in the aggregate demand curve, the Fed explained, "the level of interest rates needed to align demand with potential supply may have increased substantially." The Fed felt that it would have to raise the nominal interest rate to raise the real interest rate and rein in aggregate demand to bring real GDP back into equality with potential GDP. In the spring and summer of that year, the Fed did raise the federal funds rate to $6\frac{1}{2}$ percent from $5\frac{1}{2}$ percent. At its last summer meeting that year (August 22, 2000), the Federal Open Market committee decided that $6\frac{1}{2}$ percent was enough for the time being, and it issued a statement explaining its decision. Here is the statement, along with a hint of what the risks looked like:

> The Federal Open Market Committee at its meeting today decided to maintain the existing stance of monetary policy, keeping its target for the federal funds rate at $6\frac{1}{2}$ percent. Recent data have indicated that the expansion of aggregate demand is moderating. . . . Nonetheless, the Committee remains concerned about the risk of a continuing gap between the growth of demand and potential supply. . . . The Committee believes the risks continue to be weighted mainly toward conditions that may generate heightened inflation pressures in the foreseeable future.

Observe how the *AD-IA* diagram captures six key elements in the Fed's analysis in this case study:

1. Real GDP rose above potential GDP because aggregate demand had shifted.

2. Aggregate demand shifted as a result of a shift in consumption spending.

3. With real GDP above potential GDP, inflation was predicted to rise.

4. But inflation had not yet risen, because it adjusts slowly.

5. The Fed increased interest rates to bring real GDP back to potential GDP.

6. After increasing the interest rate, the Fed took a breather and reported that aggregate demand was moderating.

■ **The Inherent Uncertainty in Monetary Policy.** This case study also illustrates that, in practice, it is not easy for the Fed to keep real GDP near potential GDP by varying the interest rate. Although the Fed increased interest rates to rein in aggregate demand, there was concern that real GDP would not respond as quickly as in the past. At the time, it appeared that investment and consumption might be less responsive than the Fed thought they would be to the increase in the interest rate. That is why the Fed said it was "concerned about the risk" that aggregate demand might still grow too rapidly.

In general, there is a great deal of uncertainty about how long it takes for a change in the interest rate to affect aggregate demand. Other things affect aggregate demand too, and some of those things might work in the opposite direction to the change in interest rates.

Moreover, potential GDP is very difficult to estimate. Recall that potential GDP is determined by the underlying supply of labor, capital, and technological change. In many situations, central banks do not know for sure whether real GDP is or is not equal to potential GDP. Uncertainty about potential GDP is particularly high during periods when technology seems to be changing rapidly and the path of potential GDP is changing, as it was in 2000.

The Reaction to the Gap Between Real GDP and Potential GDP

Observe that in order to bring real GDP into alignment with potential GDP in this case study, the Fed reacted to the *gap*, or the *difference*, between real GDP and potential GDP. That is, it raised the real interest rate when real GDP rose above potential GDP. Similarly, if real GDP were to fall below potential GDP, as shown in the top left graph of Figure 14.4, the Fed would lower the real interest rate.

This type of interest rate reaction to the gap between real GDP and potential GDP is typical of the Fed and many other central banks. It represents a good policy response, because it tends to move the aggregate demand curve in a way that brings real GDP back into equality with potential GDP.

This interest rate reaction is similar to the reaction of central banks to changes in the inflation rate. Recall that such reactions of the real interest rate to inflation are described by the monetary policy rule introduced in Chapter 11. In fact, it is possible to combine both reactions—the reaction to inflation and the reaction to the gap—into one monetary policy rule, and thereby obtain a more accurate description of central bank behavior. Remember that a monetary policy rule is a description of a central bank's behavior in the same sense that a microeconomic demand curve is a description of a person's consumption behavior. Just as a person's purchase decisions may depend on two variables, (1) price and (2) income, so too the central bank's real interest rate decisions may depend on two variables, (1) the inflation rate and (2) the gap between real GDP and potential GDP.

Table 14.1 shows a numerical example of this type of policy rule. On the left is the inflation rate. On the top is the gap between real GDP and potential GDP. The entries

Table 14.1
Real Interest Rate Reaction to Inflation and to the Gap Between Real GDP and Potential GDP (Compare with Table 11.1 on page 262.)

| | | Percent Gap Between Real GDP and Potential GDP | | |
		−2	0	2
Inflation Rate	0	0	1	2
(percent)	2	1	2	3
	4	2	3	4
	6	3	4	5
	8	4	5	6

(The entries in the shaded area show the real interest rate for each inflation rate and gap between real GDP and potential GDP.)

in the shaded part of the table show the real interest rate. For example, the blue entry shows that when inflation is 2 percent and real GDP is equal to potential GDP (the percent gap between real GDP and potential GDP is zero), the real interest rate is 2 percent. When inflation rises to 4 percent, the real interest rate rises to 3 percent. Each column of Table 14.1 tells the same story: When inflation rises, the central bank raises the real interest rate. Note that in order to raise the real interest rate, the nominal interest rate has to rise by more than inflation rises.

Now observe in Table 14.1 that the central bank's response also depends on what happens to real GDP. When real GDP rises above potential GDP—and the gap increases—the central bank raises the real interest rate. And when real GDP falls below potential GDP, the central bank lowers the real interest rate.

The monetary policy rule in Table 14.1 is a more accurate description of monetary policy than the rule in Table 11.1 because central banks do react to the gap between real GDP and potential GDP, as the case study of the Fed makes clear. Hence, financial market analysts use monetary policy rules like this one to predict interest rate changes in many different countries.

> The **Taylor Rule,** a form of the monetary policy rule described by Table 14.1, is used by economists to describe the behavior of the Federal Reserve.

REVIEW

- Monetary policy is a constant struggle to keep aggregate demand from getting too high or too low. The Fed carries out this policy by trying to keep the aggregate demand curve in a position where real GDP is equal to potential GDP and the inflation rate is equal to the target inflation rate.

- The Fed and other central banks increase the real interest rate when real GDP grows above potential GDP and lower the real interest rate when real GDP falls below potential GDP.

- In early 2000, the Fed increased the real interest rate because it thought real GDP was greater than potential GDP.

- The response of the real interest rate to the gap between real GDP and potential GDP can be combined with the response to inflation in order to get a monetary policy rule that accurately describes central bank behavior.

Money and Other Instruments of Monetary Policy

> **Look back for a quick review:** Chapter 9, pages 209–210, defines open market operations and shows how the Fed uses them to make changes in the supply of bank reserves. Chapter 11, page 263, shows how the Fed increases or decreases the federal funds rate through such changes in the supply of bank reserves.

So far, we have focused entirely on the Fed's decisions about the interest rate, and in particular about the overnight interest rate called the federal funds rate. Recall from Chapter 11 that the Fed changes the overnight interest rate by increasing or decreasing the supply of bank reserves in the overnight market where the federal funds rate is determined. Recall that the federal funds rate is the interest rate on overnight loans of reserves between banks. The Fed changes the supply of bank reserves by *open market operations*, which, as defined in Chapter 9, are purchases or sales of bonds by the Fed. Purchases of bonds increase the supply of bank reserves and thus lower the overnight interest rate. Sales of bonds decrease the supply of bank reserves and thus raise the overnight interest rate.

The overnight interest rate is now the main instrument of monetary policy at central banks around the world, but it is not the only instrument. The money supply, the discount rate, and reserve requirements are other potential instruments of policy. In this section we examine how the changes in the interest rate have important implications for the amount of money that the Fed supplies. We also define the discount rate and show how it and reserve requirements fit into monetary policy decisions.

Money Demand, the Interest Rate, and the Money Supply

The quantity of money in the economy is closely related to the interest rate decisions of the central bank. To show this, we first look at the demand for money and show that it depends on the nominal interest rate.

money demand: a relationship between the nominal interest rate and the quantity of money that people are willing to hold at any given nominal interest rate.

■ **Money Demand.**   **Money demand** is defined as a relationship between the interest rate and the quantity of money people are willing to hold at any given interest rate. As shown in Figure 14.5, the amount of money demanded is negatively related to the nominal interest rate. One reason people hold money is to carry out transactions: to buy and sell goods and services. People will hold less money if the nominal interest rate is high. That is, a higher interest rate reduces the amount of money people want to carry around in their wallets or hold in their checking accounts. Conversely, a lower nominal interest rate will increase the amount of money people want to hold. Why is money demand negatively related to the nominal interest rate?

Money (currency plus checking deposits) is only part of the wealth of most individuals. People also hold some of their wealth in financial assets that pay interest. For example, some people have time deposits at banks. Others hold securities, such as Treasury bills. If you bought Treasury bills in 2000, they paid 6 percent interest. Holding money is different from holding time deposits or Treasury bills because currency does not pay interest and checking deposits pay low, or no, interest. If you hold all your money in the form of cash in your wallet, clearly you do not earn any interest. Thus, an individual's decision to hold money is best viewed as an alternative to holding some other financial asset, such as a Treasury bill. If you hold money, you get little or no interest; if you hold one of the alternatives, you earn interest.

The interest rate on the vertical axis in Figure 14.5 is the average nominal interest rate on these other interest-bearing assets that people hold as alternatives to money. Now, if the interest rate on these alternatives rises, people want to put more funds in the alternatives and hold less as money. If they hold the funds as currency, they get no interest on the funds. If they hold the funds in a checking account, they may get a small amount of interest, but certainly less than they would get from other financial assets. There is a lower quantity of money demanded at higher interest rates because putting the funds in interest-bearing assets becomes more attractive compared to keeping the funds in a wallet.

The interest rate on the alternatives to holding money is the *opportunity cost* of holding money. When the opportunity cost increases, people hold less money. When the opportunity cost decreases, people hold more money.

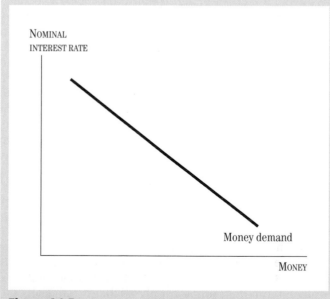

Figure 14.5
The Demand for Money
The interest rate is the opportunity cost of holding money. A higher interest rate on Treasury bills or other interest-bearing assets raises the opportunity cost of holding money and lowers the quantity of money demanded.

Figure 14.5 represents money demand in the economy as a whole. The curve is obtained by adding up the money demanded by all the individuals in the economy at each interest rate. The money held by businesses—in cash registers or in checking accounts—should also be added in.

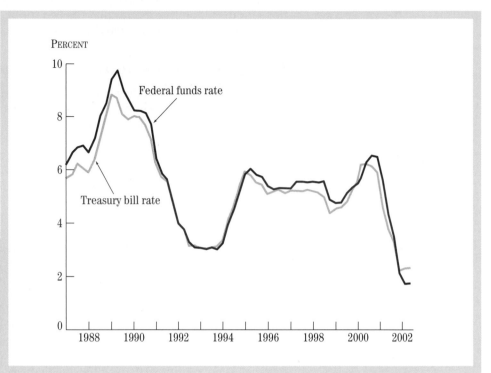

Figure 14.6
Short-Term Interest Rates
The federal funds rate is the interest rate the Fed focuses on when deliberating about policy. Other short-term interest rates, such as the Treasury bill rate, move up and down with the federal funds rate.

■ **The Interest Rate and the Quantity of Money.**   Using the money demand curve, it is possible to find the quantity of money in the economy that will be associated with any given nominal interest rate decision by the Fed. First note that there is a very close correlation between the federal funds rate set by the Fed and interest rates on Treasury bills and other interest-bearing assets that people can hold as an alternative to holding money. This close correlation is shown in Figure 14.6. Thus, when the Fed changes the federal funds rate, other interest rates tend to change in the same direction.

Now, for any given interest rate, one can use the money demand curve to find the quantity of money in the economy. This is illustrated in Figure 14.7. If the Fed lowers the federal funds rate, then the lower interest rate increases the quantity of money demanded and, as shown in the left panel, the quantity of money in the economy rises. Or, if the Fed raises the interest rate, the quantity of money in the economy decreases, as shown in the graph on the right of Figure 14.7.

■ **What About Focusing on the Money Supply?**   One question you might ask about Figure 14.7 is, "Where is the money supply?" Recall from Chapter 9 that the Fed controls the quantity of money supplied in the economy. Does the quantity of money supplied equal the quantity of money demanded? Yes, of course it does. The demand and supply of money is no different from any other demand and supply model. As monetary policy now works in the United States and most other countries, the central bank automatically adjusts the money supply so that it intersects the money demand curve at the nominal interest rate chosen by the central bank. For example, as the interest rate falls in the left graph of Figure 14.7, the money supply is automatically increased so that the intersection of money demand and money supply moves as shown. Figure 14.8 shows how the money supply shifts in both cases shown in Figure 14.7.

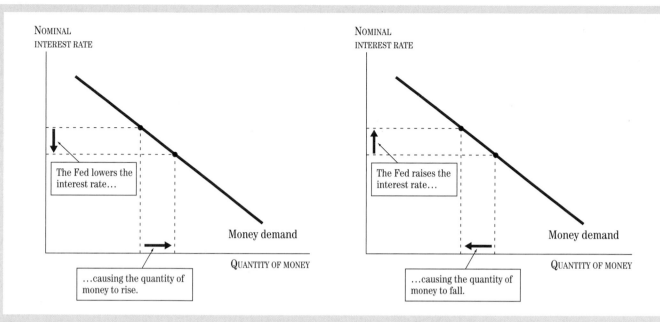

**Figure 14.7
When the Fed Changes the
Interest Rate, the Quantity
of Money Changes**

When the Fed lowers the interest rate, people want to hold more money. When the Fed raises the interest rate, people want to hold less money.

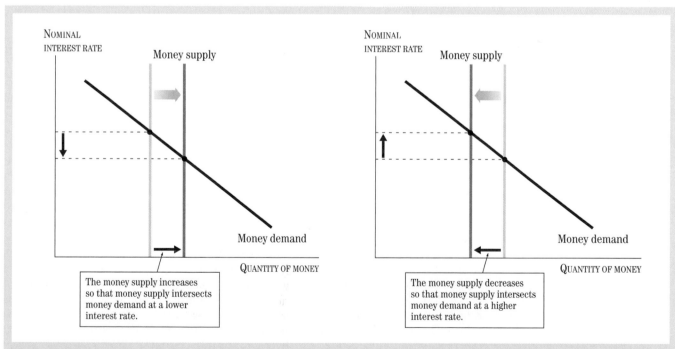

**Figure 14.8
Money Supply Changes
Implied by Interest Rate
Changes**

When the Fed lowers or raises the interest rate, the money supply must also change.

> **Review:** Recall the connection between reserves and the money supply:
>
> Monetary base = currency + reserves
>
> Money supply = $m \times$ (monetary base)
>
> where m is the money multiplier. Thus, when reserves change, so does the monetary base and so does the money supply.

Such movements in the money supply occur as the Fed makes open market purchases or sales to change the interest rate. When the Fed lowers the interest rate, for example, it must increase reserves. And we know from Chapter 9 that when the Fed increases reserves, the money supply increases. Thus, the increase in the money supply in the left graph of Figure 14.8 is exactly what the analysis in Chapter 9 tells us will happen when the central bank increases reserves. Whether you focus on the interest rate or the money supply, the story is the same.

Then why doesn't the Fed simply focus on the money supply? Because the money demand curve tends to shift around a lot; if the Fed simply kept the money supply constant, there would be fluctuations in the interest rate as money demand shifted back and forth. These fluctuations in the interest rate would cause fluctuations in real GDP—perhaps large enough to cause a recession—and thus would not be good policy.

Some economists, such as Milton Friedman, have argued that the Fed should simply hold the growth of the money supply constant, a policy that is called a *constant money growth rule*. However, central banks now feel that money demand shifts around too much for a constant money growth rule to work well. Nevertheless, an inflationary monetary policy—such as the gain then pain scenario—would mean that there would be an increase in money growth. Money growth would increase as the Fed lowered the interest rate. As we saw (in Chapter 9), throughout history higher money growth has been associated with higher inflation.

Those who object to the constant money growth rule do not object to keeping inflation low. They feel that a constant money growth rule will lead to more and larger fluctuations in real GDP and inflation than other policies would. That is why they recommend that the Fed and other central banks focus more on interest rates.

Two Other Instruments of Monetary Policy

In addition to the federal funds rate and the money supply, two other instruments are sometimes used in conducting monetary policy.

discount rate: the interest rate that the Fed charges commercial banks when they borrow from the Fed.

■ **The Discount Rate.** The **discount rate** is the rate the Fed charges commercial banks when they borrow from the Fed. To understand why commercial banks borrow from the Fed, we must consider another role of central banks: the role of *lender of last resort*. During recessions and depressions in the nineteenth and early twentieth centuries, there were frequently "runs" on banks, in which people scrambled to withdraw their deposits for fear that the bank was going under. Rumors caused runs even on sound banks. By agreeing to lend to banks if they experience a run, the Fed can bolster confidence in the bank. The mere existence of a central bank that is willing to lend reduces the chances of runs by raising confidence. That is why the Fed stands ready to make loans to banks.

However, if the discount rate fell much below the federal funds rate, then banks would save on interest costs by borrowing from the Fed rather than borrowing in the federal funds market. Thus, the Fed must make sure that the discount rate does not depart too much from the federal funds rate. When the Fed changes the federal funds rate, it thus frequently changes the discount rate so that the two rates stay near each other. The federal funds rate is the main focus of monetary decisions. The discount rate is usually adjusted when the federal funds rate changes.

■ **Reserve Requirements.** Another tool of monetary policy is the reserve requirement. If the Fed decreases the required reserve ratio—that is, decreases reserve requirements—then the banks will demand fewer reserves and the federal funds rate will fall.

In practice, however, the Fed very rarely changes reserve requirements, and when it does so, its aim is not to change the federal funds rate, because open market operations are sufficient to achieve any desired change in that rate. Sometimes the Fed changes reserve requirements in order to affect the profits of banks. For example, in 1990, the Fed lowered reserve requirements in order to raise banks' profits and thereby reduce the chance that some banks would become insolvent during the 1990–1991 recession. Banks do not receive interest on reserves; thus, lower reserve requirements mean that they can make more profits by making more interest-earning loans.

In 1990, when the Fed lowered reserve requirements, it used open market sales to reduce the supply of reserves. This action exactly offset the effect of the reserve requirement change on the interest rate.

REVIEW

- The Fed affects the short-term nominal interest rate by changing reserves through open market operations.

- Money demand depends negatively on the nominal interest rate.

- When the Fed changes the interest rate, the quantity of money changes.

- Changes in the quantity of money supplied automatically match these changes. Changes in reserves mean changes in the money supply.

- The Fed also has two other instruments: the discount rate and reserve requirements. But the main instrument of monetary policy is the federal funds rate.

The Exchange Rate and Monetary Policy

Quick review: The *exchange rate* is the rate at which one country's currency is exchanged for another country's currency. For example, one U.S. dollar could be exchanged for 9.53 Mexican pesos on May 26, 2000. An *appreciation* of the dollar—say from 9.53 to 10.00 pesos— means that it can be exchanged for more pesos.

flexible exchange rate policy: a policy in which exchange rates are determined in foreign exchange markets and governments do not agree to fix them.

fixed exchange rate policy: a policy in which a country maintains a fixed value of its currency in terms of other currencies.

The exchange rate is another important economic variable that is influenced by monetary policy. When the Fed increases the interest rate, the dollar tends to appreciate in value. The reason is that the higher U.S. interest rate makes dollar assets more attractive and this bids up the price of dollars. Conversely, when the Fed lowers the interest rate, the dollar depreciates.

These changes in the exchange rate affect net exports. For example, an appreciation of the dollar makes imported goods more attractive to Americans and makes U.S. exports less attractive to foreigners. Thus, imports rise and exports fall, causing net exports (exports minus imports) to decline. The decline in net exports in turn causes real GDP to decline. Such changes in exchange rates are an essential part of the impact of monetary policy in the economic fluctuations model explained in Chapters 11 and 12, because the United States follows a **flexible exchange rate policy,** allowing the exchange rate to fluctuate in this way.

But what if the Fed did not want the exchange rate to change? Or what if the U.S. government and another country, such as Japan, agreed to fix the exchange rate? Such a policy is called a **fixed exchange rate policy.** How would that affect monetary policy?

Such questions are not simply hypothetical. Throughout history, governments have decided from time to time to adopt fixed exchange rate policies. The United States and most developed countries were part of a fixed exchange rate system— called the Bretton Woods system—from the end of World War II until the early 1970s. Most recently, eleven countries in Europe have permanently fixed their exchange

A Single Currency and a Single Central Bank
The euro is the new single currency in the European Monetary Union. The central banks of countries in the European Monetary Union have combined to form the European Central Bank (shown at right).

rates by forming a monetary union with a single currency, the euro. Until recently, Argentina fixed its exchange rate to the U.S. dollar. Other countries, like Ecuador, have adopted the U.S. dollar as their currency, and some people have suggested that the other countries in the Western hemisphere join in with the United States in a permanently fixed exchange rate system, with countries in Asia joining in a fixed exchange rate system with Japan. There would then be three large fixed exchange rate systems in the world—centered around the dollar, the euro, and the yen. Some have even imagined a whole world with fixed exchange rates—with the dollar, the yen, and the euro all fixed together. Thus, it is important to look at the implications of a fixed exchange rate for monetary policy, as we do in this section, not only to understand what is happening in different countries today but also to understand proposals that would affect the United States and the whole world in the future.

The Effects of a Fixed Exchange Rate System on Monetary Policy

Suppose the United States decided to set up or join a fixed exchange rate system with Japan. Suppose also that after the United States joins the system, inflation starts to rise in the United States, and monetary policymakers want to raise the interest rate. Such an increase in the interest rate will tend to raise the value of the dollar relative to the Japanese currency. But if the dollar were fixed in value, as it would be with a fixed exchange rate policy, such a rise in the dollar would not be possible. Hence, if exchange rates were fixed, the Fed could not raise the interest rate in the United States relative to the interest rates in Japan. The fixed exchange rate would impose a serious restriction on U.S. monetary policy because interest rates in the United States could not be changed.

In general, if two countries have a fixed exchange rate and people are free to move funds back and forth between the two countries, then the interest rates in the two countries must move together. If, in the example of the United States and Japan, the Fed wanted to raise interest rates, then the Bank of Japan would have to raise interest rates by the same amount. But that might not be in the best interests of Japan, especially if the Japanese economy was in a recession. Like the two steering wheels of a driver's training car, which move in tandem, interest rates in any two countries with a fixed exchange rate must move together.

The connection between interest rates in different countries is very visible to people in smaller countries that fix their currencies to the dollar, as Argentina painfully found out over the last year. In 1991, Argentina chose to fix the value of the peso to the dollar, thus forcing its central bank to give up an independent monetary policy. When interest rates in the United States fell in the mid-1990s, this was beneficial to Argentina, as its interest rates fell as well. However, when U.S. rates rose very rapidly in the year 2000 as the Fed battled inflation, Argentina was forced to raise its interest rates as well, pushing the weakened economy into a recession.

Ever since the eleven countries in the European Monetary Union permanently fixed their exchange rates with each other, there has effectively been only one overnight interest rate in Europe. The central banks of Germany, France, Italy, Spain, and other countries in the European Monetary Union have had to band together into a new European Central Bank. The overnight interest rates in France, Germany, Italy, and the other countries move together, so there is really only one interest rate to decide about. With the European Monetary Union, there cannot be separate monetary policies in Germany and in France. They have only one monetary policy. If real GDP fell below potential GDP in France and remained equal to potential GDP in all the other countries, then a reduction in the interest rate by the European Central Bank, which would be right for France, would be wrong for Europe as a whole, so it probably would not occur. In such a circumstance it might be necessary to use countercyclical *fiscal* policy in France—spending increases or tax cuts—as described in the previous chapter because monetary policy would not be changed.

A real-life example of the effect of fixed exchange rates on monetary policy arose in Britain in 1992. At that time, interest rates were rising in Germany because the German inflation rate was rising. But policymakers in Britain, which was facing hard economic times, did not want British interest rates to rise. The British faced a decision: Either they could raise their interest rates to keep them near Germany's, or they could let their interest rates fall below Germany's. In the latter case, their exchange rate would depreciate. For much of 1991 and 1992, the British kept their exchange rate stable, and that required a rise in British interest rates. But by the end of 1992, increasingly poor economic conditions in Britain forced the British to give up the fixed exchange rate. Then interest rates in Britain could fall.

Interventions in the Exchange Market

Why wasn't it possible for the British government to go into the exchange market and buy and sell foreign exchange and thereby prevent these changes in the exchange rate? For example, if the British government purchases British pounds, this increases the demand for pounds and thereby raises the pound exchange rate. Thus, if the high interest rates in Germany were reducing the value of the British pound, why couldn't the British government buy pounds to offset these pressures? Such buying and selling of foreign currency by governments is called **exchange market intervention.** Such intervention does occur, and it can affect the exchange rate for short periods of time. However, the world currency markets are so huge and fast-moving that even governments do not have the funds to affect the exchange rate for long by buying and selling foreign exchange.

exchange market intervention: purchases and sales of foreign currency by a government in exchange markets with the intention to affect the exchange rate.

In December of 2001, Argentina abandoned the rigid fixed exchange rate system that had pegged the value of the Argentinean peso at a 1-to-1 rate with the U.S. dollar. This decision came in the face of a deepening recession that threatened to reverse years of economic progress made by Argentina in the 1990s. This article, taken from the *Economist* of December 20, 2001, describes the dire straits of the Argentinean economy.

When reading the article, you should think about how the increase in U.S. interest rates in 2000 would affect Argentina's economy. Without the fixed exchange rate, would Argentina have chosen to raise interest rates when the economy was contracting by 11 percent and unemployment was as high as 20 percent? Did the government make the right decision when it dismantled the currency board about a week later, and eventually let the peso's value fluctuate freely?

Patience Wears Thin

Dec 20th 2001 | BUENOS AIRES

From the *Economist* print edition

In 1989, Raul Alfonsin was forced to step down as Argentina's president when mobs began to loot supermarkets amid hyperinflationary chaos. That event is burnt into the country's political memory. So it looked like a grim augury for Fernando de la Rua, the current president who, like Mr Alfonsin, is a member of the Radical party, when looters attacked supermarkets in several cities recently to obtain food. A one-day general strike on December 13th attracted more support than had seven previous stoppages during Mr de la Rua's term. After 42 months of recession, the patience of some Argentines has snapped.

Since July, Argentina's economy has contracted at an annual rate of 11%, according to Miguel Angel Broda, a local economic consultant. The latest official survey says that in October unemployment exceeded 18% (it is now probably 20%). And that was before the government this month imposed limits on cash withdrawals from banks, which have hit retail sales and the informal economy hard.

The looting is still isolated. But it comes as Mr de la Rua and Domingo Cavallo, his economy minister, try to persuade Congress, dominated by the opposition Peronists, to approve a stern budget, aimed at restoring $2.7 billion in loans suspended by the IMF and other multilateral bodies. Those loans

Argentina's economic woes

are the government's last hope of avoiding a unilateral debt default and the collapse of the currency board which pegs the peso at par to the dollar.

Though much-delayed, the budget is still vague on details. It includes no estimate for economic growth, but does recognise that tax revenues will fall (by 3.8%). To reach the government's balanced-budget target, spending is to fall by $9.2 billion, or almost a fifth, compared with this year. Mr Cavallo claims that $5 billion will be saved in lower interest payments as a result of debt restructuring. Some $3 billion will be saved by maintaining for a full year the cuts in provincial finances and in public-sector salaries introduced in August.

The potential benefits of getting new loans and exercising fiscal restraint

If there is a substantial interest rate advantage in favor of one currency, funds will flow into that currency, driving up its value; exchange market intervention by governments cannot do much about this. Empirical studies have shown that exchange market intervention—if it is not matched by a change in interest rates by the central bank—can have only small effects on the exchange rate.

Another possibility is to prevent funds from flowing between the countries. If there were a law restricting the flow of funds into and out of a country, then that country could have both a fixed exchange rate and a separate interest rate policy.

Such controls on the flow of capital were discussed intensely after the collapse of fixed exchange rates in Asia in 1997, and Malaysia did institute some restrictions on financial capital flows. However, such restrictions have disadvantages. They are difficult to enforce and can reduce the amount of foreign capital a country needs for development.

Why Fixed Exchange Rates?

If fixed exchange rates lead to the loss of a separate monetary policy, then why do countries form fixed exchange rate systems? One reason to adopt a fixed exchange rate is that exchange rate volatility can interfere with trade. This is certainly one of the reasons the European countries set up the European Monetary Union. Firms may not develop long-term relationships and contacts with other countries if they are worried about big changes in the exchange rate.

Another, perhaps more important, reason is that some countries have had a history of very poor monetary policies. For example, Italy had very high inflation before it decided to join with the other countries of Europe in a monetary union. And Argentina had many years of hyperinflation before it fixed its exchange rate with the United States and gave up having its own monetary policy.

The goal of fixing the exchange rate in these cases is to adopt the good monetary policy of a country whose central bank has a history of good policy: the Fed in the case of Argentina, and the central banks of Germany and France in the case of Italy. In these cases, the benefits of a fixed exchange rate system may outweigh the loss of a separate monetary policy. However, the evidence is mixed. In the case of Italy, the policy seems to have worked: Inflation has been in single digits for many years. However, in Argentina, where the policy seemed to work well initially in bringing inflation down, restricting the hand of monetary policymakers seemed to make it very tough for the country to recover from its recession of the late 1990s.

REVIEW
- Interest rates must move together in countries with fixed exchange rates and with a free flow of funds between the countries.

- With a fixed exchange rate, there can be no separate monetary policy for each country.

- By permanently fixing exchange rates, a country can adopt the monetary policy of another country.

Conclusion

Monetary policymaking is a powerful, but difficult, job. Central bankers like to say that the job is like driving a car by looking only through the rear-view mirror. They have to take actions that greatly affect the economy without knowing where the economy is going, only where it has been.

In this chapter, we have seen exactly why the job is difficult. It is difficult to resist political pressure to raise inflation for short-term benefits at the expense of long-term costs. And it is difficult to keep aggregate demand in line with potential GDP in a world where potential GDP is hard to estimate and policy effects on aggregate demand are uncertain.

We have also learned that while monetary policy has a powerful effect, it cannot do everything. It cannot lower unemployment permanently, and trying to do so will only raise inflation. And a country cannot have both a fixed exchange rate and the ability to adjust interest rates to control inflation and prevent recessions.

All these ideas are useful for understanding the frequent headlines and news stories about the Fed. And they help take some of the mystique out of what many people feel is the most mysterious institution in the world.

KEY POINTS

1. Central bank independence is a way to avoid political business cycles and the temptation to raise inflation for short-term gain.

2. The gain then pain scenario illustrates that a monetary policy shift to high inflation has short-run benefits but long-run costs.

3. An important task of monetary policy is to manage aggregate demand so that real GDP equals potential GDP.

4. In early 2000, the Fed raised the real interest rate to reduce aggregate demand.

5. A good monetary policy rule is responsive to real GDP as well as to inflation.

6. The demand for money is negatively related to the interest rate.

7. The Fed changes the quantity of money when it changes the interest rate.

8. Reserve requirements are rarely changed.

9. Fixed exchange rates restrict monetary policy.

KEY TERMS

central bank independence
political business cycle
time inconsistency

money demand
discount rate

flexible exchange rate policy
fixed exchange rate policy

exchange market
intervention

QUESTIONS FOR REVIEW

1. What are the advantages and disadvantages of central bank independence?

2. What is an example of a political business cycle?

3. Why would the Fed raise real interest rates if real GDP were above potential GDP?

4. Why is it important that real GDP be close to potential GDP?

5. What is the Phillips curve?

6. Why is the demand for money inversely related to the interest rate?

7. What is the opportunity cost of holding money?

8. Why is there a loss of monetary policy independence with fixed exchange rates?

9. Why would a country adopt a fixed exchange rate policy?

PROBLEMS

1. In recommending central banking reforms for Eastern European economies, the *Economic Report of the President, 1990,* p. 202, asserted, "It is widely agreed that the central bank should have a high degree of independence from the central government so that it can resist political pressures." Explain the reasoning behind this assertion. What are some counterarguments?

2. The original Federal Reserve Act of 1913 allowed the secretary of the Treasury to be a member of the Federal

Reserve Board, but a later amendment prohibited this. How would allowing the secretary of the Treasury to be a member affect the conduct of monetary policy?

3. Suppose the Fed wants to raise the federal funds rate. Describe in detail how it accomplishes this policy. What happens to the quantity of money?

4. What is the discount rate? How does it differ from the federal funds rate? Describe how the Fed affects each of these interest rates.

5. Suppose there is an increase in money demand at every interest rate. Show this in a diagram. What effect will this have on the interest rate if the Fed does not increase the money supply?

6. Suppose there are two countries, identical except for the fact that the central bank of one country lets interest rates rise sharply when real GDP rises above potential GDP and the other does not. Draw the aggregate demand curve for each country. What are the benefits and drawbacks of each country's policy?

7. During the early 1990s in Japan, there was deflation and real GDP was below potential GDP.
   a. Draw a diagram showing the situation in which there is deflation at potential GDP.
   b. Suppose the Japanese central bank decides that it must reinflate and sets a target inflation rate of 2 percent. How does it accomplish this? Show the short-, medium-, and long-run effects.
   c. Is it possible that the central bank can have a fully credible reinflation? What are the benefits of immediate increases in the inflation rate?

8. Using the aggregate demand curve and the inflation adjustment line, show what the Fed should do if real GDP is below potential GDP and inflation is equal to the target inflation rate.

9. Real GDP, consumption, and investment in the United States all declined from 1990 to 1991 and increased in 1992.
   a. Using an aggregate demand curve and an inflation adjustment line, show how a change in monetary policy in 1991 could explain these developments.
   b. Net exports increased from 1990 to 1991. Is the explanation in part (a) consistent with this development? If not, what other factors may have explained the behavior of net exports?

10. Sweden and the United Kingdom did not join the European Monetary Union (EMU) at the start. Explain why the central banks of these two countries would no longer be able to make separate interest rate decisions if they joined the EMU.

11. Explain why restricting flows of funds into or out of a country can give that country's central bank the ability to conduct monetary policy even with a fixed exchange rate. What are some of the disadvantages of such a restriction?

CHAPTER 15

Financial Markets

Winning a million dollars on *Who Wants to Be a Millionaire?*, one of the most popular TV shows in history, seems pretty easy. All the contestants need to do is answer a selection of multiple-choice questions. The show's host, Regis ("Is that your final answer?") Philbin, even allows contestants to call a friend for help. This may sound like an easy way to make a million. But, in reality, it is hard. First you have to be chosen from among 250,000 people who want to be on the show, and then you need to reach the final one-on-one with Regis. The chances are really not in your favor.

But, don't despair—there are more certain ways to become a millionaire. "As any decent financial adviser will tell you, almost anyone can do it," according to the *Wall Street Journal*, "If a 25-year-old earning $30,000 invests 10% a year and realizes an annual return of 6%, he or she will accumulate about $1.1 million by age 65. . . . [W]hen you weigh the odds of even getting on to *Millionaire* against those of a steady investment plan, you might say [Regis] makes it look harder than it really is."

This comparison of a TV show with a regular investment plan indicates that one can do very well over the long term by investing in stocks and other assets. The gains can be even greater when stock prices rise rapidly, as they did in the 1980s and 1990s. But stock prices do not always rise so rapidly. In fact, stock prices did not rise much at all in the 1970s, and they fell sharply in the 1930s. More recently, the twenty-first century has not been kind to the stock market, as there was a 30 percent decrease in the Dow Jones stock index in less than six months in 2002, and a more than 70 percent decrease in the Nasdaq stock index in less than three years. Stock prices are volatile, and thus stocks can be very risky.

In this chapter, we extend our analysis of different types of markets to financial markets, which include not only the exciting stock market, but also

340

other fast-moving markets such as the bond market and the foreign exchange market.

To examine financial markets, we will use some of the basic tools of economics, including the supply and demand model. However, because prices in financial markets are very volatile and uncertain, to study these markets we need to consider some new tools to handle risk and uncertainty.

Financial Market Terminology

Some basic terminology about the distinction between physical and financial capital is useful in studying financial markets.

Physical Capital

Physical capital refers to all the machines, factories, oil tankers, office buildings, and other physical resources used in the production of goods or services. In previous chapters on the behavior of firms, we simply used the term *capital* when referring to "physical capital" because we were not contrasting it with financial capital. Firms combine physical capital with labor inputs to produce goods and services. Businesses obtain physical capital by either building it, buying it, or renting it. For example, McDonald's might hire a construction firm to build a new facility near a highway, buy an old Burger King and renovate it, or rent a storefront in a mall.

Residential housing—single-family homes, apartments, trailers—is also a form of physical capital. It provides productive services in the form of living space that people can enjoy year after year. Government-owned roads, schools, and military equipment are also physical capital. It is useful to think of government capital as helping to produce services, whether transportation services, educational services, or national security.

An important characteristic of physical capital is that it lasts for a number of years. However, it does not remain in new condition permanently. Rather, it depreciates each year. *Depreciation* is the gradual decline in the productive usefulness of capital. Trucks, trailers, and even buildings wear out and must eventually be either replaced or refurbished.

depreciation: the decrease in an asset's value over time; for capital, it is the amount by which physical capital wears out over a given period of time. (Ch. 5)

Financial Capital: Debt and Equity

When a firm starts up or expands, it needs to obtain funds. These funds are an example of *financial capital.* A firm needs these funds in order to purchase, rent, or build physical capital. It may also need funds to pay workers for a while until the firm starts to earn a profit. Older existing firms also need to obtain funds in order to expand or to buy physical capital.

Firms can obtain financial capital in two different ways: by issuing debt and by issuing equity. Examples of debt are bank loans and bonds. Loans and bonds are a type of contract called a **debt contract** in which the lender agrees to provide funds today in exchange for a promise that the borrower will pay back the funds at a future date with interest. The amount of interest is determined by the *interest rate.* If the amount borrowed is $10,000 and is due in one year and the interest rate is 10 percent

debt contract: a contract in which a lender agrees to provide funds today in exchange for a promise from the borrower, who will repay that amount plus interest at some point in the future.

per year, then the borrower pays the lender $11,000 at the end of the year. The $11,000 includes the *principal* on the loan ($10,000) plus the *interest payment* ($1,000 = .1 times $10,000). Firms typically obtain loans from banks, but larger firms also issue *corporate bonds*.

Firms are not the only issuers of debt. Most people who buy a house get a *mortgage*, which is a loan of funds to purchase real estate. In addition, many people get loans from banks to buy cars and consumer appliances. The biggest single issuer of debt in the United States is the federal government. The federal government borrows funds by selling *government bonds*.

Firms also obtain financial capital by issuing *stock*, or shares of ownership in the firm. Shares of ownership are a type of contract called an **equity contract.** In contrast to a debt contract, where the payment by the firm (the interest payment) does not depend on the profits of the firm, in an equity contract the payment by the firm does depend on the firm's profits. Sometimes the payment is a *dividend*, but shareholders can also benefit if the firm increases in value and their shares are worth more when they are sold.

Once bonds or stocks have been issued, they can be exchanged or traded. There are highly organized financial markets for trading stocks and bonds. The government and corporate bond markets are located in New York City, London, Tokyo, and other large financial centers. The stock markets include the New York Stock Exchange, the American Stock Exchange, several regional stock exchanges in the United States, and many stock exchanges in other countries.

equity contract: shares of ownership in a firm; payments to the owners of the shares depend on the firm's profits.

REVIEW

- Physical capital and financial capital are distinct but closely related. To expand their physical capital, firms need to raise financial capital in some way.

- Debt contracts, such as bonds or loans, specify interest payments that do not depend on the profits of the firm. Equity contracts, such as stocks, pay dividends or earn capital gains that do depend on the profits of the firm.

- The bonds or stocks that firms issue can be traded. Organized markets for trading bonds and stocks are found in all the world's financial centers

---

Stock and Bond Markets

return: the income received from the ownership of an asset; for a stock, the return is the dividend plus the capital gain.

capital gain: the increase in the value of an asset through an increase in its price.

capital loss: the decrease in the value of an asset through a decrease in its price.

Stocks and bonds are also called securities. Once firms issue stocks or bonds, these securities can be traded on the financial markets. Their prices are determined by the actions of buyers and sellers, like prices in any other market.

Stock Prices and Rates of Return

The prices of the stocks of most large firms can be found in daily newspapers as shown in the box on the next page, which focuses on the listing for Hewlett-Packard stock. The annual **return** from holding a stock is defined as the *dividend* plus the *capital gain* during the year. The dividend is the amount the firm pays out to the owners of the stock each year. The **capital gain** during the year is the increase in the price of the stock during the year. A **capital loss** is a negative capital gain: a decrease

Newspaper stock tables, such as this one from the *Wall Street Journal* (August 8, 2002), summarize information about firms and the stocks that they issue. The table here is part of a much bigger table called "New York Stock Exchange Composite Transactions," in which all stocks traded on the New York Stock Exchange are listed in alphabetical order. Other tables provide information about stocks traded on other stock exchanges, such as the American Stock Exchange or the Nasdaq, in exactly the same way.

To understand how to read this table, focus on one company, such as the computer firm Hewlett-Packard, which was started in a garage by David Packard and William Hewlett in the 1930s and is now run by Carleton (Carly) Fiorina. A big part of her job is to keep Hewlett-Packard's stock price strong, which means finding ways to continue to grow the earnings of the company. For example, in 2001 Hewlett-Packard and Compaq decided to merge, with the intention of improving their joint position in a rapidly changing technology sector.

The information in the table pertains to a single day, August 7, 2002. As can be seen from the table, the price of Hewlett-Packard stock increased by 0.27 dollars to 12.92 on that day.

Key terms introduced in this chapter—such as dividend, dividend yield, and price-earnings ratio—are highlighted. To check your understanding, you can see if the *Wall Street Journal* has calculated the dividend yield correctly (as we have done for Hewlett-Packard in the margin on the opposite page) for one of the other firms in the table, such as Hershey, the maker of Hershey's Kisses. Or take a look at today's *Wall Street Journal* or focus on a stock on another stock exchange.

Carly Fiorina is the Chief Executive Officer of Hewlett-Packard and is ultimately responsible for the performance of Hewlett-Packard's earnings and stock price.

Ytd % Chg	52 weeks Hi	Lo	Stock	Sym	Div	Yld %	PE	Vol 100s	Close	Net Chg
1.2	13.70	6.50	Hercules	HPC		...	dd	2115	10.12	0.11
−15.2	30.55	22.50	HertgPropn	HPG	2.55	10.1	dd	111	25.15	−0.01
−2.8	26.98	22.30	HeritageProp	n	.36e	1.5	...	3314	24.35	...
6.2	79.49	56.45	Hershey	HSY	1.31f	1.8	44	25866	71.89	−1.11
−1.9	24.50	21.20	Hewitt	HEW n		...	...	674	23.05	−0.05
−37.1	**25.45**	**10.75**	**HewlettPk**	**HPQ**	**.32**	**2.5**	**28**	**104175**	**12.92**	**0.27**
22.4	8.59	1.98	Hexcel	HXL		...	dd	624	3.77	−0.02
14.7	20.85	14.06	Hibernia	HIB	.56	2.7	18	7458	20.40	0.19

Stock price percentage change for the calendar year to date	High and low price for previous year	Stock exchange symbol	Yearly dividend	Dividend as a percent of price	Price-earnings ratio	Number of shares traded (in hundreds)	Closing price of stock	Change in price from previous days

Ytd % Chg	52 weeks Hi	Lo	Sym	Div	Yld %	PE	Vol 100s	Close	Net Chg
−37.1	25.45	10.75	HewlettPk HPQ	.32	2.5	28	104175	12.92	0.27

rate of return: the return on an asset stated as a percentage of the price of the asset.

Check the result. The dividend was $.32. The closing price was $12.92. Dividing .32 by 12.92 gives .024 or 2.4 percent.

dividend yield: the dividend stated as a percentage of the price of the stock.

earnings: the accounting profits of a firm.

price-earnings ratio: the price of a stock divided by its annual earnings per share.

in the price. The **rate of return** is the return stated as a percentage of the price of the stock.

The **dividend yield** is defined as the dividend stated as a percentage of the price. For example, the dividend for Hewlett-Packard in 2002 was $.32 per year. The dividend yield was 2.5 percent. The rate of return equals the percentage capital gain plus the dividend yield. For example, if the price of Hewlett-Packard stock went from $10 to $11 in a year, then the percentage capital gain would be $1 divided by $10, or 10 percent. Combined with a dividend yield of 2.5 percent, this would be a rate of return of 12.5 percent. In this example, the capital gain is a much bigger portion of the rate of return than the dividend; this is a defining characteristic of "growth stocks," of which Hewlett-Packard is an example.

Earnings is another word for the accounting profits of a firm. Firms do not pay out all of their profits as dividends; some of the profits are retained and invested in physical capital or research. Stock tables also list the **price-earnings ratio:** the price of the stock divided by the annual earnings per share. Observe in the box on the next page that the price-earnings ratio for Hewlett-Packard is 28. With the price of the stock at $12.92, this means that earnings for the year were $0.4614 per share ($12.92/$0.4614 = 28). A firm's earnings ultimately influence the return on the firm's stock, so the price-earnings ratio, or its inverse, which is 1/28, or 3.6 percent, for Hewlett-Packard, is closely watched.

Bond Prices and Rates of Return

Bond prices for both corporate and government bonds can also be found in the financial pages of the newspaper. The box "Reading the News About Bond Prices" on page 345 shows newspaper reports from two different dates on bonds issued by the U.S. government. These bond reports illustrate quite a bit about how bonds and bond markets work.

coupon: the fixed amount that a borrower agrees to pay to the bondholder each year.

maturity date: the date when the principal on a loan is to be paid back.

face value: the principal that will be paid back when a bond matures.

■ **Face Value, Maturity, Coupon, and Yield.** There are four key characteristics of a bond: *coupon, maturity date, face value*, and *yield*. The **coupon** is the fixed amount that the borrower agrees to pay the bondholder each year. The **maturity date** is the time when the coupon payments end and the principal is paid back. The **face value** is the amount of principal that will be paid back when the bond matures. Observe that the bond boldfaced in the box has a maturity date of November 2021 and a coupon equal to 8 percent of the face value of the bond. That is, 8 percent, or $80 a year on a bond with a face value of $1000, will be paid until 2021, and in November 2021, the $1000 face value will be paid back. (The coupon is called a "rate" because it is measured as a percentage of the face value.)

Once bonds have been issued by the government, they can be sold or bought in the bond market. In the bond market, there are bond traders who make a living buying and selling bonds. The bond traders will *bid* a certain price at which they will buy, and they will *ask* a certain price at which they will sell. The bid price is slightly lower than the ask price, which enables the bond traders to earn a profit by buying at a price that is slightly lower than the price at which they sell. For example, on August 7, 2002, the bid price on the bond in the box "Reading the News About Bond Prices" was $107 27/32, slightly lower than the ask price, which was $107 29/32. (Note that bond prices are rounded to the nearest thirty-second of a dollar.)

yield: the annual rate of return on a bond if the bond were held to maturity.

The **yield,** or yield to maturity, is defined as the annual rate of return on the bond if the bond were held to maturity. When people refer to the current interest rate on bonds, they are referring to the yield on the bond. Observe that the yield on the bold-faced bond maturing in November 2021 was 5.31 percent on August 7, 2002, somewhat below the 8 percent coupon.

Once bonds have been issued by a firm or by a government, they are traded in bond markets. The prices of bonds in these markets are reported in the daily newspapers. Examples of such reports are given in the two tables below. The examples are part of larger tables in the *Wall Street Journal* called "Treasury Bonds, Notes and Bills," which list prices for many other government bonds issued by the U.S. Treasury. (Bonds have the longest maturities, followed by notes and then bills.)

The two tables refer to two different dates—August 2002 and April 1997—and come from two different issues of the paper. Observe that bonds with exactly the same coupon rate and maturity date are listed in the two tables. The two different dates enable you to see what happens to the price and the yield on these bonds over time.

Focus on the highlighted bond; it has a coupon rate of 8 percent and matures in November 2021. Thus, in November 2002, there were 19 years to maturity on this bond. Both the price that is *bid* for bonds by bond traders and the price that is *asked* for bonds by the traders are given in the table, but the bid and ask are very close to each other. (There is enough of a difference to give the traders some profit; note that the price asked by the trader is always greater than the price bid.)

Now look at what happened to the yield and the price between the two dates. In August 2002, the price was about $132, while in April 1997, it was about $107. Thus the price has risen. But the yield has declined, from 7.30 percent to 5.31 percent. This inverse relationship occurs for all the bonds listed in the tables and is necessarily true for all other bonds as well. Can you explain why?

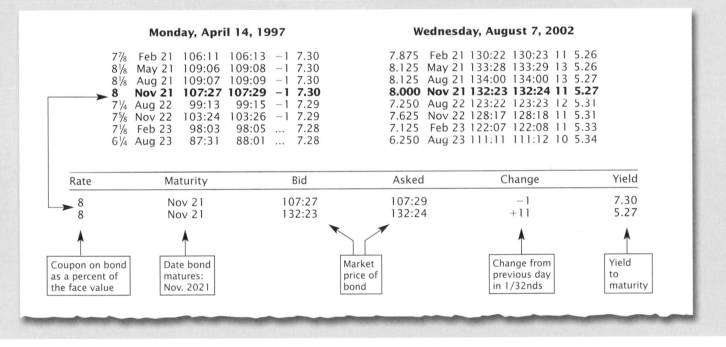

Monday, April 14, 1997

7⅞	Feb 21	106:11	106:13	−1	7.30
8⅛	May 21	109:06	109:08	−1	7.30
8⅛	Aug 21	109:07	109:09	−1	7.30
8	**Nov 21**	**107:27**	**107:29**	**−1**	**7.30**
7¼	Aug 22	99:13	99:15	−1	7.29
7⅝	Nov 22	103:24	103:26	−1	7.29
7⅛	Feb 23	98:03	98:05	...	7.28
6¼	Aug 23	87:31	88:01	...	7.28

Wednesday, August 7, 2002

7.875	Feb 21	130:22	130:23	11	5.26
8.125	May 21	133:28	133:29	13	5.26
8.125	Aug 21	134:00	134:00	13	5.27
8.000	**Nov 21**	**132:23**	**132:24**	**11**	**5.27**
7.250	Aug 22	123:22	123:23	12	5.31
7.625	Nov 22	128:17	128:18	11	5.31
7.125	Feb 23	122:07	122:08	11	5.33
6.250	Aug 23	111:11	111:12	10	5.34

Rate	Maturity	Bid	Asked	Change	Yield
8	Nov 21	107:27	107:29	−1	7.30
8	Nov 21	132:23	132:24	+11	5.27

Coupon on bond as a percent of the face value

Date bond matures: Nov. 2021

Market price of bond

Change from previous day in 1/32nds

Yield to maturity

■ **Bond Prices and Bond Yields.** There is an inverse, or negative, relationship between the yield and the price. To see this, look at the bonds in the two columns in the box. On August 7, 2002, the price of all the bonds listed is higher and the yield is lower than on April 14, 1997. Why is there an inverse relationship? Consider a simple example. Suppose you just bought a 1-year bond for $100 that says that the government will pay 5 percent of the face value, or $5, plus $100 at the end of the 1-year period. Now suppose that just after you bought the bond, interest rates on bank deposits suddenly jumped to 10 percent. Your bond says that you earn 5 percent per year, so if you hold it for the entire year, your rate of return is less than you could get on a bank deposit. Suddenly the bond looks much less attractive. You would probably want to sell it, but everyone else knows the bond is less attractive, also. You would not be able to get $100 for the bond. The price would decline until the rate of return

Table 15.1
Bond Price Formula

One-year maturity: $\quad P = \dfrac{R}{1+i} + \dfrac{F}{1+i}$

Two-year maturity: $\quad P = \dfrac{R}{1+i} + \dfrac{R}{(1+i)^2} + \dfrac{F}{(1+i)^2}$

Three-year maturity: $\quad P = \dfrac{R}{1+i} + \dfrac{R}{(1+i)^2} + \dfrac{R}{(1+i)^3} + \dfrac{F}{(1+i)^3}$

For very long term: $\quad P = \dfrac{R}{i}$

| P = price of bond |
| R = coupon |
| F = face value |
| i = yield |

on the bond just equaled the interest rate at the bank. For example, if the price fell to $95.45, then the payment of $105 at the end of the year would result in a 10 percent rate of return [that is, $.10 = (105 - 95.45)/95.45$]. In other words, the yield on the bond would rise until it equaled 10 percent rather than 5 percent.

Based on these considerations, there is a formula that gives the relationship between the price and the yield for bonds of any maturity. Let P be the price of the bond. Let R be the coupon. Let F be the face value. Let i be the yield. The formula relating to the price and the yield in the case of a 1-year bond is indicated in the first row of Table 15.1.

For a 1-year bond, a coupon payment of R is paid at the end of 1 year together with the face value of the bond. The price P is what you would be willing to pay *now, in the present,* for these future payments. It is the *present discounted value* of the coupon payment plus the face value at the end of the year. By looking at the formula in the first row of Table 15.1, you can see the negative relationship between the price (P) of the bond and the yield (i) on the bond. The higher the yield, the lower the price; and conversely, the lower the yield, the higher the price.

A 2-year-maturity bond is similar. You get R at the end of the first year and R plus the face value at the end of the second year. Now you want to divide the first-year payment by $1 + i$ and the second-year payment by $(1 + i)^2$. The formula still shows the inverse relationship between the yield and the price. A bond with a 3-year or longer maturity is similar. Computers do the calculation for the news reports, so even 30-year bond yields can easily be found from their price.

There is a convenient and simple approximation method for determining the price or yield on bonds with very long maturity dates. It says that the price is equal to the coupon divided by the yield: $P = R/i$. This is the easiest way to remember the inverse relationship between the price and the yield. It is a close approximation for long-term bonds like the 30-year bond.

REVIEW

- Stocks and bonds are issued in order to obtain funds. Once issued, they are traded in stock and bond markets.

- The return from holding stock is the dividend plus the change in the price. The rate of return is equal to the return measured as a percentage of the price of the stock.

- The return from holding bonds is the coupon plus the change in the price of the bond. The rate of return measures this return as a percentage of the price of the bond.

- Bond yields and bond prices move in opposite directions.

Risk versus Return

The long-run average trend in stock prices has been up, but there have been significant declines from time to time, and the prices of individual stocks traded in the financial markets are very volatile. The price of a share of Hewlett-Packard, for example, declined from $31 to $20 a share in 2001, but the price of a share of Genesis Microchip rose from $9 to $66 during the same year—before dropping to $6 by August 2002. A change in price of 10 or 20 percent in one day is not uncommon. Because of such variability, buying stocks is a risky activity. The price of bonds can also change by a large amount. For example, from mid-1996 to mid-1997, the price of government bonds rose by nearly 20 percent, but from mid-1993 to mid-1994, the price of government bonds *fell* by nearly 20 percent! Thus, government bonds are also a risky investment.

In this section we show that the riskiness of stocks and bonds affects their return. To do so, we first examine how individuals behave when they face risk.

Behavior Under Uncertainty

Most people do not like uncertainty. They are *risk averse* in most of their activities. Given a choice between two jobs that pay the same wage, most people will be averse to choosing the riskier job where there is a good chance of being laid off. Similarly, given a choice between two investments that pay the same return, people will choose the less risky one.

Let us examine this idea of risk aversion further. To be more precise, suppose that Melissa has a choice between the two alternatives shown in Table 15.2. She must decide what to do with her life savings of $10,000 for the next year. At the end of the year, she plans to buy a house, and she will need some money for a down payment. She can put her $10,000 in a bank account, where the interest rate is 5 percent, or she can buy $10,000 worth of a stock that pays a dividend of 5 percent and will incur either a capital gain or a loss. In the bank, the value of her savings is safe, but if she buys the stock, there is a 50 percent chance that the price of the stock will fall by 30 percent and a 50 percent chance that the price of the stock will rise by 30 percent. In other words, the risky stock will leave Melissa with the possibility of a return of $-\$2,500$ (a loss) or a return of $3,500 (a gain). (Here's the calculation: $\$10,000 \times .05 - \$10,000 \times .30 = -\$2,500$ and $\$10,000 \times .05 + \$10,000 \times .30 = \$3,500$.) The bank account leaves her with a guaranteed $500 return.

If Melissa is a risk-averse person, she will choose the less risky of these two options. It is easy to see that Melissa might be miserable in the event of a loss, so she

Table 15.2
Two Options: Different Risks, Same Expected Return

Low-Risk Option	High-Risk Option
A bank deposit with	*A corporate stock with*
5 percent interest	5 percent dividend and either a 30 percent price decline or a 30 percent price increase

expected return: the return on an uncertain investment calculated by weighting the gains or losses by the probability that they will occur.

would want to avoid it completely and take the safe option. This example illustrates the fundamental difference between more risky and less risky investments. Because the prices of stocks fluctuate, they are riskier than bank accounts when held for short periods like a year.

Both the options in Table 15.2 have the same **expected return.** The expected return on an investment weighs the different gains or losses according to how probable they are. In the case of the safe bank account, there is a 100 percent chance that the return is $500, so the expected return is $500. In the case of the stock, the expected return would be $-$2,500 times the probability of this loss (1/2) plus $3,500 times the probability of this gain (also 1/2). Thus, the expected return is $500 ($-2,500/2 + 3,500/2 = -1,250 + 1,750 = 500$), the same as the return in the bank account.

The expected return is one way to measure how attractive an investment is. The word *expected* may appear misleading, since in the risky option $500 is not "expected" in the everyday use of the word. You do not expect $500; you expect either a loss of $2,500 or a gain of $3,500. If the term is confusing, think of the expected return as the average return that Melissa would get if she could take the second option year after year for many years. The losses of $2,500 and gains of $3,500 would average out to $500 per year after many years. (The term *expected return* has been carried over by economists and investment analysts from probability and statistics, where the term *expected value* is used to describe the mean, or the average, of a random variable.)

Although it is clear that Melissa would choose the less risky option of the two in Table 15.2, perhaps there is some compensation that Melissa would accept to offset her risk aversion. Although most people are averse to risk, they are willing to take on some risk if they are compensated for it. In the case of a risky financial investment, the compensation for higher risk could take the form of a higher expected return.

How could we make Melissa's expected return higher in the risky investment? Suppose Melissa had the choice between the same safe option as in Table 15.2 and a high-risk stock that paid a dividend of 20 percent. This new choice is shown in Table 15.3; the difference is that the risky stock now offers a dividend of 20 percent, much greater than the 5 percent in the first example and much greater than the 5 percent on the bank account. With the greater chance of a higher return on the stock, Melissa might be willing to buy the stock. Even in the worst situation, she loses just $1,000, which may still leave her with enough for the down payment on her new house. The expected return for the high-risk option is now $2,000, much greater than the $500 for the bank account ($2,000 = -1,000/2 + 5,000/2 = -500 + 2,500$).

In other words, Melissa would probably be willing to take on the risky investment. And if the 20 percent dividend in the example is not enough for her, some

---

Table 15.3
Two Options: Different Risks, Different Expected Returns

Low-Risk Option	High-Risk Option
A bank deposit with	*A corporate stock with*
5 percent interest	20 percent dividend and either a 30 percent price decline or a 30 percent price increase

higher dividend (25 percent? 30 percent?) would be. This example illustrates the general point that risk-averse people are willing to take risks if they are paid for it.

Before we develop the implication of our analysis of individual behavior under uncertainty, we should pause to ask about the possibility that some people might be risk lovers rather than risk avoiders. The billions of dollars that are made in state lotteries in the United States and in private gambling casinos in Las Vegas, Atlantic City, and Monte Carlo indicate that some people enjoy risk. However, with few exceptions, most of the gambling on lotteries, slot machines, and even roulette wheels represents a small portion of the income or wealth of the gambler. Thus, you might be willing to spend $.50 or even $5 on lottery tickets or a slot machine for the chance of winning big, even if the odds are against you. Many people get enjoyment out of such wagers; but if the stakes are large compared to one's income or wealth, then few people want to play. For small sums, some people are risk lovers, but for large sums, virtually everybody becomes a risk avoider to some degree or another.

Risk and Rates of Return in Theory

What are the implications of our conclusion that investors will be willing to take risks if they are compensated with a higher return on the stock or bond? In the stock market, the prices of individual stocks are determined by the bidding of buyers and sellers. Suppose a stock, QED, had a price that gave it the same expected rate of return as a bank account. Now QED, being a common stock, clearly has more risk than a bank account because its price can change. Hence, no risk-averse investor will want to buy QED. Just as Melissa will prefer to put her funds in a bank account in the example of Table 15.2 rather than into the risky option, investors will put their funds in a bank rather than buy QED. People who own shares of QED will sell and put their funds into a bank. With everybody wanting to sell QED and no one wanting to buy it, the price of QED will start to fall.

Now, the price and the expected rate of return are inversely related—recall that for a stock the rate of return is the return divided by the price. Thus, if the price falls and the dividend does not change, the rate of return will rise. This fall in the price will drive up the expected rate of return on QED. As the expected rate of return increases, it will eventually reach a point where it is high enough to compensate risk-averse investors. In other words, when the expected rate of return rises far enough above the bank account rate to compensate people for holding the risk, the price fall will stop. We will have an equilibrium where the expected rate of return on the stock is higher than the interest rate on the safe bank account. The higher rate of return will be associated with the higher risk.

Now some stocks are more risky than others. For example, the risk on the stocks of small firms tends to be higher than the risk on the stocks of larger firms, because small firms tend to be those that are just starting up. Not having yet proved themselves, small firms have a higher risk. People like Melissa will sell the more risky, smaller company stocks until the expected rate of return on those stocks is high enough compared with the less risky stocks of larger companies.

In equilibrium, we therefore expect to see a positive relationship between risk and the expected rate of return on securities. Securities with higher risks will have higher returns than securities with lower risks. Figure 15.1 shows the resulting **equilibrium risk-return relationship.**

equilibrium risk-return relationship: the positive relationship between the risk and the expected rate of return on an asset, derived from the fact that, on average, risk-averse investors who take on more risk must be compensated with a higher return.

There is probably no more important lesson about capital markets than this relationship. Individual investors should know it well. It says that to get a higher rate of return *on average over the long run,* you have to accept a higher risk. Again, the market

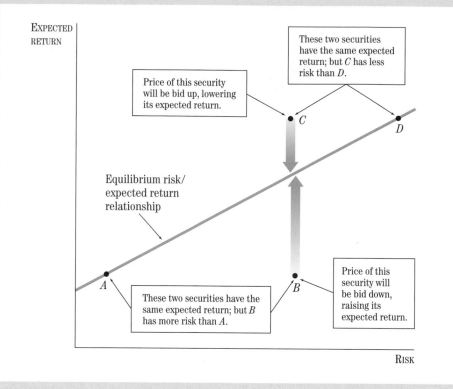

Figure 15.1
The Equilibrium Relationship Between Return and Risk
More risky securities tend to have higher returns on average over the long term. For example, bank deposits are low risk and have a low expected return. Corporate stocks are higher risk—their price fluctuates—but on average over the long term have a higher return. The higher return is like a compensating wage differential in the labor market. It compensates those who take on more risk.

forces at work are the same as the ones that led to the compensating wage differentials in the labor market. In the labor market, the higher wage in some jobs is the price that workers accept to take on the greater risk, or, more generally, the less pleasant aspects of the job.

Risk and Return in Reality

How well does this theoretical relationship work in reality? Very well. A tremendous amount of data over long periods of time on the financial markets support it. Table 15.4 presents data on the average return over 70 years for the four important types of securities we have mentioned in the theoretical discussion. The most risky of the four—the stocks of small firms—has the highest rate of return. Next highest in risk is the common stocks of large firms. The least risky—short-term Treasury bills that are as safe as bank deposits—has the smallest rate of return. Long-term bonds, where price changes can be large, have a rate of return greater than that of Treasury bills. Although the relative risks of these four types of securities may seem obvious, a measure of the differences in the sizes of their price volatility is shown in the second column and confirms the intuitive risk rankings.

Table 15.4
Average Rates of Return for Different Risks, 1926–2000

	Average Rate of Return per Year (percent)	Risk (average size of price fluctuations)
U.S. Treasury bills	3.9	3.2
Long-term corporate bonds	6.0	8.7
Large-company stocks	13.0	20.2
Small-company stocks	17.3	33.4

Note: These rates of return are not adjusted for inflation. The average rate of inflation was about 3 percent, which can be subtracted from each of the average returns to get the real return. The risk is the "standard deviation," a measure of volatility commonly used in probability and statistics.

Source: Data from Ibbotson Associates, *Stocks, Bonds, Bills and Inflation*, 2001 yearbook, Table 6–7.

In general, Table 15.4 is a striking confirmation of this fundamental result of financial markets that higher expected rates of return are associated with higher risk.

Diversification Reduces Risk

The familiar saying "Don't put all your eggs in one basket" is particularly relevant to stock markets. Rather than a basket of eggs, you have a portfolio of stocks. A *portfolio* is a collection of stocks. Putting your funds into a portfolio of two or more stocks, whose prices do not always move in the same direction, rather than one stock is called **portfolio diversification.** The risks from holding a single stock can be reduced significantly by putting half your funds in one stock and half in another. If one stock falls in price, the other stock may fall less, may not fall at all, or may even rise.

portfolio diversification: spreading the collection of assets owned in order to limit exposure to risk.

Holding two stocks in equal amounts is the most elementary form of diversification. With thousands of stocks to choose from, diversification is not limited to two. Figure 15.2 shows how sharply risk declines with diversification. By holding 10 different stocks rather than 1, you can reduce your risk to about 30 percent of what it would be with 1 stock. If you hold some international stocks, whose behavior will be even more different from that of any one U.S. stock, you can reduce the risk even further. Mutual fund companies provide a way for an investor with only limited funds to diversify by holding 500 or even 5,000 stocks along with other investors. Some mutual funds—called *index funds*—consist of all the stocks in an index like the Standard and Poor's (S&P) 500 Index, a weighted average of the stocks of 500 major companies. The Dow Jones Industrial Average of 30 companies, which draws headlines every time it passes through a 1,000-point mark, is less frequently used as an index for mutual funds because it has a smaller number of stocks.

If you do not diversify, you are taking unneeded risks. But diversification cannot eliminate risk. A certain amount of risk cannot be diversified away. **Systematic risk** is what remains after diversification has reduced risk as much as it can. It is due to the ups and downs in the economy, which affect all stocks to some degree.

systematic risk: the level of risk in asset markets that investors cannot reduce by diversification.

Efficient Market Theory

The shares of firms' stock on the market can be traded quickly at any time of day. For most large and medium-sized companies, some people are always willing to buy and

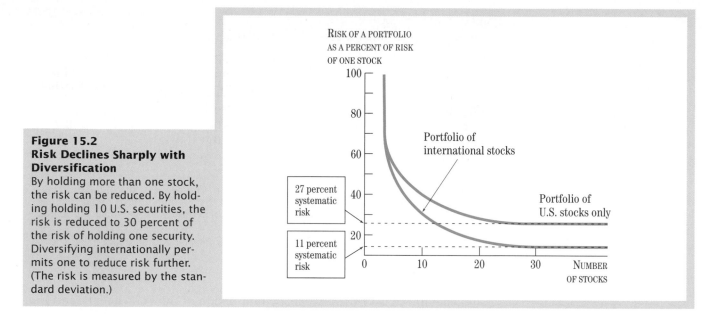

Figure 15.2
Risk Declines Sharply with Diversification
By holding more than one stock, the risk can be reduced. By holding holding 10 U.S. securities, the risk is reduced to 30 percent of the risk of holding one security. Diversifying internationally permits one to reduce risk further. (The risk is measured by the standard deviation.)

sell. If people hear that Intel made a discovery that is expected to raise its profits, they rush to buy Intel stock. If people suddenly learn about a decline in a company's profits or losses, then people rush to sell that company's stock, as in the case of Genesis Microchip, described in the box on page 353. This rush to buy and sell changes prices instantaneously, so that the price adjusts rapidly to good news or bad news. The rapid adjustment means that there are rarely any unexploited profit opportunities for regular investors without inside information or a special ability to anticipate news, whether good or bad. The **efficient market hypothesis** is that there is an elimination of profit opportunities in financial markets as stock prices adjust quickly to new information. Rates of return greater than those due to the price of risk disappear soon after any good news about a stock appears.

Many tests over the years have found the efficient market hypothesis to be a close approximation of security price determination. It has led to the growth in popularity of index funds, where investors do not pay advisers to tell them when to buy and sell stock. They simply invest in a fund that includes a large number of stocks.

efficient market hypothesis: the idea that markets adjust rapidly enough to eliminate profit opportunities immediately.

REVIEW

- Risk-averse investors require compensation to hold risky assets. This compensation may take the form of a higher expected return.

- When buyers and sellers trade stocks or bonds in the market, a relationship between return and risk emerges: Higher risk is associated with higher returns.

- Diversification reduces risk, but not below a bare minimum called systematic risk.

- The efficient market hypothesis predicts that stock prices adjust to eliminate rates of return in excess of those required to compensate for systematic risk.

The following excerpt from *The Daily Deal* (February 28, 2002) shows how fast prices adjust to new information in the stock market. As soon as Genesis Microchip—a company that designs, develops, and markets integrated circuits—revealed financial information that made the acquisition of another company not as profitable, its stock price dropped 41 percent in one day.

If you held Genesis stock and heard about the financial news and the drop in the price, you might have thought about selling the stock the next day. But that might not have been such a good idea, because the price already reflected the bad news.

Another type of news that affects stocks is new data about the state of the economy, collected and released by the U.S. government. Because of the impact of these data on markets, the government publishes a calendar that states in advance the date and exact time—precise to the minute—when inflation and unemployment statistics will be publicly released. The government distributes the news at the specified time to ensure that nobody has an unfair advantage.

Unexpected external factors can also affect the stock market. For example, the Dow Jones stock index dropped over 7 percent when the market reopened after September 11, 2001.

Strong Sales Make Sage Deal a Liability

The 41% slide in the share price of display chip maker Genesis Microchip Inc. on Feb. 27 proves that stellar financial performance is not always good for a company that just closed a major acquisition.

The Silicon Valley semiconductor company, which completed its $315 million purchase of smaller rival Sage Inc. on Feb. 20, told investors in a conference call Wednesday after the markets closed that the enlarged company will produce sales of $55 million in the first quarter of 2002, and $60 million in the second quarter.

Good news, it would seem, compared to pro forma projections before the merger closed last month. Yet the projections also revealed that Genesis so exceeded its own financial expectations in the last half of 2001 (while the Sage acquisition was still pending) that a deal which was supposed to be accretive to earnings was instead dilutive. The upshot: SoundView Technology Group Thursday reduced its earnings-per-share estimates for the upcoming fiscal year, which ends in March 2003, to $1.64 from $1.81 per share. "The company's definition of accretion will likely differ from what most investors expected," said SoundView analyst Scott Randall in the report.

Genesis' unexpectedly strong performance while the acquisition was pending—the San Jose, Calif.–based company reported 70% and 38% sequential revenue growth in the third and fourth periods of last year, respectively—clearly transformed the transaction from a financial enhancement, as it was billed when announced Sept. 28, to a drag on earnings, analysts said.

"Financially and in the near-term, Genesis would be better off if they wouldn't have done this deal," said Needham & Co. analyst Dan Scovel. Several other analysts downgraded Genesis stock Thursday morning. Trading in the shares was temporarily halted as the stock plummeted to a morning low of $24.35.

Genesis' recent strong performance also hurt it on another front. Its shares took an additional beating from news that the company would face a higher tax rate. During the Wednesday conference call, Genesis chief financial officer Peter Mangam said the company has revised its tax bracket from the 15% to 20% range upwards to 22% for the current fiscal year.

A major factor in this upward revision is Genesis having used up more tax credits than expected due to improved profitability in the second half of the fiscal year, Mangam said.

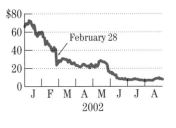

PRICE OF
GENESIS MICROCHIP STOCK
(IN DOLLARS)

February 28

$80, 60, 40, 20, 0

J F M A M J J A
2002

The Foreign Exchange Market

foreign exchange market: a market in which one currency (such as Japanese yen) can be exchanged for another currency (such as U.S. dollars).

exchange rate: the price of one currency in terms of another in the foreign exchange market. We express the exchange rate as the number of units of foreign currency that can be purchased with one unit of domestic currency. (Ch. 6)

The foreign exchange market is larger than the stock and bond markets combined. The **foreign exchange market** is where currencies of different countries are exchanged for one another. Foreign exchange traders—located at different financial centers around the world but linked together electronically—buy and sell an average of $1.5 trillion a day on this market. The prices on the foreign exchange market are the *exchange rates* between currencies, defined as the price of one currency in terms of another, for example, the number of yen per dollar.

Like any price, the exchange rate between two currencies depends on demand and supply. If the demand for dollars goes up, then the price for dollars in terms of foreign currency will rise. For example, if the demand for dollars goes up, the dollar may rise from about 107 yen per dollar to 138 yen per dollar. In practice, however, it is virtually impossible to determine the slopes and positions of supply and demand curves for foreign currency and use them to predict exchange rates. Thousands of currency traders are interested in obtaining foreign currency—not only to buy foreign goods, but also to hold foreign currency to speculate that its price might rise or fall. For example, you can exchange $1,000 for 100,000 yen if the exchange rate is 100 yen per dollar. Then if the dollar falls from 100 yen per dollar to 50 yen per dollar, you can trade your yen in for $2,000. That is a big rate of return. The supply and demand curves shift around by a large amount as expectations change. Exchange rate changes are difficult to predict and explain.

In fact, the foreign exchange market shares a very important similarity with stock and bond markets: *The exchange rate is greatly affected by people's expectations of rates of return from holding one currency compared with another.* The rate of return from holding one currency compared with another depends on the difference between the interest rates in each country and on whether the exchange rate is expected to appreciate or depreciate. When the rate of return changes, the exchange rate changes rapidly. For example, suppose that a high-ranking government official in Japan gives a speech with information that the yen is going to appreciate relative to the dollar; then people who heard the speech will buy yen anticipating a higher rate of return. But that buying will bid up the price of yen very quickly. A large sudden change in the exchange rate is observed. The story is much the same as when the president of a private corporation gives a speech announcing higher earnings at the corporation. People who hear the speech will buy that corporation's stock, expecting a higher rate of return, and the buying will bid up the price immediately. A large sudden change in the price of the stock is observed.

But exchange rates are also affected by other things in addition to rates of return. Because foreign currency is used to buy goods (such as cars) and services (such as vacations) in other countries, *the exchange rate is greatly affected by the price of goods and services in one country compared to another.* For example, if the average price of goods and services decreases in Japan compared to the United States—say because of a deflation in Japan—then more Americans will want to buy Japanese goods and services. The demand for yen to buy Japanese goods and services will thus increase, causing the yen to appreciate in value.

In this section we look at these two influences on the foreign exchange market— the differences in rates of return and differences in the average price of goods and services. Because the average price of goods and services moves more slowly than rates of return, the effects of average price differences tend to be spread out over longer periods of time. We first look at this slower moving, longer-term influence.

The table here is drawn from a larger table called "Currency Trading," published daily in the *Wall Street Journal*. The table shows the exchange rate (the price of foreign exchange) on the foreign exchange market on two days—the current day and the day before.

Observe that, for convenience, the exchange rate is stated in two equivalent ways: (1) the number of U.S. dollars for each unit of foreign currency, and (2) the number of foreign currency units for each U.S. dollar. One is the mathematical inverse of the other. For example, 120.35 yen per dollar is the same exchange rate as $1/(120.35)$ dollars per yen, or .0083091 dollar per yen, as stated in the table for Thursday, August 8, 2002.

The exchange rate in the table is the price at which banks traded large amounts of foreign currency with other banks. If you went to a bank or to an automatic teller machine at an airport, you would get fewer units of foreign currency for each of your U.S. dollars, so that the banks can earn some profit on the service they provide to you.

Observe the brand new European currency—the euro—created in January 1999. The euro has replaced the German mark, the French franc, the Italian lira, and the currencies of other European countries that now form a single currency area.

Thursday, August 8, 2002
EXCHANGE RATES

The New York foreign exchange mid-range rates below apply to trading among banks in amounts of $1 million and more, as quoted at 4 p.m. Eastern time by Reuters and other sources. Retail transactions provide fewer units of currency per dollar.

Country	U.S. $ equiv.		Currency per U.S. $		Country	U.S. $ equiv.		Currency per U.S. $	
	Wed	Tue	Wed	Tue		Wed	Tue	Wed	Tue
Argentina (Peso)	.27700831	.27700831	3.61	3.61	Jordan (Dinar)	1.41843972	1.41843972	.705	.705
Australia (Dollar)	.53694158	.53103924	1.8624	1.8831	Malaysia (Ringitt)-b	.26315789	.26315789	3.8	3.8
Brazil (Real)	.33167496	.32467532	3.015	3.08	Mexico (Peso)	.10270104	.10269049	9.737	9.738
Britain (Pound)	1.5376	1.5398	.6504	.6494	New Zealand (Dollar)	.45599635	.45199783	2.193	2.2124
Canada (Dollar)	.63411541	.63079543	1.577	1.5853	Pakistan (Rupee)	.01679966	.01679966	59.525	59.525
China (Renminbi)	.12081818	.12081964	8.2769	8.2768	Poland (Zloty)	.23860654	.23724792	4.191	4.215
Ecuador (US Dollar)-e	1	1	1	1	Russia (Ruble)-a	.03166561	.03168367	31.58	31.562
Hong Kong (Dollar)	.12820513	.12820513	7.8	7.8	Saudi Arabia (Riyal)	.26660268	.26660268	3.7509	3.7509
India (Rupee)	.02055498	.02054232	48.65	48.68	Singapore (Dollar)	.56721497	.56468462	1.763	1.7709
Indonesia (Rupiah)	.00011038	.00011007	9060	9085	South Africa (Rand)	.09560229	.09430404	10.46	10.604
Israel (Shekel)	.21244954	.21290185	4.707	4.697	South Korea (Won)	.00082988	.00082305	1205	1215
Japan (Yen)	**.0083091**	.00827335	**120.35**	120.87	Sweden (Krona)	.10461564	.10332927	9.5588	9.6778
					Taiwan (Dollar)	.02967359	.02955956	33.7	33.83
					Turkish (Lira)	.00000061	.00000061	1633000	1652500
					Euro	**.9745**	**.9666**	**1.0262**	**1.0346**

Exchange rate stated two ways:
.0083091 dollars per yen is the same exchange rate as 120.35 yen per dollar, because $1/(120.35) = .0083091$.

U.S. dollar fell slightly from 1.0346 euros per dollar on Tuesday to 1.0262 euros per dollar on Wednesday.

Differences in the Price of Goods and Services in Different Countries

To understand the influence of differences in the price of goods and services on the exchange rate, first suppose that the same exact good is sold in two countries and that transportation costs between countries are negligible compared to the price of the good. In this case, one would predict that the price of the good—after using the exchange rate to convert to the prices to the same currency—in the two countries should be the same. If the prices were not the same, then people could buy the good at the low price location and sell it at the high price location, making an easy profit. The principle that the prices of the same good in two locations should be equal in the absence of transportation costs is called the law of one price. The idea that the exchange rate between two countries is determined in such a way that the law of one price holds is called **purchasing power parity (PPP).**

purchasing power parity: the theory that exchange rates are determined in such a way that the prices of goods in different countries are the same when measured in the same currency.

Consider a good with a price that is much higher than its transportation cost—expensive vintage wine, for example. Suppose that, in August 2002, the wine cost 1,500 dollars per case in the United States and 1,000 pounds per case in Britain. Then, according to purchasing power parity, the exchange rate should be 1.5 dollars per pound.

In fact, the exchange rate was 1.54 dollars per pound in August 2002, so in this example, purchasing power parity works quite well. If purchasing power parity did not hold closely for tradable goods, people would either buy wine in Britain and ship the wine to the United States in order to make a nice profit, or vice versa. This would shift either supply or demand until purchasing power parity held. Hence, the exchange rate is such that the price of wine in the two countries is almost the same.

If goods are not so easily transported, then purchasing power parity does not always work as well. Suppose, for example, you tried to ship a McDonald's Big Mac purchased in the United States across the ocean. It would not be pleasant to eat. Even if you used an airplane, the Big Mac would be stale and decayed by the time it arrived at its destination. The transport costs in this case are prohibitive, and purchasing power parity does not always hold. Let us compare the price of a Big Mac in the United States with the price of a Big Mac in Europe. In April 2002, the average price of a Big Mac in the United States was about $2.49, while in Europe it was 2.67 euros. If the Big Macs were to cost exactly the same in the two locations, the exchange rate would have to be 1.072 euros per dollar. (To get this, divide 2.67 euros by 2.49 dollars to get 1.072 euros per dollar.) The actual exchange rate was 1.12 euros per dollar in April 2002. In this example, the Big Mac index implies that the dollar was overvalued against the euro in April 2002. However, by August 2002 the actual exchange rate was 1.03 euros per dollar—the dollar had depreciated so much that it was now undervalued against the euro, according to the Big Mac index.

To see how PPP is applied in practice, it is helpful to introduce some notation. Let P be the average price of goods in the United States and P^* the average price of goods in Japan. Then the purchasing power exchange rate (E) would be given by $E \times P = P^*$. For example, if the average price in the United States is $10 and the average price in Japan is 1,000 yen, then the purchasing power exchange rate is 100 yen per dollar, because $E \times P = (100 \times 10) = 1,000$ when $E = 100$. Now suppose that there is more inflation in the United States than in Japan, so that P rises to $20 and P^* stays constant; then, according to purchasing power parity, E must fall from 100 yen per dollar to 50 yen per dollar so that $E \times P = (50 \times 20)$ stays equal to P^*, which still equals 1,000 yen. Thus, an increase in prices in the United States will be matched by a depreciation of the dollar.

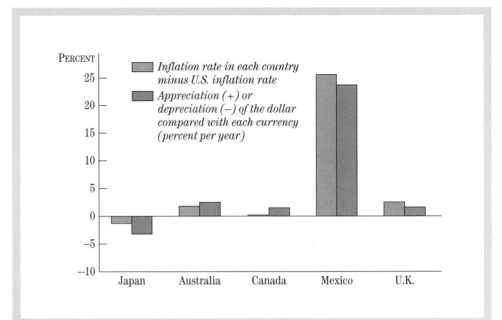

Figure 15.3
Purchasing Power Parity, 1970–2001
As predicted by purchasing power parity, the U.S. dollar has appreciated against the currencies of countries with high inflation (Australia, Canada, Mexico, the United Kingdom) and depreciated against the currencies of countries with low inflation (Japan).

Such an association between changes in average prices and the change in the exchange rate is exactly what happens over long periods, as shown in Figure 15.3. This figure shows (1) the percent increase in average prices—or the *inflation rate*—in several large countries compared to that in the United States, and (2) the percent change in the exchange rates of those different countries' currencies with that of the United States. For example, over this period from 1975 to 1995, the inflation rate in Italy was higher than that in the United States. Over the same period of time, the dollar appreciated relative to the lira, the Italian currency. The United Kingdom also had a higher inflation rate than the United States, and the dollar appreciated relative to the pound. Japan and Germany, on the other hand, had inflation rates that were on average lower than that in the United States, and, as purchasing power parity would predict, the dollar depreciated relative to the yen and mark. Purchasing power parity works well in explaining exchange rates over this time span.

Over shorter periods of time, however, the purchasing power parity theory does not work very well. For example, in the mid-1980s, the U.S. dollar was much higher than could be explained by purchasing power parity. To explain such events, we need to look at another important factor affecting exchange rates: differences in rates of return.

Differences in Rates of Return

International investors operating in the global foreign exchange market decide where to place their funds in order to get the highest return. The capital they invest is

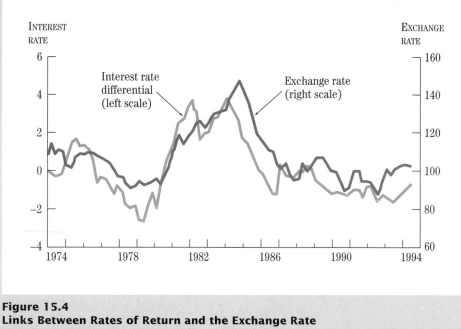

Figure 15.4
Links Between Rates of Return and the Exchange Rate
Note the correlation between the difference in interest rates in the United States and Japan (percent a year, green line) and the exchange rate (yen per dollar, blue line).

highly mobile. The movement of funds around the world to receive the highest return creates a link between the rate of return and the exchange rate that can explain the departures from purchasing power parity.

For example, if the interest rate on bonds in the United States rises relative to interest rates abroad, then the U.S. dollar becomes more attractive to international investors. Or, if the dollar exchange rate is expected to rise, then dollars will be in greater demand. For an investor deciding whether to put funds in a bank in the United States or Japan, a rise in the U.S. interest rate compared to that of Japan makes the United States more attractive, and this raises the price of the dollar. Similarly, if the U.S. interest rate falls relative to Japan's, the dollar will depreciate relative to the yen as international investors move their funds from the United States to Japan.

Figure 15.4 shows how the exchange rate correlates with the interest rate differential in Japan. The rise of the dollar relative to other countries in the early 1980s and its subsequent decline in the late 1980s are highly correlated with the interest rate differential. In the early 1980s, interest rates in the United States rose relative to those in other countries, and then in the mid-1980s, interest rates in the United States declined relative to those in other countries.

REVIEW

- The exchange rate is determined in the foreign exchange market, where different countries' currencies are bought and sold.

- Purchasing power parity is helpful in explaining exchange rates, but it does not explain everything.

- Another factor influencing exchange rates is the difference in rates of return between countries. When the interest rate in the United States rises relative to that in another country, the exchange rate rises. When news of an exchange rate appreciation spreads, people buy up the currency immediately.

- The relationship between rates of return and the exchange rate occurs because investors in the global foreign exchange market shift their funds in response to interest rate differentials.

Conclusion and Some Lessons

In this chapter we have seen how to employ some basic economic tools to analyze financial markets. In reviewing the lessons learned, it is helpful to see how they may apply to you personally.

First, by diversifying a portfolio of stocks, you can reduce risk substantially. Conversely, by holding an undiversified portfolio, you are needlessly incurring risk.

Second, be aware of the efficient market hypothesis that profit opportunity disappears quickly in financial markets. Trading securities frequently to seek out profits can result in high transaction costs. Diversification in a mutual fund—perhaps an index fund—can reduce the transaction costs of frequent buying and selling.

Third, if you do try to pick your own portfolio rather than use a mutual fund, concentrate on areas you are familiar with. If you go into a medical career, you may know more than even the best investors about the promise of a new medical device or drug.

Fourth, over the short run, holding corporate stocks is more risky than putting your funds in a bank account, but over the long term, the higher rate of return on stocks outweighs the risks for most people. However, if you need money in the short term—to pay next year's tuition, for example—stocks may not be worth the risk.

Fifth, exchange rates can fluctuate by large magnitudes and are very difficult to predict. If you are worried about a depreciation of the currency in a country you are about to travel to, then you can wait until the last minute to buy the currency, but speculating in foreign exchange is very risky.

KEY POINTS

1. Physical capital is a form of capital used to produce goods and services. Financial capital, including the stocks and bonds traded on the exchanges, is used by firms to obtain funds to invest in physical capital.

2. Once stocks and bonds are issued by firms, the shares trade on financial markets.

3. The rate of return on stocks is equal to the dividend plus the change in the price as a percentage of the price. The rate of return on bonds is the coupon plus the change in the price as a percentage of the price.

4. Risk-averse investors will buy more risky stocks or bonds only if the expected rate of return is higher.

5. In market equilibrium, there is a positive relationship between risk and rate of return. If you want to get a higher rate of return, you have to accept higher risk. In any case, diversification reduces risk.

6. Purchasing power parity explains changes in exchange rates due to large changes in the price of goods and services in different countries.

7. The price of a country's currency rises when interest rates in that country rise compared to those in other countries.

KEY TERMS

debt contract

equity contract

return

capital gain

capital loss

rate of return

dividend yield

earnings

price-earnings ratio

coupon

maturity date

face value

yield

expected return

equilibrium risk-return relationship

portfolio diversification

systematic risk

efficient market hypothesis

foreign exchange market

purchasing power parity

QUESTIONS FOR REVIEW

1. Why are the price and yield on bonds inversely related?

2. What is the rate of return on stocks? On bonds?

3. Why do stocks have higher rates of return than bank deposits over the long term?

4. What is the effect of diversification on risk?

5. Of what use is purchasing power parity as a theory of the price in foreign exchange markets?

6. Why does the difference between the interest rate in Japan and the United States matter for an American deciding how many Japanese yen to buy?

PROBLEMS

1. Which of the following are physical capital, and which are financial capital?
   a. A Toyota Camry at Avis Car Rental
   b. A loan you take out to start a newspaper business
   c. New desktop publishing equipment
   d. A bond issued by the U.S. government
   e. A pizza oven at Pizza Hut

2. The U.S. government issues a 1-year bond with a face value of $1,000 and a zero coupon. If the market interest rate is 10 percent, what will the market price of the bond be? Now suppose you observe that the bond price falls by 5 percent. What happens to its yield?

3. You are considering the purchase of stocks of two firms: a biotechnology corporation and a supermarket chain. Because of the uncertainty in the biotechnology industry, you estimate that there is a 50-50 chance of your either earning an 80 percent return on your investment

or losing 80 percent of your investment within a year. The food industry is more stable, so you estimate that you have a 50-50 chance of either earning 10 percent or losing 10 percent. Suppose that both stocks have equal expected returns. Which stock would you buy? Why? What do you think other investors would do? What would be the effect of these actions on the relative prices of the two stocks?

4. What is the expected return of the following stock market investment portfolio?

	Good Market	Bad Market	Disastrous Market
Probability	.50	.30	.20
Rate of return	.25	.10	−.25

   a. Would you choose this expected return or take a safe return of 7 percent from a savings deposit in your bank? Why?
   b. Suppose your teacher chooses the safe return from the bank. Is your teacher risk-averse? How can you tell?

5. Graph the data on risk and expected return (in percent) for the following securities.

Asset	Expected Rate of Return	Risk
Bank deposit	3	0
U.S. Treasury bills	4	3
Goodcorp bonds	9	10
ABC stock	11	24
XYZ stock	13	24
Riskyco stock	16	39

Draw an equilibrium risk-return line through the points. Which two assets should have changes in their prices in the near future? In which direction will their prices change?

6. a. Suppose a 2-year bond has a 5 percent coupon and $1,000 face value, and the current market interest rate is 5 percent. What is the price of the bond?

    b. Now suppose that you believe that the interest rate will remain 5 percent this year, but next year will fall to 3 percent. How much are you willing to pay for the 2-year bond today? Why?

7. What are the benefits of buying a mutual fund? Is there any risk in this investment?

8. Suppose that the average price of goods in Europe rises from 100 in the year 2000 to 130 in the year 2010. Suppose that the average price of goods in the United States rises from 120 in the year 2000 to 140 in 2010. Suppose that the exchange rate in 2000 was 1 euro per dollar. If purchasing power parity held in 2000, what would purchasing power parity predict for the exchange rate in 2010?

Present Discounted Value

A dollar in the future is worth less than a dollar today. This principle underlies all economic decisions involving actions over time. Whether you put some dollars under the mattress to be spent next summer, whether you borrow money from a friend or family member to be paid back next year, or whether you are a sophisticated investor in stocks, bonds, or real estate, that same principle is essential to making good decisions. Here we explain why the principle is essential and derive a formula for determining exactly *how much* less a dollar in the future is worth than a dollar today. The formula is called the *present discounted value formula.*

Discounting the Future

First let's answer the question, why is the value of a dollar in the future less than the value of a dollar today? The simplest answer is that a dollar can earn interest over time. Suppose a person you trust completely to pay off a debt gives you an IOU promising to pay you $100 in one year; how much is that IOU worth to you today? How much would you be willing to pay for the IOU today? It would be less than $100, because you could put an amount less than $100 in a bank and get $100 at the end of a year. The exact amount depends on the interest rate. If the interest rate is 10 percent, the $100 should be worth $90.91 because, if you put $90.91 in a bank earning 10 percent per year, at the end of the year you will have exactly $100. That is, $90.91 plus interest payments of $9.09 ($90.91 times .1 rounded to the nearest penny) equals $100.

The process of translating a future payment into a value in the present is called **discounting.** The value in the present of a future payment is called the **present discounted value.** The interest rate used to do the discounting is called the **discount rate.** In the preceding example, a future payment of $100 has a present discounted value of $90.91, and the discount rate is 10 percent. If the discount rate were 20 percent, the present discounted value would be $83.33 (because if you put $83.33 in a bank for a year at a 20 percent interest rate, you would have, rounding to the nearest penny, $100 at the end of the year). The term *discount* is used because the value in the present is *less* than the future payment; in other words, the payment is "discounted," much as a $100 bicycle on sale might be "discounted" to $83.33.

Finding the Present Discounted Value

The previous examples suggest that there is a formula for calculating present value, and indeed there is. Let

the present discounted value be PDV

the discount rate be i

the future payment be F

The symbol i is measured as a decimal, but we speak of the discount rate in percentage terms; thus we would say "the discount rate is 10 percent" and write "$i = .1$."

Now, the present discounted value PDV is the amount for which, if you put it in a bank today at an interest rate i, you would get an amount in the future equal to the future payment F. For example, if the future date is one year from now, then if you put the amount PDV in a bank for one year, you would get PDV times $(1 + i)$ at the end of the year. Thus, the PDV should be such that

$$PDV \times (1 + i) = F$$

Now divide both sides by $(1 + i)$; you get

$$PDV = \frac{F}{(1 + i)}$$

which is the formula for the present discounted value in the case of a payment made one year in the future. That is,

$$\text{Present discounted value} = \frac{\text{payment in one year}}{(1 + \text{the discount rate})}$$

For example, if the payment in one year is $100 and the discount rate $i = .1$, then the present discounted value is $90.91 [$100/(1 + .1)], just as we reasoned previously.

To obtain the formula for the case where the payment is made more than one year in the future, we must recognize that the amount in the present can be put in a bank and earn interest at the discount rate for more than one year. For example, if the interest rate is 10 percent, we could get $100 at the end of 2 years by investing $82.64 today. That is, putting $82.64 in the bank would give $82.64 times (1.1) at the end of one year; keeping all this in the bank for another year would give $82.64 times (1.1) times (1.1), or $82.64 times 1.21, or $100.00, again rounding off. Thus, in the case of a future payment in 2 years, we would have

$$PDV = \frac{F}{(1 + i)^2}$$

Analogous reasoning implies that the present discounted value of a payment made N years in the future would be

$$PDV = \frac{F}{(1 + i)^N}$$

For example, the present discounted value of a $100 payment to be made 20 years in the future is $14.86 if the discount rate is 10 percent. In other words, if you put $14.86 in the bank today at an interest rate of 10 percent, you would have about $100 at the end of 20 years. What is the present discounted value of a $100 payment to be made 100 years in the future? The above formula tells us that the PDV is only $.00726, less than a penny! All of these examples indicate that the higher the discount rate or the further in the future the payment is to be received, the lower the present discounted value of a future payment.

In many cases, we need to find the present discounted value of a *series* of payments made in several different years. We can do this by combining the previous formulas. The present discounted value of payments F_1 made in 1 year and F_2 made in 2 years would be

$$PDV = \frac{F_1}{(1 + i)} + \frac{F_2}{(1 + i)^2}$$

For example, the present discounted value of $100 paid in one year and $100 paid in 2 years would be $90.91 plus $82.64, or $173.55. In general, the present discounted value of a series of future payments $F_1, F_2, \ldots, F_N$ over N years is

$$PDV = \frac{F_1}{(1 + i)} + \frac{F_2}{(1 + i)^2} + \cdots + \frac{F_N}{(1 + i)^N}$$

Key Points

1. A dollar to be paid in the future is worth less than a dollar today.

2. The present discounted value of a future payment is the amount you would have to put in a bank today to get that same payment in the future.

3. The higher the discount rate, the lower the present discounted value of a future payment.

Key Terms and Definitions

discounting: the process of translating a future payment into a value in the present.
present discounted value: the value in the present of future payments.
discount rate: an interest rate used to discount a future payment when computing present discounted value.

Questions for Review

1. Why is the present discounted value of a future payment of $1 less than $1?

2. What is the relationship between the discount rate and the interest rate?

3. What happens to the present discounted value of a future payment as the payment date stretches into the future?

4. Why is discounting important for decisions involving actions at different dates?

Problems

1. Find the present discounted value of
   a. $100 to be paid at the end of 3 years.
   b. $1,000 to be paid at the end of 1 year plus $1,000 to be paid at the end of 2 years.
   c. $10 to be paid at the end of 1 year, $10 at the end of 2 years, and $100 at the end of 3 years.

2. The Disney Company issued corporate bonds, sometimes called "Mickey Mouse" bonds, that simply promised to pay $1,000 in 100 years, with no payments of interest. What is the present discounted value of one of these bonds on the date issued if the interest rate is 10 percent? How about 5 percent?

3. Suppose you win $1,000,000 in a lottery and your winnings are scheduled to be paid as follows: $300,000 at the end of 1 year, $300,000 at the end of 2 years, and $400,000 at the end of 3 years. If the interest rate is 10 percent, what is the present discounted value of your winnings?

Trade and Global Markets

CHAPTER 16

Economic Growth Around the World

Half a million foreign students are now studying in colleges and universities in the United States. Maybe you know some of these students. Maybe you *are* one of these students. There are also about half a million foreign students studying in Germany, France, Japan, and other countries. Many of those foreign students are Americans. Studying abroad is one of the ways in which technical knowledge is spread around the world. Thanks to improvements in telecommunications, including the Internet, the ability to spread information is increasing rapidly.

This highly visible diffusion of information raises some fundamental questions about economic theory, especially about economic growth theory. While economic growth theory tells us how technology and capital have provided people with the means to raise their productivity, there is something disquieting about the theory when we look around the world. As we compare living standards, it is clear that people in some countries are much better off than people in other countries. Why has the theory applied so unevenly to different countries around the world, with some growing rapidly and some stuck in poverty, not growing at all? Why hasn't the spread of technological information allowed poor countries to grow faster?

In this chapter, we look for answers to these crucial questions about the uneven patterns of economic growth in different countries. We begin our quest for the answers by looking at economic growth performance in different parts of the world.

Catching Up or Not?

growth accounting formula:
Productivity growth rate =
$\frac{1}{3}\left(\begin{array}{l}\text{growth rate of capital}\\ \text{per hour of work}\end{array}\right) +$
(growth rate of technology)

(Ch. 8)

catch-up line: the downward-sloping relation between the level of productivity and the growth of productivity predicted by growth theory.

If technological advances can spread easily, as seems reasonable with modern communications, then poorer regions with low productivity and low income per capita will tend to catch up to richer regions by growing more rapidly. Why? If the spread of new technology is not difficult, then regions with lower productivity can adopt the more advanced technology of other regions to raise their productivity. Recall from the *growth accounting formula* that an increase in the growth of technology leads to an increase in productivity growth.

Investment in new capital would also tend to cause poor regions to catch up to the rich. Consider a relatively poor region in which both capital per worker and output per worker are low. Imagine several hundred workers constructing a road with only a little capital—perhaps only a few picks and shovels, not even a jackhammer. With such low levels of capital, the returns to increasing the amount of capital would be very high. The addition of a few trucks and some earthmoving equipment to the construction project would bring huge returns in higher output. Regions with relatively low levels of capital per worker would therefore attract a greater amount of investment, and capital would grow rapidly. The growth accounting formula tells us that productivity grows rapidly when capital per worker grows rapidly. Thus, productivity would grow rapidly in poorer regions where capital per worker is low.

A rich region where the capital per worker is high, however, would gain relatively little from additional capital. Such a region would attract little investment, and the growth rate of capital would be lower; therefore, the growth of productivity would also be lower.

In summary, economic growth theory predicts that regions with low productivity will grow relatively more rapidly than regions with high productivity. Regions with low productivity will tend to catch up to the more advanced regions by adopting existing technology and attracting capital.

Figure 16.1 illustrates this catch-up phenomenon. It shows the level of productivity on the horizontal axis and the growth rate of productivity on the vertical axis. The downward-sloping line is the **catch-up line.** A country or region on the upper left-hand part of the line is poor—with low productivity and, therefore, low income per capita—but growing rapidly. A country on the lower right-hand part of the line is rich—with high productivity and, therefore, high income per capita—but growth is relatively less rapid. That the catch-up line exists and is downward-sloping is a prediction of growth theory.

Catch-up Within the United States

Let us first see how the catch-up line works when the regions are the states within the United States. Figure 16.2 presents the data on real income per capita and the growth rates of real income per capita for each of the states. Because productivity and real income per capita move closely together, we can examine the accuracy of the catch-up line using the real income per capita data. (Again, the adjective *real* means that the income data are adjusted for inflation.) Real income per capita in 1880 is on the horizontal axis, and the growth rate of real income per capita from 1880 to 1980 is on the vertical axis. Each point on the scatter diagram represents a state, and a few of the states are labeled. If you pick a state (observe Nevada, for example, down and to the right), you can read its growth rate by looking over to the left scale, and you can read its 1880 income per capita level by looking down to the horizontal scale.

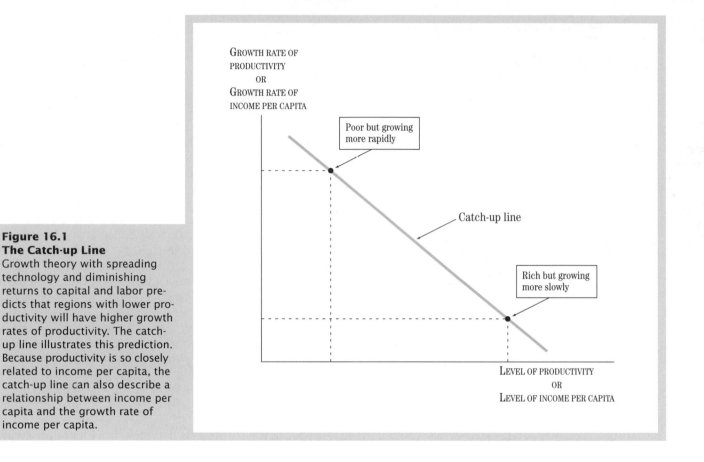

Figure 16.1
The Catch-up Line
Growth theory with spreading technology and diminishing returns to capital and labor predicts that regions with lower productivity will have higher growth rates of productivity. The catch-up line illustrates this prediction. Because productivity is so closely related to income per capita, the catch-up line can also describe a relationship between income per capita and the growth rate of income per capita.

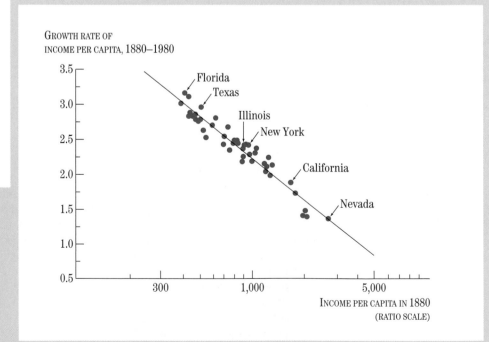

Figure 16.2
Evidence of Catch-up Within the United States
In the United States, those states that had low real income per capita in 1880 grew relatively rapidly compared to states that had high income per capita. The poor states tended to catch up to the richer states. A catch-up line is drawn through the dots.

The diagram clearly shows a tendency for states with low real income per capita in 1880 to have had high growth rates since then. The state observations fall remarkably near a catch-up line. Southern states like Florida and Texas are in the high-growth group. On the other hand, in states that had a relatively high income per capita in 1880, income per capita grew relatively slowly. This group includes California and Nevada.

Thus, the theory of growth works quite well in explaining the relative differences in growth rates in the states of the United States. There is a tendency for relatively poor regions to grow more rapidly than relatively rich regions.

Catch-up in the Advanced Countries

What if we apply the same thinking to different countries? After all, communication is now global. Figure 16.3 is another scatter diagram with growth rate and income per capita combinations. It is like Figure 16.2 except that it plots real GDP per capita in 1960 against growth in real GDP per capita from 1960 to 1990 for several advanced countries.

Observe in Figure 16.3 that the richer countries, such as the United States, grew less rapidly. In contrast, relatively less rich countries, such as Greece, Portugal, Spain, and Italy, grew more rapidly. Canada and France are somewhere in between. These countries tend to display the catch-up behavior predicted by the growth theory. Apparently, technological advances are spreading and capital-labor ratios are rising more rapidly in countries where they are low and returns to capital are high. So far, our look at the evidence confirms the predictions of growth theory.

Catch-up in the Whole World

However, so far we have not looked beyond the most advanced countries. Figure 16.4 shows a broader group of countries that includes not only the more advanced

Figure 16.3
Evidence of Catch-up in More Advanced Countries, 1960–1990
For the advanced countries shown in the diagram, GDP per capita growth has been more rapid for those that started from a lower level of GDP per capita. Thus, there has been catching up, as shown by the catch-up line drawn through the points.

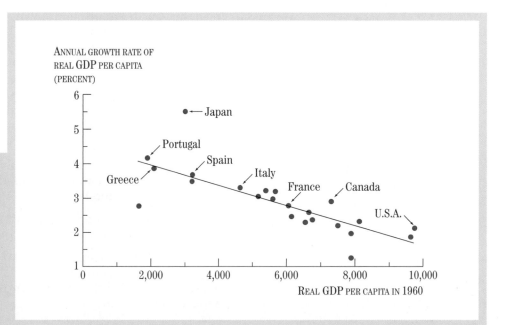

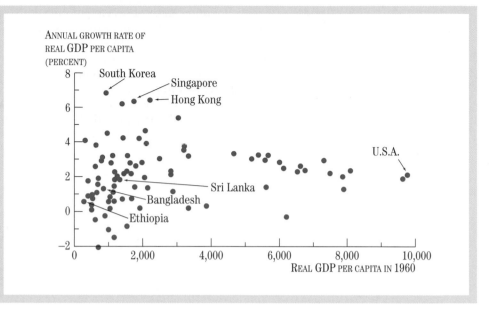

Figure 16.4
Lack of Catch-up for Developing Countries, 1960–1990
Unlike the states in the United States or the advanced countries, there has been little tendency for poor countries to grow more rapidly than rich countries. The gap between rich and poor has not closed.

countries in Figure 16.3 but also countries that are still developing. It is apparent that there is little tendency for this larger group of countries to fall along a catch-up line.

The countries with very low growth rates, such as Bangladesh and Ethiopia, are also the countries with very low GDP per capita. On the other hand, many countries with higher growth rates had a much higher GDP per capita. Singapore and Hong Kong had higher growth rates than Sri Lanka and Ethiopia even though their GDP per capita was above that of these countries.

Comparing countries like Singapore and South Korea with countries like Bangladesh and Sri Lanka is striking. South Korea and Singapore had about the same real GDP per capita as Sri Lanka and Bangladesh in 1960, but South Korea and Singapore surged ahead with a more rapid growth rate over the next 30 years, leaving Bangladesh and Sri Lanka behind. And this is not the exception. Contrary to the predictions of the economic growth theory, which says that technological advances should spread and capital per hour of work should rise from low levels, Figure 16.4 shows little tendency for relatively poor countries to grow relatively rapidly. It appears that something has been preventing either the spread and the adoption of new technology or the increase in investment needed to raise capital-labor ratios. We examine possible explanations as this chapter proceeds.

REVIEW
- Economic growth theory predicts that poorer regions will tend to catch up to richer ones. The flow of technology around the world and investment in new capital will bring this about.

- Data for the states in the United States and for the more advanced countries show that such catch-up exists and is quite strong.

- However, there has been little evidence of catch-up in the world as a whole. Many of the poor countries have fallen even further behind the developed countries, while other poor countries, in particular those in East Asia, have grown very rapidly.

Economic Development

As well as raising questions about economic growth theory, the lack of catch-up evidenced in Figure 16.4 presents a disturbing situation. There are huge disparities in world income distribution, and billions of people in low-income countries lack the necessities that those in high-income countries frequently take for granted.

Billions Still in Poverty

The richest countries in the world, with more than $10,000 income per capita, account for about 700 million people. The United States, with 275 million people, is among the richest, along with Japan and most of Western Europe. Another 600 million people live in countries that have an income per capita between $5,000 and $10,000. But the vast majority of the world's people—about three-fourths—live in countries with an income per capita of less than $5,000 per year. This is below the poverty level in advanced countries. Income per capita in South Korea, Venezuela, and Malaysia is only about one-third that in the United States. In China and Sri Lanka, income per capita is only one-eighth that in the United States. Income per capita for Ethiopia is a mere 2 percent of that in the United States.

Low income per capita is a serious economic problem, but the implications go well beyond economics. Large differences in income per capita and vast amounts of poverty can lead to war, revolution, or regional conflicts. Will these differences persist? Or is the lack of catch-up that has left so many behind a thing of the past?

Geographical Patterns

Figure 16.5 shows the location of the relatively rich and the relatively poor countries around the world. Notice that the higher-income countries tend to be in the northern part of the world. An exception to this rule is the relatively high income per capita in Australia and New Zealand. Aside from these exceptions, income disparity appears to have a geographical pattern—the North is relatively rich and the South relatively poor. Often people use the term *North-South problem* to describe world income disparities.

But whether it is North versus South or not, there do appear to be large contiguous regions where many rich or many poor countries are located together. The original increase in economic growth that occurred at the time of the Industrial Revolution started in northwestern Europe—England, France, and Germany. It then spread to America, which industrialized rapidly in the nineteenth and twentieth centuries. It also spread to Japan during the late-nineteenth-century Meiji Restoration, one of the main purposes of which was to import Western technology into the Japanese economy.

economic development: the process of growth by which countries raise incomes per capita and become industrialized; also refers to the branch of economics that studies this process.

developing country: a country that is poor by world standards in terms of real GDP per capita.

Terminology of Economic Development

Economic development is the branch of economics that endeavors to explain why poor countries do not develop faster and to find policies to help them develop faster. Economists who specialize in economic development frequently are experts on the problems experienced by particular countries—such as a poor educational system, political repression, droughts, or poor distribution of food. The term **developing country** describes those countries that are relatively poor. In contrast, the term

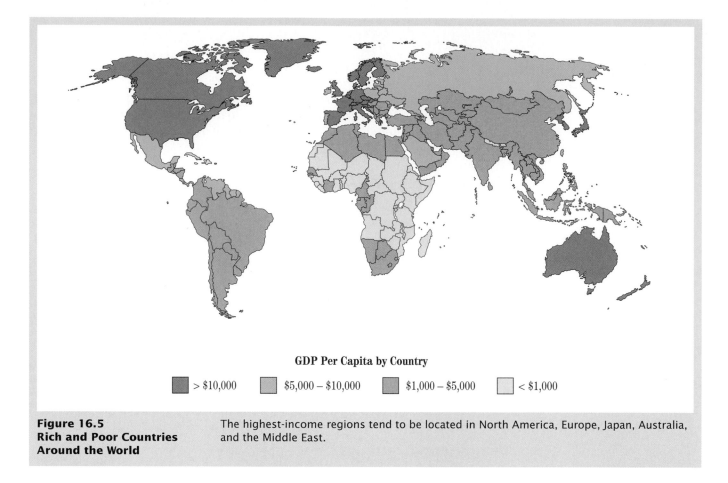

GDP Per Capita by Country

▇ > $10,000   ▇ $5,000 – $10,000   ▇ $1,000 – $5,000   ▢ < $1,000

Figure 16.5
Rich and Poor Countries
Around the World

The highest-income regions tend to be located in North America, Europe, Japan, Australia, and the Middle East.

industrialized country or *advanced economy* describes relatively well-off countries. Sometimes the term *less-developed country (LDC)* is used rather than *developing country*. There are also terms to distinguish between different developing countries. *Newly industrialized countries* such as Korea and Singapore are relatively poor countries that are growing rapidly. *Countries in transition* are relatively poor countries, such as Russia and Poland, that are moving from central planning to market economies.

Table 16.1 shows the shares of world GDP produced by advanced economies, developing countries, and countries in transition. Thus, this table looks at aggregate income (which equals GDP) rather than at income per capita. Over 50 percent of world GDP comes from industrialized countries.

Most striking is the nearly 22 percent share of world GDP in Asia outside of Japan. This large share is due to the newly industrialized countries and to China. China's GDP is already larger than Japan's. Although income per capita is less, China is already a major force in the world economy.

Economic development economists working at universities, the World Bank, the International Monetary Fund, the United Nations, and of course in the developing countries themselves focus their research on reasons why poor countries have grown so slowly. We now proceed to examine these reasons; in doing so, we will touch on some of the central issues of economic development. Our examination will consider the two key determinants of increasing productivity—improvements in technology and higher capital per worker. We consider technology in the next section and then go on to consider capital in the following section.

Table 16.1
Shares of World GDP Produced by Different Countries

	Number of Countries	Percent of World GDP
Advanced Economies	**29**	**56.3**
Major industrialized countries	7	44.7
United States		21.4
Japan		7.3
Germany		4.5
France		3.2
Italy		3.1
United Kingdom		3.1
Canada		2.0
Other advanced economies	22	11.6
Developing Countries	**125**	**37.6**
By region		
Africa	51	3.2
Asia	25	22.2
Middle East and Europe	16	4.0
Western Hemisphere	33	8.2
Countries in Transition	**28**	**6.2**
Central and Eastern Europe	16	2.3
Russia	1	2.6
Transcaucas and Central Asia	11	1.2

Source: From *World Economic Outlook*, October 1999, p. 159. Updated by the author. Reprinted by permission of International Monetary Fund.

REVIEW

- The slow productivity growth in poor countries has resulted in extreme income inequality around the world. The growth miracle has spread to parts of the world, but productivity in many developing countries of the world has remained low.

- With a few exceptions, most of the rich countries are in the northern regions of the globe and most of the poor countries are in the southern regions, thus giving rise to the term *North-South problem*.

- About 75 percent of the world's population lives in countries with less than $5,000 income per capita.

Spreading and Using Technology

There are two important facts to remember about economic growth. First, a large and persistent increase in economic growth began during the Industrial Revolution about 200 years ago, and this increase in economic growth raised income per capita in some countries to levels experienced only by royalty throughout most of human history. Second, economic growth did not spread throughout much of the world, leaving people in many countries hardly better off than their ancestors. Could these two facts be linked? Could they have the same explanation? A number of ideas have been put forth to explain the increase in economic growth in the late 1700s, and some of these may help explain why growth has not accelerated in many developing countries.

Empowering Entrepreneurs

Some economists and historians have pointed to developments in science as the explanation of the rapid increase in economic growth in Europe in the 1700s. But if that is the explanation, why did the Industrial Revolution not begin in China or in the Islamic nations, where scientific knowledge was far more advanced than in Europe? Others note the importance of natural resources, but these were available in many other countries where there was no Industrial Revolution; also, growth in Japan has been high since the mid-nineteenth century, yet Japan has almost no natural resources. Still others have focused on exploitation, slavery, colonialism, and imperialism, but these evils existed long before the Industrial Revolution.

What, then, is the reason for this increase in economic growth that we associate with the Industrial Revolution? Historians of capitalist development from Karl Marx onward have stressed that in the 1700s, for the first time in human history, entrepreneurs were gaining the freedom to start business enterprises. Economic historian Angus Maddison shows in an influential book, *Phases of Capitalist Development*, that the Dutch were the first to lead in productivity, with the British and then the United States soon catching up. He also shows that in the 1700s many Dutch farmers owned their land, the feudal nobility was small and weak, and the potential power was in the hands of entrepreneurs. Hence there was greater freedom to produce and sell manufactured and agricultural products. By the late 1700s and early 1800s, similar conditions existed in the United Kingdom and the United States. Firms could ship their products to market and hire workers without political restrictions.

Moreover, these firms were able to earn as much as they could by selling whatever they wanted at whatever price the market determined. They began to invent and develop products that were most beneficial to individuals. The business enterprises could keep the profits. Profits were no longer confiscated by nobles or kings. Individual property rights—including the right to earn and keep profits—were being established and recognized in the courts.

Karl Marx—although known more for his critique of capitalism—saw earlier than others that the unleashing of business enterprises and entrepreneurs was the key to economic growth. He credited the business and entrepreneurial class—what he called the bourgeois class—with the creation of more wealth than had previously been created in all of history.

In sum, the sudden increase in technology and productivity may have occurred when it did because of the increased freedom that entrepreneurs had to start businesses, to invent and apply new ideas, and to develop products for the mass of humanity where the large markets existed.

Remaining Problems in Developing Countries

If true, the idea that the economic growth surge in the late 1700s and 1800s was caused by the removal of restrictions on business enterprises may have lessons for economic development. In many developing countries, there are restrictions on entrepreneurial activity and weak enforcement of individual property rights.

■ **Regulation and Legal Rights.**   Good examples of these restrictions have been documented in the research of economist Hernando de Soto on the economy of Peru. De Soto showed that there is a tremendous amount of regulation in the devel-

informal economy: the portion of an economy characterized by illegal, unregulated businesses.

oping countries. This regulation has been so costly that a huge informal economy has emerged. The **informal economy** consists of large numbers of illegal businesses that can avoid the regulations. Remarkably, de Soto found that 61 percent of employment in Peru was in the informal, unregulated, illegal sector of the economy. In the city of Lima, around 33 percent of the houses were built by this informal sector. About 71,000 illegal vendors dominated retail trade, and 93 percent of urban transportation was in the informal sector.

This large informal sector exists because the costs of setting up a legal business are high. It takes 32 months—filling out forms, waiting for approval, getting permission from several agencies—for a person to start a retail business. It takes 6 years and 11 months to start a housing construction firm. Hence, it is essentially impossible for someone to try to start a small business in the legal sector. Therefore, the informal sector grows.

Why does it matter if the informal sector is large? How does this impede development? Precisely because the sector is informal, it lacks basic legal rights such as the enforcement of the laws of property rights and contracts. These laws cannot be enforced in a sector that is outside the law. Bringing new inventions to market requires the security of private property so that the inventor can capture the benefits from taking the risks. Without this, the earnings from the innovation might be taken away by the government or by firms that copy the idea illegally. For example, if a business in the informal sector finds that another firm has reneged on a contract to deliver a product, that firm has no right to use the courts to enforce the contract because the business itself is illegal.

Some economists feel that weak enforcement of individual property rights is at the heart of the poor economic performance of Russia. The explanation given earlier for why the Industrial Revolution occurred in Western countries seems to point to this as a reason. In Europe in the 1700s, a new freedom for businesses to operate in the emerging market economy led to new products and technology. Laws to prevent theft or fraud gave people more certainty about reaping the returns from their entrepreneurship.

■ **Lack of Human Capital.**   In order for existing technology to be adopted—whether in the form of innovative organizational structures of firms or as new products—it is necessary to have well-trained and highly skilled workers. For example, it is hard to make use of sophisticated computers to increase productivity when there are few skilled computer programmers.

Recall that human capital refers to the education and training of workers. Low investment in human capital is a serious obstacle to increasing productivity because it hampers the ability of countries that are behind to use new technology.

In fact, economists have found that differences in human capital in different countries can explain why some countries have been more successful at catching up than others. The developing countries that have been catching up most rapidly—in particular the newly industrialized countries like South Korea, Hong Kong, Taiwan, and Singapore—have strong educational systems in grade school and high school. This demonstrates the enormous importance of human capital for raising productivity.

REVIEW   ▪ The removal of restrictions on private enterprise and enforcement of individual property rights may have been the key factors unleashing the growth of productivity at the time of the Industrial Revolution. Similar restrictions in developing countries may have tended to stifle development in recent years.

- An educated work force is needed to adopt technology. Better-educated and more highly skilled workers—those with human capital—can also use available capital more efficiently.

Increasing Capital per Worker

In addition to obstacles to the spread and adoption of new technology, there are obstacles to the increase in capital per worker that can prevent poor countries from catching up.

Population Growth

In order for the capital to labor ratio to increase, it is necessary to invest in new capital. However, the amount of investment in new capital must be larger than the increase in labor, or capital will increase by less than labor and the ratio of capital to labor—the factor influencing productivity—will fall. Thus, high population growth raises the amount of investment needed in order to increase, or even maintain, the level of capital per worker. High population growth rates can, therefore, slow down the increase in capital per worker.

Population growth rates have declined substantially in countries where income per capita has risen to high levels, such as Europe, Japan, and the United States. Economic analysis of the determinants of population indicates that the high income per capita and resulting greater life expectancy may be the reason for the decline in population growth. When countries reach a level of income per capita where people can survive into their old age without the support of many children, or where there is a greater chance of children reaching working age, people choose to have fewer children. Hence, higher income per capita in developing countries would probably reduce population growth in these countries.

National Saving

Capital accumulation requires investment, which requires saving. From our national income accounting equation, $Y = C + I + G + X$, we get the equation $Y - C - G = I + X$, which states that national saving is equal to the sum of investment plus net exports. Recall that national saving is the sum of private saving and government saving. In some developing countries where income per capita is barely above subsistence levels, the level of private saving—people's income less their consumption—is low. Government saving—tax receipts less expenditures—is also often low, perhaps because there is little income to tax and because governments have trouble controlling expenditures. Figure 16.6 shows the very low saving rates in the poorest countries of Africa and south Asia compared with the highest-saving countries.

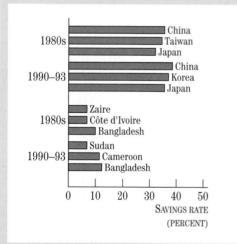

Figure 16.6
The Highest- and Lowest-Saving Countries
Very low national saving rates in poor countries impede capital accumulation and growth.

National saving =
   investment + net exports
$S = I + X$

Foreign Investment from the Advanced Economies

foreign direct investment: investment by a foreign entity of at least a 10 percent direct ownership share in a firm.

Investment from abroad can come in the form of **foreign direct investment,** such as when the U.S. firm Gap Inc. opens a store in Mexico. Technically, when a foreign firm invests in more than 10 percent of the ownership of a business in another country, that investment is defined as direct investment.

Foreign investment also occurs when foreigners buy smaller percentages (less than 10 percent) of firms in developing economies. For example, foreign investment in Mexico takes place when a German buys newly offered common stock in a Mexican firm. In that case, the foreign investment from abroad is defined as **portfolio investment,** that is, less than 10 percent of ownership in a company.

portfolio investment: investment by a foreign entity of less than a 10 percent ownership share in a firm.

World Bank: an international agency, established after World War II, designed to promote the economic development of poorer countries through lending channeled from industrialized countries.

Another way investment can flow in from abroad is through borrowing. Firms in developing economies or their governments can borrow from commercial banks, such as the Bank of America, Dai-Ichi Kangyo, or Crédit Lyonnais. Sometimes the governments of developing economies obtain loans directly from the governments of industrialized economies. Borrowing from government-sponsored international financial institutions, such as the International Monetary Fund (IMF) and the World Bank, can also occur

International Monetary Fund (IMF): an international agency, established after World War II, designed to help countries with balance of payments problems and to ensure the smooth functioning of the international monetary system.

■ **The Role of International Financial Institutions.**   The **World Bank** and the **International Monetary Fund (IMF)** were established after World War II as part of a major reform of the international monetary system. Both institutions make loans to the developing countries. They serve as intermediaries, channeling funds from the industrial countries to the developing countries.

Many of the World Bank's loans are for specific projects—such as building a $100 million dam for irrigation in Brazil and a $153 million highway in Poland. Although

Anti-Globalization Protests
In recent years, the annual meetings of the World Bank and the IMF have attracted thousands of demonstrators protesting the poverty and pollution they associate with the drive for globalization. Many demonstrators have called for the reduction of the debt that poor countries owe to rich ones.

ECONOMICS IN ACTION

Has World Saving Shifted Down?

Has there been a downward shift worldwide in people's desire to save?

On average, national saving rates around the world have declined from about 25 percent to about 23 percent from the 1970s to the 1990s. But that might reflect a drop in the demand for investment rather than a shift in saving. If it were due to a downward shift in saving, then policies to stimulate saving around the world might be appropriate.

To determine whether there has been a shift in saving or investment, we can look at what happened to interest rates and utilize the saving-investment diagram introduced in Chapter 6 and shown here. The world interest rate is measured on the vertical axis, and world saving or investment as a share of world GDP is on the horizontal axis. Recall that, along the green saving curve, the saving rate rises as the interest rate rises because a higher interest rate gives people a greater incentive to save. Recall also that, along the purple investment curve, the investment rate declines as the interest rate rises because a higher interest rate discourages businesses from investing in plant and equipment. For the whole world, net exports must be zero, so the world investment rate must equal the world saving rate; hence, the equilibrium interest rate is found at the intersection of the two curves. We can conveniently ignore net exports in the analysis because $X = 0$.

The interest rate/saving rate observations are shown in the diagram. It turns out that when the world saving rate fell from 25 to 23 percent, the average world real interest rate rose, as shown in the diagram. Observe how these observations can be explained by a leftward shift of the world saving rate in the direction of lower world saving. Such a shift *raises* the equilibrium interest rate and lowers the equilibrium investment and saving rate. In contrast, a shift in the world investment curve toward lower investment, perhaps because of a decline in investment demand in developing countries, would *lower* the equilibrium interest rate. Hence, we can use the interest rate/saving rate observations to identify a shift in the world saving curve. We can conclude that world saving shifted down in the 1990s, at least compared with the 1970s. What are the implications of this shift for growth in less developed countries?

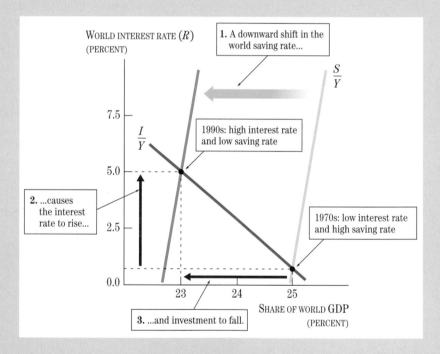

these project loans have been helpful, they are much smaller in total than private investment in these countries.

In recent years, the IMF has tried to use its loans to encourage countries to implement difficult economic reforms. Frequently, it tries to induce countries to make these reforms by making the loans conditional on the reforms; this is the idea of *conditionality*. Under conditionality, the IMF gives loans to countries only if the countries undertake economic reform—such as eliminating price controls or privatizing firms. This conditionality is viewed as a way to encourage reforms that are difficult to put into effect because of the various vested interests in each country.

However, the IMF has been heavily criticized in recent years for going too far with its conditions and actually giving bad economic advice to developing countries. For example, during the financial crisis in East Asia in 1997 and 1998, the IMF insisted that the countries in crisis implement politically controversial reforms before it would agree to make loans to deal with the crisis. This criticism has led to the creation of several commissions to suggest reforms of the IMF.

■ **Are the Advanced Countries Saving Enough?**   Despite the existence of these channels by which capital can flow to developing economies, there is a serious question as to whether the advanced economies are saving enough to provide the increased capital to developing countries. When an individual country saves more than it invests at home, it makes foreign investment abroad. A country can invest more than it saves by borrowing from abroad. In the whole world economy, saving must equal investment, because (as of this writing) there seems to be no one in outer space to borrow from.

In fact, national saving rates have shifted down around the world. The large trade deficit in the United States in recent years means that investment is greater than national saving. Hence, the United States is a net user rather than a supplier of saving. Countries with large trade surpluses (such as Japan) are the only net suppliers of saving to the rest of the world.

REVIEW

- High rates of population growth and low national saving rates are two of the obstacles to raising capital per worker in developing economies.

- The International Monetary Fund makes loans to developing countries. The loans are frequently conditional on an economic reform program, a practice that came under heavy criticism in the Asian financial crisis of the 1990s.

- The World Bank makes loans mainly for specific projects.

Conclusion

In this chapter, we have shown how productivity has increased in many countries because of higher capital per worker and technological change. In some cases there has been a convergence of productivity, with the poorer countries moving closer to the richer countries. However, for many developing countries, productivity has not been catching up, and income per capita remains very low. The many countries in Africa are still in extreme poverty.

Among the possible explanations for the lack of catch-up are obstacles to the spread of technology, such as government restrictions on entrepreneurs and a shortage of human capital, and obstacles to higher capital per worker, such as low saving rates and low foreign investment. The removal of similar obstacles in Western Europe in the eighteenth century may have been the cause of the Industrial Revolution. Their removal today may result in another great growth wave in the developing economies.

In fact, there are already signs of the removal of such obstacles to economic growth. Hence, in the absence of retrenchments or setbacks from ethnic and military conflicts, we may see higher productivity growth in the poorer countries in the future than we have seen in the past. If so, the economic landscape of the world will be transformed.

Suppose, for example, that real GDP in the industrialized countries grows at a 2.5 percent pace for the next 50 years. Suppose that real GDP in all the other countries of the world grows at 5 percent per year. With these growth rates, the countries we now classify as developing or in transition would produce 75 percent of world GDP in the year 2050, and the countries we now classify as industrialized would produce 25 percent—a complete about-face from the current situation. This, of course, is an example, not a forecast, but it hints at some of the amazing possibilities for the future.

HEY POINTS

1. Economic growth theory pinpoints capital accumulation and technological change as the two key ingredients of productivity growth. In a world without obstacles to the spread of technology or to investment in new capital, growth theory predicts that poor regions will catch up to rich regions.

2. Catch-up has occurred in the states of the United States and among the industrialized countries but is distressingly absent from developing countries.

3. Low incomes and poverty have persisted for the vast majority of the world's population while other countries have become richer.

4. Insufficient capital accumulation in the poor countries, due to high population growth, low saving rates, or insufficient capital flows from the advanced countries, is part of the problem.

5. Higher population growth means that more investment is required in order to raise capital per worker.

6. Some countries may have poor growth performance because of restrictions on markets and a lack of property rights. The lifting of those restrictions in Europe in the 1700s was a cause of the economic growth associated with the Industrial Revolution.

7. The removal of such restrictions may be a key to increased productivity and economic development.

8. Low investment in human capital is another reason for low productivity growth.

9. In many countries today, especially in Latin America and China, there is a great potential for higher economic growth as the market system is being encouraged and restrictions on entrepreneurs are being removed.

10. Another great growth wave would change the economic landscape of the whole world.

HEY TERMS

catch-up line
economic development
developing country

informal economy
foreign direct investment

portfolio investment
World Bank

International Monetary
Fund (IMF)

QUESTIONS FOR REVIEW

1. Why does economic growth theory predict that productivity and real income per capita will grow relatively more rapidly in poor countries?

2. In what way does the catch-up line describe more rapid growth in poor countries?

3. Why is catch-up observed among the industrialized economies but not for the whole world?

4. Why is the identity that investment plus net exports equals saving important for understanding the flow of capital around the world?

5. What is the difference between foreign direct investment and portfolio investment?

6. Why is human capital important for the spread of technology?

7. What is the significance of conditionality for IMF loans?

8. What do government restrictions on entrepreneurs have to do with economic growth?

9. What harm does an informal economy cause?

PROBLEMS

1. Plot on a scatter diagram the data for the Asian countries that appear below. Does there appear to be a catch-up line in the scatter diagram?

Country	Per Capita Real GDP in 1965 (1984 U.S. dollars)	Average Annual Rate of Growth from 1965 to 1985 (%)
Thailand	360	4.0
Pakistan	210	2.4
Philippines	380	1.9
China	110	5.1
Malaysia	330	4.3
Indonesia	190	4.6

2. In 1997 and 1998, there was a financial crisis in some of the countries listed in problem 1 that caused recessions, apparently temporary deviations of real GDP from potential GDP. How do you think the crisis will affect the catch-up phenomenon in the future?

3. The states of the United States have moved toward one another in real income per capita over the past 100 years, but the countries of the world have not. What differences are there between state borders and country borders that might explain this problem?

4. Suppose a developing country does not allow foreign investment to flow into the country and, at the same time, has a very low saving rate. Use the fact that saving equals investment plus net exports and the growth accounting formula to explain why this country will have difficulty catching up with the industrialized countries. What can the country do to improve its productivity if it does not allow capital in from outside the country?

5. Which of the following will increase the likelihood of poor countries catching up to rich countries, and which will decrease the likelihood? Explain.
   a. Industrial countries do not allow their technology to be bought or leased by firms in developing countries.
   b. Worldwide saving rates shift up.
   c. The legal system in developing countries is improved to protect property rights.
   d. Governments in developing countries make use of their international aid to buy armaments from developed countries.
   e. Investment in human capital increases in the developing countries.

6. Most developing countries have low saving rates and governments that run budget deficits. What will be required for such countries to have large increases in their capital stocks? What will happen if industrialized countries' saving rates decline as well? How does this affect the developing countries' prospects for catching up?

7. What would be the effect of a decrease in the Japanese saving rate on the growth rate of developing countries? Why?

8. The rule of 72 gives the approximate doubling time of a variable if you know its rate of growth. For example, if the population of a country is 200 million and the rate of growth of the population is 2 percent per year, then it will take approximately 35 years for the country's population to reach 400 million. Suppose real income per capita does not grow at all in the United States in the future, and suppose that the per capita growth rate in China is 4 percent per year. About how long will it take for China to catch up with the United States? What is likely to happen to the growth rates before this period of time passes? Assume that per capita income is now $32,000 in the United States and $3,400 in China.

9. The International Monetary Fund (IMF) estimates that a decline in the world saving rate by 1 percentage point would increase the world interest rate by about 75 basis points. Using a diagram like the one in the box on page 378, explain the reasoning behind the IMF's estimate. How large an increase in the interest rate would you predict from the diagram in the box?

CHAPTER 17

The Gains from International Trade

On July 4, 1993, an explosion in a single factory in Japan sent the price of computer memory chips soaring by 50 percent all over the world.

Why was there such a big change in price? Because this one factory made 65 percent of the world's supply of a special epoxy used to seal computer memory chips in their cases. When investigative reporters asked why the market was so concentrated at one firm, they found that the company, Sumitomo, was a very low cost producer; despite the small demand for this epoxy in Japan or in any other single country, by producing for the world market, this factory could specialize, invest heavily in research, and achieve low-cost production. Such concentration and specialization are not unusual. The semiconductor firm Intel dominates the world market for the computer memory chip.

Later on that same day in the United States, Americans celebrated Independence Day. Many listened to tapes and CDs on electronic equipment made in Malaysia. Others played tennis wearing Nike shoes made in Korea or went swimming in Ocean Pacific swimsuits made in Sri Lanka. Still others looked at their Casio digital watches made in Mexico to be sure they would not miss the fireworks. A few even drove to the celebration in German cars. In the meantime, the people in other countries who made the products the Americans imported—such as the Malaysians, Koreans, Sri Lankans, Mexicans, and Germans—were buying American products: Caterpillar tractors, Motorola cellular phones, Microsoft Windows, Boeing 747s, and Merck pharmaceuticals to remove parasites from livestock or treat heart attacks.

These two stories—one about a single firm selling its product around the world and the other about people consuming goods made in other countries—illustrate two different reasons why people benefit from international trade. First, international trade allows firms such as Sumitomo and Intel to reduce costs by selling products to larger markets throughout the world. Second, international trade allows different countries to specialize in producing what they are relatively efficient at producing, such as pharmaceuticals in the United States and digital watches in Mexico.

gains from trade: improvements in income, production, or satisfaction owing to the exchange of goods or services. (Ch. 1)

This chapter explores the reasons for these *gains from trade* and develops two models that can be used to measure the actual size of these gains. We begin with a brief look at recent trends in international trade.

Recent Trends in International Trade

international trade: the exchange of goods and services between people or firms in different nations. (Ch. 1)

International trade is trade between people or firms in different countries. Trade between people in Detroit and Ottowa, Canada, is international trade, whereas trade between Detroit and Chicago is trade within a country. Thus, international trade is just another kind of economic interaction; it is subject to the same basic economic principles as trade between people in the same country.

tariff: a tax on imports.

quota: a governmental limit on the quantity of a good that may be imported or sold.

commerce clause: the clause in the U.S. Constitution that prohibits restraint of trade between states.

International trade differs from trade in domestic markets, however, because national governments frequently place restrictions on trade, such as **tariffs** or **quotas,** between countries that they do not place on trade within countries. For example, the Texas legislature cannot limit or put a tariff on the import of Florida oranges into Texas. The **commerce clause** of the U.S. Constitution forbids such restraint of trade between states. But the United States can restrict the import of oranges from Brazil. Similarly, Japan can restrict the import of rice from the United States, and Australia can restrict the import of Japanese automobiles.

International trade has grown much faster than trade within countries in recent years. Figure 17.1 shows the trade in goods and services between countries for all

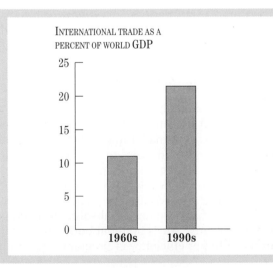

INTERNATIONAL TRADE AS A PERCENT OF WORLD GDP

**Figure 17.1
Rapidly Expanding
International Trade**
International trade has increased faster than GDP as trade restrictions and the cost of transportation have gone down. By 2002, international trade accounted for a 24 percent share of GDP.

countries in the world as a percentage of the world GDP. International trade has doubled as a proportion of the world GDP during the last 30 or so years. Why has international trade grown so rapidly?

One reason is that the cost of transportation and communication has been reduced dramatically. The cost of air travel fell to 9.5 cents per mile in 2000 from 87 cents per mile in 1930, while the cost of a three-minute phone call from New York to London fell to $0.24 in 2002 from $315 in 1930 (adjusting the 1930 prices for general inflation). E-mail and the Internet, unheard of in 1930, reduce costs even further.

However, the most important reason that trade has expanded so rapidly is that government restrictions on trade between countries have come down. Western European countries are integrating into a single market. Canada, Mexico, and the United States have agreed to integrate their economies into a free trade area, where the term *free* indicates the elimination of restrictions on trade. Previously closed economies have opened themselves to world trade through major political and economic reforms. The formerly closed economies in Eastern Europe, Russia, and China, for example, are anxious to join the world trading system. Export-oriented countries in Asia are growing rapidly, and governments in South America such as Argentina and Chile are opening their economies to competition and foreign trade.

These countries are making these changes in an effort to help people. But how do people gain from international trade? Let's now consider that question.

REVIEW

- The basic principles of economics apply to international trade between people in different countries.

- There is a greater tendency for governments to interfere with trade between countries than with trade within their own country.

- International trade has grown rapidly in recent years because of reduced transportation and communication costs and, especially, lower government barriers to trade.

Comparative Advantage

comparative advantage: a situation in which a person or country can produce one good at a lower opportunity cost than another person or country. (Ch. 1)

According to the theory of *comparative advantage,* a country can improve the income of its citizens by allowing them to trade with people in other countries, even if the people of the country are less efficient at producing all items.

Getting a Gut Feeling for Comparative Advantage

First, consider a parable that conveys the essence of comparative advantage. Rose is a highly skilled computer programmer who writes computer-assisted drawing programs. Rose owns a small firm that sells her programs to architects. She has hired an experienced salesman, Sam, to contact the architects and sell her software. Thus, Rose specializes in programming, and Sam specializes in sales.

absolute advantage: a situation in which a person or country is more efficient at producing a good in comparison with another person or country.

You need to know a little more about Rose. Rose is a friendly, outgoing person and, because she knows her product better than Sam does, she is better at sales than Sam. We say that Rose has an **absolute advantage** over Sam in both programming and sales because she is better at both jobs. But it still makes sense for Rose to hire Sam because her efficiency at programming compared to Sam's is greater than her efficiency at sales compared to Sam's. We say that Rose has a *comparative advantage* over Sam in programming rather than in sales. If Rose sold her programs, then she would have to sacrifice her programming time, and her profits would fall. Thus, even though Rose is better at both programming and sales, she hires Sam to do the selling so that she can program full time.

All this seems sensible. However, there is one additional part of the terminology that may at first seem confusing but is important. We said that Rose has the comparative advantage in programming, not in sales. But who does have the comparative advantage in sales? Sam does. Even though Sam is less efficient at both sales and programming, we say he has a comparative advantage in sales because, compared with Rose, he does relatively better at sales than he does at programming. A person cannot have a comparative advantage in both of only two activities.

■ Opportunity Cost, Relative Efficiency, and Comparative Advantage.

opportunity cost: the value of the next-best forgone alternative that was not chosen because something else was chosen. (Ch. 1)

The idea of comparative advantage can also be explained in terms of *opportunity cost*. The opportunity cost of Rose or Sam spending more time selling is that she or he can produce fewer programs. Similarly, the opportunity cost of Rose or Sam spending more time writing programs is that she or he can make fewer sales.

Observe that, in the example, Sam has a lower opportunity cost of spending his time selling than Rose does; thus, it makes sense for Sam to do the selling rather than Rose. In contrast, Rose has a lower opportunity cost of spending her time writing computer programs than Sam does; thus, it makes sense for Rose to write computer programs rather than Sam.

Opportunity costs give us a way to define comparative advantage: A person with a lower opportunity cost of producing a good than another person has a comparative advantage in that good. Thus, Rose has a comparative advantage in computer programming, and Sam has a comparative advantage in sales.

Comparative advantage can also be explained in terms of relative efficiency: A person who is relatively more efficient at producing good X than good Y compared to another person has a comparative advantage in good X. Thus, again, we see that Rose has a comparative advantage in computer programming because she is relatively more efficient at producing computer programs than at making sales compared to Sam.

■ From People to Countries.

Why is this story about Rose and Sam a parable? Because we can think of Rose and Sam as two countries that differ in efficiency at producing one product versus another. In the parable, Rose has a comparative advantage over Sam in programming, and Sam has a comparative advantage over Rose in sales. In general, *country A has a comparative advantage over country B in the production of a good if the opportunity cost of producing the good in country A is less than in country B*, or, alternatively but equivalently stated, *if country A can produce the good relatively more efficiently than other goods compared to country B*. Thus, if you understand the Rose and Sam story, you should have no problem understanding comparative advantage in two countries, which we now examine in more detail.

Productivity in Two Countries

Consider the following two goods: (1) vaccines and (2) TV sets. Different skills are required for the production of vaccines and TV sets. Vaccine production requires knowledge of chemistry and biology, and the marketing of products where doctors make most of the choices. Producing TV sets requires knowledge of electrical engineering and microcircuitry, and the marketing of goods where consumers make most of the choices.

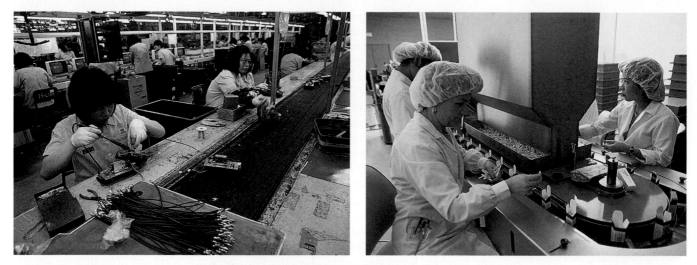

Electronics versus Pharmaceuticals
In the example used in this chapter, Korea has a comparative advantage in an electronic good (TV sets), and the United States has a comparative advantage in a pharmaceutical (vaccines). Thus, with trade, the electronic good will be produced in Korea, as shown in the left-hand photo, and the pharmaceutical good will be produced in the United States, as shown in the right-hand photo.

Table 17.1 provides an example of productivity differences in the production of vaccines and TV sets in two different countries, the United States and Korea. Productivity is measured by the amount of each good that can be produced by a worker per day of work. To be specific, let us suppose that the vaccines are measured in vials, that the TVs are measured in numbers of TV sets, and that labor is the only factor of production in making vaccines and TV sets. The theory of comparative advantage does not depend on any of these assumptions, but they make the exposition much easier.

According to Table 17.1, in the United States it takes a worker one day of work to produce 6 vials of vaccines or 3 TV sets. In Korea, one worker can produce 1 vial of vaccine or 2 TV sets. Thus, the United States is more productive than Korea in producing both vaccines and TV sets. We say that a country has an *absolute advantage* over another country in the production of a good if it is more efficient at producing that good. In this example, the United States has an absolute advantage in both vaccine and TV set production.

However, the United States has a comparative advantage over Korea in the production of vaccines rather than TV sets. To see this, note that a worker in the United

Table 17.1
Example of Productivity in the United States and Korea

	Output per Day of Work	
	Vials of Vaccine	*Number of TV Sets*
United States	6	3
Korea	1	2

States can produce 6 times as many vials of vaccine as a worker in Korea but only 1.5 times as many TV sets. In other words, the United States is relatively more efficient in vaccines than in TV sets compared with Korea. Korea, being able to produce TV sets relatively more efficiently than vaccines compared to the United States, has a comparative advantage in TV sets.

Observe also how opportunity costs determine who has the comparative advantage. To produce 3 more TV sets, the United States must sacrifice 6 vials of vaccine; in other words, *in the United States, the opportunity cost of 1 more TV set is 2 vials of vaccine*. In Korea, to produce 2 more TV sets, the Koreans must sacrifice 1 vial of vaccine; in other words, *in Korea, the opportunity cost of 1 more TV set is only ¹/₂ vial of vaccine*. Thus, we see that the opportunity cost of producing TV sets in Korea is lower than in the United States. By examining opportunity costs, we again see that Korea has a comparative advantage in TV sets.

■ **An American Worker's View.**   Because labor productivity in both goods is higher in the United States than in Korea, wages are higher in the United States than in Korea in the example. Now think about the situation from the point of view of American workers who are paid more than Korean workers. They might wonder how they can compete with Korea. The Korean workers' wages seem very low compared to theirs. It doesn't seem fair. But as we will see, comparative advantage implies that American workers can gain from trade with the Koreans.

■ **A Korean Worker's View.**   It is useful to think about Table 17.1 from the perspective of a Korean worker as well as that of a U.S. worker. From the Korean perspective, it might be noted that Korean workers are less productive in both goods. Korean workers might wonder how they can ever compete with the United States, which looks like a productive powerhouse. Again, it doesn't seem fair. As we will see, however, the Koreans can also gain from trade with the Americans.

Finding the Relative Price

To measure how much the Koreans and Americans can gain from trade, we need to consider the *relative price* of vaccines and TVs in Korea and the United States. The relative price determines how much vaccine can be traded for TVs and, therefore, how much each country can gain from trade. For example, suppose the price of a TV set is $200 and the price of a vial of vaccine is $100. Then 2 vials of vaccine cost the same as 1 TV set; we say the relative price is 2 vials of vaccine per TV set. The next few paragraphs show how to determine the relative price from data on the costs of production.

> **Another example of relative prices may be helpful:**
> Price of Phish concert
> = $45
> Price of Phish T-shirt = $15
> Relative price = 3 T-shirts per concert

■ **Relative Price Without Trade.**   First, let us find the relative price with no trade between the countries. The relative price of two goods should depend on the relative costs of production. A good for which the cost of producing an additional quantity is relatively low will have a relatively low price.

Consider the United States. In this example, a day of work can produce either 6 vials of vaccine or 3 TV sets. With labor as the only factor of production, 6 vials of vaccine cost the same to produce as 3 TV sets; that is, 2 vials of vaccine cost the same to produce as 1 TV set. Therefore, the relative price should be 2 vials of vaccine per TV set.

Now consider Korea. Electronic goods should have a relatively low price in Korea because they are relatively cheap to produce. A day of work can produce either 1 vial of vaccine or 2 TV sets; thus 1 vial of vaccine costs the same to produce as 2 TV sets in Korea. Therefore, the relative price is ¹/₂ vial of vaccine per TV set.

■ **Relative Price with Trade.**   Now consider what happens when the two countries trade without government restrictions. If transportation costs are negligible and markets are competitive, then the price of a good must be the same in the United States and Korea. Why? Because any difference in price would quickly be eliminated by trade; if the price of TV sets is much less in Korea than in the United States, then traders will buy TV sets in Korea and sell them in the United States and make a profit; by doing so, however, they reduce the supply of TV sets in Korea and increase the supply in the United States. This will drive up the price in Korea and drive down the price in the United States until the price of TV sets in the two countries is the same. Thus, with trade, the price of vaccines and the price of TV sets will converge to the same levels in both countries. The relative price will therefore converge to the same value in both countries.

If the relative price is going to be the same in both countries, then we know the price must be somewhere between the prices in the two countries before trade. That is, the price must be between 2 vials of vaccine per TV set (the U.S. relative price) and $\frac{1}{2}$ vial of vaccine per TV set (the Korean relative price). We do not know exactly where the price will fall between $\frac{1}{2}$ and 2. It depends on the *demand* for vaccines and TV sets in Korea and the United States. *Let us assume that the relative price is 1 vial of vaccine per TV set after trade*, which is between $\frac{1}{2}$ and 2 and is a nice, easy number for making computations. The calculation of the price with trade is summarized in Table 17.2.

Measuring the Gains from Trade

How large are the *gains from trade* due to comparative advantage? First, consider some examples.

■ **One Country's Gain.**   Suppose that 10 American workers move out of electronics production and begin producing pharmaceuticals. We know from Table 17.1 that these 10 American workers can produce 60 vials of vaccine per day. Formerly, the 10 American workers were producing 30 TV sets per day. But their 60 vials of vaccine can be traded for TV sets produced in Korea. With the relative price of 1 vial per TV set, Americans will be able to exchange these 60 vials of vaccine for 60 TV sets. Thus, Americans gain 30 more TV sets by moving 10 more workers into vaccine production. This gain from trade is summarized in Table 17.3.

■ **The Other Country's Gain.**   The same thing can happen in Korea. A Korean manufacturer can now hire 30 workers who were formerly working in vaccine pro-

---

Table 17.2
The Relative Price (The relative price—vials of vaccine per TV set—must be the same in both countries with trade)

	United States	**Korea**
Relative price before trade:	2 vials of vaccine per TV set	$\frac{1}{2}$ vial of vaccine per TV set
Relative price range after trade:	Between $\frac{1}{2}$ and 2	Between $\frac{1}{2}$ and 2
Relative price assumption:	1	1

Table 17.3
Changing Production and Gaining from Trade in the United States and Korea

	United States (10 workers)		
	Change in Production	*Amount Traded*	*Net Gain from Trade*
Vaccines	Up 60 vials	Export 60 vials	0
TV sets	Down 30 sets	Import 60 sets	30 sets
	Korea (30 workers)		
	Change in Production	*Amount Traded*	*Net Gain from Trade*
Vaccines	Down 30 vials	Import 60 vials	30 vials
TV sets	Up 60 sets	Export 60 sets	0

duction to produce TV sets. Vaccine production declines by 30 vials, but TV production increases by 60 TV sets. These 60 TV sets can be traded with Americans for 60 vials of vaccine. The reduction in the production of vaccine of 30 vials results in an import of vaccine of 60 vials; thus, the gain from trade is 30 vials of vaccine. The Koreans, by moving workers out of vaccine production and into TV set production, are getting more vaccine. This gain from trade for Korea is summarized in Table 17.3. Observe that the exports of TV sets from Korea equal the imports of TV sets to the United States.

■ **Just Like a New Discovery.** International trade is like the discovery of a new idea or technique that makes workers more productive. It is as if workers in the United States figured out how to produce more TV sets with the same amount of effort. Their trick is that they actually produce vaccines, which are then traded for the TV sets. Like any other new technique, international trade improves the well-being of Americans. International trade also improves the well-being of the Koreans; it is as if they discovered a new technique, too.

A Graphical Measure of the Gains from Trade

The gains from trade due to comparative advantage can also be found graphically with production possibilities curves, as shown in Figure 17.2. There are two graphs in the figure—one for the United States and the other for Korea. In both graphs, the horizontal axis has the number of TV sets and the vertical axis has the number of vials of vaccine produced.

■ **Production Possibilities Curves Without Trade.** The solid lines in the two graphs show the production possibilities curves for vaccines and TV sets in the United States and in Korea before trade. To derive them, we assume, for illustrative purposes, that there are 10,000 workers in the United States and 30,000 workers in Korea who can make either vaccines or TV sets.

If all the available workers in the United States produce vaccines, then total production will be 60,000 vials of vaccine (6 × 10,000) and zero TV sets. Alternatively, if

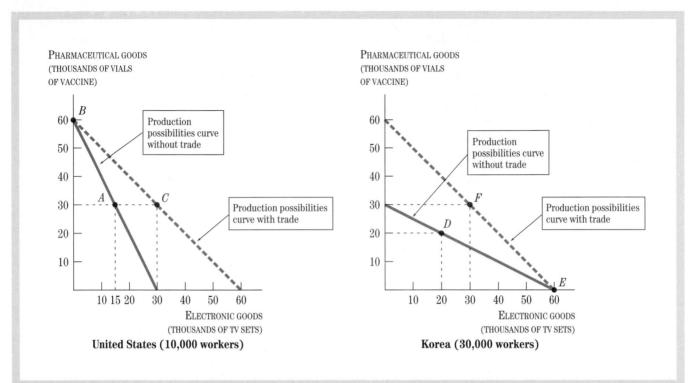

**Figure 17.2
Comparative Advantage**

On the left, Americans are better off with trade because the production possibilities curve shifts out with trade; thus, with trade, Americans reach a point like *C* rather than *A*. The gains from trade due to comparative advantage are equal to the distance between the two production possibilities curves—one with trade and the other without trade. On the right, Koreans are also better off because their production possibilities curve also shifts out; thus, Koreans can reach point *F*, which is better than point *D*. To reach this outcome, Americans specialize in producing at point *B* and Koreans specialize in producing at point *E*.

5,000 workers produce vaccines in the United States and 5,000 workers produce TV sets, then total production will be 30,000 vials of vaccine (6 × 5,000) and 15,000 TV sets (3 × 5,000). The solid line in the graph on the left of Figure 17.2 shows these possibilities and all other possibilities for producing vaccines and TV sets. It is the production possibilities curve without trade.

Korea's production possibilities curve without trade is shown by the solid line in the graph on the right of Figure 17.2. For example, if all 30,000 Korean workers produce TV sets, a total of 60,000 TV sets can be produced (2 × 30,000). This and other possibilities are on the curve.

The slopes of the two production possibilities curves without trade in Figure 17.2 show how many vials of vaccine can be transformed into TV sets in Korea and the United States. The production possibilities curve for the United States is steeper than that for Korea because an increase in production of 1 TV set reduces vaccine production by 2 vials in the United States but by only ½ vial in Korea. The slope of the production possibilities curve is the opportunity cost; the opportunity cost of producing TV sets in the United States is higher than it is in Korea.

■ **Production Possibilities Curves with Trade.**   The dashed lines in the two graphs in Figure 17.2 show the different combinations of vaccine and TV sets avail-

Doing Politics and Economics

David Ricardo was a man of action. He went to work as a stockbroker at age 14 and eventually accumulated a vast fortune, including a beautiful country estate. He then became one of the most influential economists of all time. He also ran for and won a seat in the British Parliament from which to argue his economic position.

As an economist, Ricardo continued the tradition of Adam Smith. In fact, he got interested in economics after reading Smith's *Wealth of Nations* during a vacation. But Ricardo greatly extended and improved on Smith's theories and made them more precise. Along with Smith and Thomas Robert Malthus—who was Ricardo's close friend but frequent intellectual opponent—Ricardo is considered by historians to be in the classical school, which argued for laissez-faire, free trade, and competitive markets in eighteenth- and nineteenth-century Britain.

Ricardo grappled with three of the most important policy issues in economics: inflation, taxes, and international trade. But Ricardo's most famous contribution is to international trade—in particular, his theory of comparative advantage. Ricardo used this theory when he was in Parliament to argue for repeal of the restrictions on agricultural imports known as the corn laws.

Ricardo's theory of comparative advantage is a good example of how he improved on the work of Adam Smith.

Smith used common-sense analogies to illustrate the gains from trade; one of his examples was "The tailor does not attempt to make his own shoes, but buys them from the shoemaker." As with this tailor and shoemaker example, Smith focused on cases in which one person had an absolute advantage in one good and the other person had an absolute advantage in the other good. But Ricardo showed how there were gains from trade even if one person was better at producing both goods. Here is how Ricardo put it way back in 1817:

Two men can both make shoes and hats, and one is superior to the other in both employments; but in making hats, he can only exceed his competitor by one-fifth or 20 per cent., and in making shoes he can excel him by one-third or 33 per cent.;—will it not be for the interest of both that the superior man should employ himself exclusively in making shoes, and the inferior man in making hats?

DAVID RICARDO, 1772–1823

Born: London, 1772

Education: Never attended college

Jobs:
Stockbroker, 1786–1815
Member of Parliament, 1819–1823

Major Publications:
The High Price of Bullion, 1810;
On the Principles of Political Economy and Taxation, 1817;
A Plan for a National Bank, 1824

able in Korea and the United States when there is trade between the two countries at a relative price of 1 vial of vaccine for 1 TV set. These dashed lines are labeled "production possibilities curve with trade" to contrast them with the "production possibilities curve without trade" label on the solid line. The diagram shows that the production possibilities curves with trade are shifted out compared with the curves without trade.

To see how the production possibilities curve with trade is derived, consider how the United States could move from point *A* to point *C* in Figure 17.2. At point *A*, without trade, Americans produce and consume 15,000 TV sets and 30,000 vials of vaccine by having 5,000 workers in each industry. Now suppose all U.S. workers move out of TV set production into vaccine production, shifting U.S. production to zero TV sets and 60,000 vials of vaccine, as shown by point *B*. Then by trading some of the vaccine, Americans can obtain TV sets. As they trade more vaccine away, they move down the production possibilities curve with trade: 1 less vial of vaccine means 1 more TV set along the curve. If they move to point *C* in the diagram, they have traded 30,000 vials of vaccine for 30,000 TV sets. Americans now have 30,000 TV sets and are left with 30,000 vials of vaccine. By producing more vaccine, the Americans get to purchase more TV sets. The distance from point *A* (before trade) to point *C* (after trade) in Figure 17.2 is the gain from trade: 15,000 more TV sets.

It would be possible, of course, to choose any other point on the production possibilities curve with trade. If Americans prefer more TV sets and fewer vials of vaccine, they can move down along that dashed line, trading more of their vaccine for more TV sets. In general, the production possibilities curve *with* trade is further out than the production possibilities curve *without* trade, indicating the gain from trade.

Observe that the slope of the production possibilities curve with trade is given by the relative price: the number of vials of vaccine that can be obtained for a TV set. When the relative price is 1 vial per TV set, the slope is -1 because 1 less vial gives 1 more TV set. If the relative price were $1/2$ vial per TV set, then the production possibilities curve with trade would be flatter.

The gains to Korea from trade are illustrated in the right-hand graph of Figure 17.2. For example, at point *D*, without trade, Koreans produce 20,000 TV sets with 10,000 workers and, with the remaining 20,000 workers, produce 20,000 vials of vaccine. With trade, they shift all production into TV sets, as at point *E* on the right graph. Then they trade the TV sets for vaccine. Such trade allows more consumption of vaccine in Korea. At point *F* in the right diagram, the Koreans could consume 30,000 vials of vaccine and 30,000 TV sets, which is 10,000 more of each than before trade at point *D*. As in the case of the United States, the production possibilities curve shifts out with trade, and the size of the shift represents the gain from trade.

This example of Americans and Koreans consuming more than they were before trade illustrates the *principle of comparative advantage: By specializing in producing products in which they have a comparative advantage, countries can increase the amount of goods available for consumption.* Trade increases the amount of production in the world; it shifts out the production possibilities curves.

■ **Increasing Opportunity Costs: Incomplete Specialization.** One of the special assumptions in the example we have used in Table 17.2 and Figure 17.2 to illustrate the theory of comparative advantage is that opportunity costs are constant rather than increasing. It is because of this assumption that the production possibilities curves without trade in Figure 17.2 are straight lines rather than the bowed-out lines that we studied in Chapter 1. With increasing opportunity costs, the curves would be bowed out.

The straight-line production possibilities curves are the reason for *complete* specialization, with Korea producing no vaccines and the United States producing no TV sets. If there were increasing opportunity costs, as in the more typical example of the production possibilities curve, then complete specialization would not occur. Why? With increasing opportunity costs, as more and more workers are moved into the production of vaccine in the United States, the opportunity cost of producing more vaccine will rise. And as workers are moved out of vaccine production in Korea, the opportunity cost of vaccine production in Korea will fall. At some point, the U.S. opportunity cost of vaccine production may rise to equal Korea's, at which point further specialization in vaccine production would cease in the United States. Thus, with increasing opportunity costs and bowed-out production possibilities curves, there will most likely be incomplete specialization. But the principle of comparative advantage is not changed by increasing opportunity costs. By specializing to some degree in the goods they have a comparative advantage in, countries can increase world production. There are still substantial gains from trade, whether between Rose and Sam or between America and Korea.

REVIEW

- Comparative advantage shows that a country can gain from trade even if it is more efficient at producing every product than another country. A country has a comparative advantage in a product if it is relatively more efficient at producing that product than the other country.

- The theory of comparative advantage predicts that there are gains from trade from increasing production of the good a country has a comparative advantage in and reducing production of the other good. By exporting the good it has a comparative advantage in, a country can increase consumption of both goods.

- Comparative advantage is like a new technology in which the country effectively produces more by having some goods produced in another country.

Reasons for Comparative Advantage

What determines a country's comparative advantage? There are some obvious answers. For example, Central America has a comparative advantage over North America in producing tropical fruit because of weather conditions: Bananas will not grow in Kansas or Nebraska outside of greenhouses.

In most cases, however, comparative advantage does not result from differences in climate and natural resources. More frequently, comparative advantage is due to decisions by individuals, by firms, or by the government in a given country. For example, a comparative advantage of the United States in pharmaceuticals might be due to investment in research and in physical and human capital in the areas of chemistry and biology. An enormous amount of research goes into developing technological know-how to produce pharmaceutical products.

In Korea, on the other hand, there may be less capital available for such huge expenditures on research in the pharmaceutical area. A Korean comparative advantage in electronic goods might be due to a large, well-trained work force that is well suited to electronics and small-scale assembly. For example, the excellent math and technical training in Korean high schools may provide a large labor force for the electronics industry.

Comparative advantages can change over time. In fact, the United States did have a comparative advantage in TV sets in the 1950s and early 1960s, before the countries of east Asia developed skills and knowledge in these areas. A country may have a comparative advantage in a good it has recently developed, but then the technology spreads to other countries, which develop a comparative advantage, and the first country goes on to something else.

Perhaps the United States's comparative advantage in pharmaceuticals will go to other countries in the future, and the United States will develop a comparative advantage in other, yet unforeseen areas. The term *dynamic* comparative advantage describes changes in comparative advantage over time because of investment in physical and human capital and in technology.

Labor versus Capital Resources

To illustrate the importance of capital for comparative advantage, imagine a world in which all comparative advantage can be explained through differences between countries in the amount of physical capital that workers have to work with. It is such a world that is described by the Heckscher-Ohlin model, named after the two Swedish economists, Eli Heckscher and Bertil Ohlin, who developed it. Ohlin won a Nobel Prize for his work in international economics. The Heckscher-Ohlin model provides a particular explanation for comparative advantage.

capital abundant: a higher level of capital per worker in one country relative to another.

labor abundant: a lower level of capital per worker in one country relative to another.

capital intensive: production that uses a relatively high level of capital per worker.

labor intensive: production that uses a relatively low level of capital per worker.

Here is how comparative advantage develops in such a model. Suppose America has a higher level of capital per worker than Korea. In other words, America is **capital abundant** compared to Korea, and—what amounts to the same thing—Korea is **labor abundant** compared to America. We noted that pharmaceutical production uses more capital per worker than electronics production; in other words, pharmaceutical production is relatively **capital intensive,** while electronics production is relatively **labor intensive.** Hence, it makes sense that the United States has a comparative advantage in pharmaceuticals: The United States is relatively capital abundant, and pharmaceuticals are relatively capital intensive. On the other hand, Korea has a comparative advantage in electronics because Korea is relatively labor abundant, and electronics are relatively labor intensive. Thus, the Heckscher-Ohlin model predicts that if a country has a relative abundance of a factor (labor or capital), it will have a comparative advantage in those goods that require a greater amount of that factor.

The Effect of Trade on Wages

An important implication of the Heckscher-Ohlin model is that trade will tend to bring factor prices (the price of labor and the price of capital) into equality in different countries. In other words, if the comparative advantage between Korea and the United States was due only to differences in relative capital and labor abundance, then trade would tend to increase real wages in Korea and lower real wages in the United States.

factor-price equalization: the equalization of the price of labor and the price of capital across countries when they are engaging in free trade.

More generally, trade tends to increase demand for the factor that is relatively abundant in a country and decrease demand for the factor that is relatively scarce. This raises the price of the relatively abundant factor and lowers the price of the relatively scarce factor. Suppose the United States is more capital abundant than Korea and has a comparative advantage in pharmaceuticals, which are more capital intensive than electronics. Then with trade, the price of capital will rise relative to the price of labor in the United States. The intuition behind this prediction—which is called **factor-price equalization**—is that demand for labor (the relatively scarce factor) shifts down with trade as the United States increases production of pharmaceuticals and reduces its production of electronic goods. On the other hand, the demand for capital (the relatively abundant factor) shifts up with trade. Although there is no immigration, it is as if foreign workers competed with workers in the labor-scarce country and bid down the wage.

Because technology also influences wages and productivity, it has been hard to detect such movements in wages due to factor-price equalization. Wages of workers in the developed world with high productivity due to high levels of technology remain well above wages of workers in the less-developed world with low productivity due to low levels of technology.

In other words, changes in technology can offset the effects of factor-price equalization on wages. If trade raises technological know-how sufficiently, then no one has to suffer from greater trade. In our example of comparative advantage, American workers are paid more than Korean workers both before and after trade; that is because their overall level of productivity is higher. Workers with higher productivity will be paid more than workers with lower productivity even in countries that trade.

Factor-price equalization can explain another phenomenon: growing wage disparity in the United States during the past 25 years, in which the wages of high-skilled workers have risen relative to the wages of less-skilled workers. The United States is relatively abundant in high-skilled workers, and developing countries are relatively abundant in low-skilled workers. Thus, high-skilled workers' wages should rise and low-skilled workers' wages should fall in the United States, according to factor-price equalization. In this application of factor-price equalization, the two factors are high-skilled workers and low-skilled workers.

In the next section, we show that there are gains in efficiency and lower cost from trade that can benefit all workers.

REVIEW
- Comparative advantage changes over time and depends on the actions of individuals in a country. Thus, comparative advantage is a dynamic concept.

- International trade will tend to equalize wages in different countries. Technological differences, however, can keep wages high in high-productivity countries.

Gains from Expanded Markets

In the introduction to this chapter, we mentioned the gains from trade that come from larger-sized markets. Having discussed the principle of comparative advantage, we now examine this other source of the gains from trade.

An Example of Gains from Trade Through Expanded Markets

Let us start with a simple example. Consider two countries that are similar in resources, capital, and skilled labor, such as the United States and Germany. Suppose there is a market in Germany and the United States for two medical diagnostic products—magnetic resonance imaging (MRI) machines and ultrasound scanners. Suppose the technology for producing each type of diagnostic device is the same in each country. We assume that the technology is identical because we want to show that trade will take place without differences between the countries.

Figure 17.3 illustrates the situation. Without trade, Germany and the United States each produce 1,000 MRIs and 1,000 ultrasound scanners. This amount of production meets the demand in the two separate markets. The cost per unit of producing each MRI machine is $300,000, while the cost per unit of producing each ultrasound scanner is $200,000. Again, these costs are the same in each country.

■ **Effects of a Larger Market.** Now suppose that the two countries trade. Observe in Figure 17.3—and this is very important—that the *cost per unit* of producing

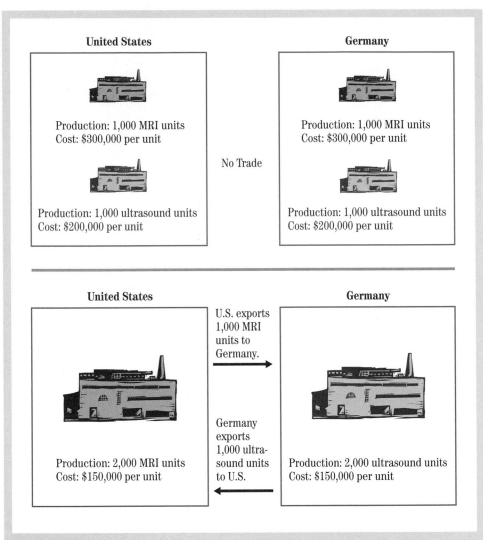

Figure 17.3
Gains from Global Markets
In this example, the technology of producing magnetic resonance imaging (MRI) machines and ultrasound scanners is assumed to be the same in the United States and Germany. In the top panel, with no trade between the United States and Germany, the quantity produced in each country is low and the cost per unit is high. With trade, the U.S. firm increases its production of MRIs and exports to Germany; the German firm increases its production of ultrasound scanners and exports to the United States. As a result, cost per unit comes down significantly.

MRIs and ultrasound scanners *declines as more are produced*. Trade increases the size of the market for each product. In this example, the market is twice as large with trade as without it: 2,000 MRIs rather than 1,000 and 2,000 ultrasound scanners rather than 1,000. The production of MRIs in the United States can expand, and the production of ultrasound scanners in the United States can contract. Similarly, the production of ultrasound scanners in Germany can expand, and the production of MRIs in Germany can contract. With the United States specializing in production

Writing "Talking Points" for the President

To promote trade and reduce trade barriers, the president of the United States and other executive branch officers must make speeches and hold meetings with members of Congress and other interested groups. Many of their "talking points"—short phrases that people can easily remember and repeat—are developed by their economic advisers and give examples of the gains from trade through larger markets. Here are some examples of the actual talking points used to promote the North American Free Trade Agreement that reduced trade barriers between the United States and Mexico and Canada in the 1990s. This agreement was a high priority in the administrations of both President George H. W. Bush and President Bill Clinton.

Observe how these talking points are related to the model illustrated in Figure 17.4, which shows the gains from trade through expanded markets. The term *economies of scale* refers to the decline in cost per unit. *Product rationalization* refers to locating production in fewer factories in order to reduce cost per unit. *Internal distortions* means that trade barriers had caused factories to be too small.

Talking Points on Gains from Trade

- The further integration of North American manufacturing facilities and the resulting product rationalizations would increase trade and the competitiveness of U.S. producers.

- U.S. companies operating in both Mexico and the United States will be able to reduce costs through product rationalization. They will no longer have to make the same vehicles, or the same parts for those vehicles, in two countries.

- Removal of internal distortions and economies of scale would enhance the international competitiveness of the North American automotive industry.

---

of MRIs, the cost per unit of MRIs declines to $150,000. Similarly, the cost per unit of ultrasound scanners declines to $150,000. The United States exports MRIs to Germany so that the number of MRIs in Germany can be the same as without trade, and Germany exports ultrasound scanners to the United States. The gain from trade is the reduction in cost per unit. This gain from trade has occurred without any differences in the efficiency of production between each country.

Note that we could have set up the example differently. We could have had Germany specializing in MRIs and the United States specializing in ultrasound scanner production. Then the United States would have exported ultrasound scanners, and Germany would have exported MRIs. But the gains from trade would have been exactly the same. Unlike the comparative advantage motive for trade, the expanded markets motive alone cannot predict what the direction of trade will be.

■ **Intraindustry Trade versus Interindustry Trade.** MRIs and ultrasound scanners are similar products; they are considered to be in the same industry, the medical diagnostic equipment industry. Thus, the trade between Germany and the United States in MRIs and ultrasound scanners is called **intraindustry trade,** which means trade in goods in the same industry.

intraindustry trade: trade between countries in goods from the same or similar industries.

interindustry trade: trade between countries in goods from different industries.

In contrast, the trade that took place in the example of comparative advantage was **interindustry trade,** because vaccines and TV sets are in different industries. In that example, exports of vaccines from the United States greatly exceed imports of vaccines, producing a U.S. industry trade surplus in vaccines. Imports of TV sets into the United States are much greater than exports of TV sets, producing a U.S. industry trade deficit in TV sets.

These examples convey an important message about international trade. Trade due to comparative advantage tends to be interindustry, and trade due to expanded markets tends to be intraindustry. In reality, a huge amount of international trade is intraindustry trade. This indicates that creating larger markets is an important motive for trade.

Measuring the Gains from Expanded Markets

The medical equipment example illustrates how larger markets can reduce costs. To fully describe the gains from trade resulting from larger markets, we need to consider a model.

■ **A Relationship Between Cost per Unit and the Number of Firms.**   Let us examine the idea that *as the number of firms in a market of a given size increases, the cost per unit at each firm increases.* The two graphs in Figure 17.4 are useful for this purpose. In each graph the downward sloping line shows how cost per unit (or average total cost) at a firm decreases as the quantity produced at that firm increases. Cost per unit measured in dollars is on the vertical axis and the quantity produced and sold is on the horizontal axis. Observe that cost per unit declines through the whole range shown in the graph. Cost per unit declines because the larger quantity of production allows a firm to achieve a greater division of labor and more specialization.

Focus first on the graph on the left. The total size of the market (determined by the number of customers in the market) is shown by the bracket on the horizontal axis. We assume that the firms in the market have equal shares of the market. For example, if there are 4 firms in the market, then each firm will produce 1/4 of the market. Suppose that there are 4 firms; then, according to Figure 17.4, the cost per unit at each firm will be $30. This is the cost per unit for the quantity labeled by the box "1 of 4" which means that this is the quantity produced by each 1 of the 4 firms.

Now, suppose that there are 3 firms in the market and each firm produces 1/3 of the market, then the cost per unit at each firm will be $25 as shown by the box labeled "1 of 3" in Figure 17.4. Cost per unit at each firm is lower with 3 firms than with 4 firms in the market because each firm is producing more: That is, 1/3 of the market is

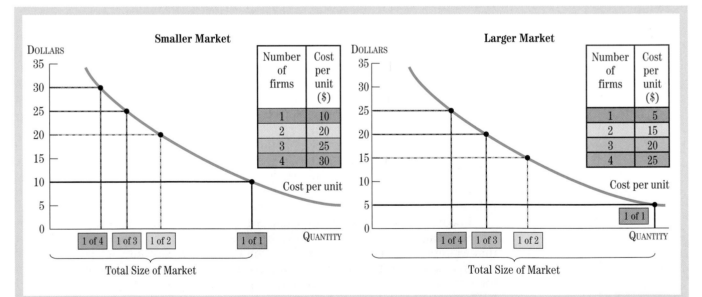

Figure 17.4
Cost per Unit: The Number of Firms and Market Size
(1) The market on the right is larger than the market on the left. Hence, cost per unit is lower on the right with the larger market. (2) Regardless of the size of the market, cost per unit declines as the number of firms declines.

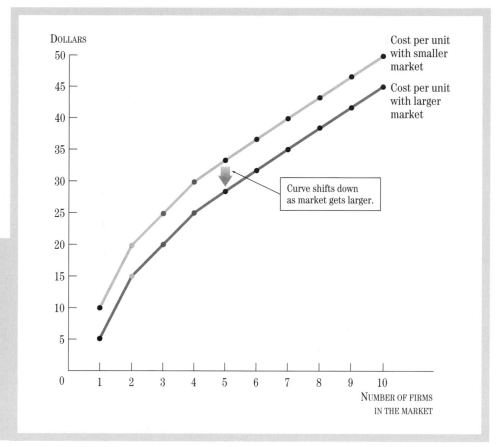

Figure 17.5
The Relationship Between Cost per Unit and the Number of Firms
The first four points on each curve are plotted from the two tables in Figure 17.4 for 1 to 4 firms; the other points can be similarly obtained. Each curve shows how cost per unit at each firm rises as the number of firms increases in a market of a given size. The curve shifts down when the size of the market increases.

more than 1/4 of the market. Continuing in this way, we see that with 2 firms in the market, the cost per unit is $20. And with 1 firm in the market, the cost per unit is $10. In sum, as we decreased the number of firms in the market, each firm produced more and cost per unit decreased. If the number of firms in the market increased, then cost per unit at each firm would increase.

■ **The Effect of the Size of the Market.**   Now compare the graph on the left with the graph on the right of Figure 17.4. The important difference is that the graph on the right represents a larger market than the graph on the left. The bracket in the right-hand graph is bigger to show the larger market.

By comparing the graph on the left in Figure 17.4 (smaller market) with that on the right (larger market), we see that an increase in the size of the market reduces cost per unit at each firm, holding the number of firms in the industry constant. For example, when there is one firm in the market, cost per unit is $5 for the larger market compared with $10 for the smaller market. Or with four firms, cost per unit is $25 for the larger market compared with $30 for the smaller market. Compare the little tables in Figure 17.4. As the market increases in size, each firm produces at a lower cost per unit.

Figure 17.5 summarizes the information in Figure 17.4. It shows the positive relationship between the number of firms in the market, shown on the horizontal axis, and the cost per unit at each firm. As the figure indicates, more firms mean a higher cost per unit at each firm. (Be careful to note that the horizontal axis in Figure 17.5 is the *number* of firms in a given *market*, not the quantity produced by a given firm.) When the size of the market increases, the relationship between the number of firms in the market and the cost per unit shifts down, as shown in Figure 17.5. In other words, as the market increases in size, cost per unit declines at each firm if the number of firms does not change.

■ **A Relationship Between the Price and the Number of Firms.** A general feature of most markets is that as the number of firms in the market increases, the price at each firm declines. More firms make the market more competitive. Thus, there is a relationship between the price and the number of firms, as shown in Figure 17.6. As in Figure 17.5, the number of firms is on the horizontal axis. The curve in Figure 17.6 is downward-sloping because a greater number of firms means a lower price.

■ **Equilibrium Price and Number of Firms.** In the long run, as firms either enter or exit an industry, price will tend to equal cost per unit. If the price for each unit were greater than the cost per unit, then there would be a profit opportunity for new firms, and the number of firms in the industry would rise. If the price were less than the cost per unit, then firms would exit the industry. Only when price equals cost per unit is there a long-run equilibrium. Because price equals cost per unit, the curves in Figure 17.5 and 17.6 can be combined to determine the price and the number of firms in long-run equilibrium. As shown in Figure 17.7, there is a long-run equilibrium in the industry when the downward-sloping line for Figure 17.6 intersects the upward-sloping line (for the smaller market) from Figure 17.5. At this point, price equals cost per unit.

Corresponding to this long-run equilibrium is an equilibrium number of firms. More firms would lower the price below cost per unit, causing firms to leave the industry; fewer firms would raise the price above cost per unit, attracting new firms to the industry. Figure 17.7 shows how the possibility of entry and exit results in a long-run equilibrium with price equal to cost per unit.

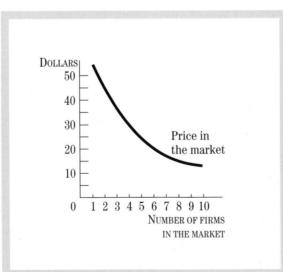

Figure 17.6
The Relationship Between the Price and the Number of Firms
As the number of firms increases, the market price declines. This curve summarizes this relationship.

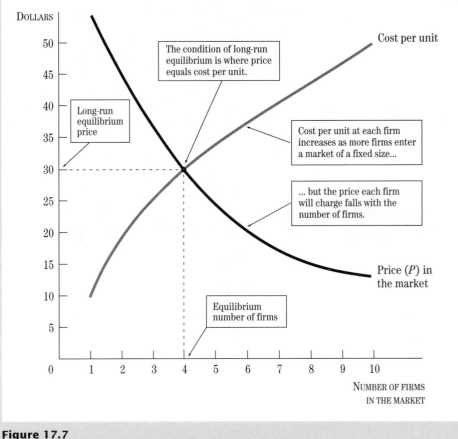

Dollars

The condition of long-run equilibrium is where price equals cost per unit.

Long-run equilibrium price

Cost per unit

Cost per unit at each firm increases as more firms enter a market of a fixed size...

... but the price each firm will charge falls with the number of firms.

Price (*P*) in the market

Equilibrium number of firms

NUMBER OF FIRMS IN THE MARKET

Figure 17.7
Long-Run Equilibrium Number of Firms and Cost per Unit
A condition for long-run equilibrium is that price equals cost per unit. In this diagram, this condition is shown at the intersection of the two curves.

■ **Increasing the Size of the Market.**   Now let us see how the industry equilibrium changes when the size of the market increases due to international trade. In Figure 17.8, we show how an increase in the size of the market, due perhaps to the creation of a free trade area, reduces the price and increases the number of firms. The curve showing the cost per unit of each firm shifts down and out as the market expands; that is, for each number of firms, the cost per unit declines for each firm. This brings about a new intersection and a long-run equilibrium at a lower price. Moreover, the increase in the number of firms suggests that there will be more product variety, which is another part of the gains from trade.

■ **The North American Automobile Market.**   The gains from trade due to larger markets arise in many real-world examples. Trade in cars between Canada and the United States now occurs even though neither country has an obvious comparative advantage. Before 1964, trade in cars between Canada and the United States was restricted. Canadian factories thus had to limit their production to the Canadian market. This kept cost per unit high. When free trade in cars was permitted, the production in Canadian factories increased, and the Canadian factories began to export cars to the United States. With more cars produced, cost per unit declined.

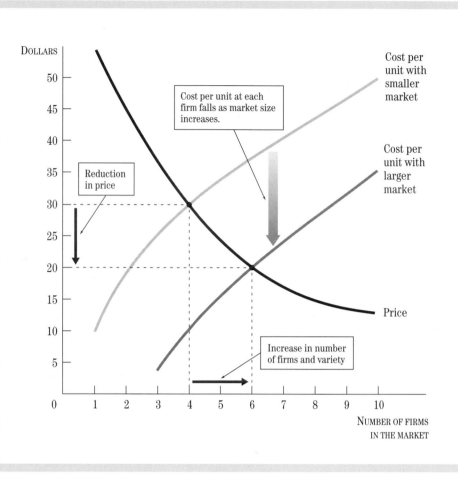

Figure 17.8
Gains from Trade Due to Larger Markets
When trade occurs, the market increases from the size of the market in one country to the combined size of the market in two or more countries. This larger market shifts the upward-sloping line down because cost per unit for each firm is lower when the market is bigger. In the long-run equilibrium at the intersection of the two new curves, the price is lower and there are more firms. With more firms, there is more variety. Lower price and more variety are the gains from trade.

REVIEW
- Lowering cost per unit through the division of labor requires large markets. International trade creates large markets.

- A graphical model can be used to explain the gains from international trade; the model shows that a larger market reduces prices.

Conclusion

In this chapter, we have focused on the economic gains to the citizens of a country from international trade. We have mentioned two reasons for such gains: comparative advantage and larger markets that reduce cost per unit. Both reasons apply to trade within a country as well as to international trade. Most of the chapter was spent showing how to measure the gains due to comparative advantage and larger markets.

In concluding this chapter, it is important to point out that the benefits of international trade go well beyond economic gains.

International trade sometimes puts competitive pressure on governments to deliver better policies. Within the United States, competition between states can make regulatory and tax policies more efficient. Similarly, competition can make regulatory policies in countries more efficient.

International trade can also improve international relations. Trade enables Americans to learn more about Southeast Asians or Europeans or Latin Americans. This improves understanding and reduces the possibilities for international conflict. Developing international trade with Russia and the other countries of the former Soviet Union might even reduce the possibility of another cold war or new international conflict in the future. If many people have an economic stake in a relationship, they will not like a military action that threatens that relationship.

KEY POINTS

1. The principles of economics can be used to analyze international trade just as they can be used to analyze trade within a country.

2. International trade is different from within-country trade because national governments can place restrictions on the trade of goods and services between countries and on immigration.

3. According to the principle of comparative advantage, countries that specialize in producing goods that they have a comparative advantage in can increase world production and raise consumption in their own country.

4. The gains from trade due to comparative advantage can be shown graphically by shifting out the production possibilities curve.

5. The relative price of two goods with trade is between the relative prices in the two countries without trade.

6. Comparative advantage is a dynamic concept. If people in one country improve their skills or develop low-cost production methods through research, they will alter the comparative advantage.

7. If differences in the relative abundance of capital and labor are the reason for differences in comparative advantage, then international trade will tend to equalize real wages.

8. Lower cost per unit in larger markets is another key reason for gains in trade.

9. When the size of the market increases, the price declines, there are more firms, and there is greater variety of products.

KEY TERMS

tariff	absolute advantage	capital intensive	intraindustry trade
quota	capital abundant	labor intensive	interindustry trade
commerce clause	labor abundant	factor-price equalization	

QUESTIONS FOR REVIEW

1. Why has international trade grown so rapidly in recent years?

2. What is the difference between absolute advantage and comparative advantage?

3. If the relative price of two goods is 4 in one country and 6 in another country before trade, in what range will the relative price be after trade?

4. What is the difference between the production possibilities curve before trade and after trade?

5. In what sense is comparative advantage a dynamic concept?

6. Why does trade take place even if one country does not have an absolute advantage over another?

7. What is the difference between capital abundant and capital intensive?

8. Why might costs per unit decline when the market increases in size?

9. What is the difference between interindustry trade and intraindustry trade?

PROBLEMS

1. Suppose the production of wheat and strawberries per unit of labor in the United States and Mexico is as follows:

	Wheat	**Strawberries**
Mexico	1 bushel	3 pints
United States	2 bushels	3 pints

   a. Which country has a comparative advantage in wheat production? Why?

   b. With free trade between the United States and Mexico, is it possible that 1 bushel of wheat will trade for 1 pint of strawberries? Why or why not?

   c. Suppose the free trade price is 1 bushel of wheat for 2 pints of strawberries. Draw a diagram indicating the production possibilities curve with and without trade if the United States has 200 million units of labor. What is the maximum amount of wheat the United States can produce?

2. What is the shape of the production possibilities curve in problem 1? What does this shape imply about the nature of the tradeoff between wheat and strawberries? Is this a realistic assumption? Explain.

3. Suppose there are two goods, wheat and clothing, and two countries, the United States and Brazil, in the world. The production of wheat and clothing requires only labor. In the United States, it takes 1 unit of labor to produce 4 bushels of wheat and 1 unit of labor to produce 2 items of clothing. In Brazil, it takes 1 unit of labor to produce 1 bushel of wheat and 1 unit of labor to produce 1 item of clothing.

   a. Suppose the United States has 100 units of labor and Brazil has 120. Draw the production possibilities curve for each country without trade. Which country has the absolute advantage in each good? Indicate each country's comparative advantage.

   b. In what range would the world trading price ratio lie when these countries open up to free trade? Will both countries be better off? Why? Show this on your diagram.

4. Suppose France has 250 units of labor and Belgium has 100 units of labor. In France, 1 unit of labor can produce 1 shirt or 3 bottles of wine. In Belgium, 2 units of labor can produce 1 shirt or 3 bottles of wine. Draw the production possibilities curve for each country. If these countries open up to trade, what will happen? Why?

5. Suppose an economics professor can type 15 pages in an hour or write half an economics lecture in an hour. Will she ever have a reason to hire an assistant who can type 10 pages per hour? Use the idea of comparative advantage to explain.

6. "Developing countries should exploit their own comparative advantage and quit trying to invest in physical and human capital to develop high-tech industries." Comment.

7. How does the relative abundance of factors of production affect comparative advantage? Suppose you found that imports to the United States from China were mainly goods, such as airplanes, that require much capital compared to labor, and that exports from the United States to China were mainly goods, such as toys, that require much labor compared to capital. Would your finding constitute evidence against the theory of comparative advantage?

8. Comparative advantage explains interindustry trade in different goods between countries. How do economists explain intraindustry trade, that is, trade in the same industry between countries? Why might people in the United States want to buy German cars, and Germans want to buy cars from the United States?

9. Suppose that each firm in an industry has the total costs shown at the top of the next column.

Quantity of Output	Total Costs (dollars)
1	50
2	54
3	60
4	68
5	80
6	90
7	105
8	112

a. Suppose that the quantity demanded in the market is fixed at 4. Calculate the average total cost for each firm when there are 1, 2, and 4 firms in the industry. Draw a diagram indicating the relationship between average total cost and number of firms.

b. Suppose the quantity demanded in the market expands because of an opening of trade and is now fixed at 8. Draw a diagram similar to the one in part (a) indicating the relationship between average total cost and the number of firms. Why does this opening of trade cause this shift in the curve?

10. The following relationship between price, cost per unit, and the number of firms describes an industry in a single country.

Number of Firms	Cost per Unit ($)	Price ($)
1	10	90
2	20	80
3	30	70
4	40	60
5	50	50
6	60	46
7	70	43
8	80	40
9	90	38
10	100	36

a. Graph (1) the relationship between cost per unit and number of firms, and (2) the relationship between price and number of firms. Why does one slope up and the other slope down?

b. Find the long-run equilibrium price and number of firms.

c. Now suppose the country opens its borders to trade with other countries; as a result, the relationship between cost per unit and the number of firms becomes as follows:

Number of Firms	Cost per Unit ($)
1	5
2	10
3	15
4	20
5	25
6	30
7	35
8	40
9	45
10	50

Find the long-run equilibrium price and number of firms.

d. What are the gains from expanding the market through the reduction in trade barriers?

11. Compare and contrast the following: international trade versus trade within a country, absolute advantage versus comparative advantage, tariff versus quota, labor abundant versus labor intensive, intraindustry trade versus interindustry trade.

CHAPTER 18

International Trade Policy

The violent riots in Seattle in December 1999 made newspaper headlines all over the world and were shown on TV news hour after hour.

The riots grew out of what was expected to be a peaceful protest of a big meeting of the World Trade Organization (WTO), an organization that includes most countries in the world. The WTO was founded in 1993. Its purpose is to develop policies to reduce the many barriers to international trade that still exist and to keep countries from enacting new barriers. The WTO's specific goal for the Seattle meeting was to negotiate a new plan to reduce trade barriers. This goal is in keeping with the economic findings of Chapter 17 that people gain from international trade.

The protesters objected to many things about the WTO. Some objected to reducing trade barriers because they thought this would reduce jobs in certain industries. Others objected to a lack of concern for the environment on the part of the members of the WTO. Still others felt that the WTO was not doing enough to promote higher labor standards in poor countries. Many were suspicious of the WTO, believing that it had too much power; they said that the WTO was run by international bureaucrats who did not have to answer to anyone.

It is not clear how and why the riots got started, but they were brutal; stores were looted, the police used tear gas, and delegates to the WTO could not leave their hotel rooms. The riots were a reminder that the reduction of trade barriers is still strongly opposed by some people for many different reasons. As the twenty-first century began, many worried that a powerful political movement demanding higher trade barriers could arise.

This chapter considers both the economics and the politics of international trade policy. It examines the economic impact of the trade barriers that currently exist, reviews the political history of past trade barriers in the United States, and considers the political-economic arguments given in favor of trade barriers, including some of the arguments made by the protesters in Seattle. It then goes on to evaluate alternative international trade policies in terms of their effectiveness in reducing trade barriers.

Tariffs, Quotas, and VRAs

Governments use many methods to restrict international trade. Policies that restrict trade are called *protectionist policies* because the restrictions usually protect industries from foreign imports. In addition to reducing imports, these policies raise prices, as we show next.

Tariffs

ad valorem tariff: a tax on imports evaluated as a percentage of the value of the import.

specific tariff: a tax on imports that is proportional to the number of units or items imported.

The oldest and most common method by which a government restricts trade is the *tariff*, a tax on goods imported into a country. The higher the tariff, the more trade is restricted. An **ad valorem tariff** is a tax equal to a certain percentage of the value of the good. For example, a 15 percent tariff on the value of goods imported is an ad valorem tariff. If $100,000 worth of goods are imported, the tariff revenue is $15,000. A **specific tariff** is a tax on the quantity sold, such as 50 cents for each kilogram of zinc.

The economic effects of a tariff are illustrated in Figure 18.1. We consider a particular good—automobiles, for example—that is exported from one country (Japan, for example) and imported by another country (the United States, for example). An *import demand curve* and an *export supply curve* are shown in Figure 18.1. The *import demand curve* gives the quantity of imported goods that will be demanded at

Seattle, 1999
The goal of the WTO is to reduce trade barriers. But not everyone agrees with the goal, as the protest against the WTO meeting in Seattle reminds us.

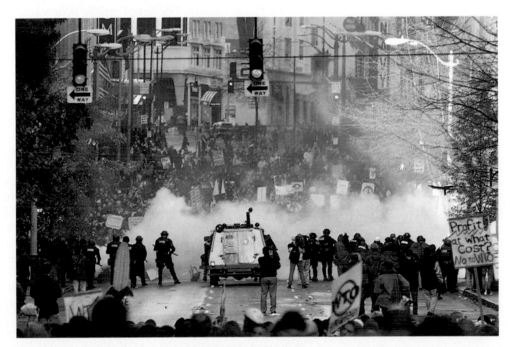

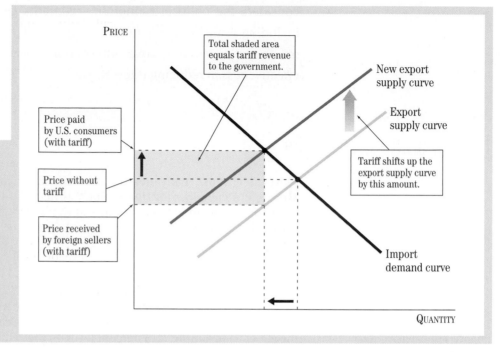

Figure 18.1
The Effects of a Tariff
A tariff shifts the export supply curve up by the amount of the tariff. Thus, the price paid for imports by consumers rises and the quantity imported declines. The price increase (upward-pointing black arrow) is less than the tariff (upward-pointing blue arrow). The revenue to the government is shown by the shaded area; it is the tariff times the amount imported.

each price. It shows that a higher price for imported goods will reduce the quantity of the goods demanded. A higher price for Nissans and Toyotas, for example, will lead to a smaller quantity of Nissans and Toyotas demanded by Americans. Like the standard demand curve, the import demand curve is downward-sloping.

The *export supply curve* gives the quantity of exports that foreign firms are willing to sell at each price. In the case of Nissans and Toyotas, the export supply curve gives the quantity of Toyotas and Nissans that Japanese producers are willing to sell in the United States. The supply curve is upward-sloping, just like any other supply curve, because foreign producers are willing to supply more cars when the price is higher.

In equilibrium, for any single type of good, the quantity of exports supplied must equal the quantity of imports demanded. Thus, the intersection of the export supply curve and the import demand curve gives the amount imported into the country and the price.

When the government imposes a tariff, the supply curve shifts up, as shown in Figure 18.1. The tariff increases the marginal cost of supplying cars to the United States. The amount of the tariff in dollars is the amount by which the supply curve shifts up; it is given by the length of the blue arrow in Figure 18.1.

The tariff changes the intersection of the export supply curve and the import demand curve. At the new equilibrium, a lower quantity is imported at a higher price. The price paid for cars by consumers rises, but the increase in the price is less than the tariff. In Figure 18.1, the upward-pointing black arrow shows the price increase. The blue arrow, which shows the tariff increase, is longer than the black arrow along the vertical axis. The size of the price increase depends on the slopes of the demand curve and the supply curve.

The price received by suppliers equals the price paid by consumers less the tariff that must be paid to the government. Observe that the price received by the sellers declines as a result of the tariff.

The amount of revenue that the government collects is given by the quantity imported times the tariff, which is indicated by the shaded rectangle in Figure 18.1.

For example, if the tariff is $1,000 per car and 1 million cars are imported, the revenue is $1 billion. Tariff revenues are called *duties* and are collected by customs.

The tariff also has an effect on U.S. car producers. Because the tariff reduces imports from abroad and raises their price, the demand for cars produced by import-competing companies in the United States—General Motors or Ford—increases. This increase in demand will raise the price of U.S. cars. Thus, consumers pay more for both imported cars and domestically produced cars.

Quotas

Another method of government restriction of international trade is the *quota*. A quota sets a limit, a maximum, on the amount of a given good that can be imported. The United States has quotas on the import of ice cream, sugar, cotton, peanuts, and other commodities. Foreigners can supply only a limited amount to the United States.

The economic effect of a quota is illustrated in Figure 18.2. The export supply curve and the import demand curve are identical to those in Figure 18.1. The quota, the maximum that foreign firms can export to the United States, is indicated in Figure 18.2 by the solid purple vertical line labeled "quota." Exporters cannot supply more cars than the quota, and, therefore, American consumers cannot buy more

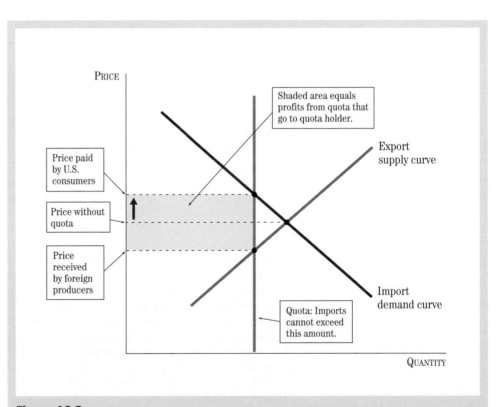

Figure 18.2
The Effects of a Quota
A quota can be set to allow the same quantity of imports as a tariff. The quota in this figure and the tariff in Figure 18.1 allow the same quantity of imports into the country. The price increase is the same for the quota and the tariff. But, in the case of a quota, the revenue goes to quota holders, not to the U.S. government.

than this amount. We have chosen the quota amount to equal the quantity imported with the tariff in Figure 18.1. This shows that if it wants to, the government can achieve the same effects on the quantity imported using a quota or a tariff. Moreover, the price increase in Figure 18.2, represented by the black arrow along the vertical axis, is the same as the price increase in Figure 18.1. Viewed from the domestic market, therefore, a quota and a tariff are equivalent: If the quota is set to allow in the same quantity of imports as the tariff, then the price increase will be the same. Consumers will pay more for imports in both cases, and the demand for domestically produced goods that are substitutes for imports will increase. The price of domestically produced cars will also increase if there is a quota on foreign cars.

Then what is the difference in the effects of a tariff and a quota? Unlike the situation with a tariff, no revenue goes to the government with a quota. The difference between the price that the foreign suppliers get and the higher price that the consumers pay goes to the holders of the quota—the ones who are allowed to import into the country. Frequently foreign countries hold the quotas. The revenue the quota holders get is indicated by the shaded rectangle in Figure 18.2. It is equal to the quantity imported times the difference between the price paid by the consumers and the price received by the producers. The size of that rectangle is identical to the size of the rectangle showing the revenue paid to the government in the case of the tariff in Figure 18.1.

Voluntary Restraint Agreements (VRAs)

voluntary restraint agreement (VRA): a country's self-imposed government restriction on exports to a particular country.

A relatively new alternative to tariffs and quotas is the **voluntary restraint agreement (VRA).** Such a restraint is similar to a quota except that one country, such as the United States, asks another country to "volunteer" to restrict its firms' exports to the United States. Although a tariff or a quota must be passed by Congress, VRAs can be negotiated by the president without Congress approving.

The United States negotiated VRAs with Japan for automobiles in the early 1980s. The Japanese government agreed to limit the number of automobiles Japanese firms exported to the United States to 2.8 million. There are also VRAs on machine tools and textiles exported to the United States. These voluntary agreements usually occur because of pressure that one country, such as the United States, exerts on the other country. Hence, they are not actually voluntary. For example, a foreign government might agree to a VRA because the other country was about to impose steep tariffs. Or there may be diplomatic pressures unrelated to economics that one country can use to pressure another country into these so-called voluntary actions.

What is the economic effect of a VRA? Figure 18.3 examines the impact. The supply and demand curves are identical to those in Figures 18.1 and 18.2. The amount of the VRA chosen for illustration is the same as the quota in Figure 18.2 and the quantity resulting from the tariff in Figure 18.1. This shows that the effect of the VRA on price and quantity can be made identical to that of the quota and the tariff. Consumers pay more under tariffs, quotas, or VRAs. The difference between VRAs and quotas is the recipient of the equivalent of the tariff revenue. In the case of the VRA, these revenues go to the foreign firms. As firms reduce their production, the price rises, and their profits rise. Thus, what would have been tariff revenue to the U.S. government in the case of a U.S. tariff becomes increased profits for foreign firms in the case of a VRA.

Studies show that the VRAs used in the United States in the 1980s for automobiles did lead to a higher price and additional revenue to the Japanese automobile producers. The price of Japanese cars sold in the United States rose by about $1,000, and the increase in demand for U.S. cars led to their price increasing by about $1,400 for the average car.

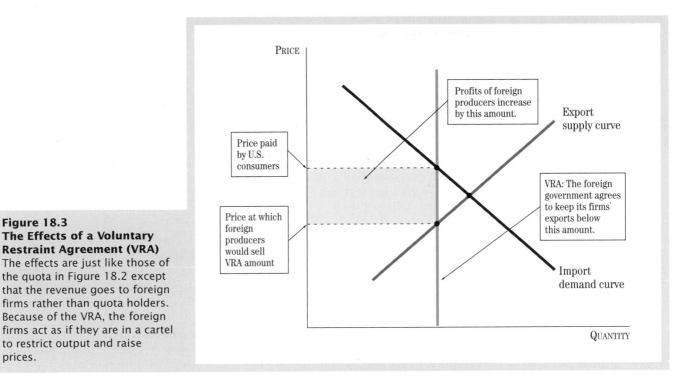

Figure 18.3
The Effects of a Voluntary Restraint Agreement (VRA)
The effects are just like those of the quota in Figure 18.2 except that the revenue goes to foreign firms rather than quota holders. Because of the VRA, the foreign firms act as if they are in a cartel to restrict output and raise prices.

The Costs of Trade Restrictions

Trade barriers such as tariffs, quotas, and VRAs distort prices and reduce the quantity consumed, benefiting domestic producers at the expense of domestic consumers and foreign producers. For example, the United States imposes quotas on sugar to increase the price of domestic sugar beets and sugar cane. Producers receive $1 billion a year in additional surplus as a result of higher prices, but U.S. consumers lose $1.9 billion, for a net loss of welfare of $.9 billion to the United States.

Another trade restriction with big implications for U.S. consumers is the Multifiber Agreement, a set of quotas on textiles and apparel that resulted in an estimated reduction of consumer surplus of $24.4 billion in 1990, and that generates over $10 billion a year in deadweight loss for the United States. Most of this loss comes from transferring the quota rents—the shaded area in Figure 18.2—to foreign producers. Using tariffs instead of quotas would have reduced the cost to the United States to about $2.5 billion a year. The Multifiber Agreement is supposed to disappear in 2005.

REVIEW
- The most common ways for government to restrict foreign trade are tariffs, quotas, and voluntary restraint agreements. Each has the same effect on price and quantity.

- With a tariff, the revenue from the tariff goes to the government. With a quota, that revenue goes to quota holders. With a VRA, that revenue goes to foreign producers.

- Trade restrictions alter the allocation of resources in the economy and are significant sources of deadweight loss.

The History of Trade Restrictions

revenue tariff: an import tax whose main purpose is to provide revenue to the government.

As stated earlier, tariffs are the oldest form of trade restriction. Throughout history, governments have used tariffs to raise revenue. **Revenue tariffs,** whose main purpose is raising revenue, were by far the most significant source of federal revenue in the United States before the income tax was made constitutional by the 16th amendment to the U.S. constitution in 1913 (see Figure 18.4). Revenue tariffs are still common in less-developed countries because they are easy for the government to collect as the goods come through a port or one of a few checkpoints.

U.S. Tariffs

Tariffs are a big part of U.S. history. Even before the United States was a country, a tariff on tea imported into the colonies led to the Boston Tea Party. One of the first acts of the U.S. Congress placed tariffs on imports. Figure 18.5 summarizes the history of tariffs in the United States since the early 1800s.

■ **From the Tariff of Abominations to Smoot-Hawley.**   Tariffs were high throughout much of U.S. history, rarely getting below 20 percent in the nineteenth century. In addition to raising revenue, these tariffs had the purpose of reducing imports of manufactured goods. The tariffs offered protection to manufacturers in the North but raised prices for consumers. Since the South was mainly agricultural and a consumer of manufactured goods, there was a constant dispute between the North and the South over these tariffs.

The highest of these tariffs was nicknamed the "tariff of abominations." This tariff, passed in 1828, brought the average tariff level in the United States to over 60 percent. The tariff made purchases of farm equipment much more expensive in the southern states. It almost led to a civil war before the actual Civil War, as the southern states threatened to secede. However, because the tariff was so high, it was soon

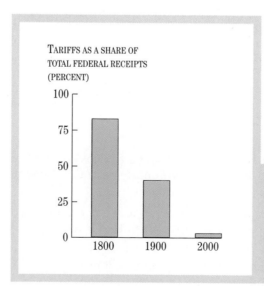

TARIFFS AS A SHARE OF TOTAL FEDERAL RECEIPTS (PERCENT)

Figure 18.4
Tariffs as a Share of Total Federal Revenue
The first tariff, passed in 1789, represented nearly all of the federal government's revenue; 200 years later, tariff revenues were only about 1 percent of the total.

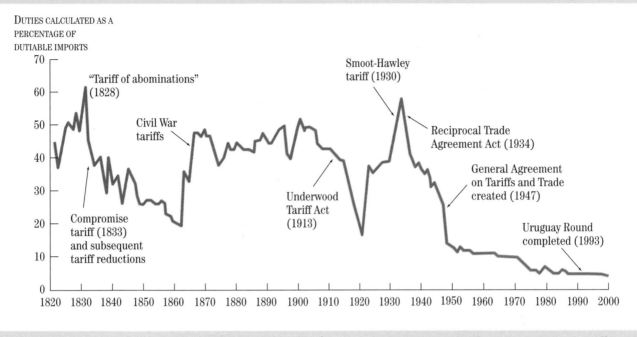

DUTIES CALCULATED AS A PERCENTAGE OF DUTIABLE IMPORTS

"Tariff of abominations" (1828)

Civil War tariffs

Compromise tariff (1833) and subsequent tariff reductions

Underwood Tariff Act (1913)

Smoot-Hawley tariff (1930)

Reciprocal Trade Agreement Act (1934)

General Agreement on Tariffs and Trade created (1947)

Uruguay Round completed (1993)

**Figure 18.5
History of Tariffs in the
United States**

The chart shows the ratio of tariff revenues to the value of imports subject to tariffs measured as a percentage. This percentage is a measure of the average tariff excluding goods not subject to any tariff.

repealed, and for the next 10 years tariffs were relatively low by nineteenth-century standards.

The most devastating increase in tariffs in U.S. history occurred during the Great Depression. The **Smoot-Hawley tariff** of 1930 raised average tariffs to 59 percent. Congress and President Hoover apparently hoped that raising tariffs would help stimulate U.S. production and offset the Great Depression. But the increase had precisely the opposite effect. Other countries retaliated by raising their tariffs on U.S. goods. Each country tried to beat the others with higher tariffs, a phenomenon known as a **trade war.** The Smoot-Hawley tariff had terrible consequences. Figure 18.6 is a dramatic illustration of the decline in trade that occurred at the time of these tariff increases during the Great Depression. The Smoot-Hawley tariff made the Great Depression worse than it would have otherwise been.

■ **From the Reciprocal Trade Agreement Act to the WTO.** The only good thing about the Smoot-Hawley tariff was that it demonstrated to the whole world how harmful tariffs can be. In order to achieve lower tariffs, the Congress passed and President Roosevelt signed the *Reciprocal Trade Agreement Act* in 1934. This act was probably the most significant event in the history of U.S. trade policy. It authorized the president to cut U.S. tariffs by up to 50 percent if other countries would cut their tariffs on a reciprocating basis. The reciprocal trade agreements resulted in a remarkable reduction in tariffs. By the end of World War II, the average tariff level was down from a peak of 59 percent under Smoot-Hawley to 25 percent. The successful approach to tariff reduction under the Reciprocal Trade Agreement Act was made permanent in 1947 with the creation of a new international organization, the *General*

Smoot-Hawley tariff: a set of tariffs imposed in 1930 that raised the average tariff level to 59 percent by 1932.

trade war: a conflict among nations over trade policies caused by imposition of protectionist policies on the part of one country and subsequent retaliatory actions by other countries.

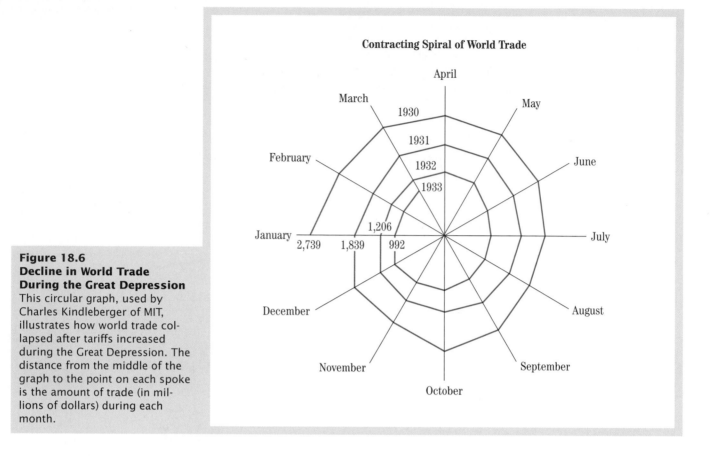

Figure 18.6
Decline in World Trade During the Great Depression
This circular graph, used by Charles Kindleberger of MIT, illustrates how world trade collapsed after tariffs increased during the Great Depression. The distance from the middle of the graph to the point on each spoke is the amount of trade (in millions of dollars) during each month.

World Trade Organization (WTO): an international organization that can mediate trade disputes.

antidumping duty: a tariff imposed on a country as a penalty for dumping goods.

Agreement on Tariffs and Trade (GATT). GATT was set up to continue the process of tariff reduction. During the half century since the end of World War II, tariffs have continued to decline on a reciprocating basis. By 1992, the average U.S. tariff level was down to 5.2 percent.

In 1993, GATT was transformed into the **World Trade Organization (WTO),** which will continue to promote reciprocal reductions in tariffs and other trade barriers. But the WTO also has authority to resolve trade disputes between countries. For example, if the United States complains that Europe is violating a trade agreement by restricting U.S. beef imports in some way, then the WTO will determine whether the complaint has merit and what sanctions should be imposed on Europe. This dispute resolution authority has led to complaints, such as those made by the protesters in Seattle in 1999, that the WTO represents a loss of sovereignty for individual countries. On the other side of the argument, by resolving disputes, the WTO can avoid misunderstandings that otherwise can lead to trade wars between countries when trade disputes occur.

■ **Antidumping Duties.** No history of U.S. tariffs would be complete without a discussion of antidumping duties. **Antidumping duties** are tariffs put on foreign firms as a penalty for dumping. When a firm sells products in another country at prices below average cost or below the price in the home country, it is called *dumping*. Dumping can occur for many reasons. For example, the firm might want to sell at a lower price in the foreign market than in the home market because the demand in the foreign market is more elastic. If so, consumers in the foreign market benefit. But some people argue that dumping is a way for foreign firms to drive domestic firms out of business and thereby gain market share and market power. In any case, in the United States and other countries, dumping is illegal; the penalty is a high tariff—the antidumping duty—on the good that is being dumped. Steel is one of the industries protected with antidumping duties in the United States, at a cost to consumers of as much as $732,000 per job protected, about 10 times what a steelworker earns. President Bush's increase in steel tariffs in 2002 provoked retaliation by the European Union and Japan, adding to the deadweight loss caused by trade barriers.

Many economists are concerned that antidumping duties, or even the threat of such duties, are serious restrictions on trade. They reduce imports and raise consumer prices. Moreover, they are frequently used for protectionist purposes. Firms in industries that desire additional protection can file dumping charges and request that tariffs be raised. Frequently, they are successful. Thus, an important issue for the future is how to reduce the use of antidumping duties for restricting trade.

■ **The Rise of Nontariff Barriers.** As tariffs were being reduced in the post–World War II period, a conflicting trend began to emerge. Some of the other methods of restricting trade—called **nontariff barriers** to trade—grew in popularity. Nontariff barriers include anything from quotas to quality standards aimed at reducing the import of foreign products. Nontariff barriers may have arisen as a replacement for tariffs in response to political pressure for protection of certain industries.

nontariff barrier: any government action other than a tariff that reduces imports, such as a quota or a standard.

Quality and performance standards are sometimes nothing more than barriers to trade. Some standards may have a good purpose, such as safety or compatibility with other products, but others do not. Consider the Canadian plywood standards for building construction, which keep out U.S. plywood. The Canadians argue that the standards are needed to satisfy building requirements in Canada, but Americans argue that plywood that does not meet the Canadian standards works just as well. A safety restriction against American-made baseball bats in Japan during the 1980s is another example. Most Americans viewed the bats as perfectly safe and viewed the Japanese safety standard as a restriction on trade.

Quality and performance standards, therefore, are a tricky problem because governments can argue that they are for the purpose of improving economic conditions in their own country. The U.S. Food and Drug Administration does not allow untested drugs into the United States even though foreign governments deem them safe. The FDA argues that the restriction is necessary to protect consumers, but foreign governments view it as a trade restriction. Such a standard does seem like a trade barrier, but in reality it is a matter of dispute.

REVIEW
- Tariffs were used by governments to raise revenue long before income taxes were invented.

- Tariffs have also been used for protectionist purposes in several important instances in U.S. history. Manufacturing firms in the North were protected by tariffs at the expense of consumers of manufactured goods, many of whom were in the South.

- The Smoot-Hawley tariff of the 1930s was one of the most harmful in U.S. history. It led to a trade war in which other countries raised tariffs in retaliation.

- Tariffs have come down since the 1930s. However, in recent years, nontariff barriers to trade have gone up.

Arguments for Trade Barriers

Are there any good economic arguments for trade barriers? Let's examine some of the arguments that are typically made.

High Transition Costs

When an industry shrinks as a result of the removal of restrictions on trade, the cost of adjustment in the short run may be quite large, even if other industries grow. Those who lose their jobs in the protected industry, even temporarily, suffer. In the short run, it is difficult to retrain workers. Workers who are laid off as the industry shrinks cannot move easily to another industry. Many have to retire early. Retraining is possible, but it takes time and is difficult for older workers.

■ **Phaseout of Trade Restrictions.**   Some people argue that these costs are so high that we should not reduce trade barriers. But there is a better approach. These costs of adjustment are a reason for a slow phaseout of trade barriers. *Phaseout* means that trade barriers are reduced a little bit each year. A slow phaseout of trade barriers was part of the North American Free Trade Agreement between Canada, Mexico, and the United States. This agreement called for a phaseout period of 10 to 15 years, depending on the product. For example, some tariffs were scheduled to be cut by 25 percent in the first year, 50 percent after 5 years, and 100 percent after 10 years. The purpose of the slow phaseout was to allow production to shift from one industry to another slowly. The intention was to adjust the work force through attrition as workers normally retired.

■ **Trade Adjustment Assistance.**   Another approach is to use *trade adjustment assistance*, which refers to transfer payments to workers who happen to be hurt because of a move to free trade. Unemployment insurance and other existing transfer programs may go a long way toward providing such assistance. However, because society as a whole benefits from free trade, some increased resources can be used to help the workers who bear the brunt of the adjustment. In other words, the extra income that can be obtained by trade may be used to ease the adjustment.

Transition costs are not a reason to avoid free trade. They are a reason to phase out the restrictions on trade gradually and to provide trade adjustment assistance to workers as needed.

The Infant Industry Argument

infant industry argument: the view that a new industry may be helped by protectionist policies.

One of the earliest statements of the **infant industry argument** in favor of trade restrictions was put forth by Alexander Hamilton in 1791 in his *Report on Manufactures*. Hamilton argued that manufacturing firms in the newly created United States should be protected from imports. Once the industries were established, they could compete with foreign imports. But as they got started, they needed protection until they reached a certain scale.

A danger with the infant industry argument is that the protection may last long after it was initially justified. In Latin America, for example, infant industry arguments were used to justify import protection in the 1950s. However, these barriers to trade lasted long after any kind of reasonable infant industry argument could be made.

The National Security Argument

A nation's security is another argument for trade restrictions. The national security argument is that there are certain goods, such as special metals, computers, ships, or aircraft, that the country needs to be able to produce in time of war. If it does not have an industry that produces them, it could be at a severe disadvantage.

However, national security arguments can be used by firms seeking protection from foreign imports. Japanese rice farmers, for example, made national security arguments for protection from rice imports. In fact, the rice restriction has little to do with national security because rice can be imported from many different countries. In the United States, the textile industry has argued on national security grounds that it needs protection because it provides military uniforms made from U.S. textiles.

It is important to examine whether there are alternatives to trade restrictions before applying the national security argument and restricting trade. For example, rather than restricting rice imports, the Japanese could store a large amount of rice in case of a war emergency. Or the United States could store millions of extra uniforms rather than restrict textile imports if it was really thought that uniforms were a national security issue. In fact, the United States does have stockpiles of many rare minerals and metals needed for national defense production.

The Retaliation Argument

Threatening other countries or retaliating against them when they have trade restrictions is another possible reason to deviate from free trade. If the United States threatens the Japanese by saying it will close U.S. markets, this may encourage Japan to open its markets to the United States. Thus, by retaliating or threatening, there is a possibility of increasing international trade around the world.

However, the retaliation argument can also be used by those seeking protection. Those in the United States who are most vocal about retaliation against other countries are frequently those who want to protect an industry. Many economists worry about threats of retaliation because they fear that other countries will respond with further retaliation, and a trade war will occur.

The Foreign Subsidies Argument

If foreign governments subsidize their firms' exports, does this justify U.S. government subsidies to U.S. firms to help them compete against the foreign firms?

Foreign subsidies to foreign producers are a particularly difficult issue. If foreign subsidies lower the price of U.S. imports, then U.S. consumers benefit. If Europe wants to use taxpayer funds to subsidize aircraft manufacturers, then why not enjoy the lower-cost aircraft? However, foreign subsidies enable industries to thrive more for political reasons than for economic ones. From a global perspective, such government intervention should be avoided, since it hurts consumers.

Environment and Labor Standards Arguments

During the 1990s a new type of argument against reducing trade barriers emerged: that tariffs or quotas should not be removed against countries with weak or poorly enforced environmental protection laws and labor standards, such as child labor laws and workplace safety laws. Because such laws and standards are generally weaker in developing countries than in developed countries, this argument frequently opposes reducing trade barriers to the imports of goods from relatively poor countries. For example, this argument is made by people who are against reducing tariffs on imports of Brazilian oranges into the United States.

Environmental and labor standard arguments are of two main types. First, some argue that holding back on the reduction of trade barriers until countries change their environmental and labor policies is a good way to persuade these countries to change. However, there is an important counterargument: Low trade barriers themselves lead to improvements in environmental and working conditions. History has shown that as their income grows, people become more concerned with the environment and their working conditions; people in deep poverty do not have the time or resources to deal with such issues. Thus, by raising income per capita, lower trade barriers can improve the environment and the workplace. Moreover, more effective and cheaper technologies to improve the environment or increase safety become available through trade.

A second type of argument is that it is difficult for workers and firms in the advanced countries to compete with those in less developed countries who do not have to pay the costs of complying with environmental protection laws. However, by keeping trade barriers high, income growth may not be sufficient to address the environmental problems in developing countries, so the differences in the law will persist.

The Political Economy of Protection

Firms seek protection from foreign competition simply because the protection raises their profits. But the firms may use any of the above arguments to justify their case. In a famous satire of firms seeking protection from foreign competitors, a French economist, Frédéric Bastiat, wrote more than 150 years ago about candlemakers complaining about a foreign rival—the sun! The candlemakers in Bastiat's satire petitioned French legislators to pass a law requiring the closing of all shutters, curtains, and blinds during the day to protect them from this competition. The behavior Bastiat described seems to apply to many modern producers who seek protection from competition.

One reason that firms seeking protection are frequently successful is that they spend a lot more time and money lobbying the Congress than do the people who would be hurt by the protection. Even though consumers *as a whole* benefit more from reducing trade barriers than firms in the protected industry are harmed, each consumer benefits relatively little, so spending a lot of time and money lobbying is not worthwhile. It is difficult to get enough votes to remove trade barriers when a few firms each have a lot to lose, even though millions of consumers have something to gain.

REVIEW

- Transition costs, environmental and labor standards, national security, infant industry, and retaliation are some of the arguments in favor of trade restrictions. Each has the possibility of being used by protectionists.

- Although many arguments in favor of trade barriers have been put forth over the years, in each case there are better ways to deal with the problems raised. The case for free trade holds up well in the debates when the economic rationale for the gains from trade is applied correctly and understood.

How to Reduce Trade Barriers

Viewed in their entirety, the economic arguments against trade restrictions seem to overwhelm the economic arguments in favor of trade restrictions. The economic arguments in favor of free trade have been in existence for over 200 years. The recommendation of early economists such as Adam Smith and David Ricardo was simple: Reduce trade barriers.

However, it was not until many years after Smith and Ricardo wrote that their recommendations were translated into a practical trade policy. Then, as now, political pressures favoring protection made the repeal of trade barriers difficult. Hence, a carefully formulated trade policy is needed in order to reduce trade barriers. There are a variety of approaches.

Unilateral Disarmament

One approach to removing trade barriers in a country is simply to remove them unilaterally. Making an analogy with the arms race, we call this policy *unilateral disarmament*. When a country unilaterally reduces its arms, it does so without getting anything in arms reduction from other countries. With unilateral disarmament in trade policy, a country reduces its trade barriers without other countries also reducing their trade barriers. Unilateral disarmament is what Smith and Ricardo recommended for England.

The problem with unilateral disarmament is that some individuals are hurt, if only temporarily, and it is hard to compensate them. Of those who gain, each gains only a little. Of those who lose, each loses a lot. The political pressures they exert are significant. As a result, unilateral disarmament is rarely successful in the developed countries today as a means of reducing trade barriers.

Multilateral Negotiations

multilateral negotiation: simultaneous tariff reductions on the part of many countries.

An alternative to unilateral disarmament is **multilateral negotiation,** which involves simultaneous tariff reductions by many countries. With multilateral negotiations, opposing political interests can cancel each other out. For example, import-competing domestic industries that will be hurt by the reduction of trade barriers, such as textiles in the United States or agriculture in Europe and Japan, can be countered by export interests that will gain from the reduction in trade barriers. Since consumers will gain, they are also a potential counter to protectionism, but they are too diffuse to make a difference, as we just discussed. With multilateral negotiations, interested exporters who gain from the reduction in barriers will push the political process to get the reductions.

Multilateral negotiations also balance international interests. For example, to get less-developed countries to remove their barriers to imports of financial and telecommunications services, the United States had to agree to remove agricultural trade barriers in the United States.

■ **The Uruguay Round.**   Multilateral trade negotiations have taken place in a series of negotiating rounds, each of which has lasted several years. During each round, the countries try to come to agreement on a list of tariff reductions and the removal of other trade restrictions. There have been eight rounds of negotiations since 1947. The most recent was the **Uruguay Round,** named after the country where

Uruguay Round: the most recent round of multilateral negotiations, completed in 1993.

the first negotiations occurred in 1986. The Uruguay Round negotiations ended in 1993.

The reduction in tariffs through multilateral negotiations under GATT has been dramatic. Tariffs are expected to go below 3 percent on average in the United States with the implementation of the Uruguay Round agreement. Recall that this compares with nearly 60 percent in the mid-1930s.

■ **Most-Favored Nation Policy.**   Multilateral negotiations are almost always conducted on a *most-favored nation (MFN)* basis. MFN means that when the United States or any other country reduces its tariffs as part of a multilateral trade agreement, it reduces them for everyone. Since the late 1990s the term *normal trade relations (NTR)* has frequently been used in place of MFN because it is a more accurate description of the policy. Today, if a country is not granted MFN or NTR status, the United States imposes very high tariffs on the country. For example, concern about human rights in China has led some to argue that the United States should not grant MFN or NTR status to China. Without MFN/NTR, tariffs on Chinese imports to the United States would be about 60 percent.

Regional Trading Areas

Creating regional trading areas is an increasingly popular approach to reducing trade barriers. For example, the free trade agreement between the United States, Canada, and Mexico removes all trade restrictions among those countries. An even wider free trade area covering the whole Western Hemisphere has been proposed.

Regional trading areas have some advantages over multilateral approaches. First, fewer countries are involved, so the negotiations are easier. Second, regional political factors can help offset protectionist pressures. For example, the political goal of European unity helped establish grassroots support to reduce trade barriers among the countries of Europe.

■ **Trade Diversion versus Trade Creation.**   But there are disadvantages to regional trading areas in comparison with multilateral reductions in trade barriers under GATT. **Trade diversion** is one disadvantage. Trade is diverted when low-cost firms from countries outside the trading area are replaced by high-cost firms within the trading area. For example, as a result of NAFTA, producers of electronic equipment in Southeast Asia have to pay a U.S. tariff, while producers of the same equipment in Mexico do not have to pay the tariff. As a result, some production will shift from Southeast Asia to Mexico; that is viewed as trade diversion from what might otherwise be a low-cost producer. The hope is that **trade creation**—the increase in trade due to the lower tariffs between the countries—will outweigh trade diversion.

trade diversion: the shifting of trade away from the low-cost producer toward a higher-cost producer because of a reduction in trade barriers with the country of the higher-cost producer.

trade creation: the increase in trade due to a decrease in trade barriers.

free trade area (FTA):   an area that has no trade barriers between the countries in the area.

customs union: a free trade area with a common external tariff.

■ **Free Trade Areas versus Customs Unions.**   There is an important difference between two types of regional trading areas: **free trade areas (FTAs)** and **customs unions.** In both, barriers to trade between countries in the area or the union are removed. But external tariffs are treated differently: Under a customs union, such as the European Union (EU), external tariffs are the same for all countries. For example, semiconductor tariffs are exactly the same in France, Germany, and the other members of the EU. Under a free trade area, external tariffs can differ for the different countries in the free trade area. For example, the United States's external tariffs on textiles are higher than Mexico's. These differences in external tariffs under an FTA cause complications because a good can be shipped into the country with the low tariff and then moved within the FTA to the country with the high tariff. To prevent such external tariff avoidance, *domestic content restrictions* must be incorporated

Ending the Corn Laws

Corn laws, recorded as far back as the twelfth century, restricted imports of grains, including wheat, rye, and barley, into England. Adam Smith devoted an entire chapter of his 1776 *Wealth of Nations* to the corn laws, arguing that "the praises which have been bestowed upon the law . . . are altogether unmerited."* But legislation introduced in 1791 raised the grain import tariff even further. The corn laws were unpopular with everyone except landowners and farmers.

The Anti-Corn League, founded in 1839 by Richard Cobden, was the most significant pressure group in nineteenth-century England. The Anti-Corn League used the economic arguments of Smith and Ricardo that the corn laws were an economic disaster and a moral tragedy: The laws impoverished and even starved the working class, constrained the growth of manufacturing, and provided government support to the wealthy. The catalyst was the Irish potato famine of 1845, which raised agricultural prices even further.

Robert Peel was the Tory prime minister from 1841 to 1846. Until 1845, he was against repeal of the corn laws, primarily because of strong support for them from landowners in the Tory party. But under pressure from Cobden and the Anti-Corn League, he changed his position after the potato famine and argued for the repeal of the corn laws.

In February 1846, Peel introduced a package of measures abolishing duties on imported corn over a three-year period. Only a minority of his party supported him, but the package passed. The split in the Tory party ended Peel's career, and the party did not win another election until 1868.

Thus, Peel paid a high political price for his policy of reducing trade protection, a policy that many feel helped make the British economy strong for the rest of the nineteenth century. How do you think he would have fared had he used one of the other methods (such as multilateral negotiations) to reduce protection rather than "unilaterally disarming"?

*Adam Smith, *Wealth of Nations* (New York: Modern Library, 1994), p. 560.

---

into the agreement. These restrictions say that in order for a product to qualify for the zero tariffs between the countries, a certain fraction of the product must be made within the FTA. For example, under NAFTA, the majority of parts in television sets and automobiles must be manufactured in Canada, Mexico, or the United States in order for the television or car to qualify for a zero tariff.

REVIEW
- There are many different approaches to removing restrictions on international trade, including unilateral disarmament, multilateral negotiations, and regional trading areas—FTAs and customs unions.

- Of all these approaches, unilateral disarmament is the most difficult politically. Multilateral and regional approaches are both more common and more successful in lowering trade barriers and keeping them low.

Conclusion

Very few economists disagree with the proposition that tariffs, quotas, and other trade barriers reduce the economic well-being of a society. In fact, polls of economists show that they disagree less on this proposition than on virtually any other in economics. This unanimity among economists was reflected in the debate over the North American Free Trade Agreement in the United States. Every living Nobel

Prize–winning economist endorsed the agreement to eliminate tariffs and quotas among Canada, Mexico, and the United States.

This chapter has shown that despite this unanimity, many restrictions on international trade still exist. There is continued political pressure to erect new trade barriers or prevent the existing ones from being removed.

Thus, the need for good trade policies to reduce trade barriers is likely to increase rather than decrease in the future. The challenge is to develop a means for conducting international trade policy in a world with many sovereign governments, each of which is free to formulate its own policy.

KEY POINTS

1. Despite the economic arguments put forth in support of free trade, there are still plenty of restrictions on trade in the world.

2. Tariffs and quotas are the two main forms of restricting international trade. They are equivalent in their effects on prices and imports.

3. Tariffs were originally a major source of government revenue but are relatively insignificant sources of revenue today.

4. Quotas do not generate any revenue for the government. The quota holders get all the revenue.

5. Voluntary export restraints are much like quotas except that they can be negotiated without an act of Congress, and the revenue usually goes to the foreign producer in the form of increased profits.

6. National security and infant industry are two arguments frequently put forth in support of trade barriers. In most cases, they are overwhelmed by the arguments in favor of reduced trade barriers.

7. Eliminating restrictions on trade unilaterally is difficult because of the harm done to those who are protected by the restrictions.

8. Regional trading areas and multilateral tariff reductions endeavor to reduce trade barriers by balancing export interests against import-competing interests.

9. Free trade areas and customs unions both create trade and divert trade.

KEY TERMS

ad valorem tariff

specific tariff

voluntary restraint agreement (VRA)

revenue tariff

Smoot-Hawley tariff

trade war

World Trade Organization (WTO)

antidumping duty

nontariff barrier

infant industry argument

multilateral negotiation

Uruguay Round

trade diversion

trade creation

free trade area (FTA)

customs union

QUESTIONS FOR REVIEW

1. In what sense are a tariff and a quota equivalent?

2. Why might a tariff raise the price of the imported product by less than the amount of the tariff?

3. How does a voluntary restraint agreement encourage the restriction of supply in the foreign country?

4. What are some examples of quality standards being used as trade barriers?

5. Why is unilateral disarmament a difficult way to reduce trade barriers?

6. How do multilateral negotiations or regional trading areas make the reduction of trade barriers easier politically?

7. Why might a free trade area cause trade diversion?

8. What is the infant industry argument in favor of trade protection?

9. What are the disadvantages of using retaliation in trade policy?

PROBLEMS

1. India has a 70 percent tariff on imported chocolate.
   a. Sketch a diagram to show the impact of this tariff on the price of imported chocolate in India.
   b. Suppose India cuts the tariff to zero but imposes a quota that results in the same price for imported chocolate. Show this in a diagram. What happens to the government's tariff revenue?

2. Use a supply and demand diagram to show what happens to the price and quantity of sugar in the United States when the quotas on sugar are removed.

3. Estimates show that the voluntary export restraints through which the government of Japan restricted automobile exports to the United States in the mid-1980s raised the price of Japanese cars in the United States by about $1,000. Sketch a diagram to show how this occurred and briefly explain the price increase.

4. Suppose French wine suddenly becomes popular in the United States. How does this affect the price and quantity of imports of French wine? Suppose the U.S. wine industry lobbies for protection. If the government imposes a tariff in order to restore the original quantity of imports, what will happen to the price of French wine in the United States? Show how much tariff revenue the government will collect.

5. Suppose that in order to encourage tourism, a Caribbean country subsidizes hotel construction. Draw an export supply and demand curve to show what will happen. Is the United States better off? Might the hotel owners in Florida ask the U.S. government to complain about this?

6. Suppose the U.S. government has decided that for national security reasons, it must protect the machine tools industry. Name two ways in which the government can accomplish this goal. Which policy would you recommend? Why?

7. Suppose the North American Free Trade Agreement (NAFTA) causes the United States to import lumber from Canada instead of Finland, even though Finland is a lower-cost producer than Canada. Identify and explain this phenomenon.

8. Suppose the United States decides to withdraw most-favored nation treatment from China. What will happen to the price and quantity of U.S. imports from China? Use a diagram to explain your answer.

9. Suppose the president of a nation proposes a switch from a system of import quotas to a system of tariffs, with the idea that the switch would not affect the quantity of goods imported. Who will be in favor of the switch? Who will oppose it? Would you expect the proponents and the opponents to have the same political influence on the president?

10. Assume that several hundred independent farmers in Argentina are the only producers of a rare plant used for medicinal purposes around the world.
    a. Graphically show the world demand and supply for this plant when there are no trade restrictions. Show the equilibrium quantity and price.
    b. Imagine you are an economic adviser to the Argentine government. The president asks you to find a way to capture some of the economic rents from the production of this rare plant, so that more profits stay in Argentina. Your job is to design a trade policy that accomplishes the president's goal. Explain verbally and graphically what your trade policy would be, how it would affect quantity and price in the market, and how it would affect the profits and surpluses of all the players in this market. Make sure your policy is designed in such a way that it will have support from the Argentine voters. Include any potential drawbacks of this policy in your analysis.

19

Emerging Market Economies

In 1998, the announcement by the Russian government that it would stop paying interest on its foreign debt (that is, that it would default on the debt) sent shock waves throughout the world. The default raised concerns that similar defaults would occur in other countries; as a result interest rates rose worldwide. The global impact of the Russian decision was a reminder of how integrated the world economy had become, but it also underscored how slow the transition from communism to a market economy had been. Although nearly 10 years had passed since the end of communism and central planning, the Russian economy was still struggling to emerge as a market economy. The economy was in trouble; the Russian people were suffering; foreign debts could not be paid.

There is perhaps no greater economic policy challenge in the twenty-first century than the difficult emergence of market economies in countries that used central planning throughout much of the twentieth century. A common feature of these countries—Russia, China, Poland, Ukraine, and others—is that a major transition is occurring, from a *command economy*, or a centrally planned economy in which the government sets prices and decides *what, how,* and *for whom* goods should be produced, to a *market economy* that is based much more on markets and freely determined prices, in which most of these decisions are left to individuals.

The problems of moving to a market economy have proved very difficult in many cases. Economic growth has faltered in some countries that are trying to make a transition from central planning to a market economy, especially countries that were formerly part of the Soviet Union. In contrast, progress has been faster in Poland and in Hungary.

In this chapter, we take a special look at the emerging market economies in those countries that are making a transition from central planning. To understand what is happening now, we need to look back at what economic life was like under central planning. We first show how central planning grew out of the communist revolutions that were induced by the Marxist criticism of market economies. We then examine the aim of market reforms, alternative approaches to reform, and the experience of several economies during the transition.

What Were Centrally Planned Economies Like?

socialism: an economic system in which the government owns and controls all the capital and makes decisions about prices and quantities as part of a central plan.

capitalism: an economic system based on a market economy in which capital is individually owned, and production and employment decisions are decentralized.

communism: an economic system in which all capital is collectively owned.

With a few exceptions, such as North Korea and Cuba, centrally planned economies no longer exist. But it is important to remember essential economic lessons from the experience of countries that tried central planning during the twentieth century. A well-known expert on communism and socialism, Robert Heilbroner, summarizes the lessons this way: "The Soviet Union, China and Eastern Europe have given us the clearest possible proof that capitalism organizes the material affairs of humankind more satisfactorily than socialism."[1]

Under **socialism** the government owns the capital—factories, stores, farms, and equipment—and decisions about production and employment are made by those who run the government as part of a central plan for the economy. In contrast, in a market economy, also called **capitalism,** individuals own the capital, and decisions about production and employment are decentralized and made by many individuals buying and selling goods in markets. The term **communism** refers to a theoretical situation in which all the people of a country *collectively* own the capital and the land without direct government ownership. Those who advocated communism viewed collective ownership by the people as a long-term goal: A socialist economy would evolve into communism, with the government gradually withering away. However, today most economists and historians use the word *communism* to mean the same thing as *socialism*, as that term is defined here.

Not all socialist economies are the same; there are different degrees of government ownership and centralization. For example, in some socialist economies, farmers could sell a portion of their agricultural output and use the proceeds to buy farm equipment or even consumer goods. Similarly, not all market economies are the same; in most market economies, the government owns the public infrastructure capital, such as roads and bridges, and is involved in the production of education, health services, and other goods. The degree of government involvement differs from market economy to market economy. For example, a much larger fraction of medical care is produced by the government in the United Kingdom than is produced by the government in the United States.

However, in reality, the differences between socialist economies as a group and market economies as a group are much larger than the differences among the economies within each group. In other words, there is a "night-and-day" distinction between centrally planned economies with government ownership of firms that do not have to compete and market economies with private ownership of firms that do have to compete. To understand this distinction, we need to examine how centrally planned economies worked.

---

1. See Robert Heilbroner, "The Triumph of Capitalism," *The New Yorker*, January 1993, pp. 98–109.

Central Planning in the Soviet Union

V. I. Lenin and the Bolshevik party (also known as the Communist party) gained control of the government of Russia in the October Revolution of 1917. At this time, the Russian economy was much less developed than most of Western Europe. GDP per capita in Russia was less than one-third that in the United Kingdom or the United States. The economy was mostly agricultural. Although large-scale manufacturing industries were growing, they were still much smaller than those in Germany, the United Kingdom, or the United States. For more than 1,000 years before the communists gained control, Russia had been ruled by tsars, who held enormous power and resisted economic and political change.

nationalization: the taking over of private firms by the government.

For those reasons, the Russian people were dissatisfied with both their economy and their political system. Lenin and the Bolsheviks seized the opportunity, forcing through a completely new economic system. Most significantly, Lenin decreed that private firms would be taken over by the government, a process called **nationalization.** The Bolsheviks immediately nationalized the banking system, and by mid-1918, a massive nationalization of large- and small-scale industry was under way. Although the alleged reason for the Bolshevik takeover was to give the workers control of the economy, Lenin soon rejected worker control. He argued that people like himself were needed to run the economy on behalf of the workers. He began controlling production from the center, appointing administrators to run each industry from offices in Moscow. In doing so, he laid the foundation of a command economy, in which government *diktats*, or commands, rather than prices and decentralized markets, would determine what was produced. In 1921, **Gosplan,** the state planning commission, was established. In 1922, the Communist party established the Soviet Union, incorporating Ukraine and other countries along with Russia into one large command economy.

Gosplan: the planning agency of the Soviet Union.

At the very start, the experiment in central planning was unsuccessful. Production fell and inflation rose dramatically. Much of the blame for the early lack of success could be placed on the civil war between the communists (the Reds) and the anticommunists (the Whites). Moreover, Lenin had little guidance on how to set up a socialist economy. Karl Marx, whose analysis of capitalism provided the intellectual support for the communist revolution, wrote virtually nothing about how a socialist economy or central planning would work (see the box Starting a Revolution). In any case, the early 1920s saw a retreat from central planning and a partial reinstatement of the market economy under Lenin's New Economic Policy. But with Lenin's death in 1924 and Joseph Stalin's becoming leader of the Communist party in 1928, central planning was reinstated with even more force than previously.

■ **The Five-Year Plans.**   The goal of catching up with Western Europe and the United States quickly came to dominate Stalin's thinking about the economy. Catching up required raising the level of investment in factories and industrial equipment, increasing labor hours, and shifting workers out of agriculture into industry. Stalin wanted to do this rapidly and on a massive scale. To do so, he needed to raise investment in heavy industry and reduce consumption. He saw a command economy as the only way to accomplish his goal.

five-year plan: a document that stated production goals for the entire Soviet economy for the succeeding five years.

Stalin, therefore, gave Gosplan much more authority to run the economy from the center. In 1928, Gosplan issued a **five-year plan** stipulating production goals for the entire economy. This turned out to be the first of a succession of many more five-year plans, and the methods of central planning that would last for 60 years were put in place. Gosplan, under the command of the Communist party leaders, controlled production not only for Russia but for the entire Soviet Union, which was spread over eleven time zones and covered one-sixth of the world's land area.

state enterprise: an organization, analogous to a firm in a market economy, that is owned and controlled by the government.

Production of most goods took place at **state enterprises**—organizations similar in function to business firms in market economies but owned and controlled by the

Starting a Revolution

What led to the rejection of markets and the acceptance of socialism in Russia, China, and Eastern Europe in the twentieth century? The economic writings of Karl Marx in the nineteenth century played a key role.

Karl Marx was an economist and social philosopher. He was an outspoken critic of the existing economic and political system in Europe. He spent much of his adult life in London, studying and writing in the archives of the British Museum. Marx eked out a modest living—his wife and children struggled at the brink of poverty—through his journalistic writings and through financial assistance from his long-time friend and collaborator, Friedrich Engels.

Marx's polemical writings were influential. The widely read and often-quoted *Communist Manifesto* was a short pamphlet written in 1848 by Marx and Engels. It was a stirring call for a revolution:

> A specter is haunting Europe—the specter of communism. . . . Let the ruling classes tremble at a Communist revolution. The proletarians have nothing to lose but their chains. They have a world to win. Working men of all countries, unite!

Surprisingly, Marx and Engels found much to admire in capitalism. They wrote that the bourgeoisie—the class that owned or ran the business firms—

> has accomplished wonders far surpassing the Egyptian pyramids. Roman aqueducts, and Gothic cathedrals. . . . [D]uring its rule of scarcely one hundred years, [it] has created more massive and more colossal productive forces than have all preceding generations together.

It is in Marx's economic writings—longer and more ponderous—that his detailed criticism of capitalism is found. In particular, his treatise *Das Kapital* aimed to show why Adam Smith and David Ricardo were wrong in their praise of the market economy. Referring to Smith's idea that workers would benefit from the increased labor productivity resulting from the division of labor or more machinery, Marx wrote in *Das Kapital*:

> Adam Smith, by a fundamentally perverted analysis, arrives at [this] absurd conclusion. . . .

In truth, Adam Smith breaks his investigation off, just where its difficulties begin.

Marx argued instead that increases in labor productivity would not benefit workers; capitalists, trying to maintain their profits, would keep workers' wages from rising. But history shows that wages have increased by huge amounts in the 150 years since Marx wrote.

Although socialism may have originally seemed like an attractive alternative to the market system, socialism's own severe problems eventually became obvious. Surprisingly, however, Marx wrote almost nothing about how a socialist economy would work. His writings focused entirely on capitalism.

KARL MARX, 1818–1883

Born: Trier, Germany, 1818

Education:
University of Bonn, 1835; University of Berlin, 1836–1841; University of Jena, doctorate in philosophy, 1841

Jobs:
Editor, freelance journalist, Cologne, Paris, Brussels, 1842–1848; independent study, freelance journalist, London 1849–1883

Major Publications:
Communist Manifesto (with Friedrich Engels), 1848; *Das Kapital*, 1867 (Vol. I); Russian translation, 1868; English translation, 1886

collectivized farm: a farm in a planned economy that is in theory collectively owned by peasants, but is controlled by the government.

production target: a goal set for the production of a good or service in a planned economy.

government. Stalin also virtually abolished private property in agriculture in the Soviet Union. He created **collectivized farms,** through which the government took ownership of most farmland, farm equipment, and livestock.

By setting **production targets** for millions of products throughout the Soviet Union, Gosplan tried to control what and how much should be produced at each state enterprise and collectivized farm. Through this method, Stalin was successful in raising the level of investment and reducing people's consumption, thereby rapidly expanding the number of machines and factories devoted to manufacturing. In order to make sure that the labor force was sufficient for this rapid industrialization, the communist government also placed restrictions on workers. For example, new graduates were assigned jobs in different parts of the country, and restrictions on moving to and living in certain areas made it difficult for workers to change jobs if they wanted to.

■ **Centrally Controlled Prices.** Prices for individual goods were also set at the center, but Gosplan rarely set these prices at levels that would equate the quantity supplied with the quantity demanded. Shortages were typical. Food prices were set very low, resulting in food shortages. The managers of state enterprises frequently found themselves having to wait for parts or inputs to production. At other times they produced an excess supply that no one could use. To be sure, when shortages got very severe, markets would develop: Enterprise managers who were in desperate need of materials would offer side payments, or bribes, to other managers or workers in order to get the materials. These markets operated outside of the normal central planning process and were called *gray* or *black markets*. Some economists feel that by reducing crucial shortages, these markets enabled central planning to function.

Recall from Chapter 1 that prices have three roles: They transmit information, coordinate actions by providing incentives, and affect the distribution of income. In a market economy, a change in demand or supply causes a change in the price, which transmits information throughout the economy. Such changes in prices were thwarted by central planning. Central planners simply did not have enough information to know how to change the prices. Thus, the information transmission role of prices did not exist.

The coordination role of prices was deemphasized, although the central planners recognized that prices affected incentives. The managers of the state enterprises were given rewards for hitting production targets, but the rewards were not designed in a way that encouraged efficient management practices. To poke fun at Gosplan, a famous cartoon showed a picture of a nail factory producing *one* large but useless 500-ton nail in order to meet the factory's production target for 500 tons of nails. There were also few rewards for inventing new products or even for finding more efficient ways to produce the existing products. State enterprises thus became very inefficient. Competition between enterprises was discouraged, and production became highly concentrated in a few firms in each industry.

Gosplan did not ignore the role of prices in affecting the distribution of income. Prices were held low on most staple items and high on the few consumer durable items that were produced. By setting prices this way, Gosplan tried to make the distribution of goods and services more equal. But income distribution was by no means egalitarian under central planning. Communist party officials and enterprise managers were given extra payments in the form of better housing, transportation, and the opportunity to shop in stores that contained consumer goods unavailable to ordinary consumers. Because virtually all prices were set by the government, there was no measured inflation, although because prices for many products were set too low, the economy was frequently in a condition of shortage. The central bank (Gosbank) was the only bank in the country. It provided loans to state enterprises and collectivized farms in the amounts Gosplan instructed. Gosbank also issued currency (rubles) and accepted deposits from consumers.

Gosplan did not have to worry much about taxes because it could set the price of everything. For example, to finance the production of military goods, the central planners could set the price of inputs to defense production low and the price of defense goods high. They could also simply order increased production of military goods and reduced production of some other goods.

Trade Between the Soviet Union and Eastern Europe

After World War II, when communist governments were installed in Poland, Hungary, Czechoslovakia, East Germany, Romania, and Bulgaria, Soviet-style central planning was extended to each of these countries. How did international trade take place between the Soviet Union and its close neighbors in the Soviet bloc?

Trade among these countries and the Soviet Union took place through a trading organization called the *Council for Mutual Economic Assistance*. The trade did not take place at world market prices. For example, the Soviet Union, which was rich in energy resources such as oil and natural gas, would supply energy to the Eastern European countries at prices well below the market prices prevailing throughout the world. The prices were established through political negotiations between the governments, which undoubtedly involved noneconomic considerations such as the placement of military troops and weapons. In exchange for the low-priced energy, the Eastern European countries would provide manufactured goods, although those were lower in quality than similar goods produced in the West. Prices for trade between the countries of Eastern Europe were similarly negotiated. Thus, neither domestic trade nor international trade between the centrally planned economies was market-based.

Technological Change and the Quality of Goods

By most accounts, Stalin's forced investment and forced labor strategy did increase economic growth in the 1930s in the Soviet Union. In the years after World War II, both the Soviet Union and Eastern Europe grew rapidly. However, it eventually became apparent that the great inefficiencies associated with central planning were starting to offset the high levels of investment and labor force participation. The growth of technology began to slow down. Investment rates and labor force participation rates had reached their limits, and technology growth was lagging seriously. Environmental pollution was severe in cities such as Warsaw and Bucharest.

State-owned retail shops had few consumer goods, and those that they had were of very poor quality. Long lines were evident at stores, especially those selling anything special, such as candy bars or gasoline. The availability of goods was also poor.

One of the apparent puzzles about central planning was its success in certain areas. The space exploration achievements of the Soviet Union, for example, were outstanding enough for the United States to get involved in the space race. They were the source of President Kennedy's goal of a manned flight to the moon.

One explanation for this success was that an enormous amount of resources was put into defense production. Just as East German athletes dominated the Olympics because of all the resources that went into their training, a centrally planned economy could excel at certain things. Students with talents useful for defense production—mathematics, science, and engineering—were given excellent training in the Soviet Union. Even inefficiency can be offset by enough resources. Moreover, as mentioned previously, economists have found that managers in defense production had ways to go outside the central planning system, essentially using gray markets to obtain parts or equipment that was in short supply. Such markets were tolerated more frequently in the defense industry than in consumer goods industries.

From Perestroika to the End of the Soviet Union

Pressures to reform the central planning system began in the 1960s and 1970s and gained momentum in the 1980s. In 1985, Mikhail Gorbachev became the leader of the Communist party. To deal with the problems of inefficiency, poor quality, and

perestroika: the restructuring of the Soviet economy by reforming the central planning process.

slow technology growth, he tried to change central planning through a process called **perestroika,** which translates as "restructuring." Perestroika changes were put into the twelfth five-year plan, formulated in 1985. For example, enterprise managers were to be made more accountable for their actions through worker and public criticism. By 1989, however, it was clear that perestroika was doing little to increase economic growth. Economists complained that perestroika was piecemeal because it continued to rely on the central planning process to set prices. An alternative plan, called the Shatalin Plan, after one of Gorbachev's advisers, would have used the market much more. However, it was rejected by Gorbachev because it would have initiated a transition to a market economy and thereby done away with central planning.

But perestroika started a process that could not easily be stopped. The open criticism of the central planning process made it acceptable to criticize the political authorities. Soon people in Eastern Europe were criticizing their own governments and their close ties with the Soviet Union. Gorbachev decided to "let go" of the Eastern European countries in 1989, and by 1990 the republics of the Soviet Union also wanted their freedom. Gradually the Russian Republic began to take over the responsibility for the Soviet Union. After an aborted military coup in 1991, Gorbachev resigned and the Soviet Union ceased to exist. Boris Yeltsin, the president of Russia, disbanded central planning and began to follow a more radical series of reforms aimed at creating a market economy. Many of Yeltsin's reforms were opposed by the Russian parliament, and the reforms that were put in place (discussed below) were not sufficient to avoid serious problems for the Russian economy, evidenced by the default on foreign debt in 1998. In 2000 Vladimir Putin became president of Russia, marking the first democratic transition between leaders in Russian history.

Soviet-Style Central Planning in China

The Chinese communists under Mao Zedong gained control of China in 1949. Mao's goals were similar to those of the Soviet Union—to rapidly industrialize. In fact, Mao originally viewed the Soviet Union as an economic model. He imported Soviet-style central planning to China. Under Mao and the Communist party, most economic production was controlled by the central government, just as in the Soviet Union. In the 1950s, growth was rapid due to heavy investment.

Starting in 1958, Mao began the "Great Leap Forward," which briefly raised economic growth by promoting a warlike work effort throughout the country and calling for a massive expansion of production. But the Great Leap Forward could raise economic growth for only a short period. The communist spirit was not enough to make people work hard year after year. The Great Leap Forward ended in a huge decline in production.

A misguided attempt to revive the spirit of the communist revolution took place in the late 1960s with the Cultural Revolution. But the Cultural Revolution ended up severely hurting the Chinese economy. Productive managers and technicians were forced to leave their jobs and do manual labor. Universities were closed. By the late 1970s, it was clear that economic reform was necessary in China, a subject we will return to later in the chapter.

REVIEW   ▪ Central control of the economy began in Russia soon after the Bolsheviks rose to power. Central planning grew and dominated the Soviet economy under Stalin in the 1920s and 1930s and spread to Eastern Europe and China after World War II.

> - Although the high investment and high labor force participation led to strong growth initially, central planning eventually broke down. Inefficiency, poor-quality goods, and slow growth of technology were the most obvious problems.

Economic Transition in Theory

The Elements of Reform

How does a country change from central planning to a market economy? There is general agreement that in any successful transition from central planning to a market economy, a legal system specifying property rights and enforcing the law must be set up, and a system of tax collection must be put in place. And, of course, the government must stop controlling prices, and let prices be determined in decentralized markets. Enforcing competition among firms—including the former state enterprises—is also important. Finally, if there is a large government budget deficit, it must be substantially reduced so that the government is not forced to print money in order to finance the deficit, causing inflation.

As is true of many areas of economics, however, there is disagreement about how to achieve these goals of a transition.

Shock Therapy or Gradualism?

A major question about the transition to a market economy is how fast it should be. The two basic alternatives are **shock therapy** and **gradualism.** Under shock therapy, or the *big bang* approach, all the elements of the market economy are put in place at once. Under gradualism, the reforms are phased in slowly.

shock therapy: the abrupt introduction of free markets in a formerly centrally planned economy.

gradualism: the slow phasing in of free market reforms.

One of the most remarkable aspects of the transition from central planning in the countries of Eastern Europe was the strong commitment to the move to market economies on the part of government policymakers and the general public at the start of the reforms in 1989 and 1990. Most officials went out of their way to emphasize that they were not looking for a third way and to recognize the need to move to a Western-style market-based economic system in order to raise living standards.

Such positive attitudes toward reform were part of the motivation behind shock therapy. Those in favor of a shock-therapy approach argue that such positive attitudes are probably temporary, creating a brief window of opportunity for reform. The enthusiasm for reform may diminish if, as is likely, the reforms do not bring noticeable improvements quickly. Thus, rather than see the reform movement aborted in midstream, it is better to sweep through the reforms quickly. This was one of the arguments for the shock-therapy approach that was used in Poland.

Another argument in favor of shock therapy is that all the elements of reform are interrelated. Making state enterprises private without enforcing competition, for example, could make things worse by creating monopolies.

The arguments against shock therapy are that people require time to adjust to new circumstances. Even though the production of low-quality black and white television sets in Warsaw is inefficient compared with importing televisions from Malaysia, it might be better to move gradually to free trade. This would give firms time to move into some other business and workers time to find other jobs.

> **REVIEW**
> - The goals of a transition to a market economy are much easier to state than to achieve; the goals can be defined in terms of the key ingredients of a market economy.
> - Shock therapy and gradualism are two different paths to a market-based economy.

Economic Transition in Practice

What has been the experience of those countries trying to make a transition from central planning to a market-based economy? Table 19.1 presents data on real GDP growth in the formerly centrally planned economies of central and Eastern Europe and the former Soviet Union in the first few years following reform. A quick glance at this table shows how difficult the transition has been. Although these countries had slow economic growth under communism, the period of transition has seen deep recession. In some countries the decline in real GDP has been nearly as large as the decline in real GDP during the Great Depression in the United States. In contrast, the transition to a market economy in China was not associated with such large declines in real GDP. But Russia and many of the central Asian countries continue to suffer transition problems. Real GDP in Ukraine in 1999 was only 35 percent of Ukraine's real GDP in 1989. Real GDP in Russia in 1999 was about 55 percent of Russia's real GDP in 1989.

However, by the late 1990s the economies of Eastern Europe, especially Poland and Hungary, had shown considerable improvement after their shaky start. Real GDP in Hungary and Poland in 1999 was 99 percent and 128 percent of their respective real GDP levels in 1989.

To understand the problems of transition, we must look more carefully at the countries undertaking the transition. Consider two countries—Poland and China—that have been undergoing a transition for several years and that have achieved positive economic growth.

Reforms in Poland

Poland was the first country in Eastern Europe to start a transition to a market economy. The Polish program has typified the shock-therapy approach.

Four months after the reform program was put in place in Poland, there were many visible signs of its effects, including a decline in inflation and a reduction of shortages. Inflation, which averaged 420 percent in 1989 and 1990, had fallen to 25 percent by 1992, but the adjustment costs, as evidenced by large declines in production and employment, were painful. Real GDP declined by 12 percent in 1990 and another 7 percent in 1991. However, by 1992 real GDP had stopped falling and showed a small increase. By 1994 economic growth was 6 percent, as shown in Table 19.1, and it was still strong in the late 1990s.

Table 19.1
Real GDP Growth in the Early Years of Transition from Central Planning to a Market Economy

	Real GDP Growth (percent)	
	1992	1994
Central and Eastern Europe		
Albania	−9.7	7.4
Estonia	−21.6	6.0
Hungary	−4.3	2.6
Latvia	−35.2	2.0
Lithuania	−56.6	1.5
Poland	2.6	6.0
Romania	−10.1	3.4
Ukraine	−17.0	−23.0
Russia	−19.0	−15.0
Caucasus and Central Asia		
Azerbaijan	−22.1	−21.9
Georgia	−42.7	−10.0
Kazakhstan	−14.0	−25.0
Tajikistan	−30.0	−16.3
Uzbekistan	11.1	−2.6

Source: From *World Economic Outlook*, May 1995. Reprinted with permission of International Monetary Fund.

The Polish stabilization program made use of several policy initiatives. Government expenditures and the budget deficit were reduced sharply, largely through a reduction in government subsidies to state enterprises and a halting of public infrastructure investment. Most prices were deregulated at once and were left to be determined by state enterprises or private firms. Coal prices increased significantly, but internal transportation prices and rents remained low. Wage growth was controlled by government guidelines.

The result of these policies was a substantial decline in demand. There was also a reduction in shortages—the lines of people waiting to be served in butcher shops disappeared, for example. This reduction was brought about partly by the decline in demand, but also because free prices began to bring the quantity supplied into equality with the quantity demanded. Goods started appearing on the shelves, and firms could get intermediate inputs without long delays. Imported consumer goods, most noticeably fruits and vegetables, were more available. The trade account went into surplus in 1990, with exports increasing rapidly and imports declining rapidly.

At the start of the reform program, employment declined surprisingly little despite the large declines in production. The unemployment rate increased only to about 2 percent of the work force in the first few months of the program, but then unemployment increased sharply. Many workers were laid off because the state enterprises needed to reduce wage costs in order to avoid losses as the demand for their products dropped.

privatization: the process of converting a government enterprise into a privately owned enterprise.

In order for a market economy to take root, it is necessary that existing state enterprises become privately owned, a process called **privatization,** and that new private firms be able to start up. Moreover, private investment from abroad provides technological know-how. Privatization helps provide managers with the incentive to allocate resources efficiently and increase productivity.

The Polish government submitted a privatization bill to the Parliament after the economic reforms began in 1990, but it moved slowly because of extensive debate. The main controversial issue was over who owned the state enterprises that were being sold. Hence, privatization was one part of the Polish reform program that was gradual.

A useful assessment of the Polish economic reforms comes from the person who implemented them firsthand on a day-to-day basis. Leszek Balcerowicz, who was the Polish finance minister in charge of the reforms, put it this way in 1993:

> Even successful economic reforms generate some dissatisfaction. Such reforms transform hidden unemployment into open unemployment and produce shifts in the relative pay and prestige of many groups. New entrepreneurs, managers, lawyers, accountants, etc., are on the way up and—as a result—some powerful groups such as miners are on the way down. Not everybody can make a direct use of radically enlarged economic freedom, and those who can't often look with envy at the new ingroups.
>
> But it is a mistake to reject the radical economic reforms simply because they produce these side effects. Postponing difficult steps is even more costly and risky socially, as a look at Ukraine or Russia shows. Radical reforms, as distinct from muddling through, also produce economic dynamism.[2]

Reforms in China

Market-based reforms began earlier in China than in Poland. The first reforms were in the agriculture sector. By the late 1970s, the Chinese government was leasing land back to individual farmers in order to give them more incentive to produce. The reform resulted in a huge increase in the growth rate of farm output. Agricultural production grew by 3 percent per year from 1952 to 1978; from 1978 (when the reforms began) to 1981, the growth rate was about 6 percent per year. Moreover, the increased efficiency in agriculture increased the supply of labor in the industrial sector.

By the mid-1980s, about the same time as perestroika was starting in the Soviet Union, economic reforms were already spreading beyond the farm sector. Individual state enterprises were first given more discretion to experiment with new products and to use the profits generated from those products. As in the case of agriculture, industrial enterprises were leased to the managers, who could then keep part of the profits. As a result of these reforms, real GDP growth increased rapidly. Economic growth averaged a remarkably rapid 9.6 percent per year from 1987 to 1994. Real GDP growth in China remained strong throughout the 1990s.

China also reduced restrictions on foreign trade. In fact, much of China's growth has come from producing goods for foreign trade. Exports grew even more rapidly than real GDP.

To summarize, the overall reform in China has been much more gradual than in Poland. However, after more than a decade of reforms, both Poland and China appear to be growing rapidly, suggesting that either shock therapy or gradualism may work, as long as a comprehensive set of reforms is implemented. In the meantime, the transition in Russia and other countries is still floundering. The comparison with Poland suggests that in these countries it is not the speed of the reforms that has been crucial, but rather that the reforms have been incomplete. In particular, poor enforcement of private property rights, large budget deficits, and high inflation have impeded the transition to a market economy thus far in Russia. Nevertheless, economists continue to debate whether the gradual reform is better or worse than shock therapy.

---

2. "Why the Leftists Won the Polish Election," *Wall Street Journal*, September 28, 1993, Section A, p. 10.

REVIEW
- Poland took the lead in major economic reform in Eastern Europe. Its reform program is the prototype of shock therapy.

- The transition has been hard on the Polish economy. However, real GDP growth started increasing in 1992 and was strong in most of the 1990s. Institutions have been put in place that will help foster the market economy in the future.

- China started its market-based reforms in the late 1970s by selling off a large amount of land to the farmers. Controls on state enterprises have been lifted more gradually.

Conclusion

It was the economic failure of central planning and strict state control that led to socialism's demise. The failure of the centrally planned economy in East Germany in comparison with the success of the market economy in West Germany was as close as the real world ever gets to a controlled experiment. But if the emerging market economies do not deliver economic success for the people of these regions—a success that will be as obvious as was the failure of socialism—it is likely that there will be more changes, perhaps for the worse.

As we have seen in this chapter, the countries that are attempting a transition to a market economy have a difficult task. There have been setbacks, and there are likely to be more. But high economic growth in the formerly centrally planned economies of Poland, China, and Hungary indicate hope for others, such as Russia, that are still struggling to set up a strong market economy.

KEY POINTS
1. The economies of the countries in transition from central planning to a market economy are emerging market economies.

2. Central planning and state control grew out of the communist revolutions under Lenin in Russia in 1917 and under Mao in China in 1949. Central planning was extended to Eastern Europe after World War II. At communism's height, over one-third of the world's population lived in centrally planned economies.

3. By mounting an intellectual criticism of the classical economists' model, Marx spearheaded the communist revolutions that eventually led to central planning.

4. Most centrally planned economies grew rapidly in their early stages because of heavy investment, but eventually productivity growth slowed down sharply and even declined.

5. The transition from central planning to a free market economy is much more difficult than the reverse transition. The road from socialism to free markets will be long, with the gains perhaps not noticeable for many years in some cases.

6. There are two different approaches to transition: shock therapy and gradualism.

KEY TERMS

socialism	Gosplan	collectivized farm	shock therapy
capitalism	five-year plan	production target	gradualism
communism	state enterprise	perestroika	privatization
nationalization			

QUESTIONS FOR REVIEW

1. When did central planning begin, and why?

2. What led to dissatisfaction with central planning and the end of socialism in Russia?

3. What comparison of countries is most useful for demonstrating the inefficiencies of central planning?

4. What are the elements of an economic reform program?

5. What is the difference between shock therapy and gradualism in the transition to a market economy?

6. What political argument favors shock therapy?

7. In what sense was the Polish reform program shock therapy, and in what sense was it more gradual?

PROBLEMS

1. In 1960, Mao Zedong wrote, "The whole Socialist camp headed by the Soviet Union . . . now accounts for nearly 40 percent of the world's . . . gross industrial output . . . and it will not be long before it surpasses the gross industrial output of all the capitalist countries put together." Explain why such a statement was believable at the time, and why the prediction turned out to be so inaccurate.

2. Why was central planning successful in increasing real GDP growth for a while? Why did real GDP growth eventually falter under central planning?

3. Explain why it may be easier to move from a market economy with private property to a command-and-control economy without private property than the other way around. Give a real-world example to prove your point.

4. Describe Gosplan's role during the period of central planning in the Soviet Union.

5. Has Poland or China had an easier time with the transition from central planning? Why do you think this is the case?

6. Could state-owned firms be made to operate as if they were private firms? For example, suppose that the managers of state enterprises were instructed to maximize profits with prices and wages set by the central planners. According to the Hungarian economist Janos Kornai, the answer to this question is no. In *The Road to a Free Economy*, he writes, "It is futile to expect a state-owned unit to behave as if it were privately owned." Provide an argument supporting Kornai's view. Be sure to mention the role of prices as well as the role of private property and incentives.

7. Compare and contrast how the three key questions—*how, what,* and *for whom* goods and services should be produced—are dealt with in a centrally planned economy and in a market economy.

8. Comment on the validity of the following statement in the *New York Times Book Review* on March 30, 1997. Support your answer with historical examples and economic reasoning: "Capitalism was and is a destructive and revolutionary phenomenon. It leveled European feudalism and aristocracy, then proceeded, in this century, to destroy statism, both fascist and communist. It has created a dynamic, materialistic, and dominating global culture with an aspiring middle class at its helm."

Glossary

absolute advantage a situation in which a person or country is more efficient at producing a good in comparison with another person or country. (17)

ad valorem tariff a tax on imports evaluated as a percentage of the value of the import. (18)

aggregate demand the total demand for goods and services by consumers, businesses, government, and foreigners. (4)

aggregate demand (*AD*) curve a line showing a negative relationship between inflation and the aggregate quantity of goods and services demanded at that inflation rate. (11)

aggregate hours the total number of hours worked by all workers in the economy in a given period of time. (7)

aggregate supply the total value of all goods and services produced in the economy by the available supply of capital, labor, and technology (also called potential GDP). (4)

antidumping duty a tariff imposed on a country as a penalty for dumping goods. (18)

asset something of value owned by a person or a firm. (9)

automatic stabilizers automatic tax and spending changes that occur over the course of the business cycle that tend to stabilize the fluctuations in real GDP. (13)

balanced budget a budget in which tax revenues equal spending. (13)

bank a firm that channels funds from savers to investors by accepting deposits and making loans. (9)

budget deficit the amount by which government spending exceeds tax revenues. (13)

budget surplus the amount by which tax revenues exceed government spending. (13)

capital the factories, improvements to cultivated land, machinery and other tools, equipment, and structures used to produce goods and services. (4)

capital abundant a higher level of capital per worker in one country relative to another. (17)

capital gain the increase in the value of an asset through an increase in its price. (15)

capital income the sum of profits, rental payments, and interest payments. (5)

capital intensive production that uses a relatively high level of capital per worker. (17)

capital loss the decrease in the value of an asset through a decrease in its price. (15)

capitalism an economic system based on a market economy in which capital is individually owned, and production and employment decisions are decentralized. (19)

Cartesian coordinate system a graphing system in which ordered pairs of numbers are represented on a plane by the distances from a point to two perpendicular lines, called axes. (2A)

catch-up line the downward-sloping relation between the level of productivity and the growth of productivity predicted by growth theory. (16)

central bank independence a description of the legal authority of central banks to make decisions on monetary policy with little interference by the government in power. (14)

ceteris paribus all other things being equal; refers to holding all other variables constant or keeping all other things the same when one variable is changed. (2)

checking deposit an account at a financial institution on which checks can be written; also called checkable deposit. (9)

choice a selection among alternative goods, services, or actions. (1)

circular flow diagram a diagram illustrating the flow of funds through the economy as people buy and sell in markets. (2)

collectivized farm a farm in a planned economy that is in theory collectively owned by peasants, but is controlled by the government. (19)

command economy an economy in which the government determines prices and production; also called a centrally planned economy. (1)

commerce clause the clause in the U.S. Constitution that prohibits restraint of trade between states. (17)

communism an economic system in which all capital is collectively owned. (19)

comparative advantage a situation in which a person or country can produce one good at a lower opportunity cost than another person or country. (1, 17)

complement a good that is usually consumed or used together with another good. (3)

compound growth applying the growth rate to growth from the previous period; analogous to compound interest. (4A)

consumer price index (CPI) a price index equal to the current price of a fixed market basket of consumer goods and services relative to a base year. (5)

consumption   purchases of final goods and services by individuals. (5)

consumption function   the positive relationship between consumption and income. (10)

consumption share   the proportion of GDP that is used for consumption; equals consumption divided by GDP, or *C/Y*. (6)

consumption smoothing   the idea that, although their incomes fluctuate, people try to stabilize consumption spending from year to year. (10A)

controlled experiments   empirical tests of theories in a controlled setting in which particular effects can be isolated. (2)

Council of Economic Advisers   a three-member group of economists appointed by the president of the United States to analyze the economy and make recommendations about economic policy. (2)

countercyclical policy   a policy designed to offset the fluctuations in the business cycle. (13)

coupon   the fixed amount that a borrower agrees to pay to the bondholder each year. (15)

crowding out   the decline in private investment owing to an increase in government purchases. (6)

currency   money in its physical form: coin and paper money. (9)

currency to deposit ratio   the proportion of currency that people in the economy want to hold relative to their deposits; it equals currency divided by deposits. (9)

Current Population Survey   a monthly survey of a sample of U.S. households done by the U.S. Census Bureau; it measures employment, unemployment, the labor force, and other characteristics of the U.S. population. (7)

customs union   a free trade area with a common external tariff. (18)

cyclical unemployment   unemployment due to a recession, when the rate of unemployment is above the natural rate of unemployment. (7)

debt contract   a contract in which a lender agrees to provide funds today in exchange for a promise from the borrower, who will repay that amount plus interest at some point in the future. (15)

debt to GDP ratio   the total amount of outstanding loans the federal government owes divided by nominal GDP. (13)

deflation   a decrease in the overall price level, or a negative inflation rate. (12)

demand   a relationship between price and quantity demanded. (3)

demand curve   a graph of demand showing the downward-sloping relationship between price and quantity demanded. (3)

demand schedule   a tabular presentation of demand showing the price and quantity demanded for a particular good, all else being equal. (3)

demand shock   a shift in one of the components of aggregate demand that leads to a shift in the aggregate demand curve. (12)

depreciation   the decrease in an asset's value over time; for capital, it is the amount by which physical capital wears out over a given period of time. (5, 15)

developing country   a country that is poor by world standards in terms of real GDP per capita. (16)

diffusion   the spreading of an innovation throughout the economy. (8)

diminishing returns   a situation in which successive increases in the use of an input, holding other inputs constant, will eventually cause a decline in the additional production derived from one more unit of that input. (8)

discount rate   an interest rate used to discount a future payment when computing present discounted value. (15A)

discount rate   the interest rate that the Fed charges commercial banks when they borrow from the Fed. (14)

discounting   the process of translating a future payment into a value in the present. (15A)

discretionary fiscal policy   changes in tax or spending policy requiring legislative or administrative action by the president or Congress. (13)

disinflation   a reduction in the inflation rate. (12)

dividend yield   the dividend stated as a percentage of the price of the stock. (15)

division of labor   the division of production into various parts in which different groups of workers specialize. (1)

dual scale   a graph that uses time on the horizontal axis and different scales on the left and right vertical axes to compare the movements of two variables over time. (2A)

earnings   the accounting profits of a firm. (15)

economic development   the process of growth by which countries raise incomes per capita and become industrialized; also refers to the branch of economics that studies this process. (16)

economic fluctuations   swings in real GDP that lead to deviations of the economy from its long-term growth trend. (4)

economic growth   an upward trend in real GDP, reflecting expansion in the economy over time. (4)

economic interaction   exchanges of goods and services between people. (1)

economic model   an explanation of how the economy or part of the economy works. (2)

economic variable any economic measure that can vary over a range of values. (2)

economics the study of how people deal with scarcity. (1)

efficiency wage a wage, higher than that which would equate quantity supplied and quantity demanded, set by employers in order to increase worker efficiency— for example, by decreasing shirking by workers. (7)

efficient market hypothesis the idea that markets adjust rapidly enough to eliminate profit opportunities immediately. (15)

employment-to-population ratio the ratio (usually expressed as a percentage) of employed workers to the working-age population. (7)

equilibrium interest rate the interest rate that equates the sum of the consumption, investment, and net export shares to the share of GDP available for non-government use. (6)

equilibrium price the price at which quantity supplied equals quantity demanded. (3)

equilibrium quantity the quantity traded at the equilibrium price. (3)

equilibrium risk-return relationship the positive relationship between the risk and the expected rate of return on an asset, derived from the fact that, on average, risk-averse investors who take on more risk must be compensated with a higher return. (15)

equity contract shares of ownership in a firm; payments to the owners of the shares depend on the firm's profits. (15)

exchange market intervention purchases and sales of foreign currency by a government in exchange markets with the intention to affect the exchange rate. (14)

exchange rate the price of one currency in terms of another in the foreign exchange market. We express the exchange rate as the number of units of foreign currency that can be purchased with one unit of domestic currency. (6, 15)

expansion the period between the trough of a recession and the next peak, consisting of a general rise in output and employment. (4)

expected return the return on an uncertain investment calculated by weighting the gains or losses by the probability that they will occur. (15)

expenditure line the relation between the sum of the four components of spending ($C + I + G + X$) and aggregate income. (10)

experimental economics a branch of economics that uses laboratory experiments to analyze economic behavior. (2)

exports the total value of the goods and services that people in one country sell to people in other countries. (5)

face value the principal that will be paid back when a bond matures. (15)

factor-price equalization the equalization of the price of labor and the price of capital across countries when they are engaging in free trade. (17)

federal budget a summary of the federal government's proposals for spending, taxes, and the deficit. (13)

federal debt the total amount of outstanding loans owed by the federal government. (13)

federal funds rate the interest rate on overnight loans between banks that the Federal Reserve influences by changing the supply of funds (bank reserves) in the market. (11)

Federal Open Market Committee (FOMC) the committee, consisting of the seven members of the Board of Governors and the twelve presidents of the Fed district banks, that meets about eight times per year and makes decisions about the supply of money; only five of the presidents vote at any one time. (9)

Federal Reserve System (the Fed) the central bank of the United States, which oversees the creation of money in the United States. (9)

final good a new good that undergoes no further processing before it is sold to consumers. (5)

five-year plan a document that stated production goals for the entire Soviet economy for the succeeding five years. (19)

fixed exchange rate policy a policy in which a country maintains a fixed value of its currency in terms of other currencies. (14)

flexible exchange rate policy a policy in which exchange rates are determined in foreign exchange markets and governments do not agree to fix them. (14)

foreign direct investment investment by a foreign entity of at least a 10 percent direct ownership share in a firm. (16)

foreign exchange market a market in which one currency (such as Japanese yen) can be exchanged for another currency (such as U.S. dollars). (15)

45-degree line the line showing that expenditure equals aggregate income. (10)

forward-looking consumption model a model that explains consumer behavior by assuming that people anticipate future income when deciding on consumption spending today. (10A)

free trade area (FTA) an area that has no trade barriers between the countries in the area. (18)

freely determined price a price that is determined by the individuals and firms interacting in markets. (1)

frictional unemployment unemployment arising from normal turnover in the labor market, such as when people change occupations or locations, or are new entrants. (7)

gains from trade   improvements in income, production, or satisfaction owing to the exchange of goods or services. (1, 17)

GDP deflator   nominal GDP divided by real GDP; it measures the level of prices of goods and services included in real GDP relative to a given base year. (5)

Gosplan   the planning agency of the Soviet Union. (19)

government failure   a situation in which the government makes things worse than the market, even though there may be market failure. (1)

government purchases   purchases by federal, state, and local governments of new goods and services. (5)

government purchases share   the proportion of GDP that is used for government purchases; equals government purchases divided by GDP, or *G/Y*. (6)

gradualism   the slow phasing in of free market reforms. (19)

gross domestic product (GDP)   a measure of the value of all the goods and services newly produced in an economy during a specified period of time. (2)

growth accounting formula   an equation that states that the growth rate of productivity equals capital's share of income times the growth rate of capital per hour of work plus the growth rate of technology. (8, 16)

human capital   a person's accumulated knowledge and skills. (8)

imports   the total value of the goods and services that people in one country buy from people in other countries. (5)

incentive   a device that motivates people to take action, usually so as to increase economic efficiency. (1)

increasing opportunity cost   a situation in which producing more of one good requires giving up an increasing amount of production of another good. (1)

infant industry argument   the view that a new industry may be helped by protectionist policies. (18)

inferior good   a good for which demand decreases when income rises and increases when income falls. (3)

inflation adjustment (*IA*) line   a flat line showing the level of inflation in the economy at a given point in time. It shifts up when real GDP is greater than potential GDP, and it shifts down when real GDP is less than potential GDP; it also shifts when expectations of inflation or raw materials prices change. (11)

inflation rate   the percentage increase in the overall price level over a given period of time, usually one year. (4)

informal economy   the portion of an economy characterized by illegal, unregulated businesses. (16)

innovation   application of new knowledge in a way that creates new products or significantly changes old ones. (8)

insider   a person who already works for a firm and has some influence over wage and hiring policy. (7)

interest rate   the amount received per dollar loaned per year, usually expressed as a percentage (*e.g.*, 6 percent) of the loan. (4)

interindustry trade   trade between countries in goods from different industries. (17)

intermediate good   a good that undergoes further processing before it is sold to consumers. (5)

International Monetary Fund (IMF)   an international agency, established after World War II, designed to help countries with balance of payments problems and to ensure the smooth functioning of the international monetary system. (16)

international trade   the exchange of goods and services between people or firms in different nations. (1, 17)

intraindustry trade   trade between countries in goods from the same or similar industries. (17)

invention   a discovery of new knowledge. (21)

investment   purchases of final goods by firms plus purchases of newly produced residences by households. (5)

investment share   the proportion of GDP that is used for investment; equals investment divided by GDP, or *I/Y*. Sometimes called investment rate. (6)

job rationing   a reason for unemployment in which the quantity of labor supplied is greater than the quantity demanded because the real wage is too high. (7)

job search   a reason for unemployment in which uncertainty in the labor market and workers' limited information requires people to spend time searching for a job. (7)

job vacancies   positions that firms are trying to fill, but for which they have yet to find suitable workers. (7)

Keynesian multiplier   the ratio of the change in real GDP to the shift in the expenditure line; the formula is $1/(1 - \text{MPC})$, where MPC is the marginal propensity to consume. (10A)

labor   the number of hours people work in producing goods and services. (4)

labor abundant   a lower level of capital per worker in one country relative to another. (17)

labor demand curve   a downward-sloping relationship showing the quantity of labor firms are willing to hire at each wage. (7)

labor force   all those who are either employed or unemployed. (7)

labor force participation rate   the ratio (usually expressed as a percentage) of people in the labor force to the working-age population. (7)

labor income   the sum of wages, salaries, and fringe benefits paid to workers. (5)

labor intensive   production that uses a relatively low level of capital per worker. (17)

labor supply curve   the relationship showing the quantity of labor workers are willing to supply at each wage. (7)

law of demand   the tendency for the quantity demanded of a good in a market to decline as its price rises. (3)

law of supply   the tendency for the quantity supplied of a good in a market to increase as its price rises. (3)

learning by doing   a situation in which workers become more proficient by doing a particular task many times. (8)

liability   something of value that a person or firm owes to someone else. (9)

life-cycle model   a type of forward-looking consumption model that assumes that people base their consumption decisions on their expected lifetime income rather than on their current income. (10A)

linear   a situation in which a curve is straight, with a constant slope. (2A)

liquidity constraint   the situation in which people cannot borrow to smooth their consumption spending when their income is low. (10A)

macroeconomics   the branch of economics that examines the workings and problems of the economy as a whole—GDP growth and unemployment. (2)

marginal propensity to consume (MPC)   the slope of the consumption function, showing the change in consumption that is due to a given change in income. (10)

marginal propensity to import (MPI)   the change in imports because of a given change in income. (10A)

market   an arrangement by which economic exchanges between people take place. (1)

market economy   an economy characterized by freely determined prices and the free exchange of goods and services in markets. (1)

market equilibrium   the situation in which the price is equal to the equilibrium price and the quantity traded equals the equilibrium quantity. (3)

market failure   any situation in which the market does not lead to an efficient economic outcome and in which there is a potential role for government. (1)

maturity date   the date when the principal on a loan is to be paid back. (15)

medium of exchange   something that is generally accepted as a means of payment. (9)

microeconomics   the branch of economics that examines individual decision-making at firms and households and the way they interact in specific industries and markets. (2)

minimum wage   a wage per hour below which it is illegal to pay workers. (3, 7)

mixed economy   a market economy in which the government plays a very large role. (2)

monetary base   currency plus reserves; the monetary base can be tightly controlled by the Fed. (9)

monetary policy rule   a description of how much the interest rate or other instruments of monetary policy respond to inflation or other measures of the state of the economy. (11)

money   that part of a person's wealth that can be readily used for transactions; money also serves as a store of value and a unit of account. (9)

money demand   a relationship between the nominal interest rate and the quantity of money that people are willing to hold at any given nominal interest rate. (14)

money multiplier   the multiple by which the money supply changes as a result of a change in the monetary base. (9)

money supply   the sum of currency (coin and paper money) held by the public and deposits at banks. (9)

movement along the curve   a situation in which a change in the variable on one axis causes a change in the variable on the other axis, but the position of the curve is maintained. (2A)

multilateral negotiation   simultaneous tariff reductions on the part of many countries. (18)

national saving   aggregate income minus consumption minus government purchases. (5)

national saving rate   the proportion of GDP that is saved, neither consumed nor spent on government purchases; equals national saving (S) divided by GDP, or S/Y. (6)

nationalization   the taking over of private firms by the government. (19)

natural unemployment rate   the unemployment rate that exists when there is neither a recession nor a boom and real GDP is equal to potential GDP. (7)

negative slope   a slope of a curve that is less than zero, representing a negative or inverse relationship between two variables. (2A)

negatively related   a situation in which an increase in one variable is associated with a decrease in another variable; also called *inversely related*. (2)

net exports   the value of exports minus the value of imports. (5)

net exports share the proportion of GDP that is equal to net exports; equals net exports divided by GDP, or X/Y. (6)

new economy a term used to describe the period of high productivity growth, attributed largely to better computer and information technology. (8)

nominal GDP gross domestic product without any correction for inflation; the same as GDP; the value of all goods and services newly produced in a country during some period of time, usually a year. (5)

nominal interest rate the interest rate uncorrected for inflation. (4)

nontariff barrier any government action other than a tariff that reduces imports, such as a quota or a standard. (18)

normal good a good for which demand increases when income rises and decreases when income falls. (3)

normative economics economic analysis that makes recommendations about economic policy. (2)

open market operation the buying and selling of bonds by the central bank. (9)

opportunity cost the value of the next-best forgone alternative that was not chosen because something else was chosen. (1, 17)

outsider someone who is not working for a particular firm, making it difficult for him or her to get a job with that firm even though he or she is willing to work for a lower wage. (7)

peak the highest point in real GDP before a recession. (4)

perestroika the restructuring of the Soviet economy by reforming the central planning process. (19)

permanent income model a type of forward-looking consumption model that assumes that people distinguish between temporary changes in their income and permanent changes in their income; the permanent changes have a larger effect on consumption. (10A)

political business cycle a business cycle caused by politicians' use of economic policy to overstimulate the economy just before an election. (14)

portfolio diversification spreading the collection of assets owned in order to limit exposure to risk. (15)

portfolio investment investment by a foreign entity of less than a 10 percent ownership share in a firm. (16)

positive economics economic analysis that explains what happens in the economy and why, without making recommendations about economic policy. (2)

positive slope a slope of a curve that is greater than zero, representing a positive or direct relationship between two variables. (2A)

positively related a situation in which an increase in one variable is associated with an increase in another variable; also called *directly related*. (2)

potential GDP the economy's long-term growth trend for real GDP determined by the available supply of capital, labor, and technology. Real GDP fluctuates above and below potential GDP. (4, 10)

present discounted value the value in the present of future payments. (15A)

price refers to a particular good and is defined as the amount of money or other goods that one must pay to obtain the good. (3)

price ceiling a government price control that sets the maximum allowable price for a good. (3)

price control a government law or regulation that sets or limits the price to be charged for a particular good. (3)

price elasticity of demand the percentage change in the quantity demanded of a good divided by the percentage change in the price of that good. (3)

price elasticity of supply the percentage change in quantity supplied divided by the percentage change in price. (3)

price floor a government price control that sets the minimum allowable price for a good. (3)

price level the average level of prices in the economy. (5)

price shock a change in the price of a key commodity such as oil, usually because of a shortage, that causes a shift in the inflation adjustment line; also sometimes called a supply shock. (12)

price-earnings ratio the price of a stock divided by its annual earnings per share. (15)

privatization the process of converting a government enterprise into a privately owned enterprise. (19)

production function the relationship that describes output as a function of labor, capital, and technology. (4)

production possibilities alternative combinations of production of various goods that are possible, given the economy's resources. (1)

production possibilities curve a curve showing the maximum combinations of production of two goods that are possible, given the economy's resources. (1)

production target a goal set for the production of a good or service in a planned economy. (19)

productivity output per hour of work. (8)

productivity curve a relationship stating the output per hour of work for each amount of capital per hour of work in the economy. (8A)

property rights rights over the use, sale, and proceeds from a good or resource. (1)

purchasing power parity the theory that exchange rates are determined in such a way that the prices of goods in different countries are the same when measured in the same currency. (15)

quantity demanded   the quantity of a good that people want to buy at a given price during a specific time period. (3)

quantity equation of money   the equation relating the price level and real GDP to the quantity of money and the velocity of money: The quantity of money times its velocity equals the price level times real GDP. (9)

quantity supplied   the quantity of a good that firms are willing to sell at a given price. (3)

quota   a governmental limit on the quantity of a good that may be imported or sold. (17)

rate of return   the return on an asset stated as a percentage of the price of the asset. (15)

real business cycle theory   a theory of macroeconomics that stresses that shifts in potential GDP are a primary cause of fluctuations in real GDP; the shifts in potential GDP are usually assumed to be caused by changes in technology. (10,12)

real gross domestic product (real GDP)   a measure of the value of all the goods and services newly produced in a country during some period of time, adjusted for changes in prices over time. (4, 5)

real interest rate   the interest rate minus the expected rate of inflation; it adjusts the nominal interest rate for inflation. (4)

real wage   the wage or price of labor adjusted for inflation; in contrast, the nominal wage has not been adjusted for inflation. (7)

recession   a decline in real GDP that lasts for at least six months. (4)

recovery   the early part of an economic expansion, immediately after the trough of the recession. (4)

reinflation   an increase in the inflation rate caused by a change in monetary policy. (12)

relative price   the price of a particular good compared to the price of other things. (2)

rent control   a government price control that sets the maximum allowable rent on a house or apartment. (3)

required reserve ratio   the fraction of a bank's deposits that it is required to hold at the Fed. (9)

reserves   deposits that commercial banks hold at the Fed. (9)

return   the income received from the ownership of an asset; for a stock, the return is the dividend plus the capital gain. (15)

revenue tariff   an import tax whose main purpose is to provide revenue to the government. (18)

scarcity   the situation in which the quantity of resources is insufficient to meet all wants. (1)

scatter plot   a graph in which points in a Cartesian coordinate system represent the values of two variables. (2A)

shift of the curve   a change in the position of a curve, usually caused by a change in a variable not represented on either axis. (2A)

shock therapy   the abrupt introduction of free markets in a formerly centrally planned economy. (19)

shortage (excess demand)   the situation in which quantity demanded is greater than quantity supplied. (3)

slope   a characteristic of a curve that is defined as the change in the variable on the vertical axis divided by the change in the variable on the horizontal axis. (2A)

Smoot-Hawley tariff   a set of tariffs imposed in 1930 that raised the average tariff level to 59 percent by 1932. (18)

socialism   an economic system in which the government owns and controls all the capital and makes decisions about prices and quantities as part of a central plan. (19)

specific tariff   a tax on imports that is proportional to the number of units or items imported. (18)

spending balance   the level of income or real GDP at which the 45-degree line and the expenditure line cross; also called equilibrium income. (10)

stagflation   the situation in which high inflation and high unemployment occur simultaneously. (12)

state enterprise   an organization, analogous to a firm in a market economy, that is owned and controlled by the government. (19)

store of value   something that will allow purchasing power to be carried from one period to the next. (9)

structural surplus   the level of the government budget surplus under the scenario where real GDP is equal to potential GDP; also called the full-employment surplus. (13)

structural unemployment   unemployment due to structural problems such as poor skills, longer-term changes in demand, or insufficient work incentives. (7)

substitute   a good that has many of the same characteristics as and can be used in place of another good. (3)

supply   a relationship between price and quantity supplied. (3)

supply curve   a graph of supply showing the upward-sloping relationship between price and quantity supplied. (3)

supply schedule   a tabular presentation of supply showing the price and quantity supplied of a particular good, all else being equal. (3)

surplus (excess supply)   the situation in which quantity supplied is greater than quantity demanded. (3)

systematic risk   the level of risk in asset markets that investors cannot reduce by diversification. (15)

target inflation rate   the central bank's goal for the average rate of inflation over the long run. (11)

tariff   a tax on imports. (17)

Taylor Rule   a monetary policy rule used by economists to describe or recommend how a central bank like the Federal Reserve should set short-term interest rates as economic conditions change to achieve both the bank's short-run goal for stabilizing the economy and its long-run goal for inflation. (14)

technological change   improvement in technology over time. (8)

technology   anything that raises the amount of output that can be produced with a given amount of labor and capital. (4, 8)

time inconsistency   the situation in which policymakers have the incentive to announce one economic policy but then change that policy after citizens have acted on the initial, stated policy. (14)

time-series graph   a graph that plots a variable over time, usually with time on the horizontal axis. (2A)

trade balance   the value of exports minus the value of imports. (5)

trade creation   the increase in trade due to a decrease in trade barriers. (18)

trade diversion   the shifting of trade away from the low-cost producer toward a higher-cost producer because of a reduction in trade barriers with the country of the higher-cost producer. (18)

trade war   a conflict among nations over trade policies caused by imposition of protectionist policies on the part of one country and subsequent retaliatory actions by other countries. (18)

trough   the lowest point of real GDP at the end of a recession. (4)

unemployment rate   the percentage of the labor force that is unemployed. (4, 7)

unit of account   a standard unit in which prices can be quoted and values of goods can be compared. (9)

Uruguay Round   the most recent round of multilateral negotiations, completed in 1993. (18)

value added   the value of the firm's production minus the value of the intermediate goods used in production. (5)

velocity   a measure of how frequently money is turned over in the economy. (9)

voluntary restraint agreement (VRA)   a country's self-imposed government restriction on exports to a particular country. (18)

working-age population   persons over 16 years of age who are not in an institution such as a jail or hospital. (7)

World Bank   an international agency, established after World War II, designed to promote the economic development of poorer countries through lending channeled from industrialized countries. (16)

World Trade Organization (WTO)   an international organization that can mediate trade disputes. (18)

yield   the annual rate of return on a bond if the bond were held to maturity. (15)

Index

Credits

Wall Street Journal, February 1, 2002. Reprinted by permission of The Wall Street Journal.
Chapter 16: p. 368, Figure 16.2 source, *Historical Statistics of the United States: Colonial Times to 1970,* U.S. Department of Commerce, and *State Personal Income,* U.S. Department of Commerce, l989; pp. 369, 370, Figures 16.3 and 16.4 source, International Comparison Project administered by the United Nations, World Bank, and International Monetary Fund. The data for 1960 are measured in 1985 dollars; p. 372, Figure 16.5 source, 1990 data from International Comparison Project administered by the United Nations, World Bank, and International Monetary Fund; p. 376, Figure 16.6 source, *World Economic Outlook,* May 1995. By permission of International Monetary Fund.
Chapter 17: p. 391, source of quotes in feature box, David Ricardo, *On the Principles of Political Economy and Taxation,* 1817, pp. 152-153, in *The Works and Correspondence of David Ricardo,* ed. Piero Sraffa (Cambridge University Press, 1962).

Chapter 18: p. 412, Figure 18.4 source, *Historical Statistics of the United States, Colonial Times to 1957,* series Y, 259-260, and *Budget of the U.S. Government,* 2000; p. 413, Figure 18.5 source, *Historical Statistics of the United States, Colonial Times to 1970* and *Statistical Abstract of the United States,* 1999; p. 414, Figure 18.6 source, "Contracting Spiral of World Trade," from Kindleberger, Charles, *The World of Depression 1929-39* (Berkeley, California: University of California Press, 1973). Data reprinted by permission from League of Nations, *Monthly Bulletin of Statistics,* February 1934.
Chapter 19: p. 427, source of quotes in feature box, Karl Marx and Friedrich Engels, *Communist Manifesto,* 1848, in *Essential Works of Marxism,* ed. A. P. Mendel (New York: Bantam Books, 1961), pp. 1, 44, and 16-17, and Karl Marx, *Capital: A Critique of Political Economy* (New York: Modern Library, 1906), p. 647.